W9-BRY-659

World Armaments and Disarmament

SIPRI Yearbook 1981

sipri

Stockholm International Peace Research Institute

SIPRI is an independent institute for research into problems of peace and conflict, especially those of disarmament and arms regulation. It was established in 1966 to commemorate Sweden's 150 years of unbroken peace.

The Institute is financed by the Swedish Parliament. The staff, the Governing Board and the Scientific Council are international. As a consultative body, the Scientific Council is not responsible for the views expressed in the publications of the Institute.

sipri

Stockholm International Peace Research Institute

Bergshamra, S-171 73 Solna, Sweden
Cable: Peaceresearch, Stockholm
Telephone: 08-55 97 00

World Armaments and Disarmament

SIPRI Yearbook 1981

sipri

Stockholm International Peace Research Institute

Taylor & Francis Ltd
London
1981

Oelgeschlager, Gunn & Hain, Inc.
Cambridge, Mass.

First published 1981 by Taylor & Francis Ltd, London
and Oelgeschlager, Gunn & Hain, Inc., Cambridge, Mass.

ISBN 0-89946-090-9
ISSN 0347 2205

Typeset by The Lancashire Typesetting Co. Ltd,
Bolton, Lancashire BL2 1DB
Printed and bound in the United Kingdom by
Taylor & Francis (Printers) Ltd, Rankine Road,
Basingstoke, Hampshire RG24 0PR

Previous volumes in this series:

SIPRI Yearbook of World Armaments and Disarmament 1968/69
SIPRI Yearbook of World Armaments and Disarmament 1969/70
World Armaments and Disarmament, SIPRI Yearbook 1972
World Armaments and Disarmament, SIPRI Yearbook 1973
World Armaments and Disarmament, SIPRI Yearbook 1974
World Armaments and Disarmament, SIPRI Yearbook 1975
World Armaments and Disarmament, SIPRI Yearbook 1976
World Armaments and Disarmament, SIPRI Yearbook 1977
World Armaments and Disarmament, SIPRI Yearbook 1978
World Armaments and Disarmament, SIPRI Yearbook 1979
World Armaments and Disarmament, SIPRI Yearbook 1980

World Armaments and Disarmament, SIPRI Yearbooks 1968–79, Cumulative Index

PREFACE

The twelfth issue of the *SIPRI Yearbook* continues our analysis of the world's arms races, and the attempts to stop them, up to 31 December 1980. As in all SIPRI publications, information has been obtained from open sources only.

Attributions

Introduction	Frank Barnaby
Chapter 1	Frank Blackaby
Chapter 2	Allan Krass
Chapter 3	Signe Landgren-Bäckström
Chapter 4	Thomas Ohlson
Chapter 5	Bhupendra Jasani
Chapter 6	Frank Blackaby, assisted by Elisabeth Sköns and Rita Tullberg
Chapter 7	Signe Landgren-Bäckström, assisted by Evamaria Loose-Weintraub and Thomas Ohlson
Chapter 8	Frank Barnaby and Bhupendra Jasani
Appendix 8A	Randall Forsberg
Chapter 9	Bhupendra Jasani, assisted by Carol Stoltenberg-Hansen
Chapter 10	Jozef Goldblat and Macha Levinson
Chapters 11–14 and 18	Jozef Goldblat, assisted by Ragnhild Ferm
Chapter 15	Nicholas Sims
Chapter 16	Alessandro Corradini
Chapter 17	Sverre Lodgaard, assisted by Ragnhild Ferm and Per Berg

The Yearbook was produced under the direction of Frank Barnaby. The editorial work was done by Connie Wall, assisted by Billie Bielckus and Gillian Stanbridge.

Acknowledgements

The Yearbook team wish to thank the Institute's librarians, the press cutters and the secretarial staff for their assistance in preparing the Yearbooks. Special thanks are also extended to Kimmo Persson for his considerable help in establishing the computer data-storage systems.

CONTENTS

Part I. The 1970s, developments of the past decade

Part II. Developments in world armaments in 1980

Part III. Developments in arms control in 1980

FOREWORD

Taken together, the last ten Yearbooks are a record of an alarming increase in world armaments, resulting in an ever accelerating Soviet–American nuclear arms race and new regional arms races. Tragically, there has been virtually no real progress in negotiations for disarmament. Because of the huge resources devoted to it by the great powers, military science, an activity now essentially out of the control of the political leaders, has succeeded in developing weapons which will be perceived to be more suitable for fighting a nuclear war than for nuclear deterrence. This, in my opinion, is the most alarming factor emerging from the SIPRI Yearbooks. Unless military science is brought back under political control there is an increasing risk of a nuclear world war which, in the words of a recent UN report, would be the "ultimate human madness".

In spite of the depressing nature of the topics, responsibility for the production of the past ten SIPRI Yearbooks has been a very rewarding and worthwhile experience. It has required much labour by a relatively small number of people, and I would like to record my personal gratitude to all of them.

Frank Barnaby

Introduction

I. *World military spending*

During the past decade the world has spent about $4 million million, at constant (1978) prices and dollars, on the military. But, in spite of this enormous expenditure of resources, few nations feel more secure now than they did ten years ago. On the contrary, most populations feel increasingly insecure. Money spent on military activities can, therefore, be regarded as an unjustifiable and tragic waste of our limited resources.

If the raw materials, productive capacity and, above all, human skill and ingenuity now spent on the world's military were directed to civilian ends, the effect on the living standard of the average citizen would be considerable. The diversion of scientific and intellectual effort is particularly tragic. In the military field, enormously complex technological and organizational problems have been solved. If that same effort were devoted to problems of, say, world health or world food production, the results could be impressive.

For many years now, world military spending, in real terms, has increased at a rate of about 2 per cent a year. Total world military spending is now in excess of $500 thousand million, at current (1980) prices.

NATO and the WTO have dominated in the field of military expenditure throughout the 1970s, and will no doubt continue to do so throughout the next decade. However, the military spending of the Third World countries has nearly doubled during the past decade, illustrating the wasteful use of limited resources adding to world instability.

NATO and the WTO

NATO and the Warsaw Treaty Organization (WTO) account for the bulk of world military expenditure. NATO countries have committed themselves to a 3 per cent annual real growth in military spending. But most NATO European countries (with the exception of the UK, Luxembourg and Portugal) have failed to reach this goal.

In the USA there will be sharp rises in the military budget. The budget which ex-President Carter left provided for a 4.6 per cent volume increase in military spending in fiscal year 1981, and indeed for further years. Such an increase would mark a sharp change from the trend of the 1970s. From 1971 to 1976, after the Viet Nam War, US military spending

Figure 1. World military expenditure, 1960–80

US $ thousand million, in constant (1978) prices and exchange-rates[a]

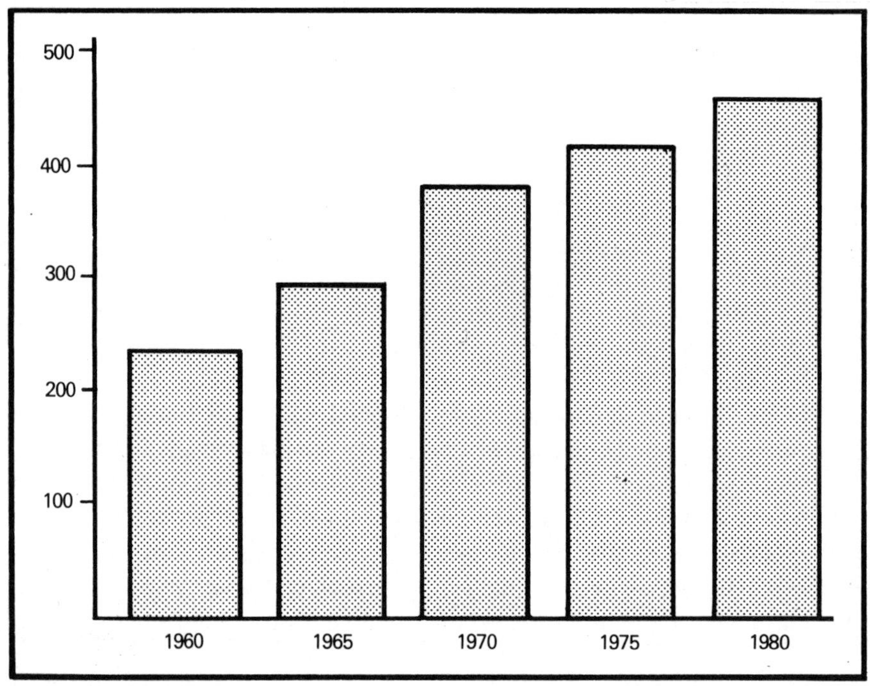

[a] The figure for 1980 corresponds to $500 thousand million in 1980 prices.

decreased in real terms; from 1976 to 1980 it was moving up at about 1.5 per cent a year.

The outgoing Carter Administration proposed military outlays, at current prices, of $158 000 million in fiscal year 1981, rising to $293 000 million in 1986. The Reagan Administration plans in addition to ask Congress for an extra $1 300 million in fiscal year 1981, $7 200 million in 1982, $20 700 million in 1983, $27 000 million in 1984, $50 200 million in 1985 and $63 100 million in 1986.

US military spending accounted for 44 per cent of the federal budget in 1962. This percentage decreased to 24 in 1981. But the Reagan Administration wants to increase it to 32 per cent in 1984.

New emphasis will be placed on the US Rapid Deployment Force (to get military equipment for troop pre-positions in unstable regions before a crisis occurs) and on expanding the US Navy.

The Soviet Union may also be having difficulty in persuading its allies in the Warsaw Treaty Organization (WTO) to share more of the defence

Figure 2. Distribution of world military expenditure, 1971 and 1980

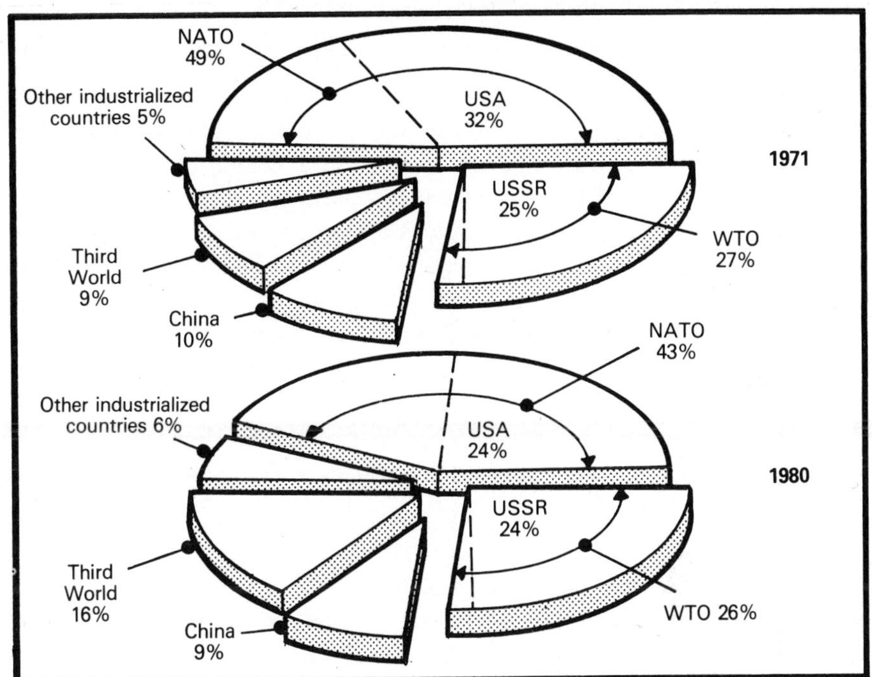

burden. The only other WTO country which increased its military spending significantly is the German Democratic Republic. Between 1977 and 1980, East German military expenditure appears to have risen, in real terms, some 25 per cent. The figures for the other WTO countries seem roughly constant—except for Poland, where there may have been a fall.

The military budget of the USSR itself remains a mystery, due to Soviet secrecy about most military matters. On the one hand, there is the CIA dollar estimate, which claims that Soviet military expenditure is about 50 per cent higher than that of the United States. On the other hand, there is the Soviet official figure in roubles which, when converted into dollars at the official exchange-rate (64 kopecks to the dollar), implies that Soviet military spending is between one-fifth and one-sixth of that of the United States. Neither of these figures provides a credible comparison of the military spending of the two countries. Given the roughly equal size of their arsenals, the best assumption is that they each use about the same amount of resources. The USSR is also, like the USA, using some of its resources to improve its Navy.

II. Arms production and trade

During the past decade the international trade in conventional armaments increased dramatically. New suppliers and new recipients entered the arms market, the weapons supplied became more sophisticated and expensive, and the chances of controlling the arms trade diminished. In fact the global arms trade went out of control during this period.

It is estimated that about 130 wars or armed conflicts have taken place in the world since 1945. Approximately 50 of these took place during the past decade. Furthermore, these armed conflicts were fought almost exclusively in the Third World and, with few exceptions, using weapons supplied by the industrialized countries.

The major suppliers of arms are the United States and the Soviet Union. They alone accounted for some 75 per cent of the total export of major weapons (aircraft, missiles, armoured vehicles and warships) during the 1970s.

Figure 3. Value of world major weapon[a] exports, 1961–80
Values are in US $ thousand million, at constant 1975 prices

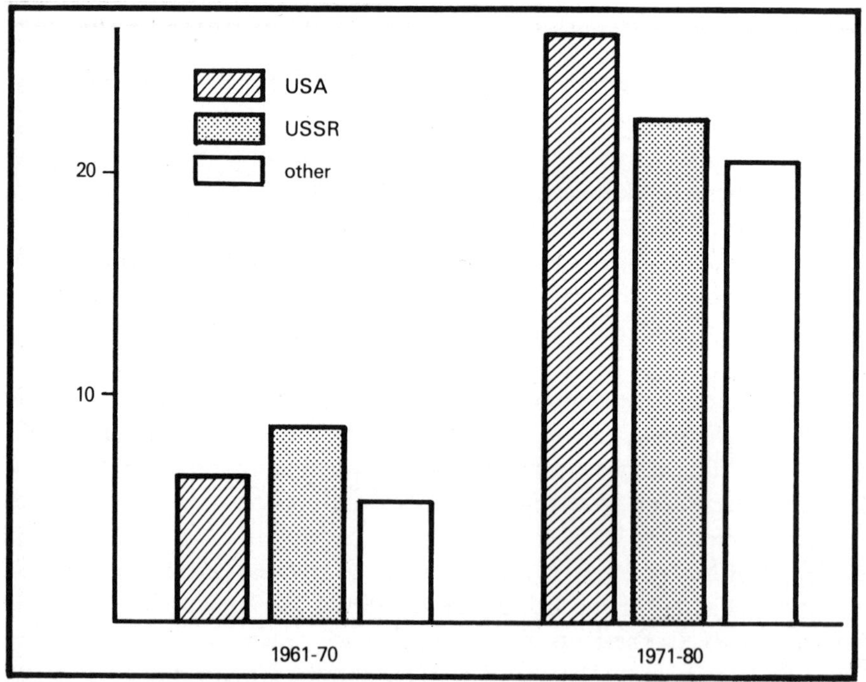

[a] The SIPRI arms production and trade data cover the four categories of major weapons—that is, aircraft, missiles, armoured vehicles and warships.

The share of the other suppliers in the arms trade is steadily increasing. France, Italy, FR Germany and the United Kingdom accounted for approximately 22 per cent of the total arms exports during the past decade—a substantial increase compared to previous post-war decades.

Another new trend is a marked increase in production in and export from Third World countries. Arms transfers between Third World countries still very often consist of the re-export of arms originating from an industrialized country. The arms industries of the Third World are as yet relatively new. But licence production agreements and various forms of technological assistance allowed some Third World countries to acquire the design capacity necessary for large-scale arms production. The main Third World weapon producers are currently Israel, Brazil, South Africa and Argentina.

At present, the Third World contribution to the global export of major arms is small—2 or 3 per cent of the total. But the share is rising. Owing to relatively small production costs, major arms produced in Third World countries are particularly attractive to other Third World countries. Third

Figure 4. Shares of the major-weapon exporters and Third World importers, 1977–80[a]

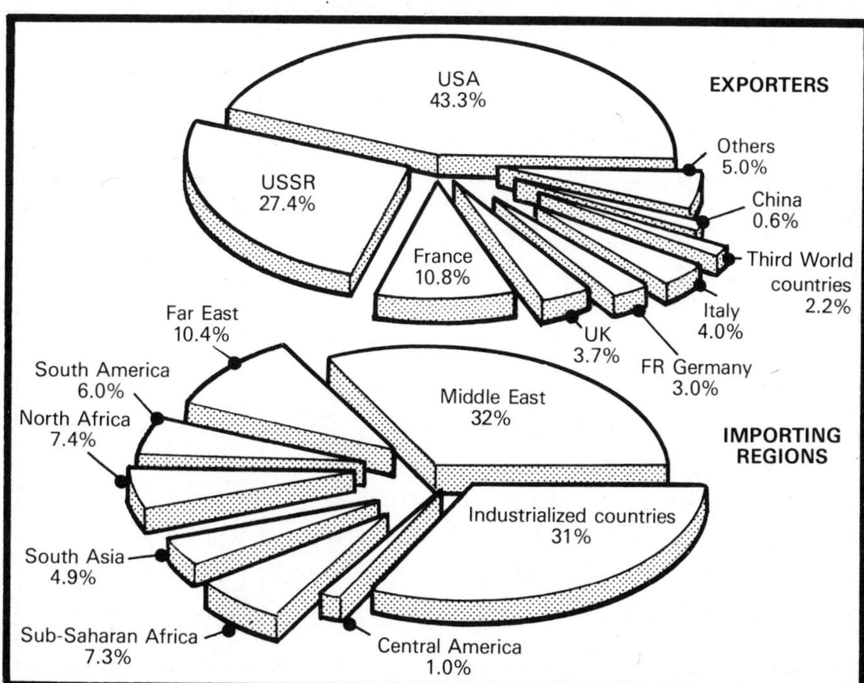

[a] The values include licences sold for the production of major weapons.

World countries, therefore, usually export arms to other Third World countries.

The Middle East was by far the largest arms importing region, accounting for 48 per cent of total Third World arms imports. In this region, conflicts coincide with great power interests in the strategic position and oil resources of the region. The wealth of many Middle Eastern countries also facilitates the purchase of the most sophisticated weapon systems. Six of the eight largest Third World arms importing countries during the decade are in the Middle East.

In summary, the main trends in the global arms trade over the past decade were: more arms were traded than ever before, they were of a higher level of technological sophistication, and they were imported by more countries. There is, however, some evidence that the rate of increase in arms imports will in the future be higher for industrialized countries than for Third World countries. Between 1977 and 1980, for example, the share of the industrialized countries increased to about 30 per cent, while that of Third World countries decreased to about 70 per cent.

III. Developments in nuclear weapons

During 1980, the qualitative developments of a number of US and Soviet strategic and tactical nuclear weapon systems continued. These improved nuclear weapons pose an increased threat of nuclear war. By their very nature, some are likely to be seen as more suitable for fighting a nuclear war than deterring it. Increased accuracy and larger numbers of warheads per launcher put an increased premium on a first strike.

If a nation could add to its offensive capabilities an effective defence against retaliation, a first strike will become even more probable. The current revival of interest in ballistic missile defence (BMD) can, therefore, be considered as a significant weapon trend of the 1980s.

US strategic nuclear weapon developments

In the USA, the deployment of the Mark 12A warhead on Minuteman III intercontinental ballistic missiles (ICBMs) and the conversion of Poseidon strategic nuclear submarines to carry Trident I submarine-launched ballistic missiles (SLBMs) continued in 1980, as did the development of air-launched cruise missiles, MX mobile ICBMs and Trident II SLBMs. There were also renewed demands for the development of a new strategic bomber, to follow the B-52.

Four Poseidon nuclear submarines were converted in 1979 and 1980 to carry Trident I SLBMs. A total of 12 Poseidons will be re-fitted to carry 16 Trident I missiles each.

Sea trials for the first of the Trident nuclear strategic submarines are scheduled to begin in 1981. The initial plan is to deploy 8 Trident submarines (these 8 have already been ordered), but this number may be increased to 25.

US theatre nuclear weapon developments

The development of the ground-launched cruise missile (GLCM) and the Pershing II missile continued during 1980. In October 1980, however, the Pentagon announced a six months' delay in the testing of the GLCM. The missiles should, however, be ready for deployment in December 1983. According to a decision made by NATO in December 1979, the deployment of 464 US GLCMs and 108 Pershing II missiles should begin in five West European countries in 1983. The UK, Italy and the Federal Republic of Germany have agreed to deploy GLCMs. It is unclear whether or not Belgium will fully participate in the programme. The Netherlands will decide at the end of 1981 whether to accept GLCMs on its territory.

Soviet strategic nuclear weapon developments

The Soviet Union is developing a new nuclear strategic submarine, the Typhoon, in the 25 000- to 30 000-ton class, significantly heavier than the 18 700-ton weight of the US Trident submarine. One Typhoon, said to be fitted to carry about 20 SLBMs, has been launched and three others are under construction.

According to former US Secretary of Defense Harold Brown, in his 1981 annual report, the new Soviet Typhoon solid-propellant SLBM, the SS-NX-20, will almost certainly be MIRVed. The SS-NX-20 is expected to be deployed after the mid-1980s.

There are reports that the USSR is testing two new types of solid-fuelled ICBM. One is said to be a large mobile system like the proposed US MX ICBM. This is in addition to the mobile ICBM, the SS-16, which has already been developed but may not be deployed.

The deployment of the SS-20 continues. By the end of 1980, about 180 SS-20s were deployed. These missiles are aimed at targets in Europe and China.

Ballistic missile defence

Much research is being carried out in the field of high-energy lasers for application as anti-satellite weapons based on the Earth as well as in space. When placed on satellites in outer space, high-energy lasers might be usable as a BMD system to destroy ballistic missiles during their boost phase.

A number of problems need to be solved before high-energy lasers can be used in practicable weapons or a BMD system. For example, there is the problem of tracking and aiming at a fast-moving target. Some success has already been achieved against targets at short ranges. But although it may be some time before this can be done at long range, many experts do not doubt that the problem will eventually be solved. This will have major ramifications for the stability of the strategic nuclear balance between the USA and the USSR.

This balance is, in any case, in jeopardy. During the 1970s progress in military technology was not characterized by dramatic breakthroughs or revolutionary new weapon concepts, but rather by steady, incremental, across-the-board improvements in all the various systems that constitute a counterforce or nuclear war-fighting capability. These, as we have seen, include advances in missile accuracy, warhead efficiencies and cruise missiles, but also in systems for anti-submarine warfare, anti-satellite warfare and command, control, communications and intelligence.

These developments have undermined the notion of a stable nuclear deterrence. The continued efforts to perfect counterforce technologies derive from an undiminished desire to extract maximum political utility from nuclear weapons, something a deterrence strategy cannot provide.

The improvement of counterforce capabilities may, therefore, not be the result of blind technological momentum but instead of a conscious and reasonably well-managed effort by each side to achieve and maintain a politically usable superiority over the other in war-fighting capabilities.

IV. Other military developments in space

In 1980, 103 military satellites were launched—14 by the USA and 89 by the Soviet Union. Of these, some 40 per cent were photographic reconnaissance satellites, and most of these were launched by the Soviet Union. The USSR launched more of these satellites simply because US photographic reconnaissance satellites remain in orbit for a very long time, while the majority of the Soviet satellites have lifetimes of only 13 days. Some of the reconnaissance satellites launched in 1980 were used to monitor the Iran–Iraq war.

During 1980 the Soviet Union launched an ocean surveillance satellite similar to the one which crash-landed in Canada in early 1978. This satellite presumably also carried a nuclear reactor since, after a few weeks, it was manoeuvred into a higher orbit where it will remain for some hundreds of years.

In April 1980, two satellites, a target and a hunter–killer satellite, were launched by the Soviet Union. These were part of an anti-satellite (ASAT) programme in which some 35 target and interceptor satellites have been launched by the Soviet Union. The USA has a similar ASAT programme. But the United States may also test soon a system in which non-nuclear warheads will be launched from a high-speed aircraft flying at high altitude. The warhead would be guided onto the target by an infra-red homing device.

V. Arms control

The main arms control event in 1980 was the Second Conference to review the operation of the Non-Proliferation Treaty (the NPT). The first Review Conference, held in 1975, reached agreement on a final document. The second failed to do so. The unfavourable political climate which contributed to this failure was due to: the uncertain future of the strategic arms limitation talks, the inability of the US government to take major decisions during a presidential campaign, the international reaction to the Soviet intervention in Afghanistan, the acute conflict in the Persian Gulf area, the controversy over Eurostrategic missiles, and in general the unabated build-up of military strength, especially nuclear, the continued nuclear weapon testing, and the total lack of progress in disarmament.

One major controversy was related to the application of safeguards under Article III of the NPT. All the participants in the Review Conference agreed, in principle, that full-scope NPT safeguards should be applied also to non-parties. But there was no agreement as to whether such safeguards should be required as a *condition* of supplies. Continued supplies to non-parties, especially to those having unsafeguarded facilities, constitute a direct danger to the survival of the NPT. Such countries are, after all, the most likely next proliferators. If further proliferation does take place, withdrawals from the Treaty may be unavoidable. The inability to settle the question of safeguards was a regrettable setback.

The majority of states argued for a strengthening of the NPT, improvement of nuclear safeguards as well as other appropriate international arrangements to minimize the risk of nuclear proliferation. In that this attitude will provoke action, the Conference may not have been useless.

Most delegates at the NPT Review Conference expressed concern at the failure of the USA, the USSR and the UK to negotiate a comprehensive nuclear test ban. At least 1 271 nuclear explosions have been conducted between 1945 and 1980, 783 of them after the signing in 1963 of the Partial Test Ban Treaty (PTBT) prohibiting atmospheric tests.

In 1980 the USSR carried out 20 nuclear explosions, the USA 14, France 11, the UK 3 and China 1.

Figure 5. Nuclear explosions during 1945–80 (known and presumed)

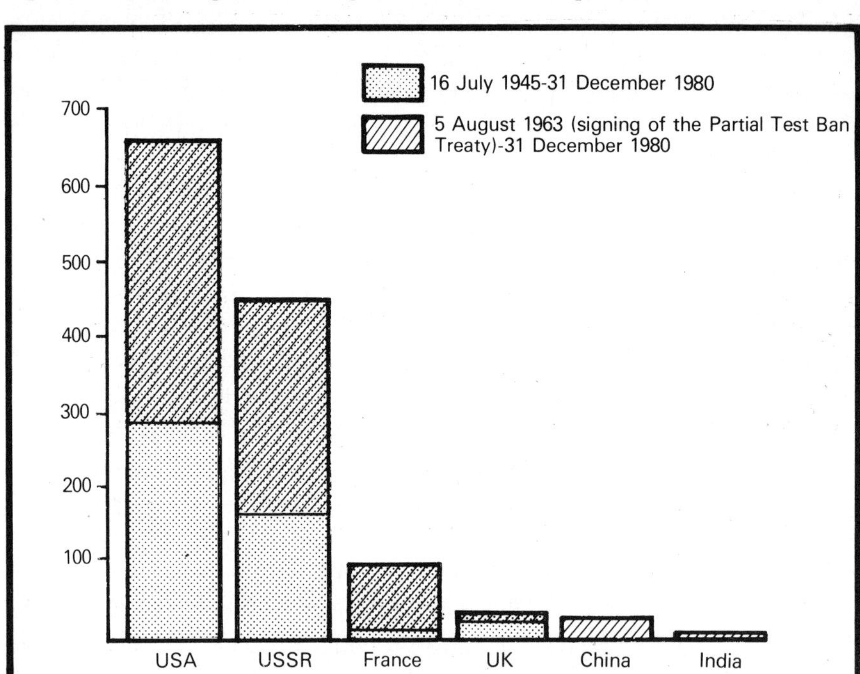

VI. Conclusions

The greatest disappointment in 1980 for those interested in controlling the nuclear arms race was the failure of the US Senate to ratify the SALT II Treaty, signed by the USA and the USSR in 1979. Without SALT, or at least significant progress in the SALT process, it is hard to see any real progress being made in any other arms control negotiations, such as a comprehensive test ban. In the absence of the ratification of SALT II, it is to be hoped that both the USA and the USSR will take no action inconsistent with the SALT treaties.

In the current international climate, and given the planned and probable increases in military budgets over the next few years, we can expect the East–West nuclear and conventional arms races to accelerate. New nuclear weapons and weapon systems will be developed and deployed, some of which will increase the probability of a nuclear world war, because they will provoke continuing moves away from nuclear deterrence policies to nuclear war-fighting strategies.

The international arms trade, which has for some time now been out of control, continues to spread world-wide the most sophisticated weapons. More and more Third World countries are establishing significant defence industries and will, if past experience is any guide, begin to sell the weapons they produce. Third World countries are already participating in arms exports to a significant extent.

The non-proliferation regime has not been strengthened sufficiently to prevent the spread of nuclear weapons. Because of this, countries in some unstable regions are becoming increasingly nervous when their neighbours acquire nuclear power reactors and other elements of the nuclear fuel cycle for peaceful purposes. The inability of the current nuclear weapon powers to control the nuclear arms race encourages the proliferation of nuclear weapons to countries which do not now have them.

The current situation in arms control and disarmament and the acceleration of the nuclear arms race emphasize the importance of achieving some disarmament in Europe. It is in Europe, after all, that the armies of the two sides are face to face. At least 10 000 nuclear weapons are deployed for use against targets in Europe. And there are plans on both sides for the deployment of new types of nuclear weapon in Europe which will be seen as suitable for fighting rather than deterring a nuclear war. There are, therefore, many reasons for convening a disarmament conference of European states. Hopefully, this will soon be done.

Part I. The 1970s, developments of the past decade

Chapter 1. World military expenditure, the past decade
Introduction / The great powers / The rest of the world / Economic consequences / The prospects for military expenditure

Chapter 2. The evolution of military technology and deterrence strategy
Introduction / Developments in counterforce technology / The impact on deterrence / Technology and doctrine / Some consequences for the 1980s

Chapter 3. World production of conventional weapons in the 1970s
Introduction / The established arms producers / Third World arms producers / The weapons produced in the 1970s / Future trends in conventional arms development

Chapter 4. World trade in major conventional weapons in the 1970s
Introduction / Background / Arms trade in the 1970s / The determinants of demand and supply / Conclusions

Chapter 5. A decade of military uses of outer space
Introduction / Some specific advances / The future

1. World military expenditure, the past decade

Square-bracketed numbers, thus [1], *refer to the list of references on page* 18.

I. Introduction

The graph of world military expenditure in the past decade suggests, at first sight, nothing particularly dramatic—indeed it continues the rather familiar pattern of the whole post-war period. The pattern is for a ratchet effect: for spending to go up fast when there is a major war or crisis, such as the Korean War or the Viet Nam War. Then there is a flattening off for a year or two, but at or near the new high figure. After a few years, a gradual rise begins again. This is the pattern of the 1970s as well (see figure 1.1).

In eleven successive Yearbooks, research staff at SIPRI have been charting the course of military expenditure. In this twelfth Yearbook, this chapter picks up some of the themes developed during the past decade.

Figure 1.1. World military expenditure, 1949–80

US $ thousand million, in constant (1978) prices and exchange-rates

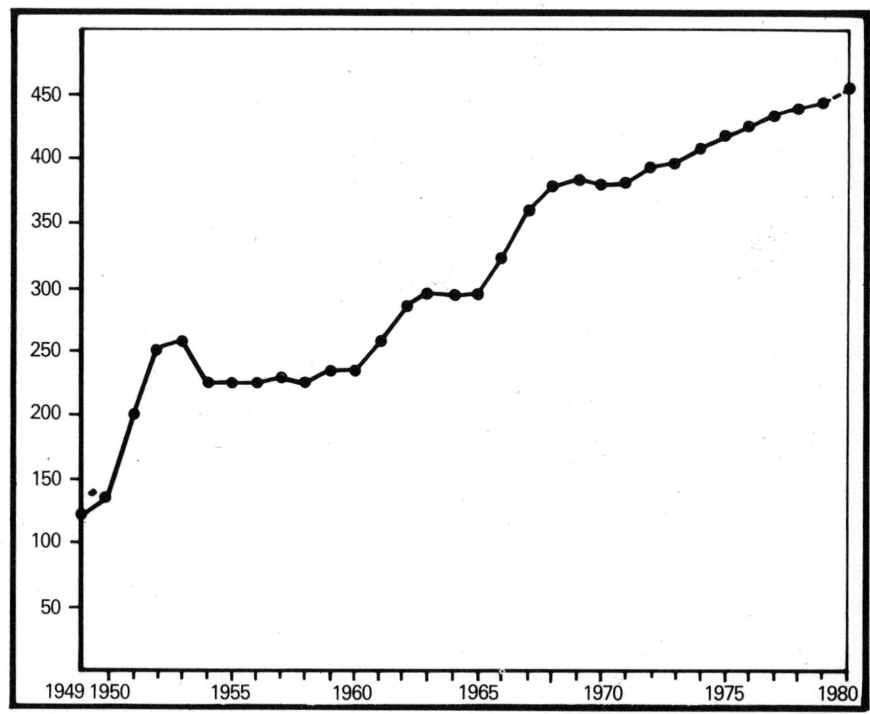

It asks in particular what the driving forces have been behind this enormous and essentially pointless diversion of resources: pointless because this expenditure has singularly failed to achieve its objective. Each individual country will state, in justifying its military budget, that its objective is to improve its own security. Over the last ten years the nations have spent (at current, 1980 prices) some $5 000 thousand million to this end. At the end of it, it is doubtful whether there is any single nation which does not consider itself less secure than it was ten years ago. The evidence of surveys in a large number of countries shows that ordinary people are feeling (with considerable justification) increasingly insecure.

The driving forces behind this self-defeating search for security through military expenditure have varied in different countries and regions. The sections which follow discuss the trend and the determinants of that trend, first in the two great power blocs—NATO and the Warsaw Treaty Organization (WTO); then in Third World countries. There are concluding sections on the economic consequences of military spending, and on the prospects for the 1980s.

II. The great powers

At the beginning of the 1970s, there seemed to be some hope that the process of competitive armament between the great powers might be checked.

First of all, the United States was disengaging itself from Viet Nam, and US military spending there was coming down fast. The estimated 'incremental cost' of the Viet Nam War reached a peak of rather over $20 thousand million (in current dollars) in 1969, and was down to $6 thousand million in 1973; and there was discussion at that time in the United States of the way in which the 'peace dividend' might be used.

Secondly, the first moves were being made to attempt to set some kind of ceiling on US and Soviet strategic weapons. These moves were possible because the Soviet Union appeared to be at last approaching some kind of rough parity with the United States. Throughout the 1960s, any such attempt had been impossible because the United States had such a wide margin of superiority. It is of some interest to consider how that wide margin came about, for it is a good illustration of one of the ways in which the competitive process goes on. What happened is described by former US Secretary of Defense McNamara, speaking in 1967:

> In 1961 when I became Secretary of Defense, the Soviet Union possessed a very small operational arsenal of intercontinental missiles. However, they did possess the technological and industrial capacity to enlarge that arsenal very substantially over the succeeding several years.

Now we had no evidence that the Soviets did in fact plan to fully use that capability. But . . . a strategic planner must be 'conservative' in his calculations: that is he must prepare for the worst plausible case and not be content to hope and prepare merely for the most probable.

Since we could not be certain of Soviet intentions . . . we had to insure against such an eventuality by undertaking ourselves a major build-up of the Minuteman and Polaris forces. . . .

Thus, in the course of hedging against what was then only a theoretically possible Soviet build-up, we took decisions which have resulted in our current superiority in numbers of warheads and deliverable megatons. But the blunt fact remains that if we had had more accurate information about planned Soviet strategic forces, we simply would not have needed to build as large a nuclear arsenal as we have today. . . .

Furthermore, that decision in itself—as justified as it was—in the end could not possibly have left unaffected the Soviet Union's future nuclear plans. . . .

It is precisely this action–reaction phenomenon that "fuels an arms race". [1]

The enormous lead which the United States established in intercontinental ballistic missiles (ICBMs) during the 1960s made any kind of US–Soviet agreement on the matter impossible: superior strength is no basis for successful agreements. It was only at the end of the 1960s, when the Soviet Union was approaching some kind of parity, that an agreement to stop at that point seemed conceivable. This hope may have been unrealistic—indeed the following chapter suggests that there were very strong forces militating against any stable plateau of mutual deterrence. Nonetheless, the hope was there.

In addition to these two apparently optimistic developments—the de-escalation of the Viet Nam War and the possibility of an agreed plateau of some kind in US and Soviet strategic weapons—there was a third development which appeared to hold promise for the future. In the early 1970s the first moves were made towards some kind of détente in Europe. In 1970, for the first time since the division of Germany, substantive and formal discussions were held between representatives of the two German states, and a basic treaty was signed between them in December 1972 which led on to the general diplomatic recognition of the German Democratic Republic by Western countries. At around the same time there was the first Helsinki meeting, to plan a conference on European security. At the beginning of the next year, talks began in Vienna between NATO and WTO countries on the possibility of force reductions in Europe.

Thus at the beginning of the 1970s, there were hopeful signs. By the end of the 1970s, those hopeful signs had disappeared. What went wrong?

What went wrong?

There is no simple answer to this question. Each side, of course, claims that it was simply reacting to an increased threat from the other side: that is not particularly helpful.

Chapter 2 discusses some of the forces which pushed the strategic arms race on from any stable plateau of mutually assured destruction. Here we are concerned with two other themes, to which the Yearbook has constantly recurred: the theme of escalating military technology, and the theme of the 'presentation of the threat'.

The first theme concerns the extremely rapid rate of technological advance in the military field, which arises from the immense quantum of research resources devoted to weapon development and the very large number of research institutions engaged in this field. There is a two-way process here. If the military policy-makers decide that they wish to push out the technological frontier in some particular field, they have the resources at their command to do so. At the same time they have presented to them, coming up from below, a very large menu of suggestions for 'product improvement' in a very wide range of weapons.

The process of the development of any particular weapon can be, in a certain sense, self-propelled and independent of any actual observation of what a potential enemy might be doing. Once a new weapon has been developed, it is automatically assumed that a potential enemy will get to work on counter-measures, so the best thing to do is to begin work at a very early stage on the next generation of that weapon. This process can continue without any hard information that the potential enemy is doing anything at all.

There is a current example in cruise missile development. The head of R&D & Acquisition for the United States Air Force, Lt. Gen. Kelly H. Burke, says that he expects that some of the Soviet defences against the cruise missile will become effective "by the end of the eighties". To counter the expected Soviet cruise missile defence effort, the Air Force has an advanced cruise missile technology programme "which begins to look toward what a second generation cruise missile would look like, to be able to cope with what we would expect in the reactive threat from the Soviet Union" [2]. (Note the use of the word "threat" to describe the development of a cruise missile defence effort.)

These institutional structures and these habits of mind lead inevitably to a technological arms race, and that in turn means that the military are pushing against the limits of virtually any military budget, however generously it might have been set. The rapid rate of technological advance in the military sector is a very strong force pushing up military budgets in real terms—that is, in terms of the real civil resources which are forgone.

This phenomenon—the fact that the rate of technological change in the military sector far exceeds the rate in the civil sector—can be documented in a number of ways. One way is to look at the figures of research and development (R&D) input, per unit of output, in the two sectors. Table 1.1

Table 1.1. Research and development input per unit of output: civil and military sectors compared

Country	Year	Military R&D expenditure as % of value of production of military equipment	R&D expenditure as % of value of manufacturing output
FR Germany	1975–76	32	1.9
UK	1975–76	34	1.3
USA	FY 1975	43	2.3
Japan	1975	5	1.2

Sources: Research and development figures for the manufacturing sector are taken from *International Statistical Yearbook 1975* (OECD, Paris, March 1979). Values of gross output of the manufacturing sector are taken from *Statistical Yearbook 1978* (United Nations, New York, 1978).

Military R&D:

FR Germany *Die Wehrstruktur in der Bundesrepublik Deutschland* (the Wehrstruktur-Kommission together with the Government of FR Germany, Bonn, 1972/73).

UK *Research and Development Expenditure and Employment* (HMSO, London, 1976). Military R&D for the UK is intra- plus extra-mural gross expenditure on natural science R&D for defence.

USA 'US defence budget for fiscal year 1981', *International Defense Business*, January/February 1980.

Japan *Defense of Japan 1978* (Defense Agency, July 1978).

Military production:

FR Germany As above.

UK *Defence in the 1980s, Statement on the Defence Estimates 1980* (HMSO, London, April 1980). Production is acquisition of equipment only, plus net exports.

USA As above.

Japan As above.

Arms exports and imports:

FR Germany, USA and Japan *World Military Expenditures and Arms Transfers 1968–77* (ACDA, Washington, D.C., October 1979).

UK As above.

presents calculations of this kind, showing for the military sector the value of military R&D expenditure as a percentage of an estimate of the value of the production of military equipment. For the civil sector, it shows the value of R&D expenditure as a percentage of the value of manufacturing production. The military figures shown in the table have a fairly strong downward bias: published figures of military R&D will tend to understate the total, since expenditure on military R&D projects is often concealed in other parts of the national budget. By this measure of research intensity, the average military product is some 20 times as research-intensive as the average civil product.

Another way of looking at the same phenomenon is to compare the rate of increase in the costs of different types of military hardware with the general rise in prices in various countries. That also can be taken as a measure of the extent to which product improvement in the military sector exceeds that in the civil sector. To provide a civil comparison—the cost of a typical automobile has in most countries and over most periods risen more slowly than the consumer price index. Table 1.2 shows that the real cost of a typical military product, in terms of real civil resources forgone, has been rising by anything from 5 to 10 per cent a year.

As long as this rate of technological change persists, sooner or later it is bound to force up the real cost of military spending. It is not only the rapid rise in the cost of the weapons themselves; as they become more complex, the cost of maintaining them will tend to rise rapidly as well. The skills, and consequently the cost of operating the weapons, also tend to go up fast. This is one of the constant driving forces behind the rise in military expenditure in the NATO–WTO area.

The second theme, to which the Yearbook has constantly returned, is the 'presentation of the threat'. If there is no threat—actual or potential—then of course the justification for military expenditure is gone. The problem arises because the presentation of the threat is in the hands of the military sector itself (if, as seems reasonable, intelligence agencies are included in the military sector). The military sector has almost exclusive possession of the information which can be used to justify its demands. No other pressure group is in such a powerful position. If the military can make the threat appear greater and more immediate, then it is of course more likely to be successful in increasing its claim on resources. The outsider who studies the military presentation may indeed wonder whether there may not be some bias; given that he has very little independent access to the basic information, he is in a very weak position.

At the beginning of the 1970s, the 'statement of the threat' in the United States concentrated fairly heavily on the build-up of Soviet missile strength. In the second half of the 1960s, the Soviet Union had been making an enormous effort to close the gap which the United States had opened up. Between 1 October 1966 and 1 October 1968 it added 550 ICBMs to its stock. A simple way, therefore, of presenting the threat was to extrapolate the rate of increase. The US Secretary of Defense in 1969 said: "If the Soviets were to continue to deploy ICBMs at the rate they deployed them in 1967–68, they could have as many as 2 500 by the mid-1970s" [3]. Charts were presented to Congress showing linear extrapolations of the number of Soviet missiles. The same kind of exercise was conducted later in the 1970s with the Soviet launching of nuclear submarines. In 1973 a UK defence spokesman pointed out that the Soviet Union was launching one nuclear submarine every three and a half weeks—the implication being that it would continue to do so into the indefinite future.

It was in the mid-1970s that more attention began to be paid to estimates

Table 1.2. Measures of 'product improvement' in the military sector[a]

Product	Cost and date	Product	Cost and date	Annual average change in cost (%)	Annual average change in consumer prices (%)	Annual rate of 'product improvement'[a] (%)
F-104 G Starfighter	DM 5.0 mn 1965	Tornado MRCA	DM 40.3 mn 1980	15	4	10.5
Canberra medium bomber	US $0.6 mn[b] 1951	Buccaneer bomber	US $2.0 mn[b] 1962	—	—	12
Hunter fighter	US $0.8 mn[b] 1954	Jaguar fighter–bomber	US $4.0 mn[b] 1972	—	—	9
M-47 tank	DM 0.5 mn 1956	Leopard-2 tank	DM 3.8 mn 1980	9	3	6
Morecambe bay frigate	£0.500 mn 1949	Ariadne frigate	£7.403 mn 1973	12	4	8
Defender destroyer	£2.280 mn 1952	Sheffield destroyer	£26.438 mn 1975	11	5	6

[a] The rate of 'product improvement'—or, more precisely, the extent to which the rate of product improvement in the military sector exceeds that in the civil sector—is roughly indicated by the extent to which the cost of military products rises faster than the cost of consumer products.
[b] At 1973 constant prices. Costs are SIPRI estimates of what it would have cost in 1973 to build the aircraft in the USA.

Sources: Anti-militarismus Information, Vol. 3, 1980; Kaldor, M., 'Defence cuts and the defence industry', *Military Spending and Arms Cuts* (Croom-Helm, London, 1977).

of Soviet military expenditure. The US Central Intelligence Agency's method of producing this estimate proved to be something of a free gift to those who wished to lay great stress on the Soviet threat. The CIA estimates what it would cost, in the United States and in US dollars, to reproduce the Soviet military effort. It is well known that, used by itself, this is a wholly illegitimate method of international comparison. In the Soviet Union's military sector, with a long period of conscription, military manpower is extremely cheap; the Soviet armed forces are therefore profligate with the number of men they use. When the dollar cost of Soviet military expenditure is computed, these men are valued at the high wages paid to US servicemen. This is the main reason why the CIA get their enormous dollar figure for Soviet military spending. There is no reasonable doubt that if a proper attempt were made to value US military expenditure at what it would cost the Soviet Union, in roubles, to reproduce, then the US military budget (measured in roubles) would considerably exceed the Soviet military budget. This is because the rouble cost of reproducing US advanced military technology would be very high indeed.

The CIA do indeed themselves say that dollar valuations should not be used as a measure of the relative effectiveness of US and Soviet forces. However, these qualifications are totally ignored in the use made of these figures by those who lobby for a larger military establishment. Here were simple summary figures which could be used to push home the message of the Soviet threat. Detailed comparisons of weapon systems and force levels are complex exercises, likely to bewilder both legislators and the public at large. The message that "the Soviet Union is outspending us by 50 per cent" is an apparently simple message, and it requires intricate and laborious exposition to explain why a dollar comparison of this kind is a wholly misleading figure.

The CIA presented the proponents of a massive Soviet threat with another gift, in 1976, when they raised their estimate of the share of defence in Soviet gross national product (GNP) from 6–8 per cent to 11–13 per cent. They did indeed couple this with an explanation that they had not revised their view about Soviet military programmes in any way—there was no doubling of their estimate of the rate of actual Soviet defence spending, which had not changed. What happened was that they changed their view of the efficiency of the Soviet military production sector. Previously they had credited this sector with a high degree of productive efficiency; they then came to the conclusion that it was not very efficient after all. So it was using up a much greater share of Soviet GNP than had previously been supposed.

Once again, the complex explanation of what had happened was ignored. The change clearly implies that the Soviet Union was weaker, not stronger, than previously thought, with its military sector acting as a greater burden on the civil economy. The message that reached the public, and the legislators, was the exact opposite of this—that the CIA had doubled its estimates of Soviet military expenditure. Even an ex-President of the United States, it seems, failed to understand what had happened. In his recent book, *The Real War*, Nixon writes: "In 1976 the CIA estimates of Russian military spending for 1970–75 were doubled overnight . . . When the first concrete steps towards arms control were taken, American presidents were being supplied by the CIA with figures on Russian military spending that were only half of what the agency later decided spending had been. Thanks, in part, to this intelligence blunder we will find ourselves looking down the nuclear barrel in the mid-1980s" [4]. This is an astonishing assertion for an ex-President of the United States. As President, one of his main concerns should have been to come to a correct assessment of the Soviet Union's military effort. Yet here he is saying that the US intelligence agencies doubled their estimate of Soviet military spending, when they did no such thing.

It is not only these essentially erroneous figures for the comparative *levels* of military expenditure which have been extensively used; the other comparison which turns up almost universally in threat presentations is the figure for the *rate of growth* of military expenditure, in real terms, in the two countries. Here again there is the apparent advantage of a single, simple figure comparison. As an illustration of its use, President Carter, in an interview in 1980, said: "We have a very serious concern about the build-up rate of Soviet military capability over the last 15 years. They have been increasing their expenditures for military capability at an average annual compounded rate of 3 or 4, sometimes 5 per cent; whereas up until 1977, our own nation's expenditure for defense in real terms has been going downward" [5].

First of all, this is a good example of cavalier use of figures: the average annual compounded rate over 15 years can hardly be "sometimes 5 per cent". The more important criticism of the use of these figures is that those who use them have no concept of the statistical problems of constructing a volume index for a collection of products and services where quality change is very rapid. How precisely does one measure the *volume* change in military expenditure, when an SS-20 missile replaces an SS-4? The method of estimating the volume change for military expenditure in Western countries is different from the method used for the Soviet Union. The crucial problem in constructing a volume index is to make proper allowance for quality changes. There is reason to believe that the estimates published in the West for the rise in the volume of Soviet military expenditure make considerable allowance for quality changes. On the other hand, the method used for constructing volume indices for the United States and other Western countries embodies a much less satisfactory way of taking quality change into account. Again, we have simple, appealing statistical comparisons whose statistical basis is inadequate.[1]

Here, then, in the presentation of the threat is a powerful force pushing up military expenditure in the two great power blocs. In the Western countries, information is provided; but the military sector, which is the ultimate source of the information, has a strong incentive towards bias. In the United States the presentation of the threat, helped substantially by the extensive use of misleading expenditure comparisons, has been highly effective. A poll taken in October 1980 indicated that seven US voters out of ten believed that "the United States is not keeping pace with Soviet power and influence" [6]. This is one reason why the majority of Americans are now supporting a very substantial acceleration in US military expenditures.

The position in East European countries is rather different. There is very little hard factual information about military matters in the public domain. In the one main power bloc, the public is misinformed. In the other great power bloc it is not informed at all. These are hardly the ideal conditions for effective public pressure against military competition.

III. The rest of the world

There are some countries and areas outside the two great power blocs whose trends in military expenditure are, in one way or another, closely related to those in NATO or the WTO.

The neutral and non-aligned countries in Europe obviously react to the state of tension in Europe, and to the trends in military expenditure on either side of the dividing line between East and West. Their expenditure has moved up fairly much in line with that of European NATO and WTO, taken together. Since the break with the Soviet Union at the end of the 1950s, China has considered itself (rightly or wrongly) predominantly threatened by the Soviet Union, and—latterly—by Viet Nam's moves to control Indo-China.

Japan's position in the matter of military expenditure has changed somewhat in the past decade. The share of the Japanese national product devoted to military purposes has always been very low—with great

[1] The CIA volume estimates of Soviet military expenditure are built up from figures for actual production runs of different items of equipment; when there is a quality change, then full allowance is probably made for it. The estimates of volume changes for military expenditure in Western countries are obtained by dividing military expenditure figures, at current prices, by price indices. Price indices are notoriously bad at incorporating the effects of quality changes, and as a consequence normally tend to overstate the 'quality-corrected' price rise. This method therefore will tend to have prices rising too fast, and volume figures consequently rising too slowly.

advantage to its economic stature. However, through the 1970s there have been changes. First, Japan has come under increasing pressure from the United States to shoulder more of the burden of countering the Soviet military deployment in the Far East; indeed, latterly, it seems that a trade has been suggested—the United States would refrain from putting up further barriers against Japanese exports if Japan's military effort were intensified. There has in any case in Japan itself been some move away from an essentially non-military stance. With the Soviet military assistance to Viet Nam, and Soviet refusal to discuss the return of territory ceded to the Soviet Union after World War II, Japanese defence White Papers have begun to stress the Soviet threat. Although as yet the share of military spending in the Japanese national product has stayed very low, the rise in that national product has been such that the Japanese military budget is now the seventh largest in the world. Japan, however (see table 1.1), has not yet entered on its own account into the technological arms race to any significant extent: Japanese military R&D expenditure is still very small.

Australia and New Zealand have been linked in a military alliance with the United States since the beginning of the 1950s; both countries assisted the USA in Viet Nam. Their defence systems have become increasingly integrated into the US Pacific defence system. However, so far as military expenditure is concerned, both countries were fairly passive partners during the 1970s; in real terms, their military spending did not rise significantly.

It has been a common observation throughout the past decade that military expenditure in Third World countries, although very small by comparison with that of the great powers, has been rising relatively fast. As a proportion of the total, it has risen from 8 per cent in 1970 to 15 per cent in 1979. The figures for Third World countries have, admittedly, a high margin of error; the margin of error, however, is not such as to invalidate this general conclusion—that in Third World countries as a whole, military expenditure has been rising rapidly.

The forces making for rapidly rising military expenditure in Third World countries are rather different from those in the Northern industrial world. First of all there are the conflict areas: some (like North and South Korea) the result of the temporary arrangements rapidly reached at the end of World War II; others the consequence of boundaries hastily and arbitrarily drawn in the colonial period. In many of these areas, military expenditure would probably have risen fast even without the intervention of the great powers. However, in most of these potential conflict areas the great powers have intervened, supporting one side or the other with training and with supplies of arms. This second force has radically changed the nature of the potential conflicts, and changed the pattern of military spending. The third force is simply the desire of newly independent nations to build up their armed forces; armed forces are generally regarded as one of the symbols of statehood and they can be used as a unifying force in countries troubled by tribal divisions. Fourth, in countries with military or quasi-military regimes, the military rulers will naturally ensure that the armed forces (on which they rely for maintaining power) are well supplied and well paid. Their position is much like that of the later Roman emperors, who knew that they would stay in power only so long as they had the loyalty of the legions, and that loyalty would remain only so long as the legions were well paid. Finally, the enormous increase in wealth of the Middle East countries members of OPEC since the quadrupling of oil prices in 1973–74 must be regarded as an independent factor. Most of the states which received large increases in their income since 1973 have spent a significant proportion of that increase on weapons which the major arms suppliers were only too enthusiastic to sell.

These, then, are the various forces which we see at work in the military expenditure trends in Third World countries over the past decade—and there are indeed very few countries or areas where one or other of these forces has not been at work.

The tension between North and South Korea, each side with backing from one of the great powers, has kept military expenditure rising fast there. In the Far East, at the beginning of the 1970s US and Soviet supplies were flowing into North and South Viet Nam. However, when that war was over, the tension was not relaxed. China took the place of the United States as Viet Nam's opponent, and Viet Nam in turn set itself to establish hegemony over the area which once comprised French Indo-China. As a consequence, the neighbouring states—Thailand, Malaysia and Singapore—have also been expanding their military budgets rapidly.

In the conflict between Ethiopia and Somalia, the two great powers have, somewhat cynically, changed sides; there again, there has been a massive inflow of arms initially from the United States and then from the Soviet Union. As in the Far East, the neighbouring states have reacted to the tension by building up their own armed forces. Kenya, for example, which ten years ago had a very small military budget, has in recent years been increasing its military spending rapidly.

In Southern Africa, it is the military budget of South Africa itself which has been dominant. This has little to do with the intervention of the great powers; South Africa is arming itself against the internal and external threat caused by the existence of a white minority government.

In the Middle East, three of the factors have come together to bring about the phenomenal rise in military expenditure which is evident in the 1970s. There was the basic conflict between Israel and the Arab states, and in addition the latent conflict, which became actual at the end of the period, between Iraq and Iran over the control of their joint outlet to the sea. There is the involvement of the great powers, taking sides in the conflict between Israel and the Arab states, and supplying massive quantities of weaponry. Third, there is the oil price factor; after 1973, the oil-producing states in this region were in a position to buy virtually any non-nuclear weapons which they wanted.

In the Indian sub-continent, there is of course the long-standing hostility between India and Pakistan; there was also, at the beginning of the period, nervousness in India about China's intentions, although possibly by the end of the period this was becoming less acute. However, the general upward trend of military expenditure in this region was substantially lower than in either the Middle East or the Far East.

Finally, in Latin America border disputes between states were a relatively unimportant force in leading to increases in military spending. It was the prevalence of military or quasi-military regimes, whose main concern was the internal suppression of dissent, which was a much more important force in moving up the total of military spending in this region through the 1970s. This is a region where it is often difficult to draw a clear distinction between military forces and police forces; both are often engaged in the armed suppression of internal dissent.

IV. Economic consequences

The basic economic consequence of the militarized world in which we live is simply stated. It is a waste of the world's limited resources. If the resources of raw materials, productive capacity, and above all human skill and ingenuity which are now engaged in the world war industry were directed to civil economic ends, the effect on the living standard of the average world citizen would be profound. The diversion of intellectual effort is particularly important. In the military field, enormously complex problems have been solved; if that same intellectual effort were devoted to problems of, say, world health or world agricultural production, the results could be remarkable.

Standards of living can rise only if output rises; the rise in output normally requires an increase in productivity (output per man or woman); and behind the long rise in productivity since the Industrial Revolution lies technological advance. It stands to reason that the enormous diversion of technological expertise to military ends must be to the detriment of technological advance in the civil sector.

Further, the industrial world may be moving (for the first time) into a period when economic growth will be held back by inadequate supplies of certain primary inputs—notably energy. Military expenditure is energy-intensive; here, too, there is an obvious potential gain to the civil sector if military spending were cut back.

There is no doubt that the rate of growth of the world's output of goods and services for civil needs could be raised significantly, if the burden of military spending could be lifted. The deleterious economic consequences of military spending have been extensively documented in reports of United Nations study groups, and in the Brandt Commission (for example, references [7, 8]).

Some commentators have gone further, and have blamed military expenditure for the worsening of the economic situation both in the Western industrial world and in the Socialist countries during the last decade. This is a proposition which it is hard to sustain. The Western industrial world presented a picture of remarkable economic success from 1945 to 1973, with real growth rates in aggregate national product of 4–5 per cent a year, with an average level of unemployment in the OECD region as a whole of only about 3 per cent and with an average rate of inflation also only of the order of 3–4 per cent. Since 1973, that economic performance has deteriorated badly; the growth rate has been halved, the unemployment rate has doubled, and the rate of inflation at the end of the period in the Western industrial world as a whole was still around 10 per cent.

It does not appear valid to attribute this worsening economic performance to any change in the trend of military expenditure—for the very good reason that there has been no significant change in that trend. The reasons for the deteriorating economic performance lie elsewhere.

There is here a curious doctrinal paradox. In a number of Western countries—including the United States and Great Britain—a new conservative (or monetarist) economic doctrine has come to the fore, in policy, which lays heavy stress on excessive public expenditure, and on the size of the public sector's financial deficits, as one of the major causes of current difficulties. Yet this conservative approach to economic policy is joined—in both countries—with a policy of accelerating the increase in military spending. This produces a certain schizophrenia in public pronouncements and public policy. On the one hand, excessive public deficits are blamed both for inflation and for increasing unemployment. On the other hand, there is this strong conservative pressure for higher military spending, and we find military spokesmen claiming that increased military expenditure (which of course increases public sector deficits) will help *reduce* unemployment.

The 'excessive public expenditure' view of the causes of inflation in the Western industrial world seems difficult to sustain: it implies that it is an excessive sum total of demand in the economic system which is driving up prices. This is a proposition which it is difficult to reconcile with the rising figures of unemployment: there is no easy way of matching the proposition that demand is excessive with a doubling of unemployment in the last seven years. The alternative to the conservative (or monetarist) view, which is the Keynesian view, does not attribute the difficulties of the Western industrial world to excessive public expenditures. Indeed, at the moment Keynesians would argue that if public expenditure were increased (or if taxes were reduced) unemployment would come down, and the effect on inflation would be fairly small. However, there is of course no reason why any increase in public expenditure should be in military form: there is no shortage of social needs, in health or education.

The economic consequences of military expenditure, therefore, remain what they have been all along—an enormous waste of resources in a world where resources are limited. It is most unfortunate that the Western industrial world is now running with a substantial degree of unemployment, and that consequently military expenditure can be put forward as a way of reducing unemployment. If indeed it were the case that full employment in the Western industrial world could be brought about only by rising military expenditure, that would be a basic condemnation of the Western world's economic system. However, that is not the case.

V. The prospects for military expenditure

The prognosis for the 1980s is not good. Perhaps one way of validating this rather depressing proposition is to consider the kind of world which would make optimism about the future reasonable. It would be, first, a world in which the United States and the Soviet Union had come to some reasonably permanent agreement to moderate their military rivalry. Secondly, it would be a world in which the general acceptance of the status quo in Europe had begun to lead to some significant reductions in the massive amount of weaponry, and the massive number of armed soldiers, on either side of the border. Thirdly, it would be a world in which both NATO powers and the USSR had begun to limit the flow of arms to Third World countries. If any of these developments were in train, it could be counted a hopeful sign. There are no such hopeful signs.

So far as agreement between the United States and the Soviet Union is concerned, the lesson of the 1960s is that some kind of agreement might be possible on the basis of parity: it is not possible as a way of establishing—and, as it were, legalizing—a superior position. This lesson, it appears, is now being unlearnt; the United States, under the old and foolish rubric of 'negotiating from strength', appears to be about to try to establish once again the kind of superiority which it possessed in the 1960s. It is not likely to be successful, in that there is bound to be a Soviet response; and in any case there is no chance of successful negotiations which, as it were, freeze the Soviet Union into a position which might be regarded as permanent inferiority.

Secondly, over seven years the negotiations in Vienna about force reductions in Europe have not come near to reaching any agreement. Further, now that it is proposed to install in Western Europe medium-range nuclear missiles which could reach Soviet territory (in response, it is claimed, to the installation in the Soviet Union of the SS-20 missile and the development of the Backfire bomber), any possible agreement seems likely to have been put back even further.

Thirdly, as chapter 4 shows, the rate of increase in the flow of arms from the major industrial countries to Third World countries is not decelerating, but accelerating.

Such few signs of optimism as there may be are not to be found in the decisions of governments. They are to be found rather in the growing concern among ordinary citizens, in West European countries in particular, about the apparent drift towards war. The popular movements opposed to increased military expenditure in general, and to nuclear weapons in particular, have grown in importance in recent years. This is the one sign of hope.

References

1. *USA Bulletin*, United States Information Services, 19 September 1967.
2. *Soviet Aerospace*, 21 December 1980, p. 121.
3. *Safeguard Antiballistic Missile System*, Hearings before a Subcommittee of the Committee on Appropriations, House of Representatives, 91st Congress, first session (US Government Printing Office, Washington, D.C., 22 May 1969).
4. Nixon, R. M., *The Real War* (Warner Books, New York, 1980).
5. *Baltimore Sun*, 14 October 1980.
6. *Newsweek*, 27 October 1980, pp. 48–50.
7. *Economic and Social Consequences of the Armaments Race and its Extremely Harmful Effects on World Peace and Security* (UN, New York, 1971).
8. *North–South, A Program for Survival*, A Report of the Independent Commission on International Development Issues under the Chairmanship of Willy Brandt (MIT Press, Cambridge, Mass., 1980).

2. The evolution of military technology and deterrence strategy

Square-bracketed numbers, thus [1], *refer to the list of references on page 63.*

I. Introduction

The purpose of this chapter is to examine the technological developments in strategic weaponry which occurred in the 1970s and to ask what effect these have had on the concept of deterrence.

This concept has clearly undergone changes over the past two decades which have made it fundamentally different from the originally simple, defensive form it assumed in the 1950s. It can in fact be argued that the strategies of flexible counterforce and extended deterrence which have now evolved are hardly distinguishable from the coercive strategies of threat and counterthreat which have characterized the politics of the industrialized world for over a century. It would seem that both the purpose and effect of military technological efforts since 1945 have been to overcome the notions that nuclear weapons are unusable and that nuclear war is unthinkable. The 1970s in particular have produced technological solutions to many of the limitations which in past years have inhibited national leaders from using nuclear weapons as instruments of political coercion and military power.

A parallel theme will consider whether these developments have been the result of rational decisions and conscious intention or instead are the product of uncontrolled technology or bureaucratic momentum. The evidence favours the conclusion that most of the developments have been pursued consciously and rationally by decision makers who were aware of the probable consequences of their decisions. An analogy can be drawn between the logic of escalation in the strategic arms race and the US escalation strategy in Viet Nam. In this analogy the bureaucratic–technological 'system' can be seen to be working reasonably effectively in pursuing policies which promise nothing but an open-ended commitment to unattainable goals.

It is possible to identify three axioms which seem to underlie the arms race and to be accepted by all participants in it, as well as most of those in the arms control community who are trying to stop it (see section V). As long as these axioms remain unquestioned, the arms race will most likely continue in more or less its current form. It is therefore possible to suggest some extrapolations of technology and doctrine into the 1980s and derive some implications for the future of arms control efforts.

II. Developments in counterforce technology

The significance of the many innovations of the past decade can be clarified if they are placed in the context of a strategic counterforce posture. Such a posture contemplates a wide range of strategic options: from the capability to carry out a massive, pre-emptive first strike down to lesser capabilities to carry out limited nuclear wars or credibly threaten to do so.

The requirements for a pre-emptive first strike are stringent. Most of an enemy's retaliatory capability must be destroyed quickly, efficiently and without warning. This requires offensive weapons which either reach their targets very quickly or can approach their targets without detection. It requires highly accurate and reliable weapons which possess a high one-shot kill probability. It requires a wide variety of weapons, since the retaliatory systems also represent a wide variety, ranging from stationary, well-hardened missile silos, through bombers held on quick alert status, to missile submarines roaming freely over wide and deep volumes of ocean. It requires extensive reconnaissance, surveillance and communications facilities for assessing the success of the attack and rapid retargeting of weapons for subsequent strikes. No first strike could possibly be 100 per cent effective, so preparations must be made for defence of both military and civilian targets against those retaliatory forces which do remain and for the mitigation of damage resulting from those weapons which do reach their targets. This implies a need for survivable and reliable communications, active and passive defence systems, and a preparation of the population for evacuation, shelter and post-war recovery.

For the fighting of limited nuclear wars most of these same capabilities are needed, but depending on the length and scope of the contemplated war they would not necessarily all be needed at the same time or in the same quantities. Minimal requirements are weapons which are reliable, accurate and survivable; command, control and communications networks which are efficient, accurate and redundant; anti-submarine weapons capable of neutralizing missile submarines; and defensive systems to protect military installations. Protection of cities and civilian populations may be desirable, but if it is genuinely believed that the mutual self-interest and rationality of the adversaries can be counted on to preserve a 'no-cities' understanding (either tacit or explicit), then this protection can be less extensive and primarily passive (e.g., fall-out shelters but no massive evacuations or area-defence anti-ballistic missile systems).

The requirements for pre-emptive strikes or flexible counterforce options should be kept in mind during the following review of the technological developments of the 1970s and the research and development prospects for the 1980s. Not all aspects of the posture have been pursued with the same intensity or success, and relative emphasis on various aspects differs between the USA and the USSR. But the patterns of technological progress over the past decade are consistent with a deliberate development of counterforce capabilities on both sides.

Accuracy and lethality of nuclear weapons

Table 2.1 summarizes the quantitative comparison between the US and Soviet strategic nuclear arsenals over the decade of the 1970s. The major quantitative changes which have occurred are the substantial increases in the numbers of Soviet submarine-launched ballistic missiles (SLBMs) (mainly resulting from the steady deployment of the Delta-class missile submarine), and the enormous increases in the numbers of deliverable warheads on both sides resulting from the installation of multiple independently targetable re-entry vehicles (MIRVs) on both land-based missiles (ICBMs) and SLBMs.

Table 2.1. US and Soviet nuclear arsenals, 1970 and 1980

	1970	1980
ICBMs		
USA	1 054	1 052
USSR	1 487	1 398
SLBMs		
USA	656	576
USSR	248	950
Long-range bombers		
USA	512	348
USSR	156	156
Total warheads		
USA	4 000	9 200
USSR	1 800	6 000

Sources: SIPRI Yearbooks 1979, p. 422, and *1981*, p. 273.

The history of warhead deployment shows a levelling off of US numbers toward the end of the decade (MIRV deployment on Minuteman III was completed in 1975 and on Poseidon in 1978) but a continuing upward trend in Soviet deployments as heavily MIRVed SS-18 and SS-19 missiles replace older versions and as more and more SS-N-18 SLBMs go to sea on Delta III-class submarines.

These numbers, both in their absolute magnitudes and in their rates of change, are disturbing enough in themselves, but even more disturbing are the changes that have occurred in the past 10 years in the capabilities of these weapons. Large numbers of weapons might with some justice still be thought of as contributing to a deterrence strategy, but this rationalization rapidly evaporates when one examines the refinements which have been made possible by technological progress in the 1970s.

The first is accuracy. In 1972 the best US missiles had circular error probabilities (CEPs) of about 500 metres, and the best Soviet missiles were under 1 500 metres [1]. These accuracies could be achieved only from fixed, land-based launching sites, and submarine-launched missiles had substantially lower accuracies. Even an optimistic assessment of the hard-target counterforce capabilities of the USA in 1970 would have found the ICBMs only marginally effective and the SLBMs far less so. The Soviet Union could not have been considered to possess any significant hard-target potential at all.

At the end of the 1970s the situation had changed considerably, with US installation of the NS-20 guidance system on the Minuteman III, reducing the CEP to 200 metres [2a]. This increase in accuracy, coupled with design improvements which have more than doubled the yield of the warhead, have increased the single-shot kill probability against a well hardened (1 000 p.s.i.) Soviet missile silo to 80 per cent.

Evidence on the accuracies of Soviet missiles is available only from Western sources, which have been known to exaggerate Soviet capabilities. However, a CEP comparable to that of the Minuteman III has been attributed to the Soviet SS-18 [3], and the question of whether or not this number is accurate seems less important than the evidence that the Soviet Union has significantly improved the accuracy of its missiles since 1970. There is no reason to doubt either the intention or capability of the USSR to make further improvements in the 1980s.

The problem of making long-range ballistic missiles more and more accurate has been a major preoccupation of military scientists and engineers since World War II, but the most dramatic and strategically significant progress has occurred in the 1970s. Intensive efforts to achieve greater accuracies were well under way already in 1970 when General Ryan, Chief of Staff of the US Air Force, was quoted as saying: "We have a programme we are pushing to increase the yield of our warheads and decrease the circular error probable, so that we have what we call a hard-target killer, which we do not have in the inventory at the present time" [4]. This statement was quickly repudiated by President Nixon, who denied that such a programme was in existence. However, subsequent years have shown that General Ryan's statement was correct.

Improvements in accuracy have required technological advances in all of the following areas: (*a*) precision mapping of both missile launching sites and targets; (*b*) improved guidance systems, which not only utilize highly sophisticated guidance technology, but also benefit from extremely accurate mapping of the Earth's gravitational field; (*c*) improvements in re-entry vehicle design to decrease the disturbing effects of re-entry and local weather conditions; and (*d*) terminal guidance systems which are intended for the next generation of warheads, and which promise both to increase accuracy and to make defence more difficult.

Precision location of launch points and targets has been achieved through satellite mapping, in the case of land-based missiles, and greatly improved inertial navigation systems and radio navigation aids for submarines [2b]. New electrostatically supported gyroscopic monitors can permit a submarine to navigate accurately while submerged for several weeks, thereby improving survivability. If extremely accurate fixes are needed, the submarine can determine its position within an accuracy of about 15 metres using the Loran-C radio navigation system. It has also been suggested that Soviet submarines may be using the US Loran-C system for their own navigation [2c].

Improvements in guidance systems have resulted from better designs in missile inertial guidance and from the use of satellite and astronomical navigational aids. The US Global Positioning System is evolving into the NAVSTAR system which will by the mid-1980s consist of 18 satellites in three rings at altitudes of 20 000 kilometres [5]. This system, along with the Stellar Inertial Guidance System which has been developed for the Trident SLBM, can provide extremely precise guidance information to both land-based and sea-based missiles as well as the MIRV 'buses' which carry the warheads through space [6].

The 1970s have also seen the development and deployment of re-entry vehicles which can be much better controlled in their trajectory towards the target, and tests are well advanced on manoeuvrable re-entry vehicles equipped with terminal guidance systems. These use any of a number of possible terrain-matching or map-recognition systems which could lead to accuracies of well under 100 metres [7].

All of these developments have removed the single most important technological obstacle which prevented the use of strategic nuclear weapons against hardened targets in 1970. Improvements in accuracy have now given military leaders more confidence that they can select and destroy well-protected targets at long range with 'surgical' precision.

Anti-submarine warfare (ASW)

If a credible threat to fight a nuclear war is to be maintained, then something must be done to neutralize an enemy's missile-launching submarines. Since each submarine carries between 12 and 24 long-range missiles, and since each missile can deliver anywhere from 3 to 14 accurate, independently targetable warheads, it is clear that even one submarine represents what most people would consider an effective deterrent capability. But one or a small number of submarines would not be effective

Figure 2.1. A Soviet Backfire bomber, as photographed over the Baltic Sea by a Swedish aircraft

Swedish Air Force, first published in FLYGvapenNytt, *No. 2, 1980*

Pershing II. However, doubt concerning the validity of this justification has come from two directions: one asserting that the capabilities of the SS-20 are considerably less spectacular than has been advertised [12] and the other suggesting that the development of strategic counterforce weapons by the US Army has been motivated by military and bureaucratic concerns quite detached from any demonstrated or projected Soviet capabilities [13].

The Pershing II is a product of a number of technological advances, including more rapid means of targeting and launching and a highly accurate, terminally guided warhead. The latter also possesses an earth penetrator capability making it useful for attacks on hardened targets while minimizing collateral damage [14].

The long-range cruise missile in its various forms (air-, sea-, and ground-launched) certainly represents one of the major technological developments of the 1970s. In this system at least three strands of technological development have come together to produce a system which can greatly enhance the counterforce and war-fighting capabilities of any nation which possesses it. Advances in jet engine technology produced small, lightweight and highly efficient engines. More energetic liquid fuels allowed for more payload and longer range in a small missile. And solid-state electronics led to new guidance and control systems which substantially increase the accuracy, reliability and versatility of the missile [7].

The role of the cruise missile in the strategic counterforce strategies of the USA and the USSR is not yet clear. The relatively slow speed of the missile reduces its effectiveness as a surprise first-strike weapon. However, its ability to evade defensive radars, its relatively low cost, which allows for the stockpiling of large numbers, and above all its exceptionally high accuracy suggest that it is intended to play an important role in limited nuclear war.

However, it would be premature to discount the full strategic counterforce implications of the long-range cruise missile. The high accuracy and mobility of cruise missiles and their ability to confuse and overwhelm defences suggest that they could play an important role in a first strike if they could be launched reasonably close to their targets, and if their launching could be co-ordinated with strikes by long-range missiles in such a way as to bring them all to their targets within a relatively short time. Such co-ordination is a problem for command and control systems, discussed in section V. The usefulness of the cruise missile as a strategic first-strike weapon could be enhanced if its flight time to the target could be substantially reduced. This could be achieved by making much faster (supersonic) cruise missiles; research and development on such a system, the Martin-Marietta ASALM, is under way in the USA [15a]. However, the same result could be achieved if existing subsonic cruise missiles could be brought within close range of their targets without being detected. This seems to be the most ominous implication of the new 'stealth' technologies, which purport to make aircraft much more difficult to detect with existing radar or infra-red warning systems.

The full significance of the development of stealth technologies remains to be analysed, but an example of military thinking about it is seen in the title of a recent article in a military publication which hails the arrival of "virtually invisible aircraft" [16].

Dr Harold Brown, US Secretary of Defense, has been quoted in a slightly less euphoric tone: "Dr Brown conceded . . . that in the strict sense of the word these stealth technologies don't result in an 'invisible airplane', adding that the Soviets would be able to know that it was coming, 'but too late to intercept you' " [17].

It is difficult to distinguish the hard facts from the self-serving promotion and election-year politics of the claims made for these developments, but if there is a reasonable measure of truth in them, then technological progress has made a major step in restoring to manned aircraft the counter-force role they seemed to have lost in the missile age.

Anti-satellite technologies

A wide range of military activities in space contribute to the capacity to fight wars, whether conventional or nuclear. Most of these have been reviewed elsewhere [18], so in the interest of brevity only anti-satellite technologies (ASAT) will be discussed here.

Anti-satellite warfare presents a set of problems which are in some degree the opposite of those in anti-submarine warfare. In the latter the major problem is detection and tracking, after which destruction is relatively easy. In the former the detection and tracking of satellites are not difficult, but attacking them presents severe problems, especially if it must be done quickly and in co-ordination with other military manoeuvres.

Efforts to solve these problems have been going on for many years. For example, in 1969 the US Secretary of Defense testified: "As described in previous years, we have a capability to intercept and destroy hostile satellites within certain ranges. The capability will be maintained throughout the program period [1970–74]" [19a]. This assertion was based on the rather limited experience gained from a direct-ascent ASAT missile tested at Johnston Island in the 1960s. The knowledge gained from this programme and the SAINT programme, which experimented with orbital rendezvous tactics, seems to have convinced the United States that direct-ascent methods are more promising. Current efforts are to produce an air-launched ASAT interceptor with a non-nuclear kill mechanism guided to its target by a long-wavelength infra-red homing device [15b]. Meanwhile the Soviet Union seems to have opted for the orbital rendezvous technique, and the 1970s have witnessed a revival in Soviet testing of such systems [18a].

A particularly interesting ramification of the search for anti-satellite technologies has been the continuous progress towards anti-ballistic missile (ABM) systems. Indeed the similarities between many aspects of the two missions, especially in the US direct-ascent systems, suggest that the capabilities are being developed in parallel. ABM deployment was prohibited by the SALT I Agreements, but research and development have continued, and as the 1970s drew to a close, there was renewed interest in exploiting new technological developments (particularly in electronics and data-processing) for a revival of ABM development [20].

There has been much discussion in the latter part of the decade of new developments in high-energy lasers (HEL) and particle beam weapons. This has led many people to believe that these technologies are already well along in development, but a closer examination shows this to be only partially true. Particle beam weapons may or may not show promise of ultimate usefulness, but in any event much work remains to be done before they could become operational systems [21]. However, high-energy lasers have already been shown capable of delivering energy with sufficient accuracy and concentration to destroy both aircraft and missiles in flight. And there is no question of their ability to disable many types of satellite [2f].

Command, control, communications and intelligence (C^3I)

As impressive as each of the previously described systems may sound, none of them is sufficient to threaten a first strike against a nation with as varied and sophisticated a deterrent capability as the United States or the Soviet Union. Only a massive and carefully co-ordinated employment of the full range of these systems (listed at the beginning of this section) would even begin to fulfil the stringent conditions for such a strike. Only with a highly sophisticated, redundant and flexible C^3I system could such co-ordination be achieved. Indeed, such a system would also be the essential cornerstone of any nuclear war-fighting strategy, no matter how 'limited'.

Any war creates endless opportunities for mistakes, miscalculations and misapprehensions, but the stakes involved in containing any limited nuclear conflict would be far larger than those of past wars. A nation entering a nuclear war with any confidence of confining its scope to limited objectives would require considerable confidence that weapons would be delivered to intended targets and not to unintended targets, that close control could be maintained over all forces in the field, that rapid and reliable damage assessment of both the enemy's and one's own forces could be maintained, and that channels of communication to the enemy were always open to the rapid transmission of accurate and unambiguous messages.

The most significant technological progress of the 1970s has taken place in two areas essential to the execution of these missions. The first is the development of 'packet-switching' techniques for handling the vast amounts of information which must be gathered from sensors and other devices. Enormous quantities of data must be quickly transmitted to computers for processing, so that tactical decisions can be made rapidly. This is particularly important in anti-submarine warfare, but will also be necessary for orchestrating other kinds of attack as well.

Packet-switching involves the breaking down of data into conveniently sized packages which can then be sent to their destination by the most rapid of several possible routes. The data can then be reassembled in the proper order by a computer at the receiving end [2g]. The US Navy seems to have taken the lead in developing this concept, but it is destined to be used by all of the services as strategic C^3I capabilities are integrated across service lines [22].

The second major set of technological innovations contributes to the security and reliability of communications. These are the so-called 'spread spectrum' technologies for transmitting coded messages in a form which can be both extremely difficult to jam and virtually impossible to detect by an unintended listener [23]. These concepts have actually been used for over 20 years, but only the recent development of new digital components and devices has made the techniques inexpensive enough to be considered for widespread applications.

The two developments together constitute a major step forward in the ability to carry out a counterforce attack. The vastly greater data-handling ability provided by packet-switching means that information on target location and damage assessment can be gathered, processed and evaluated much more quickly than before. The ability to transmit uninterceptable and unjammable messages will greatly increase the reliability and flexibility of control over deployed weapons.

The objective of monitoring the 'battlefield' in real time for target acquisition and identification and for damage assessment is being pursued largely by improving space-based reconnaissance systems. Steady progress was made in the 1970s in improving electromagnetic sensors for satellites, so that pictures can be obtained in both the infra-red and visible portions of the spectrum. Improved data-processing and -transmitting technologies promise much more rapid transmission and interpretation of these pictures.

The relevance of this rapid acquisition of information for tactical decision making has been enhanced by substantial improvements in the ability to retarget missiles. The early 1970s saw the introduction in the USA of the Command Data Buffer System, which allows the retargeting of land-based ICBMs in a few minutes rather than the hours or days it previously required.

Considered by themselves these developments are quite impressive, even more so when they are combined with the vast proliferation of ground-, sea- and space-based communications facilities which allow the nation which operates them to be informed rapidly and in graphic detail of militarily significant events anywhere in the world. But in the larger sense of the mission they are intended to perform, these developments fall far short of their goals. In addition, there was evidence at the end of the decade that existing systems of reconnaissance, communications and control may be far less effective than was supposed, making the distance between existing capabilities and objectives even larger.

In recent years there have been a number of surprising revelations about the inadequacies of the world-wide C^3I system employed by the US military. A prominent example of the failure of this system to operate properly was the attack by Israeli aircraft on the US ship *Liberty* during the 1967 Middle East War [24]. There have also been recent revelations of problems with US attack warning systems which seem to be prone to false alert warnings, a situation which will become progressively more dangerous as the two great powers move away from a stable deterrent posture and towards an unstable counterforce posture. Finally, there was the event of 22 September 1979 in which a US reconnaissance satellite may or may not have detected a clandestine nuclear explosion. Whether the ambiguity of this observation is largely technological or largely political remains an open question at this date. But if it is the former, then further doubt has been cast on the ability of existing (and, by implication, proposed) systems to accomplish the missions they have been designed to perform.

In addition to these problems of reliability, the problem of survivability is probably even less amenable to solution. There is an inherent 'softness' associated with C^3I facilities which, along with their absolute necessity for effective war fighting, makes them prime targets for early attack in war. This vulnerability problem is highly relevant to the deterrence counterforce question; the more vulnerable one's C^3I system is, the stronger is the incentive to strike first.

In summary, it can be said that the C^3I problem generated a great deal of technological ingenuity and creativity in the 1970s, but that the goal of reliable and survivable world-wide, real-time C^3I systems remains far from being achieved. Plans for remedying this situation are discussed below in section V.

Summary

This description of technological advances of the 1970s has considered the full spectrum of strategic weapons. It has identified a number of areas in which quite remarkable advances have taken place as well as some others in which progress has been much slower and in which significant problems remain to be solved. But whatever the variations in rates of progress, there can be no mistaking the overall direction in which progress on both sides is moving: towards ever more sophisticated, flexible and accurate weapon systems, designed and deployed for the purpose of credibly threatening, and if necessary fighting and winning, nuclear wars.

For many years each new system and each new capability were advertised as enhancing deterrence. Over the years this emphasis on deterrence in public statements has evolved into a combined emphasis on deterrence plus 'second-strike counterforce', where the latter is always accompanied by the reassurance that its purpose is to enhance deterrence. As the arsenals of the two great powers have grown, and as counterforce capabilities have increased relative to those necessary for deterrence, the counterforce tail has begun to wag the deterrence dog. Yet the world is still assured that the purpose of counterforce capabilities is to enhance deterrence.

It seems clear that the concept of deterrence has been stretched far beyond the meaning it once had, and beyond the meaning it still has in the minds of many people. The essentially defensive connotation of the concept has for many years served as a useful cover for essentially offensive purposes. The military leaders of both great powers have always advocated, and have generally succeeded in, integrating nuclear weapons into traditional conceptions of the uses of military force. Obviously this includes defensive as well as offensive uses, but there has never been any question in military minds that the balance should lean as far to the offensive side as technology would permit. Civilian leaders have approached the issue more cautiously, but with only one or two possible exceptions they have also understood and supported development of nuclear weapons as politically usable instruments.

Only in the arms control community has the notion of a stable deterrence system exerted any lasting influence. It has been accepted by many as the only possible solution to the problem of living with nuclear weapons in a world divided by conflict. It is seen as an evil, but as the least evil alternative one can realistically hope for. But after 35 years of failure in achieving this limited objective, there would seem to be ample justification for a searching reexamination of this concept. The possibility must be considered that deterrence died long ago, and that all the effort which is going into keeping it breathing by artificial means might be better exerted in other directions.

III. The impact on deterrence

What is deterrence?

A strategic policy of deterrence is one of hindering or discouraging other nations by means of credible threats.

The popular conception of deterrence remains fundamentally defensive in character. It has been reinforced in many ways by many writers, but one statement of the doctrine stands out as historically significant:

> The way to deter aggression is for the free community to be willing and able to respond vigorously at places and with means of its own choosing. . . . to depend primarily on a great capacity to retaliate instantly, by means and at places of our choosing. [25]

This statement implies a defensive posture, based on threats of retaliation and punishment. In modern systems jargon it specifies a way of ensuring that the enemy's cost–benefit analysis always comes out negative when he considers an aggressive move. It is not difficult to find similar statements on the Soviet side: "If, however, the aggressive circles, relying on atomic weapons, should decide on madness and seek to test the strength and might of the Soviet Union, then it cannot be doubted that the aggressor would be crushed by that very weapon . . ." [26a].

These statements leave no doubt that deterrence is a system based on threat. But to understand what has happened to the concept of deterrence since Dulles and Malenkov made these statements in 1954, it is essential to understand the dual nature of threats. Threat can be used for both defensive and offensive purposes; it can be deterrent or coercive.

The ambiguities and intricacies of this connection, and the ramifications of a strategy based on threats, have been thoroughly explored by Thomas Schelling. He points out that "violence is most purposive and most successful when it is threatened and not used" [27a]. And to make a threat effective "one needs to know what the adversary treasures and what scares him and one needs the adversary to understand what behavior of his will cause the violence to be inflicted and what will cause it to be withheld" [27b].

It is in this context that the modern concept of deterrence must be understood. The development of modern nuclear weapons and the systems needed to deliver them cannot be explained if one insists on defining deterrence in an essentially defensive and reactive form. Instead, the modern concept of deterrence has evolved into something much closer to the traditional understanding of the role of military force in the pursuit of national objectives. Deterrence is now seen as 'flexible' or 'extended', and a 'second-strike counterforce' capability is defended as part of a deterrent on the grounds that a credible (i.e., non-suicidal) response must be available if deterrence fails.

The word 'deterrence' survives even though (or perhaps because) it obscures more than it clarifies. Consider, for example, the following definition:

> . . . it is a fairly safe prediction that from now on neither side will be able seriously convincingly to use for political ends threats of strategic nuclear attack, or anything that in scale is even close to it. What one *can* threaten are lesser actions that *could* start events moving in that direction. The opponent cannot at any stage be deprived of the choice within his capabilities, of making the situation more dangerous or less so; but we can reasonably hope and expect to influence his choices appropriately. This is what we must henceforth mean by deterrence, or by containing aggression militarily. [28]

The following authors are willing to go even further, and in their words can be heard the echoes of Schelling's prescriptions reverberating without inhibition:

> the West needs to devise ways in which it can employ strategic nuclear forces coercively, while minimizing the potentially paralyzing impact of self-deterrence. U.S. strategic planning should exploit Soviet fears insofar as is feasible from the Soviet perspective . . . [29]

One final example will serve to illustrate just how broad the spectrum of definitions of deterrence has become as the 1980s begin:

> The political power of nuclear weapons is based on:
> —the yield
> —the number available
> —the number of launch vehicles and the certainty of their availability
> —hit and kill probabilities
> —the credibility of their use.
> As long as *superiority* really exists in all the parameters, the risk for the user is small and the *deterrent* concept is credible, as was demonstrated with Hiroshima and Nagasaki. [30]

These quotes represent US interpretations of deterrence. Soviet views are more difficult to ascertain, but they seem to have been much more consistent and much less ambiguous (at least on the surface) than US views. A wide range of interpreters of Soviet nuclear doctrines seem to be in essential agreement that the USSR has never made much of an intellectual effort to distinguish between the concepts of deterrence and war fighting. The Soviet Union has certainly recognized the deterrent value of its military power, but has appeared to assume that the power to deter arises ultimately out of the power to fight and win wars. Whether a

Western interpreter chooses to focus on the deterrent aspect of the war-fighting aspect seems to depend more on the political preferences of the observer than on any inherent doctrinal distinction or preference in Soviet thinking. In summary, whatever meaning the concept of deterrence may once have had in the minds of the public has been stretched beyond any recognition by the technological and doctrinal evolution of the past 20 years, most dramatically in the past 10. This raises the question of why a doctrine which seemed at one time to be the only viable solution to living with nuclear weapons in a divided world did not survive.

The contradictions of deterrence

Pure deterrence has never been practised, so in analysing its shortcomings it is necessary to deal with abstractions. The closest either the USA or the USSR ever came to adopting a pure deterrent posture occurred in the 1950s when the economic, political and technological problems associated with counterforce strategies seemed to many people to be insurmountable. This was the period in the USA during which the doctrine of massive retaliation was formulated by the Eisenhower Administration. During the same period the Soviet leadership which emerged after the death of Josef Stalin attempted to rationalize a shift in emphasis from military to civilian production by a reliance on nuclear deterrence and the mutually suicidal nature of nuclear war. The attacks which were made on these doctrines by proponents of counterforce strategies exposed many of the contradictions of deterrence, and the attacks from the other side advocating total nuclear disarmament exposed the rest.

Two of the deepest contradictions in a deterrent strategy have already been suggested by quotes in the previous section. One is the essentially defensive or reactive character of a deterrent posture, a strategy that leaves all the initiative to the adversary. It is this posture which results in the loss of any real political value in the possession of nuclear weapons; in a purely deterrent posture, nuclear weapons become useless as coercive implements.

In the United States, this criticism was well known to President Eisenhower and to Secretary of State Dulles, and it had already been the subject of much analysis and argument by the time massive retaliation was publicly enunciated. Indeed, in the very same speech, Dulles took pains to reassure his audience that the new doctrine did not abandon the initiative to the enemy:

> Now the Department of Defense and the Joint Chiefs of Staff can shape our military establishment to fit . . . *our* policy, instead of having to try to be ready to meet the enemy's many choices. That permits . . . a selection of military means instead of a multiplication of means . . . [25]

But these reassurances were not convincing, ultimately even to Dulles himself, who changed his position substantially in 1957:

> . . . the resourcefulness of those who serve our nation in the field of science and weapon engineering now shows that it is possible to alter the character of nuclear weapons. It now seems that their use need not involve vast destruction and widespread harm to humanity. Recent tests point to the possibility of possessing nuclear weapons, the destructiveness and radiation effects of which can be substantially confined to predetermined targets. [31]

A second contradiction inherent in deterrence was suggested by the requirement that, to be deterred, the enemy must "understand what behavior of his will cause the violence to be inflicted and what will cause it to be withheld" [27a]. In other words a deterrent threat must be both unambiguous and credible. But by being explicit about just what is being deterred, and by committing himself irrevocably to carrying out the threat, a national leader has totally lost his *flexibility*, a position in which no political leader will ever willingly place himself.

The credibility criterion proved too full of logical flaws to survive analysis. Simply stated, the problem is how a nation credibly commits itself to retaliation by suicide. Attempts to resolve this problem led to some of the more bizarre proposals of the 1950s in the form of 'doomsday machines' or the holding of hostage cities in such a way that the attacked party would have no choice but to carry out the retaliation it was committed to. Early on it was recognized that by assigning the retaliatory task to computers the unpredictable factors of human fear, remorse or compassion could be eliminated.

Such proposals, by carrying the concept of deterrence to its full technological and logical implications, exposed a third contradiction in the theory: its utter moral repugnance. Naturally this contradiction was exposed more often in the beginning by advocates of disarmament than by advocates of counterforce, but the latter also have often relied on moral objections to the holding of hostages and mass murder to support their arguments for a counterforce strategy. It is a measure of the degree to which the entire spectrum of debate has shifted that advocates of disarmament now find themselves forced to defend on practical political grounds a strategy of minimal deterrence which conflicts fundamentally with their own moral convictions.

A fourth contradiction of deterrence is its effect on the morale of the political leadership, the military establishment and the civilian population. The morale of political leaders cannot help but be reduced by a policy which puts the vital issues of national security effectively beyond their control, and the morale of the civilian population must certainly be undermined by the constant threat of massive destruction against which no defence is possible—or even desirable if the doctrine is taken seriously.

But equally important would be the effect on military morale, which no political leader can take lightly.

A posture of minimal deterrence would put the military into an impossible position. It would recognize the possibility of war; indeed it postulates the predilection of one's adversary toward aggression. But it also leaves all the initiative to the adversary in deciding when, where and how the war will be fought. The doctrine would deny the possibility of defence against nuclear attack and, in effect, say to military officers: you must sit and wait for the enemy to attack first. Then you must stand by and watch while his missiles destroy your planes, ships, missiles, communications facilities, and so on. Then you must gather together what is left and send them off to kill as many defenceless civilians in his country as you can.

If one believes that there is any dignity at all in the military profession, and there certainly is a great deal, then one cannot ask a military officer to carry out such a strategy. The good ones will not do it and the incompetent and unprincipled ones will do it badly.

It is important to emphasize in this context the very real differences between a deterrent and a defensive posture. Many countries are able to maintain a credible military posture and high military morale with a strategy based entirely on the defence of the homeland against attack: Sweden, Switzerland and Japan come to mind as examples. But in these countries the soldiers know that they will be fighting other soldiers and that they will in truth be defending themselves and their country. Nuclear deterrence does not admit the possibility of defence and directs its destructive power against civilians rather than soldiers.

There is good evidence that these arguments about the impact of deterrence on military and civilian morale were instrumental in Nikita Khrushchev's successful efforts to oust Premier Malenkov and head off a Soviet minimal deterrence strategy. Khrushchev argued forcefully, and with the full support of the Soviet Army, that such a strategy would lead to "complacence" and "defeatism" and that it was essential to future Soviet foreign policy to maintain the idea that not only was defence possible but that it was also possible to win a nuclear war. But Khrushchev's early commitment to these notions was quickly followed by a return to his own version of deterrence. It cannot be determined whether this was a genuine attempt on his part to establish the doctrine or a concession to Soviet technological limitations [26b].

The final contradiction in a strategy of deterrence is its instability with regard to technological advance. A credible deterrent requires an invulnerable retaliatory striking force which can inflict 'unacceptable' damage upon an attacker even after absorbing a full first strike, whose primary purpose can only be the total destruction of the deterrent. If the attacker has also deployed active and passive defences, then the remaining retaliatory force must be large enough to carry out its mission even though further degraded by the defences.

This statement of the deterrent mission raises many more questions than it answers. What level of damage is unacceptable? How does one estimate one's own invulnerability? How effective are the enemy's defences? How big should the margin of safety be? Should a launch-on-warning option be maintained as a hedge against miscalculation? Each of these questions may have an acceptable answer at any given time, but technological advances constantly render old answers obsolete and demand new ones. The submarine deterrent which was thought to be totally invulnerable for many years now seems to be losing this invulnerability. Doubts about the survivability of communications engendered by anti-satellite technologies and the ability to make selective attacks on C^3I facilities raise questions about being able even to order, much less plan and co-ordinate, a second strike. Each new technological advance by the offence demands a response by the deterrent, so there seems to be no fixed answer to the now famous question: how much is enough? [32].

These contradictions constitute a powerful indictment against a strategy of nuclear deterrence. But if the arguments of this section are correct and deterrence is unworkable, then what are the alternatives? They are clearly either nuclear disarmament or preparation for nuclear warfare. There can be little doubt about which course the major powers of the world have chosen.

The lure of counterforce

The pursuit of a nuclear counterforce strategy derives from a continuing desire to make nuclear weapons useful as instruments of war, coupled with an understanding, either explicit or implicit, of the inadequacies of pure deterrence. So the attractions of counterforce are to some extent the mirror images of the deficiencies of deterrence, but there is a significant additional set of motivations which have to do with an undiminished belief in the utility of military force in international affairs and an unquestioned faith that the most powerful weapon ever invented must be capable of making a major contribution to this utility.

The desire to make nuclear weapons militarily useful is as old as the weapon itself. The first major doctrinal battles within the US government were being fought even as the public was adjusting to the new idea that nuclear weapons had made future wars 'unthinkable'. In fact they were as thinkable as ever, and the discussion of how nuclear weapons were to be employed quickly accommodated itself to the political environment of the US military. The battle lines were drawn between air power enthusiasts in the Air Force and the traditional Army–Navy hierarchy.

The argument was not about counterforce versus deterrence, but about different conceptions of the best counterforce applications of the new weapons. The US Air Force attempted to gain a monopoly control over nuclear weapons by stressing their usefulness in strategic attacks on the enemy heartland, while the Army emphasized their potential for battlefield use.

However ardently the US Air Force may have wished for a counterforce mission in the 1940s and 1950s, technological, economic and political constraints produced a strategic posture which looked much more like deterrence. But the deterrence doctrine was then, as it has been ever since, a doctrine of necessity, enforced more by technological constraints than by any desire to renounce counterforce as a viable military posture. The persistence of the search for a counterforce capability can be traced through all US Administrations. In the Kennedy Administration Robert McNamara promoted his 'no-cities' doctrine, and when he came to understand the technological limitations which made it unworkable, he set in motion a purposeful effort to overcome them [31]. (The evidence for this is discussed in the next section.)

Richard Nixon came to Washington advocating 'superiority' over the USSR, and the subsequent softening of this word to 'sufficiency' had more of a cosmetic than an operational significance. The leadership of Melvin Laird and James Schlesinger in the Pentagon carried on the development of counterforce capabilities, leading to a declaration of a limited options policy by Schlesinger in 1974. The Carter–Brown military policies did not change this basic thrust, and counterforce thinking, planning and weapons procurement were modified only in detail. Only the technical means of achieving the mission have been re-evaluated from time to time; the mission itself has not been questioned. There seems very little likelihood that it will be questioned by the Reagan Administration.

The Soviet Union moved along a similar course, one which may or may not have been promoted by Khrushchev in the 1950s, but which was certainly pushed by the Brezhnev–Kosygin government in the 1960s and 1970s. The Soviet pursuit of limited options cannot be inferred from their statements, and it may be that their reliance on deterrence is still heavier than that of the USA, but there is no solid evidence that this is any less a concession to technological limitations than it was for the USA. The USSR shows every sign of working to overcome these limitations and achieve a full counterforce capability.

However, it may still be possible to identify important differences between US and Soviet counterforce doctrines. The growing US emphasis on limited counterforce wars was well stated by Secretary of Defense Schlesinger in 1975:

> In answering the question "Do you think it is possible to have a limited nuclear war, just to exchange a couple of weapons?" the Secretary said "I believe so". He added it

is easier to think of the circumstances in which limited use might occur than it would be to think of a massive all-out strike against the urban industrial base of another nation, which has the capability of striking back. [33]

It is clear that a preponderance of US military and civilian strategists favour such a doctrine, but no similar tendency can be identified in Soviet strategic declarations. Instead:

Soviet military writings continue to assert that in any nuclear engagement, theater or global, Soviet nuclear forces will strike simultaneously at the strategic capabilities, political–military command infrastructure, and economic–administrative centers of the adversary. Moreover, they reveal no trace of interest in the notions of intrawar bargaining, graduated escalation, and crisis management which play a heavy role in current US strategic theorizing. [34a]

This Soviet refusal to play the controlled counterforce game is a matter of some concern to US strategists. The hope seems to be that as Soviet technology improves, Soviet military strategists will be as attracted by the virtues of this new game as are the US strategists. As two influential US analysts have argued:

Russian commentators once scoffed at the idea that there could be a substantial conflict in the NATO area that would not immediately become nuclear. After much invective on the subject, they eventually admitted the need to plan for nonnuclear engagements. For good reason, we might witness the same phenomenon with respect to other forms of limitation, for example, within nuclear conflict. Now a great deal of Soviet rhetoric flows about the absurdity of the notion of limiting the use of nuclear weapons; on the other hand there is no real evidence that the Soviets would abandon all caution in a nuclear or any other conflict. [34b]

Indeed there is "no real evidence" to support any of this theorizing, planning, procuring, deploying and posturing. The word "hope" was used above advisedly, not facetiously. The strategy of limited counterforce is built entirely on hope: hope that the weapons will work as they are supposed to, hope that control can be maintained, hope that once a war starts both sides will be able to recognize a common point at which all cost–benefit calculations balance and they can stop it, but above all hope on both sides that when 'the time comes', when 'it's eyeball to eyeball', 'they' will blink first and 'we' will win without a shot being fired. These hopes have extremely fragile foundations.

The contradictions of counterforce

An analysis of a counterforce strategy should begin with an understanding that it is not in any sense the opposite of a deterrence strategy. Deterrence always has been and is still very much a part of any war-fighting capability. However, as the capability to fight becomes more flexible, versatile and controllable, the deterrent function becomes more and more incidental to the primary function: the employment of military force for coercive ends. For example, a nation may move aggressively against the interests of another in one area, while using its military strength to deter counter-moves by the opponent in some other area. In such a situation deterrence is certainly being used, but the essential purpose is coercion.

Both civilian and military leaders recognize the advantage in being so strong that no one dares to attack or threaten their interests. But it is quite another matter to allow the deterrence to become mutual, that is, to allow others to become so strong that one is afraid to threaten or attack them. At such a point deterrence ceases to be a useful strategy.

But is an emphasis on flexible nuclear counterforce a useful strategy? The answer is almost certainly no, since such a strategy is at least as riddled with contradictions, uncertainties and even absurdities as deterrence.

The first defect in a counterforce posture is the high premium it puts on a first strike. As section II has shown, the weapons and support systems needed to carry out a flexible counterforce strategy are indistinguishable from those needed for a disarming first strike. The numbers and accuracies of weapons, the rapid acquisition of detailed intelligence, and the redundancy for assurances that the assigned mission will be accomplished are all required for both postures. So an adversary can never be certain of what is intended once the political situation has deteriorated to the point where nuclear war is imminent.

Probably the most important contributor to this instability problem is the MIRV concept, which deploys large numbers of accurate, independently targetable nuclear weapons on relatively few delivery systems. For example, each US Polaris–Poseidon submarine carries about 160 nuclear warheads, and the Trident may carry as many as 250 or more. But it takes only one weapon (not necessarily nuclear) to destroy a submarine, and if a number of submarines happen to be in port when war starts, an attacker could destroy many hundreds of warheads with one well-placed shot.

Table 2.1 has shown the relative strengths of the two sides in terms of warheads: a ratio of 9 000 to 6 000. But the high premium on a first strike is illustrated by a different ratio: the number of independently targetable warheads on one side divided by the number of militarily significant targets on the other. ("Militarily significant" is used to refer only to the retaliatory striking force.) The USA's 9 000 strategic warheads could be destroyed by only about 1 200 well-aimed Soviet warheads, while the Soviet Union could lose all their strategic nuclear weapons as the result of about 1 500 successful US shots. So the United States has six times the number of weapons necessary to destroy the Soviet deterrent, while the USSR has five times the necessary number. The calculation is complicated in the case of the USSR by US nuclear weapons deployed in Europe and Asia, but even if these are taken into account the Soviet overkill ratio is not reduced a great deal.

The significance of this ratio should not be overstressed. Obviously a disarming first strike is an enormously complicated and risky undertaking whose success depends on far more than a simple ratio of warheads to targets. But what the ratio does reveal is a growing disparity between the potential losses which will be suffered by the party which strikes first and the one which strikes second. The stability of any crisis decreases as this ratio increases, because the incentive for a first strike, or at least a launch-on-warning posture, is increased. The contradiction is clear: the more the capability for flexibility is increased by increasing the variety and reliability of possible attacks, the less amenable the psychological atmosphere will be to the calm, rational restraint required to exercise the flexibility judiciously.

The second major contradiction of a counterforce strategy is its dependence on the theory of intra-war bargaining or controlled escalation, a theory that has fundamental logical flaws. It has already been noted that "the opponent cannot at any stage be deprived of the choice within his capabilities, of making the situation more dangerous or less so" [28]. More specifically:

> It is the nature of escalation that each move passes the option to the other side, while at the same time the party which seems to be losing will be tempted to keep raising the ante. To the extent that the response to a move can be controlled, that move is probably ineffective. If the move is effective, it may not be possible to control—or accurately anticipate—the response. Once on the tiger's back we cannot be sure of picking the place to dismount. [35a]

In spite of such warnings, theories of crisis bargaining in a nuclear world continue to be fashionable and influential, especially in the United States. These theories have a superficially scientific quality which derives from their association with the quantitative analytical methods of game theory and systems analysis and their use by prestigious institutions such as the RAND Corporation.

But the apparent scientific nature of these techniques is spurious [36]. They rely totally on mechanistic or economic definitions of human rationality, which have shown only limited usefulness in predicting economic behaviour and virtually none at all in predicting political or military behaviour. It hardly needs to be added that these theories have never been tested under the pressure of nuclear warfare.

A third flaw in the logic of counterforce can be found in the requirement that the weapons used must be able to carry out their missions efficiently, reliably and quickly. No national leader would order a counterforce strike if he doubted the ability of his military forces to execute it, and in spite of remarkable progress in the capabilities of counterforce weapons, such doubts must still remain. Reminders of military and technological fallibility recur with alarming regularity, for example, the failure of the US rescue mission in Iran, and the recent revelation that for 18 months in the 1960s most of the warheads deployed on Polaris submarines were inoperative [37]. It can safely be assumed that similar problems exist on the Soviet side.

The high accuracy of missiles is essential if surgical counterforce strikes are to be carried out with economy of force and a minimum of collateral damage. All estimates of achievable accuracies are based almost entirely on information released by the US military establishment, and the very real possibility exists that this information is exaggerated. Such is the thesis of a recent article based on interviews with a number of knowledgeable former officials in the US military establishment [38a]. Although the argument is somewhat overstated (both the counterforce capabilities and the potential vulnerability of nuclear submarines are dismissed too easily), there does seem to be good reason to question the public claims for both accuracy and reliability made by the military.

Perhaps the most telling point is the fact that ICBMs have never been tested over the courses they would be expected to fly in wartime. US missiles are tested over the Pacific from California to the Marshall Islands, and Soviet missiles are shot from west of the Urals to targets on the Kamchatka Peninsula or beyond [38b]. It follows that guidance systems have all been calibrated over regions of the Earth which may have significantly different gravitational anomalies from the regions over which the missiles would fly in a real war. It is true that US and Soviet geodetic and other satellites have been engaged in mapping the gravitational field for many years, but it still requires a substantial leap of faith to believe that all that is necessary to give a missile pinpoint accuracy at a range of 10 000 km on the very first shot is to programme this information into its guidance computer.

It may be true at present that operational accuracies are significantly worse than claimed, but the problem of improving accuracy is purely technical and therefore amenable to ultimate, if not imminent, technical solution. But reliability is another matter. The history of military technology is a history of poorly designed equipment, slovenly and incompetent maintenance, and breakdowns in communication and control. In addition the stakes involved in ordering a nuclear strike, no matter how limited, are so high that it is extremely difficult to imagine a national leader making such a move unless the situation were already desperate. But if the situation is desperate, thoughts will turn to preventive and massive strikes rather than to surgical, limited strikes. Saturation is the traditional military remedy

Figure 2.2. Six unarmed MIRV warheads approaching their targets near Kwajelein Atoll in the Western Pacific Ocean. Estimates of missile accuracies are based on the results of tests such as this one

US Air Force

Figure 2.3. The military answer to doubts about bomb or missile accuracy in saturation bombing. This photograph of Dresden in 1951 shows the lingering results of such saturation bombing 6 years after it occurred

ADN-ZB

for doubts about reliability and accuracy, as was demonstrated in the bombing campaigns of World War II. It is this military imperative which invalidates all claims of superior morality for counterforce over deterrence.

This analysis of counterforce can be summarized by noting that the entire 'posture' (a word which seems particularly apt in this context) is built on weapons and theories which have never stood the test of empirical verification under the conditions in which they will have to be employed. Generals have been accused with considerable condescension of always preparing to fight the last war. However, now that that conservative mould has been broken, preparations are being made to fight a war in which the old process of learning by trial and error is unacceptable. This is certainly one of the major reasons why nuclear weapons have not been used since Nagasaki, over 35 years ago. As time passes this non-use precedent grows stronger and presents even greater obstacles to the plans of military leaders for controlled use of nuclear weapons. It is an essential part of the 'self-deterrence' which most of the world finds comforting, but which many analysts find inconvenient.

IV. Technology and doctrine

Is technology out of control?

The previous two sections have described an intense and enormously expensive programme to develop new technologies whose purposes are to implement strategic theories which possess neither empirical nor logical validity. How can such behaviour be explained?

It is convenient for the purposes of this discussion to organize efforts to explain this phenomenon into two categories: those which see technology as determining doctrine and those which have doctrine determining technology. The first sees technology (in particular military technology) as progressing according to its own dynamical laws, which have at some time in the past escaped from human control [39, 40]. Human institutions in this model are hardly more than mechanisms for adapting to the dynamics of technology, and in this context strategic doctrines must all be seen as doctrines of necessity, dictated by the availability and imperatives of technology rather than by autonomous human intentions.

The second class of explanations sees human beings and their institutions as being in control of technology, but within this class of theories there is a wide divergence of opinion as to *which* human beings or institutions are in control [41]. One variant of this class will be examined in the next section. This section will consider the proposition that the arms race is a product of science and technology out of control.

This theory has many advocates, and one of the latest and most prestigious of them is the Group of Experts who have studied the nuclear arms race for the United Nations.

The development of nuclear weapon technology has created an important dimension to the arms race. It is clear that in many cases technology dictates policy instead of serving it and that new weapons systems frequently emerge not because of any military or security requirement but because of the sheer momentum of the technological process. In particular, the successively enhanced accuracy of the strategic delivery systems fuels the arms race by creating a duelling situation between these systems. This general trend, that technology rather than policy leads, carries with it an intrinsic danger. Technology by itself is blind to the dangers of the arms race; it leads to wherever the principles of science and engineering may carry. In this situation it is imperative that statesmen and political leaders accept their responsibility. If they do not, the arms race is certain to go out of control. [42]

Here there is a suggestion that application of responsibility might bring technology under control, but there are others who are not even this optimistic: "The unremitting buildup of the atomic arsenal represents just another example of the technological imperative—when technology beckons, men are helpless" [43].

This theme is not confined to the arms control community, but also plays an important role in the arguments of many counterforce advocates. For example:

In any case, these developments are not at all likely to be stopped. The technologies of information processing are pervasive in industrialized societies; many of these developments are being fostered by applications in the civil sector, and they will diffuse among advanced industrial states. [34c]

Even the popular media find the concept of uncontrolled technology attractive. In a recent US television documentary on the MX missile the narrator stated:

But the real author of this scenario is technology. Simply by the momentum of technology we have been conducted to a new level of uncertainty and danger. . . . Will we ever be able to wrest back our destiny from this blind propulsion of technology? [44]

Many more examples could be found of the widespread currency of the idea that technology, and in particular military technology, is out of control. However, it will be sufficient here to use just one more, both to illustrate the almost unconscious acceptance of this idea and to serve as a point of departure for a critique of it. In an analysis of two disarmament scenarios and their verification requirements the author adopts the following procedure:

In order to indicate the role of military technology, which is a factor of special significance during strategic disarmament, two scenarios were designed; one where technology is *kept frozen* during the process of disarmament; and the other where technology is *allowed to develop unhindered.* [45]

In the context defined by these models it is impossible to understand why the governments of the world have invested incredibly vast sums of money and enormous quantities of scientific, engineering and managerial talent in military research and development over the past 40 years. Why is all of this expenditure of money, resources and talent necessary to maintain the 'momentum' of something which if not frozen will develop unhindered?

The need for lavish governmental financial support of science and technology is clear: "None of the support of basic science by defense ministries is accidental. It is quite rational and purposeful, and its aim is not primarily the support of scientific research *per se*. It must, however, feed the goose to obtain the golden egg" [46a].

That the goose would have to be fed, and fed well, was recognized even before the greatest golden egg of all was laid at Alamogordo in July of 1945. For example, Vannevar Bush, Director of the Office of Scientific Research and Development under President Franklin Roosevelt, wrote a report in July 1945 which outlined a programme for a revolutionary change in the relationship between the US government and science and technology. As far as military R&D was concerned: "There must be more—and more adequate—military research in peacetime. It is essential that the civilian scientists continue in peacetime some portion of those contributions to national security which they have made so effectively during the war" [47]. Military leaders came to the same conclusion. General Dwight D. Eisenhower, then Chief of Staff of the US Army, recognized the need for close co-operation between the military and civilian scientists and engineers:

> The armed forces could not have won the war alone. Scientists and businessmen contributed techniques and weapons which enabled us to outwit and overwhelm the enemy. . . . In the interest of cultivating to the utmost the integration of civilian and military resources and of securing the most effective unified direction of our research and development activities, this responsibility is being consolidated in a separate section on the highest War Department level. [48]

These two people, in positions of substantial power in the United States, obviously did not believe that technology was autonomous or unmanageable. But perhaps they wrote too early in the process; perhaps it was the enormous impetus they and their colleagues gave to science and technology in the 1940s which created the 'momentum' of today. It is possible to imagine a system which begins under political control but becomes so large and ramified that it ultimately comes to dominate those who are supposed to control it. But if this was the case it must surely have happened by 1973, by which time many observers had already called attention to the phenomenon.

How then can one account for the following concerns expressed by a prominent scientist and administrator in 1973?

What are the steps that should be taken to acquire the technological strength needed to stabilize international security?

To be most effective, we believe R&D requires more vigorous action in at least five major areas: strategic planning, tactical needs, technology base, prototypes, testing. [49]

These words were written at a time when US public sentiment against the war in Viet Nam had given rise to a more sceptical attitude toward military expansion, resulting most prominently in the defeat of the ABM system. In this environment military technology did not seem to many policy-makers to be a Juggernaut out of control. Quite the contrary, it seemed to be winding down for lack of support, both from the public as represented in Congress and from the scientific and technical communities, in particular the academic scientists.

The above is an example of an attitude at least as prevalent as the notion of technological determinism, that is, the concern that innovation is either slowing down or misdirected. Instead of the image of a car on a steep hill which will accelerate out of control if the brakes are not applied, such concerns suggest a sailing-ship which will change direction with shifts in the wind and even find itself becalmed if the wind stops blowing altogether.

This second image seems much more accurately to convey the real nature of modern military technology. To conclude that technology is ungoverned or ungovernable, one must ignore or explain away not only the vast financial and human investment which is required to sustain it, but also more than two generations of intellectual effort and the creation of a massive literature, both scholarly and practical. The 'management of innovation' is now as much a part of the vocabulary of both Eastern and Western academics, bureaucrats and technocrats as are 'systems analysis' and 'technology assessment'.

In view of this it seems more promising to examine the hypothesis that technology is doing more or less what those who control its budgets want it to do. Then if this hypothesis turns out to be at variance with the evidence, one can feel more justified in moving on to the autonomous technology hypothesis.

There is not enough space here to marshal even a small portion of the evidence which supports the argument that technology is indeed under control. It will have to suffice to consider one example of a weapon system which is highly relevant to both the pursuit of a counterforce targeting doctrine and the question of political control of technology. The system is MIRV.

Herbert York, Director of Defense Research and Engineering (DDR&E) during the Eisenhower Administration, has written:

... during the development phase, the MIRV program was almost entirely technologically determined in the sense that the key decisions were made by technologists who were either attempting to solve problems posed by nature or responding to their perceptions of the technological challenges posed by the Soviet missile and space programs. [50a]

and

For all practical purposes, the decisions to deploy the two MIRVs [Minuteman and Poseidon] were inevitable consequences of the decisions to develop them. [50b]

These two statements constitute a clear example of the technological imperative at work.

Much of what York writes is certainly true, but it leaves out or de-emphasizes evidence which supports a much more purposeful interpretation of the process. In a thorough and well-documented study of the evolution of the MIRV system, Ted Greenwood has come to a different conclusion:

In that these programs did not simply move ahead propelled by their own bureaucratic momentum but were actively encouraged, fostered and supported by senior decision-makers, they provide an example of fairly successful control, in the sense of management of technological innovation. In that the systems have been deployed and that efforts to prevent deployment were unsuccessful, they provide an example of unsuccessful control, in the sense of limitation of qualitative improvements. [51a]

The most telling piece of evidence Greenwood presents in support of his conclusion is the 1964 decision to give the Poseidon MIRV a counterforce capability. He first points out that McNamara's reorganization of the Pentagon administrative system gave civilian officials much more authority to involve themselves in what had previously been considered purely military matters [51b]. He goes on to discuss the general reluctance of the US Navy to take on a counterforce mission, a stand challenged by only one office in the Navy bureaucracy, the Office of Special Projects. The Navy hierarchy was overruled when the Secretary of Defense himself intervened and ordered that accuracy improvements as well as warhead design improvements be incorporated into the new missile [51c].

Greenwood argues that "to the military . . . the important question is not *whether* to introduce technical innovations but *how to choose* from a wide assortment of possibilities, what the costs will be, and how fast to proceed" [51d]. In other words, technological momentum is taken for granted, but its magnitude and direction are not. This is the purpose of doctrine, and doctrine is the expression of political purpose. As Henry Kissinger has emphasized:

Strategic doctrine transcends the problem of selecting weapons systems. It is the mode of survival of a society. For a society is distinguished from an agglomeration of individuals through its ability to act purposefully as a unit. It achieves this by reducing most problems to a standard of average performance which enables the other members of the group to take certain patterns of behavior for granted and to plan their actions accordingly. [52]

It is remarkable how neatly and plausibly this dovetails with Greenwood's claim that

... the research scientist must anticipate future military needs and prepare the groundwork so that the need can be satisfied when recognized. Only more recently has the other side of this process been recognized, namely that in doing that the technical community can generate a requirement and sell a weapon that might otherwise have been needed only later, or not at all. [51e]

Here is an apparent concession on Greenwood's part to the autonomous technology model, and it is an important one. The R&D goose lays many golden eggs, and no doctrine is so unambiguous and all-inclusive as to dictate the proper decision on each one. Unnecessary weapons are developed and deployed, and it is undeniable that a new weapon can affect doctrines; one need look no further than the atomic bomb for an example of this. But both of these phenomena tend to be isolated events, and once they have happened either the unnecessary weapon is allowed to die a quiet, bureaucratically muffled death, or the new doctrine assumes command over the 'patterns of behaviour' of the technical community.

But the developments of the past 20 years in missile accuracy, anti-submarine warfare, anti-satellite warfare and C^3I have not been of this inadvertent or revolutionary character. They have been incremental and persistent, and the more or less steady advances in all of them can be seen as following an identifiable doctrinal path—the flexible counterforce path. Obviously it cannot be argued that all of the technological developments in these areas have been planned. There is a constant feedback between technology and policy. But this feedback has operated at the level of operational capabilities and options, not as a determinant of general strategic objectives.

It remains to ask why the concept of autonomous technology is still so widely believed by both advocates and opponents of the arms race. For the advocates the answer is easy: the idea that technology proceeds according to its own dynamics is convenient and self-serving.

The conjunction of 'progress cannot stop', and 'we do not want it to stop' is frequent and hardly accidental. The continuity, for political reasons, of the process of research–development–device procurement then itself becomes the claimed proof of the thesis that 'science can't be stopped', as if this were a somehow ordained or predetermined process ... rather than what it actually is, a well organized, and highly successful goal-oriented effort. [46b]

For advocates of arms control the explanation must be more complex and speculative, but it seems to arise out of the perennial frustration of their efforts and a certain reluctance to face political reality. The frustration is understandable; it is not surprising that people who have worked for years to stop the arms race only to see it continue to accelerate would begin to attribute their failures to 'supernatural' forces.

The reluctance to face political reality is more serious. It leads many critics of military policy into attacking symptoms of the problem rather than causes. The politically neutral plea to bring technology under control avoids confronting the real possibility that technology is being promoted and manipulated for the benefit of some groups at the expense of others. Such suggestions may be considered impolite, but it is difficult to see how they can be avoided indefinitely.

The irony of the arms race—the system works

To assert that technology is under control raises some obvious questions, in particular how, by whom, and for what purposes is it controlled? It is not possible to develop here even partial answers to these questions, even if attention were to be focused only on military technology. What will be done instead is to suggest one model which seems to offer some prospects of giving a coherent explanation of the particular phenomenon under discussion in this chapter—the strategic arms race. The model is based on an analogy between US and Soviet escalation behaviour in this race and the US policies of controlled escalation in the Indo-China War.

Two things must be kept in mind in reading what follows. First, this is an analogy and must be treated with the same caution as any analogy. It can be a useful guide to further study, but can also be misleading if pushed too far. Secondly, the choice of US policies in Indo-China as the analogue must not be interpreted as implying any judgement about who is responsible for the strategic arms race. It seems clear that the leaders of both major powers accept the basic premises of this competition, and the Soviet involvement in Afghanistan indicates that Soviet leaders may not have learned the lessons of Viet Nam any better than have US leaders.

Most analyses of the US experience in Viet Nam have seen it as a failure of the US decision-making system. Two such explanations seem analogous to the autonomous technology theory of the arms race which was discussed above. These are the 'bureaucratic politics' model and the 'slippery slope' or 'quagmire' model, both of which suggest that the apparently futile progression of escalations in Indo-China could not have been made intentionally by rational people. Each model portrays the decision makers as being carried along by forces beyond their control, that is, by bureaucratic momentum or misinformed and misguided optimism, following a course which they never would have chosen had they known how hopeless it was.

There is much evidence which contradicts these hypotheses. Leslie Gelb and Richard Betts have pointed out "that the *foreign policy* failed, but the *domestic decision making system worked.* Vietnam was not an aberration of the decision making system but a logical culmination of the principles that leaders brought with them into it" [35b].

Most of the elements of this same paradox are present in the strategic arms race. Just as no responsible US decision maker ever really believed the USA could 'win' the Indo-China War, it seems highly unlikely that any responsible US or Soviet leader believes his country can 'win' the arms race, in the sense of acquiring a credible first-strike or usable limited-options capability against the other.

Of course, there were people who believed that the USA could and should win in Viet Nam, just as there are some on both sides of the arms race who believe their country can find ways to use nuclear weapons coercively. Such people are generally contemptuous of 'artificial restraints' or 'self-deterrence' and advocate that clear objectives should be defined and that forces capable of achieving these objectives should be developed and deployed. But such strategies are both extremely dangerous and extremely costly. For example, the US leadership always feared that a truly massive escalation of the Indo-China War involving widespread bombing and possibly an invasion of North Viet Nam might bring China and/or the Soviet Union into the war. Similarly, open public advocacy and unbridled pursuit of a first-strike capability would be politically indefensible both domestically and in world opinion. And it would be enormously, even prohibitively, expensive.

So those who manage the arms race have followed the same principle as those who pursued the Indo-China War, a strategy Gelb and Betts have labelled "the minimum necessary and the maximum feasible" [35c]. This strategy is pursued by doing enough to keep the game going but not enough to win it. However, such a strategy presents problems when it comes to measuring progress:

> Administration leaders persistently failed to clarify US objectives in concrete and specific terms. Uncertainty and ambiguity in reports were therefore bound to emerge, for no one could be certain what he was measuring progress against or how victory could be defined.
>
> Indeed the direction of the curve seemed more important than the point on the curve; the sense of moving toward or away from the goals usually established the measure of improvement more than did the estimate of how much longer it would take to attain the goals. [35d]

In Viet Nam progress came to be measured in body counts, bomb tonnage dropped and numbers of pacified hamlets. In the arms race, progress is measured in terms of improvements in missile accuracies, kill probabilities, numbers of warheads, and so on. None of these measures has any understandable relation to the goals of the enterprise, which remain at least as elusive and ambiguous as those of the Indo-China War. Each side is striving for deterrence or sufficiency or even superiority, but there is no consensus on what the operational definitions of these abstract concepts really are, just as no US Administration had any coherent idea of what victory in Viet Nam would really mean. Eventually the goals become little more than demonstrating commitment or maintaining credibility—in simple terms, not losing.

The dilemma posed by open-ended commitments to undefined goals is clearly evident in the following exchange between a US Senator and an Admiral:

Senator Brooke: What I am getting at, Admiral, is, as we improve our capability, then the Soviets respond by trying to catch up with us, and as they begin to catch up with us we find it necessary to improve our capability beyond that. I am just wondering where this ends.

Admiral Moorer: Well, I think it is a function of technology, Senator, and I do not think it ever ends. I mean this has been going on since the stone age. [19b]

But the war in Indo-China ended, or at least the US involvement in it did. And the strategic arms race will also end. The Admiral's prediction of the future is as short-sighted as his understanding of the past. The important question is *how* it will end, and here one is free to be as optimistic or pessimistic as one wishes. But, if one is willing to carry the analogy with the Indo-China War a bit further, some hints can be found of how it might turn out.

The fundamental problem faced by policy makers in an open-ended commitment is the inexorable way in which the stakes keep getting higher, constantly increasing the apparent gap between winning and losing. Each new escalation must be bigger and more expensive and more risky than the previous ones, otherwise one is not demonstrating commitment. But, as the levels of expense and danger rise, so does the number of people who begin to doubt the wisdom of the commitment. These people can be convinced to support the policy only if the costs of raising the ante seem clearly lower than the alternative. So the threat must be made to seem greater than ever, but this cannot be done without increasing the instability of the political confrontation. The result is a system which becomes less and less stable over time, and more and more susceptible to strong reactions to small disturbances.

The Indo-China War provides an excellent example of this phenomenon in the Tet Offensive. Such an offensive would not have had the same devastating effect on US public opinion if it had occurred in 1960 instead of 1968. But by 1968 the ante had been raised many times, and in doing so the US public had been fed larger and larger doses of official optimism. The result was an emotional reaction against the war which could have been overcome only by an even greater escalation which the Johnson Administration was not willing to undertake, having itself become riddled with disillusion and doubt by this time.

The escalation of the strategic arms race can only lead to similar instabilities. Growing frustration and anxiety are already quite apparent in the

United States. Meanwhile, events in the Middle East, Afghanistan and Poland contribute to a heightened perception of threat in the Soviet Union as it prepares for its own imminent change of leadership. The temptation is strong in such situations for leaders to exploit the threatening atmosphere to consolidate their power. Even responsible leaders attempting to maintain balance and stability can find that as the scale of threat increases, the middle road looks less like a broad boulevard and more like a high wire without a net.

It seems paradoxical to argue that decision-making systems which can produce such a situation are working, but there seems to be no other explanation. Systems are supposed to implement policies, and in doing this they seem quite successful. As one prominent arms control advocate has noted:

> Criticism of the military procedures for developing new weapons has often been intense in the US, particularly from congressional committees and from the general public. For the most part, however, the criticism seems to be wrongly directed. Starting at the identification of operational needs, the military services are in fairly complete control of the decision process that leads to new weapons, and in the main their procedures seem at least as rational as those applied to industrial research. The real difficulties, difficulties that are not looked at seriously by most critics, lie elsewhere. They lie in the establishment of the policies that guide the basic military programs. [53]

This statement could apply equally well to the Soviet military–technological system. On both sides these systems are responding rationally to a set of policies which can only lead to irrational and unacceptable outcomes.

V. Some consequences for the 1980s

Any extrapolation of this analysis into the future must be based on the assumption that the mechanisms described above will continue to operate. It is possible to identify three basic axioms which have been accepted, largely without challenge, by the United States and the Soviet Union and which suffice to explain the way the arms race has developed through 1980:

1. The confrontation between the USA and the USSR—the so-called central balance—is fundamental and essentially irreducible for the foreseeable future.

2. Military power and the credible determination to use it if necessary are essential to the successful pursuit of national interests. War remains the continuation of politics by other means.

3. Nuclear weapons are a central and an indispensable component of military power.

These are the assumptions that make stable deterrence unworkable and counterforce doctrines attractive; they lead logically to the conclusion that massive investments in military research and development are essential, and that military spending must grow as rapidly as the traffic will bear.

Starting from these axioms it is possible to make some predictions about future developments in military technology, strategic doctrine, and arms control. However, to the extent that the axioms are susceptible to modification, the predictions must be viewed with caution. It should be kept in mind that as the scale and instability of the arms race continue to increase, extrapolation of current trends becomes much less reliable. The confrontation is approaching a situation in which the mathematical technique of extending smooth curves is probably less useful than some newer concepts, appropriately named 'catastrophe theory'.

Technology in the 1980s

Missile accuracy

In the USA the installation of the NS-20 guidance system and Mark 12-A warhead on the Minuteman III is in progress, giving this missile an unprecedented accuracy. There are two apparent choices for future improvements in the land-based ICBM systems. One is a further refinement of the Minuteman system, including manoeuvrable re-entry vehicles (MaRV) and possibly a hard site anti-ballistic missile system called LoADS (Low Altitude Defense System). The other choice is the MX mobile missile, about which there has been much discussion but little in the way of irrevocable commitment.

For the sea-based missile force, the Trident II missile, utilizing stellar inertial guidance and possibly the advanced manoeuvrable re-entry vehicle (AMaRV) warhead, is expected to enter engineering development in 1982 or 1983 and to be deployable by the end of the decade. It should be just as accurate as the MX or the Minuteman and will multiply by a large factor the counterforce capability of the USA [54].

Deployment of all versions of the cruise missile is scheduled for the 1980s. The coupling of the air-launched cruise missile with a new penetrating bomber, presumably incorporating the recently revealed reduced visibility or 'stealth' technologies, promises to add yet another facet to counterforce capability. In Europe the Pershing II missile remains a strong possibility, but with some hope remaining that its deployment can be prevented by an agreement between the United States and the Soviet Union or by increased resistance by West European governments.

Soviet efforts seem to be focused on continuing improvements in guidance systems for both their land-based and sea-based missiles. One new missile under development has been described as carrying 10 MIRV

Figure 2.4. The US SSBNs *Georgia* (on pier) and *Ohio* (in water between piers). These vessels will carry 24 Trident missiles, each at least as accurate as current ICBM systems

US Navy

warheads, each with a yield of 500 kt, a range of 10 000 km, and a CEP of 260 metres. The missiles will be stored in silos reputed to be hardened to withstand 6 000 p.s.i. overpressure [55]. As usual, such statements must be viewed with caution, but even after applying reasonable discounts to the numbers there is no reason to doubt that the Soviet counterforce capability is increasing rapidly. The same can be said for Soviet sea-based missiles, IRBMs and cruise missiles.

Anti-submarine warfare

Progress toward the goal of real-time surveillance of submarine activity will require more extensive development and application of the data-gathering and -processing technologies discussed in section II. Long-range goals are stated by the US Defense Advanced Research Projects Agency (DARPA) as follows:

> Program objectives, (a number of which have been attained) include order-of-magnitude improvements in the performance of passive acoustic systems and signal processing strategies, development of (long-range, low frequency) active acoustic surveillance technologies, exploration of sensor concepts exploiting non-acoustic submarine signatures, and evaluation of all-source surface and subsurface targeting strategies on ocean basin scales. [56]

The purpose of all of this effort is to "continue converting our advantage in computers and signal processing technology into a growing advantage in submarine detection, so that our submarines will be able to detect Soviet submarines (and take appropriate action) long before the Soviet submarine is aware of our presence" [57].

Because of its geography, the Soviet Union faces much more severe obstacles in pursuing such a programme, particularly in the ability to deploy fixed acoustic arrays. For this reason it is likely that the USSR will rely more heavily on mobile and non-acoustic technologies, such as satellites, aircraft, submarines and surface ships utilizing infra-red, optical or magnetic sensing devices. The current asymmetry in submarine detection and tracking ability strongly favours the USA. This suggests that the development of these technologies will be a high priority for the USSR.

Satellite warfare and ABM

The increasing importance of space-based reconnaissance and C³I satellites implies a greater emphasis by each side on an ability to destroy an enemy's capabilities in these areas:

> As we plan for the future, it becomes very clear that the US must be able to defend and protect its space assets. To meet this objective we are developing an anti-satellite capability. The Soviets already have one. The alternative to not having this capability or the ability to respond to an enemy attack on our space systems would limit our political or military choices. [58]

The implication here is that the most effective defence of one's own satellites is the ability to threaten those of the other side, in other words, deterrence as usual. Some efforts are being made to make satellites less vulnerable to attack, but weight and size limitations and the lack of concealability of satellites imply that there are definite limits to how far this can be pushed. So the development of offensive ASAT technologies is the more likely path.

In the area of ballistic missile defence (BMD), deployment, but not research and development, were prohibited by the SALT I Agreements. Since much of BMD technology is similar to ASAT, continued progress in the latter will certainly further revive interest in the former.

C³I

It was pointed out in section II that C³I systems remain the weakest element in the complex of technologies needed to execute a counterforce strategy. This situation was recognized explicitly, for example, by the Carter Administration, as part of the process leading up to the refinements of counterforce doctrine promulgated in Presidential Directive 59: "Hence the issue of Presidential Directives 53 and 58 and a wide range of other measures intended to improve the *survivability* and the *endurance* of the US C³ system" [59a].

It is possible to argue quite convincingly that the search for a C³I system sufficiently survivable, reliable and flexible to fight nuclear wars is futile. C³I systems are inherently soft compared to other military target systems, some crucial elements cannot be made redundant, others cannot be made mobile, and many are extremely difficult to camouflage because of their electronic emissions [59b]. But it should be clear by now that the apparent futility of an ultimate objective is not a reliable predictor of its abandonment. Since the axioms demand a vastly improved and expanded C³I capability, this is most likely what will be pursued.

All of this seems to imply that the 1980s will be much like the 1970s, simply transposed to higher levels of technical sophistication and much higher levels of military expenditures. It cannot be doubted that technological sophistication will continue to increase, but there are reasons to wonder whether military expenditures can continue to grow as fast as they have in the past and as fast as many are suggesting for the future.

One prosperous Western country after another is watching its economic growth falter and its trade balances decline, while unemployment and inflation rise. Economic problems have already created considerable tension in the NATO alliance as West European countries find more reasons to resist US pressure to increase their military spending faster than inflation and faster than their overall economic growth rates. There is no evidence to suggest much slack in the Soviet economy which could be taken up by added military expenditures, but there is much evidence to suggest that the argument over military versus civilian priorities has been a chronic irritant in Soviet internal politics. Even the USA will find it much more difficult than in the past to raise military spending substantially without risking major domestic political conflicts. Meanwhile Japan stands out more and more clearly as an example of the economic advantages of low military budgets.

Strategic doctrine in the 1980s

The doctrines of counterforce and deterrence by threat of victory are solidly entrenched on both sides in the arms race, and, unless fundamental changes occur in the axioms from which they are derived, it is not possible to see anything but continuing refinements in these doctrines in the next decade.

The Carter Administration's PD-59 indicates the continuing evolution of these concepts, and it looks as if theories of coercion are becoming much more explicit in US declaratory policy. One of the drafters of PD-59 was quoted as saying:

> In the past nuclear targeting has been done by military planners who have basically emphasized the efficient destruction of targets. But targeting should not be done in a political vacuum.
>
> Some targets are of greater psychological importance to Moscow than others, and we should begin thinking of how to use our strategic forces to play on these concerns. [60]

The historical continuity of Soviet doctrine gives no expectation that dramatic changes will occur. Soviet policy will continue to stress a reliance on the full range of strategic military power consistent with its geographical and economic constraints. And it can be expected that both sides will continue to drop enough hints of possible pre-emptive strike or launch-on-warning postures to keep the other side's analysts quite busy during the 1980s.

A major problem which has already arisen for strategic doctrine and which will continue to grow in the 1980s is the adaptation of notions of deterrence and flexible counterforce to an increasingly multipolar world. Although the significance of the 'central balance' (see axiom 1) to the overall situation remains extremely important, more centres of independent power and initiative are evolving. In this changing environment the nature of strategic doctrine must be dynamic, but in the absence of challenge to the basic axioms it is most likely that answers to constantly arising new problems will be sought in new technologies and new variations on old doctrinal themes.

Implications for arms control

Unfortunately, ordinary extrapolation techniques cannot be used to make predictions about arms control in the 1980s. A straightforward extension of the downward trend in the record of success of these efforts cannot be made, since the level has already approached a value indistinguishable from zero. This is not intended in any way to belittle the efforts of the many people who have worked for so many years in an attempt to restrain the arms race. But however much one may respect the intelligence, commitment and persistence with which they have worked, there is no other word than failure to describe the result.

For the past decade almost all hope for limiting the arms race has focused on the SALT process, a process which has never promised very much and which has delivered even less. But as the 1980s begin, even this inadequate mechanism seems to have collapsed entirely. Of course, the resumption of some kind of dialogue between the USA and the USSR on strategic arms management is virtually inevitable. The SALT process has been too useful to both sides in keeping open channels of communication, legitimizing and regulating new weapons initiatives, and co-opting nascent political pressures for disarmament to be abandoned. But as long as the SALT process maintains its self-contradictory purposes of attempting both to stop the arms race and keep it going, it can lead to no genuine stability or security.

Opponents of the arms race have given up a great deal in committing themselves to SALT. The great majority of the arms control community has for the past 20 years accepted the basic axioms of the arms race and has therefore been unable to maintain a logically consistent case for nuclear disarmament. Efforts have therefore had to be focused on attempting to moderate or control the pace of the competition, and for this purpose arms controllers have found it necessary to depend heavily on the dubious concept of stable deterrence to support their arguments. The result has been a series of battles against particular weapon systems which are seen as destabilizing combined with an acceptance of others which are seen as stabilizing. But these definitions are just as ambiguous as the concept of deterrence itself, and technological progress keeps changing the definitions as new interactions among systems are recognized. Given this reliance on an unsound and perennially shifting intellectual base, it is not so surprising that the arguments of arms controllers lack both the force of conviction and the power to persuade.

It is clear that if an effective opposition to the arms race is to be mounted, a fresh look must be taken at the basic assumptions and objectives of the effort. In particular it seems that there is little hope of achieving meaningful results as long as opponents of the arms race continue to accept without challenge its axiomatic basis.

APN

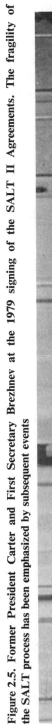

Figure 2.5. Former President Carter and First Secretary Brezhnev at the 1979 signing of the SALT II Agreements. The fragility of the SALT process has been emphasized by subsequent events

chapter 5, Part II, Arms control implications of antisubmarine warfare (ASW) programs, pp. 109–10.
10. *World Armaments and Disarmament, SIPRI Yearbook 1974* (Almqvist & Wiksell, Stockholm, 1974, Stockholm International Peace Research Institute), pp. 317–18.
11. *World Armaments and Disarmament, SIPRI Yearbook 1980* (Taylor & Francis, London, 1980, Stockholm International Peace Research Institute), pp. 178–79.
12. Pincus, W., 'Debut of Soviet missiles could color U.S. NATO policies', *Washington Post*, 26 June 1980, p. 2.
13. Paine, C., 'Pershing II: the Army's strategic weapon', *Bulletin of the Atomic Scientists*, Vol. 36, No. 8, October 1980, pp. 25–31.
14. Berry, Jr., F. C., 'Pershing II: first step in NATO theatre nuclear force modernization?' *International Defence Review*, Vol. 12, No. 8, 1979, pp. 1303–308.
15. *World Armaments and Disarmament, SIPRI Yearbook 1978* (Taylor & Francis, London, 1978, Stockholm International Peace Research Institute).
(a) —, p. 453.
(b) —, p. 127.
16. Schemmer, B. F., 'U.S. has been flying virtually invisible aircraft for over two years', *Armed Forces Journal International*, Vol. 118, No. 1, September 1980, pp. 30–31.
17. Ulsamer, E., 'The "invisible airplane" issue', *Air Force Magazine*, Vol. 63, No. 10, October 1980, p. 18.
18. *Outer Space, Battlefield of the Future?* (Taylor & Francis, London, 1978, Stockholm International Peace Research Institute).
(a) —, pp. 175–76.
19. *Authorization for Military Procurement Research and Development, FY 1970, and Reserve Strength*, Hearings before the Committee on Armed Services, US Senate, 91st Congress, 1st session on S.1192 and S.2407 (US Government Printing Office, Washington, D.C., 19 March 1969).
(a) —, p. 37.
(b) —, p. 673.
20. Robinson, Jr., C. A., 'Ballistic missile defense emphasis urged', *Aviation Week & Space Technology*, Vol. 113, No. 15, 13 October 1980, pp. 18–20.
21. Bekefi, G., Feld, B. T., Parmentola, J. and Tsipis, K., 'Particle beam weapons—a technical assessment', *Nature*, Vol. 284, 20 March 1980, pp. 219–25.
22. *US Department of Defense Annual Report, Fiscal Year 1981*, Report of Secretary of Defense Harold Brown to the Congress on the FY 1981 Budget, FY 1982 Authorization Request and FY 1981–1985 Defense Programs (US Government Printing Office, Washington, D.C., 29 January 1980), pp. 140–44.
23. Cameron, A. G., 'Spread spectrum technology effecting military communication', *Naval Research Reviews*, Vol. 30, No. 9, spring 1977, pp. 19–36.
24. 'Spy ship got no warning', *Science*, Vol. 208, No. 4450, 20 June 1980, p. 1354.

25. Head, R. G. and Rokke, E. J., eds., *American Defense Policy* (Johns Hopkins University Press, Baltimore, 1973), reprint of speech by J. F. Dulles before the Council on Foreign Relations, 12 January 1954.
26. Dinerstein, H., *War and the Soviet Union* (Praeger, New York, 1962), quoting G. M. Malenkov, Chairman of the Council of Ministers of the USSR, 27 April 1954.
   (a) —, p. 74.
   (b) —, chapter 3.
27. Schelling, T., *Arms and Influence* (Yale University Press, New Haven, 1966).
   (a) —, p. 10.
   (b) —, p. 2.
28. Brodie, B., *Escalation and the Nuclear Option* (Princeton University Press, Princeton, 1966), p. 101.
29. Gray, K. S. and Paine, K., 'Victory is possible', *Foreign Policy*, No. 39, summer 1980, p. 14.
30. Hanning, Lt. Gen. N. (ret.), 'Essential equivalence: the end of the nuclear deterrent myth', *International Defense Review*, Vol. 12, No. 2, 4 April 1979, p. 179 (emphasis added).
31. Kaufmann, W. W., *The McNamara Strategy* (Harper & Row, New York, 1964), p. 26.
32. Enthoven, A. C. and Smith, K. W., *How Much is Enough?* (Harper & Row, New York, 1971).
33. *World Armaments and Disarmament, SIPRI Yearbook 1975* (Almqvist & Wiksell, Stockholm, 1975, Stockholm International Peace Research Institute), p. 44.
34. Holst, J. F. and Nerlich, U., eds., *Beyond Nuclear Deterrence: New Aims, New Arms* (Crane, Russak & Co., New York, 1977).
   (a) —, B. Lambeth, 'Selective nuclear operations and Soviet strategy', p. 87.
   (b) —, H. S. Rowen and A. Wohlstetter, 'Varying response with circumstances', pp. 226–27.
   (c) —, H. S. Rowen and A. Wohlstetter, 'Varying response with circumstances', p. 237.
35. Gelb, L. H. and Betts, R. K., *The Irony of Vietnam: The System Worked* (Brookings Institution, Washington, D.C., 1979).
   (a) —, p. 111.
   (b) —, p. 2.
   (c) —, pp. 249–98.
   (d) —, p. 307.
36. Green, P., *Deadly Logic, The Theory of Nuclear Deterrence* (Mershon Center, Columbus, 1966).
37. Pincus, W., 'Fault in Polaris, found in 1966, disclosed in U.S.', *International Herald Tribune*, 4 December 1978.
38. Cockburn, A. and Cockburn, A., 'The myth of missile accuracy', *New York Review of Books*, 20 November 1980.
   (a) —, pp. 40–43.
   (b) —, p. 41.

39. Ellul, J., *The Technological Society* (Knopf, New York, 1964).
40. Winner, L., *Autonomous Technology: Technics Out of Control as a Theme in Political Thought* (MIT Press, Cambridge, 1978).
41. Allison, G. T., *Essence of Decision: Explaining the Cuban Missile Crisis* (Little Brown & Co., Boston, 1971).
42. *Report of the Group of Experts on a Comprehensive Study on Nuclear Weapons*, United Nations Conference Room, Paper No. 9 (UN, New York, 23 July 1980), p. 199.
43. Lapp, R. E., *Arms Beyond Doubt: The Tyranny of Weapons Technology* (Cowles Book Co., New York, 1970).
44. Unger, A., 'The apocalypse game—an "ABC closeup" must-see', *Christian Science Monitor*, 16 October 1980, p. 18.
45. *Strategic Disarmament, Verification and National Security* (Taylor & Francis, London, 1977, Stockholm International Peace Research Institute), p. 105 (emphasis added).
46. Leitenberg, M., 'The dynamics of military technology today', *International Society of Science Journal*, Vol. 25, No. 3, 1978.
   (a) —, p. 349.
   (b) —, p. 351.
47. Bush, V., 'Science, the endless frontier', *Report to the President on a Program for Postwar Scientific Research* (US Government Printing Office, Washington, D.C., 1945), p. 12.
48. Melman, S., *Pentagon Capitalism* (McGraw-Hill, New York, 1970), pp. 231–34.
49. Seitz, F. and Nichols, R. W., *Research and Development and the Prospects for International Security* (Crane, Russak & Co., New York, 1973), pp. 16–18.
50. *The Origins of MIRV*, SIPRI Research Report No. 9 (Almqvist & Wiksell, Stockholm, 1973, Stockholm International Peace Research Institute).
   (a) —, p. 22.
   (b) —, p. 20.
51. Greenwood, T., *Making the MIRV: A Study of Defense Decision Making* (Ballinger, Cambridge, Mass., 1975).
   (a) —, p. xiii.
   (b) —, p. 25.
   (c) —, chapter II.
   (d) —, p. 14.
   (e) —, p. 36.
52. Kissinger, H., *Nuclear Weapons and Foreign Policy* (Harper, New York, 1957), p. 403.
53. Long, F. A., 'The process of new weapons development', Paper prepared for the 36th Pugwash Symposium, London, 10–12 December 1980, p. 5.
54. Robinson, Jr., C. A., 'Space-based systems stressed', *Aviation Week & Space Technology*, Vol. 112, No. 9, 3 March 1980, pp. 26–27.
55. Robinson, Jr., C. A., 'Soviets testing new generation of ICBMs', *Aviation Week & Space Technology*, Vol. 113, No. 18, 3 November 1980, p. 28.

56. *Fiscal Year 1981 Program for Research and Development, Statement by the Director of the Defense Advanced Research Projects Agency to the 96th Congress, second session, 1980* (US Department of Defense, Washington, D.C., February 1980), pp. I-11, 12.
57. *Perry, W. J., Under Secretary of Defense Research and Engineering, Statement to the 96th Congress, Hearings on Military Posture*, Committee on Armed Services, US House of Representatives (US Government Printing Office, Washington, D.C., 1980), Part 4, Book 1, p. 25.
58. Slay, Gen., A. D., 'Space and the U.S. Air Force', *Spaceflight*, Vol. 21, No. 12, December 1979, p. 513.
59. Ball, D. J., 'PD-59: a strategic critique', *F.A.S. Public Interest Report*, October 1980.
    (a) —, p. 5.
    (b) —, p. 6.
60. *New York Times*, 16 December 1977.

3. World production of conventional weapons in the 1970s

Square-bracketed numbers, thus [1], *refer to the list of references on page* 103.

I. Introduction

The 1970s, proclaimed by the United Nations as the Decade of Disarmament, became instead another Decade of Armaments, witnessing a new momentum in the build-up of conventional armed forces throughout the world, in parallel to that of the nuclear arsenals. The race towards new technological frontiers is common to both nuclear and conventional weapon development and constitutes what is generally known as the 'qualitative' or 'technological' arms race. There has been no attempt to curb the research, development and production of conventional arms; on the contrary, while national governments may hold widely differing opinions as to the desirability of and the need for nuclear weapons, there is unanimous acceptance of the need for increasingly sophisticated conventional weapons. In the 'nuclear age', the possession of adequate conventional armed forces, preferably equipped for protection in the event of use of nuclear, biological or chemical (NBC) weapons, has become a universal strategy irrespective of political ideology. The majority of the ground mobile weapon systems which entered production during the 1970s in the technologically leading nations, for example, are equipped with extremely effective filtration, aeration and decontamination systems—generally described as NBC protection systems—to withstand nearly anything but a direct hit by a nuclear warhead.

There are several indicators of the waste of resources which this vast military production capacity represents. The report of the 1980 United Nations Environment Program (UNEP), for example, concluded that the market for military products is one of the fastest expanding markets of the world; that the military establishment is the largest user of valuable natural resources such as metals and oil; and that, in some regions of the world, conventional weapons have damaged the environment even more than a limited use of nuclear weapons would have done.[1]

Some 400 000 leading scientists, or 40 per cent of the world total, are

[1] Since 1977 the annual reports of the Director of UNEP (Mr Mostafa Kamal Tolba) have taken up precise subjects related to environmental problems. UNEP was set up by the UN in 1972, with its seat in Nairobi. The Tolba report of 1980 views the consequences of military activities as a threat to the physical and biological environment and denounces these activities, both as consequences of past wars and as preparation for future wars.

employed in military research and development tasks in countries of the developed world—that is, first of all, the USA, the UK, France, the Federal Republic of Germany, Italy, and a few other West European countries with established defence industries such as Sweden, as well as the Soviet Union, Czechoslovakia and China. In a decade of economic recession, military industries constituted the most expansive sector in many countries, of course with some exceptions. This fact makes the absence of international attempts to curb the conventional arms race even more conspicuous.

In the most technologically advanced countries, four major factors underlie decisions to invest in the research and development of new types of conventional armaments: (*a*) the perception of the military strength of the USA and the USSR, as reflected in the forces of NATO and the Warsaw Treaty Organization (WTO); (*b*) the actual testing of new weapons in wars such as that in Indo-China and the Middle East;[2] (*c*) the practical opportunities for new weapon developments offered by advances in technology and availability of funds; and (*d*) changes in the political and social structures of Third World countries which have created a demand for a special class of weapons whose name reflects the mode of use—the COIN (counter-insurgency) weapons.

The first factor, the great power contest, is clearly the main motivating force behind the ever-advancing weapon technology. At regular intervals, alarming reports appear, usually emanating from the US intelligence community or defence department or from NATO, of a 'gap' suddenly created between WTO and NATO forces through a rapid Soviet advancement in one area or the other of weapons capacity. Such reports are behind the decisions to develop new systems or increase the military strength in general of the Western alliance, for example, the NATO decision of December 1978 to increase military spending by 3 per cent. One typical example of this type of argument was given by the Western European Union, which at its meeting in December 1980 endorsed a report calling for a boost in the region's armament in the face of an alleged Soviet military expansion. The report said that the Soviet Union was becoming "the world's leading military power" and that its lead was growing, and concluded that "NATO, and particularly its European component, must make a major effort to make up for the time it has lost in the last 10 years in the power and modernization of its armaments, both conventional and nuclear" [2]. However, when comparing the individual conventional

[2] It is by no means only the products from the leading European, US and Soviet arms industries that profit from experience in the Middle East wars—the Israeli Military Industries, for example, advertise their Galil machine-gun as being "more than an entire *combat-proven* weapons system" [1].

weapon systems, it remains impossible to establish any Soviet technological 'lead'. Rather, it remains clear that the United States retains the leading position it has held ever since 1945. The information on Soviet and Chinese weapon production, such as it is, ultimately always emanates from the Western intelligence community, and there are no means of checking the information. Often, conflicting information is given without any explanation —for example, vastly exaggerated reports have been made on Chinese aircraft production. The mere fact that there is no information from the Soviet Union itself on arms production cannot justify the assumptions of Soviet technological leadership (see also chapter 1).

Typical developments of the 1970s

During the 1970s an increasing portion of defence production in the developed world consisted of weapons for export, in order to recover at least a share of the soaring costs for research, development, testing and evaluation (RDT&E). When adjusted for inflation, the overall cost of the production of new weapons is influenced by the costs of advanced technology such as developments in optics and laser technology, refinements in avionics and ballistics, and so on. In 1977, for example, the RDT&E cost for all three military services in the United States was $10 942 thousand million. Towards the end of the 1970s, missile guidance systems reportedly averaged approximately 50 per cent of the total cost of the missile, and an average of 30 per cent of the cost of aircraft was for avionics equipment [3].

A RAND report [4] points out that the cost per ton of tanks, when adjusted for inflation, shows no upward or downward trend from 1918 to 1960, but since then, the cost has increased two or three times.

The effect electronics has had on the development of conventional military arms and equipment is tremendous, covering a large range of aspects such as improved communications, millimetre-wave technology, fibre optics, next-generation night-vision equipment, and so on. The growing power of integrated circuit electronics may prove to have the biggest influence on human history since the Industrial Revolution [5]. The development of military electronics in the 1970s, as well as future trends, was well illustrated in October 1980 at the Military Electronics Defence Expo 80 in Wiesbaden, where the products of 15 countries in fields of radar, anti-submarine warfare, electro-optics, computer technology, communications, electronic countermeasures, remotely piloted vehicles and simulation were displayed. The increasing use of electronics in tanks is one of the major causes of the cost escalation; it also entails increased testing requirements, decreased reliability and more complicated maintenance problems.

Given the technological leadership of the powers mentioned above, one of the net results of the ever growing spread of new conventional weapons to areas outside Europe, the USA and the USSR is that an increasing number of armed forces throughout the world find themselves more or less adequately equipped with weapons designed for a war in Europe. Another, more sinister aspect of developments in conventional weaponry may well be that they will in the end make the use of nuclear weapons 'acceptable' in a limited war—since conventional forces are being equipped and trained to withstand an attack with nuclear weapons.

By the end of the 1970s, the borderline between conventional and nuclear weaponry was becoming blurred through the development of the neutron bomb, although no decision on its deployment had as yet been taken. But the wording of various statements and forecasts indicated that preparations had been made to influence the public to accept nuclear weapons, that is, the neutron bomb, as a natural ingredient among the new anti-tank weapons deployed in Europe during the first half of the 1980s. The neutron bomb is referred to by the non-committal abbreviation 'ER-weapon' (enhanced radiation), for example, in the following study:

> It is a basic premise of this analysis that ER (enhanced radiation) technology is capable of being adapted to 155 mm HE guided projectiles and could become an integral part of NATO's weaponry. While the stated US policy is to refrain from production of ER warheads, development of systems which could ultimately carry such warheads *is, nevertheless, ongoing*. The following discussion of the effects of ER weapons and the reasons *pro* and *con* are enumerated to demonstrate that NATO is defense-oriented and that ER weaponry would *increase the credibility of deterrence* and *decrease the probability of a conflict escalating to a nuclear confrontation* [6].

Various surveys of anti-tank weapons in NATO openly include the neutron bomb, without comment, for example: "The role of anti-tank weapons is given considerable thought in Western Europe and the USA in the European war context facing a large number of WTO tanks. One strand in this thought is that NATO must have the Neutron Bomb to cope with an enormous mass attack of tanks". [7]

The overall tendency to condone the continuous qualitative arms race in conventional weaponry is reflected in the use of language which speaks of 'generations' and 'families' of weapons—the 'Scorpion' family of armoured vehicles, for example, consists of first-generation armoured cars, a second generation armed with anti-tank missiles, and so on. Such terminology not only expresses acceptance of the phenomenon but indeed also implies that this type of development is natural and inevitable, which of course is not the case.

II. The established arms producers

The technologically most advanced weapon-producing nations by the end of the 1970s were the USA, the USSR, France, the UK, FR Germany,

Italy, Japan and Sweden. These countries had the capacity to independently design and develop practically the entire range of non-nuclear weaponry. In addition, a number of other countries possessed domestic defence industries capable of producing some specialized types of weapon, e.g., Belgium and Czechoslovakia (small arms), the Netherlands (transport aircraft and ships), Switzerland (small arms) and Spain (ships and training aircraft); in other countries, the domestic defence industries concentrated on licensed production of weapons, for example, Canada and Australia as well as Poland and Czechoslovakia.

A distinctive feature in the traditional arms-producing countries of the West during the 1970s has been the continuing process of amalgamating the arms industries into single, big corporations. This process has been at work most typically in the aerospace industry, as is witnessed by the forming of the Rockwell International Corp. and McDonnell-Douglas Aircraft Co. Inc. in the USA, the SNIAS (also known as Aérospatiale) and Dassault-Breguet companies in France, Messerschmitt-Bölkow-Blohm in FR Germany, and Aeritalia in Italy.

The most heavily concentrated defence industry is seen in Japan where, according to claims by the General Council of Trade Unions of Japan (Sohyo), nearly half of the arms and defence equipment used by the Self Defence Forces is designed and produced in Japan by seven major enterprises, including large, well-known industrial enterprises such as Mitsubishi, Kawasaki and Fuji (the other half consists of weapons produced under US licences).

In the UK, the integration process came relatively late with the establishment of British Aerospace (BAe) in 1977. In Sweden the Saab-Scania company was formed in 1968.

Multinational production

Multinational production in the defence sector normally takes the form of *licence production*, where the selling company often acquires a share of the producing company. The seller often builds the entire production facility, particularly in the non-industrialized countries. Lockheed Aircraft Corporation, for example, is building up an aerospace industry in Greece; Vosper Thornycroft has established a shipbuilding industry in Singapore, and so on.

The multinationalization of defence industries is also reflected in the growth of *co-production* projects—normally involving industrialized countries but increasingly also Third World countries. In fact, multinational co-operation is often claimed to be necessary in view of the rising costs of arms technology. In 1975 the US Department of Defense was engaged in some 40 large co-production projects abroad, valued at a total of $8 500 million [8]. US arms industries are connected by commercial agreements to at least 50 military projects abroad. Most of this co-production occurs between US companies and arms industries in Europe and Japan. Most of the West European licence production and co-production occurs with the Third World. The Soviet Union has granted production licences to a comparatively small number of countries: to Poland, Czechoslovakia, North Korea and India. China is providing aid for arms industries in Pakistan.

During the latter half of the 1970s, a process towards more integration even across national borders was visible, although related to specific *ad hoc* projects rather than as a result of any grand overall design: so, for example, Irano British Dynamics Ltd was set up in 1977 to manufacture the Rapier missile in Iran, and Arab-British Dynamics Ltd was set up the same year by BAC and AOI for the production of the Swingfire anti-tank missile in Egypt. The Panavia consortium was created as early as 1969 to produce the Tornado fighter for the UK, FR Germany and Italy in the 1980s. One of the most successful ventures so far has been the Euromissile agency, set up to develop anti-tank missiles for France and FR Germany as a contribution to the recommended NATO standardization. It is, however, also a fact that virtually all the consortium projects—with the exception of the above-mentioned Euromissile anti-tank systems—have received serious criticism over the years, mostly for the cost escalations involved but also for the performance of the weapons. This type of criticism has been addressed to the F-16 as well as to the Tornado, although both of these aircraft have only just come into service. One extreme view on consortium-produced weapons was given in the British House of Lords in a debate in April 1980:

> We have set up consortia among our European allies bilaterally, trilaterally and quadrilaterally. But I think that it is generally agreed among producers of sophisticated arms in this country. . . that it is not the ideal way to produce the best weapon and the weapon that will sell the most and make the most profit. . . . If it is said that a camel looks like a horse designed by a committee, I must say that a sophisticated weapon produced by a European consortium very often looks like a machine designed by a committee. No wonder the United States manages to outbuild us, outpace us scientifically, and outsell us in this extremely important market. [9]

During the 1970s the growth of the West European arms industries marked a significant departure from dependence on US arms and has created a competitive market for conventional arms. A nationalistic desire to become 'self-sufficient' in arms procurement had by 1979 resulted for the NATO countries in 35 different types of tactical combat aircraft, 10 tank models, 4 types of anti-tank missile and 28 types of howitzer, as well 6 unrelated tactical communications systems under development. The significance of this trend for future arms projects was clearly described by a high-level US official as follows:

The war-torn economies we once bolstered have now become major competitors with us in the arms industry. For US manufacturers, a growth of European industry translates into a loss of assured markets and, especially in the aerospace industry, competition with international consortia of companies backed by European governments. This trend to consortia-produced systems reflects the high cost and technological complexity involved, among other factors. Faced with the political and economic realities of modern Europe, we must conclude that we have two choices: Either we cooperate in some way, through licensing, shared research and development, and coproduction or we try to go it alone on both sides of the Atlantic. The days of wholesale acceptance of American finished products, utilizing advanced and unmatchable technology, have just about ended in Europe and even elsewhere around the world. Everyone wants a piece of the pie and will strike the deal that gives him the biggest slice. But I would remind you that the pie is a large and expanding one—the NATO market accounts for over 60% of the free world total of military expenditures. [10]

The model for the NATO drive to standardize its weapon systems is obviously provided by the WTO inventories, which are standardized on Soviet equipment, with a few exceptions. A certain division of labour is evident in the WTO organization—in principle, licence production of Soviet aircraft and tanks is undertaken by Poland and Czechoslovakia, and a local trainer has been developed in both of these countries (the Czech L-29 Delfin and L-39 Albatross, accepted as WTO standard, and the Polish TS-11 Iskra). Warships are produced independently in the German Democratic Republic and Poland.

In other European countries, a policy of non-alignment or neutrality has traditionally incorporated investments in local defence industries to ensure independence, for example, in Sweden and Yugoslavia.

China

In January 1980 US Secretary of Defense Harold Brown said that the military hardware of the People's Republic of China was more than a decade behind that of the United States and the Soviet Union. It is expected that the Chinese military industry will see major developments in the 1980s, investing in know-how rather than directly importing Western weapons. According to Mr Brown, the Chinese leadership intended to avoid a weapons policy like that of the ousted Shah of Iran, under which large orders of US arms were shipped to Iran and then had to be operated by a small army of US civilians [11]. Other reports claim that Chinese aerospace technology, for instance, is at least 20 years behind that of the West. China maintains at least six aircraft construction factories, the largest being the Shenyang Aircraft Factory [12].

The main Chinese project has for two decades been the Shenyang F-6, which first flew in 1961. This plane was the licensed MiG-19 Farmer, which continued in production throughout the 1960s. An improved version appeared in the early 1970s, designated F-6bis or Fantan. The MiG-21 copy, known as Shenyang F-7, did not remain in production during the 1970s, and two further planes—the F-9 and F-10—apparently never entered production. In 1975, China concluded an agreement with Rolls-Royce for the licence production of the Spey jet engine, and by 1979 there were unconfirmed reports about the first flight of an aircraft designated the F-12 with the British engine. By late 1980, reports appeared in several Chinese newspapers that the F-12 had entered full-scale production, having reached Mach 2 in March 1980. According to the pictures published in China, the F-12 has the same delta wing as the MiG-21.

The bombers in production in China are still quite old—the B-5, which is a copy of the Soviet Il-28 Beagle of the 1950s, and the B-6, which is a copy of the Soviet Tu-16. In the field of armoured vehicles and missiles, China has been restricted to production of 'copies' of Soviet types. The AT-3 Sagger copy is, for example, the only anti-tank guided weapon in service with the People's Liberation Army. The SA-2 Guideline copy is deployed at at least 50 sites, according to US intelligence, and at 100 sites, according to WTO sources. Towards the end of the 1970s, Chinese purchases of Western military know-how seemed to mark the beginning of a new development phase which in 10 years or so may profoundly change the conventional arms inventory of China.

During the 1970s, in fact, most of the Chinese resources spent on conventional weapons were devoted to the build-up of its navy, which doubled in size in 10 years. The Luda-class destroyers, Kiang Hu frigates and Hai Dua-class fast patrol boats are all equipped with a Chinese-designed ship-to-ship missile.

Self-sufficiency in arms production

The existence of domestic defence industries is not the same as being self-sufficient in arms procurement. Real self-sufficiency is achieved only by the technologically most advanced nations with a capacity for development of *all* the various categories of major weapons, small arms and components. Some vital components are virtually monopolized by a handful of US and West European companies such as those producing aero-engines and military electronics. Some producers traditionally lead in certain fields, such as the anti-aircraft and naval guns produced by Bofors in Sweden and Oerlikon in Switzerland, naval engines produced by MTU and MAN in FR Germany, the FN infantry weapons produced by Fabrique Nationale in Belgium, and so on.

Those countries closest to self-sufficiency in weapons production are obviously the USA, the USSR, France, the UK and Sweden. For these countries, the import of a weapon or weapon components does not necessarily reflect any inability to produce a certain type of equipment but rather results from economic considerations, co-production agreements, and so on. The UK, for example, is importing the Milan anti-tank missile for local production from Euromissile, and the USA has purchased the Roland surface-to-air missile from Euromissile. Sweden produces the Israeli Galil 5.56-mm machine-gun under licence and with the designation FFV-890C [13].

III. Third World arms producers

The 1970s witnessed a spectacular rise of new arms projects in the Third World, competing with the traditional arms companies in the industrialized world. Already by the end of the 1960s, a total of 27 Third World countries produced some equipment for their own armed forces, if only rifles, other small arms and ammunition. Eleven Third World countries had established aircraft industries; six Third World nations produced missiles and six produced armoured vehicles, while nine countries possessed domestic shipbuilding industries (see reference [14]). Most of the projects consisted of licence production.

By the end of the 1970s, the number of countries possessing domestic defence industries had not increased so much as the number of advanced projects in these new industries, which in some cases had reached a level where they were actively competing with the established suppliers. For example, when the Iranian regime in 1981 began to look around for weapons, Taiwan, a new producer, offered some products. Taking account of turnover and diversification, the following Third World countries today possess the most developed domestic defence industries: Israel, India, Brazil and South Africa, all producing a range of aircraft, armoured vehicles, missiles and warships. A second and fast growing group includes Argentina, Taiwan, South Korea, the Philippines, Indonesia, Egypt, North Korea and Singapore. Most of the weapons in these countries are still produced domestically under licence, which takes place within a range from the mere assembly of imported sub-assemblies to the full-scale manufacture of components from locally produced raw materials, but according to an imported blueprint.

Given the continuing advances in weapon technology in the leading industrialized countries, a considerable effort is needed today in order to establish a viable domestic defence industry. This effort must include the investment of financial and manpower resources for the build-up of related basic industries and relevant infrastructure. The build-up of an indigenous arms production capacity follows, in principle, a common pattern: first, a repair and overhaul plant is established with aid from one or more of the established arms-producing companies. Then, licence assembly of imported sub-assemblies is undertaken, followed by the assembly of imported components, which in turn gives rise to the manufacture of components from imported raw materials. The final stage, ideally if not in reality, is the complete manufacture of an entire weapon system from domestic raw materials. The advance of this process is measured in terms of indigenization of a weapon project, either in percentage of value or percentage of content. Needless to say, hardly any project ever reaches a stage of 100 per cent self-sufficiency, even in industrialized countries and certainly not in new producer nations. For example, the locally designed armoured car EE-9 Cascavel in Brazil, which is becoming an export success and is sold to several nations in the Middle East, contains the following imported components or components produced in Brazil by foreign companies: a Hispano-Suiza H-90 turret (France, on the first production models), the Mercedes-Benz diesel engine (FR Germany), Detroit Diesel Allison gears (USA), and the Cockerill 90-mm gun (Belgium).

The motivating force behind the decision to build up domestic arms industries in the Third World has been the political demand for independence from foreign arms suppliers, just as in the case of the neutral or non-aligned nations in Europe. While some nations, notably South Africa, have reached a stage of political independence, meaning that they are no longer dependent on the political goodwill of a foreign arms supplier, the pattern of economic dependence on foreign suppliers remains and is even strengthened as the domestic arms projects proceed, since the most vital components and often the most vital raw materials have to be imported. This is best illustrated by the fact that virtually all aero-engine industries in the Third World consist of licensed projects—no single company has yet been able to construct an indigenous design beyond the test stage.

For the suppliers of arms production licences, an economic incentive may play a part insofar as the low labour costs in a developing country are attractive—components for Alouette helicopters are produced in India and resold to France; the Israeli Aircraft Industries are producing components for the F-15 Eagle fighter re-exported to the USA. For the suppliers, the sale of licences may also offer an opportunity to circumvent arms export restrictions—for example, the FR German-designed TAM tank is produced in Argentina and exported to Pakistan.

The advances made by the Israeli arms industry—with such weapons as the Kfir fighter-bomber, the Gabriel ship-to-ship missile, the Merkava main battle tank, and the Reshef-class missile patrol boat—are rather well known. The Brazilian Xavante COIN aircraft and the Engesa armoured cars are also among the products of the new producers capable of competing on the arms market, the latter being developed precisely for export. It is estimated that the value of arms and military equipment produced in Third World countries has increased from less than $1 000 million in 1970 to over $5 000 million in 1979 (excluding China) [15].

The Middle East

A closer look at the second group of Third World producers reveals some ambitious programmes: in the Middle East, only *Israel* has, for the entire period since World War II, concentrated on building up a domestic defence industry. (The advanced plans for arms industries with US, British and Italian aid in *Iran* all came to an end with the fall of the Shah's regime.) But *Egypt* is slowly being transformed into a modern industrialized society, and renewed interest in military production will also make Egypt an arms producer of some standing in time. For the entire period 1967–76, Egypt exported military equipment and weapons valued at $24 million. In January 1979, the Egyptian Defence Minister could announce that Egypt planned to export about $10 million worth of arms in 1979 alone, most of it to Sudan, Somalia and Yemen. This second attempt to attain a military production capacity was started in 1975, when the Arab Organization for Industrialization was set up by Egypt, Saudi Arabia, Kuwait, Qatar and the United Arab Emirates with an initial capital valued at more than $1 000 million and with an additional $9 000 million in reserve capital. AOI signed several co-production project agreements with Westland, Rolls-Royce, Dassault-Breguet and America Motors Ltd, all of which were halted when the AOI was disbanded in 1979. The first Egyptian-assembled Lynx helicopter was due to fly in 1980, but following the signing of the peace treaty between Egypt and Israel, work had been stopped. A number of British personnel remained in Egypt waiting for refinancing of the project.

French co-production projects in Egypt were also halted; these involved, for example, the Alpha Jet, the Mirage-2000 and the Matra airborne missile. But some projects have survived, such as the production of the British Swingfire anti-tank missile. The Italian firm IRET has helped to build a factory in Egypt to manufacture transceivers for use in the T-54/55 and T-62 tanks of Soviet origin. Another Egyptian-made modification to these tanks is the provision for a twin-missile launcher on each side of the turret, originally reported to be for the Swingfire but now intended for the DM-80 rockets indigenously manufactured by the firm SAKR. Meanwhile, Egypt hopes to receive US financing to continue the AOI work alone.

In 1980 it was reported that discussions had begun on the possibility of setting up a factory in Egypt to manufacture the US FX fighter. This plane will eventually replace the F-5 in the arsenals of the less developed nations around the world. This would therefore make Egypt an important arms exporter for the first time.

Egypt is also reportedly planning for the licence production of the

US F-5 fighter and the M-113 armoured personnel carrier. It is also capable of building light naval craft: in the mid-1970s a batch of nine October-class missile-armed fast patrol boats were built at the Alexandria shipyard, based on the Soviet Komar design. Egypt already produces most types of ammunition, with US co-operation, including that for the M-60 main battle tank. In 1981 Egypt received offers for licence production from BAe for the Hawk trainer and from Dassault/Dornier for the Alpha Jet.

In an interview in 1980, the Minister of Defence and Military Production, Lt Gen Badaoui, said that "the domestic defense industry will be built up in order to become as little dependent as possible on foreign powers and reach selfsufficiency in arms and ammunition. Egypt will cooperate with some Arab and African states in this field" [16].

Latin America

In Latin America, Brazil and Argentina continue to invest in domestic defence industries. *Brazil* has interestingly pursued what might be called an intermediate-technology course, producing comparatively simple designs for use in Third World countries. By 1980, however, Brazil had embarked on an ambitious and far-reaching programme aimed at full-scale development of the arms industry with Italian co-operation. Negotiations were proceeding both at the industry and the government levels. The main co-production programme under discussion was the Italian AMX Close Air Support aircraft, undertaken by Aeritalia and Macchi, now joined by the Brazilian firm EMBRAER. The air forces of Italy and Brazil signed a Memorandum of Understanding in 1980, providing for the supply of information and technical data on the project. Brazil will probably purchase a "share" of the project, rather than a production licence, and assume part of the R&D costs. The aircraft will then be produced in Brazil both for its own air force and for export. This agreement further includes the Sauro-class conventional-powered submarine, of which two units will be produced in Brazil, and one purchased from Italy with five more on option. Negotiations were under way in 1980 for an unspecified number (but at least six to eight) of the Mini Lupo-class frigates, plus a training vessel based on the British Niteroi-class frigate hull, both to be built in Brazil. The ship deals, including shipyard reorganization and manpower training, were reported to be worth around $3 000 million. In the field of artillery and small arms, a new subsidiary was recently set up in Brazil by the Italian firm OTO-Melara, called OTO-Brazil.

Argentina has expanded its indigenous military industrial base ever since the Europa Plan of 1967 was passed, aimed at expanding the domestic defence industry. A range of light aircraft was produced during the 1970s, including the IA-58 Pucara COIN fighter and the licensed production of the

Hughes Model OH-6 helicopter. By 1980 discussions were under way with Dornier of FR Germany to licence-produce the Alpha Jet advanced jet trainer.

The Argentinian shipyards have built destroyers, corvettes, survey ships and oceanographic ships, and assembled submarines. As for armoured vehicles, the AMX-13 has been licence produced since 1969, followed by the FR German 33-ton TAM tank, produced for both indigenous use and export. Another TAM version, the VCI, was also in production by 1980.

By 1976, the country's armament factories sold over $7 million worth of arms, of which $225 000 were made up of exports to other Latin American countries. Domestic ordnance factories are expected to supply the bulk of the armed forces' requirements in Argentina during the 1980s. Among new achievements were a naval supersonic radio-guided missile, a wire-guided anti-tank missile and a 'fire-and-forget' rocket, all developed by the Armed Forces Scientific and Technical Research Centre. Of the anti-tank missiles, 68 per cent were reportedly assembled in Argentina, the rest presumably imported from FR Germany.

Africa

In Africa, the *Republic of South Africa* is the only sub-Saharan country possessing any military industrial base. The arms production capacity was firmly established during the 1960s, and during the 1970s South Africa actually became the largest arms producer in the Southern Hemisphere, surpassing even Brazil and Australia. The local arms industry has relied heavily on adapting manufacturing licences obtained from abroad before the UN arms embargo. Specific items produced in South Africa by 1980 included the French Mirage F-1C fighter; the Italian Aermacchi MB-326 armed trainer, known as Impala-2 and well suited for counter-insurgency roles; French-designed Panhard armoured cars known as Eland-2 to Eland-4; Israeli-designed Reshef-class fast missile boats; a derivative of the French Crotale surface-to-air missile originally funded by South Africa and known as Cactus; air-to-air missiles; artillery pieces; infantry weapons; and a wide range of ammunition.

South Asia and the Far East

In South Asia, *India* has a well-established domestic arms industry, with Pakistan lagging far behind. India, one of the few countries outside the WTO allowed to purchase Soviet military know-how, in 1980 acquired production licences for the T-72 main battle tank and the MiG-23. India will also produce conventional submarines under licence from FR Germany.

The newest group of arms producers, established during the past 10 years, are made up of the ASEAN countries, as was demonstrated at the Asian Defence Expo 80 in Kuala Lumpur. Massive resources have during the past few years been devoted to the construction of a local defence industry infrastructure. Two main arguments have been quoted in this connection: first, the acquisition of a manufacturing capacity will keep a considerable amount of money in the country for goods which would otherwise have to be purchased abroad; and secondly, it has the political advantage of ensuring a constant supply of spares and equipment.

The Philippines has assumed a leading position as a supplier of smaller equipment for ground troops. The M-16-A1 rifle is produced under US licence, and a small cross-country vehicle has been mass-produced for the army. The Philippines has also succeeded in setting up the nucleus of an electronics industry, which produces tactical communications equipment and ancillaries for the armed forces as well as for export.

The competitiveness of local defence production in Far Eastern countries is reflected particularly in small arms production: for the period 1980–82, for example, the Malaysian local requirement for 7.62-mm and 5.56-mm ammunition is estimated at 260 million rounds. European and US industries can offer such ammunition at a price of $160–165 per thousand rounds. But Taiwan's ammunition industry offers the same ammunition for $128, while South Korea offers the reduced price of $123.5. Taiwan and South Korea possess the most advanced defence industries in the Far East.

In *Taiwan*, reliance on US technology has always been strong, but the local production capacity is being expanded. The industrial base was by 1980 capable of producing propellants and ammunition, overhauling warships and combat aircraft, producing military vehicles and tactical communications equipment, licence-producing modern fighter aircraft, and indigenously designing primary trainer aircraft and helicopters, air-to-air missiles, surface-to-surface missiles and helicopter engines. In 1977 a government administrative report claimed that Taiwan had made a breakthrough in military R&D. By 1980 a new surface-to-surface missile was under development, designated Coral, managed by the Chun Shan Institute of Science and Technology. (There were also unconfirmed reports about licence production of the Israeli Gabriel ship-to-ship missile.) Already in 1974, Taiwan began licence production of the improved version of the AIM-9 Sidewinder.

The licence production in Taiwan of the F-5E Tiger-2 remained the biggest programme by the end of the 1970s, worth $230 million under the initial contract signed in 1973. The total number of aircraft produced in Taiwan will reach 180.

Like Taiwan, *South Korea* established its domestic arms industry with US aid and was by the end of the 1970s capable of producing all types of equipment, from combat aircraft to small arms. In late 1979, the USA approved a requirement from South Korea for licence production of the F-5E Tiger-2, while the request for the more sophisticated F-16 was refused. It has been claimed that by 1980 South Korea was able to meet all the requirements of its armed forces from local sources, with the exception of some highly sophisticated electronic equipment and high-technology combat aircraft.

In December 1979 a special fund of $195 million for the development of the national defence industry was created by the government. Other measures to encourage investment in military production would be to waive stamp and business income taxes for military-related projects. The statute for encouragement of investment would be revised to bolster military-related production.

Thailand has created an arms industry mostly for the manufacture of non-sophisticated weapons. In December 1977, Prime Minister General Chamanan said that future plans included the establishment of a number of new arms factories, both government and privately owned. According to the Thai Defence Ministry, about $225 million was invested in the country's arms manufacturing base between 1969 and 1976. In 1978, the Thai Navy alone was planning a $275 million shipyard on the Gulf of Thailand near Bangkok with substantial aid from the USA and Japan. The plans included the future construction of fast missile-armed patrol boats. Indigenous production of hovercraft was also planned. The Air Force Directorate of Armament has undertaken the construction of trainer aircraft such as the RTAF-4 Chandra, which entered service in 1974, and the RTAF-5 advanced trainer, now under development. The Air Force has also modified and developed many types of explosive weapon, such as all-purpose mines and fragmentation bombs, and, as a result, the air force claims that it has been able to save a significant amount of money each year.

Singapore has a growing domestic arms production capacity, initially centred on the Vosper Thornycroft Singapore shipyard. There, fast patrol boats are produced to meet not only the requirements of Singapore but also of Malaysia, Hong Kong, Sabah and Brunei. The servicing of combat aircraft is performed by Lockheed Aircraft Singapore, set up in 1970. The Swedish company Bofors has also set up a subsidiary in Singapore.

The new arms industries in Third World countries all have one thing in common: their existence and growth are never disputed and never mentioned in connection with disarmament efforts. During the 1980s, the existing Third World arms industries will continue to be enlarged, and other countries will embark on military projects. They will, however, not 'catch up' with the latest technology in the industrialized world.

IV. The weapons produced in the 1970s

Tables 3.1 and 3.2, showing the production of selected military aircraft and non-nuclear missiles, illustrate the technological capacity of the producers. The picture would remain much the same if other weapon categories were also listed, such as warships, armoured fighting vehicles, ammunition, small arms, and so on. These two particular categories were chosen because by tradition the aerospace industries, together with the missile industries, illustrate incorporation of the latest advances in science.

Combat aircraft

The 1970s witnessed the largest expenditure ever made by the world's air forces on modernization and the purchase of new equipment. The arms race really gathered momentum during the second half of the decade, after a temporary recession brought about by the oil crisis following the 1973 Arab–Israeli war.

The constant reports that the Soviet Union was overtaking the West in air power, and the lack of any real progress in the SALT talks, were the main features behind the further orders to the aircraft industries of the West. According to Defence Ministry sources in the UK, the WTO countries were producing 1 500 military aircraft a year, of which 1 000 were combat types, including 500 of the latest swing-wing design. After the introduction of the Tu-26 Backfire bomber, which first flew in 1969, the NATO countries decided, in principle, to deploy the Boeing AWACS early-warning aircraft, capable of "looking over the horizon". Table 3.1 shows the most typical combat aircraft of the 1970s, and it is evident from the chronological development of the projects, despite claims to the contrary, that the USA and other Western countries continue to retain the technological leadership.

The latest generation of fighter aircraft deployed in the second half of the 1970s is represented by the US F-14, F-15 and F-16, which are technologically more advanced than those available to the USSR. The MiG-25 Foxbat set down in Japan by a Soviet defector pilot caused a prolonged dispute in the West as to the real capabilities of the Soviet aircraft industry—the plane was thoroughly examined by US experts and described in detrimental terms. A more balanced view would be that the MiG-25—a considerably older design than the US F-14 or F-15—provided an adequate capacity for its originally intended purpose of intercepting the US B-1 bombers, which, however, never entered production. This illustrates one aspect of the action–reaction pattern in weapons design—countermeasures may be developed to a certain weapon system which never materializes. If

Table 3.2. Tactical missiles in production or under development during the 1970s[a]

Country/ missile type	Designation	Manufacturer	Warhead weight (kg)	Range (km)	Design begun	In production
1. Air-to-air						
USA	AIM-9H Sidewinder	Raytheon	. .	. .	1970	1970–
	AIM-9J Sidewinder	Raytheon	. .	. .	1970	1970–
	AIM-54A Phoenix	Hughes	60	165	1960	1970–
	AIM-7E Sparrow	Raytheon	30	. .	. .	1975–
	AIM-9L Sidewinder	Raytheon	11	18	1972	1977–
	AIM-7F Sparrow	Raytheon	40	100	1975	1977–
	AIM-54C Phoenix	Hughes	60	200	1978	(1982)
	AMRAAM[b]	. .	14–22	. .	1976	. .
	Brazo	Raytheon	. .	. .	1972	. .
USSR	AA-3 Anab	State Arsenal	. .	16	. .	(1960)
	AA-5 Ash	State Arsenal	. .	30	. .	(1965)
	AA-2 Adv. Atoll	State Arsenal	11	7	. .	(1970)
	AA-6 Acrid	State Arsenal	100	50	. .	(1973)
	AA-7 Apex	State Arsenal	40	33	. .	(1974)
	AA-8 Aphid	State Arsenal	6	7	. .	(1976)
France	R-530	Matra	27	18	1958	1963–79
	R-550 Magic	Matra	125	10	1968	1974–
	Super 530	Matra	. .	35	1971	1977–
UK	SRAAM[c]	BAe	10	. .	1972	1976–
	Sky Flash	BAe	30	50	1973	1977–
Japan	AAM-1	Mitsubishi	. .	7	. .	1969–
	AAM-2	Mitsubishi	. .	. .	. .	. .
Italy	Aspide-1A	Selenia	35	100	1969	1977–
Sweden	RB-72	Saab-Scania	. .	. .	1973	. .
Third World						
Israel	Shafrir-2	Raphael	11	5	1965	1969–
	Shafrir-3	Raphael	. .	. .	1978	. .

2. Air-to-surface/Air-to-ship

USA	AGM-45A Shrike-9/10	Texas Instruments	66	16	1962	1963–
	Standard ARM AGM-76C/D/D2	General Dynamics	. .	27	1962	. .
	AGM-62-2 Walleye	Martin Marietta	907	. .	1968	1974–
	AGM-65B Maverick	Hughes	59	22	1970	1976–
	AGM-65C Laser Maverick	Hughes	59	53	1972	1977–
	AGM-84A Harpoon	MDD	238	145	1972	1977–
	AGM-65D IIR Maverick[d]	Hughes	59	87	1976	(1981)
	AGM-88A HARM	Texas Instruments	. .	. .	1972	(1981)
	WASP	. .	9	. .	1975	(1982)
France	AM-39 Exocet	Aerospatiale	165	50	1970	1976–
	AM-10 LASSO	Aerospatiale	28	11	1977	. .
	AS-15 TT	Aerospatiale	28	15	1976	. .
	AS-20	Aerospatiale	30	7	. .	–1978
	AS-30L	Aerospatiale	250	12	1977	. .
	ASMP	Aerospatiale	. .	100	1978	(1985)
USSR	AS-5 Kelt	State Arsenal	. .	180	. .	. .
	AS-6 Kingfish	State Arsenal	. .	220	. .	1975–
	AS-7 Kerry	State Arsenal	. .	10	. .	. .
	AS-8	State Arsenal	. .	. .	. .	1977–
	AS-9	State Arsenal	. .	90	1978	. .
Sweden	RB-05A	Saab-Scania	. .	9	1960	1969–77
	RB-04E	Saab-Scania	. .	20	1968	1973–77
	RB-83	Saab-Scania	20	10	1977	. .
UK	P3T	BAe	. .	100	1977	1980–
	Sea Skua	BAe	35	14	1970	1980–
FR Germany	AS-34 Kormoran	MBB	160	37	1964	1974–
Italy	Seakiller/Marte	Sistel	70	20	. .	1978–
Japan	ASM-1	Mitsubishi	. .	. .	1973	1979–
International						
France/FR Germany	NATO ASSM	Euromissile	. .	. .	1977	. .
Third World						
Argentina	ASM	CITEFA	40	7	1978	. .
Brazil	MAS-1 Carcara	AVIBRAS	9	. .	1973	. .

Country/ missile type	Designation	Manufacturer	Warhead weight (kg)	Range (km)	Design begun	In production
3. Anti-tank: man-portable, vehicle-launched or airborne						
USA	BGM-71A TOW	Hughes	3	4	1968	1969–
	FGM-77A Dragon	MDD	2	1	1966	1972–
	Hellfire	Rockwell	9	6	1971	(1981)
	Copperhead	Martin-Marietta	22.5	16	1971	(1983)
UK	Swingfire	BAe	6	4	1958	1968–
	Sabre	BAe	. .	6	1978	. .
	Beeswing	BAe	6	. .	1978	. .
USSR	AT-3 Sagger	State Arsenal	11	3	. .	1964–
	AT-4 Spigot	State Arsenal	. .	2	. .	1975–
	AT-5 Spandrel	State Arsenal	. .	. .	. .	. .
China	AT-3 (AT-3 Sagger)	. .	11	3	. .	1968–
FR Germany	Mamba	. .	2	2	1972	1974–
Italy	Sparviero	Breda-Meccanica	4	3	1978	(1982)
Japan	KAM-9	Kawasaki	1	2	1964	1980–
Sweden	RB-53 Bantam	Bofors	7	2	1956	1963–
International						
France/FR Germany	MILAN	Euromissile	3	2	1962	1972–
	HOT	Euromissile	6	4	1964	1975–
France/UK/FR Germany	ATEM	Aerospatiale/BAe/MBB	. .	. .	1977	. .
Third World						
Argentina	ATM	CITEFA	. .	. .	1974	1978–
4. Surface-to-air/Surface-to-surface						
USSR	SCUD-B	State Arsenal	. .	270	. .	1960–
	SA-4 Ganef	State Arsenal	. .	70	. .	1964–
	Scaleboard	State Arsenal	. .	800	. .	1965–
	SA-7 Grail	State Arsenal	1	3	. .	1966–
	SA-2 Impr Guideline	State Arsenal	. .	7	. .	1967–
	SA-6 Gainful	State Arsenal	80	60	. .	1967–

	SA-9 Gaskin	State Arsenal	. .	8	. .	1974–
	SA-8 Gecko	State Arsenal	. .	16	. .	1975–
	SCUD-C	State Arsenal	. .	450	. .	1977–
USA	MGM-52C Lance	LTV	454	120	1962	1971–
	MIM-23B Hawk	Raytheon	. .	41	1964	1972–
	Chaparral	Ford	50	8	1970	1976–
	Patriot	Raytheon	. .	100	1965	(1981)
	Stinger	General Dynamics	. .	5	1973	1978–
UK	Rapier	BAe	. .	7	1963	1967–
	Tigercat	Short Brothers	. .	4	. .	1969–
	Blowpipe	Short Brothers	2	6.5	1966	1973–
	Impr Rapier	BAe	. .	. .	1978	1980–
Italy	Indigo	Sistel	21	10	. .	1971–
	Aspide/Spada	Selenia	. .	50	1975	1978–
	Indigo-Mei	Sistel	. .	. .	1971	. .
China	SA-2 (SA-2 Guideline)	State Arsenal	130	50	. .	. .
	FROG Type	State Arsenal	. .	40	. .	. .
France	Crotale	Thomson/Matra	15	11	1964	1968–
	Shahine	Thomson/Matra	. .	. .	1975	1980–
Japan	TAN-SAM	Toshiba	. .	. .	1977	1979–
	XSSM-2	. .	. .	. .	1978	. .
Sweden	RBS-70	Bofors	1	5	1969	1976–
International						
France/FR Germany	Roland-2	Euromissile	6	6	1964	1977–
Third World						
Brazil	SAM	. .	. .	. .	1976	. .
5. Ship-to-ship/Ship-to-air						
USA	Seasparrow	Raytheon	. .	. .	1968	1973–
	RGM-84A Harpoon	MDD	232	90	1971	1976–
	RIM-67C/SM-2	General Dynamics	. .	96	1976	1978–
	RIM-66C/SM-2	General Dynamics	. .	48	1978	. .

Country/ missile type	Designation	Manufacturer	Warhead weight (kg)	Range (km)	Design begun	In production
USSR	SSN-11 Adv Styx	. .	. .	40	1968	. .
	SSN-3 Shaddock	. .	. .	550	. .	. .
	SSN-9	. .	. .	275	. .	1969–
UK	Sea Dart Mk-2	BAe	. .	80	. .	. .
	Sea Wolf	BAe	150	5	1965	1977–
Italy	Seakiller-2	Sistel	70	25	1965	1972–
	Aspide/Albatros	Selenia	. .	. .	1969	1977–
	Vanessa	Oto Melara	. .	. .	1978	(1985)
	. .	Oto Melara/Sistel	. .	200	1978	. .
France	MM-38 Exocet	Aerospatiale	165	42	1967	1972–
	Naval Crotale	Thomson/Matra	15	8	1974	1978–
	MM-40 Exocet	Aerospatiale	165	70	1977	. .
Australia	Ikara-3	. .	. .	20	1970	. .
Norway	Penguin-2	Kongsberg	120	25	1969	1974–
International						
France/Italy	OTOMAT-2	Matra/Oto Melara	. .	100	. .	1975–
Third World						
Israel	Gabriel-2	IAI	180	41	. .	1972–

[a] Countries are listed according to the number of projects undertaken in the 1970s. Projects are listed in chronological order, according to the years in which they entered production.
[b] Advanced Medium-Range Air-to-Air Missile.
[c] Short-Range Air-to-Air Missile.
[d] Imaging Infra-Red.

the US B-1 bomber programme is resurrected by the Reagan Administration, the USSR in turn may feel obliged to develop a next-generation MiG-25.

Table 3.1 also reveals that the technological lead was held in the 1970s by a very small number of countries in the West: apart from the USA, only France, the UK, Japan and Sweden were capable of designing modern fighter aircraft on their own in the 1970s.

The outdated technology of China is evident from the data on aircraft production. The sole modern project is the F-12, with the licence-built powerplant. Yugoslavia produced one fighter in the 1960s and early 1970s, now being replaced by a joint programme with Romania for the Orao fighter.

In the new trend towards multinationalization of the aircraft projects described above, the most advanced fighter programme is the Tornado, jointly designed and produced by FR Germany, Italy and the UK for deployment in the 1980s. So far, only one project represents the move towards co-production between Third World countries and industrialized countries—the Italian–Brazilian AMX project.

In the Third World, only India and Israel have designed fighter aircraft, the Israeli Kfir actually being the only successful programme from the manufacturer's point of view.

The time span of an aircraft project is also evident from table 3.1—the first-generation jet combat aircraft, designed in the 1950s, were still in production in the 1970s. The most representative of these are the F-5A/B Freedom Fighter produced by Northrop, the Mirage-3 and the F-4 Phantom, both of which made first flights in 1956, and the first-generation MiG-21.

The Northrop F-5E/F was developed for export and has been sold to some 30 nations. When McDonnell-Douglas produced the last F-4 Phantom in 1978, sales had reached 5 000. The export success of the 1980s may well be the F-16 produced by General Dynamics, which won substantial export orders during the 1970s. The French Mirage-3E was further developed into the Mirage-50, with an engine with a 20 per cent increase in thrust. The two planes share 90 per cent commonality of airframe parts, 95 per cent of various systems such as flying controls, hydraulics and electrical circuits, and 45 per cent of the engine components. The latest addition to the Mirage family during the past decade is the Mirage F-1. By the end of 1979, total sales amounted to 614, of which 255 were to the French Air Force.

The British Harrier and the Swedish Viggen, which made their first flights in 1966 (Harrier-3) and 1967, respectively, are both examples of very high technology projects that have failed to win any large export orders. The British Harrier is the only V/STOL fighter in the NATO inventory, and it was sold to the USA as the AV-8A to be further developed for the US

Marine Corps as the AV-8B. The Swedish Viggen participated in the competition for the 'deal of the century' to four NATO countries; its manufacturer also tried unsuccessfully to sell it to Australia, Austria and India. Viggen uses a canard layout instead of a swing wing design.

The most complicated and hence most expensive fighter produced during the 1970s is perhaps the F-15 (first flight in 1972) which is exported to Japan, Israel, Egypt and Saudi Arabia. The improved F-15 Strike Eagle, with a modified radar, will eventually get a unit fly-away price for a 300-aircraft production run at $13.5 million (in 1979 prices).

The first-generation Soviet MiG-21 made its first flight in 1955. The final production version resulted from a competition between four prototypes, the requirements for a relatively light day fighter having arisen from the experience of the air war over Korea. Series production of the MiG-21F, with two Atoll infra-red-guided air-to-air missiles, started in 1959, followed in the early 1960s by the MiG-21PF all-weather fighter. The upgraded MiG-21MF entered service with the Soviet Air Force from 1970, followed by the MiG-21SMT from 1973. Upgraded trainer and reconnaissance versions have also been deployed. The third-generation MiG-21 of the late 1970s is technologically much improved over the first versions, and over 10 000 planes have been exported.

Compared to the MiG-21, the MiG-23 Flogger is a very different plane, being a much heavier weapon platform. The MiG-27 Flogger version has begun to be exported. As is also evident from table 3.1, very few bombers are designed nowadays. The Soviet Tu-126 Backfire and the outdated Chinese types were actually the only types in production during the past decade. According to official US sources, by 1980 there were 125 Backfire bombers in service in the Soviet Air Force.

The Tornado fighter programme was begun in 1967, and the service entry date was to be 1975. The project was delayed due to various complications in the multirole requirements, and the drawn-out programme has been badly hit by inflation. It involves more than 70 000 workers in more than 500 companies in the UK, FR Germany and Italy. By mid-1980 the fly-away unit cost had reached $38.5 million, which was more than four times the original estimate. (The fly-away unit cost was originally estimated at DM 7–8 million but by the end of 1979 had risen to DM 35.26 and to DM 70 million by the end of 1980. It is further expected to rise to DM 100 million [17–18].) Delivery started in 1980, and total production will be 809 aircraft, of which 385 are for the UK, 324 for FR Germany, and 100 for Italy. In addition, the Tornado has been entered in the contest to find a new tactical aircraft for the USAF for the mid-1980s.

Helicopters

In addition to the new tactical aircraft, a considerable deployment of helicopters has taken place during the 1970s, mostly for anti-tank missions. The first generation in Europe was represented by the British Scout and the French Alouette helicopters, armed with the wire-guided SS-11 anti-tank missile. The United States developed the armed attack helicopter AH-1G Huey Cobra, based on the experience in Indo-China, followed by the AH-1Q and AH-1S versions, which carry eight TOW anti-tank missiles. In the context of an East–West conflict in Europe, the helicopter would have an anti-armour mission. Other uses include anti-submarine warfare (ASW), observation, liaison and rapid transport of weapons and troops. An example of a heavy-lift helicopter is the Boeing Vertol CH-47C Chinook, with a payload of some 10 tons, which means that it carries 44 troops, or one Lance surface-to-surface missile, or one 155-mm gun, or one M-113 armoured personnel carrier, or 26 casualties. The Mil Mi-24 Hind-D is a Soviet gunship helicopter, tested in practice in Afghanistan. At sea, naval helicopters have during the 1970s changed the concept of operations in ASW roles. Most frigates and larger ships are by now capable of operating helicopters which carry anti-submarine torpedoes or air-to-surface missiles. The British, Dutch, German, French and Norwegian navies all use the British Lynx naval helicopter; the US Navy uses the Kaman Seasprite; Spain uses an ASW version of the Hughes Model 500; and the Italian Navy will get a naval version of the Agusta A-109. France uses the large ASW helicopter SA-321G Super Frelon. From this list it can be inferred that a relatively small group of aerospace companies produce helicopters, the largest being Bell and Sikorsky in the USA, the Mil Design Bureau in the USSR, Westland in the UK, and Aerospatiale in France, the latter producing the whole range of 14 different models from light to medium/heavy-lift types. By contrast, FR Germany, for example, produces only one model: the light liaison, observation and anti-tank helicopter MBB Bo-105.

After Viet Nam, helicopters also became a typical COIN weapon and have additional use for purposes of riot control and border security. Generally speaking, the status of the aerospace industries is commonly seen as a reflection of a country's technological achievements, because of the high-technology demands not only for the aircraft as such but for the related equipment, engines and armaments. By the end of the 1970s, the world markets for aerospace equipment and systems in the air as well as on the ground had reached such proportions that they were more important creators of employment and spin-off technology than the airframe industry. The UK has Western Europe's largest aerospace industry, and by 1979 only 15 000 out of the total work force of 80 000 worked directly with airframe construction. The proportion is probably similar in other West European and US aerospace industries. In terms of *value*, the manufacture of equipment ranked roughly on a par with that of engines and airframes as a contribution to the cost of a complete aircraft.

Aero-engines

The aero-engine manufacturers of the West are involved in the same competition to win new orders as their airframe manufacturer counterparts. Generally, the aero-engine element is estimated to amount to about a quarter of the basic fly-away unit cost of an aircraft, rising to one-third if initial spares are included. Over the lifespan of the aircraft, which is 15–20 years, at least another one-quarter is spent on spares. Some of the largest aero-engine producers are AVCO Lycoming, Detroit, Diesel Allison (a division of the General Motors Corp, which is the world's largest industrial organization), Garrett AiResearch and General Electric in the USA, Fiat in Italy, Rolls-Royce and Lucas Aerospace in the UK, Turbomeca and SNECMA in France, and MTU in FR Germany. In the USSR, Tumansky is one of the biggest aero-engine producers. In the *Third World*, manufacture of aero-engines is undertaken only with support from one or more of the established industries, for example, in Israel (Turbomeca and General Electric), India (Turbomeca, Rolls-Royce and Tumansky), South Africa (Fiat, Rolls-Royce), Egypt (Rolls-Royce), and Brazil (Turbomeca).

Missiles

During the 1970s, the capabilities of tactical missiles were multiplied through the deployment of the second generation of the various types on the major weapon platforms—fighter aircraft normally carry at least one type of missile, the air-to-air dogfight missile, and often an air-to-surface missile system for anti-tank use or ground attack missions, and in the case of naval fighters, for ASW or anti-ship use. In the case of ground forces, missiles are deployed for air defence for anti-tank use and for tactical surface-to-surface missions. The anti-tank missiles are either man-portable or vehicle-mounted, or helicopter-borne. In the case of navies, virtually all new fast patrol boats are equipped with ship-to-ship missiles, while frigates and large vessels normally carry ship-to-air missiles.

Table 3.2 lists the various categories of tactical missiles in production during the 1970s. From this list it is evident that missile design capacity reflects the technological capacity even better than aircraft production. Air-to-air missiles are designed only by the USA, the USSR, the UK, France, Italy and Israel, for example.[3] In fact, Israel stands out as the sole

[3] Missile construction in FR Germany was by 1980 confined to these Euromissile joint ventures with France. The much publicized undertakings of the West German rocket and space company OTRAG (Orbital Transport und Raketen-AG) on its leased territory in Zaire were still shrouded

Third World country with a manifested capacity to design and produce missiles. The dividing line between the three generations of missiles currently in existence or coming into existence has more to do with the types of guidance than with anything else: the first generation consists of wire-guided missiles, where the operator keeps both the missile and the target in sight and manually guides the missile by sending steering commands down a wire which the missile trails behind it. The second-generation missiles are fitted with infra-red (IR) emitters; an automatic tracker at the launcher receives the IR emissions from the missile and then a computer generates commands to bring the missile into line automatically along the trailing wire. The third generation is fully automatic and not wire-guided. It is designed so that the operator only has to launch it, hence the description 'fire-and-forget' weapon. The missile seeks its own target and homes onto it, guided by radar, laser or IR-homing.

The most advanced air-launched missiles under development by the end of the 1970s were the British Sea Skua anti-ship missile, which will arm Lynx helicopters and weighs only a tenth of the Exocet; the Sea Eagle, which is based on the Anglo–French Martel and which will arm Buccaneer, Tornado and Sea Harrier fighters; and Sky Flash, which recently entered service on British Phantoms and the Swedish Viggen. Sky Flash is the first air-to-air missile to have a monopulse radar seeker. It can be launched within two seconds of the firing button being pressed.

In 1980, the first reports appeared of a Soviet operational 'look-down shoot-down' air-to-air missile developed to counter penetrating bombers and cruise missiles. The weapon is expected to arm the modified MiG-25 Foxbat [17]. The USA had been working on its advanced medium-range air-to-air missile (AMRAAM) of the same type for approximately the same time, but this missile will not be deployed until 1985. Meanwhile, work was proceeding on the new Wasp air-launched missile that will be able to seek out and destroy enemy armour without guidance or other commands from the launch aircraft. The Wasp is being developed by Hughes and will have a 'look on after launch' capacity. The aircraft crew will not need to see or designate the target before weapon release. Both IR and millimetre-wave radar are being evaluated. According to the project manager, the missile will be the first ever to possess its own built-in target location and selection mechanism.

---

in secrecy when Zaire, in 1980, cancelled the lease agreement which would have run until the year 2000. Whether the company's activities were in reality confined to commercial satellite development, as claimed, or in fact had something to do with the development of military missiles and rockets may perhaps be clarified in the future, since the company during 1980 moved from Zaire to Libya. According to unconfirmed reports in the West German press, OTRAG obtained from the Libyan government the lease of a territory 600 km from Tripoli, where it will commence its rocket testings again.

The British Seawolf is so far the only naval anti-missile missile system. It uses the same type of guidance as the Rapier surface-to-air missile (SAM). Target acquisition, missile launch and in-flight guidance are all fully automatic. The final cost remains unknown, but one single round is reported to cost some $132 000.

The long-range Sea Dart ship-to-air missile system is now being developed in a Mk-2 version, for deployment in the late 1980s and 1990s. A vectored thrust solid-propellant boost motor will be used, and the guidance will be miniaturized, using the latest electronic techniques such as large-scale integration (LSI). Flight performance will be improved, as will the electronic counter-countermeasures (ECCM).

Among the surface-to-surface missile systems produced and deployed during the 1970s, some of the missiles listed can use both a conventional high-explosive (HE) warhead or a nuclear warhead: that is, the US Lance and Patriot, and the Soviet SCUD and Scaleboard. Among the most widely used and most exported SAM systems are the French–South African Crotale, the US MIM-23B Hawk, the Soviet SA-6 Gainful, and the British Rapier. More than 12 000 rounds of Rapier have been delivered. The Blindfire radar allows Rapier to be used at night or in conditions of poor visibility. The Tracked Rapier is mounted on a US vehicle, which carries an optical tracker and eight standard Rapier rounds. The system was originally developed for Iran.

The role of anti-tank weapons has been given considerable thought in Western Europe and the USA in the context of a war in Europe, with NATO forces facing a large number of WTO tanks. The first-generation anti-tank missiles still in use by the end of the 1970s were the French SS-11, the British Swingfire and Vigilant, the FR German Cobra and Mamba, the Italian Mosquito, and the US Dragon. The second generation is represented by the Euromissile MILAN and HOT systems and the US BGM-71A TOW. TOW has been delivered to over 30 countries, and Hughes will develop an improved version. Euromissile has delivered 100 000 MILAN rounds and more than 3 000 launchers to 22 countries. MILAN will be improved to a third-generation system either by being given a bigger or more lethal warhead or a new night-sight. HOT has been delivered to 12 customers and can be launched from various types of platform. For the future, the Euromissile Dynamics Group, set up in December 1979, has started a two-year study for a heavy long-range anti-tank missile, involving BAe, Aérospatiale and MBB.

In the USA, the Rockwell Hellfire anti-tank missile system is being developed to arm the AH-64 attack helicopter. Hellfire will be automatically guided. The US Army will receive 536 systems between 1984 and 1992. Testing of another US third-generation system will be completed in 1982 under the Infantry Man-portable Anti-Armour Assault Weapon System

(IMAAWS) programme, to produce a shoulder-launched 16-kg all-weather weapon suitable for anti-tank use and for military operations in cities. Raytheon and Ford are tendering for the design of this laser-guided missile. The most widely used Soviet anti-tank missile remains the AT-3 Sagger, dating from the early 1960s. Apart from the AT-4 and AT-5, first seen in 1975, no new anti-tank missiles have been deployed. (The WTO has rather countered NATO anti-tank missile efforts by improving the armour of the tanks.) No Third World country has designed an anti-tank missile.

Small arms

In contrast to the four categories of major weapon system, small arms have a much longer service lifetime. Towards the end of the decade, both NATO and the Soviet Union presented new automatic gun designs. The most common guns now in use, both in the West and in the East, use 7.62-mm calibre ammunition—the most well-known guns being the US M-16 and the Soviet AK-47 Kalashnikov. The AK-47 has been identified in use with the rebel troops in Afghanistan, originating from 18-year-old licence production in China, according to information supplied by the rebels to Western reporters. A total of at least 30 million AK-47s are in use in the world today—or 40 million, according to other reports. A common saying among US soldiers in Viet Nam with experience of attacks with the AK-47 was that if "political power really grows out of the barrel of a gun, it is a Kalashnikov gun" [19].

The Israeli experiences of the AK-47 in combat led them to develop the 5.56-mm Galil, based on the Kalashnikov. The new Soviet model, which bears the designation AK-74 and is presently being introduced, uses 5.45-mm ammunition, while the recently tested new gun for NATO is of the 5.56-mm calibre.

V. Future trends in conventional arms development

The market forecasts that existed by 1980 for the various weapon categories all assumed that no drastic changes would take place in the next decade, insofar as the continued development of armaments was concerned. Plans for the armaments of the 1990s were well advanced.

Aircraft

Military aircraft manufacturers throughout the world expect the market for combat aircraft of all kinds to remain buoyant during the 1980s, despite some pressure for a reduction in arms sales. The aerospace industries collectively believe that more than 5 000 new combat aircraft are likely to be ordered during the 1980s, since several current types, such as over 5 000 Phantoms and over 1 000 Starfighters, will need replacement. Most of the orders will be placed in the USA, which is the biggest Western aircraft producer. The total market value is estimated at more than $100 000 million, including spares and support. The shares of different categories of aircraft are estimated as follows: (*a*) light strike trainers, such as Hawk, Alpha Jet and Macchi 339, could be worth up to $7 800 million or 16 per cent; (*b*) ground attack aircraft, such as Harrier, could be worth up to $12 700 million or 25 per cent; (*c*) larger strike and air superiority aircraft, such as the F-16 and F-18, would comprise $15 750 million or 36 per cent; and (*d*) complex multirole aircraft, such as the F-15 and Viggen, could be worth $10 200 million or 23 per cent of the world aircraft market [20].

The number of projects will, however, not be very large—the Tornado programme alone is expected to cost about $8 000 million through the 1980s. In the USA, several new tactical aircraft are planned. One related project is the AFTI (Advanced Fighter Technology Integration) programme, conducted by General Dynamics. It uses a F-16A to test some of the technologies likely to be incorporated in tomorrow's fighters, such as advanced manoeuvring capability, digital flight controls, integrated flight and weapons fire control systems, and advances in the ever critical area of pilot–aircraft interaction.

The Eurofighter programme may eventually surpass that of the Tornado. Initial studies undertaken since September 1979 by BAe, Dassault-Breguet and MBB suggested that a single design could meet the three-country requirements. The French ACT.92 and the British AST 403 requirements were quite similar, specifying a multirole aircraft with a slight emphasis on strike capability. The FR German TKF.90 requirement was more oriented toward the interceptor role. All three companies recommended the use of canard surfaces, similar to that of the Swedish Viggen. The ECA (European Combat Aircraft) would have to fly in 1984/85 to meet British demands. Alternatives might be to buy most of the ECA avionics from the USA, or to purchase a US design to avoid funding problems, but FR Germany and the UK agreed as a baseline for the ECA that it must be 20 per cent better than the most advanced-technology aircraft of its size available in 1980. The programme unit cost would be $20 million (in constant 1980 prices), and sales could total some $20 000 million—FR Germany and the UK will need 300 and 200 planes respectively, France could buy 200, and Italy and other countries might bring total sales to 1 000. If the ECA fails, the respective countries will fall back on their national programmes.

The future for Sweden's aircraft industry is even more hazardous, considering the fact that no big export market is readily available—an industrial group was set up in 1980 to conduct a two-year project definition study for the future so-called JAS fighter aircraft. Some type of collaboration with other industries is being sought, and talks had been held at an early stage with BAe (UK), MBB (FR Germany), Rockwell (USA) and IAI (Israel). The requirement was established as 300 aircraft from 1990 onwards.

In the USA, the FX fighter project, approved by the Carter Administration in January 1980, will be developed for export only, for a market of 500–1 000 planes, in spite of the previous US policy of export restraint. Northrop is participating in the FX contest with its F-5G, with first prototype due to fly in 1982, and General Dynamics is presenting a re-engined F-16, the F-16/79. The FX is described as an intermediate-technology or low-performance fighter, or a 'defensive interceptor', and its development is considered necessary to prevent an increasing number of countries turning to more sophisticated combat aircraft to fill their needs [21].

The expected value of military helicopters produced in the Western world alone during the 1980s is estimated at $7 500 million, or about 15 000 units. The US UH-60A Black Hawk programme alone calls for the production of 1 107 helicopters until the end of 1986 at a total cost of $3 400 million. This gives a unit cost of $3 046 million per helicopter, twice the price of the Bell UH-1 Huey. A European co-operative helicopter project is being planned.

In addition to the continued development of the above categories of aircraft, all aircraft manufacturers have begun research into alternative fuels and more efficient aerodynamic shapes.

Armoured vehicles

The future production of tanks in Western Europe may also be a co-operative effort, according to a formal letter of intent signed by France and FR Germany in 1980, but financial constraints have cast doubts on the feasibility of the project in its envisaged form. Until recently a battle tank consisted simply of an armoured shell, a gun and mechanical components, but by 1980 electronic systems accounted for 30 per cent of the cost of a tank and within 10 years can be expected to reach 40 per cent. Hence, a co-operatively produced main battle tank is expected to result in savings of approximately 30–40 per cent in R&D due to cost sharing. In 1980 it was reported that the UK would order 240 new tanks for its forces in FR Germany. The new tank will be the version first developed for Iran as Shir-2, and later known as the P4030 Challenger. However, each decade since 1945 has seen the failure of collaboration in tank production—in the 1950s, a first French–FR German effort failed, followed by a joint project between France, FR Germany and Italy which also came to nothing. In the 1960s, the FR German–US project for the XM-803/KPz-70 tank failed. In the 1970s, a second FR German–US joint project was cancelled and instead resulted in two new tanks, XM-1 (USA) and Leopard-2 (FR Germany).

With these new battle tanks, plus others such as the Israeli Merkava and the Soviet T-80, entering service or completing trials, it is obvious that the armies of the world remain convinced of the need for such weapons in the future, despite advances in anti-tank missiles and armour-piercing guns. During the 1970s tank designs reverted to the heavier type, as new types of armour were developed. The Leopard-1, for example, weighs 40 tons, and the Leopard-2, which entered service in 1979, weighs 55 tons. The development of spaced high-performance steel armour in the 1970s made the Chobham armour possible. Then the composite armour was developed, reported to be three times as effective against shaped charges as steel armour of the same weight. The US Secretary of the Army stated publicly that the XM-1 tank was impervious to any known anti-tank missile, including the TOW with a 127-mm warhead and the Shillelagh with a 152-mm warhead. The new armour was incorporated in the British Shir-1 and the FR German Leopard-2. The Soviet T-72, first paraded in Moscow in November 1977, does not use composite armour, but this tank is in effect much older and was already in troop use in 1969–70. The US Army assumed that the Soviet Union must have a tank with the latest armour, however, even before reports had appeared of the new Soviet T-80 main battle tank, and therefore increased the warhead of its new Hellfire guided anti-tank missile from 152-mm to 178-mm.[4]

New technologies

During the 1970s the advent of laser rangefinders and of electronic ballistic computers has improved the tank gun systems, in combination with a number of sensors used to locate the targets. A further development will be the introduction of carbon dioxide lasers. The single-shot hit probability which is obtained with the latest fire control systems is close to the theoretical maximum. When this maximum has been reached, technology will perhaps advance only through the development of an entirely new type of gun. This might be the magnetic railgun, which by the end of the 1970s was reportedly taking shape in Los Alamos, supported by the US Army and the Defense Department's Defense Advanced Research Projects Agency. According to US officials engaged in this project, the Soviet Union is also at work on

[4] Reporters of the advancements in conventional weaponry are occasionally carried away into describing their own weapons utopia. The following example concerns future anti-tank weapons: "It would be ideal if every infantryman, every home guard, every guerilla fighter, every policeman and even every civilian could be armed with his own personal weapon capable of knocking out a tank. He would sleep with it under his bed, take it with him when he went out, put it under his table when he eats and treat it like a soldier should treat his rifle" [7].

railguns, and has reportedly conducted 150 railgun firings as compared to 40 test firings in the USA. The relatively small railguns could blast through the thickest armour of a tank or battleship at about 10 times the speed of the fastest gun projectiles now in existence, which is comparable to the speed of a spacecraft. Railguns could also lift objects into orbit and launch space missions [22].

The increase in the share of electronics and computer techniques in all weapon systems is behind the concept of the 'intelligent weapon'. For example, a new type of minehunter is being developed by Belgium, the Netherlands and France around a minehunting data handling system. Very few industries have worked on this technology, and the system which samples and processes all data coming from the minehunting sonars, radio navigational systems, radar, and so on will make the tripartite minehunter into a 'clever ship'.

The advances in counter-radar-detection techniques announced in 1980 point towards future 'invisible' aircraft and missiles—US Secretary of Defense Brown said at a press conference on 22 August 1980 that a new technology had been invented which will have great military significance, namely, a technology to render aircraft invisible to radar detection. In the same year the UK announced a developed version of a Polaris missile which cannot be detected by enemy radar. The missile is called Chevaline and has cost $1 000 million to develop. With microminiature radars no bigger than a coin, the possibility of intelligent weapons begins to look immense.

One remaining problem for the 1980s will be that of man–machine relationships and how to adjust and fully integrate man with a very complex machine. Research is already being conducted to define the limits of man's own responses and to specify how man can be kept functioning at peak efficiency when in command of an intelligent weapon where the danger of an overload of information on the human factor is greatest.

Disarmament aspects

While the future trends in conventional weaponry may include computerized pilots, electronic soldiers, invisible aircraft and intelligent weapons, including guns that fire the ammunition into space, there have been very few attempts at intelligent ways of reversing the upward spiral in weapon developments during the 1970s.

The UN General Assembly's 1978 Special Session devoted to Disarmament did take up the issue of conventional in addition to nuclear disarmament. Yugoslavia advocated a ban on the development, production and deployment of all new types of conventional weapon and new systems of such weapons. Norway proposed that states should adopt a procedure by which budget requests for major weapons and weapon systems should be accompanied by an evaluation of the impact of such weapons on arms control and disarmament. The Final Document of the Special Session states that countries with the largest military arsenals have a special responsibility for pursuing the process of conventional armaments reductions, and further stresses the importance of agreements reached on a regional basis, specially mentioning Europe and Latin America.

The conversion of military industries to civilian, that is, alternative production, became a much debated issue during the 1970s. The early 1960s marked a certain breakthrough for the conversion idea at the UN level, when a group of East–West experts in a 1962 report agreed on the feasibility of conversion in all economic systems. Since then, a vast body of literature has been published, a further inspiration occurring when military production for the Viet Nam war began to decrease. About one-third of the workers in aerospace industries lost their jobs from 1968 to 1972. At the end of the 1970s some 75 per cent of all assessments of the conversion problem originated in the USA [23a].

But one of the most publicized initiatives for alternative production in a military industry came from the UK, with the programme presented by the shop stewards of Lucas Aerospace, called the Corporate Plan. It remains to be seen in the 1980s whether this was just a shortlived exception or if it signalled a new trend by which a demand for more power over production by the defence industry workforce will lead to more civilian production.

A Soviet contribution was noted in Leonid Brezhnev's speech to the Central Committee of the Communist Party in October 1980, calling upon the defence industry of the Soviet Union to pay more attention to providing for the production of civilian goods. He also claimed that in recent years, the defence industry had done a great deal to increase the production of such commodities as TV-sets, refrigerators, washing machines, and so on. Over the next five years it is expected that not only the 'hands' of the defence industry but also the 'brains' will be concerned with peaceful production. There are plans to draw more widely on the knowledge and experience of engineers and designers of the defence industry to develop civilian branches [24].

Alternative production is closely related to the debate on disarmament and development, which has been of concern to the United Nations since 1960. During the 1970s, several important UN-sponsored studies in this field were published [23, 25]. A UN study initiated prior to the 1978 Special Session devoted to Disarmament, prepared by experts under the Chairmanship of Inga Thorsson, dealt with the relationship between disarmament and development. This study will also take up various aspects related to conventional disarmament, such as the alternative production in military production.

References

1. *Military Technology* (Bonn), No. 16, 1980.
2. Assembly of the Western European Union, *Proceedings*, Second Part (WEU, Paris, December 1980).
3. Gervasi, T., *Arsenal of Democracy, American weapons available for export: what they cost, what they do, who makes them, who has them* (Grove Press, New York, 1977).
4. Alexander, A. J., *Armor Development in the Soviet Union and the United States*, Rand R-1860-NA, A report prepared for the Director of New Assessment, Office of Secretary of Defense (RAND, Santa Monica, September 1976).
5. Richardson, D., 'The importance of electronics in defence', *Military Technology* (Bonn), No. 18, 1980, p. 53.
6. *The NATO Standardization Market for Ground-Launched Missiles and Missile Air Defense Systems* (*Is Shared Technology of Missiles in NATO a Valid Marketing Strategy?*), A special study prepared and published by Forecast Associates Inc., Analysis A (Forecast Associates, Ridgefield, 1979), pp. 3–4.
7. Eliot, C., 'Man portable anti-tank weapons', *Military Technology* (Bonn), No. 7, January–February 1979, p. 18.
8. Klare, M. T., 'La multinationalisation des industries de guerre', *Le Monde Diplomatic*, 4 February 1977.
9. *Defence Equipment: Policy on Overseas Sales*, Parliamentary debates (Hansard), House of Lords Official Report, Motions, Col. 779, Vol. 408, No. 117, 23 April 1980 (HMSO, London, 1980).
10. 'Arms coproduction', an address by Matthew Nimetz, Under Secretary of State for Security Assistance, Science and Technology, before the American Defense Preparedness Association in Rosslyn, Virginia, on July 15, 1980, *Current Policy*, No. 200, 15 July 1980.
11. 'UPI from Wuhan, China', *International Herald Tribune*, 11 January 1980.
12. 'Chinese pushing aerospace technology', *Aviation Week & Space Technology*, 11 June 1979.
13. *Afrique Défense*, November 1979.
14. *World Armaments and Disarmament, SIPRI Yearbook 1979* (Taylor & Francis, London, 1979, Stockholm International Peace Research Institute), chapter 2.
15. *Defense Daily*, 6 January 1981 (quoting the latest ACDA issue of *World Military Expenditures and Arms Transfers*).
16. 'Egypte: le lieutenant-générale Badaoui: "Nous avons trés fortement dévéloppé nos armement" ', *Afrique Défense*, November 1980, p. 55.
17. *Government Business Worldwide*, 8 December 1980.
18. *Dagens Nyheter* (Stockholm), 8 December 1980.
19. Jacobson, P., 'Kalashnikov—vapnens Volkswagen' ['Kalashnikov—the Volkswagen of weapons'], *Dagens Nyheter* (Stockholm), 22 February 1981.
20. 'Combat aircraft projections', *Financial Times*, 4 June 1980, p. vii.

majority of arms transfers from the two major powers were in this period in the form of military aid; that is, both the USA and the USSR gave away second-hand (mostly war surplus) weapons.

In the 1950s, US foreign policy also strongly emphasized the importance of the so-called forward defence areas in the Third World, that is, pro-Western countries bordering on the Soviet Union or China. A similar change in Soviet policy towards Third World countries can be observed from the mid-1950s, when the two-camp theory was abandoned in favour of the policy of 'peaceful co-existence', enabling the USSR to expand relations with the non-aligned countries. These policies resulted in an increasing flow of arms to Third World countries, mainly in the form of gifts of relatively unsophisticated material. Thus, the giving away of second-hand military equipment to allied and friendly nations, often with political conditions attached, was characteristic of arms transfers from the major powers during the 1950s and the early 1960s.

Two new and important trends emerged during the first half of the 1960s. The first was a marked shift from aid to trade; that is, instead of giving them away, the suppliers began to sell arms under a variety of cash, credit or loan arrangements. The main motivation for this trend was purely economic. Coupled with this trend was a change from the transfer of obsolete to more sophisticated weapons: it became obvious that an increasing number of countries could afford to pay for the weapons they required, hence the demand for more sophisticated equipment (see figure 4.1).

The second emerging trend was that an increasing share of the global arms trade was with Third World countries. The reasons for this were several. Most importantly, as the arms industries of Western Europe were reconstructed, the European market for US arms became smaller. Competition grew among the weapon exporters as more countries entered the arms business, so the need to create new export markets became important, not least to the two great powers. At the same time, the demand for weapons was rising among the newly independent states in the Third World for reasons of both national security and national prestige.

These two main trends are still distinctive features of the global arms trade. The shift from aid to trade can be exemplified using figures from the United States. During 1949–61 the cost of the Military Assistance Program (MAP) amounted to $25 701 million, while weapon sales represented an income of $161 million [2]. During the 1970s, weapon sales were 2.3 times larger than military assistance. Figure 4.2 compares the revenues from Foreign Military Sales (FMS) deliveries and MAP expenditures during the 1970s.

The other main trend, the shift towards the Third World, has given underdeveloped countries a 75 per cent share of the world-wide trade in

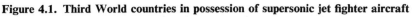

Figure 4.1. Third World countries in possession of supersonic jet fighter aircraft

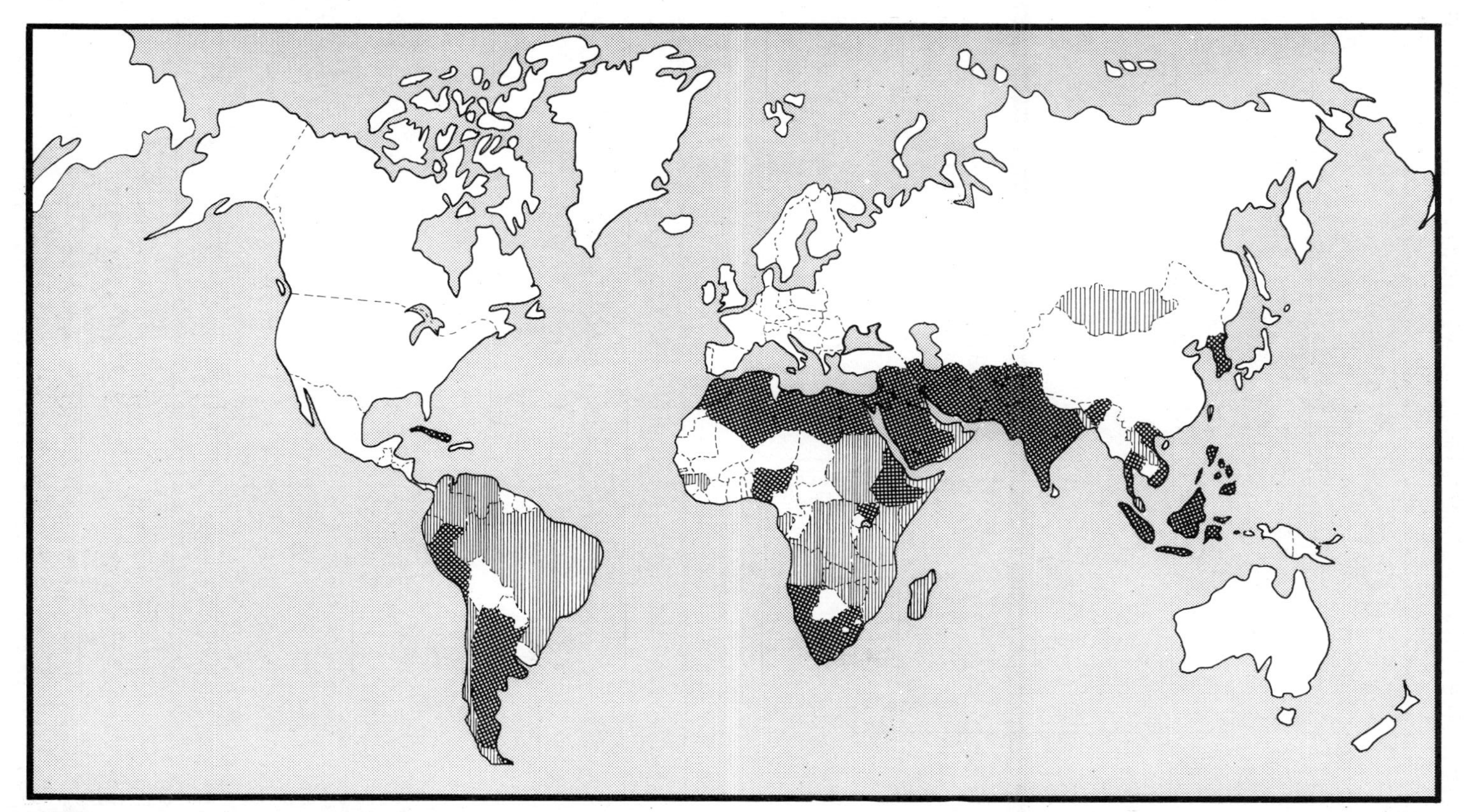

Figure 4.2. FMS revenues and MAP expenditures for the United States, 1970–79

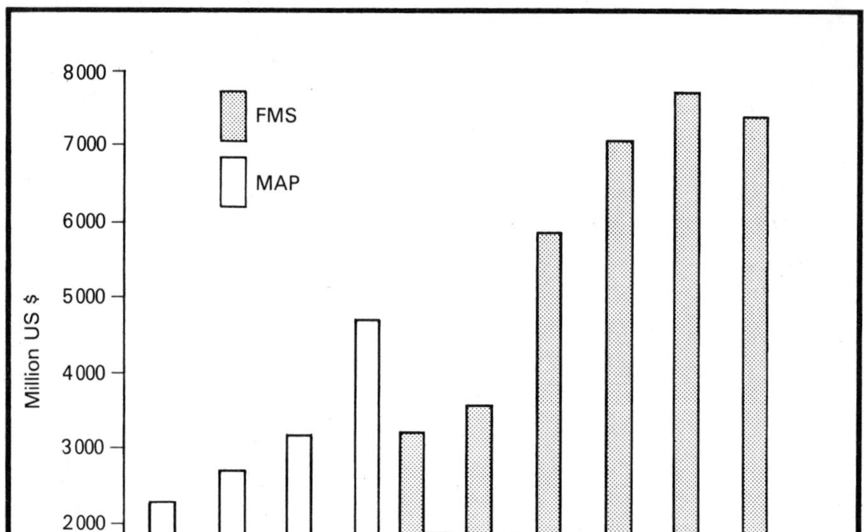

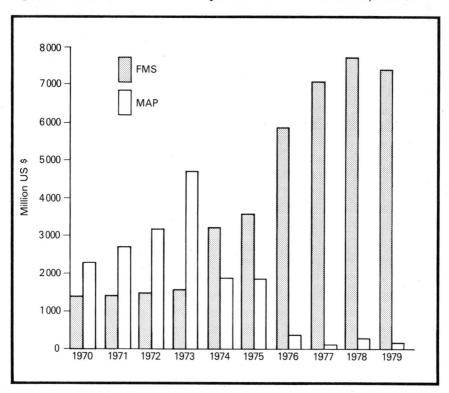

Note: The high MAP expenditures during 1970–73 are explained by the Viet Nam War, but otherwise the trend towards sales is a prominent one.
Source: Reference [3].

major conventional weapons (while the industrialized countries account for 85 per cent of world military expenditure).[1]

The yearly rate of increase in the global trade in arms is notable. During the first half of the 1960s it was 5 per cent, in the next five years 10 per cent and during 1970–75 about 15 per cent. The most explosive increase has occurred from 1973–74 onwards, mainly due to the rise in crude oil prices, the Middle East conflicts, the Viet Nam War and, paradoxically, its termination.

[1] The SIPRI arms trade data cover transfers of major weapons only (that is, aircraft, missiles, armoured vehicles and warships). The SIPRI figures and percentages in this chapter refer to SIPRI trend indicator values of the arms transactions, unless stated otherwise.

Figure 4.3. The 15 leading Third World importers and the 7 leading exporters of major arms in the 1970s

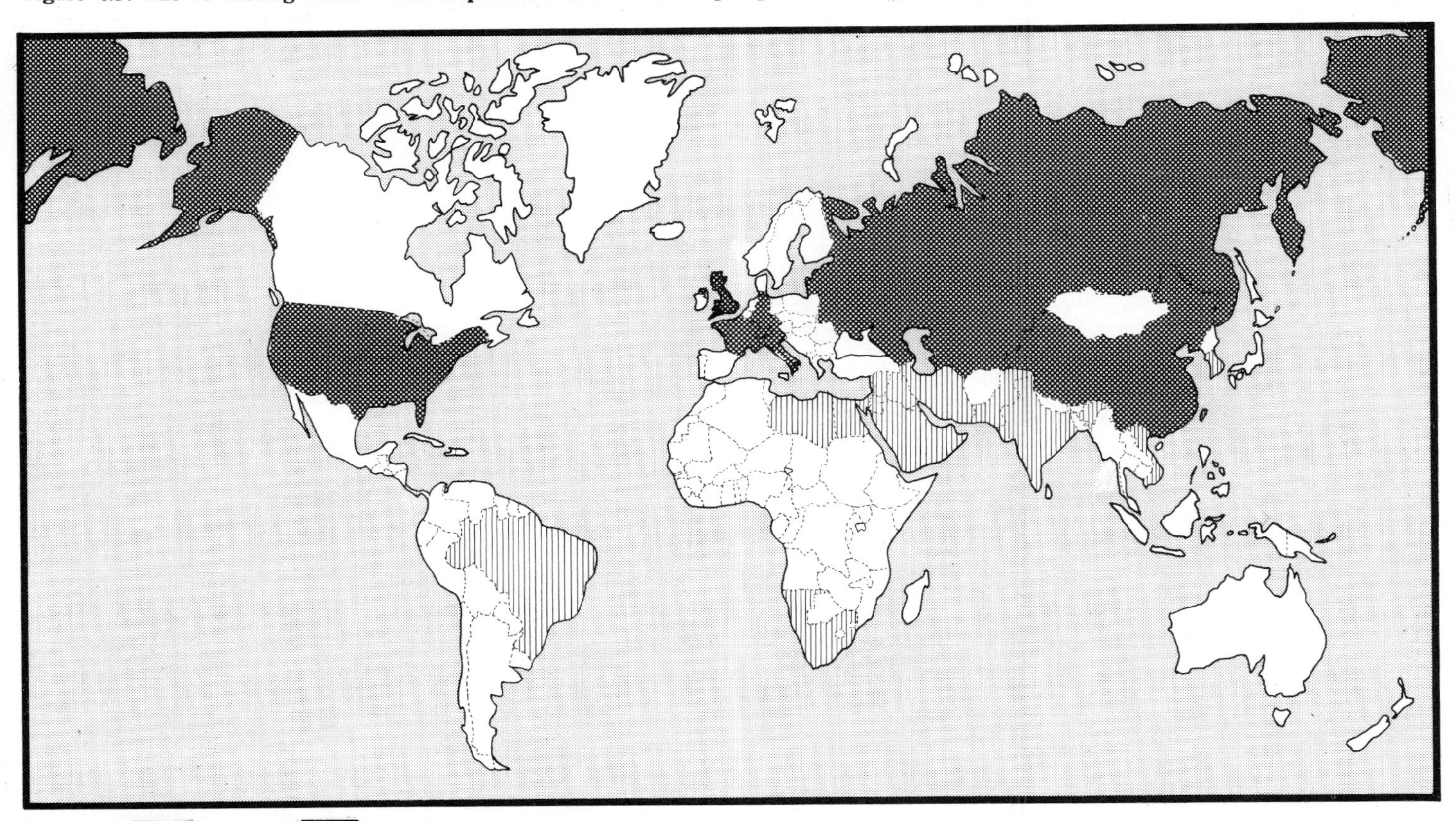

Source: Derived from table 4.1.

III. Arms trade in the 1970s

The trade with the Third World

Roughly 75 per cent of the global trade in major conventional weapons during the 1970s consisted of deliveries from industrialized countries to the Third World. This flow is illustrated on the map in figure 4.3, which also clearly shows the concentration of recipient states in an area which is both strategically important vis à vis big power interests and one of the most flagrant conflict areas of the world during this period. It is also possible to see the emergence of regional great powers in the Third World, mirrored in arms trade patterns. The largest importing countries are listed in table 4.1, with the most prominent supplier countries in each case.

Table 4.1. The 15 leading Third World importers of major weapons, 1970–79

Recipient country	Percentage of Third World total imports	Largest supplier to each country
Iran	13.6	USA
Libya	6.2	France, USSR[a]
Israel	6.1	USA
Syria	5.7	USSR
Viet Nam[b]	5.6	USA, USSR[a]
Saudi Arabia	5.1	USA
Iraq	4.5	USSR
Jordan	4.4	USA
South Korea	4.4	USA
India	3.8	USSR
Egypt	3.6	USSR
South Africa	2.4	France
Brazil	2.0	USA
Taiwan	1.7	USA
Pakistan	1.7	China, France[a]
Others	*29.2*	

[a] The first country was the main supplier in 1970–74 and the second in 1975–79.
[b] The figure for Viet Nam includes transfers to North and South before 1976.

Figure 4.4 shows the share of each of the Third World regions in the global imports of major weapons during the past decade.

The Middle East

During the 1970s, the Middle East was the largest arms-importing region in the Third World, accounting for 48 per cent of all Third World imports of major weapons. This trend is consistent with the two overriding determinants of arms transfers: the conflict determinant, and the promotion of the interests of the great powers, mainly the USA and the USSR. The

Figure 4.4. Regional shares of the major weapons supplied to the Third World, 1970–79

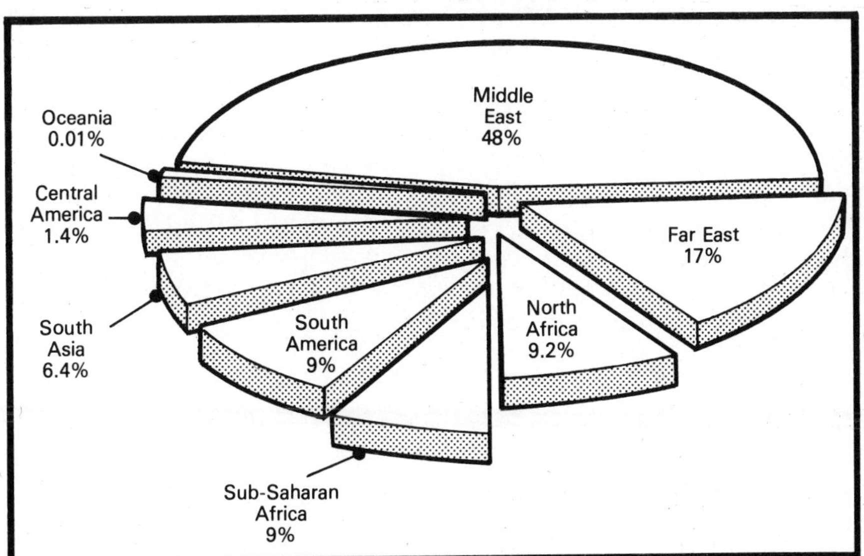

sources of conflict in this region are many: for example, the hostility between Israel and the Arab states, which has caused a major war to break out in every decade since World War II; antagonism between some Arab states and civil wars involving several different minority groups; the ambitions for power of national leaders and individual nations, exemplified by the late Shah of Iran's ambition for Iran to become the 'guardian of the Gulf'; and the Palestine problem. These and several other potential or armed conflicts have ensured a constant demand to secure new weapons for the armed forces or to replace damaged or destroyed equipment.

The interests of the supplier nations, on the other hand, are directed towards the region by its strategic geographic position in the world and, not least, by the oil resources there.

The conflicts and the strategic position of the region, coupled with the fact that the capacity of many oil-exporting countries to absorb capital is often low in relation to the amount of capital available for investments, have had a strong impact on the propensity for the region to buy arms. This was accentuated by the 400 per cent rise in crude oil prices in 1973–74. By 1976 the military expenditures of Iran and Saudi Arabia, two of the main oil producers, ranked seventh and eighth respectively, among the countries of the world. Ten years earlier, in 1967, their positions were 25th and 33rd. Also in 1976, these two countries, together with Israel, accounted for 37 per cent of the military expenditure of the Third World. During the period from 1973 until the fall of the Shah in 1979, approximately two-thirds of all US arms exports went to these three countries.

The main suppliers of arms to the region have shifted: in 1970–74 the Soviet Union accounted for 51 per cent of all deliveries to the region and the United States for 34 per cent. During 1975–79, the US share rose to 61 per cent; the Soviet share fell to 15–20 per cent; and France and the UK switched positions so that France ranked as third largest exporter and the UK fourth.

Notable shifts in the positions of the individual importers have also occurred. During the first half of the 1970s, Syria and Egypt were the largest recipients, both dependent on deliveries from the Soviet Union. While Iran then ranked third, in the second half of the decade it became by far the largest importer in the region, receiving well over twice as much as the second largest recipient, Saudi Arabia. This reflected the nearly unconditional support Iran enjoyed from the United States.

Egypt's share of imports to the region sharply diminished with the shift from the Soviet Union to the United States for arms supplies. However, large-scale arms deliveries from the USA are now under way, to a large extent the result of the Camp David Peace Treaty signed by Israel and Egypt. The two countries were promised $4 500 million in military grants and loans from the United States—a notable illustration of an international political role arms transfers can play, that is, 'arms for peace'. The following observation on the Middle East scene summarizes the present situation:

> The interaction of local tensions and conflicts, ready availability of cash, appetite for sophisticated arms and the opportunity for political influence through arms transfers lends little prospect of success for attempts to achieve regional arms control . . . It is one of the grim ironies of the Middle East that few parties to those conflicts seem willing to contemplate compromise without the assurance of massive military backing. [4]

The Far East

The conflict determinant has also steered arms transfer developments in this region. The many conflicts represent a mix of historical and ethnic controversies, on the one hand, and the involvement of the great powers on the other. The Indo-China wars explain a large share of the region's total import of major arms: North and South Viet Nam accounted for 62 per cent during the first half of the decade. The end of the Viet Nam War, however, led to an increased flow of weapons to the region. The so-called Nixon Doctrine—whereby the USA should strive to assist other countries to assume greater responsibility for their own defence—implied that the United States should give or preferably sell military equipment in such quantities that these countries could themselves resist external or internal threats. In 1970, Secretary of Defense Melvin Laird stated:

> The challenging aspects of our new policy can, therefore, best be achieved when each partner does its share and contributes what it best can to the common effort. In the

majority of cases, this means indigenous manpower organized into properly equipped and well trained armed forces with the help of material, training, technology and specialized skills furnished by the United States through the Military Assistance Program or as Foreign Military Sales. [5]

Arms supplies from the USA, as well as from West European countries, have consequently increased to countries such as the Philippines, Singapore, Thailand and Malaysia. But the main arms importers of the region during the second half of the 1970s were South Korea, Viet Nam and Taiwan. Viet Nam re-emerged as a major importer from 1978 because of the wars with China and Kampuchea, and was dependent on the Soviet Union for arms supplies, much of which was in the form of gifts. South Korea's and Taiwan's dominant positions have been due to their rapid economic growth in the 1970s. One aspect of this growth is their emergence as strong regional military powers: together they account for 51 per cent of the region's import of major arms during 1975–79. In addition, both countries have bought production licences for sophisticated weapon systems—for example, Taiwan has since 1974 produced the F-5E jet fighter under licence from the USA. The effects of the normalization between the United States and China on US policy towards Taiwan are as yet uncertain, but will probably have some impact.

Africa

Africa had a relatively low military profile until the 1970s, when the conflict determinant began to play a role: there were the liberation wars in the Portuguese colonies, fighting in the Horn of Africa over the Ogaden province, liberation movement conflicts in South Africa and Rhodesia which also affected the front-line states Angola, Zambia and Mozambique, and the West Saharan conflict. In addition, growing awareness of the importance of the strategic raw materials in many African countries attracted the involvement of the great powers in the region. While before the 1970s the traditional arms suppliers to Africa had been the former colonial powers France and the UK, in the second half of the 1970s this near-monopoly was broken primarily by the Soviet Union. During 1975–79 the USSR was the largest single arms supplier to Algeria, Libya, Angola, Mozambique and Ethiopia. Furthermore, it was during the same period the largest supplier to the North African as well as the Sub-Saharan African states as a whole. US arms sales to the region also increased, in particular to Morocco, Tunisia, Kenya and Sudan.

South Africa acquired large numbers of weapons during the decade, mainly by licence production agreements but also by means of loopholes in the UN embargoes. One of the most spectacular transfers to South

Africa during the 1970s was its acquisition of the GC-45 long-range howitzer, supplied through the Space Research Corporation, a Canadian company on the US–Canadian border.

In summary, Africa is no longer a virgin market for arms suppliers: adding North and Sub-Saharan Africa together, they now account for approximately 21 per cent of all Third World arms imports, making Africa the second largest importing region in the Third World.

Latin America

This region exhibits a somewhat different arms procurement pattern. Historically, Latin American defence policies have to a large extent been dictated by the needs of the United States. US policy towards the continent has from the beginning of the 1960s been concentrated on internal security matters and, therefore, US arms exports since that time have largely consisted of counterinsurgency (COIN) equipment such as helicopters, COIN aircraft and armoured personnel carriers. Furthermore, the United States has throughout much of the 1970s refused to sell sophisticated major weapon systems such as jet fighter aircraft, advanced missile systems and modern warships.

On the other hand, the 1970s is the first full decade in which the larger Latin American countries have been able to formulate their national security needs on a more independent basis. This has led to increasing coherence and co-ordination within and between the armed services and, not least, to a strong demand for major weapon systems. The acquisition of large and small modern warships in particular can probably to some extent be seen in connection with the overall extension of the territorial waters to 12 nautical miles and the international recognition of a 188-nautical mile exclusive economic zone beyond.

Due in part to the restrictive arms export policy of the United States, leading European arms producers were able to enter the Latin American market and deliver sophisticated weapon systems. In the first half of the 1970s, France ranked as the largest supplier, the USA second, the UK third and FR Germany fourth. From 1973 the United States in successive stages lifted some restrictions on arms exports to the region, which led to the transfer of some major weapon systems and a growing US share of the market. During 1975–79 the USA was the largest single supplier to the region, but European suppliers added together still accounted for by far the greatest share. This is due largely to the agreements for licence production or co-production negotiated with the UK, FR Germany, France and Italy. Consequently the two greatest powers in the region, Brazil and Argentina, now produce COIN aircraft, helicopters, tanks, anti-tank missiles, frigates, corvettes and submarines of European design. Another notable fact is that

Israel sold major weapon systems to 10 Latin American countries during the 1970s.

Arms transfers to the region are mainly a Western affair, with the exception of Cuba, which is dependent on Soviet supplies.

South Asia

In the rank order of Third World arms-importing regions, South Asia ranked third in the first half of the 1970s and sixth in the second half. The largest importing country was India, accounting for approximately two-thirds of the region's arms imports during the 1970s. Similar to Brazil in the Latin American region, India, as the dominant power in South Asia, attempted to become less dependent on a great power (i.e., the UK), has a large indigenous arms production capacity and produces many major weapons under licence.

In seeking to free itself from British influence, India turned to the Soviet Union for arms supplies but seemingly found itself in a similar position of dependence: in the period 1970–74 the USSR accounted for 70 per cent of India's arms imports and in 1975–79 for 57 per cent. However, India seems to have been fairly successful in diversifying its sources of major weapons.

Pakistan is the second largest importer in the region, securing most of its arms from France and China. Relations between the United States and Pakistan are complicated in terms of arms transfers. The United States has turned down some Pakistani requests for arms, but Pakistan has also refused to accept arms transfers offered by the USA. It is possible that the recent events in Iran and Afghanistan will both open the market to the USA and generally increase arms transfers to the region.

The suppliers

Two facts about the arms-supplying countries are illustrated in figure 4.5: first, the arms trade with the Third World is dominated by transfers from the United States and the Soviet Union, reflecting their dominant positions in the two alliances. Second, when grouping the suppliers on a political basis, the arms trade is dominated by transfers from Western countries, whose share throughout the 1970s amounted to 65–70 per cent.

There are strong, dynamic elements underlying these figures. Many new elements have come into evidence during the 1970s, notably the rapidly increasing weapon exports from France, Italy and FR Germany. This is primarily explained by two factors: (*a*) the economic imperative, i.e. the need to cover research and development costs and secure employment in the arms industries (see also section IV) and (*b*) the fact that these countries,

technical assistance, maintenance, training and education throughout the life span of the weapon. This increases military efficiency but generates dependence on the weapon supplier, thus reinforcing the overall political and economic dependence on the supplier countries. Diversified supply and licensed production by many countries, especially in the Third World, are regarded as a means to counteract dependence. It is doubtful whether licensed production significantly alters the situation. On the contrary, it may be argued that the vast technological assistance required to set up a sophisticated production plant in an otherwise not so technologically advanced country will reinforce dependence on the supplier country.

Arms exports can also jeopardize the industrialized countries, both economically and politically. Unforeseen events have caused sudden changes in arms transfers. For example, after the recent revolution in Iran, defence contracts with the USA worth $15 000–20 000 million were cancelled, as were $4 000 million worth of contracts with the UK. Similarly, Saudi Arabia withdrew funding for a planned licence production agreement between Egypt and the UK when Egypt signed the Camp David Treaty.

The political and economic repercussions of such events, seen in the context of arms trade relationships among states, are many. Employment in the arms industries and the sub-contractor firms in the supplier countries is affected, as is the balance-of-payments situation.

Political repercussions might occur, for instance, when a sudden, radical political change takes place in a recipient country. If this country has previously acquired technologically sophisticated weapon systems, it may be able to use reverse leverage on the supplier country—for example, by threatening to disclose details of the weapon to a rival supplier country.

Summary of main trends

The most important trends in the global arms trade in conventional weapons during the 1970s are: (*a*) the quantitative increase in general and in the trade with the Third World in particular, including an increase in the number of countries buying and selling arms; (*b*) the increasing frequency of licence production agreements with Third World countries; (*c*) the emergence of Third World countries as suppliers; and (*d*) the qualitative increase, that is, in the level of technological sophistication, combined with the continuing shift from aid to trade.

IV. The determinants of demand and supply

It is useful to list the various factors which give impetus to the international trade in weapons, both for the recipients of arms and for the suppliers, but in reality these factors closely interact and are not easily definable as separate determinants of specific arms transfers.

The demand for weapons

The general motivation for importing weapons is 'to increase national security'. This implies that the country or government (*a*) is involved in an inter-state conflict or civil war, (*b*) is experiencing the threat of war or civil war, (*c*) wishes to counteract the arming of a potentially hostile neighbouring country, (*d*) is striving for regional dominance, or (*e*) seeks sophisticated weapons for reasons of national prestige. Some countries also claim that arms imports accelerate industrialization and modernization of their economies. Finally, practically every acquisition of major arms is also to some extent influenced by the major powers and the promotion of their interests.

The supply of weapons

Looking at the global determinants as opposed to those related to the national economies, the global determinants are perhaps more applicable to the USA and the USSR, while the national economy determinants apply more to the 'smaller' suppliers. Again, both types of determinants closely interact.

The global economic determinants for the supplier countries are that they wish to ensure the flow of raw materials and other basic commodities to their own countries; they wish to ensure markets for their manufactured products; and they may sometimes wish to ensure access to cheap labour.

The global political determinant is the interest in establishing or maintaining political influence in a country or a region by, for example, guaranteeing internal stability through the support of a friendly regime or increasing regional stability by backing the dominant country in a region.

The national economy determinants, which have become increasingly important during the 1970s, imply that the supplier may need arms exports (*a*) to improve the balance of payments, (*b*) as a means of spreading the R&D costs and using the advantages of economies of scale, that is, lower unit prices, and (*c*) to ensure employment in military industries.

US arms exports to Iran and Saudi Arabia provide an illustration of the interaction between the supply and demand determinants. The accumulation of so-called petro-dollars in the region after the dramatic rise in crude oil prices in early 1974 reached such proportions that they posed a potential threat to the monetary system of the entire Western world. It was vital for the United States to regain control over part of this money. On the other hand, however, Iran and Saudi Arabia were requesting arms in large quantities for 'reasons of national security'. By supplying these arms as well as civilian goods and technology, the USA managed to fulfil all their requirements, from securing oil supplies to guaranteeing employment in the arms industries. At the same time, Iran and Saudi Arabia fulfilled their demand requirements. Thus the arms trade is one important element of the complicated network of economic and political relations between and within countries.

V. Conclusions

The international trade in armaments shows no sign of restraint. Judging from recent orders made, the trends of the 1970s will continue through the beginning of the 1980s. This is serious, not least since the possibilities of controlling the arms trade seem limited. The Conventional Arms Transfer (CAT) talks between the United States and the Soviet Union failed during a time when the international situation was less tense than it is today. With this in view, it will be difficult to win support for arms control measures from other suppliers and, not least, from the major recipients. The most important step needed today would seem to be that the USA and the USSR, as the leading weapon exporters, re-open the CAT talks and thereafter urge and stimulate other exporters to follow suit.

References

1. *Strategic Survey 1978* (International Institute for Strategic Studies, London, 1979), p. 126.
2. *U.S. Overseas Loans and Grants and Assistance from International Organizations, July 1, 1945–September 30, 1978* (Agency for International Development, Washington, D.C., 1978), p. 6.
3. *Foreign Military Sales and Military Assistance Facts* (Department of Defense, Security Assistance Agency, Washington, D.C., December 1979), pp. 5 and 19.
4. Benton, G., 'The Middle East's armoury', *The Middle East Yearbook 1979* (IC Magazines Ltd, London, 1979), p. 63.
5. *Foreign Assistance and Related Agencies for 1971*, Hearings, US House of Representatives, 91st Congress, second session (US Government Printing Office, Washington, D.C., 1979), p. 307.
6. Bartlett, D., 'Standardizing military excellence—the key to NATO's survival', *AEI Defence Review*, No. 6, 1977, p. 4.
7. Sivard, R. L., *World Military and Social Expenditures 1979, World Priorities* (WMSE Publications, Leesburg, Va., 1979), p. 5.

5. A decade of military uses of outer space

Square-bracketed numbers, thus [1], *refer to the list of references on page 142.*

I. Introduction

Artificial Earth satellites are playing an increasing role in the ongoing arms race, particularly the nuclear arms race, and becoming an integral part of modern strategic and tactical nuclear weapon systems. One of the most disturbing aspects of advances in military technology is their contribution to first-strike capability, in which space technology plays a major role. During the past decade the military establishments both in the United States and in the Soviet Union have considerably increased their dependence on Earth satellites. In the same period the People's Republic of China became the third country to recover the whole or part of a satellite, having launched its first satellite in April 1970. France, the United Kingdom and NATO also use satellites for military purposes. Satellites belonging to the UK and NATO are launched by the United States. More than 1 700 military satellites or some three satellites a week have been launched by all these nations during the decade.

The extent to which satellites have been used for military purposes is shown in figure 5.1. It can be seen that over 75 per cent of all the satellites launched during the 1970s have been for military purposes. Their functions range from navigation, communications, meteorology and geodesy to reconnaissance and anti-satellite activities. The various types of orbit used for these missions are indicated in figure 5.2. In the United States some $15 thousand million, about 40 per cent of the total US space budget, have been spent on the military space programme during the last decade [1]. Although comparable information is not easily available about the Soviet space budget, it is most probably on a similar scale.

In the following sections some of the main developments in military space activities during the past decade are reviewed briefly.

II. Some specific advances

Photographic reconnaissance satellites

Both the Soviet Union and the United States have launched a number of military satellites each year. Of these, some 40 per cent have been used for photographic reconnaissance purposes from a low-altitude orbit of about

Figure 5.1. Military and civilian satellites launched during 1970–79

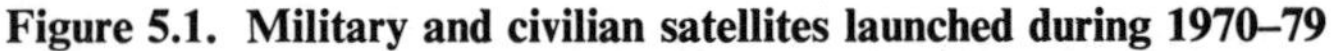

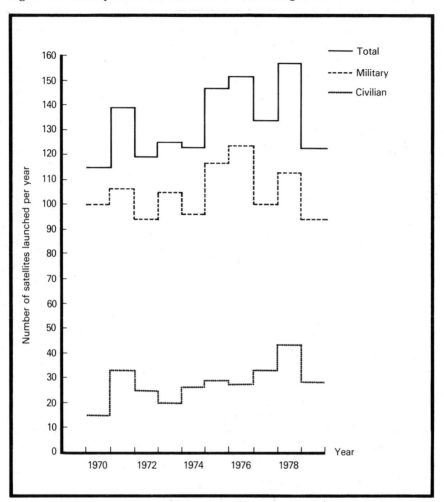

200 km (see figure 5.2). They perform two basic missions. The first requires an area-surveillance satellite, in order to scan a large area of a particular country for objects of potential interest by means of a wide-angle, low-resolution camera. For the second type of reconnaissance mission a camera with a high resolution and a relatively narrow field of vision has been used on board the satellite to re-photograph areas of particular interest located during the area-surveillance mission.

In 1971 a new-generation 'Big Bird' satellite was launched by the United States using the Titan-3D launcher. This kind of satellite is designed to perform both the area-surveillance and the close-look types of mission. While films with high-resolution images taken during the close-look missions are returned to Earth for processing and analysis, the area-

Figure 5.2. Types of orbit used for various types of satellite

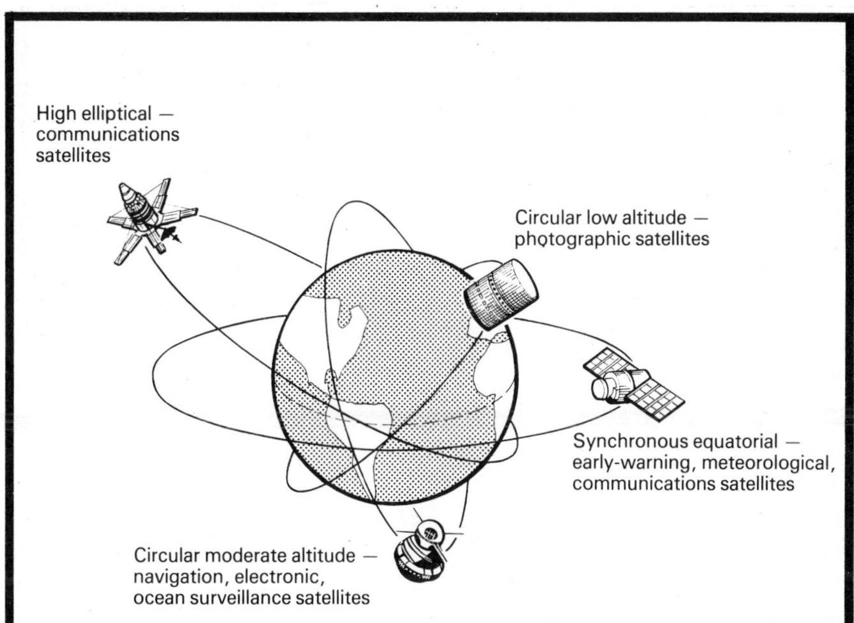

surveillance images on films are usually developed and converted into electrical signals aboard the satellite, and the electrical signals are transmitted to Earth. As advances are made in the latter technique it may become unnecessary to return films to Earth, and a trend towards long-lived satellites could be expected. This trend can be seen in figure 5.3 in which the orbital lifetimes of US photographic reconnaissance satellites launched during the past 10 years are plotted. The lifetime of Big Bird satellites is shown to have increased from 50 days to nearly 200 days. Another advantage of long-lived satellites is that fewer launchings are required.

The development of the Big Bird satellites has eliminated the use of area-surveillance satellites. No such satellites have been launched since 1972 (see figure 5.3). While the USA still continues to launch its third-generation close-look satellites (launched using Titan-3B/Agena-D), the lifetimes of even these have increased from about 20 days to about 90 days. Such satellites carry at least two recoverable film capsules [2]. The fifth and the latest generation of satellites developed by the US Central Intelligence Agency (project 1010) transmit images in real time in digital form to a ground station. These satellites (KH-11) are orbited about 50 km higher than the Big Bird satellites and have an orbital lifetime of over 700 days (see figure 5.3). The data gathered by these satellites are transmitted and

Figure 5.3. The orbital lifetimes of US reconnaissance satellites launched during 1970–80

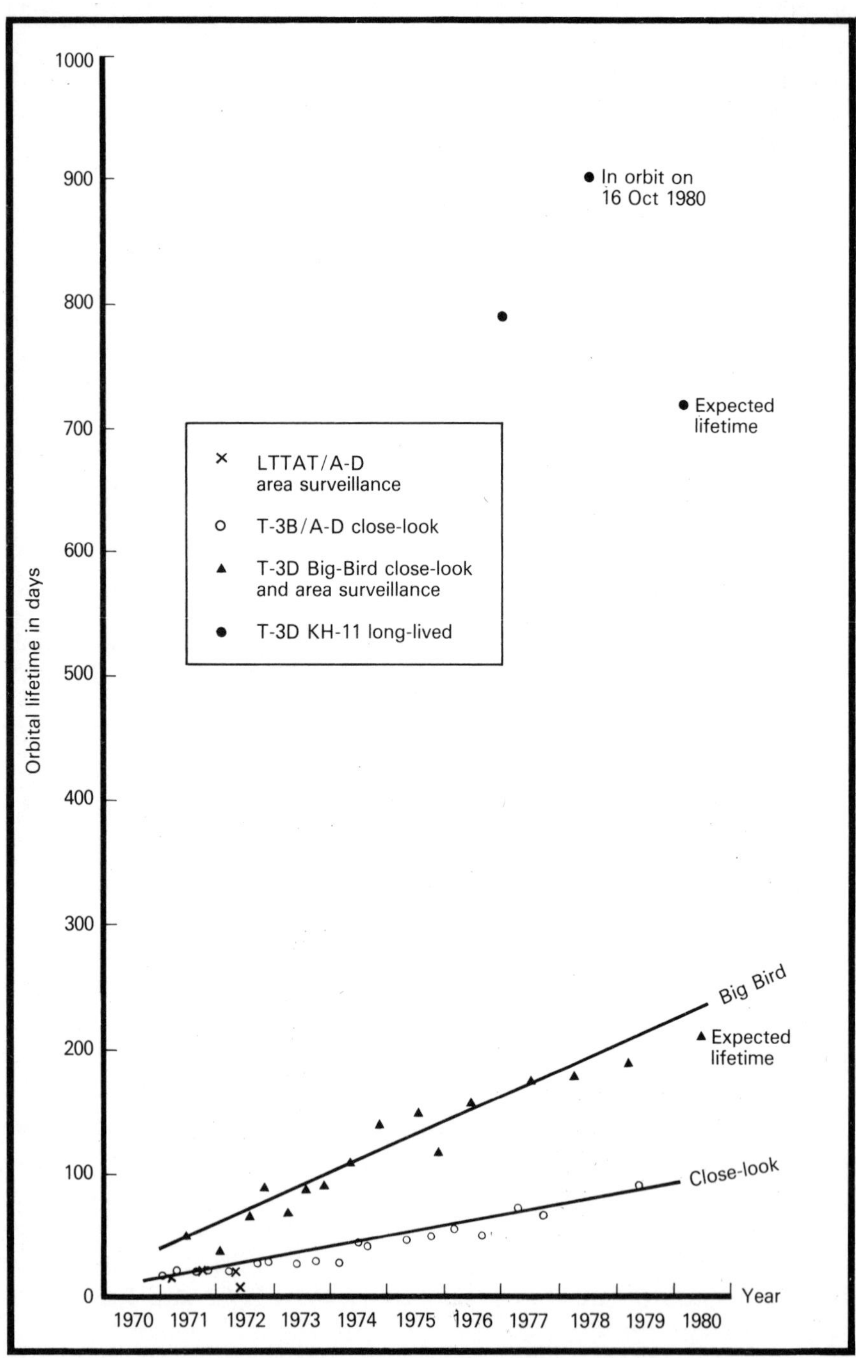

processed in the same way as is done by the Landsat satellites [2]. One of the techniques used to enhance the image quality of a photograph taken by Landsat satellites is to combine images of the same scene obtained by different sensors. For example, combining images produced by a return beam vidicon television camera with those produced by a multispectral sensor (MSS) improves the ground resolution of an MSS imagery by a factor of three [3].

This trend of orbiting long-lived photographic reconnaissance satellites has not been confined to the USA. The Soviet Union's long-lived reconnaissance programme probably began in 1975 with the launch from Plesetsk of Cosmos 758. The satellite was launched at an orbital inclination of 67 degrees—unusual for a Soviet reconnaissance satellite. Two additional such satellites, Cosmos 805 and Cosmos 844, were launched in 1976 [4]. The former manoeuvred during flight and was recovered after 20 days; the latter exploded after three days. Several of these satellites launched during 1977–79 had an orbital life of 30 days. One launched in 1980 had a lifetime of 44 days (see chapter 9).

One of the significant events of the 1970s was the emergence of the People's Republic of China as the fifth nation to launch a satellite and the third to launch a reconnaissance satellite. The first Chinese satellite was launched on 24 April 1970, and the first with an orbit characteristic of a reconnaissance satellite was China 3, launched on 26 July 1975. The ability to recover on Earth payloads ejected from a spacecraft was first demonstrated in 1975 when a capsule from China 4 was recovered. However, since 25 January 1978, when China 8 was launched, no other satellite has been orbited by the People's Republic of China.

Ocean surveillance and oceanographic satellites

During the 1970s two types of satellite were developed to monitor the oceans. One, the ocean surveillance satellite, is used to detect and track military surface ships while the other, the oceanographic satellite, is used to determine various ocean properties.

Ocean surveillance satellites

A decade or more ago surface ships were, on the whole, free to sail the oceans undetected. However, this is not the case today even if normal safety precautions to avoid detection are taken. This is because, during the 1970s, considerable progress was made in the development of space sensors to monitor the oceans. For example, radars able to detect military surface ships were developed and deployed on board satellites, and equipping satellites to monitor electronic signals from surface ships has enabled naval ships to be identified.

Although the Soviet Union appears to have launched its first ocean surveillance satellite at the end of 1967, the first operational satellite, Cosmos 651, was launched in May 1974 [5]. Such satellites perform their missions in pairs and carry radar systems. For good resolution the satellites fly in a low orbit and, at the end of the mission, the space platform, the nuclear reactor and the final stage of the rocket carrying the radar's antenna separate from each other. The nuclear reactor with its own rocket engine is moved into a higher orbit for safety reasons. In one instance, Cosmos 954, a higher orbit was not achieved and the satellite fell to the ground. Presumably the problem was that of the separation of the above three parts.

While the US Navy's interest in the problem of ocean surveillance dates from 1965, the first satellite designed to monitor locations of surface ships was launched in April 1976. The satellite carried three small sub-satellites which were released into circular orbits similar to that of the main satellite. This set of satellites was part of the Navy's White Cloud project, and the satellites have been identified as ELINT Ocean Reconnaissance Satellites (EORSATs). However, the technology of using several satellites to monitor electronic signals and determine the direction of travel of ships was demonstrated in 1971 by the launching of multiple satellites. Under the so-called Clipper Bow programme, the Navy is planning to launch satellites equipped with high resolution radar. When these satellites, the Radar Ocean Reconnaissance Satellites (RORSATs), are fully operational, the EORSATs will, from the detection of electronic signals emitted from surface ships, help identify military vessels detected by the RORSATs. Under the Navy Satellite Oceanographic Research Program (SOREP) the development and demonstration are planned of the effective use of satellites in oceanography as well as in enhancing other naval tasks [6]. The sensors used on board the US Seasat 1 satellite were developed under SOREP.

Oceanographic satellites

Detection of submerged submarines from space is still difficult, but considerable effort is being put into the development of space sensors to measure as many ocean properties as possible so as to facilitate submarine detection by non-space-based sensors. Knowledge of properties such as the departures of the ocean surface from the geoid, the height of waves, the strength and direction of ocean currents and surface winds, temperatures at and below the surface, salinity and coastal features is important both for the use of some weapons and for the detection of submarines. For example, with the satellite's radar altimeter and from the measurements of the satellite's orbital perturbations, the accurate shape of the geoid and values of the Earth's gravitational field can be determined. Such improved data would permit, for example, more accurate ballistic trajectories, resulting in smaller CEPs for submarine-launched ballistic missiles (SLBMs). Moreover, corrections to inertial guidance systems would result in smaller navigational errors, both in velocity and position. The knowledge of the salinity and the temperature distribution on the ocean surface and below it would provide quantitative data used for computing the velocity of sound in sea water, an important parameter for determining submarine locations.

Navigation satellites

Knowledge of exact position and velocity is important for most weapons, but it is particularly so for missiles launched from sea platforms. This requirement is now beginning to be met by satellites. Naval surface ships as well as submarines, aircraft and missiles determine their positions and velocities using signals emitted continually by satellites. Recent US tests using navigation satellites and some estimates from simulation experiments suggest that, even in a civilian application, positions could be fixed with an accuracy of 200 m [7]. In a military system this is about 20 m when 18 satellites are used (as in figure 5.4a). Figure 5.4b illustrates the principle of the use of satellites for navigation.

Consider, firstly, two satellites at *A* and *B* with the line *00* bisecting a line joining the satellites. If two signals are transmitted simultaneously by the satellites, then the times at which they arrive at a point *X* will be different as long as *X* is not on the plane through *00*. However, if a coded pulse is transmitted, for example, from *A*, then the lead or lag in the lapse of time of arrival of the pulse at *X* to that from *B* can be measured. This would, in turn, determine which side of *00* the point *X* lies. If this time difference is kept constant for various positions of *X*, a series of hyperboloids (the solid curves in figure 5.4b) forming well-defined lanes could be obtained. With a third satellite at *C*, a similar set of hyperboloids could be obtained between *B* and *C* and *A* and *C* (dotted curves in figure 5.4b). It can be seen that a three-dimensional grid is formed in which the position of *X* could be accurately determined. For a world-wide navigation system and for greater accuracy a number of satellites would be needed. In order to avoid ambiguity, the transmitters on various satellites must be operated at different frequencies.

Both the United States and the Soviet Union have developed such navigation systems. In the USA, the Navy Navigation Satellite System (TRANSIT) has been in operation since 1964. The TRANSIT satellites were developed to provide position fixes in two directions particularly for

Figure 5.4a. Eighteen-satellite navigation system

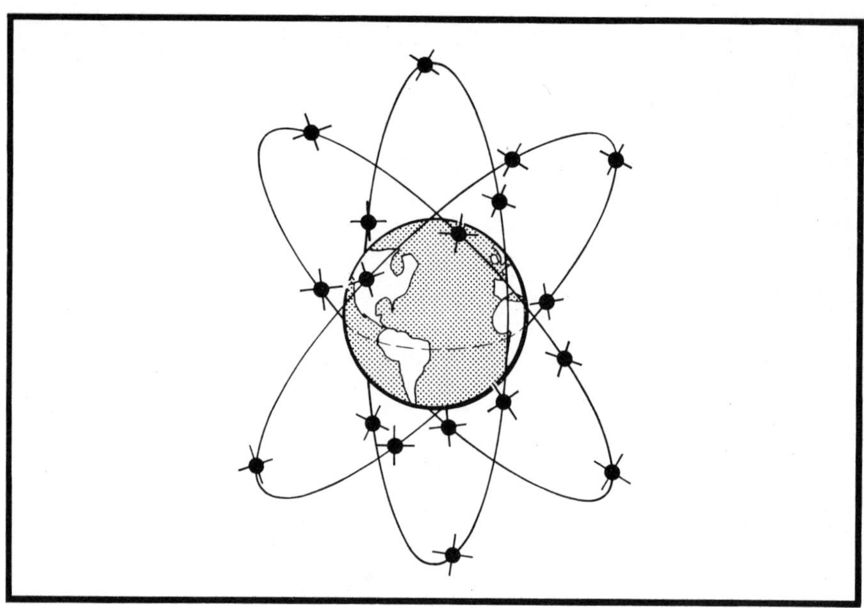

Figure 5.4b. Position-fixing by navigation satellites

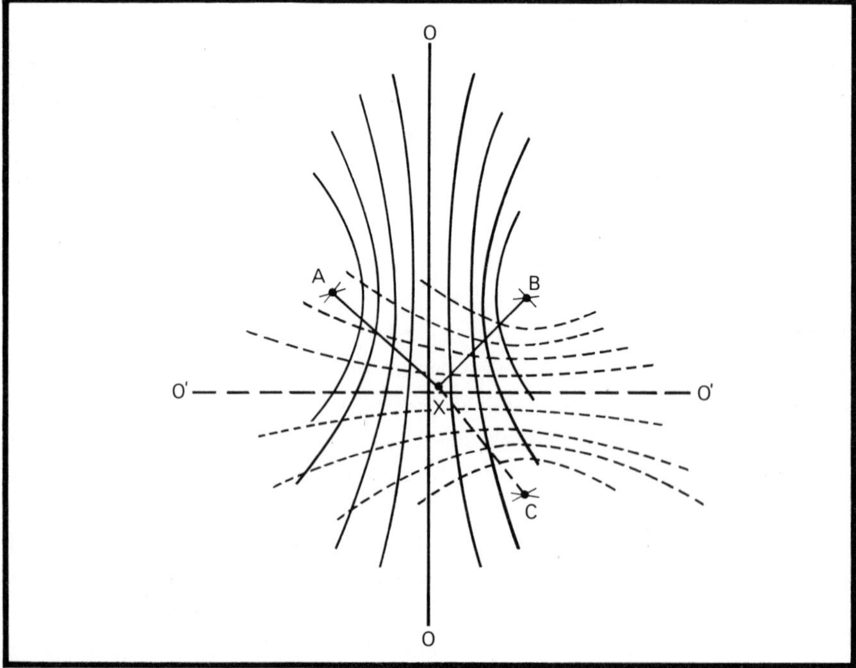

Figure 5.5. NAVSTAR Global Positioning System satellite

US Air Force

the strategic ballistic missile submarines [8]. A second-generation system, the NAVSTAR Global Positioning System (GPS), was evolved in mid-1974 under a joint service development programme. Originally, the NAVSTAR system was to consist of 24 satellites, grouped equally into three rings situated in circular orbits at altitudes of about 20 000 km, with 12-hour orbital periods and at orbital inclinations of 63 degrees. Recently the programme has been revised and now, initially, there will be 18 instead of 24 satellites in three orbital planes in the NAVSTAR system [9]. Some simulation tests have shown that with the 18-satellite system, the position fixes will be slightly inferior, to within about 20 m instead of 10 m [10]. In fact, using four satellites for demonstration, it was shown that position could be determined to within 22 m 90 per cent of the time and the velocity of a test vehicle to within 0.12 metres per second [11]. Two additional NAVSTAR satellites were launched during 1980. The GPS is expected to contribute to improvement in the accuracy of ballistic missiles under the US Navy's Trident Improved Accuracy Program [9].

The satellites in the NAVSTAR system will also carry sensors for the detection of nuclear explosions under the Integrated Operational Nuclear Detection System (IONDS). In addition, this system is intended to provide damage assessment during and after a nuclear attack [12]. Sensors for the detection of nuclear explosions are also used on board US early-warning satellites. It is interesting to note that data from an early-warning satellite do not appear to have been used to resolve the uncertainty as to whether a flash of light observed by the US Vela satellite on 22 September 1979 was due to a nuclear explosion or a natural phenomenon. In 1980, reports from South Africa, based on US intelligence information, stated that a nuclear explosion may have been conducted on 16 December 1980, again in the South Atlantic region. A subsequent report in *Defense Daily* on 23 February 1981 in the United States stated that a US early-warning satellite had registered a flash in this region, attributing it to the "flash of a large meteor entering the atmosphere".

A close examination of the orbital characteristics of Soviet navigation satellites has shown that during 1970–72, satellites launched with orbital inclinations of 74 degrees and at 105-minute orbital periods had their orbital planes spaced by 120 degrees. This meant that at least three satellites were used in a group for navigation purposes. From August 1972, the spacing of the orbital planes of such satellites was changed to 60 degrees and from November 1975 it became 30 degrees. This was the beginning of the new set which formed a six-satellite navigation system [13]. The Soviet Union first mentioned its global navigation system in May 1978, when Cosmos 1000, a navigation satellite belonging to the fourth generation of the Soviet navigation satellite system, was launched [13].

Communications satellites

Satellite-based sensors for surveillance of the Earth's land mass and the oceans and for early-warning of missile launches, and other land-based surveillance systems, for example, for deep space surveillance, generate considerable amounts of data. The transmission of this and other data for military purposes needs highly reliable communications systems. Some 80 per cent of military communications is carried out using artificial Earth satellites [14].

In the USA, the military communications programme is basically divided into three project areas: (*a*) a satellite system for command, control and communications; (*b*) a high capacity communications system for the National Command Authorities (NCA) and military commanders stationed in major headquarters around the world, including the World-Wide Military Command and Control System (WWMCCS) and the intelligence community; and (*c*) communications for mobile forces such as aircraft, ships and anti-submarine warfare aircraft [8].

For command, control and communications, the Air Force Satellite Communications System (AFSATCOM) was developed. Under this programme, AFSATCOM I, equipment for satellite communications is developed and procured for selected Department of Defense (DoD) host satellites. An important component of the AFSATCOM system is the Satellite Data System (SDS) which is a multi-purpose communications satellite. The first of two SDS experimental satellites was launched by the USA in March 1971 and, so far, six operational spacecraft have been launched in highly elliptical orbits at orbital inclinations of about 63 degrees and orbital periods of about 12 hours. The last one was launched in December 1980 [15].

Under the second US project, the Defense Satellite Communications System (DSCS) has been developed. Satellites under this programme are launched in pairs and in geosynchronous orbit. The most recent pair was launched in November 1979. The DSCS presently has four DSCS II satellites in orbit which form part of the WWMCCS. Besides relaying military communications, the satellites also relay data gathered by reconnaissance satellites on the size and activities of military forces and the deployment of weapons. Such data are also needed for the verification of some arms control treaties.

The third project uses mainly the US Navy's Fleet Satellite Communication (FLEETSATCOM) system. Four FLEETSATCOM satellites have been launched, the first one being in February 1978 and the latest one in October 1980. The satellites are orbited in geosynchronous orbit.

To meet the communications requirements of the US nuclear forces, improved survivability of satellites against potentially damaging electromagnetic radiation and physical destruction is planned for under the US Air Force's Strategic Satellite System (SSS). Two experimental satellites, LES 8 and 9, were launched in 1976 to demonstrate the use of a high-power radioisotope thermoelectric power supply to increase a satellite's resistance to nuclear attack and to eliminate the large radar cross-section of solar panels.

The US Navy and the Defense Advanced Research Project Agency (DARPA) are investigating the possibility of using blue–green lasers for communications with submarines via satellites. The only electromagnetic waves which can travel significant distances in oceans are extremely low-frequency radiation and those corresponding to visible light. The blue–green lasers fall into the latter category. An initial study was conducted by the US Navy in 1977. Two systems are being investigated under the optical strategic communications programme. In one, the transmitting laser would be placed on the ground. The signal-carrying laser beam would be aimed at a satellite in a geosynchronous orbit carrying large mirrors to reflect the beam down to parts of the ocean where submarines may be travelling. In the other system, microwave signals would be transmitted from the ground to the satellite in a conventional way and a laser on board the satellite would retransmit the signals down to the submerged submarine [16]. In either case the wavelength of the laser light will be in the range of 460 to 530 nanometers (blue–green light).

In the case of the ground-based laser transmitter, the need for clear skies means that many such transmitters would be needed so that at least one transmitter would be under clear skies. A laser beam, in this case, of an average power of a few megawatts would be needed [17]. Such a system should also have a high-precision optical system controlled by a sophisticated target acquisition, pointing and tracking system. Moreover, the optical system must be able to compensate for distortions of the laser beam as it travels through the atmosphere.

All of these problems are also common to, for example, the development of laser weapons technology. The target acquisition, pointing and tracking systems have already been under development for a decade or so and the level of precision (one microradian or less) required for the strategic optical communications system has been demonstrated [16]. Under the strategic reconnaissance data relay satellite programme (programme 405B, space communication system using lasers) accurate acquisition, pointing and tracking capabilities over, for example, intercontinental distances have been demonstrated.

Almost two decades have been devoted to solving the problem of distortions introduced by the atmosphere when a laser beam travels through it. One way of overcoming this problem is to modify the optics of the laser instrument in such a way as to compensate for atmospheric distortions. For example, a large mirror (measuring a few metres square) for a high-energy laser device is made up of many small (10-cm) mirrors. These are mounted so that each of them could be moved slightly in order to distort the wavefront of the laser beam in such a way that after it emerges through the atmosphere the distortions introduced by the atmosphere are exactly compensated for. It is claimed that this technology is now available [16].

In the case in which a laser beam is generated on board a satellite to transmit signals received by the satellite via a microwave link from the ground, the average power of the laser beam would be about one kilowatt [17]. Moreover, from this high vantage point, it is possible to get the coverage needed without a large number of transmitters.

It has been suggested that the intensity of the laser beam considered above would not only be sufficiently strong to penetrate most clouds and fogs but would also penetrate the oceans to depths at which US strategic submarines operate [16]. The most likely laser system at present seems to be the rare-gas-halide excimer, such as the xenon fluoride or xenon chloride laser, which emits in the ultraviolet region of the electromagnetic spectrum. The laser light from such a device is then passed through a material which shifts the wavelength from about 350 nm to the desired wavelength of 495 nm [17].

One of the main problems, from the point of view of the laser light receiver, is to distinguish the incoming laser light from the solar background light. One method being investigated is to pass the signal-carrying laser light beam through a solution which will fluoresce on interacting with the laser light. The fluorescent materials being tried are hot vapours of caesium or rubidium which will fluoresce emitting light in the infra-red region of the spectrum. Such fluorescence is unique to the blue–green laser light and, using a detector mainly sensitive to the infra-red radiation, detection of other sources of strong light could be avoided [17].

Under the US Navy's Optical Ranging And Detection System (ORADS) and Optical Ranging, Identification, Communications System (ORICS) programmes, two-way communication with a submerged submarine has been demonstrated [18]. Also, under the US Naval Air Development Center's Submarine Aircraft Optical Communications System (SAOCS) and Optical Satellite Communications (OPSATCOM) programmes, communication has also been made with a submerged receiver [18].

While most of the global communications satellites either planned or in use by the USA make use of geosynchronous orbits, the civilian and military communications satellites of the USSR are placed in highly elliptical orbits with periods of about 12 hours. Soviet communications satellite programmes are carried out by the Molniya series and some satellites in the Cosmos series. Under these programmes initially three satellites at a time were used, but this system has now been superseded by a four-satellite system.

The first Soviet synchronous satellite was orbited in 1974 and it was not until the end of 1975 that a new series of such synchronous satellites was launched.

Early-warning satellites

Until now, one of the main objectives of early-warning satellites has been to detect enemy missiles soon after they are launched. This mission has been fulfilled using sensors sensitive to the infra-red radiation emitted by the hot plume of a rocket. In fact, most military targets emit infra-red radiation to a varying degree.

In the USA considerable progress made during the 1970s in the field of thermal imaging sensor technology, such as focal plane infra-red mosaic devices and integrated microelectronics, will extend the mission of early-warning satellites to possible detection of aircraft and cruise missiles [19]. Such devices consist of a telescope to form an image of a scene in its focal plane, a mosaic of many small photo-sensitive sensors placed in the focal plane of the telescope, and signal processing microelectronic circuits. The latter can be mechanically and electrically coupled to the sensors or could be an integral part of the sensor system. When an image falls on the sensors it is converted into electrical signals, which in turn are processed by the microelectronic circuits attached to the sensors. For high resolution and sensitivity, it is desirable to have many sensors which are individually very small in size. It is predicted that by 1983 a mosaic array module will have between 1 024 and 4 096 elements and by 1987 this will be over 10^6 elements [20]. As mentioned above, such sensors will be used to monitor not only missile launches but also such targets as aircraft. The Teal Ruby sensor has been designed to use a large mosaic focal plane detector. The device will be launched in 1982 with an on-board signal processing system [19]. Another element of such a device is the adaptive optics, the testing of which was completed under the High Altitude Large Optics (HALO) adaptive optics programme [19].

While the above describes some of the techniques which were being developed during the 1970s for application in the 1980s, conventional telescopes mounted on board satellites are still used. For example, the US early-warning satellite system consists of three satellites placed in geosynchronous orbit. The Rhyolite satellites, the first of which was launched in 1973, perform an additional task: they also monitor telemetry of Soviet ballistic missiles when they are being tested [21].

The Soviet early-warning satellites are orbited in highly elliptical orbits. It is possible that some of the Soviet satellites launched in geosynchronous orbits during the 1970s may be performing the early-warning missions.

Anti-satellite (ASAT) developments

The importance and the sensitive nature of artificial Earth satellites were probably recognized soon after the space age began in 1957. By the early 1960s, in the USA at least, programmes existed which considered the development of the technology and possibly some hardware for intercepting and destroying satellites. Most of these were either cancelled or suspended. Until 1975, however, the USA had an operational, Earth-based, anti-satellite system which used missiles based on Johnston and Kwajalein Islands in the Pacific Ocean. Since 1975, active interest in anti-satellite weaponry has been revived. The current programme contains three separate projects, each investigating different techniques. Under a contract of the US Air Force two types of anti-satellite system are being investigated. In one, a direct-ascent system, a cylinder containing a non-nuclear warhead would be launched from a high-speed aircraft flying at high altitude. The warhead would be separated close to the target and guided to it by an infra-red homing device. Another approach being developed does not make use of any explosives. Instead, a small manoeuvrable vehicle, carrying an infra-red sensor for guidance, would ram and destroy the target. A number of such vehicles would be carried into Earth orbit by a rocket which would release them near a target satellite. This system, called the Miniature Homing Intercept Vehicle, has already been developed [9]. In fact, during the Fiscal Year 1981 alone, $175.9 million have been allocated to US anti-satellite activities. This sum includes the development and operation of ASAT, space surveillance technology and a spacetrack system but does not include such exotic anti-satellite weapons as high-energy lasers and particle beams. Moreover, considerable sums of money are being spent on making satellites less vulnerable to detection and nuclear attack.

In another scheme, the ASAT system is similar to that developed by the Soviet Union. Either an interceptor satellite would be put in the same orbit as the target and then manoeuvred towards it, or else it would be put into a different orbit but given a fast approach to the target. Three such satellites are to be built initially. The interceptor satellite would be guided by radar to the target and then exploded to destroy it.

The Soviet ASAT programme may have begun as early as 1963 but rigorous testing with targets and interceptor satellites appears to have begun in 1967. Until 1970, both the targets and the interceptors were launched from Tyuratam. However, since 1971 all the targets have been launched from Plesetsk and the interceptors from Tyuratam. It is interesting to note here that, at least as far as the Soviet photographic reconnaissance satellites are concerned, Plesetsk appears to be used as an operational launching site while the experimental or specialized flights take place from Tyuratam.

The interceptions appear to have been made basically in three ways. In a so-called fast fly-by, the interceptor satellite, usually launched at an orbital inclination of 62 degrees, makes several orbital manoeuvres to achieve an eccentric orbit. The interceptor then passes close to the target spacecraft near the perigee of the orbit of the former. Soon after the target is passed the interceptor is exploded, presumably to test the kill mechanism for the destruction of the target. In the second, the interceptor makes a slower approach to the target. The interceptor is usually launched at an orbital inclination of 65 degrees, and it is in the same orbital plane as that of the target. A third method has been tested in which the interceptor ascends close to the target. The interception is made before the interceptor

Figure 5.6. USAF anti-satellite missile

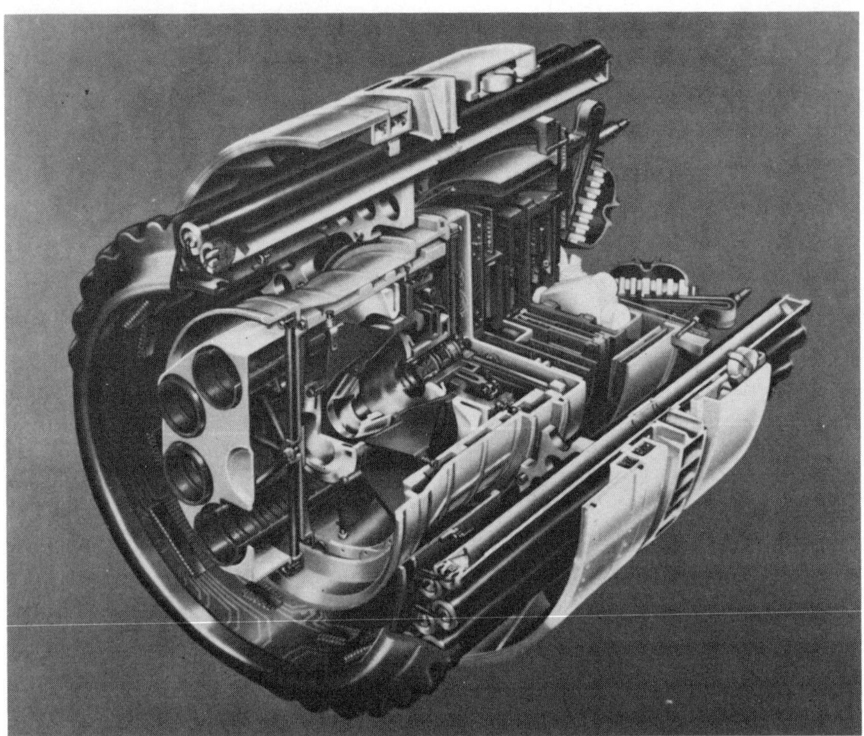

US Air Force

Figure 5.7. High-angle left-side view of an NKC-135 Airborne Laser Laboratory aircraft (laser beam is emitted from circular window on top of aircraft)

US Air Force

completes a full orbit, and it is commanded back to Earth after the interception has been made. The interceptor disintegrates on entering the Earth's atmosphere.

No target satellite has been destroyed so far. It is possible that these spacecraft carry sensing instruments to determine the success or failure of the interceptor. Often the same target is used again. Yet another suggestion is that the Soviet Union might be developing a method to inspect other satellites in order to verify compliance with the 1967 Outer Space Treaty. However, the only relevant item in this treaty which may require monitoring is the undertaking by parties to the treaty "not to place in orbit around the Earth any objects carrying nuclear weapons or any other kinds of weapons of mass destruction". It is difficult to see how the above methods tested by the Soviet Union would help them in this task.

During the 1970s, 28 Soviet satellites—13 target satellites and 15 interceptors—were launched. Some 35 target and interceptor satellites have been launched by the Soviet Union since the beginning of their programme.

Besides these conventional types of space-war weapon, more exotic weapons, the so-called directed-energy or high-energy-beam weapons for space warfare and other applications, are being developed. Although the implementation of such methods of warfare may still be somewhat futuristic, if a sound scientific basis for such systems exists then there is every chance that laser and particle-beam weapons may well be developed and even deployed. In the short period of time since the laser principle was first demonstrated in 1958, advances in this technology made it possible, in 1978, to destroy a high-speed anti-tank missile using a laser beam, making the 'war in space' concepts of science fiction seem feasible in the foreseeable future.

As a result of the initiative from the USA in March 1977, the USSR and the USA met for the first time in June 1978 in Helsinki and for the second time on 23 January 1979 in Bern to discuss the control of ASAT activities. On 19 May 1978, just before the Bern meeting, the Soviet Union launched Cosmos 1009, which passed close to Cosmos 967, a target which was launched in December 1977. This was the last ASAT test the Soviet Union conducted in the 1970s, while no further ASAT talks have been held since the Bern talks.

Space shuttle—review of its envisaged military applications

At present, artificial Earth satellites and deep space probes are launched into outer space using non-recoverable multi-stage rockets. However, a partially or fully re-usable system has now been designed. The idea of a rocket-propelled aircraft dates back to the middle of the nineteenth century in the United States as well as in the Soviet Union.

In the Soviet Union the possibilities of re-usable launch vehicles have been studied since the late 1960s but serious design development appears to have begun in the early 1970s. A vehicle, called 'Kosmolyot', has been designed with two stages, a recoverable booster and the orbiter itself [22]. The shuttle system will be launched from a vertical pad. The upper stage of the Kosmolyot has already been tested in a series of glide tests. The wings of the vehicle, launched from a Tupolev Tu-95 Bear, are delta-shaped [22].

The concept of the US space shuttle as we know it today began to take shape in 1951 when, in a study called Project Bomi, a two-stage vehicle was described [24]. In this concept, the vehicle consisted of a large delta-winged booster which carried a small upper stage. The former would glide down to an airfield while the latter continued into orbit.

The design of the present US system began in 1972 and consists of an aeroplane-like vehicle capable of gliding flight, called the Orbiter, an external fuel tank, and two booster rockets. The Orbiter and the booster rockets are re-usable while the external tank, which contains the ascent propellant to be used by the Orbiter's main engines, can either be jettisoned before the Orbiter goes into orbit or be placed in orbit and used as a space platform. The system is designed to be launched vertically.

The importance of the space shuttle system lies in the fact that it will enhance the effectiveness of the military satellites. Compared with the existing expendable boosters, the shuttle will be able to launch greater payload weight and volume. The shuttle system not only allows the recovery and refurbishing of satellites for re-use but also enables satellites to be repaired in orbit [8].

The emphasis put on the space shuttle by the military can be illustrated by the fact that, in the USA, the DoD is contributing about one-sixth of the cost of developing such a system, and some 40 per cent of the initial space shuttle's flights will be used by the DoD [25]. In fact, the US Air Force is responsible for the development of part of the US space shuttle system. It is developing the launch and landing facilities at the Vandenberg Air Force Base space complex and developing the inertial upper stage (IUS) for use on shuttle launchers to deliver DoD spacecraft to higher orbital altitudes and inclinations than the shuttle alone could provide. The IUS is a multi-stage vehicle which would use solid fuel as a propellant. The DoD version is a two-stage vehicle capable, when used on the shuttle, of delivering payloads weighing up to about 2 300 kg to geosynchronous orbit. During the early transition period, the IUS will also be used on the more conventional Titan 3 launcher [8]. The first DoD IUS launch was planned for late 1980 on a Titan 3D, but this had not taken place by the end of 1980. The first DoD Space Shuttle IUS launch (designated DoD 82-1) is scheduled for May 1982 during the sixth space shuttle flight while the first operational shuttle mission is now scheduled for March 1982 [26].

Figure 5.8. Artist's concept of US space shuttle in Earth orbit, about to deploy a satellite

National Aeronautics and Space Administration

It is possible that the DoD 82-1 payload may be launched on the fourth space shuttle flight which is one of the first four orbital flight test missions [27].

The second DoD 83-1 payload is scheduled for launch in April 1983, during the eighteenth space shuttle flight, while the third and the fourth payloads (83-2 and 83-3) are planned for launch on the nineteenth and twenty-second flights, in May and August 1983 respectively. The last in these series of DoD payloads (DoD 84-1) will be launched in July 1984 on the thirty-fifth flight. Some 39 flights are planned for launch by the end of 1984; 4 of these will be launched from the Vandenberg Air Force Base while the remaining ones will be launched from Cape Canaveral [28]. Details of the DoD space shuttle payloads are not given, but it has been stated that in November 1982 the first Air Force space shuttle launch will be the Teal Ruby experiment and in 1983 the first Air Force IUS with a DSCS Communications Satellite will be launched [29].

III. The future

During the last two decades since the beginning of the space age in 1957, artificial Earth satellite systems were developed for use in enhancing the performance of land-based weapons. However, both in the USA and in the USSR the research and development phase of space technology has now entered the operational phase. Artificial Earth satellites have become an essential element in military reconnaissance, early-warning, communications, navigation and meteorological missions.

Recently, at least in the USA, apparent changes in nuclear war-fighting doctrines are surfacing which emphasize limited nuclear war-fighting capabilities at various levels. This emphasis results from concepts such as flexible response, which may be the outcome of the capability to monitor from space the effects of nuclear strikes both within one's own territory and that of the enemy. Real-time assessment of a nuclear attack anywhere in the world can be provided by the space surveillance and communications systems [9]. Moreover, the need for precise target information and the need to strike the target accurately in the current counterforce doctrine for fighting a limited nuclear war are fulfilled by space systems. It must be noted here that whether technological advances such as those in outer space were the results of nuclear war-fighting doctrines already formulated, or whether the technological advances gave rise to such doctrines, is debatable. These issues are considered in more detail in chapter 2. It is sufficient to state here that space technology has become an important part of the strategic doctrines of both the USSR and the USA and both states depend on artificial Earth satellites considerably.

As this dependence on space systems increases, their continued availability and the ability to destroy enemy satellites become equally important [30]. In fact, in the USA the indications are that military satellites are already on targeting lists. It is known that a list has been made of most strategic weapons and weapon systems on the Earth at which weapons are aimed [31]. No doubt the Soviet Union has drawn up a similar list. The future activities of both these nations in outer space in the next decade, therefore, may include the development of systems to fulfil these goals.

Research and development in space systems has concentrated on two broad areas since before the start of the 1970s. Considerable effort is being devoted to the development of advanced sensor technologies for observing, identifying and tracking military targets both in space and on Earth, and much effort is going into the development of systems for the destruction of space-based and land-based targets. A common factor in both these areas is the need for large structures for some of the systems. With the use of the space shuttle, this problem could be overcome.

With regard to the larger space-based structures, the US DoD is studying, in co-operation with the National Aeronautics and Space Administration (NASA), the possibilities of constructing such systems in space [32]. The aim is to develop imaging and tracking radars, communications and electronic surveillance systems. The envisaged antennas range from 30 m to some 200 m in diameter. A multi-beam phased array antenna in geosynchronous orbit, for example, could enable an individual soldier to communicate from the battlefield to his command post [33]. While, on the one hand, advances in the technology of large structures in outer space will enhance the capabilities of microwave sensors, it will, on the other hand, no doubt contribute to the development of US HALO technology using advanced concepts of adaptive optics. The optical lenses of such

Figure 5.9. Artist's impression of an experimental platform to demonstrate the technologies, systems and uses for future-generation platforms

National Aeronautics and Space Administration

systems may be over 30 m in diameter [34]. In fact, during 1979 DARPA began the development of a demonstration sensor, Mini-HALO, to be launched in 1984 in geosynchronous orbit [8]. Another system expected to become operational in the 1980s is a space-based system for the detection and tracking of aircraft and cruise missiles. Under the US Teal Ruby programme, an experimental infra-red focal plane sensor has been developed which will be launched into a 750-km polar orbit by the space shuttle in late 1982.

Finally, the most important development to be expected during the coming decade or so is that of the ASAT systems. The contribution of the space shuttle system and the large structure technology to the deployment of, for example, space-based high-energy-beam weapons will be considerable. Of the two types of beam weapon, laser and particle-beam, envisaged, the former is likely to be deployed first. This system is considered in some detail in chapter 8.

While the development of offensive weapons—conventional or beam weapons—will be continued, the 1980s will see considerable effort being devoted to protecting and improving the survivability of military satellites in orbit. This will be achieved by hardening the satellite surfaces and by making their communications systems resistant to interferences. Moreover, surveillance of outer space will be increased and improved.

These are some of the technical developments expected for protecting military satellites. Another way of achieving the same result, a political approach, began in 1978 when the USA and the USSR began talks in June of that year on the control of their anti-satellite activities. The last meeting took place in June 1979 and no further discussions have taken place since. Although such control would have the advantage of stopping the arms race extending into outer space, it would nevertheless enhance the qualitative nuclear and conventional arms race on Earth. What is needed is a way to check the proliferation of military satellites in Earth orbit.

References

1. *NASA Authorization for Fiscal Year 1978*, Report of the Committee on Commerce, Science and Transportation on H.R. 4088 (US Government Printing Office, Washington, D.C., 4 May 1977), p. 63.
2. 'Space reconnaissance dwindles', *Aviation Week & Space Technology*, Vol. 113, No. 14, 6 October 1980, p. 18.
3. 'Landsat returns image of San Francisco', *Aviation Week & Space Technology*, Vol. 113, No. 14, 6 October 1980, p. 24.
4. *World Armaments and Disarmament, SIPRI Yearbook 1977* (Almqvist & Wiksell, Stockholm, 1977, Stockholm International Peace Research Institute), p. 123.

5. Perry, G. E., 'Russian ocean surveillance satellites', *The Royal Air Forces Quarterly*, Vol. 18, Spring 1978, pp. 60–67.
6. Augustine, F. J. and Lujetic, V. J., 'The Navy Satellite Oceanographic Research Program (SOREP) Plan', *Ramcor Report No. U-RC149A-002*, September 1978.
7. 'Navstar still too accurate', *Defense Electronics*, August 1980, p. 20.
8. *Perry, W. J., Under Secretary of Defense for Research and Engineering, NASA Authorization for Fiscal Year 1980, Statement to the 96th Congress, first session, Hearings before the Committee on Commerce, Science and Transportation*, 'US Department of Defense Space Activities', US Senate (US Government Printing Office, Washington, D.C., March, May and June 1979), Part 3, pp. 1715–17.
9. *Perry, W. J., Under Secretary of Defense for Research and Engineering, Department of Defense and Authorization for Fiscal Year 1981, Statement to the 96th Congress, second session, Hearings on Military Posture*, Committee on Armed Services, US House of Representatives (US Government Printing Office, Washington, D.C., February–March 1980), Part 4, Research and Development, pp. 7–301.
10. Austin, J. A., 'GPS; Global Positioning System', *Military Electronic/ Countermeasures*, Vol. 6, No. 6, June 1980, pp. 63–70.
11. *Navstar Should Improve the Effectiveness of Military Missions—Cost has Increased*, Report to the US Congress, the Comptroller General, PSAD-80-21 (US General Accounting Office, Washington, D.C., 15 February 1980).
12. *Defense Annual Report—FY 1981, Department of Defense Authorization for Appropriations for Fiscal Year 1981, Hearings on Military Posture*, Committee on Armed Services (US Government Printing Office, Washington, D.C., January, February and March 1980), Part 1, p. 190.
13. Perry, G. E., 'Soviet navigation satellites', *The Royal Air Forces Quarterly*, Autumn 1978, pp. 276–84.
14. Baker, D., 'Defense and space equation', *Jane's Defense Review*, No. 1, 1980, pp. 73–77.
15. *Martin, J. J., Department of Defense Authorization for Appropriations for Fiscal Year 1980, Statement to the 96th Congress, first session, Hearings before the Committee on Armed Services*, US Senate (US Government Printing Office, Washington, D.C., April 1979), Part 5, p. 2647.
16. *Wood, L., Department of Defense Authorization for Appropriations for Fiscal Year 1980, Statement to the 96th Congress, first session, Hearings before the Committee on Armed Services*, 'Optical Strategic Communications Systems in the 1980s', US Senate (US Government Printing Office, Washington, D.C., March–April 1979), Part 6, pp. 3326–88.
17. 'Blue-green laser link to subs', *Laser Focus*, Vol. 16, No. 4, April 1980, pp. 14–18.
18. Wiener, T. F., 'Strategic laser communications', *Signal*, Vol. 35, No. 1, September 1980, pp. 43–48.

19. *Fossum, R. R., Department of Defense Authorization for Appropriations for Fiscal Year 1981, Statement to the 96th Congress, second session, Hearings on Military Posture*, Committee on Armed Services, US House of Representatives (US Government Printing Office, Washington, D.C., February and March 1980), Part 4, pp. 578–606.
20. Lloyd, D. B., 'Starting IR sensors', *Military Electronics/Countermeasures*, Vol. 5, No. 11, November 1979, p. 61.
21. Klass, P. J., 'US monitoring capability impaired', *Aviation Week & Space Technology*, Vol. 110, No. 20, 14 May 1979, p. 18.
22. Gatland, K., 'Soviet space shuttle', *Spaceflight*, Vol. 19, No. 6, June 1977, p. 211.
23. Gatland, K., 'A Soviet space shuttle', *Spaceflight*, Vol. 20, Nos 9 and 10, September–October 1978, pp. 322–28.
24. Peebles, C., 'The origins of the US space shuttle-1', *Spaceflight*, Vol. 21, No. 11, November 1979, pp. 435–41.
25. Bell, T. E., 'America's other space program', *The Sciences*, December 1979.
26. *Bostick, Mr., NASA Authorization for Fiscal Year 1981, Statement to the 96th Congress, second session, Hearings before the Subcommittee on Space Sciences and Applications of the Committee on Science and Technology*, 'Shuttle operations planning', US House of Representatives (US Government Printing Office, Washington, D.C., February–March 1980), Vol. 5, pp. 2831–85.
27. 'DoD shuttle mission schedule threatened', *Aviation Week & Space Technology*, Vol. 113, No. 5, 8 April 1980, p. 20.
28. 'Defense shuttle flights cut in new schedule', *Aviation Week & Space Technology*, Vol. 112, No. 13, 31 March 1980, pp. 54–55.
29. *Burke, K. H., Department of Defense Authorization for Appropriations for Fiscal Year 1981, Statement to the 96th Congress, second session, Hearings on Military Posture*, Committee on Armed Services, US House of Representatives (US Government Printing Office, Washington, D.C., February–March 1980), Part 2, p. 494.
30. *Hermann, R. J., Department of Defense Authorization for Appropriations for Fiscal Year 1981, Statement to the 96th Congress, second session, Hearings on Military Posture*, Committee on Armed Services, US House of Representatives (US Government Printing Office, Washington, D.C., February–March 1980), Part 2, p. 265.
31. *Department of Defense Authorization for Appropriations for Fiscal Year 1980, Hearings before the Committee on Armed Services*, US Senate (US Government Printing Office, Washington, D.C., March–April 1979), Part 6, p. 3037.
32. Covault, C., 'Shuttle pivotal to space plans', *Aviation Week & Space Technology*, Vol. 112, No. 9, 3 March 1980, pp. 69–73.
33. 'SAMSO charts future in space', *Defense Electronics*, Vol. 11, No. 11, November 1979, pp. 43–50.
34. Smith, B. A., 'Military satellite emphasis increases', *Aviation Week & Space Technology*, Vol. 110, No. 5, 29 January 1979, pp. 164–67.

Part II. Developments in world armaments in 1980

6. World military expenditure, the current situation

Square-bracketed numbers, thus [1], *refer to the list of references on page* 155.

I. Introduction

World military spending, in real terms, has continued to move up at a rate of about 2–2.5 per cent a year. Revised figures for 1978 and 1979, and a highly provisional estimate for 1980, are all in that range; indeed 2–2.5 per cent is the trend which has persisted right through the 1970s.

At current (1980) prices, the total of world military spending will now have certainly passed the $500 thousand million mark: that is the figure which corresponds with the estimate in table 6A.1 of $450 thousand million at 1978 prices.

The recent trend—up to 1980—in world military spending has been somewhat below the figure of the mid-1950s and the 1960s, when it was moving up at about 3–3.5 per cent a year. One reason is probably the slower rate of world economic growth in the 1970s. From the early 1950s right up to 1973, world output has been rising, on average, at about 6 per cent a year. In the seven years since 1973 that figure has been halved, to about 3 per cent a year. In relation, therefore, to the rate of world economic growth, the current trend is more of a burden than the old trend. Further—as the next section suggests—it seems quite likely that in the beginning of the 1980s military expenditure may begin to rise as fast (or possibly faster) than world output.

The comments on the current situation which follow concentrate this year on the prospects for military spending in NATO, the Warsaw Treaty Organization (WTO), China and Japan—which among them account for some 80 per cent of the total. The situation in the rest of the world is discussed briefly.

II. NATO and Japan

The main fact here is the decision in the United States to 'rearm'—that is, to accelerate sharply the rate at which its military spending is rising. It was a decision taken by the previous Administration: the military budget which ex-President Carter left, and which President Reagan inherited, provided for a 4.6 per cent volume increase in military spending in the fiscal year 1981–82, and indeed for further years. Such an increase would mark a sharp change from the trend of the 1970s. From 1971 to 1976, in

again—the standardized NATO military expenditure figure divided through by the consumer price index, and correctly represents the increase in the 'civil opportunities forgone'—that is, the increase in the military burden.

Rather curiously, it appears that the United States has given up attempting to put pressure on Canada to increase its military spending. Between 1978 and 1980 Canadian military expenditure fell 8 per cent in real terms (table 6.1); yet this development appears to have elicited none of the critical comment which the US Administration addressed to FR Germany or Japan.

Table 6.1. World military spending, 1971–80

All figures based on 1978 constant dollar estimates.

	Shares in total		Rates of change (per cent a year, compound)				
	1971	1980	1971–75	1975–80	1978	1979	1980 est.
USA	32	24	−2.2	0.2	0.7	0.6	1.3
Canada	1	1	1.5	1.6	3.8	−5.2	−3.3
European NATO	16	17	3.2	1.7	2.9	2.2	1.1
Total NATO	49	43	−0.2	0.9	1.6	1.1	1.1
USSR	25	24	1.5	1.5	1.5	1.4	1.5
Other WTO	2	3	4.7	2.9	1.1	3.2	2.6
Total WTO	27	26	1.8	1.6	1.4	1.6	1.6
Other Europe	2.3	2.6	4.7	2.2	1.2	3.5	2.0
Middle East	2.9	8.3	28.3	4.5	2.6	0.5	13.3
South Asia	1.0	1.1	0.7	3.8	4.0	3.2	0.4
Far East	3.5	5.7	5.1	9.7	15.0	10.7	6.2
China	10.3	8.8	−1.2	1.5	2.4	5.3	0
Oceania	0.7	0.7	3.1	1.0	0	0.5	4.7
Africa	1.5	2.1	12.6	1.5	−2.9	4.8	−1.8
Central America	0.3	0.6	6.4	12.3	7.0	3.0	11.0
South America	1.0	1.3	7.0	3.2	1.2	0	1.6
Total rest of world	24	31	6.9	3.9	3.8	4.3	4.8
World	100[a]	100[a]	2.1	2.0	2.5	2.1	2.4

[a] Totals may not add up due to rounding.

Source: Table 6A.2.

The Secretary of Defense in the present US Administration has also indicated a certain scepticism about the use of volume percentages as a way of comparing contributions to NATO military spending. However, whether that means that there will be a relaxation of US pressure on its European allies and on Japan remains to be seen. It seems on balance probable that the pressure will still be there, although it may be expressed in a different form.

III. The WTO

On the level of Soviet military spending, there is little to add to the analysis in previous Yearbooks [4–5]. On the one hand there is the CIA dollar estimate, which suggests that Soviet military expenditure is some 50 per cent higher than that of the United States. On the other hand there is the Soviet official figure in roubles which, when converted into dollars at the official exchange-rate (of 64 kopecks to the dollar), suggests that Soviet military spending is between one-fifth and one-sixth of that of the United States. Neither of these figures provides sensible comparisons of the military spending of the two countries; the figures given in table 6A.2 suggest a rough parity between the two countries.

There is a wide range of growth-rates given in US sources for the rate of increase in Soviet military spending in real terms; the reasons for this range are revealing. On the one hand there is the CIA *dollar* estimate of Soviet military spending, which attempts to measure what it would cost to the United States, in dollars, to reproduce the Soviet military efforts. Consequently all those in the Soviet armed forces are valued according to the amount paid to US servicemen. Hence the very high dollar figure for the *level* of Soviet military spending. However, when it comes to trying to calculate the *rate of growth* of Soviet military spending, this method of calculation gives a great deal of importance (or 'weight') to any changes in the numbers in the Soviet armed forces. It is generally agreed that the numbers in the armed forces have changed little in recent years: so that the volume estimates of Soviet military spending, measured in dollars, show relatively low growth-rates: a figure as low as a 1.5 per cent volume increase, for example, in 1978 [6a].

The CIA also make an estimate of Soviet military spending in roubles. Since the pay of the Soviet conscript army is very low, when the rate of growth in Soviet military spending is calculated by this method, changes in the numbers in the armed forces have much less importance (or 'weight'), and changes in procurement have much more importance. So the growth-rates calculated by this method are higher—the figure for 1978 on this basis was a growth-rate of 3 per cent [6a].

One constantly finds, in Western discussions of Soviet military expenditure, that military spokesmen and others use the *dollar* estimate for the *level* of military expenditure, since that gives a very high figure, and the *rouble* estimate for the *rate of growth* in that expenditure, since that method gives the higher figure for the rate of growth. This is, of course, not the only problem in producing sensible, and comparable, figures for rates of growth; one of the other main problems—the measurement of quality change—is discussed on page 6. The figures given for the Soviet Union in table 6A.2

represent an attempt to present statistically the following propositions: first, that there is a rough parity of resources devoted to military purposes, as between the Soviet Union and the United States. Secondly, if the growth-rate for the Soviet Union were calculated in the same way as the growth-rate for the United States—that is, by correcting expenditure figures by a price index—the Soviet figures would show a growth-rate percentage of the order of 1–2 per cent.

Table 6A.2 also presents figures for the other WTO countries. It seems quite possible that the Soviet Union may be having the same kind of difficulty as the United States in trying to persuade the other members of the WTO to 'share more of the defence burden'. The only other WTO country which shows any willingness to shift its military spending up significantly is the German Democratic Republic. Over the last three years, from 1977 to 1980, East German military expenditure appears to have risen, in real terms, by some 25 per cent. The figures for the other countries seem roughly flat—except for Poland where there seems to have been a fall.

IV. China

Our estimate of the trend of military spending in China has changed since the last Yearbook. Sources now available suggest a change in trend from 1971 onwards [6b] (figure 6.1). From 1965 to 1971, Chinese military spending appears to have risen rapidly—the estimate is of an increase of around 10 per cent a year. This was a period when China was recovering from the cut-off in Soviet military assistance, and tensions between China and the Soviet Union were becoming more acute. Then in 1972 defence procurement appears to have been cut severely; and from then until 1978 it is estimated that there was only a very slow rate of growth, of the order of 1–2 per cent a year. It appears that there were new priorities which favoured economic development over increased military spending. Finally in 1979, defence costs probably jumped because of the war with Viet Nam, and may have levelled off again in 1980.

V. The rest of the world

The following notes on development in the rest of the world look first at what has been happening in those areas where military spending appears to have been rising fast in the last two years—the Far East, the Middle East and Central America—and then at those areas where the trend has been more moderate.

Figure 6.1. Estimated Chinese military expenditure, 1965–80

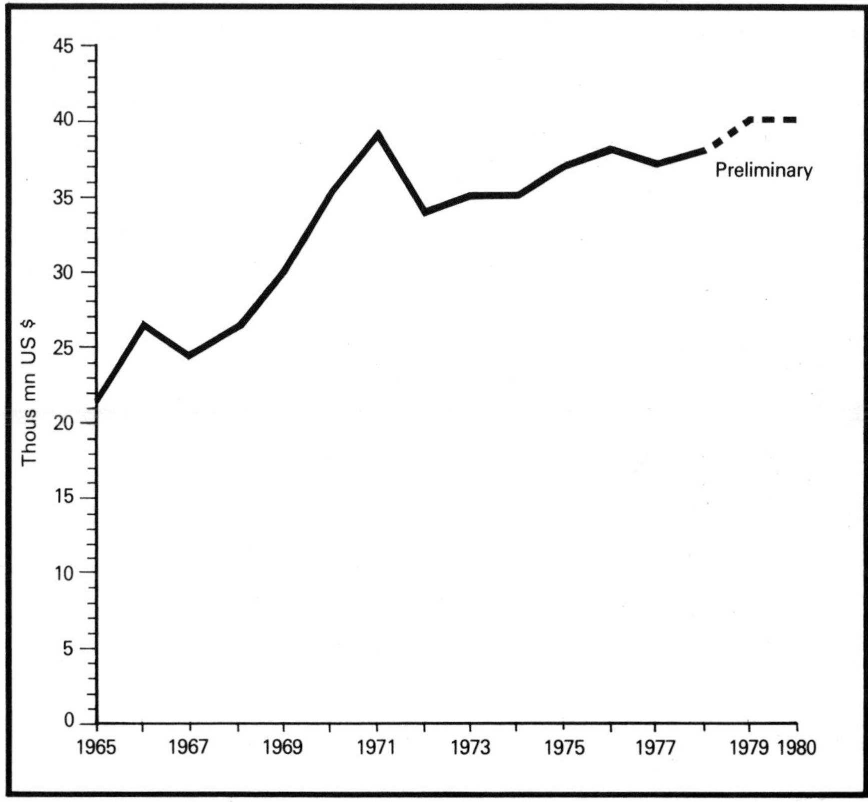

Source: Reference [6].

The SIPRI figures for military expenditure in the *Far East* are not comprehensive: there are no good numbers for Viet Nam, Laos or Kampuchea—a region where military spending must be very high. In general in the Far East, the rise in military spending is rapid. This is true in North and South Korea—military spending in South Korea nearly trebled between 1975 and 1980. It is true also in the ASEAN group; over the same period 1975–80, military spending in Malaysia and Singapore nearly doubled. Indonesia appears to provide an exception—although the Indonesian figures are very doubtful. Finally, in Taiwan the withdrawal of US recognition appears to have led to a very big increase indeed in the military budget, which in 1980 was more than four times as large as that of 1975.

In the *Middle East*, there have been in recent years a number of contrary trends, which kept the total fairly flat between 1975 and 1979: preliminary estimates for 1980 suggest a sharp rise again. Between 1975 and 1979 military spending was falling in Egypt and in Israel from the very high figures at the time of the last Arab–Israeli war. Since 1976 Iranian military spending also has been coming down. In 1976 Iran's military budget had been the sixth largest in the world; by 1979 it had halved. Now it is probably rising again.

However, there have been contrary upward trends since 1975. In both Syria and Saudi Arabia military spending has roughly trebled between 1975 and 1980. By 1980 the increase in these two countries appeared substantially to have exceeded any fall elsewhere, and the total for the area was beginning to move up significantly again.

The figures for *Central America* are dominated by Cuba and Mexico. In Cuba, the increase in military spending seems to have been fairly rapid right through the 1970s; in Mexico spending has risen steadily, presumably as some of the increasing oil revenues have been devoted to military ends.

In other areas of the world, the rise in the last two years has been less dramatic. In *South America*, the figures are bedevilled both by the rapid rates of inflation in many countries and by the difficulty of making any sensible distinction between spending on the military and spending on other armed internal security forces. Military spending appears still to be rising fast in Chile; in Venezuela and Peru it seems to have fallen in recent years. Countries like Peru which wish to borrow from the International Monetary Fund are normally enjoined by the Fund to cut total public expenditure; and this may well work through to the military budget.

In the continent of *Africa* as a whole, total military spending—which was rising fast up to 1976—seems since then to have levelled off. There are two main developments to explain this: first, military spending in Nigeria seems to have been coming down quite fast since the mid-1970s, and this is also true of Ghana. Second, in the last three years South African spending—which had nearly tripled from 1971 to 1977—levelled off. There are countries where military spending appears to be rising quite fast—Algeria and Morocco, which are still engaged in a desert war over former Spanish territory, and Ethiopia. There are no good figures for Libya since 1977.

The trends in *other European countries*—those countries which are neither members of NATO nor of the WTO—have been mixed. In both Sweden and Switzerland military spending has been virtually flat over the past four years. The two countries with fairly sizeable military budgets where there has been a rise are Spain and Yugoslavia; and in Ireland the military budget—though very small—has grown by some 18 per cent between 1977 and 1980.

Finally, the relatively long period of comparative military calm in *Oceania* appears to be over. For five years, from 1974 to 1979, military spending in real terms hardly rose at all. In 1980—possibly under some pressure from the United States—there was a volume increase of 4.5 per cent in both Australia and New Zealand.

References

1. *Baltimore Sun*, 7 January 1981, p. 1.
2. *Far Eastern Economic Review*, 16 January 1981, p. 25.
3. *New York Times*, 13 November 1980, p. 6.
4. *World Armaments and Disarmament, SIPRI Yearbook 1979* (Taylor & Francis, London, 1979, Stockholm International Peace Research Institute), pp. 27 ff.
5. *World Armaments and Disarmament, SIPRI Yearbook 1980* (Taylor & Francis, London, 1980, Stockholm International Peace Research Institute), pp. 7 ff.
6. *Allocation of Resources in the Soviet Union and China—1979*, Hearings before the Subcommittee on Priorities and Economy in Government of the Joint Economic Committee, 96th Congress, 1st session (US Government Printing Office, Washington, D.C., 1979), Part 5, 26 June and 9 July 1979.
   (a) —, p. 106.
   (b) —, p. 67.

Appendix 6A

World military expenditure, 1980

For the sources and methods for the world military expenditure data, see appendix 6B. For the conventions used in the tables and for footnotes, see page 169.

Table 6A.1. World military expenditure summary, in constant price figures

Figures are in US $ mn, at 1978 prices and 1978 exchange-rates. Totals may not add up due to rounding.

	1971	1972	1973	1974	1975	1976	1977	1978	1979	1980
USA	120 655	121 105	114 976	113 666	110 229	104 261	108 537	109 247	109 861	111 236
Other NATO	66 469	69 994	71 286	73 200	75 272	76 642	78 134	80 468	81 942	82 674
Total NATO	187 124	191 099	186 261	186 866	185 501	180 903	186 671	189 715	191 803	193 910
USSR	[93 900]	[95 400]	[96 900]	[98 300]	[99 800]	[101 300]	[102 700]	[104 200]	[105 700]	[107 300]
Other WTO	8 853	9 040	9 541	10 003	10 624	11 103	(11 444)	(11 574)	[11 943]	[12 250]
Total WTO	[102 753]	[104 440]	[106 441]	[108 303]	[110 424]	[112 403]	[114 144]	[115 774]	[117 643]	[119 550]
Other Europe	8 814	9 374	9 537	10 204	10 598	11 125	(11 064)	(11 192)	(11 587)	[11 821]
Middle East	11 189	12 569	18 943	25 007	30 350	(33 033)	(32 451)	(33 283)	[33 445]	[37 900]
South Asia	3 955	4 269	3 853	3 680	4 065	4 642	4 549	(4 731)	(4 882)	(4 902)
Far East	13 267	14 254	14 757	14 694	16 193	17 427	19 058	21 916	24 260	25 767
China	[39 000]	[33 200]	[35 100]	[35 100]	[37 100]	[38 000]	[37 100]	[38 000]	[40 000]	[40 000]
Oceania	2 839	2 797	2 871	3 106	3 203	3 193	3 204	3 203	3 218	3 369
Africa	5 679	6 064	6 259	7 750	9 138	9 796	9 859	(9 577)	[10 037]	[9 859]
Central America	953	975	1 030	1 093	1 223	(1 526)	1 786	(1 912)	(1 969)	[2 186]
South America	3 942	3 906	4 121	4 765	(5 175)	5 867	5 980	5 953	(5 953)	[6 050]
World total	**379 515**	**382 946**	**389 174**	**400 569**	**412 970**	**417 914**	**425 866**	**435 256**	**444 798**	**455 311**
Developed market economies[a]	206 322	211 395	209 078	209 627	209 354	205 570	211 660	215 257	217 989	219 690
Centrally planned economies[a]	143 268	138 796	142 698	144 776	149 112	152 368	153 456	156 237	160 304	161 296
OPEC countries[a]	8 925	10 719	12 854	20 204	25 852	29 732	28 432	31 970	31 495	35 507
Non-oil developing countries:[a]										
with (1977) GNP *per capita* <US $300	5 117	5 449	4 950	5 072	5 356	5 836	5 705	6 245	6 561	6 662
with (1977) GNP *per capita* US $300–800	6 594	6 605	8 974	9 648	10 106	10 028	10 527	8 302	8 331	9 061
with (1977) GNP *per capita* >US $800	7 889	8 687	9 320	10 161	11 560	13 332	13 892	15 992	18 955	22 717
Total non-oil developing countries	19 600	20 741	23 244	24 881	27 022	29 196	30 124	30 539	33 847	38 440
Southern Africa[a]	1 100	1 155	1 312	1 716	2 094	2 448	2 770	3 102	2 902	2 956

Table 6A.2. World military expenditure, in constant price figures

Figures are in US $ mn, at 1978 prices and 1978 exchange-rates.

	1971	1972	1973	1974	1975	1976	1977	1978	1979	1980
NATO										
North America:										
Canada	3 273	3 279	3 290	3 515	3 468	3 702	3 939	4 087	3 875	3 745
USA	120 655	121 105	114 976	113 666	110 229	104 261	108 537	109 247	109 861	111 236
Europe:										
Belgium	2 266	2 388	2 498	2 532	2 758	2 902	2 978	3 175	3 246	3 305
Denmark	1 137	1 131	1 074	1 177	1 276	1 260	1 266	1 315	1 322	(1 322)
France	14 663	15 023	15 573	15 505	16 194	16 898	17 670	18 623	19 112	19 498
FR Germany	18 024	19 255	20 010	20 885	20 791	20 641	20 561	21 417	21 730	22 003
Greece	1 044	1 114	1 112	1 065	1 705	1 665	2 015	2 071	1 882	1 673
Italy	5 457	6 027	6 018	6 025	5 607	5 580	5 990	6 246	6 642	6 324
Luxembourg	18.8	20.9	22.9	24.7	26.3	28.2	27.6	30.0	30.9	34.7
Netherlands	3 452	3 558	3 614	3 781	3 965	3 922	4 373	4 228	4 482	4 333
Norway	1 045	1 043	1 052	1 080	1 171	1 200	1 223	1 307	1 340	1 365
Portugal	1 112	1 097	1 014	1 215	836	653	616	623	631	674
Turkey[a]	1 655	1 683	1 806	1 894	2 980	3 420	3 320	2 728	2 368	2 211
UK	13 321	14 375	14 201	14 501	14 494	14 770	14 155	14 618	15 281	16 187
Total NATO (excl. USA)	63 196	66 715	67 996	69 685	71 805	72 940	74 195	76 381	78 068	78 929
Total NATO	187 124	191 099	186 261	186 866	185 501	180 903	186 671	189 715	191 803	193 910
WTO										
Bulgaria	399	440	475	538	611	664	(597)	(624)	(666)	. .
Czechoslovakia	1 721	1 739	1 831	1 948	2 008	2 115	(2 148)	(2 105)	[2 115]	. .
German DR	2 745	2 864	3 058	3 172	3 364	3 444	3 560	3 738	4 123	4 470
Hungary	721	668	651	712	766	721	750	819	780	. .
Poland	2 586	2 621	2 807	2 838	3 001	3 208	(3 412)	(3 218)	(3 195)	. .
Romania	681	708	719	795	874	951	977	1 070	(1 064)	. .
USSR	[93 900]	[95 400]	[96 900]	[98 300]	[99 800]	[101 300]	[102 700]	[104 200]	[105 700]	[107 300]
Total WTO (excl. USSR)	8 853	9 040	9 541	10 003	10 624	11 103	(11 444)	(11 574)	[11 943]	[12 250]
Total WTO	[102 753]	[104 440]	[106 441]	[108 303]	[110 424]	[112 403]	[114 144]	[115 774]	[117 643]	[119 550]
Other Europe										
Albania[b]	142	144	144	149	155	191	172	201	204	. .
Austria	472	506	511	575	642	657	679	741	767	(765)
Finland	381	435	442	455	490	499	462	485	473	532
Ireland	121	144	152	167	162	169	174	182	200	206

	1971	1972	1973	1974	1975	1976	1977	1978	1979	1980
Spain	1 718	1 868	2 042	2 217	2 308	2 472	2 478	2 461	2 672	2 784
Sweden	2 739	2 811	2 822	2 844	2 925	2 919	2 932	2 980	3 067	2 908
Switzerland	1 766	1 799	1 743	1 737	1 638	1 856	1 753	1 762	1 843	1 814
Yugoslavia	1 477	1 666	1 683	2 060	2 279	2 363	(2 414)	(2 379)	[2 363]	[2 605]
Total Other Europe	8 814	9 374	9 537	10 204	10 598	11 125	(11 064)	(11 192)	[11 587]	[11 821]
Middle East										
Bahrain	31.4	34.9	36.1	46.6	25.0	32.7	42.7	50.6	[55.5]	. .
Cyprus	16.8	16.4	15.2	21.7	23.1	22.5	29.9	23.8	[17.6]	. .
Egypt	2 972	2 911	5 367	5 927	5 756	5 004	5 238	[3 322]	[2 790]	. .
Iran	1 810	2 518	3 467	7 664	9 731	10 557	8 573	9 424	4 757	. .
Iraq[e]	862	830	1 025	2 016	2 050	2 011	2 101	1 988	2 440	. .
Israel[d]	2 166	2 134	3 880	2 900	3 160	3 159	3 079	2 676	2 783	2 218
Jordan[e]	270	292	282	250	246	411	329	311	323	. .
Kuwait[e]	353	371	396	724	865	1 064	1 183	1 076	923	[931]
Lebanon[c, d]	122	174	191	209	212	174	108	166	200	. .
Oman[b]	46.3	72.4	122	342	698	785	686	767	689	880
Saudi Arabia	2 006	2 623	3 348	(4 111)	(6 267)	(8 433)	(9 146)	(11 379)	(15 137)	(18 514)
Syria	370	427	661	624	1 116	1 110	1 111	1 165	2 018	3 186
United Arab Emirates[b]	. .	. .	13.3	20.6	32.0	80.6	611	689	1 033	[1 162]
Yemen, Arab Republic	. .	100	94.7	106	118	135	150	165	. .	. .
Yemen, Peoples' Democratic	50.4	51.6	46.2	46.6	51.5	55.1	61.3	78.5	98.1	. .
Total Middle East	11 189	12 569	18 943	25 007	30 350	(33 033)	(32 451)	(33 283)	[33 445]	[37 900]
South Asia										
Afghanistan	[33.5]	42.4	46.2	43.5	47.6	49.6	55.8	59.4	. .	. .
Bangladesh	. .	. .	46.1	52.7	68.3	117	125	113	117	121
India	3 021	3 223	2 826	2 648	2 980	3 500	3 400	3 535	3 662	3 605
Nepal	9.2	9.0	9.3	9.5	10.8	14.0	14.5	. .	. .	. .
Pakistan	874	978	914	912	943	943	937	988	1 001	(1 068)
Sri Lanka	18.0	16.5	11.8	14.5	15.2	17.8	(16.1)	(19.8)	23.8	30.9
Total South Asia	3 955	4 269	3 853	3 680	4 065	4 642	4 549	(4 731)	(4 882)	(4 902)
Far East										
Brunei	22.2	21.7	23.8	27.8	50.5	80.6	139	131	155	. .
Burma	211	220	200	170	147	149	[167]	. .	. .	. .
Hong Kong	39.5	41.7	32.9	28.7	28.3	51.3	77.1	92.9	[101]	(102)
Indonesia	. .	[1 353]	[1 268]	[1 168]	[1 621]	[1 590]	1 813	2 050	1 870	1 455

Japan	6 298	7 093	7 486	7 597	7 899	7 978	8 232	8 875	9 251	9 200
Korea, North	956	613	608	759	909	1 004	(1 034)	1 144	1 250	1 337
Korea, South	662	825	920	1 052	1 271	1 840	2 189	2 721	2 661	2 990
Malaysia	395	511	540	561	640	579	687	764	[958]	1 136
Mongolia[b]	(50.3)	(57.1)	(63.4)	(108)	(111)	(121)	(120)	(125)	(143)	(176)
Philippines	176	219	307	(355)	(395)	544	595	652	[646]	677
Singapore[e]	304	321	269	262	301	368	392	443	508	. .
Taiwan	1 101	1 162	1 254	1 069	1 199	1 398	1 665	[2 697]	4 205	5 409
Thailand	501	515	485	457	621	675	757	770	888	(859)
Total Far East, excl. Kampuchea, Laos and Viet Nam	11 966	12 954	13 457	13 614	15 193	16 377	17 867	20 658	22 849	24 271
Total Far East	13 267	14 254	14 757	14 694	16 193	[17 427]	[19 058]	[21 916]	[24 260]	[25 767]
Oceania										
Australia	2 567	2 522	2 597	2 820	2 911	2 912	2 920	2 901	2 910	3 046
Fiji	1.2	1.3	1.4	1.3	1.8	2.7	2.9	3.2	3.4	4.4
New Zealand	270	273	273	285	290	278	282	298	305	318
Total Oceania	2 839	2 797	2 871	3 106	3 203	3 193	3 204	3 203	3 218	3 369
Africa										
Algeria	221	(217)	(224)	426	371	426	473	465	524	. .
Benin[b]	5.8	5.9	6.1	6.8	7.5	7.8	11.9	(11.9)	. .	. .
Burundi	7.0	9.6	10.2	11.9	10.6	12.6	17.3	(21.3)	. .	. .
Cameroon	59.2	58.0	59.0	59.4	63.0	66.2	63.6	60.7	61.9	56.8
Central African Republic	12.8	10.7	12.4	11.7	10.8	10.5	9.3	10.1	12.7	. .
Chad	[30.0]	28.6	25.0	23.3	22.2	31.6	(35.7)	(41.3)	. .	. .
Congo	31.9	24.7	32.0	40.8	43.0	45.8	43.9	38.1	45.9	. .
Equatorial Guinea[b]	(3.6)	(3.7)	(3.8)	(3.9)	(3.9)	. .	. .	. .	. .	. .
Ethiopia	89.3	99.4	97.7	136	213	170	154	251	299	[344]
Gabon	16.1	17.3	20.3	22.0	24.3	26.9	34.9	(53.9)	(59.2)	88.2
Ghana[d]	361	299	284	370	350	312	179	133	(145)	. .
Guinea[b]	21.3	20.9	20.9	20.9	. .	. .	. .	. .	. .	. .
Ivory Coast	55.3	(57.2)	(59.8)	78.9	70.3	66.7	(65.1)	87.8	79.4	. .
Kenya	48.9	63.7	71.2	76.5	77.0	110	185	240	242	. .
Liberia	8.7	7.4	6.0	5.1	5.4	6.2	6.7	[6.9]	. .	. .
Libya	(476)	(533)	(637)	(1 010)	(1 048)	(1 603)	(1 577)	. .	. .	. .
Madagascar	26.8	29.1	30.6	34.5	33.1	41.4	50.7	52.2	67.7	. .
Malawi	2.8	2.9	4.5	5.3	10.3	10.8	15.7	21.1	19.3	. .
Mali[d]	19.0	23.4	21.1	23.6	32.3	38.6	37.6	30.9	34.9	. .

	1971	1972	1973	1974	1975	1976	1977	1978	1979	1980
Mauritania	6.1	7.9	9.6	11.2	35.1	(50.5)	(65.6)	. .	. .	. .
Mauritius	7.9	8.5	9.5	9.9	11.5	(10.7)	. .	. .	. .	. .
Morocco	241	270	311	367	538	755	867	(770)	(1 093)	. .
Mozambique[b]	. .	. .	. .	. .	14.0	(41.0)	44.3	(85.1)	87.0	. .
Niger	8.0	7.5	6.8	9.5	11.1	11.2	. .	. .	. .	. .
Nigeria	1 388	1 618	1 782	1 958	2 927	2 544	2 388	1 794	1 739	1 524
Rwanda	12.4	11.0	17.0	13.6	12.4	14.2	13.7	14.8	15.2	. .
Senegal	42.7	42.0	37.3	35.1	34.9	41.9	45.1	49.1	50.4	48.4
Sierra Leone	6.2	6.5	7.4	8.0	7.8	7.2	10.6	[11.4]	. .	. .
Somalia	25.9	30.5	31.4	35.5	31.9	31.9	34.9	(66.7)	(76.7)	. .
South Africa	701	710	869	1 164	1 429	1 768	1 999	2 179	1 916	1 989
Sudan	294	259	228	184	152	193	220	(207)	[285]	. .
Tanzania[e]	67.3	79.0	102	134	126	132	164	(265)	[247]	. .
Togo	8.6	8.9	10.2	11.5	11.9	17.2	18.3	21.2	19.7	. .
Tunisia	45.4	51.7	52.7	63.8	86.9	98.0	133	148	139	. .
Uganda[d]	447	566	409	315	315	279	199	156	. .	. .
Upper Volta	9.2	9.9	10.0	10.2	22.1	29.1	26.9	23.2	(26.2)	. .
Zaire[d]	541	501	400	635	430	(253)	(58.7)	(45.5)	(121)	. .
Zambia	[244]	[271]	[218]	[268]	[355]	[290]	[279]	[246]	[263]	. .
Zimbabwe	87.2	95.2	123	151	169	216	285	327	390	. .
Total Africa	5 679	6 064	6 259	7 750	9 138	9 796	9 859	(9 577)	[10 037]	[9 859]
Central America										
Costa Rica[e]	9.8	9.9	10.9	11.2	13.5	17.7	19.5	22.1	(19.2)	[19.2]
Cuba[b, e]	367	338	342	357	413	. .	886	992	1 065	[1 026]
Dominican Republic	64.6	64.6	59.7	68.6	72.1	78.8	78.5	87.1	145	. .
El Salvador[e]	24.4	25.1	38.8	42.1	37.8	48.0	56.8	59.0	(58.7)	. .
Guatemala	[37.5]	45.4	38.1	41.7	57.7	60.3	83.9	73.2	[64.4]	. .
Haiti	3.7	3.8	3.2	2.9	3.0	3.2	3.5	. .	. .	. .
Honduras	18.3	23.5	23.2	21.7	25.8	27.2	26.8	31.4	. .	. .
Jamaica	14.0	14.9	23.1	21.7	24.0	29.1	27.7	. .	. .	. .
Mexico	361	401	447	477	520	543	531	536	588	563
Nicaragua	22.3	28.1	22.7	27.2	32.5	43.5	43.2	. .	. .	. .
Panama	21.8	13.9	14.9	15.5	17.7	16.7	. .	. .	. .	. .
Trinidad and Tobago	7.9	7.4	5.9	6.3	7.4	8.2	8.9	. .	. .	. .
Total Central America	953	975	1 030	1 093	1 223	(1 526)	1 786	(1 912)	(1 969)	[2 186]

South America										
Argentina[d]	1 020	1 021	796	939	(1 200)	1 723	1 438	1 492	1 685	1 542
Bolivia	28.6	39.1	46.7	52.9	72.1	79.0	75.8	80.8	[87.6]	. .
Brazil[d]	1 367	1 462	1 737	1 764	1 758	2 100	1 986	2 041	1 744	. .
Chile[d]	199	199	318	554	432	430	500	630	[839]	984
Colombia	380	200	182	174	193	199	182	168	(184)	229
Ecuador	71.9	83.8	100	115	141	129	215	164	168	. .
Guyana[e]	13.6	14.4	15.2	21.9	42.0	58.5	35.0	(25.5)	. .	. .
Paraguay	30.0	29.4	28.6	26.6	33.3	34.5	37.0	38.8	35.9	. .
Peru[d]	300	280	338	359	474	537	780	599	464	469
Uruguay[d]	121	109	109	131	123	95	100	132	. .	. .
Venezuela	411	470	452	628	707	482	631	590	568	577
Total South America	3 942	3 906	4 121	4 765	(5 175)	5 867	5 980	5 953	(5 953)	[6 050]

Table 6A.3. World military expenditure, in current price figures

Figures are in local currency, current prices.

	Currency	1971	1972	1973	1974	1975	1976	1977	1978	1979	1980
NATO											
North America:											
Canada	*mn dollars*	2 131	2 238	2 405	2 862	3 127	3 589	4 124	4 662	4 825	5 130
USA	*mn dollars*	74 862	77 639	78 358	85 906	90 948	91 013	100 925	109 247	122 279	140 513
Europe:											
Belgium	*mn francs*	40 654	45 183	50 533	57 739	70 899	81 444	89 480	99 726	106 472	115 437
Denmark	*mn kroners*	3 195	3 386	3 520	4 439	5 281	5 680	6 343	7 250	7 990	(9 005)
France	*mn francs*	34 907	37 992	42 284	47 878	55 872	63 899	73 097	84 042	95 481	110 394
FR Germany	*mn marks*	25 450	28 720	31 908	35 644	37 589	38 922	40 184	43 019	45 415	48 531
Greece	*mn drachmas*	15 480	17 211	19 866	24 126	43 820	48 466	65 800	76 106	82 301	90 000
Italy	*thous mn lire*	1 852	2 162	2 392	2 852	3 104	3 608	4 533	5 301	6 468	7 450
Luxembourg	*mn francs*	442	517	601	710	836	983	1 029	1 154	1 242	1 476
Netherlands	*mn guilders*	4 394	4 886	5 360	6 144	7 119	7 662	9 092	9 146	10 106	10 409
Norway	*mn kroner*	3 022	3 239	3 505	3 938	4 771	5 333	5 934	6 854	7 362	8 248
Portugal	*mn escudos*	14 699	16 046	16 736	25 108	19 898	18 845	22 082	27 354	34 343	42 159
Turkey	*mn lire*	8 487	9 961	12 192	15 831	30 200	40 691	49 790	66 239	94 034	169 469
UK	*mn pounds*	2 815	3 258	3 512	4 160	5 165	6 132	6 810	7 616	9 029	11 306
WTO											
Bulgaria	*mn leva*	354	391	422	483	548	596	(541)	(565)	(603)	. .
Czechoslovakia	*mn korunas*	15 356	15 487	16 331	17 467	18 133	19 228	(19 795)	(19 700)	[20 550]	. .
German DR	*mn marks*	6 320	6 528	6 900	7 083	7 512	7 690	7 868	8 261	8 674	9 403
Hungary	*mn forints*	9 891	9 430	9 489	10 564	11 811	11 671	12 607	14 410	14 943	. .
Poland	*mn zlotys*	37 740	38 245	42 119	45 606	49 672	55 432	(61 865)	(63 045)	(65 725)	. .
Romania	*mn lei*	7 424	7 710	7 835	8 744	9 713	10 570	10 960	12 000	(12 000)	. .
USSR	*mn roubles*	[42 700]	[43 300]	[44 000]	[44 700]	[45 400]	[46 000]	[46 700]	[47 400]	[48 000]	[48 700]
Other Europe											
Albania	*mn leks*	580	590	589	610	635	783	705	824	835	. .
Austria	*mn schillings*	4 300	4 900	5 324	6 565	7 946	8 728	9 515	10 767	11 541	(12 260)
Finland	*mn markkaa*	692	847	956	1 148	1 455	1 695	1 767	1 996	2 093	2 612
Ireland	*mn pounds*	25.5	33.1	38.8	49.9	58.5	71.8	84.1	95.0	118	144
Spain	*mn pesetas*	47 019	55 368	67 467	84 749	103 064	127 028	158 568	188 666	236 813	286 248
Sweden	*mn kronor*	6 714	7 306	7 823	8 666	9 781	10 768	12 054	13 466	14 861	16 070
Switzerland	*mn francs*	2 232	2 426	2 556	2 795	2 813	3 242	3 110	3 151	3 415	3 496
Yugoslavia	*mn new dinars*	8 948	11 716	14 108	21 100	28 815	33 234	(38 890)	(43 530)	[52 471]	[73 463]

Middle East											
Bahrain	*mn dinars*	4.2	4.9	5.8	9.3	5.8	9.3	14.3	19.6	[22.0]	. .
Cyprus	*mn pounds*	3.8	3.9	3.9	6.7	7.2	7.3	10.4	8.9	[7.2]	. .
Egypt	*mn pounds*	650	650	1 250	1 530	1 631	1 564	1 845	[1 300]	[1 200]	. .
Iran	*thous mn rials*	55.7	82.4	125	315	451	544	563	664	385	. .
Iraq[e]	*mn dinars*	151	153	199	422	470	520	593	587	790	. .
Israel	*mn pounds*	5 399	5 990	13 080	13 636	20 723	27 218	35 724	46 749	86 660	157 850
Jordan[e]	*mn dinars*	38.0	44.1	47.3	50.2	55.2	103	94.5	95.3	130	[135]
Kuwait[e]	*mn dinars*	53.3	61.3	70.9	147	190	250	298	296	267	[286]
Lebanon	*mn pounds*	142	213	247	300	315	327	255	491	738	1 141
Oman	*mn riyals*	16.0	25.0	42.0	118	241	271	237	265	238	304
Saudi Arabia	*mn riyals*	2 379	3 246	4 830	(7 202)	(14 775)	(26 165)	(31 590)	(38 684)	(52 387)	(64 076)
Syria	*mn pounds*	676	793	1 485	1 682	3 345	3 690	4 160	4 573	8 282	15 867
United Arab Emirates	*mn dirhams*	. .	. .	51.6	79.9	124	312	2 365	2 668	4 000	[4 500]
Yemen, Arab Republic	*mn rials*	92.0	121	162	228	316	421	586	756	. .	. .
Yemen, Peoples' Democratic	*mn dinars*	8.9	9.6	10.3	12.5	15.4	17.1	20.0	27.1	36.3	. .
South Asia											
Afghanistan	*mn afghanis*	[1 343]	1 453	1 458	1 563	1 825	1 909	2 353	2 673	. .	. .
Bangladesh	*mn taka*	. .	. .	319	564	909	1 406	1 663	1 690	1 978	2 362
India	*mn rupees*	14 438	16 205	16 737	20 043	23 823	25 793	27 174	28 966	31 910	35 183
Nepal	*mn rupees*	61.7	65.9	74.9	89.2	116	148	165	. .	. .	. .
Pakistan	*mn rupees*	3 463	4 083	4 695	5 932	7 412	7 952	8 697	9 780	10 850	12 770
Sri Lanka	*mn rupees*	175	170	137	184	207	245	224	309	411	681
Far East											
Brunei	*mn dollars*	30.1	29.2	35.0	53.2	97.9	167	303	297	372	. .
Burma	*mn kyats*	572	645	732	779	891	1 099	[1 220]	. .	. .	. .
Hong Kong	*mn dollars*	113	127	118	118	117	219	348	447	[525]	(600)
Indonesia	*thous mn new rupiahs*	. .	[189]	[231]	[300]	[496]	[583]	738	906	1 028	951
Japan	*thous mn yen*	666	783	924	1 166	1 356	1 497	1 669	1 868	2 017	2 170
Kampuchea	*mn riels*	11 549	16 956	26 073	48 320	. .	. .	. .	. .	. .	. .
Korea, North	*mn won*	1 960	1 256	1 247	1 557	1 864	2 058	(2 119)	2 345	2 563	2 740
Korea, South	*thous mn won*	123	171	197	280	424	707	926	1 317	1 524	2 167
Laos	*mn kips*	9 630	10 330	12 732	[14 606]	. .	. .	. .	. .	. .	. .
Malaysia	*mn ringgits*	580	774	904	1 103	1 314	1 219	1 517	1 770	[2 300]	2 900
Mongolia	*mn tugriks*	(169)	(192)	(213)	(362)	(373)	(407)	(405)	(421)	(480)	(590)
Philippines	*mn pesos*	582	796	1 271	(1 962)	(2 360)	3 452	4 070	4 800	[5 640]	7 100
Singapore[e]	*mn dollars*	402	434	459	547	645	774	910	1 008	1 203	. .
Taiwan	*thous mn dollars*	20.3	22.1	25.8	32.4	38.3	45.7	58.3	[99.8]	170	230
Thailand	*mn baht*	5 318	5 738	6 238	7 295	10 438	11 823	13 000	15 650	19 857	(23 169)

	Currency	1971	1972	1973	1974	1975	1976	1977	1978	1979	1980
Oceania											
Australia	*mn dollars*	1 062	1 105	1 246	1 556	1 849	2 100	2 364	2 536	2 774	3 200
Fiji	*mn dollars*	0.5	0.6	0.7	0.8	1.2	2.0	2.3	2.7	3.1	4.8
New Zealand	*mn dollars*	118	128	138	160	187	210	243	288	334	409
Africa											
Algeria	*mn dinars*	491	(500)	(545)	1 088	1 030	1 288	1 600	1 843	2 318	[2 703]
Benin	*mn francs*	1 300	(1 330)	1 377	1 544	1 691	1 759	2 680	(2 680)	. .	. .
Burundi	*mn francs*	300	429	484	655	672	860	1 256	(1 915)	. .	. .
Cameroon	*mn francs*	5 921	6 274	7 052	8 334	10 023	11 582	12 766	13 700	14 875	14 925
Central African Republic	*mn francs*	1 468	1 312	1 616	1 667	1 774	1 915	1 880	2 289	2 972	. .
Chad	*mn francs*	[3 925]	3 854	3 553	3 685	4 052	5 977	(7 370)	(9 330)	. .	. .
Congo	*mn francs*	3 786	3 212	4 330	5 810	7 178	8 205	9 000	8 600	11 200	. .
Equatorial Guinea	*mn ekueles*	(255)	(260)	(265)	(270)	(275)	. .	. .	. .	. .	. .
Ethiopia	*mn birr*	91.6	95.9	102	155	259	265	280	519	722	[925]
Gabon	*mn francs*	1 514	1 682	2 107	2 556	3 612	4 807	7 107	(12 160)	(14 411)	18 616
Ghana	*mn cedis*	42.7	40.0	47.9	73.7	90.6	126	157	202	(339)	. .
Guinea	*mn syli*	418	410	410	410	. .	. .	. .	. .	. .	. .
Ivory Coast	*mn francs*	5 300	(5 500)	(6 400)	9 900	9 834	10 458	(13 000)	19 800	20 900	. .
Kenya	*mn pounds*	7.9	10.6	13.1	16.6	19.9	31.8	61.2	92.6	101	. .
Liberia	*mn dollars*	4.3	3.8	3.7	3.7	4.5	5.4	6.7	[6.9]	. .	. .
Libya	*mn dinars*	(77.0)	(86.0)	(111)	(189)	(214)	(345)	(361)	. .	. .	. .
Madagascar	*mn francs*	3 540	4 065	4 536	6 231	6 470	8 504	10 732	11 775	17 420	. .
Malawi	*mn kwachas*	1.4	1.5	2.4	3.3	7.4	8.1	12.2	17.8	18.1	. .
Mali	*mn francs*	3 175	4 195	4 890	5 600	8 100	10 456	12 751	13 966	15 341	. .
Mauritania	*mn ouguiyas*	141	200	260	340	1 200	(1 975)	(2 830)	. .	. .	. .
Mauritius	*mn rupees*	20.4	23.2	29.4	39.5	52.6	(55.3)	. .	. .	. .	. .
Morocco	*mn dirhams*	555	645	763	1 057	1 673	2 548	3 294	(3 209)	(4 937)	. .
Mozambique	*mn escudos*	. .	. .	. .	. .	600	(1 760)	1 900	(3 650)	3 733	. .
Niger	*mn francs*	775	797	816	1 173	1 501	1 859	. .	. .	. .	. .
Nigeria	*mn nairas*	293	351	408	505	1 008	1 070	1 219	1 139	1 227	1 284
Rwanda	*mn francs*	433	396	670	703	838	1 020	1 131	1 370	1 634	. .
Senegal	*mn francs*	4 570	4 824	4 715	5 188	6 780	8 233	9 913	11 073	12 554	13 563
Sierra Leone	*mn leones*	3.0	3.4	4.1	5.0	5.9	6.3	10.3	[12.0]	. .	. .
Somalia	*mn shillings*	80.7	92.0	101	135	145	165	200	(420)	(600)	. .
South Africa	*mn rands*	303	327	438	655	913	1 257	1 578	1 896	1 887	2 224
Sudan	*mn pounds*	38.0	38.0	38.6	39.2	40.2	52.0	68.9	(77.7)	[140]	. .
Tanzania[e]	*mn shillings*	217	274	391	612	728	818	1 130	(2 037)	[2 158]	. .

Togo	*mn francs*	948	1 063	1 261	1 604	1 960	3 153	4 118	4 789	4 789	4 936
Tunisia	*mn dinars*	13.0	15.1	16.1	20.3	30.3	36.0	52.2	61.7	62.5	. .
Uganda	*mn shillings*	376	462	416	535	642	835	1 123	1 200	1 800	. .
Upper Volta	*mn francs*	1 196	1 247	1 355	1 509	3 871	4 667	5 627	5 227	(6 800)	. .
Zaire	*mn zaires*	42.2	45.3	41.8	84.6	73.9	(82.0)	(31.0)	(38.0)	(200)	. .
Zambia	*mn kwachas*	[90.0]	[105]	[90.0]	[120]	[175]	[170]	[195]	[200]	[235]	. .
Zimbabwe	*mn dollars*	35.5	39.9	53.2	69.3	85.6	122	180	227	306	[355]
Central America											
Costa Rica[e]	*mn colones*	39.9	42.3	53.3	71.8	101	138	158	189	(180)	[212]
Cuba[e]	*mn pesos*	290	267	270	282	326	. .	700	784	841	[811]
Dominican Republic	*mn pesos*	31.9	34.4	36.6	47.6	57.2	67.4	75.8	87.1	158	. .
El Salvador[e]	*mn colones*	29.9	31.3	51.4	65.1	69.7	94.8	125	147	(170)	. .
Guatemala	*mn quetzales*	18.5	22.5	21.5	27.4	42.9	49.6	77.7	73.2	[71.8]	. .
Haiti	*mn gourdes*	36.6	39.1	39.9	42.3	50.9	55.8	60.9	. .	. .	. .
Honduras	*mn lempiras*	22.8	30.9	31.9	33.8	42.8	47.4	50.5	62.8	. .	. .
Jamaica	*mn dollars*	6.4	7.1	13.2	15.4	20.0	26.6	28.2	. .	. .	. .
Mexico	*mn pesos*	2 800	3 260	4 080	5 380	6 740	8 170	10 290	12 210	15 817	18 915
Nicaragua	*mn cordobas*	86.8	113	107	154	191	262	290	. .	. .	370
Panama	*mn balboas*	13.9	9.3	10.7	13.0	14.7	15.3	. .	. .	. .	. .
Trinidad and Tobago	*mn dollars*	7.8	8.0	7.3	9.5	13.0	16.0	19.3	. .	. .	. .
South America											
Argentina	*thous mn new pesos*	2.2	3.5	4.4	6.4	(23.0)	180	416	1 187	3 479	5 623
Bolivia	*mn pesos*	186	272	418	787	1 157	1 325	1 374	1 616	[2 100]	. .
Brazil	*mn cruzeiros*	4 040	5 030	6 740	8 740	11 220	19 030	25 870	36 880	48 100	. .
Chile	*mn pesos*	3.0	6.0	42.0	441	1 631	5 065	11 300	19 932	35 421	[56 777]
Colombia	*mn pesos*	3 789	2 255	2 479	2 950	4 023	4 975	6 066	6 582	(9 010)	14 237
Ecuador	*mn sucres*	742	933	1 263	1 790	2 522	2 563	4 813	4 097	4 638	. .
Guyana[e]	*mn dollars*	17.8	19.8	22.5	38.1	78.9	120	78	(65)	. .	. .
Paraguay	*mn guaranies*	1 815	1 941	2 135	2 482	3 316	3 587	4 204	4 892	5 793	. .
Peru	*mn soles*	9 500	9 500	12 557	15 605	25 464	38 527	77 246	92 514	121 000	176 000
Uruguay	*mn new pesos*	19.4	30.6	60.0	128	218	254	425	811	. .	. .
Venezuela	*mn bolivares*	1 112	1 306	1 309	1 969	2 440	1 792	2 526	2 532	2 740	(3 434)

G

Table 6A.4. World military expenditure as a percentage of gross domestic product

	1971	1972	1973	1974	1975	1976	1977	1978	1979
NATO									
North America:									
Canada	2.2	2.1	1.9	1.9	1.9	1.8	1.9	2.0	1.8
USA	7.1	6.7	6.0	6.1	6.0	5.4	5.4	5.2	5.2
Europe:									
Belgium	2.9	2.9	2.8	2.8	3.1	3.1	3.2	3.3	3.3
Denmark	2.5	2.3	2.1	2.3	2.5	2.3	2.3	2.4	(2.4)
France	4.0	3.9	3.8	3.7	3.8	3.8	3.9	3.9	3.9
FR Germany	3.4	3.5	3.5	3.6	3.6	3.5	3.4	3.4	3.3
Greece	4.7	4.6	4.1	4.3	6.5	5.9	6.8	6.6	5.8
Italy	2.9	3.1	2.9	2.8	2.5	2.3	2.4	2.4	2.4
Luxembourg	0.8	0.8	0.8	0.8	1.0	1.1	1.0	1.1	0.9
Netherlands	3.4	3.3	3.2	3.2	3.4	3.2	3.5	3.2	3.4
Norway	3.4	3.3	3.1	3.0	3.2	3.1	3.1	3.2	3.1
Portugal	7.4	6.9	5.9	7.4	5.3	4.0	3.5	3.5	3.4
Turkey	4.7	4.4	4.3	4.1	6.0	6.4	6.0	5.5	4.9
UK	4.9	5.2	4.8	5.0	4.9	5.0	4.8	4.7	4.8
WTO[f]									
Bulgaria	2.6	2.7	2.7	2.8	3.0	(2.7)	(2.8)	(2.7)	(2.7)
Czechoslovakia	3.9	3.7	3.6	3.6	3.5	3.8	(3.9)	(3.5)	(3.5)
German DR	4.4	4.4	4.4	4.3	4.3	4.2	(4.1)	(4.3)	(4.4)
Hungary	2.7	2.4	2.2	2.3	2.4	2.3	2.3	(2.2)	. .
Poland	3.8	3.4	3.2	3.0	2.9	3.0	(3.1)	(2.6)	(2.7)
Romania	2.0	1.9	1.7	1.7	1.7	1.7	1.6	. .	. .
USSR	[9.7]	[9.6]	[9.0]	[8.7]	[10.3]	[9.9]	[9.6]	[9.4]	. .
Other Europe									
Austria	1.0	1.0	1.0	1.1	1.2	1.2	1.2	1.3	1.3
Finland	1.4	1.5	1.4	1.3	1.4	1.5	1.4	1.4	1.3
Ireland	1.4	1.5	1.4	1.7	1.6	1.6	1.6	1.5	1.6
Spain	1.6	1.6	1.6	1.7	1.7	1.8	1.7	1.7	1.8
Sweden	3.7	3.7	3.6	3.5	3.4	3.3	3.4	3.4	3.4
Switzerland	2.2	2.1	2.0	2.0	2.0	2.3	2.1	2.1	2.2
Yugoslavia[g]	4.5	4.9	4.7	5.5	5.9	5.6	(5.3)	[4.7]	. .
Middle East									
Bahrain	. .	. .	3.9	3.0	1.6	1.7	2.2	. .	. .
Cyprus	1.5	1.3	1.2	2.2	2.8	2.2	2.4	1.8	[1.2]

Egypt	20.1	19.0	34.1	36.5	35.4	24.9	25.1	. .	. .
Iran	5.7	6.8	7.3	11.2	13.0	12.5	10.8	. .	. .
Iraq	10.5	10.6	12.2	12.5	11.7	10.7	10.9	. .	. .
Israel	22.9	19.8	33.9	25.1	26.7	27.1	24.8	19.8	19.2
Jordan	20.4	21.3	21.7	20.3	19.8	25.6	19.8	16.7	[19.0]
Kuwait	4.3	4.1	3.5	4.6	[5.9]	8.1	7.9	7.3	[5.0]
Lebanon	2.6	3.3	3.5	3.7	4.2	. .	3.1	. .	. .
Oman	12.8	17.8	24.8	20.8	33.3	32.8	26.9	29.7	20.3
Saudi Arabia	9.3	9.4	6.9	(6.0)	(9.7)	(14.2)	(14.7)	. .	. .
Syria	1.2	1.1	0.7	0.8	0.8	0.8	0.6	0.7	0.8
United Arab Emirates	. .	. .	0.5	0.3	0.4	0.7	4.3	5.0	. .
Yemen, Arab Republic	4.8	5.2	5.6	5.9	6.5	6.6	. .	. .	. .
Yemen, Peoples' Democratic	14.3	14.8	15.1	16.0	. .	. .	. .	. .	. .
South Asia									
Afghanistan	. .	. .	. .	. .	. .	1.4	1.6	. .	. .
Bangladesh	. .	. .	0.5	0.6	0.8	1.3	2.2	. .	. .
India	3.4	3.5	3.0	3.0	3.3	3.4	3.2	3.1	. .
Nepal	0.6	0.6	0.7	0.6	0.7	0.9	1.0	. .	. .
Pakistan	6.6	6.8	6.1	6.0	6.1	5.6	5.4	5.3	5.1
Sri Lanka	1.2	1.1	0.7	0.8	0.8	0.8	0.6	0.7	0.8
Far East									
Brunei	5.0	3.8	3.6	2.1	3.6	4.9	. .	. .	. .
Burma	5.5	6.0	6.4	4.5	4.0	4.2	[4.4]	. .	. .
Hong Kong	0.6	0.5	0.4	0.3	0.3	0.5	0.7	0.7	[0.6]
Indonesia	. .	[4.3]	[3.7]	[3.1]	[4.1]	[3.9]	4.1	4.3	3.6
Japan	0.8	0.8	0.8	0.9	0.9	0.9	0.9	0.9	. .
Korea, North	. .	. .	. .	13.0	13.9	14.1	. .	. .	. .
Korea, South	3.7	4.2	3.7	3.8	4.3	5.3	5.4	5.7	5.1
Malaysia	4.5	5.4	4.9	4.6	5.9	4.4	4.7	4.9	[5.2]
Philippines	1.2	1.4	1.8	2.0	2.1	2.6	2.6	2.7	[2.6]
Singapore	5.9	5.3	4.4	4.4	4.8	5.3	5.7	5.7	6.1
Taiwan	8.3	7.8	7.4	7.1	7.1	7.5	8.3	[12.1]	. .
Thailand	3.7	3.5	2.9	2.7	3.5	3.5	3.3	3.3	(3.5)
Oceania									
Australia	2.8	2.5	2.4	2.5	2.5	2.5	2.6	2.5	2.6
Fiji	0.2	0.2	0.2	0.2	0.2	0.3	0.3	0.3	. .
New Zealand	1.8	1.7	1.6	1.6	1.7	1.6	1.6	1.7	. .
Africa									
Algeria	2.1	(1.8)	(1.7)	2.2	1.8	1.9	2.0	. .	. .
Benin	1.8	(1.7)	1.6	1.6	1.5	1.4	1.9	(1.9)	. .

	1971	1972	1973	1974	1975	1976	1977	1978	1979
Burundi	. .	2.0	2.0	2.4	2.1	2.2	2.6	(3.4)	. .
Cameroon	1.9	1.7	1.6	1.6	1.6	1.6	. .	. .	. .
Chad	[4.0]	4.1	3.9	3.2	2.7	3.8	. .	. .	. .
Ethiopia	1.9	2.0	1.9	2.8	4.5	. .	. .	. .	. .
Gabon	. .	1.6	1.3	0.7	0.8	0.7	1.0	(2.0)	. .
Ghana	1.7	1.4	1.4	1.6	1.7	1.9	. .	. .	. .
Ivory Coast	1.2	(1.2)	(1.1)	1.3	1.2	0.9	(0.8)	1.1	. .
Kenya	. .	. .	1.6	1.6	1.7	2.2	3.3	4.5	4.5
Liberia	1.0	0.8	0.9	0.7	0.7	0.9	0.9	[1.0]	. .
Libya	(4.7)	(4.8)	(4.9)	(4.9)	(5.7)	(7.0)	(6.3)	. .	. .
Madagascar	1.3	1.5	1.5	1.7	1.6	2.0	2.4	2.5	. .
Malawi	0.4	0.4	0.6	0.7	1.3	1.2	1.6	2.1	1.8
Mali	1.9	2.4	2.8	3.0	3.5	. .	. .	. .	. .
Mauritania	. .	1.6	2.1	2.1	6.3	(8.7)	(11.6)	. .	. .
Mauritius	1.8	1.6	1.6	1.2	1.4	(1.3)	. .	. .	. .
Morocco	2.6	2.8	3.1	3.1	4.6	6.2	7.0	(6.1)	(8.5)
Niger	4.4	4.6	5.3	4.8	6.0	5.1	4.7	3.7	. .
Rwanda	2.0	1.7	2.7	2.4	1.6	1.7	1.6	. .	. .
Senegal	1.9	1.9	1.7	1.7	1.8	1.9	2.1	2.4	. .
Sierra Leone	0.9	0.9	0.9	0.9	1.0	0.9	1.3	[1.3]	. .
South Africa	2.1	2.0	2.2	2.7	3.3	4.0	4.5	4.7	3.9
Sudan	4.8	4.4	3.6	2.8	2.4	. .	. .	. .	. .
Tanzania	2.2	2.5	3.0	3.8	3.8	3.5	3.9	(6.1)	. .
Togo	1.2	1.2	1.4	1.3	1.6	2.4	. .	. .	. .
Tunisia	1.5	1.4	1.4	1.3	1.7	1.9	2.4	2.5	. .
Upper Volta	. .	1.3	1.4	1.4	3.3	3.4	3.3	2.8	. .
Zaire	4.2	4.1	2.8	4.6	3.9	(2.8)	(0.8)	. .	. .
Zambia	[7.6]	[7.8]	[5.7]	[6.3]	[11.1]	[8.8]	[9.6]	[8.9]	[9.2]
Zimbabwe	. .	2.8	3.4	3.7	4.3	5.6	8.1	9.7	11.6
Central America									
Costa Rica	0.6	0.5	0.5	0.5	0.6	0.7	0.6	(0.6)	[0.5]
Cuba[g]	4.9	4.1	3.7	3.6	[4.1]	. .	[8.1]	[8.4]	. .
Dominican Republic	1.9	1.7	1.6	1.6	1.6	1.7	1.7	1.9	3.2
El Salvador	1.1	1.1	1.5	1.7	1.6	1.7	1.8	1.9	. .
Guatemala	0.9	1.1	0.8	0.9	1.2	1.1	1.4	1.2	[1.1]
Haiti	1.6	1.6	1.2	1.2	1.1	0.9	0.9	. .	. .
Honduras	1.5	1.8	1.7	1.6	1.9	1.8	1.6	1.7	. .

Country									
Jamaica	0.5	0.5	0.8	0.7	0.8	1.0	0.9	..	..
Mexico	0.6	0.6	0.7	0.7	0.7	0.7	0.6	0.6	0.6
Nicaragua	1.5	1.8	1.4	1.5	1.7	2.0	1.8	..	..
Panama	1.2	0.7	0.7	0.7	0.8	0.8	..	..	..
Trinidad and Tobago	0.4	0.4	0.3	0.2	0.2	0.2	0.2	..	..
South America									
Argentina	1.7	1.6	1.2	1.3	(1.7)	2.5	2.0	2.1	2.3
Bolivia	1.4	1.6	1.6	1.8	2.3	2.3	2.1	2.0	[2.0]
Brazil	1.5	1.4	1.4	1.2	1.1	1.2	1.1	1.1	0.9
Chile	2.3	2.5	3.5	4.6	3.9	3.5	3.5	5.8	[9.4]
Colombia	2.5	1.2	1.0	0.9	1.0	0.9	0.8	0.7	(1.0)
Ecuador	1.8	2.0	2.0	1.9	2.3	1.9	3.0	2.2	2.0
Guyana	3.2	3.3	3.5	4.0	6.6	10.7	7.0	..	..
Paraguay	2.2	2.0	1.7	1.5	1.7	1.7	1.6	..	..
Peru	3.6	3.2	3.5	3.5	4.6	5.0	7.3	5.5	4.0
Uruguay	2.6	2.5	2.4	2.8	2.6	1.9	2.1	2.7	..
Venezuela	1.9	2.1	1.7	1.5	1.9	1.4	1.6	1.5	1.3

Conventions

.. Information not available or not applicable.
( ) SIPRI estimates, based on uncertain data.
[ ] Imputed values, with a high degree of uncertainty.

Notes

[a] *Developed market economies* include all NATO countries, Other Europe except Albania and Yugoslavia, plus Australia, New Zealand, Japan, Israel and South Africa.
Centrally planned economies include all WTO countries, Albania, North Korea, Mongolia, China and Cuba.
OPEC countries include Iran, Iraq, Kuwait, Saudi Arabia, United Arab Emirates, Indonesia, Algeria, Gabon, Libya, Nigeria, Ecuador and Venezuela. Qatar, although a member of OPEC, is not included. Oman, although it is not a member of OPEC, is included, since its position is essentially similar to that of other Arab OPEC countries.
[b] At current prices and 1978 exchange-rates.
[c] Wholesale price index used as deflator.
[d] See section on inflation in appendix 6B.
[e] Include internal security, etc.
[f] Per cent of gross national product.
[g] Per cent of gross material product.

Appendix 6B

Sources and methods for the world military expenditure data

Square-bracketed numbers, thus [1], *refer to the list of references on page* 175.

This appendix describes the sources and methods used in the preparation of the tables on military expenditure (appendix 6A). Only the main points are noted here. The tables are updated and revised versions of those which appeared in the *SIPRI Yearbook 1980.*

I. Purpose of the data

The main purpose of the SIPRI data is to give some measure of the resources absorbed by the military sector in various countries, regions and in the world as a whole—that is, the 'opportunity cost' of military spending. The purpose is *not* to provide a measure of military strength. For a large number of reasons (*inter alia*, because of differences in coverage, the difficulty in finding appropriate exchange-rates, the fact that price conditions vary widely between countries, because money may be spent on ineffective weapons, and because there is no reason to suppose that defence necessarily costs the same as offence), expenditure figures are inappropriate for this purpose.

For many small countries receiving large amounts of military aid, the military expenditure figures considerably understate the volume of military activity. This is naturally also the case for countries with a foreign military presence. Data on military aid in the form of major weapons are given in the arms trade registers (see appendices 7A and 7B).

The purpose of publishing the ratio between military expenditure and national product is to give an indication of the burden of military activities on the economies of individual countries and to provide a rough yardstick of comparison in this respect between different countries.

II. Definitions

The data for NATO countries are estimates made by NATO to correspond to a common definition. These include military research and development; include military aid in the budget of the donor country and exclude it from the budget of the recipient country; include costs of retirement pensions, costs of para-military forces and police when judged to be trained and equipped for military operations; and exclude civil defence, war pensions and payments on war debts.

The series chosen for the Warsaw Treaty Organization (WTO) countries other than the Soviet Union include for Czechoslovakia and Poland some estimates for research and development expenditure, which may not be included in their official budgets. They also exclude an estimated 'civilian' portion of internal security for the countries that publish 'defence and internal security' expenditures taken together only.

For all countries, the NATO definition is used as a guide-line, especially when choosing between alternative series. However, for most other countries, it was not possible to obtain specific definitions of their military expenditure, and consequently no adjustments were made. In the cases where major divergencies were known to exist, and information was insufficient to make a reliable alternative estimate, this has been indicated in footnotes to the tables.

For calculating the ratio of military expenditure to national product, gross domestic product (GDP) at purchasers' values has been used. GDP is defined as "the final expenditure on goods and services, in purchasers' values, *less* the c.i.f. (cost, insurance, freight) value of imports of goods and services" [1]. For the WTO countries, military expenditure is expressed as a percentage of estimates of gross national product (GNP) at market prices, which for these countries cannot be more than negligibly different from the ratio to GDP.

Coverage

Appendix 6A covers 130 countries.

The countries are presented by region in the following order: NATO (North Atlantic Treaty Organization), WTO (Warsaw Treaty Organization), Other Europe, Middle East, South Asia, Far East, Oceania, Africa, Central America and South America. The individual countries are listed alphabetically within each of these regions.

Data are provided for every year since 1971. Series for each year since 1950 are available in previous volumes of the *SIPRI Yearbook* and will also be available on request for specific countries.

III. Sources

The estimates of military expenditure for NATO countries are taken from official NATO data, published annually in, for example, *NATO Review and Atlantic News*. The estimates for WTO countries other than the USSR are taken from reference [2a] for the years 1965–76. For the years before 1965 and after 1976, the official budget figures were used to extend the series. For the Soviet Union, a 'compromise' figure has been taken, which corresponds neither with the official figures nor with the CIA estimates; the reasons are explained in the *SIPRI Yearbook 1979* (page 28).

Official figures for China for 1977, 1978, 1979 and 1980 have now been released, for the first time since 1960. Their coverage is not clear; the figures used here have been derived from estimates submitted in a report to the Joint Economic Committee of the US Congress [3].

For the remaining countries, the prime sources are the United Nations' *Statistical Yearbook* (UNSY), the United Nations' *Statistical Yearbook for Asia and the Pacific* (UNSYAP) and the *Government Finance Statistics Yearbook* (GFS) published by the International Monetary Fund for the past three years, the latest issue of which contains series of 'defence expenditure' for 100 countries. The data given are based upon a detailed definition, which reads as follows:

> This category covers all expenditure, whether by defence or other departments, for the maintenance of military forces, including the purchase of military supplies and equipment (including the stockpiling of finished items but not the industrial raw materials required for their production), military construction, recruiting, training, equipping, moving, feeding, clothing and housing members of the armed forces, and providing remuneration, medical care, and other services for them. Also included are capital expenditures for the provision of quarters to families of military personnel, outlays on military schools, and research and development serving clearly and foremost the purpose of defense. Military forces also include paramilitary organizations such as gendarmerie, constabulary, security forces, border and customs guards, and others trained, equipped, and available for use as military personnel. Also falling under this category are expenditure for purposes of strengthening the public services to meet wartime emergencies, training civil defense personnel, and acquiring materials and equipment for these purposes. Included also are expenditures for foreign military aid and contributions to international military organizations and alliances.
>
> This category excludes expenditure for nonmilitary purposes, though incurred by a ministry or department of defense, and any payments or services provided to war veterans and retired military personnel.

The GFS is considered superior to the UNSY, since it attempts to present the figures in this uniform manner, while the latter gives the figures unadjusted in the form they are notified to the United Nations by governments.

For a number of countries, estimates are made on the basis of budgets, White Papers and statistical documents published by the government or the central bank of the country concerned.

Annual reference works are usually not very useful, since they have a tendency to quote each other when giving military expenditure figures. An exception is the *Europa Year Book* (London) which is informative, especially for small nations.

The countries for which figures have been impossible to find in any of the sources so far mentioned have presented difficulties. The estimates of their military spending have been derived from other sources and are highly approximate.

The figures for the latest years in the series have mainly been obtained from journals and newspaper articles.

The regionally orientated journals most used are, for

the Middle East:	*Arab Economist* (Beirut)
	Middle East Economic Digest (London)
South Asia:	*Asian Recorder* (New Delhi)
	Asia Research Bulletin (Singapore)
Far East:	*Far Eastern Economic Review* (Hong Kong)
Asia and Oceania:	*IDSA News Reviews* (New Delhi)
Africa:	*Africa Research Bulletin* (Exeter, UK)
	Afrique Défense (Paris)
	Facts and Reports (Amsterdam)
Latin America:	*Latin America Weekly Report* (London)

The data on GDP, consumer price index and exchange-rates are taken principally from *International Financial Statistics*, published by IMF, and from the *United Nations Monthly Bulletin of Statistics*.

The GNP estimates for the USSR were obtained by converting the GNP dollar-estimate for 1975 given in reference [4a] to roubles and constructing a series by applying the percentage changes in the net material product series. For the other WTO countries, figures for the ratio of military expenditure to GNP at market prices calculated in domestic currencies were cited directly from reference [2b] for the years 1965–76, and for the other years were calculated using the NMP series.

Other periodical publications, newspapers and annual reference works used are listed in the *SIPRI Yearbook 1979*, pp. 62–63.

IV. Methods

All figures are presented on a calendar-year basis. Conversion to calendar years was made on the assumption of an even rate of expenditure throughout the fiscal year. Figures for the most recent years are budget estimates.

In order to provide time series estimates of total world military expenditure at constant prices, so as to allow for volume comparisons, two operations must be performed. First, all national expenditures must be converted into a common currency. The US dollar is the most widely used currency for this purpose, and SIPRI has adopted this practice. Second, it is necessary to adjust for the effect of price changes. The figures in this *Yearbook* are presented at 1978 price levels and 1978 exchange-rates, using, wherever available, the average for the year.

For the WTO countries other than the USSR, the exchange-rates given in reference [2b] were used. Updating was done by using the basic and non-commercial rates. For the Soviet Union, we have used the 'purchasing-power-parity' estimate derived from national product comparisons of the United States and the Soviet Union, of 1.79 dollars to the rouble [4b], updated by the change in the US consumer price index from 1975 to 1978, which brings it to 2.2 dollars per rouble.

The adjustment for changes in prices was made by applying the consumer price index in each country. In many countries this is the only price index available. As an index of the general movement of prices, it is a reasonable one for showing the trend in the resources absorbed by the military, in constant prices. For the most recent year, the estimate of the consumer price increase is based on the figures for the first 6–10 months only. For the USSR, no adjustment for prices is made, since the figure for military expenditure is so rough and inflation practically zero. For the other WTO countries, adjustments were made according to the official consumer price index.

The calculations of the ratio of military expenditure to GDP/GNP were made in domestic currencies.

V. Notes on individual countries

Inflation

The figures for 'constant price' military expenditure become more unreliable when inflation is rapid. In the following countries, prices more than trebled between 1975 and 1979.

(*Price index numbers, 1975 = 100*)

Turkey	392	Zaire	961
Israel	475	Argentina	10 721
Lebanon	322	Brazil	432
Ghana	903	Chile	1 118
Mali	(318)	Peru	485
Uganda (1978)	377	Uruguay	575

In these countries in particular, supplementary estimates are likely to be made in the course of the year, which are on occasions difficult to trace.

References

1. *Statistical Yearbook* (United Nations, New York, 1974), p. XVII.
2. Alton, T. P., Lazarcik, G., Bass, E. M. and Znayenko, W., 'Defense expenditures in Eastern Europe, 1965–76', in *East European Economies Post-Helsinki*, A compendium of papers submitted to the Joint Economic Committee, US Congress (US Government Printing Office, Washington, D.C., 1975).
3. Mitchell, R. G. and Parris, E. P., 'Chinese Defense Spending, 1965–78' submitted to the Sub-Committee on Priorities and Economy in Government of the Joint Economic Committee, US Congress (US Government Printing Office, Washington, D.C., 1980).
4. Sivard, Ruth L., *World Military and Social Expenditures* (WMSE Publications, Leesburg, Virginia, March 1978).
   (a) —, p. 21.
   (b) —, p. 30.

7. Transfers of major conventional armaments in 1980

Square-bracketed numbers, thus [1], *refer to the list of references on page* 200.

I. Introduction: typical features of the trade

The 1980s have begun with no substantial drop in world major weapon[1] purchases; indeed more countries are now exporting arms than ever before. This is clearly reflected in the number of orders for major weapons signed in 1977 (107), 1978 (150), 1979 (292) and 1980 (332) and identified in the SIPRI arms trade registers for each year. In due course, as the weapon orders are filled, this increase in sales of major weapons will also show up in the statistics for weapon deliveries.

The arms trade registers of transfers to industrialized and Third World countries and registers of licensed production appear in appendices 7A and 7B.

Large arms deals of the year

Among the largest deals concluded during the year were the Canadian order placed with the United States for 137 McDonnell-Douglas F-18A Hornet fighter aircraft, illustrating the continued US dominance of the aerospace market, previously evidenced by the large F-16 deal in Europe in 1977. In general it can be said that the competition for the next generation of fighters in the industrialized world has been narrowed down to three aircraft—namely, the McDonnell-Douglas F-18A Hornet and the General Dynamics F-16 from the USA, and the Dassault-Breguet Mirage-4000 from France. Other competing aircraft, such as the Swedish Viggen, have so far not managed to achieve a breakthrough in this market. Viggen participated in the competition for both Australia's and Austria's new fighter orders; but by the end of 1980, Australia had narrowed down the competitors to either the F-18A or the F-16, while Austria had decided to postpone the choice until 1981, although they most likely will opt for the US F-16/79. The Canadian order for the F-18A Hornet included 113 fighters and 24 trainers, worth a total of $2 500–5 000 million; Canada will also help in financing the development costs.

Another large order was signed by the Netherlands—for the first 22 F-16 fighters of an expected total of 101 planes, in addition to 102 already in the process of delivery from licensed production by Fokker. Further,

[1] SIPRI's arms trade statistics include values of the transfers of the four categories of so-called major weapons: aircraft, missiles, armoured vehicles and ships. Note that only *deliveries* are included in the statistics.

Figure 7.1. Shares of world exports of major weapons, 1977–80, by country[a]

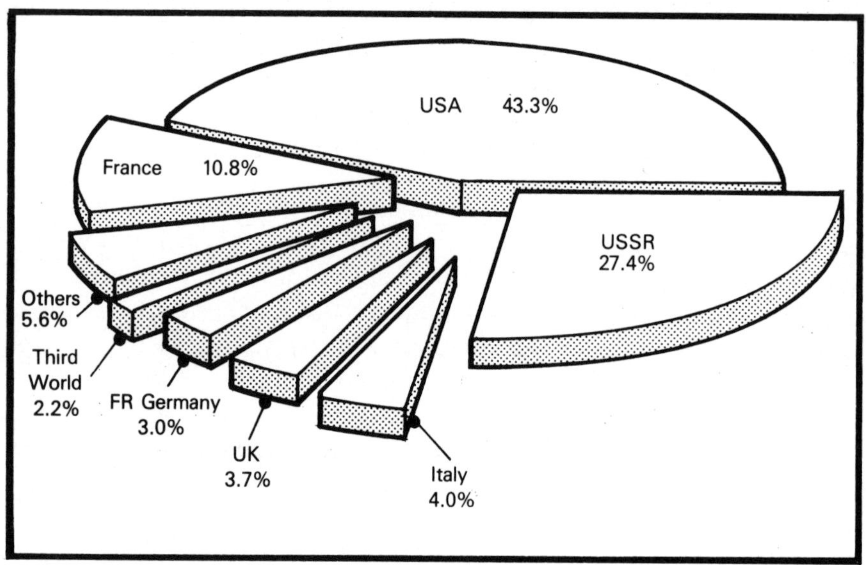

[a] Derived from table 7.3.

Figure 7.2. Shares of world imports of major weapons, 1977–80, by region[a]

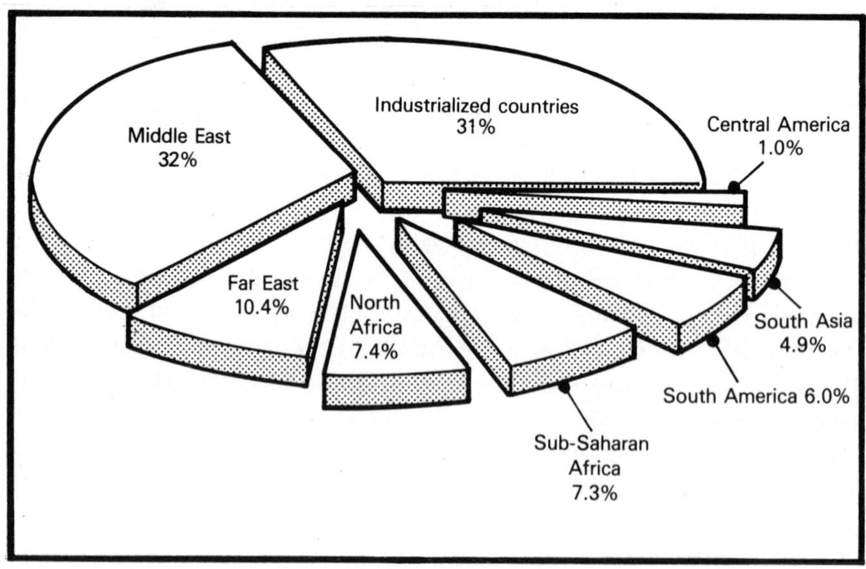

[a] Derived from tables 7.6 and 7.7.

within the NATO alliance, the UK purchased Trident-1 submarine-launched ballistic missiles (SLBMs) from the USA as part of the build-up of nuclear forces in Europe, representing one of the few new sales of nuclear weapon delivery systems. Some offset was achieved by the UK in this deal, since the USA decided to purchase the British Rapier surface-to-air missile for protection of US air bases in the UK.

Belgium purchased over 1 000 armoured vehicles from the USA, for licence production. This caused angry reactions in France, which had competed for the order with its AMX vehicles. Both Belgium and Canada signed an order for the AIM-9L Super Sidewinder air-to-air missile, for use with the F-16 and the F-18A respectively.

Within the Warsaw Treaty Organization (WTO), deliveries continued of the T-72 main battle tank and the M-1974 self-propelled howitzer, but no major new deals were concluded during the year.[2]

In the Middle East, Iraq reached an agreement with Italy for the supply of warships, some armed with missiles, at a cost of $1 800 million, and also purchased Italian helicopters. New batches of MiG-25 Foxbats and MiG-27s were also delivered from the Soviet Union. Syria concluded new deals with the Soviet Union for a large number of T-72 main battle tanks and MiG-27 fighters. South Yemen ordered MiG-23, MiG-25 and Su-22 fighters, and T-62 tanks. Egypt will receive US weapons in a large-scale build-up of the armed forces during the rest of the decade, expected to cost some $8 000–10 000 million: in 1980, agreements were reached for the supply of 550 M-113-A2 armoured personnel carriers (APCs) worth $142.4 million, bringing the total of APCs in the current aid package to 1 100. Egypt will also receive 40 F-16As and may produce 100 F-5E Tiger-2 fighters under licence.

On 14 October 1980 Saudi Arabia concluded an arms agreement for naval equipment with France worth $3 450 million. The order includes four 2 000-ton frigates armed with Matra OTOMAT ship-to-ship missiles, two 17 000-ton supply tankers and 24 SA-365N Dauphin ASW helicopters armed with AS-15TT anti-ship missiles.

In other Third World regions, India's agreement in May 1980 with the Soviet Union stands out as the largest single deal ever made by India, worth $1 630 million and covering, among other things, two squadrons of MiG-23 fighters and 700 T-72 main battle tanks, of which 600 will be licence produced.

In South Asia, Taiwan purchased large numbers of MIM-23B Hawk surface-to-air missiles and Sea Chaparrel ship-to-air missiles from the

[2] As a rule, precise statistics on the exact deliveries of arms to Eastern Europe are impossible to provide due to the general lack of information. This is also illustrated by the fact that, for example, the International Institute for Strategic Studies, in its *Military Balance 1980–1981*, has not included the WTO in its list of identified arms agreements.

USA. Thailand purchased a number of armoured vehicles and counter-insurgency aircraft from the USA.

Other exceptionally large arms orders were signed by, for example, Brazil, which in a $3 000 million deal purchased warships from Italy. Argentina signed an order for the Euromissile HOT anti-tank missile system; Chile bought two Type-209 submarines from FR Germany and is negotiating for the Alpha Jet advanced trainer from France.

Another indication of the prospering arms market was seen at the 1980 Farnborough aerospace show, which was reported as a "success" corresponding to the healthy climate reigning over the aircraft industry throughout the world. There were more than 40 French exhibitors, for example, and the return of the US exhibitors after their absence since 1978—according to the Carter Administration's decisions aimed at restraining arms exports—signalled the sharp competition between the USA and Western Europe on the military market. At the Farnborough show, British Prime Minister Thatcher made a statement exhorting the British industry to make a drive to increase its arms exports, which was another indication of this competition between the traditional arms suppliers.

Arms and scarce resources

The 1980s are likely to become a decade also of competition for world natural resources. Arms-for-oil as well as arms-for-uranium were by 1980 familiar terms of the arms trade. One of the latest examples was Iraq, which decided to give priority to its five largest arms suppliers outside the Socialist bloc, when the limited resumption of oil shipments was started in late 1980. These five countries were France, Brazil, Italy, Spain and Yugoslavia. For France, the export of arms represented one-quarter of the oil bill in 1978 [1]. Similarly, it was reported that arms industry representatives from FR Germany started negotiations in 1980 with Saudi Arabia, aimed at the supply of Leopard-2 tanks and the Tornado fighter in return for a Saudi guarantee of the supply of 40 per cent of FR Germany's oil requirements during the 1980s.

The exchange of weaponry for strategic raw materials is not a new phenomenon—the first arms-for-uranium deal was signed in the mid-1960s between France and South Africa, and has since been followed by several arms-for-oil deals between Middle East oil-producing countries and the Western arms suppliers. But a new, increasingly strategic raw material which is traded for armaments is titanium. Titanium is used both in aircraft to resist fatigue problems caused by heat and in the construction of the fuselage and turbine engine blades. The engine company Pratt & Whitney of the USA and Canada is, for example, the world's largest consumer of titanium. The scarcity of this metal has during the past few years caused a steep price rise. The Western world's production of titanium metal is currently about 30 000 tons a year, which makes the proposed Australian plant, with a 5 000-ton capacity, a significant one [2]. The USA, the USSR, the UK and Japan are so far the only countries able to process titanium, because of the advanced technology involved.

In connection with Australia's new fighter purchase, it was reported in 1980 that two US companies, General Dynamics and McDonnell-Douglas, were both offering offset arrangements with Australian titanium producers. General Dynamics announced that it had reached an agreement with Australia's Western Mining Corporation to study the feasibility of establishing a titanium processing plant if the Australian government should choose the F-16 fighter. Pratt & Whitney, the producer of the F-16 engine, is also involved in the titanium deal.

At the same time, McDonnell-Douglas is negotiating with Associated Minerals Consolidated to assist in the production of titanium if the Australian government should choose the F-18A Hornet fighter.

Simultaneously, the US Administration was active in the same field: in 1980 the Carter Administration issued 400 export licences to China, the majority of them for the export of military technology, covering radar, electronics, transport aircraft and helicopters. In return, China is willing to export from its large supplies of titanium, vanadium and tantalum [3, 4].

Arms in conflicts

Various types of armament have been constantly in the news during 1980. The Soviet Mi-24 Hind gunship helicopters have been reported in practically daily use in Afghanistan; in Thailand, US-supplied jet fighters and helicopters were used to resist the attempts in early 1980 by Vietnamese forces to cross Kampuchea's border with Thailand; in Morocco, King Hassan continues an expensive war against the Polisaro guerillas in Western Sahara, using new Mirage fighters and US-made weapons. In Zimbabwe, armed clashes occurred throughout the year between the rival liberation movements, and South African armed forces were involved in several clashes with opposing forces in Namibia, Angola and Mozambique. In the Ogaden province in Ethiopia, armed clashes have continued ever since the 1977–78 war with Somalia, involving both regular troops from both sides and Somali guerillas. Arms captured by the Ethiopians during the fighting from May until July 1980 illustrated the fact that Somalia has had no regular arms suppliers since it broke relations with the Soviet Union. The diversity of the captured weapons rather suggested that they were bought on the open market.

In Latin America, internal opposition to the ruling governments brought about the revolution in Nicaragua and nearly a civil war in El Salvador.

Throughout the continent, the use of counter-insurgency weapons remained widespread. The dispute between Chile and Argentina over the sovereignty of the Beagle Canal almost brought the two countries into armed conflict.

The war that broke out between Iraq and Iran on 22 September 1980, however, once again focused attention on the Middle East as the world's most conflict-ridden region. Furthermore, the US hostages taken by Iran brought the threat of a US intervention.

By adding to the instability of an already heavily armed and unstable area, the conflict between Iran and Iraq has increased the danger of a further war involving other states in the Persian Gulf region and, ultimately, the two great powers. Some 90 per cent of Iraq's major weapons have been supplied by the Soviet Union, and the major part of Iran's arms are from the United States. Unlike the previous Middle Eastern wars, which have been short and intense, the Iran–Iraq war drags on and has become a war of attrition, where neither side may be able to win without direct support from the USA or the USSR. Numerous reports have appeared about the supply of Soviet spare parts and ammunition to Iraq, either from the Soviet Union itself or from other Arab states, and delivered via Jordan. Simultaneously, Syria and Libya are reported to be delivering arms to Iran. The armoured vehicles which Brazil has supplied to Iraq in return for oil are now being used in a conflict which threatens to cut off half of Brazil's oil supply. In December 1980, France began to deliver Mirage F-1C fighters to Iraq in spite of the continuing war.

II. The flow

The aggregate tables 7.1 and 7.2 show the value of yearly imports and exports, respectively, of major arms to Third World countries. Since the yearly figures are often too erratic to allow an interpretation of the long-term trend, a five-year moving average is given in both tables (meaning that, for example, the figure under *B.1978* represents the average value of the years 1976 to 1980, inclusive; the figure under *B.1977* represents the average value of the years 1975 to 1979, inclusive, and so on). A look at the world total five-year average shows a steady increase through 1978. In the yearly figures (row *A*), 1978 shows up as something of a peak year; total deliveries decreased by 29 per cent in 1979, but rose again in 1980.

A larger number of new orders than ever before were signed during 1980, and it is evident that the industrialized countries are somewhat increasing their share—during the 1970s, as much as 75 per cent of the total transfers of major arms went to the Third World, whereas the share of the Third World decreased to 69 per cent during the four-year period 1977 to 1980, inclusive (see chapter 4).

Of the 1 009 single transfers identified in the registers this year, nearly half were aircraft (458); the second largest weapon category was missile systems (222), and then armoured vehicles (178) and warships (151). Of the same transfers, 92 per cent consisted of *new* systems, 5.4 per cent of *second-hand* weapons and 2.6 per cent of *refurbished* weapons. In absolute numbers, this means that very few countries accept second-hand weapons and that the majority opt for new systems, including the high-technology weapons, rather than refurbished, older models.

In real prices, according to the US Arms Control and Disarmament Agency (ACDA) estimates, global arms exports are approaching a record of $25 000 million per year for initial transfers alone [5]. The follow-on sales of spare parts (which in the sales contracts normally are guaranteed for the lifetime of the weapon), maintenance, support and training will triple those earnings. The business has been growing at roughly $5 000 million a year since 1975, and the prospects for the 1980s are for rapid expansion.

The pressures to export are spurred by the deteriorating climate between the USA and the USSR following the invasion of Afghanistan, the situation in Iran, and the Iran–Iraq war, and benefit the domestic arms industries and the continued R&D in new weapons. The drive for exports—evident in the United States even when the Carter Administration was still in power, but also in the European countries—is matched by the insecurity of the buying regimes, in particular in the Middle East, which creates the pressures to import.

III. The suppliers

Table 7.3 shows the rank order of the 20 largest arms exporters during the period 1977 to 1980, inclusive. The US share of arms exports during these four years was 43.3 per cent, whereas the Soviet Union accounted for 27.4 per cent. At the same time it can be seen that the Soviet Union exports a relatively larger share of its total to Third World countries (79.5 per cent), in comparison to the United States (60.8 per cent). This obviously reflects the relatively slow deliveries to the WTO countries, several of which still have not received the MiG-23 fighter or the MiG-25, both of which have been in use with Middle Eastern countries for some years.

Table 7.3 also shows that France has advanced substantially during the past few years, and has by now definitely left the UK behind. Italy has also delivered more major weapons than the UK during this same period.

When looking at the yearly figures in aggregate table 7.2, it is seen that the USSR and the USA had reached a parity in the size of their arms deliveries in 1980. From the peak year 1978, US deliveries declined by as much as 60 per cent but rose again quite substantially in 1980, while

Table 7.1. Values of imports of major weapons by the Third World: by region, 1961–80[a]

Figures are SIPRI trend indicator values, as expressed in US $ million, at constant (1975) prices. A=yearly figures, B[b]=five-year moving averages.

Region code	Region[c]		1961	1962	1963	1964	1965	1966	1967	1968
8	Middle East	A	196	574	393	388	441	440	1 063	1 258
		B	327	342	398	447	545	718	883	1 087
10	Far East (excl Viet Nam)[d]	A	200	356	310	392	340	497	199	266
		B	429	404	320	379	348	339	378	364
15	South America	A	205	109	72	51	110	138	128	208
		B	125	124	109	96	100	127	148	156
12	North Africa	A	15	39	34	40	81	122	135	83
		B	22	28	42	63	82	92	102	110
9	South Asia	A	289	189	221	79	213	391	271	297
		B	232	209	198	219	235	250	297	314
13	Sub-Saharan Africa (excl S. Africa)	A	56	47	47	68	95	93	81	55
		B	49	51	63	70	77	78	79	84
	South Africa	A	4	16	155	51	186	92	78	45
		B	40	46	82	100	112	90	89	68
14	Central America	A	211	298	96	34	18	21	16	8
		B	136	139	131	93	37	19	15	12
11	Oceania	A	–	–	–	–	–	–	–	–
		B	–	–	–	–	–	–	–	–
	Total (excl Viet Nam)[d]	A	**1 177**	**1 628**	**1 328**	**1 104**	**1 485**	**1 794**	**1 971**	**2 220**
		B	**1 362**	**1 344**	**1 344**	**1 468**	**1 536**	**1 715**	**1 990**	**2 195**
	Viet Nam	A	74	75	56	91	74	237	494	473
		B	50	65	74	107	190	274	315	387
	Total[e]	A	**1 251**	**1 703**	**1 384**	**1 195**	**1 559**	**2 031**	**2 465**	**2 693**
		B	**1 411**	**1 409**	**1 418**	**1 574**	**1 726**	**1 989**	**2 305**	**2 582**

[a] The values include licensed production of major weapons in Third World countries (see *SIPRI Yearbook 1979*, appendix 3C). For the values for the period 1950–56, see *SIPRI Yearbook 1976*, pp. 250–51; and for 1957–60, *SIPRI Yearbook 1978*, pp. 254–55.
[b] Five-year moving averages are calculated from the year arms imports began, as a more stable measure of the trend in arms imports than the often erratic year-to-year figures.
[c] The regions are listed in rank order according to their average values for 1970–78. The region code numbers in the first column correspond to those used in the arms trade registers (appendices 7A and 7B).
[d] Viet Nam is included in the figures for the Far East after 1975, the year the Viet Nam War ended.
[e] Items may not add up to totals due to rounding. Figures are rounded to the nearest 10.
– Nil.

Source: SIPRI computer-stored data base. Information on individual countries and arms transactions will be made available on request.

1969	1970	1971	1972	1973	1974	1975	1976	1977	1978	1979	1980
1 212	1 462	1 758	1 076	2 211	2 836	3 527	3 164	5 190	4 438	3 354	5 414
1 351	1 353	1 544	1 869	2 282	2 653	3 386	3 831	3 935	4 312	–	–
586	271	419	162	302	249	640	1 035	653	2 381	2 051	891
348	341	348	281	354	478	579	992	1 352	1 402	–	–
158	148	222	310	352	446	630	710	826	808	949	872
173	209	238	296	392	490	593	684	785	833	–	–
87	121	123	167	145	228	761	929	948	1 461	1 281	544
110	116	129	157	285	444	602	865	1 076	1 033	–	–
312	300	499	409	289	373	177	414	663	1 030	456	641
336	363	362	374	349	332	383	531	548	641	–	–
71	121	134	89	152	386	232	432	1 148	1 429	308	383
92	94	113	176	199	258	470	725	778	740	–	–
46	77	69	25	37	274	179	118	211	365	219	154
63	52	51	96	117	127	164	229	218	213	–	–
10	6	47	35	56	87	137	58	60	250	75	46
17	21	31	46	72	75	80	118	116	99	–	–
–	–	–	–	–	–	–	3	–	3	–	–
–	–	–	–	–	–	–	–	–	–	–	–
2 482	**2 506**	**3 272**	**2 273**	**3 545**	**4 878**	**6 284**	**7 312**	**9 699**	**12 165**	**8 693**	**8 945**
2 490	**2 551**	**2 816**	**3 295**	**4 050**	**4 858**	**6 344**	**8 068**	**8 831**	**9 363**	–	–
298	433	435	1 200	82	816	20	–	–	–	–	–
427	568	490	593	511	–	–	–	–	–	–	–
2 780	**2 939**	**3 707**	**3 473**	**3 627**	**5 064**	**6 304**	**7 312**	**9 699**	**12 165**	**8 693**	**8 945**
2 917	**3 118**	**3 305**	**3 762**	**4 435**	**5 156**	**6 401**	**8 109**	**8 835**	**9 363**	–	–

Table 7.2. Values of exports of major weapons to regions listed in table 7.1: by supplier, 1961–80[a]

Figures are SIPRI trend indicator values, as expressed in US $ million, at constant (1975) prices.
A=yearly figures, B=five-year moving averages.

Country[b]		1961	1962	1963	1964	1965	1966	1967	1968
USA[c]	A	393	368	514	372	540	514	481	754
	B	463	472	437	462	484	533	707	850
USSR[c]	A	511	1 029	429	375	544	970	1 545	1 116
	B	466	512	578	669	773	910	1 002	1 120
UK	A	241	124	177	179	265	193	203	294
	B	207	195	197	188	203	227	261	245
France[c]	A	50	121	194	137	96	140	68	288
	B	96	110	120	138	127	146	153	174
China[c]	A	–	–	–	51	9	47	17	5
	B	67	43	12	21	25	26	18	20
Italy	A	–	1	20	20	7	1	20	67
	B	6	10	10	10	14	23	30	37
FR Germany	A	6	2	13	26	13	83	4	11
	B	17	15	12	27	28	27	26	23
Netherlands	A	3	3	*	11	22	1	–	5
	B	3	4	8	7	7	8	11	8
Canada[c]	A	22	3	13	11	18	12	11	48
	B	28	13	13	11	13	20	22	25
Czechoslovakia	A	6	6	16	9	4	8	11	39
	B	33	19	8	9	10	14	17	22
Sweden	A	1	*	–	–	–	2	–	–
	B	–	–	–	–	–	–	–	–
Switzerland	A	–	–	2	–	1	1	1	1
	B	–	–	1	1	1	1	1	1
Japan[c]	A	14	24	1	1	6	11	30	49
	B	11	8	9	9	10	19	20	18
Third World	A	2	10	4	3	4	25	15	9
	B	4	5	5	9	10	11	15	15
Other industrialized, West	A	3	2	1	*	30	23	58	7
	B	2	2	7	11	22	24	26	20
Other industrialized, East	A	–	11	*	–	*	–	2	–
	B	9	2	2	2	–	–	1	1
Total[d]	A	**1 251**	**1 703**	**1 384**	**1 195**	**1 559**	**2 301**	**2 465**	**2 693**
	B	**1 411**	**1 410**	**1 418**	**1 574**	**1 727**	**1 989**	**2 305**	**2 581**

[a] The values include licences sold to Third World countries for production of major weapons (see *SIPRI Yearbook 1979*, appendix 3C). For the values for the period 1950–56, see *SIPRI Yearbook 1976*, pp. 252–53; and for 1957–60, *SIPRI Yearbook 1978*, pp. 256–57.
[b] The countries are listed in rank order according to their average values for 1970–78.
[c] Including exports to Viet Nam.
[d] Items may not add up to totals due to rounding.
* > $0.5 million.
– Nil.

Source: SIPRI computer-stored data base. Information on individual countries and arms transactions will be made available on request.

1969	1970	1971	1972	1973	1974	1975	1976	1977	1978	1979	1980
1 244	1 258	1 179	1 166	1 061	1 404	2 343	3 892	4 826	5 244	2 063	3 013
983	1 120	1 182	1 214	1 431	1 973	2 705	3 542	3 674	3 827	–	–
834	1 136	1 515	1 225	1 537	1 930	2 160	1 554	2 156	3 682	3 678	3 006
1 229	1 615	1 249	1 469	1 673	1 681	1 867	2 296	2 646	2 815	–	–
348	185	393	369	316	579	647	587	536	488	413	311
285	318	322	368	461	500	533	567	534	467	–	–
172	203	276	351	538	449	593	553	1 282	1 236	1 000	1 235
201	258	308	363	441	497	683	823	933	1 061	–	–
10	22	106	158	27	104	63	57	66	142	22	85
32	60	65	83	92	82	63	86	70	74	–	–
53	43	41	52	56	139	72	159	348	553	407	431
49	51	49	66	72	96	155	254	308	380	–	–
17	1	25	37	3	116	138	131	60	87	286	210
12	18	17	36	64	85	90	106	140	155	–	–
25	10	34	27	39	33	42	29	72	64	167	162
15	20	27	29	35	34	43	48	75	99	–	–
19	37	55	39	6	1	6	34	29	117	28	–
34	40	31	28	21	17	15	37	43	42	–	–
22	31	14	14	1	15	6	6	–	18	28	–
23	24	16	15	10	8	6	9	12	10	–	–
*	–	–	5	1	6	21	21	5	5	51	79
1	1	2	7	6	11	11	12	21	32	–	–
–	2	2	2	2	*	1	8	5	6	28	26
1	1	2	2	1	3	3	4	10	15	–	–
2	*	*	–	–	3	–	3	–	14	21	–
16	10	–	1	1	1	1	4	8	8	–	–
20	8	15	18	20	276	185	202	134	394	412	305
13	14	16	67	103	140	163	238	265	289	–	–
11	3	46	11	19	11	13	46	162	110	55	32
25	16	18	18	20	20	50	68	77	81	–	–
2	–	5	–	–	–	2	30	18	5	34	50
2	1	1	1	1	6	10	11	18	27	–	–
2 780	**2 939**	**3 707**	**3 473**	**3 627**	**5 064**	**6 304**	**7 312**	**9 699**	**12 165**	**8 693**	**8 945**
2 917	**3 118**	**3 305**	**3 762**	**4 435**	**5 156**	**6 401**	**8 109**	**8 835**	**9 363**	–	–

Table 7.3. Rank order of the 20 largest major-weapon exporting countries of the world, 1977–80[a]

Figures are SIPRI trend indicator values, as expressed in US $ million, at constant (1975) prices.

	Exporting country	Total value	Percentage of total exports	Percentage of total value to Third World	Largest importer per exporter
1.	USA	24 893	*43.3*	*60.8*	Iran
2.	USSR	15 755	*27.4*	*79.5*	Syria
3.	France	6 213	*10.8*	*76.5*	Morocco
4.	Italy	2 273	*4.0*	*76.6*	South Africa
5.	United Kingdom	2 141	*3.7*	*81.7*	India
6.	FR Germany	1 712	*3.0*	*37.6*	Italy
7.	Third World	1 271	*2.2*	*98.0*	–
8.	Norway	724	*1.3*	–	Sweden
9.	Netherlands	536	*0.9*	*87.0*	Peru
10.	Brazil[b]	421	*0.7*	*97.2*	Chile
11.	Israel[b]	367	*0.6*	*100.0*	South Africa
12.	Australia	361	*0.6*	*63.7*	Philippines
13.	China	333	*0.6*	*95.0*	Pakistan
14.	Sweden	277	*0.5*	*50.9*	United Kingdom
15.	Switzerland	240	*0.4*	*27.1*	Canada
16.	Canada	177	*0.3*	*98.3*	Ivory Coast
17.	South Africa[b]	116	*0.2*	*100.0*	Zimbabwe
18.	Finland	112	*0.2*	–	USSR
19.	Czechoslovakia	107	*0.2*	*43.9*	Bulgaria
20.	Libya[b,c]	98	*0.2*	*96.0*	Syria
	Others	334	*0.6*	*80.8*	–
	World total	**57 459**	**100.0**	**68.7**	

[a] The values include licences sold for the production of major weapons.
[b] Included also in the Third World group of exporters.
[c] Figures for Libya are not representative of a trend, due to the resale of aircraft and armoured vehicles in 1979.
Source: SIPRI computer-stored data base.

Table 7.4. Largest exporters of the four categories of major weapons, 1977–80

Figures are percentages of total major-weapon exports of each country, based on SIPRI trend indicator values.[a]

		Weapon category			
	Country	Aircraft	Armoured vehicles	Missiles	Ships
1.	USA	52	8	39	1
2.	USSR	60	13	24	3
3.	France	57	14	20	9
4.	Italy	36	17	34	13
5.	United Kingdom	33	19	14	34
6.	FR Germany	11	45	6	38
7.	Third World countries	34	30	10	26
8.	Norway	–	–	91	9
9.	Netherlands	43	–	–	57
10.	Brazil[b]	10	62	–	28
11.	Israel[b]	37	–	18	45

[a] Rank order according to values in table 7.3.
[b] Included also in the Third World group of exporters.
Source: SIPRI computer-stored data base.

Soviet deliveries have not varied so much and actually declined from 1979 to 1980.

SIPRI's arms export statistics for 1977–80 by political bloc show a NATO share of 68 per cent and a WTO share of 28 per cent. This indicates first, that world trade in arms still remains very much a Western affair, and second, that the two major blocs together accounted for the bulk, or 96 per cent, of all transfers during this four-year period.

The United States

The most important arms sales event in 1980 for the United States was probably the Carter Administration's turn-about in its military sales policy: in February it was announced that the US aerospace industry would be allowed to go ahead with the long-delayed development of the new lower-cost fighter aircraft designed for Third World customers, the FX fighter. The competitors for the FX are General Dynamics, with its re-engined F-16/79 aircraft, and Northrop, with an upgraded version of the F-5, called the F-5G. This contradicts the earlier policy of restraint, where one of the main points was that no weapons should be developed for export alone.

Further, the Carter Administration sought congressional approval to supply Egypt with as much as $4 000 million in US weaponry through 1984, expanding on the earlier $1 500 million arms package. The Administration also decided to give $400 million in arms aid to Pakistan, in view of the situation in Afghanistan, and to sell $235 million worth of arms to King Hassan of Morocco. This testifies to a further change in the Carter policy of restraint, aimed at curbing arms sales to areas of tension, notably the Middle East. With the Reagan Administration in power, the policy of restraint in arms sales can be regarded as shelved.

In March, the Secretary of State announced that US arms sales policy would no longer be based on annual reductions in programme activity, that is, the 'ceiling' was abandoned after two years of testing a policy that received much criticism for being both too liberal and too restrained.

The US arms industry 'blames' the Administration for the decline in US military exports—for instance, in 1978 alone, the sales of more than $1 000 million worth of arms to countries in Africa, the Middle East, Asia and even Europe were blocked. Military aerospace exports declined from $4 000 million in 1978 to $1 900 million in 1979. However, it is hardly the Carter policy alone that brought about the decline in military exports—the fact that, after the revolution, Iran cancelled its big arms orders had more significant consequences for both US and British arms industries than had the Carter policy. The United States remains far less dependent on military exports than, for example, the European nations, in particular since the domestic defence budget will rise steeply. But some of the companies have come to rely on exports for a sizeable share of their income, the most export-oriented industries being Lockheed, McDonnell-Douglas, General Dynamics, Northrop, Sperry and Raytheon.

Within the United States, there were many expressions of frustration with the lack of substantial results concerning the restraint in arms sales, and also concerning the complete lack of co-operation from the other big arms suppliers, exemplified by the following statement of Senator Proxmire:

> The administration's half-hearted efforts to interest NATO allies in mutual arms sales restraint have produced no results. In fact just the opposite seems to have occurred as other nations have aggressively entered the arms market. Emphasis on arms sales by high government officials in France and in other European countries has intensified the competition between arms manufacturing nations. Individual foreign firms have moved to the top of the foreign arms exporter lists. While Lockheed remains on top in terms of the dollar value of annual business, the next five companies are based in France, Great Britain or West Germany. Even developing nations are entering the market such as Brazil. And arms consumer Israel has a flourishing arms export business. [6]

The Soviet Union

Being the world's second largest supplier of major arms, the USSR has a more restricted number of customers than the United States. It has become the largest arms supplier to North Africa, where Libya alone is the recipient; to South Asia, where India is the single largest recipient; and to Central America, due to arms deliveries to Cuba alone. In the Middle East, the Soviet Union remains the second largest supplier after the United States, with Iraq, Syria, and North and South Yemen as the biggest customers.

The yearly figures in the aggregate table of exports in 1961–80, table 7.2, show that Soviet deliveries of major arms to Third World countries actually surpassed those of the United States in 1979 (partly reflecting the effort in Afghanistan), but levelled out again in 1980. According to a CIA report published in December 1980, almost 90 per cent of all Soviet arms sales are to the Arab world. The biggest customers are Iraq, Syria, Algeria, Libya and South Yemen. According to the report, the Soviet Union in 1978 sold arms worth $2 500 million, and in 1979 the sales reached $8 400 million [7, 8].

France

The yearly figures in table 7.2 show that since 1977 France has established itself as the world's third largest arms seller, moving increasingly ahead of the UK. Of French arms exports, 76.5 per cent went to the Third World during the period 1977–80, and during 1980 France won substantial new orders, following President Giscard d'Estaing's tour of the Middle East. Over the next decade, Avions Marcel Dassault-Breguet is expected to produce at least 450 delta-wing Mirage-2000 fighters for Arab countries alone—including Saudi Arabia and Iraq. According to unconfirmed but persistent reports, Saudi Arabia will also finance the development of the bigger Mirage-4000. French exports of military equipment, by the broadest definition, account for about 5 per cent of total exports and cover a quarter of the bill for oil imports [9].

In the past four years, according to official statistics, French arms exports in real prices have more than doubled, from $2 500 million in 1976 to an estimated $5 200 million in 1980. At constant 1968 prices, the total arms exports have increased more than fourfold during the 1970s—that is, twice as fast as the overall growth rate for French exports. Europe remains a big market for France, in spite of the loss of several important orders to the United States. In the past, two-thirds of French major arms went to other industrialized nations. But after the oil crisis in 1973, France has made a consequent effort to secure ties with the Middle Eastern oil-producing nations—mainly through the supply of arms, but also through the sales of nuclear power technology. By 1980, between 80 and 90 per cent of French arms exports were to such wealthy oil-producing countries as Iraq, Saudi Arabia, Libya and the United Arab Emirates. The commercial successes of the French arms industry are reflected in the rise of the value of the shares on the French stock exchange market—for example, the shares of the SFIM company, specialized in electronics components, rose from $155 to $300 per share in nine months. The leaders on the market are the well-known arms manufacturers Matra, Avions Marcel Dassault-Breguet and Thomson-Brandth.

French arms sales policy has been and remains one of promoting arms sales wherever possible. One of the few restraints imposed on this policy remains the arms embargo on South Africa (which, however, already produces French armaments itself). During 1980, another embargo was lifted, namely that on Angola, and prospects for the supply of French helicopters and transport aircraft to this country were created.

The French naval deal with Saudi Arabia, signed on 14 October 1980 and known as the 'Sawari' deal (named after a Muslim Byzantine battle in the year 655), is typical of French arms sales policy: the willingness to supply a large number of weapon systems, the ability to provide the related equipment, such as missiles and radar for the frigates (unlike, for example, the United States, which refused to supply sophisticated equipment for the F-15 fighters ordered by Saudi Arabia), and the persistent effort to penetrate new markets dominated by other countries in the past. Consequently, France has managed to become the third largest arms supplier, surpassing the UK and China in the Far East and the Middle East regions by 1980. France also appears as the third and the fourth largest supplier of major arms to South and Central America, respectively.

France has long dominated in arms sales to its former colonies in Africa and has in recent years also begun extensive marketing in other African countries.

Italy

During the latter part of the 1970s Italy reached the position of fourth largest arms seller, in many cases as the intermediate seller of US technology, such as the Agusta military helicopters built under US licence. The absolute majority of Italian arms exports are directed to the Third World (76 per cent), and among the single largest customers are, for example, Egypt and Libya. Latin America has become a lucrative arms market for Italy, with the large orders placed by Peru, Argentina and Brazil. In particular, Italy's rapidly expanding naval industry is dependent on exports to developing nations.

The UK

In the aggregate table 7.2 it can be seen how the trend indicator value for the UK declines steadily from 1977 through 1980.

The decline of British arms exports has been much debated, in Parliament and elsewhere; in this connection, the rise in French arms exports is always pointed out. The value of British arms exports in 1980 was, according to the Defence Sales Organization, $2 600 million. Prime Minister Thatcher called on the industry to start making simpler and cheaper weapons for export.

The loss of Iranian orders following the revolution was a hard setback for British arms industry, further aggravated by the embargo on arms supplies to Iran during 1980 (as long as the US hostages were held). Among other equipment, the delivery of the $90 million fleet replenishment ship *Kharg* was held up. Also affected by the ban was the supply of spare parts for 950 Chieftain tanks purchased by the Shah.

At the British Army Equipment Exhibition at Aldershot in June 1980, the head of the government's Defence Sales Organisation, Sir Ronald Ellis, said that British companies had conquered 5 per cent of this year's $53 000 million world market for military equipment [10].[3] He also

[3] Compare the figure for the year's total arms sales of $25 000 million quoted by US government sources (page 183). Obviously the widely differing estimates of total arms sales depend on the definition of arms and military equipment used.

declared that the drop-off in orders was not due to any restraint policy or lack of interest in British arms, but to the mass cancellation of Iranian orders.

On 15 April, the British government declared that 61 countries were buying some types of defence equipment from the UK and that military exports totalled 2.5 per cent of total exports in 1979 (which can be compared to the French share of 5 per cent of total exports mentioned above). In a parliamentary debate in the House of Lords, the arms industry and the government were called on to increase arms exports, for example, by pointing to the most gruesome consequences for the future if arms exports should continue to decrease, as in the following statement by Lord Orr-Ewing:

> If we could do half as well [as France and the USA], we should not be exporting £1100 million [$2 400 million] or £1200 million [$2 600 million] of defence equipment in the coming year but I believe we should be able to raise the figure to £1500 million [$3 300 million] and to £2000 million [$4 400 million] and perhaps even approach the level which France has succeeded in attaining. . . . *If we do not look after our own industry* (the arms industry) *we shall become a de-industrialised agricultural country again. . . . We shall have an extreme government of some sort in this country; we shall have serious unemployment and we shall no longer play a leading part in the free world.* [11a]

In a debate otherwise permeated by irony or direct ridicule of those that oppose arms sales (for example, Lord Newall: "The world is not a peaceful place . . . if anybody is against arms sales—and I am sure that there are some—they must be living in a dream world" [11b]), a more sober judgement of the causes for the British decline in weapon exports was given by Lord Bethell:

> Let us face it: we are no longer the major arms producing country that we were decades ago. We are now a medium-sized industrial country and probably a less than medium-sized military country. It is very difficult for us to produce weapons profitably—given the difficulties that face British industry at the moment—from our present industrial base. [11c]

FR Germany

In FR Germany, the issue of arms export policies was hotly debated throughout 1980. On the one hand, the Social Democratic Party (SPD) had decided, for example, by means of numerous votings at party meetings, that the export of war material has to be concluded with utmost restraint. On the other hand, Chancellor Schmidt agreed, in principle, to the sale of submarines to Chile, and the West German industries opened negotiations with Saudi Arabia for a future, large package deal including Leopard-2 tanks and the Tornado fighter. A change in the arms sales policy, described for many years as "restrictive", was made during the year, as it became known that the Foreign Ministry will not in the future define any "areas of tension" (to which arms exports were in principle prohibited), and that the motivating force behind decisions to export arms will be the national interest. In future, large orders for the Leopard-2 main battle tank, for example, are expected from Egypt, Libya, the Union of Arab Emirates and Kuwait. Given the West German dependence on oil supplies from Saudi Arabia, it can be speculated that the government may have to sell whatever Saudi Arabia wishes to buy. The Social Democrat politician Hans Jürgen Wischnewski even claims that continued arms exports to Saudi Arabia are a necessity not only for FR Germany but for the West, for securing oil supplies.

Whoever the buyer eventually may be, it is evident that the Leopard-2, which is perhaps the world's most sophisticated battle tank, is being produced for export: 1 800 units are being produced, of which the West German Army will take 1 500. An export sale of 300 such tanks, costing $2.6 million per tank, would provide additional funding for the costly Tornado project, according to Defence Minister Hans Apel [12].

By the end of 1980 it was still premature to say which direction the arms sales policy would take: towards more restriction in accordance with pressure from the ruling SPD and their coalition partners the Liberal Party (FDP), or towards an easing of the export laws in accordance with the pressure from the industry and more moderate wings of the ruling parties.

Other NATO

Norway has for the first time appeared among the 10 largest arms suppliers, according to the SIPRI statistics. But, as seen from table 7.3, no arms have been exported by Norway to Third World countries. Norwegian arms exports are in fact confined to Penguin ship-to-ship missiles to Greece, Sweden and Turkey, and fast patrol boats to Sweden.

In contrast to Norway, *the Netherlands* exports 87 per cent of its major weapon transfers to the Third World, which exports consist of Fokker aircraft and ships. *Canada*'s major arms exports are practically all (98.3 per cent) directed to Third World countries.

Other WTO

Czechoslovakia is, after the Soviet Union, the only large-scale WTO supplier of major weapons—ranked as number 19, with 43.9 per cent going to the Third World (see table 7.3). This reflects the fact that the WTO has accepted the Czech-designed L-39 Albatross advanced jet trainer as standard, and hence, over half of the Czech deliveries are made within the WTO. (If the Omnipol deliveries of small arms all over the world were included, the picture would be a different one.)

The co-ordinated East European aircraft acquisition programmes up to 1990 call for delivery of more than 3 000 L-39 trainers. The Soviet Union is the largest customer of the Czech aerospace industry, and the industry has a co-operative agreement with the Soviet Union that calls for Czech aircraft seats and other equipment. By the end of 1980, over 1 000 L-39s had been delivered to the Soviet Union and the German Democratic Republic. Omnipol, the state sales organization, nearly managed to sell the L-39 also to Nigeria, but lost out to the French–West German Alpha Jet because the L-39 (considered a second-generation trainer) could not be delivered outside the WTO until 1980.

The only other WTO country exporting major weapons is *Poland*, which sold transport aircraft to Venezuela and second-hand tanks to South Yemen.

Non-aligned European arms exporters

Sweden and *Switzerland* are ranked as fourteenth and fifteenth, respectively, in table 7.3. Roughly half of Sweden's exports of major weapons go to Third World countries, while the corresponding share of Switzerland's arms exports is 27.1 per cent. Both countries prohibit the export of arms to areas of tension, but during 1980 Swedish Bofors RBS-70 surface-to-air missiles were sold to Bahrain and Dubai, and coastal patrol boats were delivered to Oman. Switzerland has sold trainers to a large number of countries, including Argentina, Bolivia, Chile and Iraq.

In Sweden, just as in FR Germany, the debate between those in favour of and those against increased arms exports was heightened during 1980. The director of the Bofors company, Mr Claes Ulrik Winberg, called for a more generous interpretation of Swedish arms export rules in order to increase the exports and employment opportunities. He also complained that the Ministry of Foreign Affairs was working against the Swedish arms industry instead of giving the kind of support which the British and French arms industries receive from their authorities. He also argued that Swedish arms supplies would not upset the balance of power in the world but would help stabilize relations [13].

Both Commander-in-Chief Lennart Ljung and Defence Minister Eric Krönmark agree that Sweden must continue its arms exports in order to be able to distribute the R&D costs on larger production series. The limited orders from the Swedish armed forces do not secure continued production. But the parliamentary committee set up in 1979 to review the arms export regulations came up with proposals for a further strengthening of the restrictions in 1980: the committee wants more parliamentary control of arms exports and also wants to include the sale of production licences in the control system. The final report will appear during 1981. Swedish military exports were reported to take up a share of 1.41 per cent of total exports in 1979 [14].

Although not appearing in the rank order table of major arms exporters, *Austria* has during the past few years increased its sales, in particular of armoured vehicles from Steyr-Daimler Puch. In 1979, over 90 per cent of the company's output was exported, since the number of Austrian Army orders remains small. The Cuirassier tank destroyer has been sold in Africa and South America. During 1980, orders were signed with Argentina and with Bolivia. The first debate on arms sales in Austria occurred in connection with the sale of the Cuirassier to Chile in 1980, but in the end the government decided not to go through with the deal.

Third World exporters

Brazil appears in the rank order table of exporters (table 7.3) as number 10, followed by Israel as 11, and South Africa as 17. In the same table, the Third World exporters as a group occupy seventh place; the individual exporters appear by rank order in table 7.5.

Table 7.5. Rank order of the 12 largest Third World major-weapon exporting countries, 1977–80

Figures are SIPRI trend indicator values, as expressed in US $ million, at constant (1975) prices.

Exporting country	Total value	Percentage of total Third World exports	Largest importer per exporter
1. Brazil	421	*33.1*	Chile
2. Israel	367	*28.9*	South Africa
3. South Africa	116	*9.1*	Zimbabwe
4. Libya	98	*7.7*	Syria
5. Egypt	72	*5.7*	Somalia
6. South Korea	38	*3.0*	Indonesia
7. Argentina	35	*2.8*	Chile
8. Saudi Arabia	31	*2.4*	Somalia
9. Singapore	17	*1.3*	Thailand
10. Indonesia	16	*1.3*	Benin
11. Cuba	15	*1.2*	Peru
12. India	12	*0.9*	South Africa[a]
Others	33	*2.6*	–
Total	**1 271**	**100.0**	

[a] Via a company in Spain; final destination not known to Indian government.

Source: SIPRI computer-stored data base.

In the current Fiscal Year 1980/81, arms exports from Israel are expected to surpass $1 000 million, according to an official Defence Ministry announcement, which is nearly double the 1979/80 figure [15].

One area of potential growth lies in the future exports of the Kfir fighter. Shortly before the US election in 1980, the Carter Administration announced that Israel would be allowed to offer the Kfir, with its US engine, to Mexico, Colombia and Venezuela, indicating that the embargo was lifted. There are continued rumours that the Israeli fighter may be licence produced in, for example, South Africa.

Like Israel, *Brazil* has made spectacular advances on the arms market, first of all with its armoured vehicles from Engesa, a large number of which have been exported to Middle East nations, including Iraq. *Argentina* is producing the West German TAM and VCI tanks for its own use and for export. *South Africa*'s position as the third largest Third World exporter is due to its supplies of major weapons to Rhodesia before independence. In 1980, reports appeared of South African small arms being sent to Chile; at the end of the year, six fire units of the Cactus surface-to-air missile (a French–South African joint design) were delivered.

Table 7.6. Rank order of the 20 largest industrialized major-weapon importing countries, 1977–80

Figures are SIPRI trend indicator values, as expressed in US $ million, at constant (1975) prices.

Importing country	Total value[a]	Percentage of industralized world total	Largest exporter per importer
1. Italy	2 167	*12.1*	USA
2. Greece	1 900	*10.6*	USA
3. Japan	1 522	*8.5*	USA
4. Spain	1 112	*6.2*	USA
5. Netherlands	1 062	*5.9*	USA
6. Turkey	1 044	*5.8*	USA
7. Belgium	1 002	*5.6*	USA
8. Poland	899	*5.0*	USSR
9. Czechoslovakia	817	*4.6*	USSR
10. Sweden	776	*4.3*	Norway
11. FR Germany	746	*4.2*	USA
12. German DR	654	*3.7*	USSR
13. United Kingdom	582	*3.2*	USA
14. Australia	504	*2.8*	USA
15. Finland	488	*2.7*	USSR
16. Canada	485	*2.7*	USA
17. Denmark	396	*2.2*	USA
18. Romania	330	*1.8*	France
19. Switzerland	329	*1.8*	USA
20. Hungary	206	*1.1*	USSR
Others	934	*5.2*	–
Total	**17 955**	**100.0**	

[a] The values include licences sold for the production of major weapons.

Source: SIPRI computer-stored data base.

H

Table 7.7. Rank order of the 25 largest Third World major-weapon importing countries, 1977–80

Figures are SIPRI trend indicator values, as expressed in US $ million, at constant (1975) prices.

Importing country	Total value[a]	Percentage of Third World total	Largest exporter per importer
1. Iran	3 446	*8.7*	USA
2. Saudi Arabia	3 133	*8.0*	USA
3. Jordan	2 558	*6.5*	USA
4. Syria	2 311	*5.9*	USSR
5. Iraq	2 172	*5.5*	USSR
6. Libya	2 107	*5.4*	USSR
7. South Korea	1 987	*5.0*	USA
8. India	1 931	*4.9*	USSR
9. Israel	1 778	*4.5*	USA
10. Viet Nam	1 220	*3.1*	USSR
11. Morocco	1 121	*2.9*	France
12. Ethiopia	1 086	*2.7*	USSR
13. Peru	995	*2.5*	USSR
14. South Yemen	964	*2.4*	USSR
15. South Africa	950	*2.4*	Italy
16. Algeria	882	*2.2*	USSR
17. Taiwan	737	*1.9*	USA
18. Kuwait	664	*1.7*	USSR
19. Argentina	642	*1.6*	FR Germany
20. Brazil	641	*1.6*	United Kingdom
21. Egypt	594	*1.5*	USA
22. Indonesia	522	*1.3*	USA
23. Pakistan	512	*1.3*	France
24. Chile	482	*1.2*	France
25. Thailand	412	*1.0*	USA
Others	5 657	*14.3*	–
Total	**39 504**	**100.0**	

[a] The values include licensed production.

Source: SIPRI computer-stored data base.

IV. Arms control efforts

During 1980, no international attempts were made to curb the transfer of conventional armaments. No meeting took place between the United States and the Soviet Union in the so-called CAT (Conventional Arms Transfer) talks. Sharp debates took place within the United States, FR Germany and the UK on arms sales policies. In October 1980, the British Labour Party conference passed a resolution including a call for "a firm commitment to disbanding the defence sales organisation and reorganising arms industries to produce alternative products of social value" [16].

It may well be that the Carter policy of restraining arms sales deserves the criticism it has received for being "naive". It may also be that it was a premature policy, which could be regarded as a first attempt to be followed up by more mature political organizations, whether international or national, at some point in the future. There is, all the same, a widespread understanding of the inherent dangers in a continued drastic spread of conventional weapons, as expressed, for example, by an Israeli defence expert: "The conventional arms race has already led a number of Middle East states to the nuclear option" [17].

The fight for scarce resources that can be expected during the 1980s will also have implications for the military use of these resources. It may be true that a combined effort must be aimed at controlling both the production of new weapons and the traffic in arms. Meanwhile, some limited measures can also be taken in regard to arms transfers alone: for example, the British White Paper 1980 for the first time included information on arms sales, which can be regarded as a contribution to the constant demand for information needed by the disarmament community.

The nature and meaning of the arms business was well summarized by Senator Proxmire as follows:

> Arms trafficking has become a new international currency—a profitable expanding business force in the world. Under the justification of business is good for our balance of payments or if we do not sell weapons someone else will and that will cost us in jobs and we are just supplying a self-defense need, the arms merchants and their government spokesmen are turning the world into a vast armed camp. While it may be true that some weapons are for show and some are for deterrence and some are for national pride, the only responsible long-term conclusion is that most are for war. They are bought to be used. And in the numbers and sophistication that are available in the current market, the result of their use will be increased devastation and increased efficiency in killing.
>
> Our short-term greed will produce long-term disasters. The world is too populated by irrational concepts and intemperate leaders to long avoid a series of local conflagrations. [6]

Thus, the inherent danger in the present course of an unlimited build-up of the so-called conventional arsenals has been well grasped by its opponents. The prospects for the future are bleak, to say the least, in the absence of any progress on the disarmament side.

The United States is necessarily the most closely watched actor in a military scenario, being the leading military nation of the world. The prediction was made in 1980 that, with its $1 trillion defence budget for 1981–85, the United States may buy itself two things: the first is an economic decline of the sort that comes about once or twice in a century; the second is a nuclear war [18].

This prediction may as well be extended to all major arms producing countries—they are all joined in an effort that in the not too distant future may buy them a nuclear war whose battlefield is likely to be in Europe.

Proposals for reversing the arms race have also been made and have existed for a long time: proposals for alternative uses of military resources, in particular for alternative production for the arms industries, and proposals for reversing the spread of conventional weapons.

On the supply side, there have been warnings of the danger of becoming entangled in foreign conflicts and wars, in the capacity of being a large arms *supplier*. Now, on the *recipient* side, there is a growing consciousness of the potential dangers to national independence of relying heavily on a foreign arms supplier.

The Final Document adopted by the 1978 UN Special Session on Disarmament contains a recommendation that major arms supplier and recipient countries should conduct consultations on the limitation of all types of international transfer of conventional weapons. This was the first such recommendation made by the United Nations. It constitutes a very important event in itself because, until then, all attempts at curbing the spread of conventional armaments—even attempts at discussing the issue—were frustrated mainly by the resistance from Third World countries. The relevant stipulation of the Final Document (contained in paragraph 85) could be interpreted as an indication of a changing attitude in recipient countries and a realization of the dangers of an unlimited spread of conventional weapons.

However, since 1978, no practical measures have been taken to implement this important recommendation of the United Nations. It would seem natural for the Committee on Disarmament to work out appropriate procedures for the envisaged consultation.

References

1. *Le Monde*, 19 February 1980, p. 21.
2. 'US–Australia titanium study by James Forth', *Financial Times*, 28 October 1980.
3. *Military Technology*, No. 19, 1980.
4. *Defense & Foreign Affairs Daily*, 4 November 1980.
5. 'World arms, the scramble to cash in on weapons exports', *Business Week*, 24 March 1980, pp. 62–69.
6. 'Arms sales up, security down', *Congressional Record-Senate*, 3 April 1980, S 3518.
7. *Frankfurter Allgemeine*, 15 December 1980.
8. *Svenska Dagbladet* (Stockholm), 12 December 1980.
9. White, D., 'Military contracts', *Financial Times*, 4 December 1979.
10. McLain, L., 'Britain has 5% of world arms market', *Financial Times*, 24 June 1980.
11. *Parliamentary Debates* (*Hansard*), House of Lords Official Report: Motions—Defence Equipment: Policy on Overseas Sales, Vol. 408, No. 117, 23 April 1980.
    (a) —, Col. 796 (italics added).

(b) —, Col. 781.
(c) —, Col. 801.

12. *Norske Argus* (Oslo), 14 January 1981.
13. 'Boforschefen om vapenexporten: miljarder och jobb att tjäna' ['The Bofors director on weapon exports: billions and jobs to gain'], *Dagens Nyheter* (Stockholm), 4 February 1981, p. 12.
14. Karlsson, U., 'Exporten av försvarsmateriel ett led in neutralitetspolitiken' ['The export of defence material a link in neutrality policy'], *Verkstäderna* (Stockholm), No. 16, 10 December 1980.
15. Dunn, M., 'Israel's arms exports booming', *Strategy Week*, 24–30 November 1980, pp. 8–9.
16. *Newsletter*, Campaign Against The Arms Trade (London), No. 44, 22 October 1980, p. 1.
17. *Business Week*, International Business, 24 March 1980, p. 69.
18. Rothschild, E., 'The American arms boom', in E. P. Thompson and D. Smith (eds.), *Protest and Survive* (Penguin, Harmondsworth, UK, 1980), p. 170.

Appendix 7A

Register of the arms trade with industrialized and Third World countries, 1980

See the *SIPRI Yearbook 1979* for sources and methods (appendix 3C, pages 242–55) and for the key to the region codes (page 255). Countries are listed alphabetically and weapons in the order: aircraft, armoured vehicles, missiles and ships.

The following conventions and abbreviations are used in the registers of world arms trade and licensed production data (appendix 7A and 7B):

Conventions

..	Information not available
( )	Uncertain data or SIPRI estimate

Abbreviations and acronyms

AAM	Air-to-air missile
AAV	Anti-aircraft vehicle
AC	Armoured car
ADV	Advanced defence version
AEV	Armoured engineering vehicle
AEW	Airborne early-warning system aircraft
AF	Air Force
APC	Armoured personnel carrier
ARV	Armoured recovery vehicle
AShM	Air-to-ship missile
ASM	Air-to-surface missile
ASW	Anti-submarine warfare
ATM	Anti-tank missile
ATW	Anti-tank weapon
AV	Armoured vehicle
AWACS	Airborne warning and control system
Bty(s)	Battery(ies)
Cargo	Cargo vehicle
Cl	Class
COIN	Counterinsurgency
CPB	Coastal patrol boat
CPC	Command post carrier
FMS	Foreign Military Sales
FPB	Fast patrol boat

FROG	Free rocket over ground
FY	Fiscal Year
GB	Gun boat
Hel	Helicopter
ICV	Infantry combat vehicle
Landmob	Landmobile (missile)
LST	Tank landing ship
LT	Light tank
MAP	Military Assistance Program
Mar patrol	Maritime patrol aircraft
MBT	Main battle tank
MICV	Mechanized infantry combat vehicle
MRCA	Multi-role combat aircraft
MT	Medium tank
PB	Patrol boat
Port	Portable
Recce	Reconnaissance (aircraft or vehicle)
SAM	Surface-to-air missile
ShAM	Ship-to-air-missile
ShShM	Ship-to-ship missile
ShSuM	Ship-to-submarine missile
SLBM	Submarine-launched ballistic missile
SPG	Self-propelled gun
SPH	Self-propelled howitzer
t	Ton
TD	Tank destroyer

Region code/ Recipient	Supplier	No. ordered	Weapon designation	Weapon description	Year of order	Year of delivery	No. delivered	Comments
I. Industrialized countries								
11 Australia	France	1	Durance Class	Support ship	1977			For delivery 1983; total cost: $68 mn
	United Kingdom	100	Rapier	Landmob SAM	1975	1978	(20)	Order incl 20 launch units; first delivery 1978; system now operational
						1979	(40)	
						1980	(40)	
	USA	4	F-111	Fighter/bomber	(1980)			
		36	M-198	SPH	1980			Finalizing contract; incl support equipment
		90	RGM-84A Harpoon	ShShM	1976			30 launchers ordered for 2 FFG-7 Class and 3 Perth Class frigates; may buy 30 more
		1	FFG-7 Class	Frigate	1980			Fourth to be ordered soon; USA agrees to sell second-hand for $55 mn less than new ship; for delivery 1984
		3	FFG-7 Class	Frigate	1976	1981	2	Total cost incl all 3 ships; unit cost expected to be $190-230 mn
7 Austria	Italy	24	AB-212	Hel	1978	1979	4	
						1980	20	
	USA	(18)	M-109-A2	SPG	(1979)	1980	(18)	
		50	M-60-A3	MBT	1979	1980	(50)	
4 Belgium	Brazil	5	EMB-121 Xingu	Transport	1980			On order; second Brazilian contract with industrialized customer
	France	16	Alpha Jet	Trainer	1977	1978	(6)	Total order: 33, of which 50% to be licence produced
						1979	(7)	
						1980	3	
		40	SA-361 Dauphin	Hel	(1980)			Negotiating
		6000	MILAN	ATM	1979	1980	(4500)	Offset order from Euromissile; total requirement: 240 systems
	Germany, FR	55	Gepard	AAV	1973	1978	(15)	
						1979	(20)	
						1980	(20)	
	USA	(1224)	AIM-7E Sparrow	AAM	1977	1979	(60)	For 102 F-16 fighters
						1980	336	

		200	AIM-9L	AAM	1980			Pending congressional approval
		. .	MIM-23B Hawk	Landmob SAM	(1979)			To replace 2 battalions of MIM-23A
5 Bulgaria	USSR	. .	T-72	MBT	(1978)	1979	(50)	
						1980	(50)	
4 Canada	USA	. .	B-747-200F	Transport	1980			Unspecified number recently ordered; for VIP use; for delivery 1981-82
		18	CP-140 Aurora	ASW/mar patrol	1976	1980	9	Special design for Canada based on P-3C Orion and S-2A Viking
						1981	9	
		137	F-18A Hornet	Fighter/strike	1980			Order incl 113 single-seat fighters and 24 two-seat operational trainers; delivery planned for 1982-88; Canadian designation: CF-18; total cost: $2 500-5 000 mn
		14	Model 206B	Hel	1980			For pilot training
		182	AIM-9L	AAM	1980			Ordered Sep 1980; arming F-18s
3 China	United Kingdom	30	AV-8A Harrier	Recce	(1980)			Order not finalized
5 Czechoslovakia	USSR	. .	Mi 24 Hind-D	Hel	(1979)	(1980)	(12)	In service
		. .	MiG-23B	Fighter	(1979)	1980	(12)	In service
		. .	M-1974	SPH	1979	(1980)	(50)	Seen during military parade
		. .	AT-4	ATM	1979	(1980)	(480)	Seen during military parade
		. .	AT-6 Spiral	ASM	(1979)	1980	(24)	Seen on Mi-24 Hind-D helicopters; 2 missiles/hel
		. .	SA-9 Gaskin	Landmob SAM	1979	(1980)	(200)	Seen during military parade
4 Denmark	United Kingdom	7	Lynx	Hel	1977	1980	7	Delivery from May 1980
		1	Lynx	Hel	(1980)			For maritime patrol; in addition to 7 delivered 1980
	USA	46	F-16A	Fighter/strike	1977	1980	(3)	Delivery has started
		12	F-16B	Fighter/strike	1977	1980	(1)	Delivery has started
		3	Gulfstream-3	Transport	1979	1980	(1)	For maritime patrol, transport and SAR duties; final delivery 1981-82
		840	BGM-71A TOW	ATM	(1980)			DoD notified Congress; total cost incl 62 launchers
		15	RGM-84A Harpoon	ShShM	1980			Order incl support equipment; for 3 Niels Juel Class frigates
7 Finland	Iceland	2	F-27 Mk-100	Transport	(1980)	1980	2	At least 2; will probably be bought instead of An-32; to replace C-47s
		4	PA-28RT-201	Lightplane	1980	1980	4	Recently taken over

Region code/ Recipient	Supplier	No. ordered	Weapon designation	Weapon description	Year of order	Year of delivery	No. delivered	Comments
	Sweden	(60)	PBV-206	APC	1980			On order; for delivery 1981; total cost: $3.75 mn
	United Kingdom	50	Hawk T-52	Adv trainer	1977	1980	2	4 to be delivered complete from the UK, the rest scheduled for local assembly during 1981-85
	USA	3	Learjet-35A	Transport	1980			
	USSR	(7)	An-32 Cline	Transport	1979			Unconfirmed
		5	Mi-8 Hip	Hel	1980	1980	(3)	Follow-on order to 6 in service; bought in spite of AF preferences for Western types
						1981	(2)	
		20	MiG-21bis	Fighter	1978	1979	2	To replace 19 MiG-21Fs
						1980	(18)	
		180	AA-2 Atoll	AAM	1978	1979	18	Arming MiG-21bis
						1980	162	
		. .	SA-3 Goa	Landmob SAM	1977	1980	(100)	First batch delivered early 1980; to reach operational status in 1982
		. .	SA-7 Grail	Port SAM	1978			
		60	SSN-2 Styx	ShShM	1976			Arming 5 Osa-2 Class FPBs
7 Finland	USSR	5	Osa-2 Class	FPB	1976			
4 France	Brazil	35	EMB-121 Xingu	Transport	1980			Ordered Apr 1980; first industrialized customer; France expects in return order for 50 Mirage-50s and Puma hel
	Canada	2	DHC-6	Transport	(1978)	1980	2	
	United Kingdom	14	Lynx	Hel	1980			For delivery 1981-83
	USA	4	RIM-24 Tartar	ShAM	1980			Ordered Feb 1980; 4 systems
5 German DR	USSR	. .	M-1974	SPH	(1979)	(1980)	(50)	In service
		200	T-72	MBT	(1978)	1979	(50)	
						1980	(100)	
		. .	AT-4	ATM	1978	(1979)	(240)	
						(1980)	(240)	
4 Germany, FR	Israel	4	Westwind 1123	Transport	1980			Ordered May 1980
	United Kingdom	12	Lynx	Hel	1979	1980	(12)	For 6 Type 122 frigates; some sources report 22 Lynx on order

	USA	762	BGM-71A TOW	ATM	1979			Agreement signed at Paris Air Show; to arm Bo-105 hel
		(96)	NATO Seasparrow	ShAM/ShShM	1977			NATO co-production programme group in 1977
		142	RGM-84A Harpoon	ShShM	1978			
4 Greece	Austria	. .	Cuirassier	TD	(1980)			Undisclosed number ordered
	France	1	Alouette-3	Hel	(1976)	1980	1	For training ship 'Aris'
		. .	AMX-10P	AC	(1977)	(1979)	(50)	
						(1980)	(50)	
		115	AMX-30	MBT	(1978)			On order
		24	MM-38 Exocet	ShShM	1977	(1980)	16	For 8 Combattante FPBs
						(1981)	(8)	
	Germany, FR	1	Fletcher Class	Destroyer	(1980)	1980	1	NATO aid
	Italy	12	AB-212ASW	Hel	(1978)	1979	(3)	On order
						1980	4	
		6	CH-47C Chinook	Hel	1980			
	Netherlands	(15)	F-27 Maritime	Mar patrol	(1980)			Negotiating 10-15 aircr plus offset agreement
		1	Kortenaer Class	Frigate	1980	1981	1	Option on 1 more from Netherlands and on licenced production of 1 or more
	Norway	100	Penguin-2	ShShM	1976	1980	(50)	Arming 6 Combattante-3 Class FPBs being licence-produced in Greece
						(1981)	(50)	
	USA	10	CH-47C Chinook	Hel	1977			On order
		8	Model 209 AH-1S	Hel	1980			Ordered Sep 1980; armed with TOW
		10	T-37B	Trainer	1980	1980	(10)	Small batch from USAF stocks
		5	TA-7H Corsair-2	Fighter/trainer	1977	1980	5	MAP order
		11	M-109-A1	SPH	1979			
		12	M-113-A2	APC	1980			Total cost incl 10 M-728s
		10	M-728	AEV	1980			Total cost incl 12 M-113-A2s
		200	AGM-65B	ASM	1980			DoD notified Congress; bringing AFs air-to-ground capability near to NATO minimum standards
		300	AIM-9L	AAM	1977			DoD notified Congress Jul 1980; arming A-7 Corsairs
		. .	BGM-71A TOW	ATM	1980			Arming 8 Model 209s on order
		600	Chaparral	Landmob SAM	1979			Ordered Nov 1979; incl 37 launch vehicles
		32	RGM-84A Harpoon	ShShM	1979			For Navy; incl support and equipment; pending congressional approval

Region code/ Recipient	Supplier	No. ordered	Weapon designation	Weapon description	Year of order	Year of delivery	No. delivered	Comments
		1	Gearing Class	Destroyer	1980			DoD notified Congress; in addition to 5 in service
5 Hungary	USSR	(40)	MiG-23	Fighter	(1978)	1980	(20)	On order
		. .	T-72	MBT	1980			Ordered Apr 1980
4 Iceland	USA	. .	S-76 Spirit	Hel	(1979)	(1980)		Delivery reportedly started
7 Ireland	France	3	SA-330 Puma	Hel	1978	(1980)	1	Reportedly delivered for evaluation
		16	AML-90	AC	(1979)	1979	4	
						(1980)	(12)	
		. .	M3	APC	(1979)	1980	(25)	Will get a number
						(1981)	(25)	
		. .	MILAN	ATM	(1978)	1979	(100)	First shown Dec 1979
						1980	(100)	
	Sweden	. .	RBS-70	Port SAM	1979	1980	(100)	Ordered Dec 1979
	United Kingdom	1	HS-125/700	Transport	1979	1980	1	Ordered Jun 1979; for training, transport and SAR duties
		16	Scorpion FV-101	LT	(1978)	(1980)	(8)	First 4 delivered early 1980
						(1981)	(8)	
	USA	3	Super King Air	Transport	(1978)	1977	1	Will probably order 2 more; third delivered Apr 1980 for offshore patrol
						1978	1	
						1980	1	
4 Italy	Germany, FR	. .	AS-34 Kormoran	AShM	1980			To arm IAF Tornados
	USA	1	C-9B Skytrain-2	Transport	1980			
		. .	BGM-71A TOW	ATM	1979			Agreement signed at Paris Air Show; to arm A-129 hel
		2	RIM-24 Tartar	ShAM	(1980)			DoD notified Congress; 2 systems arming Audace Class
10 Japan	USA	6	C-130H Hercules	Transport	1979	1980	(3)	Will receive 6 in FY 1981
						1981	(3)	
		4	E-2C Hawkeye	AEW	1979			Additional batch of 4 to be delivered 1984-85; first 4 scheduled for delivery 1982-83

		16	F-15A Eagle	Fighter/interc	1977	1980	(8)	To be delivered prior to licence production of 84 aircraft; 8 to be bought directly from USA and 8 to be finally assembled in Japan; first delivery Jul 1980
		16	King Air C-90	Trainer	(1979)	1980	2	Incl in $13 000 mn modernization programme for 1980-84
		2	Model 209 AH-1S	Hel	(1979)	1979	1	
						1980	1	
		3	P-3C Orion	ASW/mar patrol	1977			To be delivered prior to licence production
		13	Sierra	Trainer	(1979)			For maritime patrol
		87	M-113-A2	APC	1980			Ordered Jan 1980
		. .	AGM-84A Harpoon	ASM	(1980)			Decided to buy for P-3C Orion instead of Mitsubishi ASM; funding in FY 1980 budget; Navy also wants shipborne version
		. .	AIM-7F Sparrow	AAM	(1980)	1980		Unspecified number
		2500	AIM-9L	AAM	1979			Licence production rejected by USA 1979 but off-the-shelf procurement approved; no launchers
		. .	ASROC	ShSuM	(1977)			For 4 new destroyers
		(32)	RGM-84A Harpoon	ShShM	1980			2 quadruple launchers on 2 new destroyers now under construction in Japan
		24	RGM-84A Harpoon	ShShM	1979			Ordered Oct 1979; for new frigates under construction in Japan
		. .	Seasparrow	ShAM/ShShM	1977			For new destroyers
4	Netherlands	Germany, FR	445	Leopard-2	MBT	1979		Contract signed Jun 1979; chosen instead of US XM-1; offsets to Netherlands industry at 59% of purchase value, may reach 100%; to replace 369 Centurions and 130 AMX-13s
		United Kingdom	8	Lynx	Hel	1978		For ASW frigates
		USA	13	P-3C Orion	ASW/mar patrol	1978		
			90	M-109-A2	SPG	(1978)		
			37	M-110-A2	SPH	1980		Ordered Jul 1980
			144	M-198	SPH	1980		On order
			12	AGM-84A Harpoon	ASM	(1978)		
			840	AIM-9L	AAM	1977	1979 (42)	For 102 F-16 fighters
							1980 (120)	
			(288)	NATO Seasparrow	ShAM/ShShM	1970	1978 24	NATO co-production programme
							1979 (24)	
							1980 (24)	

Region code/ Recipient	Supplier	No. ordered	Weapon designation	Weapon description	Year of order	Year of delivery	No. delivered	Comments
		(288)	RGM-84A Harpoon	ShShM	1975	1978	24	For 12 Kortenaer Class frigates
						1979	(24)	
						1980	(48)	
		. .	RIM-66A/SM-1	ShAM/ShShM	(1978)			
11 New Zealand	United Kingdom	26	Scorpion FV-101	LT	1980			On order
	USA	3	Model 421C	Trainer	1980			Ordered Nov 1980
4 Norway	France	900	Roland-2	Landmob SAM	1975			Missiles purchased from Euromissile, 40 launchers from USA
	Germany, FR	10		Submarine	(1980)			Design contract signed for 750-900t patrol subs with IKL in Luebeck
	Sweden	. .	RBS-70	Port SAM	1978			
	United Kingdom	2	Lynx	Hel	(1979)			In addition to 4 ordered in 1978; incl spares and support equipment; for Coast Guard
		4	Lynx	Hel	1978			Option on 2 more
	USA	60	F-16A	Fighter	1977	1980	(6)	To be delivered from licence production in Netherlands
		12	F-16B	Fighter/trainer	1977	1980	(2)	First delivered Jan 1980
		2	P-3B Orion	ASW/mar patrol	1980	1980	2	2 to be delivered 1980
		432	AIM-9L	AAM	1977			NATO co-production programme
5 Poland	USSR	. .	M-1974	SPH	(1979)	(1980)	(50)	In service
4 Portugal	Belgium	3	T-33A	Trainer	1980	1980	3	Purchased; maybe for spares
	Germany, FR	12	G-91R-3	Fighter/ground	1980	1980	12	Donation announced; incl spares and support; in addition to 20 delivered in 1978
	Italy	12	A-109 Hirundo	Hel	(1980)			4 to be armed with TOW
	Netherlands	1	Kortenaer Class	Frigate	1980			On order; to be delivered prior to licence production of 2
	USA	20	A-7P Corsair-2	Fighter	1980	1981	(10)	Second country to receive A-7P version; totally refurbished; payment: cash, MAP; delivery to start end-1981
		200	BGM-71A TOW	ATM	1979			Ordered Jul 1979

5 Romania	France	(100)	SA-330L Puma	Hel	1978	1979	10	
						1980	(25)	
7 Spain	Canada	7	CL-215	Amph. aircr.	1979			Follow-up order
	France	42	Mirage F-1A	Fighter/ground	1978			Order finalized after long negotiations; Spanish industry to produce 20% of planes; total cost: incl 6 F-1Bs
		6	Mirage F-1B	Trainer	1978			Total cost: incl 42 F-1As
		12	SA-330L Puma	Hel	1978	(1979)	(3)	
						(1980)	(3)	
	Germany, FR	60	Bo-105CB	Hel	1979	1980	20	60 new to be delivered 1980-82; 28 as anti-tank hel with 6 HOT ATMs each, 14 as recce, 18 as armed recce; last 50 to be assembled by CASA
		(168)	HOT	ATM	1979	1980	(60)	Arming 28 Bo-105CB hel; delivery from 1980
	Italy	12	AB-212ASW	Hel	1978	1979	(6)	For Navy
						1980	(6)	
		6	CH-47C Chinook	Hel	1978	1980	6	
		. .	Aspide/Albatros	ShAM/ShShM	1979			For installation in second batch of new F-30 Class frigates; number ordered unknown
	United Kingdom	13	Sea Harrier	Fighter/ASW	(1977)	1979	(4)	Spain has ordered total of 13 Harrier from UK; also 6 on order from USA
						1980	(5)	
		6	SH-3D Sea King	Hel	(1980)	1980	3	Terminating 20 years' production in UK
						1981	3	
	USA	6	AV-8A Harrier	Recce	1977			Ordered Aug 1977
		9	CH-47C Chinook	Hel	1977	1980	(3)	Being delivered
		3	CH-47C Chinook	Hel	1980			For Army; in addition to 9 in service; for delivery 1982
		1	KC-130H	Transport	1980			Ordered Mar 1980; in addition to 3 in use; for delivery 1981
		53	Model 205 UH-1H	Hel	(1978)	1980	(15)	Now being delivered for Army
		17	Model 300C	Hel	1978			On order
		12	OH-58A Kiowa	Hel	(1978)			On order for Army
		8	P-3C Orion	ASW/mar patrol	(1978)	(1979)	(4)	First 2 are version A
						(1980)	(2)	
		204	M-113-A2	APC	(1978)			Order incl M-577 and M-125 vehicles
		36	M-125-A2	APC	1979			
		8	M-577-A2	CPC	1979			
		108	AIM-7F Sparrow	AAM	1979			US letter of offer Apr 1979; incl 8 practice missiles, spares and support equipment
		30	AIM-9L	AAM	1977			For 5 AV-8A Harrier on order from USA

Region code/ Recipient	Supplier	No. ordered	Weapon designation	Weapon description	Year of order	Year of delivery	No. delivered	Comments
		3000	BGM-71A TOW	ATM	1978			Pending congressional approval
		. .	RGM-84A Harpoon	ShShM	1978	1978	(24)	For 4 F-30 Class frigates
						1979	(48)	
						1980	(24)	
		. .	Seasparrow	ShAM/ShShM	1976	1978	72	For 4 F-30 Class frigates; 1 octuple Selenia Albatross launcher/ship with 16 reload missiles
						1979	24	
						1980	24	
		2		LST	(1980)	1980	2	Ex-US Navy
7 Sweden	Norway	96	Penguin-1	ShShM	1975	1978	18	Being delivered for Hugin Class FPBs
						1979	30	
						1980	12	
						1981	(30)	
		16	Hugin Class	FPB	1975	1978	3	Deliveries to be completed in 1982; armed with Penguin ShShM
						1979	5	
						1980	2	
						(1981)	(5)	
	United Kingdom	(312)	Sky Flash	AAM	1978	1980	(64)	Ordered Dec 1978; arming new JA-37 Viggen
	USA	5	C-130H Hercules	Transport	1980	1981	5	Ordered May 1980
		. .	AGM-65A	ASM	(1979)	1980	128	Government decision to cancel local development RB-05B may be reconsidered in 1979; for Viggen fighter
		(624)	AIM-9L	AAM	1978	(1980)	(128)	For new JA-37 Viggen
		2000	BGM-71A TOW	ATM	1977			DoD notified Congress Oct 1980; total cost incl 100 practice missiles and associated equipment
		. .	MIM-23B Hawk	Landmob SAM	(1978)			
7 Switzerland	France	2	Mirage-3D	Trainer	1980			To replace 2 trainers lost in recent years; also designated Mirage-3BS/80
	USA	36	F-5E Tiger-2	Fighter	1980			Total cost incl 6 F-5Fs
		6	F-5F Tiger-2	Trainer	1980			Total cost incl 36 F-5Es
		207	M-109-A2	SPG	1979			

		225	M-113-A1	ICV	1979	1980 (1981)	(100) (125)	Order approved by Parliament autumn 1979
		160	M-548	Cargo	1979			Order approved by Parliament autumn 1979
		2	XM-1	MBT	1980	(1981)	2	For evaluation and trials
		(500)	AGM-65A	ASM	1980			Adopted for 140 Hunters
		(288)	AIM-9L	AAM	1977	1977 1978 1979 1980	(48) (76) (48) (48)	For 72 F-5E/F fighters
		1000	AIM-9P	AAM	1980			
		11790	Dragon FGM-77A	ATM	1978	1980 (1981)	(6000) (5790)	Order incl 3 210 practice missiles
4 Turkey	Germany, FR	3	F-104G	Fighter	1980	1980	3	NATO aid; further deliveries will follow when FR Germany starts taking delivery of its Tornados
		12	G-91T	Fighter/trainer	1980	1980	12	Ordered Feb 1980
		. .	Leopard ARV	ARV	1980			NATO aid; for delivery 1981-83
		190	Leopard-1-A3	MBT	1980			Up to 190 Leopard MBTs and some 250 MILAN ATMs ordered from FR Germany in $350 mn aid package over 3 years
		(250)	MILAN	ATM	1980			Number ordered refers to systems; NATO aid
		4	Dogan Class	FPB	1973	1977 1978 1980	1 2 1	
		1	Vegesack Class	Coastal mine-sweeper	(1979)	1980	1	Last of this class now delivered; first 5 transferred 1975-76
	Italy	12	AB-212	Hel	1980			
	Netherlands	(40)	F-104G	Fighter	1980	1980	(40)	Dutch Defence Minister announced; will be sold as they are; replaced 1980 by F-16; in Turkey replacing F-102s acc to Swedish embassy in Ankara
	USA	30	T-38 Talon	Trainer	1980	1980	30	In addition to 30 delivered in 1979
		30	T-38 Talon	Trainer	1979	1979 1980	15 (15)	Ordered Apr 1979, incl spare engines, training and support equipment; ex-USAF
		400	AIM-9J	AAM	1978	1979 1980		Ordered Aug 1978
		. .	BGM-71A TOW	ATM	(1979)			Unspecified number on order

Region code/ Recipient	Supplier	No. ordered	Weapon designation	Weapon description	Year of order	Year of delivery	No. delivered	Comments
		96	RGM-84A Harpoon	ShShM	(1976)	1977	(24)	For Dogan Class FPBs
						1978	(48)	
						1980	(24)	
		12	RGM-84A Harpoon	ShShM	1980			Pending congressional approval
		1		Destroyer	(1979)	1980	1	Delivered Jan 1980: probably for spares
		1	Tang Class	Submarine	1979	1980	1	Delivered Feb 1980; ex-USN; originally ordered by Iran
4 United Kingdom	France	120	MM-38 Exocet	ShShM	1975	1975	12	For 6 Amazon Class frigates and 4 Broadsword Class destroyers
						1976	12	
						1977	36	
						1978	12	
						1979	12	
						1980	12	
						(1981)	(12)	
	USA	33	CH-47D Chinook	Hel	1978	1980	(9)	First helicopter delivered for trials Jan 1980; regular deliveries expected to begin Sep 1980
		2	P-3C Orion	ASW/mar patrol	(1980)			On order
		18	M-109-A2	SPG	1980			Total cost incl 3 M-578s: some sources state ordered number 51
		3	M-578	ARV	1980			
		1709	AIM-9L	AAM	1977			NATO co-production programme
		(100)	Trident-1	SLBM	(1980)			
		1	Speedy	Hydrofoil FPB	1978	1980	1	Unit cost: $20.5 mn
1 USA	United Kingdom	(280)	Rapier	Landmob SAM	(1980)			To defend US airbases in the UK; will probably incl 10 systems; offset for Trident SLBM
2 USSR	Czechoslovakia	. .	L-39 Albatross	Trainer	1972	1978		Replacing L-29 Delfin
						1979		
						1980		
	Finland	2	Dubna Class	Tanker	1977	1979	1	

6 Yugoslavia	Canada	4	CL-215	Amph. aircr.	1980			Ordered Jun 1980; not known whether bought for civil or military use
	USA	13	Model 206B	Hel	(1979)			For police duties
	USSR	60	SSN-2 Styx	ShShM	1975	1977	6	For 10 Type 211 FPBs
						1978	6	
						1979	12	
						1980	(6)	

Region code/ Recipient	Supplier	No. ordered	Weapon designation	Weapon description	Year of order	Year of delivery	No. delivered	Comments
II. Third World countries								
12 Algeria	USSR	. .	T-62	MBT	1977	1979	31	
						1980	50	
		. .	T-72	MBT	(1979)	1979	(31)	First shown in military parade Nov 1979
						1980	(50)	
		9	SA-4 Ganef	Landmob SAM	(1979)	1980	(9)	Arming 1 Nanuchka Class corvette
		(12)	SSN-2 Styx	ShShM	(1979)	1980	(12)	Arming 1 Nanuchka Class corvette
		. .		FPB	1980			Contract signed Jul 1980; missile FPB; number unknown
		1	Nanuchka Class	Corvette	(1979)	1980	1	May receive more than 1
13 Angola	Netherlands	1	F-27 Maritime	Mar patrol	(1979)	1980	1	Delivered Jan 1980
		1	F-27 Maritime	Mar patrol	1980			On order in addition to 1 delivered Jan 1980
	USA	1	C-130H Hercules	Transport	(1980)	1980	1	
		2	L-100-20	Transport	(1980)			
15 Argentina	Austria	50	Cuirassier	TD	(1979)	1980	(50)	Some 120 more reportedly on order
	Belgium	13	BDX	APC	(1979)	1980	13	For evaluation
	France	7	Mirage-3E	Fighter/bomber	1978	1980	7	
		12	SA-315B Lama	Hel	1978			For Army Air Wing
		12	SA-316B	Hel	1979			Ordered Jun 1980
		12	SA-330J Puma	Hel	1978			
		3	SA-330J Puma	Hel	1980			An additional 12 on order
		14	Super Etendard	Fighter/ASW	1979			
		1000	HOT	ATM	1980	1980	(200)	Being delivered
		1	A-69 Type	Frigate	1979			New construction; in addition to 2 delivered 1979, originally purchased by South Africa but embargoed
	Germany, FR	4	Meko-360	Frigate	1978			To be built in Hamburg by Blohm & Voss
		2	Type 122	Frigate	(1978)			Frigates now under construction by Blohm & Voss
		2	Type 148	FPB	(1979)			Missile FPBs on order from Lurssen
		1	Type 1700	Submarine	1977			Prior to licence production of 3
	Italy	9	A-109 Hirundo	Hel	1977			For Army
		10	MB-339A	Trainer/strike	(1980)	1980	3	For delivery 1980-82

	Spain	5		FPB	1979			On order for Coast Guard; with hel platform
	United Kingdom	8	Lynx	Hel	1979			To be delivered over next 3 years; for ASW; in addition to 2 in use; total cost: $3 mn
	USA	3	CH-47C Chinook	Hel	(1977)	1980	3	To enter operation in 1980 Antarctic mission; order for 2 more reportedly cancelled
		2	KC-130H	Transport	(1978)			AF plans to purchase for use as tanker
		1	Learjet-35A	Transport	1980	(1981)	1	
		1	Metro-2	Transport	(1979)			Pending congressional approval; for ambulance use; delivery held up by US arms export embargo
8 Bahrain	France	110	AML-M-3-VTT	APC	(1977)	(1978)	(30)	
						(1979)	(30)	
						(1980)	(35)	
						(1981)	(15)	
		. .	MM-38 Exocet	ShShM	1980	(1980)	(12)	2 systems on 2 FPBs from FR Germany
	Germany, FR	2	Type TNC-45	FPB	1980			
	Sweden	. .	RBS-70	Port SAM	1980	1980	(200)	Order confirmed but number unknown
9 Bangladesh	China	48	F-7	Fighter	1980			On order
	Sweden	10		PB	(1979)	1980	(10)	
15 Bolivia	Austria	31	Cuirassier	TD	(1978)	(1979)	(13)	Also designated Panzerjager K; seen in La Paz during military coup Jul 1980
						(1980)	(18)	
	Brazil	12	T-25 Universal	Trainer	(1979)			Production line to be re-opened if contract is signed; requested for COIN use
	Netherlands	6	F-27 MK-400M	Transport	1979	1980	4	Delivery of last 2 aircraft withheld due to government ban on aircraft exports to Bolivia; payments stopped
	Switzerland	16	PC-7	Trainer	1977	(1980)	(16)	
	USA	1	L-100-30	Transport	1979	1980	1	To replace 1 C-130H lost in accident
13 Botswana	United Kingdom	6	Bulldog-120	Trainer	1980	1980	6	Ordered in favour of SAAB Supporter after long evaluation
15 Brazil	France	3	Mirage-3E	Fighter/bomber	1977	1980	3	Bringing total to 20 Mirage-3s incl 4 trainers

Region code/ Recipient	Supplier	No. ordered	Weapon designation	Weapon description	Year of order	Year of delivery	No. delivered	Comments
		6	SA-330 Puma	Hel	1980	1980	6	For delivery from May; will buy total of 40 of which some may be licence produced; offset to French order for Xingu trainer; order uncertain due to strained economic situation in Brazil
		. .	AS-11	ASM	1972	1974	(144)	Arming Xavantes
						1975	(144)	
						1976	(144)	
						1977	(144)	
						1978	(144)	
						1979	(144)	
						1980	(144)	
	Italy	12		Corvette	1980			Co-production agreement signed Jun 1980; total cost incl 9 Sauro Class subs; 10- to 12-year programme
		9	Sauro Class	Submarine	1980			
	United Kingdom	4	Wasp	Hel	(1979)	1980	4	From Royal Navy surplus stocks; bringing total to 14 Wasp ASW in service with Brazilian Navy; 1 or 2 lost in accidents
10 Brunei	Germany, FR	(6)	Bo-105C	Hel	1979			On order; probably version C
	United Kingdom	2	BN-2A Defender	Transport	(1979)			Planning to purchase, according to unofficial reports
		. .	Rapier	Landmob SAM	(1980)			1 battery ordered, incl Blindfire radar; total cost: $82 mn
		. .	Sabre	ATM	1979			Contract signed early 1979
		3		PB	1980			Ordered with Decca radar
	USA	10	S-76 Spirit	Hel	1980			Recently ordered
10 Burma	Australia	6	Carpentaria Class	FPB	1979			Ordered Feb 1979
	Italy	9	SF-260M	Trainer	1979	1980	(9)	Ordered Jul 1979
	Switzerland	16	PC-7	Trainer	1979	1980	(16)	Second order of 16 for delivery 1980
	USA	6	Model 180	Lightplane	(1979)			On order
15 Chile	Brazil	6	EMB-326 Xavante	Trainer/COIN	(1978)			Unconfirmed
		20	T-25 Universal	Trainer	(1979)			On order
		10	Anchova Class	PB	1977	1980	(10)	
	France	. .	Alpha Jet	Trainer	(1980)			Negotiating; Fouga-90 also requested

		16	Mirage-50	Fighter/MRCA	1979	(1980)	(16)	French government reportedly approved sale; designation also reported as Mirage-5
		(128)	R-530	AAM	1979	(1980)	(128)	For 16 Mirage-50s; designation unconfirmed
	Germany, FR	2	Type 209	Submarine	1980			Construction began in FR Germany Oct 1980 but export licence not yet granted
	Israel	6	Reshef Class	FPB	1979	(1979) (1980) (1981)	(2) (2) (2)	Unconfirmed; first pair supposedly delivered in 1979; remaining 4 to be delivered 1980-81
	South Africa	6	Cactus	Landmob SAM	(1980)	1980	6	6 fire units and 2 radars delivered via France
	Spain	. .	C-101	Trainer/strike	1980			Undisclosed number of new jet trainer ordered
	Switzerland	10	PC-7	Trainer	1979	1980	10	Delivery of first 4 in Jul 1980
15 Colombia	Germany, FR	4	FS-1500 Class	Frigate	1980			Light frigates on order
	Israel	3	IAI-202 Arava	Transport	(1979)	1980	3	
	USA	(2)	C-130H Hercules	Transport	(1980)			Surplus; negotiating
		. .	Seasparrow	ShAM/ShShM	(1980)			On order; arming 4 FS-1500 Class corvettes
13 Congo	Italy	3	Piranha Class	CPB	(1979)			Displacement: 900t
14 Cuba	USSR	1	Foxtrot Class	Submarine	(1979)	1980	1	Second of Foxtrot Class delivered
13 Djibouti	France	1	Model 172	Lightplane	1980	1980	1	Lightplane; designation unconfirmed; delivered Mar 1980
		1	Noratlas 2501	Transport	1980	1980	1	Replacing 1 delivered 1979
		1	Rallye-235GT	Lightplane	1980	1980	1	Delivered Mar 1980
		1		FPB	(1980)	1980	1	Gift; French Navy transferred for patrol duties
	Germany, FR	1		PB	(1980)			FR Germany funding; deal incl 11 military vehicles; MAP
	Iraq	1	Mystere-20	Transport	1980	1980	1	
14 Dominican Republic								
	Argentina	. .	IA-58A Pucara	Trainer/COIN	(1980)			Negotiating
15 Ecuador	Canada	1	DHC-5D Buffalo	Transport	(1980)			Incl spares
	France	16	Mirage F-1C	Fighter/interc	1977	1979 1980	(4) (12)	Ordered instead of Kfir-C2
		. .	VAB	APC	(1977)			On order

Region code/ Recipient	Supplier	No. ordered	Weapon designation	Weapon description	Year of order	Year of delivery	No. delivered	Comments
		(72)	MM-40 Exocet	ShShM	1979	1980	12	6 sextuple launchers ordered Apr 1979 for 6 Wadi Class corvettes
	Italy	. .	Aspide-1A	AAM	(1979)			Probably for Mirage
		6	Wadi Class	Corvette	1978	1980	1	Similar to Wadi Class for Libya; 3 to be built at CNR, 3 at Ancona
	USA	1	B-727-200	Transport	(1979)	1980	1	Delivered Dec 1980
		1	Super King Air	Transport	(1979)	(1981)	(1)	Total cost incl 3 T-34s; for delivery 1981
		3	T-34C-1	Trainer	(1979)	1980	3	For Navy; total cost incl 1 Super King Air
		44	M-163 Vulcan	AAV	(1979)			US DoD proposed sale of Vulcan/Chaparral air defence system
		18	Chaparral	Landmob SAM	1979			
8 Egypt	China	60	F-6	Fighter	1979	1979	30	
						(1980)	(30)	
		30	F-7	Fighter	1979			Ordered Aug 1980
		. .	SA-2 Guideline	Landmob SAM	1980			Ordered Jan 1980
	France	30	Alpha Jet	Trainer	(1980)			Letter of intent signed mid-1980; competing with Hawk; final contract reportedly signed Jan 1981
		14	Mirage-5SD	Fighter	(1979)	1980	(14)	Bringing total to 62
		60	OTOMAT-2	ShShM	1978	1980	(30)	Egypt first export customer of coastal defence version
						(1981)	(30)	
		2	Agosta Class	Submarine	1978			
	Italy	15	CH-47C Chinook	Hel	1980			On order incl spares and support
		24	OTOMAT-1	ShShM	(1978)			Arming 6 Ramadan Class FPBs under construction in the UK
		6		FPB	1980			For Coast Guard
		2	Lupo Class	Frigate	(1980)			
	United Kingdom	20	Lynx	Hel	1978			On order
		(5)	SH-3D Sea King	Hel	(1979)	(1980)	(5)	
		6	Ramadan Class	FPB	1978			
		14	SRN-6	Hovercraft	(1980)			No official confirmation
	USA	11	C-130H Hercules	Transport	(1979)			
		40	F-16A	Fighter/strike	1980	1980	(5)	Egypt requested 300, US Government offered to sell 40; order incl 250 M-60-A3s

			35	F-4E Phantom	Fighter	1979	1980	35	12 USAF F-4Es and 560 USAF personnel to train with EAF F-4Es Jul-Sep 1980
			5	S-76 Spirit	Hel	1980			On order
			50	M-106-A2	Mortar carrier	(1979)			Requested Jul 1979
			550	M-113-A2	APC	(1980)			DoD informed Congress; second batch bringing total to 1100
			550	M-113-A2	APC	1979	1980	(200)	Deal arranged Jun 1978 during War Minister Gamassi's visit to USA; several hundred reportedly on order to replace Soviet types
			50	M-125-A2	APC	(1979)			Requested Jul 1979
			50	M-548	Cargo	(1979)			Requested Jul 1979
			50	M-577-A2	CPC	(1979)			Requested Jul 1979
			43	M-578	ARV	(1980)			Total cost incl 43 M-88-A1s; pending congressional approval
			244	M-60-A3	MBT	(1980)			Order incl 40 F-16s; 250-300 more planned for delivery 1985
			67	M-60-A3	MBT	1980			Before Congress Jul 1980; in addition to 244 previously ordered
			43	M-88-A1	ARV	(1980)			Total cost incl 43 M-578; pending congressional approval
			52	M-901 TOW	ICV	1980			Improved version of M-113-A1, armed with TOW; US letter of offer
			600	AGM-65A	ASM	1980	1980	(75)	Arming F-16s
			70	AIM-7E Sparrow	AAM	1979	1980	70	Arming F-4E Phantoms
			100	AIM-9E	AAM	1979	1980	(100)	
			250	AIM-9P	AAM	1979	1980	(100)	Arming F-4E Phantoms
			. .	BGM-71A TOW	ATM	1980			Undisclosed number on order for 52 M-901 launch vehicles; pending congressional approval
			36	MIM-23B Hawk	Landmob SAM	1979	1981	12	12 btys requested Jul 1979,incl missiles, radar, spare parts and training
			12	Spectre Class	FPB	(1979)			Incl in $1.5 bn credit package
14	El Salvador	USA	6	Model 209 AH-1G	Hel	(1980)	1981	(6)	First 2 delivered Jan 1981
			3		PB	1976			
13	Equatorial Guinea	Spain	2	C-212C Aviocar	Transport	1980			On order
13	Ethiopia	USSR	. .	Mi-24 Hind-C	Hel	(1980)	1980	(10)	Transport hel now being delivered; designation unconfirmed
			200	BTR-60P	APC	(1980)	1980	(100)	APCs now being delivered; designation unconfirmed

Region code/ Recipient	Supplier	No. ordered	Weapon designation	Weapon description	Year of order	Year of delivery	No. delivered	Comments
		(50)	T-62	MBT	(1980)	1980	(25)	MBTs now being delivered; designation unconfirmed
13 Gabon	Brazil	3	EMB-110	Transport	1980			Ordered with 1 EMB-111
		1	EMB-111	Mar patrol	1980			
		12	EE-9 Cascavel	Recce AC	1980			On order; probably EE-9
	France	4	Jaguar	Fighter	(1978)	1980	4	Reportedly deployed Nov 1980
		1	SA-330 Puma	Hel	1979	1980	1	
	Italy	4	Sarzana Class	PB	1975	1977	1	First ship, 'Ngolo', delivered 1977
	USA	2	L-100-20	Transport	1980	1980	2	
13 Ghana	Germany, FR	2	Type 57M	FPB	1976	1980	2	
	Italy	9	MB-326K	Trainer	1976	1978	4	
						1979	(4)	
						1980	(1)	
14 Guatemala	Switzerland	12	PC-7	Trainer	1978	1979	(3)	On order
						1980	(4)	
14 Honduras	Israel	5		FPB	(1978)	(1980)	(5)	
	United Kingdom	. .	Scorpion FV-101	LT	1978			Ordered Mar 1978
	USA	10	Model 205 UH-1A	Hel	(1980)	1980	10	Delivered Jul 1980; on loan
		2		FPB	(1979)	(1980)	(1)	
	Yugoslavia	6	CL-13 Sabre	Fighter	(1979)	(1980)	6	Canadian-built F-86 Sabre; private affair with Yugoslavia as possible seller; unconfirmed
9 India	Germany, FR	2	Type 209	Submarine	(1980)			Finalizing order; 2 more to be built in India following setting up of production facilities
	United Kingdom	40	Jaguar	Fighter	(1979)			Delivery prior to licence production; unit cost: $7.3-9.7 mn; deal now being re-negotiated by Gandhi Administration
		18	Jaguar	Fighter	(1980)	(1980)	(18)	Delivered on loan from the RAF prior to delivery of 40 ordered 1979
		6	Sea Harrier	Fighter/ASW	1979			For use with aircraft carrier 'Vikrant'; delivery 1981-82

		2	Sea Harrier T-4	Fighter/trainer	1979			Ordered Nov 1979; total cost incl 6 Sea Harriers
	USA	2	B-737-200L	Transport	1976			Order re-approved by new Gandhi Administration; for delivery 1981; probably version L
		230	M-198	SPH	1980			Total cost incl TOW missiles and ammunition; part of $340 mn deal
		3724	BGM-71A TOW	ATM	1980			Order incl 62 launchers
	USSR	. .	Mi-8 Hip	Hel	1979	1980	(20)	Ordered Nov 1979; delivered 1980
		80	MiG-23	Fighter	1980	1980	10	Part of USSR arms package to India; some to be locally assembled
		8	MiG-25R	Recce	(1980)	1981	(8)	Negotiating; to replace aged Canberras; designation reported as Foxbat-B
		100	T-72	MBT	1980	1980	(100)	Replacing Vijayanta; an additional 600 to be licence produced; part of USSR arms package to India incl ATMs, FROGs Petya Class FPBs, MiG-23s, Atoll and Ash AAMs
		. .	AA-2 Atoll	AAM	1980			Arming MiG-23s; part of USSR arms package to India
		. .	AA-5 Ash	AAM	1980			Arming MiG-23s; part of USSR arms package to India
		. .	AT-3 Sagger	ATM	1980			
		. .	FROG-7	Landmob SSM	1980			Probably version 7
		3	Kashin Class	Destroyer	1976	1980	(3)	Modified Kashin Class; possibly with KA-26 hel
		8	Nanuchka Class	Corvette	1975	1977	1	Reported that a total of 8 are to be delivered
						1978	1	
						1979	1	
						1980	1	
		6	Natya Class	Ocean mine-sweeper	(1977)	1978	2	Last 2 delivered Jul 1980; ex-USSR Navy
						1979	2	
						1980	2	
		. .	Petya Class	Frigate	1980			Missile light frigate; part of USSR arms package to India
10 Indonesia	Australia	6	N-22L Nomad	Coast patrol	(1980)	1981	6	Ordered Apr 1980; delivery to start 1981
	Belgium	12		FPB	1980			Ordered from Belgian Shipbuilding Corporation; 12 more to be licence produced
	France	3	C-160F Transall	Transport	1979			Aerospatiale received order Sep 1979; first delivery year 1982; civil version but easily converted

Region code/ Recipient	Supplier	No. ordered	Weapon designation	Weapon description	Year of order	Year of delivery	No. delivered	Comments
		(36)	MM-38 Exocet	ShShM	1976	1980	36	For 3 corvettes purchased from the Netherlands
	Germany, FR	9		PB	(1980)			For Coast Guard and mar patrol; deliveries to begin in 1981; reportedly on order from France(3) and FR Germany(6)
		2	Type 209	Submarine	1977	1980	2	Modified enlarged version
	Israel	14	A-4E Skyhawk	Bomber	1979	1980	14	From Israeli surplus stocks; total cost incl 2 TA-4Hs; some sources report USA as seller
		2	TA-4H Skyhawk	Fighter	1979	1980	2	From Israeli surplus stocks
	Korea South	4	PSMM-5 Type	FPB	1976	1979	(2)	
						1980	2	
	Netherlands	3	Fata Hilla Cl	Frigate	1975	1980	3	Arms: Exocet ShShM and Bofors 375-mm RL
	Switzerland	20	AS-202 Bravo	Trainer	1980			
	United Kingdom	8	Hawk T-53	Adv trainer	1978	1981	(8)	Ordered Apr 1978
	USA	5	C-130S	Transport	1979	1980	5	Last 3 reported as stretched version
		12	F-5E Tiger-2	Fighter	1977	1980	12	USA agreed to sell 1978; first ordered in 1977; total cost: including 4 F-5F trainers
		4	F-5F Tiger-2	Trainer	1977	1980	4	
		2	King Air C-90	Trainer	(1978)			
		3	L-100-30	Transport	1979	1980	1	Ordered for civilian use by Pelita Air Service; first aircraft, delivered 1979, has been diverted to AF
		21	Musketeer Sport	Lightplane	(1978)			
	Yugoslavia	1		Training ship	(1978)	1980	(1)	
8 Iran	Italy	75	CH-47C Chinook	Hel	1977	(1978)	(10)	At least 20 delivered; remainder under production; will probably be transferred to Italian AF
						(1979)	(10)	
		100	Seakiller/Marte	AShM	(1978)	(1978)	(50)	Ongoing dispute concerning delay of deliveries; according to Sistel spokesman, some 50 missiles remain to be delivered
	United Kingdom	1		Support ship	1974			Ship named 'Kharg'; embargoed after taking of US hostages
8 Iraq	Argentina	(20)	IA-58A Pucara	Trainer/COIN	(1980)			Order not finalized

Brazil	. .	EE-11 Urutu	APC	(1979)	1979	(50)	Total number sold: 2 000 EE-9, EE-11 and EE-17; being delivered at rate of 10 EE-9/11/17 per month from Jul 1979
					1980	(100)	
	. .	EE-17 Sucuri	TD	1979	1980	(150)	
	. .	EE-9 Cascavel	Recce AC	(1979)	1979	(50)	
					1980	(100)	
France	4	Mirage F-1B	Trainer	1977	(1980)	4	
	24	Mirage F-1C	Fighter/interc	1979			Second order, according to French press; reduced from 36 due to wish to buy Mirage-2000
	32	Mirage F-1C	Fighter/interc	1977	1980	12	First batch of 12 delivered Dec 1980 out of total order for 60 F-1Cs
	36	SA-330L Puma	Hel	1979			Ordered Jul 1979
	(40)	SA-342K Gazelle	Hel	(1978)	(1979)	(20)	Incl in $3 000 mn package deal together with Mirage, Sagaie, AMX-30, HOT and Exocet
					(1980)	(20)	
	12	Super Frelon	Hel	1976	1976	(4)	
					1977	(4)	
					1980	(4)	
	100	AMX-30	MBT	1978	(1979)	(50)	
					(1980)	(50)	
	. .	ERC-90S Sagaie	AC	(1978)	1979	(50)	
					1980	(50)	
	360	HOT	ATM	1979	1980	(360)	Arming Gazelle helicopters now being delivered
	. .	R-440 Crotale	Landmob SAM	(1979)			
	. .	R-530	AAM	1979			On order
	(144)	R-550 Magic	AAM	1977	1980	(144)	Arming Mirage fighters
	. .	SS-11	ATM	1979			On order
Indonesia	. .	Bo-105CB	Hel	1980			Undisclosed number ordered; to be armed with French ATWs
Italy	8	AB-212ASW	Hel	1980			
	6	SH-3D Sea King	Hel	1980			Recently ordered for VIP use
	. .	Aspide/Albatros	ShAM/ShShM	1979			Arming 4 Lupo Class frigates; designation unconfirmed
	. .	Seakiller-2	ShShM	1979			Arming 4 Lupo Class frigates; designation unconfirmed
	4	Lupo Class	Frigate	1979			Armed with Aspide/Albatros ShAM and Seakiller ShShM
	. .	Sauro Class	Submarine	(1980)			Total cost: $1 200 mn; incl training and assistance in setting up shipyard in Iraq
	1	Stromboli Class	Tanker	1979			Support ship; ordered with 4 Lupo Class frigates and 6 Wadi Class corvettes

Region code/ Recipient	Supplier	No. ordered	Weapon designation	Weapon description	Year of order	Year of delivery	No. delivered	Comments
		6	Wadi Class	Corvette	1979			
	Switzerland	48	AS-202 Bravo	Trainer	1978	1979	(20)	
						1980	(20)	
		(52)	PC-7	Trainer	1979	1980	(10)	
	USSR	. .	Il-76 Candid	Transport	1978	1979	(6)	
						1980	(6)	
		. .	Mi 24 Hind-D	Hel	(1977)	1979	(20)	
						1980	(20)	
		. .	MiG-25 Foxbat-A	Fighter/interc	1979	1979	(5)	Delivered 1979-80
						1980	(5)	
		50	MiG-27	Fighter/strike	(1979)	(1979)	(7)	
						1980	(8)	
		. .	M-1973	SPH	(1980)	1980	(20)	The USSR has delivered 122-mm and 152-mm SPHs during summer 1980; probably of type M-1973 and M-1974
		. .	M-1974	SPH	1979	1980	(20)	
		600	T-62	MBT	1976	1977	(150)	
						1978	(150)	
						1979	(150)	
						(1980)	(150)	
		(150)	T-72	MBT	1980			Large batch on order; no deliveries during war with Iran
		. .	SA-6 Gainful	Landmob SAM	1979	(1980)	(90)	Believed to have received a limited number
		. .	SCUD-B	Landmob SSM	(1978)			On order in addition to 12 in service
		. .		LST	1979			Ordered Jan 1979
		3		Submarine	1979			Ordered Jan 1979
8 Israel	USA	38	F-15A Eagle	Fighter/interc	1978	1978	(5)	Incl in US sales package to Middle East; approved Feb 1978; total cost incl 75 F-16A fighters
						1979	(15)	
						1980	(3)	
		75	F-16A	Fighter/strike	1978	1980	31	First delivery Jul 1980; 8 out of 31 delivered 1980 are F-16B trainer versions; total cost incl training and test equipment
						(1981)	(44)	
		25	Model 500MD	Hel	1978	1980	25	Gunship version; armed with TOW
		(5)	RU-21E	Recce	(1979)	(1980)	(5)	Ex-USAF; estimated order number
		200	M-109-A12B	SPH	1979			
		800	M-113-A2	APC	(1979)	1980	(660)	Included in peace treaty arms package

		56	M-548	Cargo	1979			
		98	M-577-A2	CPC	1979			
		200	M-60-A3	MBT	(1980)	1980	(100)	
						1981	(100)	
		25	M-88-A1	ARV	1979			Letter of offer announced
		600	AGM-65A	ASM	1979	1980	(250)	Included in peace treaty arms package
		600	AIM-9L	AAM	1979	1980	(250)	Ordered Sep 1979; incl in peace treaty arms package; arming F-16s
		. .	BGM-71A TOW	ATM	(1979)			
		250	Chaparral	Landmob SAM	(1979)			Congress requested to approve purchase; for training and stocks
		5000	Dragon FGM-77A	ATM	1979	1980	(2500)	Ordered Jul 1980; for delivery 1980-81
						(1981)	(2500)	
		100	MIM-23B Hawk	Landmob SAM	1979			Pending congressional approval
		100	RGM-84A Harpoon	ShShM	(1979)			At least 100 ordered to complement Gabriel; also probably ordered AShM version for F-4
		2	Flagstaff-2	Hydrofoil FPB	1977			Prior to possible licence production of 10
13 Ivory Coast	France	6	Alpha Jet	Trainer	1977	1980	(4)	
						1981	(2)	
		7	ERC-90S Sagaie	AC	(1979)	1980	7	Delivered Apr 1980
		6	M3-VDA	AAV	(1979)	1980	6	
		13	VAB	APC	1979	1980	(13)	Ordered Dec 1979; delivery started mid-1980
8 Jordan	France	36	Mirage F-1C	Fighter/interc	1979			Agreed in principle to purchase instead of F-16, vetoed by USA; Saudi Arabia funding; some sources report 17 on order
	Iraq	36	M-60-A1	MBT	1980	1980	36	Captured from Iran and presented to Jordan as a gift
	United Kingdom	5	Bulldog-125	Trainer	1980			
		275	Shir-1	MBT	1979			UK hopes to sell, out of cancelled Iranian order
	USA	57	F-5E Tiger-2	Fighter	1974	1975	(8)	
						1976	(8)	
						1977	(8)	
						1978	(8)	
						1979	(8)	
						1980	(8)	
		6	F-5F Tiger-2	Trainer	1979			Pending congressional approval; deal incl AIM-9 AAMs and 20-mm guns

Region code/ Recipient	Supplier	No. ordered	Weapon designation	Weapon description	Year of order	Year of delivery	No. delivered	Comments
		10	Model 209 AH-1S	Hel	(1979)			US government approved sale but contract not final; Saudi Arabia refuses funding
		8	Model 500D	Hel	1980			
		4	S-76 Spirit	Hel	(1979)	1980	2	
		78	M-109-A2	SPG	1980			In addition to 156 in service
		29	M-110-A2	SPH	1980			Ordered Jan 1980
		100	M-113-A1	ICV	1979			US letter of offer Apr 1979, although Jordan was denied export licence in FY 1978 for M-113
		87	M-113-A2	APC	1980			Ordered Jan 1980
		100	M-60-A3	MBT	(1979)			Requested Jul 1979; US government app-roved sale; to replace M-47 and Centurion; will order another 100
		100	M-60-A3	MBT	1980			Requested in addition to 100 previously ordered
		. .	AIM-9J	AAM	1979			Contract confirmed Aug 1979; for 6 F-5Fs
		60	BGM-71A TOW	ATM	(1980)			Pending Saudi Arabia funding; for 10 Model 209 hel
		. .	Dragon FGM-77A	ATM	1980			On order; delivery delayed due to tension in Syria
10 Kampuchea	USSR	2	Mi-8 Hip	Hel	1980	1980	2	Delivered Jun 1980
		. .	MiG-21F	Fighter	(1980)	1980		Unspecified number reportedly delivered delivered
13 Kenya	United Kingdom	12	Hawk T-52	Adv trainer	1979	1980	(12)	
		40	MBT-3	MBT	1979			In addition to 38 previously ordered; probably recce and ARV versions
		38	MBT-3	MBT	1978	1979	(12)	
						1980	(26)	
		. .	Rapier	Landmob SAM	1979			Ordered Mar 1979
		4		PB	1980			On order from Vosper; will also order 4 450-t FPBs
	USA	1980	F-5F Tiger-2	Trainer	(1980)			Pending congressional approval; in addition to 2 in service

		32	Model 500MD	Hel	1979			Ordered Mar 1979; for border defence against Somalia and Uganda; Hughes received $31 mn contract from US Army for MAP to Kenya; 15 gunship and 15 TOW
		1	Navajo	Transport	1980	1980	1	For VIP transport
		2100	BGM-71A TOW	ATM	1979			Arming Model 500MD hel
10 Korea, South	USA	6	C-130H Hercules	Transport	1977			Pending congressional approval
		37	F-4E Phantom	Fighter	1977	(1979)	(19)	
						(1980)	(18)	
		14	F-5F Tiger-2	Trainer	1978	1979	14	Bringing total to 20
		27	Model 205 UH-1H	Hel	1977			On order
		56	OH-6A Cayuse	Hel	(1978)			On order
		37	M-109-A2	SPG	1978			Ordered Aug 1978
		200	AGM-65A	ASM	1977			On order
		600	AIM-9L	AAM	1975	1977	60	
						1978	200	
						1979	220	
						1980	120	
		1800	BGM-71A TOW	ATM	1979	(1980)	(360)	DoD notified Congress about planned sale Apr 1980; order incl 10 launchers
		112	RGM-84A Harpoon	ShShM	1975			For 7 PSMM-5 FPBs
		1	Gearing Class	Destroyer	(1979)			
8 Kuwait	Germany, FR	8	Type TNC-45	FPB	1980			Ordered May 1980
	Singapore	2		Landing craft	1978			Ordered in addition to 3 in service
	USA	72	M-113-A2	APC	(1980)			Pending congressional approval; 20 out of 72 ordered are ambulance version; total cost incl M-901 TOW, M-577-A2 and M-125-A2
		2	M-125-A2	APC	(1980)			
		14	M-577-A2	CPC	(1980)			
		6	M-901 TOW	ICV	1980			
		1350	BGM-71A TOW	ATM	1979			Incl 47 launchers
		32	MIM-23B Hawk	Landmob SAM	1979			Requested Sep 1979; incl containers, radar, spare parts, support equipment, training and 2 years of technical assistance
	USSR	. .	FROG-7	Landmob SSM	(1978)	(1979)	(50)	Displayed Feb 1980; also designated Luna
						(1980)	(50)	
		. .	SA-6 Gainful	Landmob SAM	1978	1979	(45)	According to local sources; total cost: incl SA-7, $100 mn
						(1980)	(45)	
		. .	SA-7 Grail	Port SAM	1979	(1979)	(250)	
						(1980)	(250)	

Region code/ Recipient	Supplier	No. ordered	Weapon designation	Weapon description	Year of order	Year of delivery	No. delivered	Comments
		. .	SCUD-B	Landmob SSM	(1978)	(1978)		Unknown number recently delivered; launchers: Maz-543 vehicle
10 Laos	USSR	(6)	Shmel Class	PB	(1980)	1980	6	River patrol boats reportedly delivered 1980
8 Lebanon	France	. .	SA-330L Puma	Hel	1978	1980	(6)	Ordered Nov 1978; total cost incl FPBs, AMX-13/30 and Gazelles
		(40)	SA-330L Puma	Hel	1980			Ordered Mar 1980
		4	SA-342K Gazelle	Hel	1979	1980	4	Armed with SS-11 and SS-12
		70	AMX-13	LT	1978			
		30	AMX-30	MBT	1978			
		(96)	SS-11	ATM	1979	1980	(96)	Arming SA-342 hel
		(96)	SS-12	ShShM	1979	1980	(96)	Arming SA-342 hel
	Hungary	(60)	T-34	LT	(1979)	1980	60	Delivered Jul 1980 for PLO; probably from USSR but channeled through Hungary
	Italy	6	AB-212	Hel	1979	(1980)	(6)	Ordered Jul 1979; follow-up order
		5		PB	1980			Ordered Feb 1980
	United Kingdom	2	Tracker Class	FPB	1980			On order from Fairey Marine; for customs duties
	USA	50	M-113-A1	ICV	(1978)			On order; in addition to 80 in use
		69	M-113-A2	APC	(1979)			Required Sep 1979; total cost incl M-125s and M-577s
		27	M-125-A2	APC	1979			
		4	M-577-A2	CPC	(1979)			
		100	BGM-71A TOW	ATM	(1979)	1980	100	Delivered Aug 1980 with 3 000 M-16 rifles
13 Lesotho	Germany, FR	1	Do-27	Transport	1980	(1980)	1	
		1	DO-28B-1	Lightplane	1980	(1980)	1	
13 Liberia	Sweden	3	Type CG-27	CPB	(1979)	1980	3	For Coast Guard; delivered Aug 1980; unarmed
12 Libya	Brazil	(200)	EE-11 Urutu	APC	1978	(1979) 1980	(100) (100)	Used in military operation 1980
	Canada	10	DHC-6	Transport	1979			

	France	. .	R-530	AAM	(1979)			On order
		10	Combattante-3	FPB	1975	1979	1	
						1980	1	
	Italy	(168)	OTOMAT-1	ShShM	1977	1978	(12)	For 10 Combattante-2G FPBs and 4 Wadi Class corvettes
						1979	(24)	
						1980	(36)	
		28	CH-47C Chinook	Hel	(1978)	(1979)	(8)	On order
						1980	(12)	
		20	G-222L	Transport	1978			On order
		. .	S-61R	Hel	1980			
		200	Leopard-1	MBT	1978	1980	75	
		. .	Type 6616M	AC	1979			On order
		4	Wadi Class	Corvette	1974	1978	1	Last of 4 launched
						1979	1	
						1980	(2)	
	Netherlands	1	F-27 MK-600	Transport	(1979)			
	Turkey	1		LST	1980			
		1	SAR-33	GB	1980			
	USA	1	Model 212	Hel	1978			On order in addition to 1 in service
	USSR	26	Mi 24 Hind-D	Hel	(1978)	1978	(10)	According to Arab sources, Libya was first non-WTO customer; reportedly flown by Soviet pilots; delivered Mar 1979
						1979	(10)	
						1980	(6)	
		3	Foxtrot Class	Submarine	1978			On order in addition to 3 in service
		. .	Osa-2 Class	FPB	1975	1980	3	Total Osa-2 deliveries: 1976-1, 1977-4, 1978-1, 1979-3, 1980-3
	Yugoslavia	50	G-2AE Galeb	Trainer/strike	1975	1978	(6)	
						1979	(14)	
						1980	(18)	
13 Madagascar	United Kingdom	2	HS-748-2	Transport	1979	1980	2	
	USSR	(1)	An-26 Curl	Transport	(1980)	1980	(1)	At least 1 delivered
		15	MiG-21F	Fighter	1980	1980	(8)	Being delivered
		2	Yak-40 Codling	Transport	(1979)	1979	1	New military and economic aid agreement signed during President's visit to Moscow in 1979; for VIP transport
						1980	1	
13 Malawi	Germany, FR	6	Do-27	Transport	(1978)	1979	3	Ex-Belgian Army; refurbished in FR Germany
						1980	3	
		12	Do-28D-2	Transport	1979	1980	(6)	Ordered Apr 1979
	United Kingdom	1	Skyvan-3M	Transport	1979	1980	1	Ordered Dec 1979; delivered Jun 1980
10 Malaysia	Germany, FR	1		Supply ship	(1978)			Launched Jul 1980
	Indonesia	12	Bo-105CB	Hel	1980			

Region code/ Recipient	Supplier	No. ordered	Weapon designation	Weapon description	Year of order	Year of delivery	No. delivered	Comments
	Spain	4	C-212C Aviocar	Transport	(1980)			On order for AF
	Switzerland	(12)	PC-7	Trainer	(1980)			Undisclosed number on order to replace Bulldog
	USA	88	A-4E Skyhawk	Bomber	1980	1980	(44)	Pending congressional approval; probably version G from USAF surplus stocks
						1981	(44)	
		3	C-130H Hercules	Transport	(1980)	1980	3	Specially equipped for maritime patrol
		1	F-5E Tiger-2	Fighter	1979			On order; replacement
		4	F-5F Tiger-2	Trainer	(1980)			US letter of offer Apr 1979; incl logistics and support equipment
		2	RF-5E Tiger-2	Recce	1980			US letter of offer; total cost incl spares and support
		. .	AIM-9J	AAM	(1978)			
14 Mexico	France	10	SA-315B Lama	Hel	1979			Ordered Nov 1979
	Spain	6		FPB	1980			On order for Coast Guard
	Switzerland	38	PC-7	Trainer	1978	1979	(6)	
						1980	(6)	
	United Kingdom	36	BN-2A Islander	Transport	1980	1980	(21)	
						(1981)	(15)	
	USA	3	HU-16A Albatros	ASW/mar patrol	1979	1980	3	Ordered Nov 1979
		1	Gearing Class	Destroyer	(1980)			
12 Morocco	France	24	Alpha Jet	Trainer	1978	1979	(4)	
						1980	(8)	
		24	SA-342K Gazelle	Hel	1980			Morocco altered decision to buy Model 500MD and chose Gazelle instead
		. .	AML-90	AC	(1978)			On order
		100	AMX-10RC	Recce AC	(1978)	1980	2	To be delivered 1980-81
						(1981)	(98)	
		(400)	VAB	APC	(1979)	1979	(100)	Delivery has started
						1980	(200)	
		6	P-32 Type	CPB	1976			On order in addition to 6 in service
		2	PR-72 Type	FPB	1976			On order in addition to 2 in service
	Germany, FR	(10)	Do-28D-2	Transport	(1979)			Decided to purchase unspecified number
	Italy	6	A-109 Hirundo	Hel	1979	1980	6	Ordered Aug 1979
		6	AB-212	Hel	1980			On order
		6	CH-47C Chinook	Hel	1977	1980	6	Option on 6 more

		19	Model 206B	Hel	1980			Transport version on order
	Spain	1	F-30 Class	Frigate	1977			Spanish designation: Descubierta Class
		4	Lazarga Class	FPB	1977			
	USA	20	F-5E Tiger-2	Fighter	1980			Incl in $245 mn package
		12	Model 209 AH-1S	Hel	1978			
		6	OV-10A Bronco	Trainer/COIN	1980			
		40	M-163 Vulcan	AAV	(1979)			40 more Vulcan cannons ordered for M-113
		. .	AGM-65A	ASM	1980			USA approved sale for use with 20 F-5Es; pending congressional approval
		. .	BGM-71A TOW	ATM	1980			For 12 of 24 Model 500MDs; order now uncertain due to Moroccan choice of Gazelles instead of 500MDs
13 Mozambique	Netherlands	2		FPB	(1978)	1980	2	2 patrol craft delivered from Rijkswerf; deal incl 2 tugs; delivered Jul 1980
	USSR	. .	MiG-23	Fighter	(1979)			
13 Niger	France	1	Noratlas 2501	Transport	(1979)	1980	(1)	Ex-French AF
	Germany, FR	2	Do-28D-1	Transport	(1979)			On order
13 Nigeria	France	12	Alpha Jet	Trainer	1979			On order
		36	MM-38 Exocet	ShShM	1977			For Combattante-3 class
		3	Combattante-3B	FPB	1977			First launched Jun 1980
	Germany, FR	1	Meko-360H	Frigate	1978	(1981)	1	Sea trials to start Mar 1981
		3	S-143 Type	FPB	1977	1980	1	First delivered in 1980; to be armed with Otomat
	Italy	(36)	OTOMAT-1	ShShM	1977	1980	(12)	For 3 S-143 Class FPBs
		15		CPB	1978			On order from Intermarine; for Coast Guard
	Netherlands	6		PB	1980			For river patrol
	United Kingdom	5	Bulldog-120	Trainer	1980			Has previously purchased 36
		18	Seacat	ShAM/ShShM	1975	1979	(9)	For Erinmi Class corvettes
						1980	9	
		2	Erinmi Class	Corvette	1975	1979	1	
						1980	1	
	USA	6	CH-47C Chinook	Hel	1977			On order
8 Oman	France	4	SA-330L Puma	Hel	(1979)	1980	4	
		. .	MM-38 Exocet	ShShM	1980			4 launchers on new FPBs on order from the UK

Region code/ Recipient	Supplier	No. ordered	Weapon designation	Weapon description	Year of order	Year of delivery	No. delivered	Comments
	Sweden	. .		CPB	1980			Karlskrona SY signed contract for delivery 1981; cost $3.1 mn; no government export permission yet; arms: 1×20mm cannon
	United Kingdom	12	Jaguar	Fighter	1980			Ordered Jul 1980; in addition to 12 in service
		10	Scorpion FV-101	LT	1980	1980	(10)	Ordered Apr 1980; for delivery 1980
		1		FPB	1980			Ordered Mar 1980
	USA	1	C-130H Hercules	Transport	(1980)			Pending congressional approval
		. .	M-60-A3	MBT	(1979)	1980	(50)	Shown in military parade Nov 1980
		250	AIM-9P	AAM	1979	1980	(250)	Requested Oct 1979; to protect Strait of Hormuz
9 Pakistan	Argentina	400	TAM	MT	1977			
	China	(65)	F-6bis	Fighter	(1979)	1980	(65)	Also designated A-5 Fantan-A
		1000	T-59	MBT	(1980)			China has delivered about 50/year
		20	CSA-1	SAM	(1979)	1980	(20)	SAMs deployed Jul 1980; designation unconfirmed
		2	Romeo Class	Submarine	(1980)	1980	2	Handed over to Pakistan in Karachi
	France	24	FT-337 Milirole	Trainer	1980			
		40	Mirage F-1C	Fighter/interc	1980			On order
		32	Mirage-3E	Fighter/bomber	1978	1980	(16)	Being delivered; Pakistan may also order 18 Mirage-3Es and 30-40 F-1Cs
		18	Mirage-5	Fighter	1980			On order
		. .	R-530	AAM	1980			Undisclosed number on order
		(192)	R-550 Magic	AAM	1978	1980	(96)	For 32 Mirage-3s ordered 1978 and now being delivered
		2	Agosta Class	Submarine	1978	1979 1980	1 1	Built for South Africa but embargoed Jan 1978
	Italy	100	SM-1019E	Lightplane	(1980)			Approved but not signed
	USA	(80)	A-7D Corsair-2	Fighter	(1980)			Order may include Redeye, Hawk and TOW missiles; USA offers to sell but Pakistani Government reluctant to accept; acc to some sources no deal now definite
		. .	M-113-A1	ICV	(1978)			On order; 550 in service
		350	AIM-9P	AAM	(1978)	1979 1980	20 330	

		2	Gearing Class	Destroyer	1980	1980	2	In addition to 2 delivered in 1977 1977
11 Papua New Guinea	Australia	2	N-22L Nomad	Coast patrol	1980	(1981)	(2)	In addition to 3 delivered in 1978; total cost incl spares and technical support
15 Paraguay	Argentina	1	C-47	Transport	1980	1980	1	Gift
	Brazil	10	EMB-110	Transport	1977			Ordered by president
		9	EMB-326 Xavante	Trainer/COIN	1979			On order
		(12)	Uirapuru-122A	Trainer/COIN	1979			In addition to 8 already delivered
	Chile	1	UH-12E	Hel	(1980)	1980	1	
15 Peru	Australia	2	N-22L Nomad	Coast patrol	(1978)			For Army
	France	(48)	MM-38 Exocet	ShShM	1977	1979	(16)	For 6 PR-72P Class FPBs
						1980	(32)	
		6	PR-72P Type	FPB	1976	1979	2	Arms: 1x76-mm Oto Melara cannon; 2x40/70-mm Breda-Bofors cannon; 2x20-mm Oerlikon cannon
						1980	4	
	Germany, FR	4	Type 209	Submarine	1976	1980	1	In addition to 2 in service
	Italy	(14)	MB-339A	Trainer/strike	1980			For delivery within 18 months
		96	Aspide/Albatros	ShAM/ShShM	1975	1978	48	For Lupo Class frigates
		96	OTOMAT-1	ShShM	1974	1978	48	For Lupo Class frigates
	Netherlands	1		Destroyer	(1978)	1980	1	ASW destroyer 'Villar'
		2	Friesland Class	Destroyer	1980	1980	2	'Amsterdam' and 'Limburg' to be re-equipped with ShAM and ShShM
	USA	5	C-130H Hercules	Transport	1980			Total cost incl 18 T-37B trainers
		18	T-37B	Trainer	1980			
	USSR	16	Su-22 Fitter-C	Fighter/bomber	1980			
		200	T-55	MBT	(1978)			On order; in addition to 250 T-54/55 in service
		100	SA-7 Grail	Port SAM	(1978)			On order
10 Philippines	Netherlands	3	F-27 Maritime	Mar patrol	1980	1981	3	Ordered Apr 1980
	USA	18	Model 205 UH-1H	Hel	1980			Ordered Jun 1980; part of base facility agreement
		18	Model 500MD	Hel	1979			Ordered Aug 1979
		18	OV-10A Bronco	Trainer/COIN	(1980)			President Carter agreed to sell; production-line to be re-opened
8 Qatar	France	6	Alpha Jet	Trainer	1979	1980	6	First sale in Middle East
		14	Mirage F-1C	Fighter/interc	1980			

Region code/ Recipient	Supplier	No. ordered	Weapon designation	Weapon description	Year of order	Year of delivery	No. delivered	Comments
		. .	SA-330 Puma	Hel	1980			Small number recently ordered
		(2)	SA-342L Gazelle	Hel	(1979)	1980	2	
		. .	VAB	APC	(1979)	1980	(10)	Delivery started
		(50)	MM-38 Exocet	ShShM	1980			Arming 3 Combattante-3 FPBs on order from France
		(50)	MM-40 Exocet	ShShM	1980			First coastal defence application of Exocet; total cost incl 3 missile FPBs armed with MM-38 Exocet
		3	Combattante-3	FPB	1980			Ordered Sep 1980; cost incl MM-38 Exocet missiles
	USA	. .	MIM-23B Hawk	Landmob SAM	1977			Unconfirmed order
14 St Vincent & the Grenadines	United Kingdom	1		FPB	1980			On order for Coast Guard; for delivery 1981
8 Saudi Arabia	Austria	. .	Panzerjager K	TD	1980			First batch to arrive in June for trials
	France	38	Mirage F-1A	Fighter/ground attack	(1980)			Possibly ordered for other Arab country; order uncertain
		(24)	SA-365N	Hel	1980			20 to be armed with AS-15TT; for use on 4 frigates on order from France
		200	AMX-10	AC	1979			Several hundred of unspecified type ordered
		650	AMX-30	MBT	1975	1975	(60)	
						1976	(60)	
						1977	(60)	
						1978	(60)	
						1979	(60)	
						1980	(60)	
		. .	AS-15TT	ASM	1980			Arming SA-365N Dauphin hel on 4 guided missile frigates
		. .	MM-40 Exocet	ShShM	1978			For coastal defence
		. .	OTOMAT-2	ShShM	1980			Arming 4 guided missiles frigates
		. .	R-440 Crotale	Landmob SAM	1980	(1980)	(50)	In addition to earlier order for Shahine version
		. .	Shahine	Landmob SAM	1974			One section delivered every third month since Jan 1980

	4	F-2000 Class	Frigate	1980			Total cost incl Otomat, Dauphin hel, AS-15TT and 2 fuel supply ships; France's most important single arms deal to date
	8	P-32 Type	CPB	1976			Displacement: 90t
	2		Support ship	1980			Fuel supply ship; displacement: 17 000t; probably Durance Class
Germany, FR	. .	Marder	APC	1977			
Spain	40	C-212A Aviocar	Transport	1979			
United Kingdom	100	Fox FV-721	AC	1974	1977	50	
USA	1	B-747-131	Transport	1977			On order
	5	C-130H Hercules	Transport	(1979)	1980	5	2 bought on behalf of North Yemen; 3 for use of official departments
	4	E-3A Sentry	AEW	1980	1980	(4)	Transferred on loan Oct 1980; Saudi Arabia has expressed interest in purchasing
	60	F-15A Eagle	Fighter/interc	1978			Incl in US sales package to Middle East; approved in Feb 1978
	2	F-15C Eagle	Fighter	1980			DoD offered to sell; to be retained in USA until needed as replacement
	2	KC-130H	Transport	(1979)	1980	2	Delivered Dec 1980
	15	TF-15A Eagle	Trainer	1978			Incl in US sales package to Middle East; approved in Feb 1978
	50	M-110-A1	SPH	(1980)			Offered as launchers for TOW ; cost incl 1 000 TOW missiles
	. .	M-163 Vulcan	AAV	(1977)			
	118	M-60-A1	MBT	1979	1980	32	Replacing 32 sent to North Yemen; order incl 86 tank chassis for air defence; to be armed with 33-mm Oerlikon AAG
	94	V-150 Commando	APC	1978			For National Guard
	579	V-150 Commando	APC	(1980)			In addition to 200 in service
	916	AGM-65A	ASM	1979			Proposed sale Dec 1979 to arm F-5 fighters; part of large package deal to Saudi Arabia
	660	AIM-9P	AAM	(1980)			Included in large proposed sale to Saudi Arabia; pending congressional approval
	1000	BGM-71A TOW	ATM	(1980)			Incl 50 M-110-A1 guided missile launchers; DoD proposed sale
	1292	Dragon FGM-77A	ATM	1979	1980	1292	Incl 172 trackers, support equipment, training and maintenance
	(1458)	MIM-23B Hawk	Landmob SAM	1974	(1978)	(400)	Replacing old Hawk systems
					(1979)	(400)	
					(1980)	(400)	

Region code/ Recipient	Supplier	No. ordered	Weapon designation	Weapon description	Year of order	Year of delivery	No. delivered	Comments
		. .	MIM-43A Redeye	Port SAM	1977			On order
		(96)	RGM-84A Harpoon	ShShM	1978	1980	(24)	For 4 Badr Class corvettes
						1981	(72)	
		(108)	RGM-84A Harpoon	ShShM	1977			For 9 As Saddiq Class FPBs
		9	As Saddiq Class	FPB	1977	1980	3	Ordered Feb 1977
						(1981)	(4)	
		4	Badr Class	Corvette	1977	1980	1	Ordered Sep 1977
13 Senegal	France	1	PR-72 Type	FPB	1979	1981	(1)	Ordered Nov 1979; for delivery 1981; arms: 2x76-mm Oto Melara cannon
11 Seychelles	Libya	1	Rallye-235GT	Lightplane	1980	1980	1	Gift
	United Kingdom	1	BN-2A Defender	Transport	1980	1980	1	Gift
10 Singapore	France	. .	T-33A	Trainer	1979	1980	(12)	Ex-French AF
		150	AMX-13	LT	1978	1980	30	
	Italy	6	SF-260W Warrior	Trainer/COIN	1979	1980	6	Follow-on order to 16 purchased in 1971
	USA	4	C-130H Hercules	Transport	(1978)	1980	4	Singapore also operates 4 C-130Bs
		6	F-5E Tiger-2	Fighter	1980			DoD notified Congress; in addition to 21 F-5E/Fs already in service; total cost incl spares and support equipment
		(250)	M-113-A1	ICV	(1978)	1979	(125)	
						1980	(125)	
		200	AIM-9P	AAM	1978	1979	40	In addition to 200 AIM-9Js delivered in 1979
						1980	160	
		. .	MIM-23B Hawk	Landmob SAM	1979			Ordered Jul 1979; 3 systems ordered
13 Somalia	China	12	F-6	Fighter	(1979)	1980	12	Unconfirmed
	Italy	4	AB-212	Hel	1980			On order
		4	G-222	Transport	(1979)	(1980)	4	Negotiating; probably for version with British engine similar to aircrafts for Libya
		4	P-166	Transport	1979	1980	4	May be for civilian use
		6	SM-1019E	Lightplane	1979			

		. .	Type 6614	APC	1979	1979 1980		On order
13 South Africa	France	. .	AS-12	ASM	1974	1975	(48)	
						1976	(360)	
						1977	(360)	
						1978	(360)	
						1979	(360)	
						1980	(360)	
	Israel	(108)	Gabriel-2	ShShM	1977			Arming 6 new Reshef Class FPBs now being built under licence in Durban
9 Sri Lanka	China	2	Shanghai-2 Cl	GB	(1979)	1980	2	Fast gunboats recently presented to Sri Lanka as gift
13 Sudan	Brazil	6	EMB-111	Mar patrol	(1979)			On order; for AF
	China	12	F-6	Fighter	(1979)	1980	12	Unconfirmed
	France	16	Mirage-5	Fighter	1977			Incl 2 trainers
		10	SA-330L Puma	Hel	1977			On order; unconfirmed
	Germany, FR	20	Bo-105C	Hel	1977	1979	(10)	Some for police force
						1980	(10)	
	USA	2	C-130H Hercules	Transport	1979			Ordered Feb 1979; 6 C-130Es in AF use
		10	F-5E Tiger-2	Fighter	1979			First requested in 1977; congressional approval received in 1978
		2	F-5F Tiger-2	Trainer	1979			
		80	M-113-A2	APC	1979			Pending congressional approval
		8	M-163 Vulcan	AAV	1980			30-mm version of the basic 20-mm air defence system; pending congressional approval
		50	M-60-A1	MBT	1979			Ordered Feb 1979
8 Syria	France	50	SA-342K Gazelle	Hel	1979	1980	(30)	Being delivered
		. .	HOT	ATM	1978	1980		For Gazelle hel
	Germany, FR	. .	AS-34 Kormoran	AShM	1977			On order; Euromissile sale
	USA	4	L-100-20	Transport	1980			
	USSR	. .	MiG-25 Foxbat-A	Fighter/interc	(1979)	1979	(12)	Large number received 1979-80 acc to Syrian newspaper 'Al Anba'; probably more on order
						1980	(50)	
		. .	MiG-27	Fighter/strike	(1980)	1980	(15)	More on order in addition to 45 in use; order incl T-72s
		(100)	BMP-1	MICV	(1979)	1980	(100)	
		500	T-72	MBT	1980	1980	(130)	

Region code/ Recipient	Supplier	No. ordered	Weapon designation	Weapon description	Year of order	Year of delivery	No. delivered	Comments
		. .	FROG-7	Landmob SSM	1979			Ordered Nov 1979; version 7 unconfirmed
		. .	SA-8 Gecko	Landmob SAM	1977			On order; possibly being delivered
10 Taiwan	Belgium	52	F-104G	Fighter	1980			USA recently approved sale of F-104G surplus offered for sale by Belgium; unit cost: $2-4 mn
	Netherlands	2	Zwaardvis Class	Submarine	1980			Government decided to sell Dec 1980 after close vote in Parliament
	USA	12	Model 500MD	Hel	(1978)	1979	(6)	
						1980	(6)	
		25	M-109-A2	SPG	1980			Delivery Mar 1983
		50	M-110-A2	SPH	1980			Pending congressional approval
		500	AGM-65A	ASM	1979	(1980)	(200)	For second batch of 48 F-5E/Fs to be produced under licence
		600	AIM-9L	AAM	(1979)	1980	(100)	Approved 1978; delivery Dec 1980-May 1981; for second batch of 39 F-5Es
						(1981)	(500)	
		1013	BGM-71A TOW	ATM	1980			DoD notified Congress; incl 49 launchers
		280	MIM-23B Hawk	Landmob SAM	(1980)			Sale approved by Congress Oct 1980
		90	MIM-23B Hawk	Landmob SAM	(1980)			DoD notified Congress; in addition to 4 battalions already purchased; to enter war reserve
		284	Sea Chaparral	ShAM	1980			Pending congressional approval
		2	Gearing Class	Destroyer	(1980)			DoD notified Congress Jun 1980
13 Tanzania	Canada	2	DHC-5D Buffalo	Transport	1980			Ordered Mar 1980
	Italy	2	CH-47C Chinook	Hel	1980			On order; for delivery 1982
10 Thailand	Indonesia	2	Bo-105CB	Hel	(1979)			
		6	C-212A Aviocar	Transport	(1979)			Option on 20 more
	Italy	2		FPB	(1980)			2 gunboats ordered in addition to 3 Ratcharit Class FPBs delivered in 1979; for delivery late 1982; displacement: 450t
	Spain	1	F-30 Class	Frigate	1980			On order
	USA	3	C-130H Hercules	Transport	1979	1980	3	US letter of offer Apr 1979; incl spares, training and support equipment
		15	F-5E Tiger-2	Fighter	1979			
		3	F-5F Tiger-2	Trainer	1979			
		8	OV-10A Bronco	Trainer/COIN	1980			

		18	S-58T	Hel	(1979)			On order in addition to 18 in service
		6	T-37B	Trainer	(1980)	1980	6	Surplus
		24	M-108	SPH	1979			Letter of offer announced; cost incl 34 M-109-A2s
		(34)	M-109-A2	SPG	1978	1980	(20)	Large number already delivered together with small arms
		40	M-113-A1	ICV	1980	1980	40	In addition to 30 delivered in 1979
		24	M-163 Vulcan	AAV	1980	1980	(12)	Ordered Feb 1980
						1981	(12)	
		(35)	M-48-A5	MBT	(1979)	1979	15	
						1980	20	
		94	V-150 Commando	APC	1978	(1980)	(20)	
		. .	AIM-9P	AAM	(1978)	1979	60	
						1980	200	
		. .	BGM-71A TOW	ATM	(1978)	1980	(215)	First batch arrived Apr 1980
		. .	Dragon FGM-77A	ATM	(1979)	1980	(630)	
13 Togo	France	5	Alpha Jet	Trainer	1977	1980	(5)	For delivery second half of 1980
	USA	1	L-100-20	Transport	(1979)	1980	1	
15 Trinidad-Tobago	Sweden	2	Spica Class	FPB	1978	(1980)	2	For Coast Guard
	United Kingdom	1	Sword Class	FPB	(1978)			On order in addition to 1 in use
12 Tunisia	France	2	C-160 Transall	Transport	(1979)	1980	(2)	
	Germany, FR	3	Type 57M	FPB	(1980)			
	Italy	18	AB-205	Hel	1979	1980	12	
		(100)	Type 6614	APC	1979	(1980)	(100)	
	Sweden	. .	RBS-70	Port SAM	1979			Agreement at Paris Air Show
	USA	1	C-130H Hercules	Transport	1980			Replacing old transport aircraft
		6	Model 212 UH-1N	Hel	1980	(1980)	6	Incl in MAP package after guerilla attack on Gafza
		60	M-113-A1	ICV	1978	1980	30	Total cost incl BGM-71A TOW and M-577
		26	M-163 Vulcan	AAV	1978			Pending congressional approval; Vulcan-Chaparral air defence system
		6	M-577-A1	Cargo	1978			Pending congressional approval
		1320	BGM-71A TOW	ATM	1978			Pending congressional approval; incl 120 practice missiles; total cost: incl M-113-A1 APCs and M-577 vehicles
		328	Chaparral	Landmob SAM	1978			Pending congressional approval; Vulcan-Chaparral air defence system
		300	Chaparral	Landmob SAM	1980			USA plans to sell; in addition to 328 already purchased; version MIM-72F Improved Chaparral

Region code/ Recipient	Supplier	No. ordered	Weapon designation	Weapon description	Year of order	Year of delivery	No. delivered	Comments
8 United Arab Emirates	Germany, FR	6	Jaguar-2 Class	FPB	1977	1979	(2)	
						1980	(2)	
		4	Type TNC-45	FPB	(1979)			First pair launched 1980
	Italy	20	Leopard-1	MBT	1978			
	Sweden	. .	RBS-70	Port SAM	(1980)	1980	(200)	Bofors negotiating via branch company in Singapore; order confirmed Feb 1980; delivery to start Jul 1980
	United Kingdom	. .	Lynx	Hel	(1979)			
		36	Scorpion FV-101	LT	1978			Ordered early 1978
13 Upper Volta	Brazil	1	EMB-110	Transport	(1980)			Reportedly sold; unconfirmed
15 Uruguay	Argentina	3	C-45 Expeditor	Transport	1980	1980	3	Gift
		. .	IA-58A Pucara	Trainer/COIN	1980			Undisclosed number on order
		9	T-28	Trainer	1980	1980	9	Gift
	Austria	. .	Cuirassier	TD	1980			Undisclosed number on order
	Belgium	. .	FN-4RM/62F	AC	1980			Ordered Apr 1980
	Brazil	1	EMB-110B	Transport	(1979)	1980	1	Bringing total to 6 Bandeirantes in service with Uruguayan AF
	France	3	Vigilante	PB	1979			
15 Venezuela	Argentina	(24)	IA-58A Pucara	Trainer/COIN	(1980)			Order incl transfer of production line; deal not finalized
	Germany, FR	2	Type 209	Submarine	1977			On order in addition to 2 in service
	Israel	3	IAI-201 Arava	Transport	1979	1980	3	Earlier delivery made to National Guard
	Italy	8	A-109 Hirundo	Hel	(1979)			Order unconfirmed
		10	AB-212ASW	Hel	(1977)	1979	1	For use on Lupo Class frigates
						1980	2	
		48	Aspide/Albatros	ShAM/ShShM	1977	1979	8	Arming 4 Lupo Class frigates
						1980	16	
		72	OTOMAT-1	ShShM	1975	1980	12	Arming 4 Lupo Class frigates

Recipient	Supplier	No. ordered	Weapon designation	Weapon description	Year of order	Year of delivery	No. delivered	Comments
		6	Lupo Class	Frigate	1975	1980	1	Being delivered; armed with Otomat and Aspide ShShM; carries 1 AB-212 ASW hel; first ship, 'Mariscal Sucre', arrived in Venezuela Jul 1980 after extensive sea trials; 3 more to arrive during 1981
	Poland	. .	An-2 Colt	Lightplane	1980			Undisclosed number on order; first sale in Latin America
10 Vietnam	USSR	1	Polnocny Class	LST	(1980)	1980	1	Ex-USSR
		1	Yurka Class	Ocean mine-sweeper	(1980)	1980	1	
8 Yemen, North	Saudi Arabia	2	C-130H Hercules	Transport	(1979)			Saudi Arabia transferred after purchase from the USA
	USSR	150	BTR-50P	APC	1979	1980	150	Delivered Feb 1980; designation unconfirmed
		(50)	T-62	MBT	1979	(1979)	(50)	Number also reported as 100
		. .	SA-2 Guideline	Landmob SAM	(1979)			Five btys on order
8 Yemen, South	Poland	200	T-55	MBT	1979	(1979)	(100)	
						(1980)	(100)	
	USSR	12	Il-28	Bomber	(1979)	(1980)	12	
		40	MiG-21MF	Fighter	(1980)	1980	(20)	At least 10; will probably receive 40 MiG-21s
		. .	MiG-23	Fighter	1980			Ordered Jun 1980
		(30)	MiG-25 Foxbat-A	Fighter/interc	(1979)	(1980)	(30)	
		20	Su-22 Fitter-C	Fighter/bomber	(1980)	1980	20	
		200	BTR-50P	APC	(1979)	(1979)	(100)	In service
						(1980)	(100)	
		(300)	T-55	MBT	(1980)	1980	300	To follow Polish deliveries of T-55
		. .	T-62	MBT	1980	1980	(50)	Ordered Jun 1980
		. .	ZSU-23-4 Shilka	SPG	(1979)	(1979)	(50)	In service
						(1980)	(50)	
		. .	SA-3 Goa	Landmob SAM	(1979)	(1979)	(50)	
						(1980)	(50)	
		. .	SA-7 Grail	Port SAM	(1979)	(1979)	(200)	
						(1980)	(200)	
		. .	SA-9 Gaskin	Landmob SAM	(1979)	(1979)	(50)	
						(1980)	(50)	
		1	Ropucha Class	LST	(1980)	1980	1	

Region code/ Recipient	Supplier	No. ordered	Weapon designation	Weapon description	Year of order	Year of delivery	No. delivered	Comments
13 Zaire	Italy	6	MB-326KG	Trainer	1979	1979	(3)	
						1980	(3)	
	USA	1	C-130H Hercules	Transport	1980			
13 Zambia	Italy	7	AB-205	Hel	1980			On order
	USSR	16	MiG-21F	Fighter	1980			Confirmed by Zambian government; part of arms package from the USSR
		. .	T-55	MBT	1980			Ordered Feb 1980

Appendix 7B

Register of licensed production of major weapons in industrialized and Third World countries, 1980

See the *SIPRI Yearbook 1979* for sources and methods (appendix 3C, pages 242–55) and for the key to the region codes (page 255).

Conventions and abbreviations used in the following register are listed on page 202.

Region code/ Country	Licenser	No. ordered	Weapon designation	Weapon description	Year of licence	Year of production	No. produced	Comments
I. Industrialized countries								
11 Australia	United Kingdom	14	Fremantle Class	FPB	1977	1980	1	First to be delivered from the UK; the rest to be produced under licence; also designated PCF-420 Class
4 Belgium	Ireland	. .	BDX	APC	1977	(1978)	(50)	Licence-produced version of Timoney
						1979	(50)	
						1980	(50)	
	USA	104	F-16A	Fighter/strike	1977	1979	5	
						1980	(40)	
		12	F-16B	Fighter/strike	1977	1979	5	
						1980	(5)	
		664	AIFV	MICV	(1980)			
		525	M-113-A1	APC	(1980)			Total number ordered: 1 189 incl 664 AIFVs; u.c.: $100 000
4 Canada	Switzerland	177	Cougar	AC	1977	1978	(10)	Canada to licence-produce 443 general purpose armoured vehicles; order incl 243 Grizzlies and 23 Huskies
						1979	(20)	
						1980	(100)	
						(1981)	(47)	
		243	Grizzly	APC	1977	1978	(60)	
						1979	(61)	
						1980	(61)	
						(1981)	(61)	
		23	Husky	ARV	1977	(1979)	(8)	
						(1980)	(8)	
						(1981)	(7)	
	USA	. .	Seasparrow	ShAM/ShShM	1970	1979	50	
						1980	(50)	
3 China	France	50	SA-365N	Hel	1980			Ordered Jul 1980; second batch to be locally assembled; for offshore oil operations; may be equipped with HOT

5	Czechoslovakia	USSR	. .	T-72	MBT	1978	(1980)	(50)	Preparing for production; direct purchase for at least 3 regiments; delivery started Apr 1979
4	France	USA	. .	FR-172K Hawk XP	Trainer	(1975)	1977	25	
							1978	25	
							1979	25	
							1980	(20)	
			. .	FT-337 Milirole	Trainer	1969	1975	12	Designation: FTB-337 Milirole; exported to Africa
							1976	12	
							1977	12	
							1978	12	
							1979	10	
							1980	3	
			. .	Model 172K	Lightplane	1976	1976	1	
							1977	(160)	
							1978	(160)	
							1979	(160)	
							1980	(160)	
			. .	Model 182	Lightplane	1975	1975	(10)	
							1976	(20)	
							1977	(20)	
							1978	35	
							1979	35	
							1980	(40)	
			. .	Model 182RG	Lightplane	1975	1978	(10)	
							1979	(10)	
							1980	30	
4	Germany, FR	USA	9000	AIM-9L	AAM	1977			NATO co-production programme
4	Greece	France	6	Combattante-3	FPB	1975	1980	3	Armed with Penguin ShShM
							(1981)	(3)	
		Netherlands	2	Kortenaer Class	Frigate	(1980)			In addition to 1 purchased directly from Netherlands; to be built at Eleusis Shipyards with Dutch assistance

Region code/ Country	Licenser	No. ordered	Weapon designation	Weapon description	Year of licence	Year of production	No. produced	Comments
4 Italy	Germany, FR	650	Leopard-1	MBT	1973	1974	(30)	
						1975	(50)	
						1976	(50)	
						1977	(75)	
						1978	(75)	
						1979	(100)	
						1980	(150)	
		. .	Cobra-2000	ATM	1974	1974	(500)	
						1975	(1000)	
						1976	(1000)	
						1977	(1000)	
						1978	(1000)	
						1979	(1000)	
						1980	(1000)	
	USA	. .	AB-205A-1	Hel	1969	1977	120	
						1978	120	
						1979	(120)	
						1980	(120)	
		. .	AB-206B-3	Hel	1972	1978	(50)	
						1979	(50)	
						1980	(50)	
		. .	AB-206B-LR	Hel	1978	1979	(50)	Long-range version at test stage
						1980	50	
		87	AB-212ASW	Hel	1975	1978	30	
						1979	30	
						1980	27	
		(126)	CH-47C Chinook	Hel	1968	1977	12	Licence production began in 1970; for Italy, Iran, Libya and Morocco
						1978	12	
						1979	(12)	
						1980	(12)	
		500	Model 500MD	Hel	1976	1977	(12)	
						1978	(12)	
						1979	(20)	
						1980	(20)	
		. .	SH-3D Sea King	Hel	1965	1977	12	In production since 1969
						1978	(12)	
						1979	(12)	
						1980	(2)	

			200	M-109	SPH	1968	1977	18
							1978	18
							1979	18
							1980	18
			. .	M-113-A1	AC	1963	1977	(150)
							1978	(150)
							1979	(150)
							1980	(150)
			. .	Seasparrow	ShAM/ShShM	1968	1978	50
							1979	(50)
							1980	(50)

10	Japan	USA	84	F-15A Eagle	Fighter/interc	1977			Ordered Dec 1977; follow-on order for 23 aircraft has been discussed
			138	F-4EJ Phantom	Fighter	1969	1974	3	First 2 purchased directly; 8 assembled and 130 locally built
							1975	22	
							1976	22	
							1977	22	
							1978	22	
							1979	22	
							1980	22	
							(1981)	(3)	
			115	KV-107/2A-4	Hel	1961	1977	(2)	
							1978	(2)	
							1979	(2)	
							1980	(4)	
			32	KV-107/2A-5	Hel	1962	1978	2	
							1979	(2)	
							1980	(4)	
			. .	Model 214ST	Hel	1980			Joint production programme for military and civilian markets; agreement signed by Bell Textron and Mitsui Oct 1980
			58	OH-6D	Hel	1977	1978	(12)	
							1979	(12)	
							1980	(12)	
			42	P-3C Orion	ASW/mar patrol	1978			Not yet in production
			102	S-61B	Hel	1965	1977	(20)	By Mar 1980, 97 out of 102 ordered were delivered
							1978	(30)	
							1979	(33)	
							1980	(14)	
			51	SH-3B	Hel	1979			On order

Region code/ Country	Licenser	No. ordered	Weapon designation	Weapon description	Year of licence	Year of production	No. produced	Comments
		. .	AIM-7E	AAM	1972	1977	(90)	Total number produced for F-4E fighters: 700; to continue in production for use with F-15 Eagle fighters
						1978	(90)	
						1979	(90)	
						1980	(90)	
		1350	AIM-7F	AAM	(1979)	1980	(50)	Production to start soon for F-15
		. .	MIM-23B Hawk	Landmob SAM	1978	1978	(100)	
						1979	(100)	
						1980	(100)	
		26	Seasparrow	ShAM	1980			Number ordered refers to systems
4 Netherlands	USA	22	F-16A	Fighter	(1980)			In addition to 102 on order; may order 71 more
		102	F-16A	Fighter	1977	1979	7	Order incl 90 F-16As and 12 F-16Bs to be produced under licence; VFW also to produce for Norway
						1980	(15)	
5 Poland	USSR	. .	An-2 Colt	Lightplane	1960	1977	200	
						1978	200	
						1979	200	
						1980	(200)	
		. .	An-28	Transport	1978			Production to start 1980-81
		. .	Mi-2 Hoplite	Hel	(1956)	1979	(200)	In production since 1957; 3000 built end 1979
						1980	(200)	
		. .	T-72	MBT	(1978)	(1980)	(50)	In production
4 Portugal	Netherlands	2	Kortenaer Class	Frigate	1980			On order; 1 to be delivered directly; 2 to be licence-produced
5 Romania	France	130	SA-316B	Hel	1971	1977	(10)	
						1978	(10)	
						1979	(10)	
						1980	(10)	
		(100)	SA-330 Puma	Hel	1977	1978	30	
						1979	35	
						1980	35	
	United Kingdom	25	BAC-111	Transport	1979	1980	(3)	Total cost: $410 mn plus $205 mn for licensed production of Rolls-Royce Spey engine; 20 aircraft for Romanian AF

7 Spain	France	4	Agosta Class	Submarine	1974			Spanish designation: S-70 Class; to be delivered 1980-83
	USA	3	FFG-7 Class	Frigate	1977			
7 Switzerland	Austria	. .	Pinzgauer	LT	1980			Will buy undisclosed number; probably to be partly built by Mowag
	United Kingdom	. .	Rapier	Landmob SAM	1980			Rapier won order after evaluation of RBS-70 and Roland-2; probably to be licence produced; for delivery 1984-87
	USA	53	F-5E Tiger-2	Fighter	1976	1978	(17)	Order number: excl 13 F-5Es and 6 F-5Fs delivered from USA
						1979	(18)	
						1980	(18)	
4 Turkey	Germany, FR	. .	Cobra-2000	ATM	1970			Has 85 systems in use; current status of production programme uncertain
		13	SAR-33 Type	PB	1976	1978	(2)	Prototype delivered from FR Germany 1977 for trials; rest of building in Turkey
						1979	(2)	
						1980	(2)	
		9	Type 209	Submarine	1974	1980	1	Built under licence in addition to 3 delivered from FR Germany
						(1981)	(1)	
	USA	100	Model 500MD	Hel	(1979)			New plant to start licence production within 1 year of contract; planned in-digenization of 30% in 1980, to increase to 80% in 1983; planned production rate: 25-30/year
4 United Kingdom	France	50000	MILAN	ATM	1976	1979	(1500)	
						1980	(3500)	
						(1981)	(5000)	
	USA	. .	Commando MK-2	Hel	1966	1978	20	A total of 239 Sea Kings and Commandos ordered by May 1980
						1979	(20)	
						1980	(20)	
		. .	SH-3D Sea King	Hel	1966	1978	20	
						1979	20	
						1980	(20)	
		17	Sea King HAS-5	Hel	(1979)	1980	2	Version 5 selected instead of version 2
		8000	BGM-71A TOW	ATM	1978			US government offer to UK Army
1 USA	France	6000	Roland-2	Landmob SAM	1974	1980	75	US Roland-2 operational in 1980; first batch incl 3 fire units and 75 missiles; total programme: 6 000
	Switzerland	. .	AU-23A	Transport	1965	1978	20	
						1979	(20)	
						1980	(20)	

Region code/ Country	Licenser	No. ordered	Weapon designation	Weapon description	Year of licence	Year of production	No. produced	Comments
	United Kingdom	336	AV-8B Harrier	Fighter	1975			Designation: Advanced Harrier, UK origin; USA continued study when UK withdrew from joint programme in 1975; for US Marine Corps
		350	Hawk-1	Adv trainer	(1980)			Version of Hawk may replace Buckeye and Skyhawk in US Navy; probably designated VTX-TS; prime contractor: MDD
6 Yugoslavia	France	132	SA-342 Gazelle	Hel	1971	1978 1979 1980	(10) (10) (10)	Estimated production rate: 10/year

II. Third World countries

Region code/ Country	Licenser	No. ordered	Weapon designation	Weapon description	Year of licence	Year of production	No. produced	Comments
15 Argentina	Germany, FR	220	TAM	MT	(1976)	1979 1980	(50) (120)	First tank off production line Jun 1979; production rate: first year 100, then 140
		300	VCI	MT	1976	(1979) 1980	(25) (100)	Similar to Marder MICV
		6	Meko-140	Corvette	1979			Order incl 4 Meko-360 frigates to be built by Blohm & Voss
		2	Type 1400	Submarine	1977			
		3	Type 1700	Submarine	1977			In addition to 1 purchased directly from FR Germany
	United Kingdom	1	Type 42	Frigate	1971			Named 'Santisima Trinidad'
	USA	. .	Arrow-3	Trainer	1977	1978 1979 1980	(10) (10) (10)	Local development of licence-produced Piper aircraft; for use as military trainer
		120	Model 500M	Hel	1972	1977 1978 1979 1980	(12) (12) (12) (12)	Assembly of knocked-down components
15 Brazil	France	200	AS-350M Esquilo	Hel	1978	1979 1980	6 (20)	Ten-year programme
		30	SA-315B Lama	Hel	1978	1979 1980	(3) (3)	France owns 45% of new company; assembly of 30 over 10 years, most for civilian market
		(34)	SA-330L	Hel	1980			On order
	Germany, FR	. .	Cobra-2000	ATM	1973	(1975) (1976)	(10) (100)	In production for Army

						(1977)	(200)	
						(1978)	(200)	
						(1979)	(200)	
						1980	(200)	
	Italy	(150)	AMX	Fighter/ground	1980			Joint production of new Italian fighter/ ground attack aircraft; production to begin in 1982
		184	EMB-326 Xavante	Trainer/COIN	1970	1971	4	AF designation: AT-26 Xavante; initial licence production contract for 112; later increased to a total of 184
						1972	24	
						1973	24	
						1974	24	
						1975	24	
						1976	12	
						1977	24	
						1978	12	
						1979	(12)	
						1980	(12)	
	USA	. .	EMB-810C	Lightplane	1974	1975	27	Designation: Piper Seneca-2; licence production contract incl 6 versions; mostly for civilian market; 10 delivered to Brazilian AF in 1978; production slowed down
						1976	23	
						1977	20	
						1978	48	
						(1979)	(48)	
						1980	(24)	
15 Chile	France	2	Batral Type	LST	1979			Announced Jan 1980 in Chile
15 Colombia	USA	. .		Lightplane	1969	1973	65	By Feb 1980 Colombia had assembled a total of 668 Cessna aircraft of various types
						1974	93	
						1975	(90)	
						1976	(90)	
						1977	(90)	
						1978	(90)	
						1979	(90)	
						1980	(92)	
8 Egypt	United Kingdom	(4000)	Swingfire	ATM	1977	1979	(100)	Arab-British Dynamics Ltd set up with 30% of the capital from BAC and 70% from AOI; initial contract value: $77.6 mn; planned production run: 7 years
						1980	(100)	
	USA	(100)	F-5E Tiger-2	Fighter	(1980)			Agreed in principle; deal may include production of Model-214ST helicopters
		. .	Model 214ST	Hel	(1980)			Egypt is trying to get production licence for Model 214 and F-5E

Region code/ Country	Licenser	No. ordered	Weapon designation	Weapon description	Year of licence	Year of pro- duction	No. produced	Comments
9 India	France	140	SA-315B Lama	Hel	1971	1973	(6)	First 40 assembly only, then licence production of 100 from local raw material
						1974	(10)	
						1975	(10)	
						1976	(10)	
						1977	(10)	
						1978	(10)	
						1979	(10)	
						1980	(10)	
		. .	SA-316B Chetak	Hel	(1962)	1978	(15)	HAL has built 221 since 1965
						1979	(15)	
						1980	(15)	
		. .	SS-11	ATM	1970	1971	100	For licence-produced B-1 Jonga AVs
						1972	500	
						1973	(1000)	
						1974	(1000)	
						1975	(1000)	
						1976	(1000)	
						1977	(1000)	
						1978	(1000)	
						1979	(1000)	
						1980	(1000)	
	Germany, FR	2	Type 209	Submarine	(1980)			Finalizing order; 2 from FR Germany and 2 from India after setting up of production plant
	United Kingdom	. .	Gnat T-2 Ajeet	Trainer	1978			Local development from licence-built Gnat; prototype flight-testing 1980-81
		80	Gnat-2 Ajeet	Fighter	1973	1976	(5)	Local development of licence-built Gnat; total requirement of some 100
						1977	(5)	
						1978	(10)	
						1979	(10)	
						1980	(10)	
		20	HS-748M	Transport	1972	1975	2	Programme to be completed 1983
						1976	2	
						1977	2	
						1978	2	
						1979	2	
						1980	(3)	

			105	Jaguar	Fighter	(1979)			Selected instead of Mirage F-1 and Viggen; contract signed on 6 Oct 1979; first 40 to be delivered from UK followed by at least 110 licence-produced; delivery of first Indian-assembled aircraft late 1981; deal now being re-negotiated by Gandhi administration
			1000	Vijayanta-2	MT	1965	1975 1976 1977 1978 1979 1980	(100) (100) (100) (100) (100) (100)	
			6	Leander Class	Frigate	1964	1980	1	Licence production of 6 Leander Class frigates now completed
		USSR	(95)	An-32 Cline	Transport	1980			Government decision to buy announced Nov 1980
			(50)	MiG-21bis	Fighter	1976	1980	(10)	
			600	T-72	MBT	1980			
10	Indonesia	Belgium	12		FPB	1980			Together with 12 FPBs ordered directly from Belgium
		France	15	SA-330L Puma	Hel	1980			Will include local assembly of SA-332 Super Puma; agreement signed May 1980
		Germany, FR	50	Bo-105CB	Hel	1975	1976 1977 1978 1979 1980	6 6 6 12 (20)	Some components are locally produced
		Spain	82	C-212A Aviocar	Transport	1975	1976 1977 1978 1979 1980	3 7 7 (8) 8	New plant set up in 1976
8	Israel	USA	10	Flagstaff-2	Hydrofoil FPB	1977			To be licence-produced after delivery of first 2 from USA
10	Korea, North	USSR	. .	MiG-21MF	Fighter	1974			First delivery was reportedly planned for 1978 but no information available

Region code/ Country	Licenser	No. ordered	Weapon designation	Weapon description	Year of licence	Year of production	No. produced	Comments
10 Korea, South	Italy	170	Type 6614	APC	1976	1977	20	Not yet in production in Italy
						1978	(20)	
						1979	(50)	
						1980	(50)	
	USA	36	F-5E Tiger-2	Fighter	1980			Negotiating; total cost incl 32 F-5Fs; some funded via FMS; co-assembly planned
		32	F-5F Tiger-2	Trainer	1980			
		. .	Model 500D	Hel	(1979)	(1979)	(50)	Some 100 delivered early 1980
						(1980)	(75)	
		48	Model 500MD	Hel	1976	1978	(10)	
						1979	(10)	
						1980	(10)	
12 Libya	Italy	(160)	SF-260W Warrior	Trainer/COIN	1977			In addition to 80 purchased directly; new assembly plant constructed with Italian assistance
14 Mexico	United Kingdom	10	Azteca Class	CPB	1975	1976	1	
						1979	4	
						1980	2	
						(1981)	(3)	
13 Nigeria	Austria	. .	Cuirassier	TD	1979			Order incl supply of complete factory from Austria
9 Pakistan	China	. .		LT	1978			
		. .		ATM	1978			
	Sweden	25	Supporter	Trainer/strike	1974	1978	5	Designation: MFI-17; first 45 delivered from Sweden; total number planned may be 100
						1979	(5)	
						1980	(10)	
	USA	. .	T-41D Mescalero	Trainer	1976			Planned production rate: 50/year
15 Peru	Italy	2	Lupo Class	Frigate	1974			In addition to first 2 delivered from Italy

Recipient	Supplier	No. ordered	Weapon designation	Weapon description	Year of order	Year of delivery	No. delivered	Comments
10 Philippines	Germany, FR	57	Bo-105C	Hel	1974	1976	9	
						1977	9	
						1978	9	
						1979	9	
						1980	9	
13 South Africa	France	32	Mirage F-1A	Fighter	1971	1979	(5)	
						1980	(10)	
		1000	Eland-2	AC	1965	1977	(100)	Designation: Panhard AML-60/90; second generation locally developed
						1978	(100)	
						1979	(100)	
						1980	(100)	
		. .	Cactus	Landmob SAM	1974	1978	(100)	
						1979	(100)	
						1980	(100)	
	Israel	6	Reshef Class	FPB	1977			To be built in Durban; in addition to 6 previously acquired
	Italy	. .	Impala-2	Trainer/COIN	1974	1974	(4)	Also designated MB-326K
						1976	(30)	
						1977	(30)	
						1978	(50)	
						1979	(50)	
						1980	(30)	
10 Taiwan	USA	39	F-5E Tiger-2	Fighter	1979	1980	(20)	Additional batch contracted Jun 1979, incl 9 F-5F trainers
		187	F-5E Tiger-2	Fighter	1973	1974	1	
						1975	5	
						1976	30	
						1977	48	
						1978	48	
						1979	48	
						1980	7	
		21	F-5F Tiger-2	Trainer	1976	1978	(5)	
						1979	(10)	
						1980	(6)	
		9	F-5F Tiger-2	Trainer	(1979)			
		(1122)	AIM-9J	AAM	1973	1974	(6)	For 187 F-5E Tiger-2 fighters produced under licence and delivered 1974-80
						1975	(30)	
						1976	(180)	
						1977	(288)	
						1978	(288)	
						1979	(288)	
						1980	(42)	

8. Developments in nuclear weapons and ballistic missile defence

Square-bracketed numbers, thus [1], *refer to the list of references on page* 271.

During 1980, the qualitative development of US and Soviet strategic and tactical nuclear weapon systems described in the *SIPRI Yearbook 1980* continued. These improved nuclear weapons, in particular the new ballistic missiles, pose a greater threat since by their very nature they are more suitable for fighting a nuclear war than deterring it; properties such as increased accuracy and larger numbers of warheads per launcher put a greater premium on a first strike. If a nation could add to its new capabilities an effective defence against retaliation, the inhibitions against such a first strike would largely be removed. It is in this light that the current revival in ballistic missile defence (BMD)—described in section II—could be considered as the most significant weapon trend of 1980. The BMD developments, as well as the qualitative nuclear weapon improvements, indicate that earlier theories on a need for mutual vulnerability appear to be changing.

For a full list of operational US and Soviet strategic nuclear forces, see appendix 8A.

I. Nuclear weapon developments

US strategic nuclear weapons

In the USA, the deployment of the Mark 12A warhead on Minuteman III intercontinental ballistic missiles (ICBMs) and the conversion of Poseidon strategic nuclear submarines to carry Trident I submarine-launched ballistic missiles (SLBMs) continued in 1980, as did the development of air-launched cruise missiles, MX mobile ICBMs and Trident II SLBMs (see figure 8.1).

There were discussions in the USA about beginning the development of a new strategic bomber, to follow the B-52 and the Trident II SLBM. According to the then Under Secretary of Defense, Dr William J. Perry, "The issue is not whether to proceed [with these new weapon programmes] but when". He pointed out that full-scale development could lead to initial operation capabilities (IOCs)[1] for these systems in the late 1980s and

[1] The IOC is the date when a new weapon is expected to be ready for deployment.

Figure 8.1. The first successful launch of a Trident missile from a submerged submarine

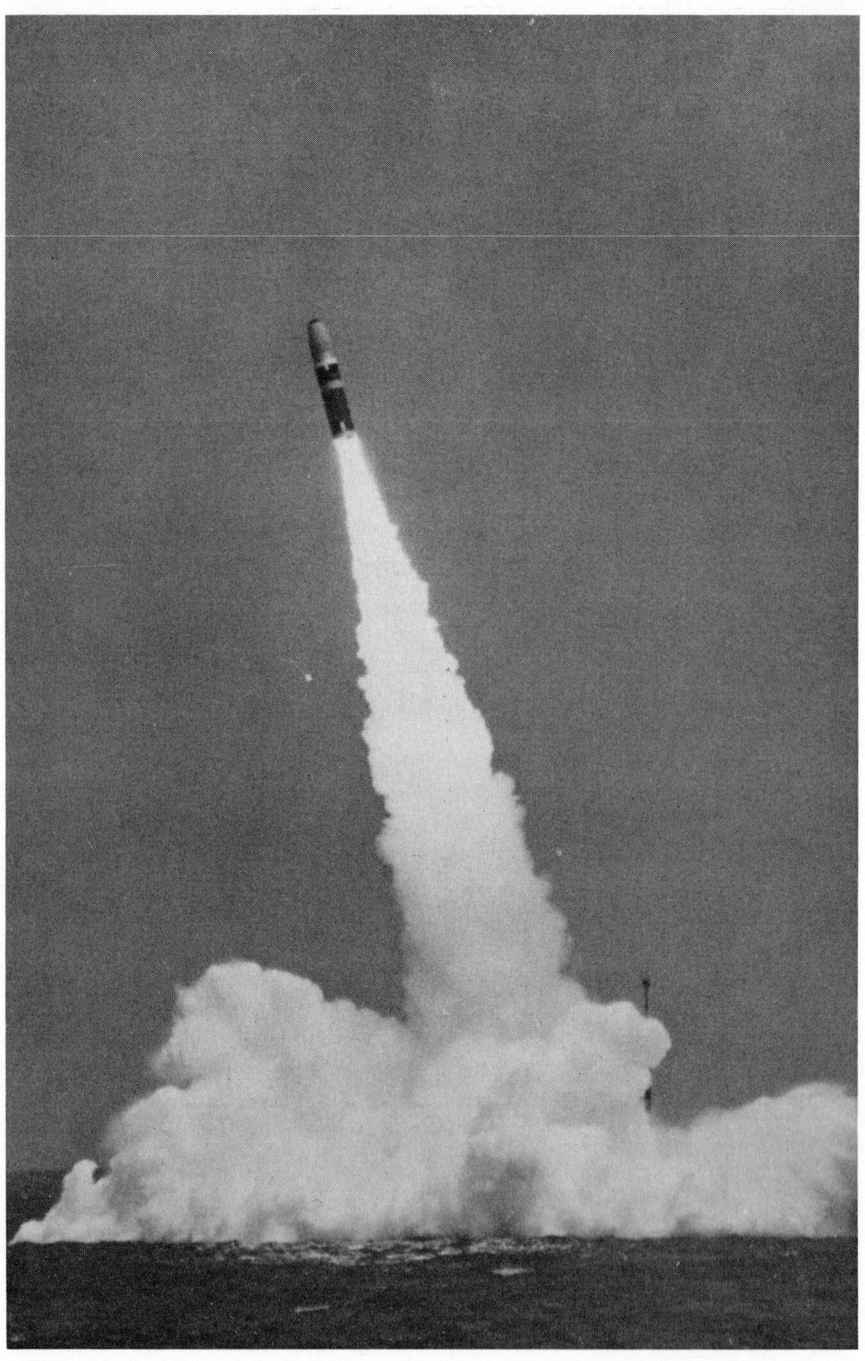

International Communication Agency

major spending "between 1983 and 1986". He said, "If we add these expenditures to the peak expenditures for MX the huge bulge that results will lead to inadequate funds and industrial resources remaining for other tactical weapons programmes. Therefore, I believe that both of these programmes should be phased three to four years later than MX, which would lead to IOCs in the early 90s". How the Reagan Administration and the US Congress will react to this suggestion remains to be seen.

In accordance with the provisions of the SALT I Treaty, two US Polaris strategic nuclear submarines will be decommissioned in 1981. Eight more Polaris submarines will have their nuclear missiles removed in 1980 and 1981 and be converted into attack submarines.

Four Poseidon nuclear submarines were converted in 1979 and 1980 to carry Trident I SLBMs. A total of 12 Poseidons will be re-fitted to carry 16 Trident I missiles each.

Sea trials for the first of the Trident submarines are scheduled to begin in 1981. The initial plan is to deploy 8 Trident submarines (these 8 have already been ordered), but this number may be increased to 25.

During 1980, the USA lost a Titan II ICBM through an accident, reducing the number of Titans from 53 to 52 and the total number of US ICBMs from 1 053 to 1 052. Each Titan II missile has a nuclear warhead with an explosive power equal to that of 9 million tons of TNT (equivalent to 700 Hiroshima bombs). The accident with the Titan missile occurred on 19 September 1980, at the missile site near Damascus, Arkansas.[2] It was caused by the explosion of the missile's very volatile liquid propellant after a technician dropped a spanner onto the missile. The nuclear warhead was blown right out of the silo, but the nuclear charge did not detonate. After the accident the US Air Force changed its maintenance procedures at ballistic missile sites, to include elementary safety precautions. One Titan site in Arizona may be closed down because 1 000 families live within one mile and many thousands live within five miles of the missiles.

Given the potential magnitude of an accident involving a Titan missile, it is amazing that such precautions were not taken before the accident. The missiles have, after all, been deployed since 1962, and there have been at least 16 accidents which may have involved various types of nuclear weapon.

Both US and Soviet military forces are very reluctant to give up obsolete nuclear weapons, even when their safety becomes questionable. The US Air Force has, for example, proposed modifications to Titan missiles

[2] For an account of nuclear weapon accidents see the *SIPRI Yearbook 1977*, pp. 52–85. According to *Flight International* (24 January 1981) the Titan II carries 15 000 US gallons of fuel (dimethyl hydrazine and hydrazine) and 17 000 US gallons of nitrogen tetroxide oxidizer which ignites the fuel on contact. The accident occurred when the fuel and oxidizer were being loaded and unloaded. (This was the second accident involving Titan IIs since 1978. Both Titans remain out of commission.)

worth about $56 million to try to keep the missiles going until the mid-1990s. However, they admit that the system is potentially hazardous and that there can be no guarantee that accidents will not happen. There is no suggestion that the missiles be scrapped.

US tactical and theatre nuclear weapons

The development of the ground-launched cruise missile (GLCM) and the Pershing II missile continued during 1980. In October 1980, however, the Pentagon announced a six months' delay in the testing of the GLCM. The missiles should, however, be ready for deployment in December 1983.

According to a decision made by NATO in December 1979, the deployment of 464 US GLCMs and 108 Pershing II missiles should begin in five West European countries in 1983. The UK, Italy and the Federal Republic of Germany have agreed to deploy GLCMs. It is unclear whether or not Belgium will fully participate in the programme. The Netherlands will decide at the end of 1981 whether to accept GLCMs on its territory.

The delay in the GLCM programme is said to have been caused by technical problems in the computers and communications equipment in the new weapon system. A final review of the first GLCM programme will take place in May 1983, instead of November 1982, as originally planned.

For the target coverage of these proposed weapons, see figure 8.2.

Soviet nuclear weapons

The Soviet Union is developing a new nuclear submarine, the Typhoon [1.] Some reports claim that it is in the 25 000- to 30 000-ton class—considerably greater than the 18 700-ton weight of the US Trident submarine. One Typhoon, said to be fitted to carry about 20 SLBMs, has been launched and three others are under construction at Severodvinsk.

According to the outgoing US Secretary of Defense Harold Brown, in his 1981 annual report, the new Typhoon solid-propellant SLBM, the SS-NX-20, will almost certainly be MIRVed. "New Soviet SLBM systems", he said, "will be qualitatively superior to those they replace—they will probably be more accurate and have greater throw-weight" [2]. The SS-NX-20 is expected to be deployed after the mid-1980s.

There is, as usual, little information about new Soviet ICBM developments. There are, however, reports that the USSR is testing two new types of solid-fuelled ICBMs. One is said to be a large mobile system like the proposed US MX ICBM. This is in addition to the mobile ICBM, the SS-16, which has already been developed but may not be deployed.

It must be expected that the Soviet Union intends to continue to increase the accuracy of its ICBMs and that of its new intermediate-range ballistic missile (IRBM), the SS-20.

Figure 8.2. Target coverage of proposed NATO theatre nuclear weapons and the Soviet SS-5[a] and SS-20[b]

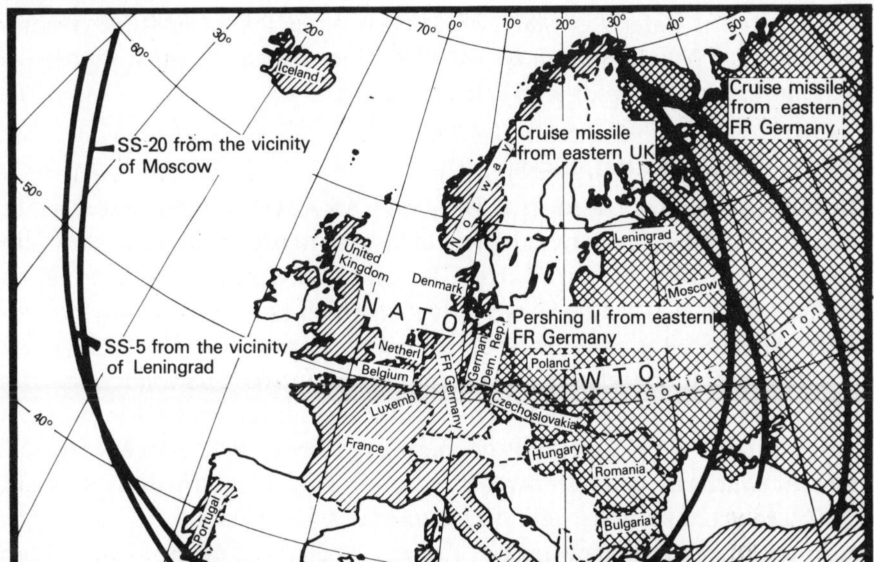

[a] The SS-5 is included for comparison.
[b] Deployed closer to the Polish border, for example, the SS-20 would have a considerably greater coverage than indicated. And if the range of the SS-20 is 5 000 km, as has been suggested, then it could be deployed well east of the Urals and still be able to reach London.

The deployment of the SS-20 continues. At the end of 1980 about 180 SS-20s were deployed [2]. The range of the SS-20 (4 000 km) is such that the whole of Europe would be within reach even if these weapons were deployed east of Moscow (see figure 8.2).

British strategic nuclear weapons

In 1980 the UK decided to build four new nuclear submarines, each equipped with 16 US Trident I SLBMs. These will replace the existing British Polaris submarines in the early 1990s.

This Trident programme in the UK will cost about $12 500 million (at 1980 prices). The UK will buy the missiles from the USA but will build its own nuclear warheads. Each missile will probably carry eight warheads.

The sale is worth about $2 500 million (in 1980 dollars) to the USA. This will include a 5 per cent surcharge to cover some US R&D costs and, in order to make an additional contribution to US R&D expenses, the UK has agreed to man—at its own cost—the British Rapier air defence system, which will be purchased by the United States to defend US air bases in the UK.

The current Polaris missiles (which carry three 200-kt multiple re-entry vehicles) are being replaced by the Chevaline warhead, which reportedly can manoeuvre to avoid anti-ballistic missiles.

Chinese strategic nuclear weapons

In May 1980 China tested an ICBM, the CSS-4, with a range estimated to exceed 13 000 km. Such missiles would be able to hit targets in the Western parts of the USA (see figure 8.3). The new ICBM has twice the range of China's other ICBM, the CSS-3, a few of which have been deployed since 1978. The CSS-4 is expected soon to become operational [1].

China is thought also to have deployed about 60 CSS-2 intermediate-range (about 3 000 km) ballistic missiles and about 50 CSS-1 medium-range (about 1 100 km) ballistic missiles. The CSS-1, which carries a nuclear warhead with an explosive power equivalent to that of about 20 000 tons (20 kilotons) of TNT, entered service in 1966.

In addition to these missiles, China operates about 60 Hong-6 medium bombers, with a range of about 3 500 km, which probably carry nuclear bombs with explosive yields equivalent to several million tons (i.e., megatons) of TNT. China also has a nuclear submarine and is building others. These are equipped with ballistic-missile launching tubes. China has not yet developed submarine-launched ballistic missiles but can be expected to do so soon.

French nuclear weapons

In June 1980 France announced that it had developed and tested the neutron bomb. According to official statements, a decision will be taken in 1982–83 whether or not to produce it.

The development of the M-4 SLBM, to carry 6 or 7 multiple independently targetable re-entry vehicles (MIRVs), each with a yield of 150 kt, is continuing. It will replace the 3 000-km range M-20 SLBM and 1-Mt warhead now deployed on French strategic nuclear submarines. The first test flight of the M-4 was made in the Pacific in December 1980.

II. Ballistic missile defence

In the debate in the late 1960s and early 1970s on strategic nuclear arms stability between the USA and the USSR, it was generally assumed that mutual vulnerability was a requirement for such stability. This was apparently one of the important reasons for concluding the Anti-Ballistic Missile (ABM) Treaty of 1972 between the two powers. The objectives of

Figure 8.3. Area of the world within range of China's CSS-3 and CSS-4 missiles

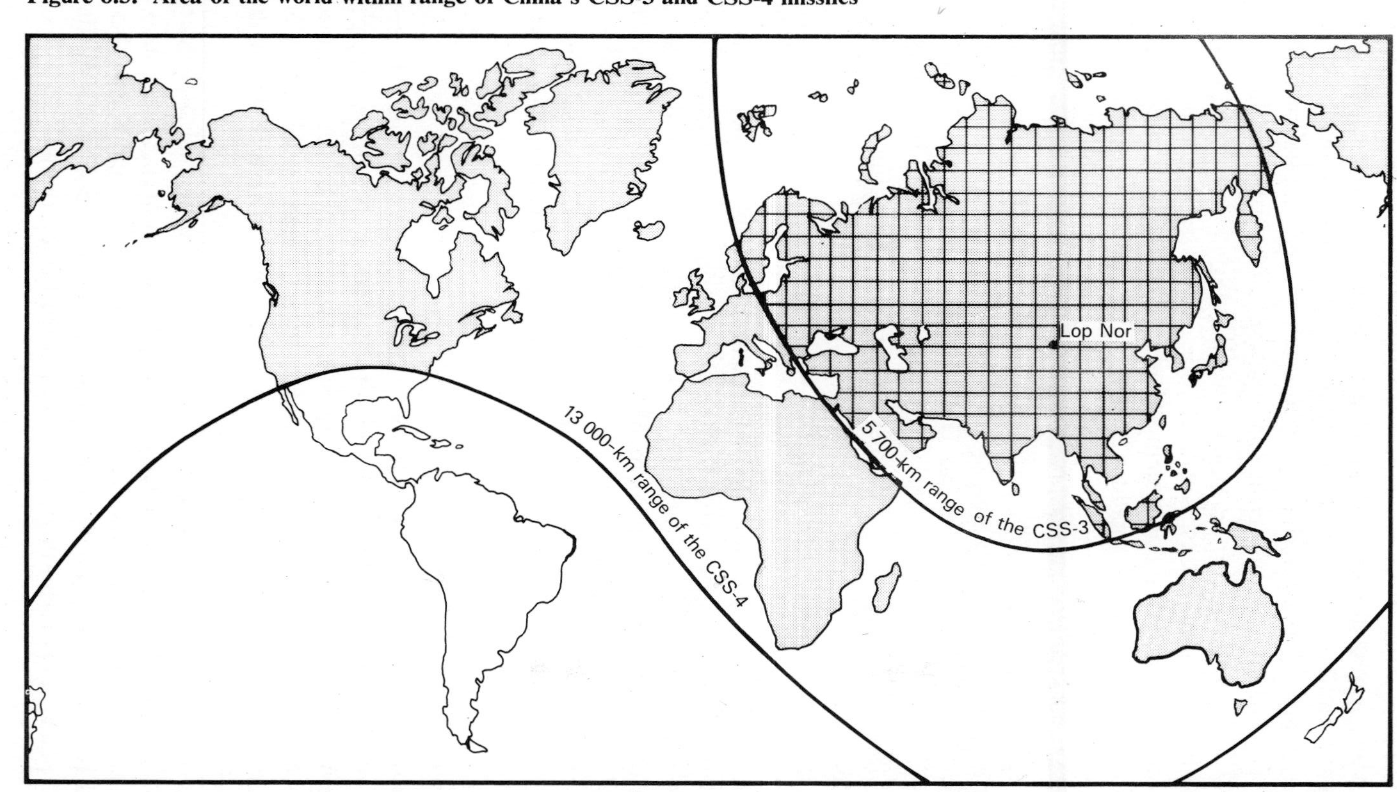

the Treaty were to stop the strategic defensive arms race by limiting the deployment of anti-ballistic missile systems designed to counter strategic missiles. The amended ABM Treaty of 1974 allows each party one limited ABM system with no more than 100 ABM launchers and no more than 100 ABM interceptor missiles at launch sites [3]. Further, the Treaty limits the number of deployed radars to 20, which can be deployed either within an area (150-km radius) centred on the party's capital or within an area (150-km radius) containing intercontinental ballistic missiles. Under the US Safeguard ABM programme, an ABM system was deployed on the ICBM field at Grand Forks, North Dakota, but it is no longer in operation. In contrast, the Soviet ABM system is deployed on the National Command Authority at Moscow; it includes 54 launchers and is operational [3].

The Treaty specifically limits ABMs in the form in which they existed in 1972. Modernization and replacement of ABM systems are allowed, although certain sophisticated systems are banned. The Treaty does not cover new ABM systems based on other physical principles, such as high-energy laser and particle beams. However, before being deployed, such systems would, according to the agreed statement between the USSR and the USA, be subject to discussion in the Standing Consultative Commission [3].

Thus, since 1972 the concept of and the approach to the ABM or, as it is now known, the BMD system, has changed considerably. Outstanding progress in a wide spectrum of BMD research and development activities resulted in a major new thrust for the BMD programme during the late 1970s and particularly during 1980 [4]. It is therefore useful to review some of the new developments in BMD systems, particularly that of the use of high-energy lasers.

In the following sections, a brief review of new BMD technologies and systems is made, and US and Soviet BMD programmes are described.

The Soviet BMD programme

As mentioned above, the USSR has a BMD system around Moscow. Considerable effort is also being devoted to research and development (R&D) on new systems. It has been suggested that the Soviet Union may be developing a rapidly deployable BMD system which would consist of a phased-array radar, a missile tracking radar and an interceptor with a high-altitude interception capability [5].

Considerable research is being carried out in the field of high-energy lasers for applications as anti-satellite weapons based on the Earth as well as in space. When placed on satellites in outer space, high-energy lasers could be used as a BMD system to destroy ballistic missiles during their boost phase. This technology is also described briefly below.

The US BMD programme

Essential elements of any BMD system are target-detection, -recognition, -tracking and -destruction. At present these tasks are being performed by ground-based radar sensors and by target interceptors armed with nuclear warheads. Such a system suffers from two main disadvantages. First, with a radar sensor, it is not possible to discriminate effectively between re-entry vehicles released halfway during an ICBM's trajectory and fragmented boosters and decoys. Although high-resolution radars such as phased-array radars have been developed, they need very large antennas to achieve the required high resolution and high beam energy for detecting targets at long ranges. Thus these systems are very large and vulnerable to enemy attack. Second, electromagnetic radiation resulting from a nuclear explosion near enemy missiles as well as clouds of chaff released by enemy re-entry vehicles could, at least temporarily, blind ground-based radars. Moreover, nuclear BMD interceptors could not be tested under realistic conditions because the Partial Test Ban Treaty prohibits nuclear explosions in the atmosphere as well as in outer space.

Table 8.1. Summary of funding for the US BMD programme

	Fundings ($ million)			
Programme	FY 1979 (actual)	FY 1980 (planned)	FY 1981 (proposed)	FY 1982 (proposed for authorization)
Advanced technology	113.5	120.8	132.8	143.5
Systems technology	114.0	120.8	133.5	176.1
Total	**227.5**	**241.6**	**266.3**	**319.6**

Source: Reference [15].

Because of these limitations, considerable efforts have been devoted to R&D on new concepts of target-detection, -recognition and -tracking systems and on non-nuclear interceptors.

Under the US Advanced Technology and System Technology Programs developing the so-called layered defence system (see figure 8.4), three types of 'non-nuclear kill' (NNK) interceptors as well as infra-red and advanced radar sensors are being investigated. For example, under a programme called Homing Overlay Experiment (HOE), tests of an infra-red telescope, in conjunction with an NNK interceptor, are expected to begin in 1982–83. During the test a Minuteman ICBM with MIRVs will be launched. This will be followed by the launching of the infra-red telescope and then of the NNK interceptor, to 'kill' the re-entry vehicles ejected from the Minuteman

Figure 8.4. Drawing of a concept of the layered BMD system

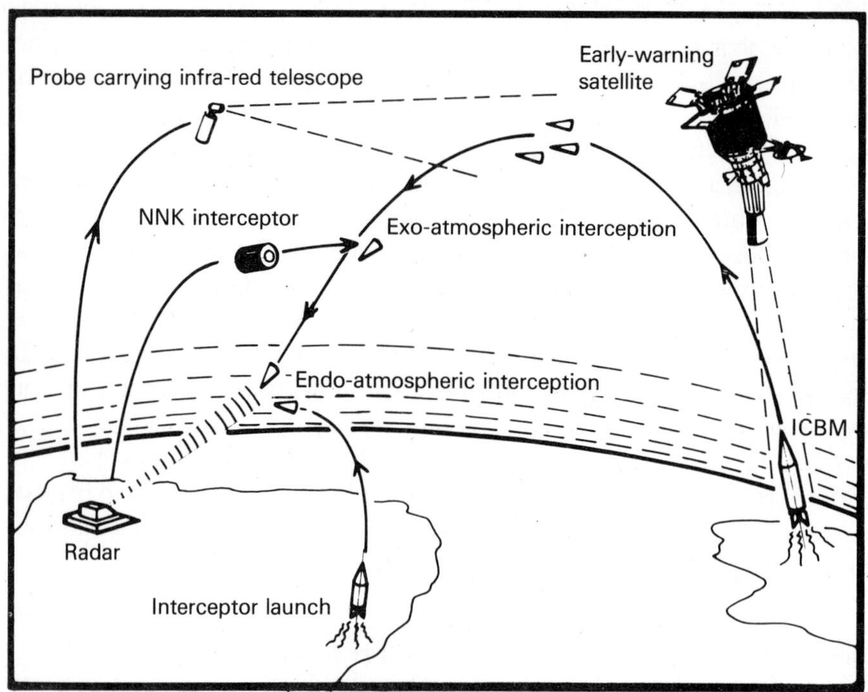

missile above the atmosphere. The telescope and its on-board data-processor, which form a system known as the Designating Optical Tracker (DOT), replace large ground-based radars and computers for acquisition, assessment, tracking and discrimination of the target. Once the infra-red telescope is above the atmosphere, the long-wavelength infra-red sensor searches for the target against the cold background of outer space. Information is relayed from the DOT to a homing infra-red sensor and data processor on board the interceptor. The latter is then aimed towards the assigned target, which it destroys by collision [6]. In another NNK interceptor, metal pellets are ejected in a controlled sequence so as to place them in concentric circles in the path of the incoming warheads. These pellets would then destroy them on impact [6]. Under operational conditions, the DOT and the NNK interceptors are launched on information received from an early-warning satellite of the launch of an enemy missile.

Two tests of DOT and NNK interceptors were made in February 1980 and in mid-September 1980, and a third one is planned for mid-1981 [4, 6, 7].

It is only recently that infra-red telescopes have become available because of advances made in semi-conductor and micro-electronic technologies. Such telescopes consist of a mosaic of a large number of small, infra-red sensors placed at the focal plane of the optical system of the telescope.

Despite the fact that infra-red sensors operated above the atmosphere provide higher resolution and better discrimination of targets from other objects than that obtained by ground radars, the development of the latter continues. In fact the current US BMD system envisages the development and deployment of both the exo-atmospheric and endo-atmospheric systems. Under the above-mentioned layered defence system (see figure 8.4), the use of radar sensors is envisaged for detection and tracking of targets that escape the exo-atmospheric infra-red sensors [4]. Under the Low Altitude Defense (LoAD) system, phased-array radars would be used. These need not be high power radars, and they would be operated at higher frequencies so as to reduce the overall size of the system. The LoAD system is designed to be used in conjunction with MX advanced ballistic missiles [4].

During the HOE test in September 1980, the ground-based phased-array radars together with the data processing systems were also tested. The US Army is now planning to build a prototype demonstration LoAD system for terminal defence [7].

As ground-based radars form an important sensor for an endo-atmospheric BMD system, considerable effort has been devoted to improving the radar system. For example, some progress has been made in reducing the effects of nuclear blasts and radiation on phased-array antennas of radars and in the development of millimetre-wave radars [6].

Another field in radar technology which is receiving much attention from the point of view of BMD is that of the laser radar. Low-energy laser beams have been used for tracking satellites and in some cases even for determining the type of optics a photographic reconnaissance satellite carries.

The NNK BMD interceptor programme dates back to the 1960s when the system was conceived as an anti-satellite (ASAT) weapon; this ASAT system could become operational in the second half of the 1980s [6, 8]. Now, a second ASAT system, one which uses high-energy lasers, is thought to be applicable as a BMD system, and is approaching the stage when realistic tests are planned for the next six years [9]. In use in a BMD system, a high-energy laser beam is most likely to cause damage[3] to an

[3] A laser beam may damage a target by thermal weakening, shock-wave propagation and ultraviolet or X-ray radiation, or a combination of these processes. In the thermal weakening process, the temperature of the target surface is raised sufficiently to soften and even melt or vaporize it. When a short pulse of high-energy laser radiation falls on the surface of a material, it causes a very rapid and substantial increase in the temperature of a thin layer of the target. The surface layer vaporizes and explodes, moving away from the target at high speed. A shock wave is propagated into the target and may tear it apart. Finally, the vaporized surface may emit a large amount of radiation such as ultraviolet radiation or X-rays. Such radiation may cause structural damage both to the target material and to the electronic equipment carried by the target.

ICBM during the boost phase of the missile. During this phase an ICBM presents itself to the beam as a large, slow-moving target and has a large amount of fuel under great pressure. Moreover, the structure is under great stress and is also heated by the atmosphere, making the ICBM both most easily detected and most vulnerable to attack at this phase. Several tests of high-energy lasers against military targets have already been carried out: for example, in 1978 the US Navy successfully tracked and destroyed high-speed BCM-71A TOW anti-tank missiles using a chemical laser [9]. The first successful test using a laser beam was made in 1973 when the US Air Force used a gas dynamic laser to destroy a drone aircraft. Again in 1976 the US Army successfully destroyed winged and helicopter drones [9] using an electric discharge laser. During January 1981, the US Air Force, for the first time, tested a laser beam at full power from its Airborne Laser Laboratory on a KC-135 aircraft. The test was conducted on the ground at Kirtland Air Force Base, New Mexico [10].

A number of problems need to be solved before high-energy lasers can be used in practicable weapons or a BMD system. For example, considerable effort is being devoted to solving the problem of tracking and aiming at a fast-moving target. Considerable success already appears to have been achieved against targets at short ranges. Under a US programme called Talon Gold, tests for high-energy laser pointing and tracking in space are being planned for the early 1980s [11, 12]. It is planned to orbit equipment for pointing and tracking a high-energy laser for satellite defence applications using the space shuttle. Another problem has been optical components suitable for use in a high-energy laser system. It has been reported that a mirror three metres in diameter has been developed in the USA to focus the laser beam on a target [12].

Implications

Despite the fact that the ABM Treaty limits the development and deployment of BMD systems, there is considerable interest and even progress being made in new BMD systems both in the USA and in the USSR. The funding in the United States for BMD research and development is shown in table 8.1. It can be seen that the efforts to develop advanced BMD concepts and technology are not frozen; the programme continues to improve old systems and evolve new ones. The impetus for such a development is derived from the fact that ASAT technology is very similar to that needed for a BMD system. Furthermore, high-energy lasers are important in other areas of research; for example, they are used for measuring the physical properties of materials at high temperatures and pressures, providing useful information for modelling some aspects of nuclear weapon design and performance.[4] Moreover, with the use of high-energy lasers, it would be possible to simulate some of the effects of nuclear weapons to study the vulnerability of, for example, missile warheads and artificial Earth satellites [13]. Another important use of high-energy lasers is in the uranium enrichment process. Therefore, more efficient and higher-energy lasers than are available today will no doubt be developed. These will in turn find use in ASAT and BMD systems. In fact, it has recently been proposed that the USA build 24 orbital laser BMD stations [14].

Thus in the absence of an ASAT treaty and with possibilities left open in the 1972 ABM Treaty for further development and deployment of new BMD systems, it is not surprising that both the USSR and the USA are developing new systems that would limit damage to their strategic weaponry. A new, effective BMD system could stimulate another round in the already perilous nuclear arms race.

References

1. Speech by the General-Secretary of the Soviet Communist Party Leonid Brezhnev, at the 26th Congress of the Communist Party of the Soviet Union, February 1981.
2. *Annual Report FY1981* (US Department of Defense, Washington, D.C., 1981).
3. 'Ballistic missile defense', *Fiscal Year 1981 Arms Control Impact Statements*, May 1980 (US Government Printing Office, Washington, D.C., 1980), pp. 219–31.
4. 'Status of the ballistic missile defense research and development program, 25 February 1980', Statement by G. D. Tate, *Hearing on Military Posture, Department of Defense Authorization for Appropriations for Fiscal Year 1981*, Committee on Armed Services, House of Representatives, Part 4, Book 1, February–March 1980 (US Government Printing Office, Washington, D.C., 1980), pp. 920–28.
5. 'The ballistic missile defense research and development program', Statement by S. C. Meyer, *Department of Defense Authorization for Appropriations for Fiscal Year 1981, Hearings before the Committee on Armed Services*, US Senate, Part 1, January–February 1979 (US Government Printing Office, Washington, D.C., 1979), pp. 309–15.
6. Klass, P. J., 'Ballistic missile defense tests set', *Aviation Week & Space Technology*, Vol. 112, No. 24, 16 June 1980, pp. 213–18.

[4] Very high pressures, densities and temperatures are produced in nuclear explosions and in inertial confinement fusion (the basis for a hydrogen bomb). To study the phenomenon connected with such conditions, it is necessary to know the equations of state—that is, the relationships between pressures, density and internal energy of materials. Such knowledge facilitates understanding the behaviour of, for example, fusion pellets in a thermonuclear weapon. Until now such studies have been carried out in underground nuclear explosions, but these have obvious limitations.

7. 'Technology milestone met in missile defense testing', *Aviation Week & Space Technology*, Vol. 113, No. 13, 29 September 1980, pp. 25–26.
8. 'Antisatellite missile flight test nears', *Defense Electronics*, Vol. 12, No. 12, December 1980, pp. 22–24.
9. Statement by W. J. Perry, *Department of Defense Authorization for Appropriations for Fiscal Year 1980, Hearings before the Committee on Armed Services*, US Senate, Part 1, January–February 1979 (US Government Printing Office, Washington, D.C., 1979), pp. 384–85.
10. 'Full-power test of anti-missile laser beam', *Interavia Air Letter*, No. 9673, 23 January 1981, p. 7.
11. Statement by P. R. Fossum, *Hearings on Military Posture, Department of Defense Authorization for Appropriations for Fiscal Year 1981*, Committee on Armed Services, House of Representatives, February–March 1980 (US Government Printing Office, Washington, D.C., 1980), pp. 580–82.
12. Robinson, C. A., Jr., 'Missile defense gains support', *Aviation Week & Space Technology*, Vol. 111, No. 17, 22 October 1979, pp. 14–17.
13. 'Inertial Confinement Fusion', *Fiscal Year 1981 Arms Control Impact Statements*, May 1980 (US Government Printing Office, Washington, D.C., 1980), pp. 460–75.
14. 'Report urges major increase in space laser weapon program', *Defense Daily*, Vol. 111, No. 27, 8 August 1980, p. 194.
15. 'Secretary of Defense Annual Report—Fiscal Year 1981', Statement by Harold Brown, *Hearing on Military Posture, Department of Defense Authorization for Appropriations for Fiscal Year 1981*, Committee on Armed Services, House of Representatives, Part 1, January–March 1980 (US Government Printing Office, Washington, D.C., 1980), p. 188.

Appendix 8A

US and Soviet strategic nuclear forces, 1972–81

Figures for 1972–76 are as of 30 June; figures for 1977–81 are as of 30 September.

For sources and notes, see page 276.

	First in service	Range (nm)	Payload	1972	1973	1974	1975	1976	1977	1978	1979	1980	1981
Delivery vehicles													
Strategic bombers													
USA B-52 C/D/E/F	1956	10 000	27 000 kg	149	149	116	99	83	83	83	83	83	83
B-52 G/H	1959	10 900	34 000 kg	281	281	274	270	265	265	265	265	265	265
(FB-111	1970	3 300	17 000 kg	66	66	66	66	66	66	66	66	65	64)
USSR Mya-4 'Bison'	1955	5 300	9 000 kg	56	56	56	56	56	56	56	56	56	56
Tu-95 'Bear'	1956	6 800	18 000 kg	100	100	100	100	100	100	100	100	100	100
(Tu-22M 'Backfire'	1975	4 000	9 000 kg	–	–	–	12	24	36	48	60	72	84)
			Long-range bomber total: USA	**430**	**430**	**390**	**369**	**348**	**348**	**348**	**348**	**348**	**348**
			USSR	**156**	**156**	**156**	**156**	**156**	**156**	**156**	**156**	**156**	**156**
Submarines, ballistic missile-equipped, nuclear-powered (SSBNs)													
USA With Polaris A-2	1962	n.a.	16 × A-2	8	8	6	3	–	–	–	–	–	–
With Polaris A-3	1964	n.a.	16 × A-3	21	13	13	13	13	11	10	10	5	5
With Poseidon C-3 conv.	1970	n.a.	16 × C-3	12	20	22	25	28	30	31	31	25	20
With Trident C-4 conv.	1979	n.a.	16 × C-4	–	–	–	–	–	–	–	–	6	11
With Trident C-4	1980	n.a.	24 × C-4	–	–	–	–	–	–	–	–	–	1
USSR 'Hotel II' conv.	1963	n.a.	3 × 'SS-N-5'	7	7	7	7	7	7	7	7	6	6
'Hotel III' conv.	1967	n.a.	6 × 'SS-N-6'	1	1	1	1	1	1	1	1	1	1
'Yankee'	1968	n.a.	16 × 'SS-N-6'	27	33	33	33	33	33	33	33	29	27
'Yankee II'	1974	n.a.	12 × 'SS-NX-17'	–	–	1	1	1	1	1	1	1	1
'Golf IV' conv.	1972	n.a.	4 × 'SS-N-8'	1	1	1	1	1	1	1	1	1	1
'Hotel IV' conv.	1972	n.a.	6 × 'SS-N-8'	1	1	1	1	1	1	1	1	1	1
'Delta I'	1973	n.a.	12 × 'SS-N-8'	–	1	7	12	18	18	18	18	18	18
'Delta II'	1977	n.a.	16 × 'SS-N-8'	–	–	–	–	–	4	4	4	4	4
'Delta III'	1978	n.a.	16 × 'SS-N-18'	–	–	–	–	–	–	2	4	10	12
			Submarine total: USA	**41**	**41**	**41**	**41**	**41**	**41**	**41**	**41**	**36**	**37**
			USSR	**37**	**44**	**51**	**56**	**62**	**66**	**68**	**70**	**71**	**71**
			Modern subs: USSR	**27**	**34**	**41**	**46**	**52**	**56**	**58**	**60**	**62**	**62**
SLBM (Submarine-launched ballistic missile) launchers on SSBNs													
USA Polaris A-2	1962	1 500	1 × 1 Mt	128	128	96	48	–	–	–	–	–	–
Polaris A-3	1964	2 500	3 × 200 kt (MRV)	336	208	208	208	208	176	160	160	80	80
Poseidon C-3	1970	2 500	10 × 40 kt (MIRV)	192	320	352	400	448	480	496	496	400	320
Trident C-4	1979	4 000	8 × 100 kt (MIRV)	–	–	–	–	–	–	–	–	96	200

USSR	'SS-N-5'	1963	700	1 × 1 Mt	21	21	21	21	21	21	21	21	18	18
	'SS-N-6 mod. 1'	1968	1 300	1 × 1 Mt	438	534								
	'SS-N-6 mod. 2' conv.	1973	1 600	1 × 1 Mt	–	–	534	534	534	534	534	534	470	438
	'SS-N-6 mod. 3' conv.	1973	1 600	2 × 200 kt (MRV)	–	–								
	'SS-N-8'	1973	4 300	1 × 1 Mt	10	22	94	154	226	290	290	290	290	290
	'SS-NX-17'	n.a.	. .	1 × 1 Mt (MIRV-cap.)	–	–	12	12	12	12	12	12	12	12
	'SS-N-18'	n.a.	4 050	3 × 200 kt (MIRV)	–	–	–	–	–	–	32	64	160	192
				SLBM launcher total: USA	**656**	**656**	**656**	**656**	**656**	**656**	**656**	**656**	**576**	**600**
				USSR	**469**	**577**	**661**	**721**	**793**	**857**	**889**	**921**	**950**	**950**
ICBMs (*Intercontinental ballistic missiles*)														
USA	Titan II	1963	6 300	1 × 10 Mt	54	54	54	54	54	54	54	53	52	52
	Minuteman I	1963	6 500	1 × 1 Mt	290	190	100	–	–	–	–	–	–	–
	Minuteman II	1966	7 000	1 × 1.5 Mt	500	500	500	450	450	450	450	450	450	450
	Minuteman III conv.	1970	7 000	3 × 170 kt (MIRV)	210	310	400	550	550	550	550	550	550	450
	Minuteman III impr.	1979	7 000	3 × 350 kt (MIRV)	–	–	–	–	–	–	–	–	–	100
USSR	'SS-7 Saddler'	1962	6 000	1 × 5 Mt	190	190	190	190	130	30	2	–	–	–
	'SS-8 Sasin'	1963	6 000	1 × 5 Mt	19	19	19	19	19	19	–	–	–	–
	'SS-9 Scarp'	1966	6 500	1 × 10–20 Mt	288	288	288	288	248	188	128	68	–	–
	'SS-11 mod. 1'	1966	5 700	1 × 1 Mt	970									
	'SS-11 mod. 2' conv.	1973	. .	1 × 1 Mt	–	970	970	970	890	800	690	580	520	460
	'SS-11 mod. 3' conv.	1973	. .	3 × 200 kt (MRV)	–									
	'SS-13 Savage'	1969	4 400	1 × 1 Mt	60	60	60	60	60	60	60	60	60	60
	'SS-11 mod. 3'	1973	. .	3 × 200 kt (MRV)	–	20	40	60	60	60	60	60	60	60
	'SS-18 mod. 1/mod. 3'	1976	5 500	1 × 10–20 Mt	–	–	–	–	60	120	180	240	308	308
	'SS-18 mod. 2' conv.	1977	. .	8 × 500 kt (MIRV)	–	–	–	–						
	'SS-19' conv.	1976	5 000	6 × 500 kt (MIRV)	–	–	–	–	80	120	180	240	300	360
	'SS-17' conv.	1977	. .	4 × 500 kt (MIRV)	–	–	–	–	–	50	100	150	150	150
				ICBM total: USA	**1 054**	**1 054**	**1 054**	**1 054**	**1 054**	**1 054**	**1 054**	**1 053**	**1 052**	**1 052**
				USSR	**1 527**	**1 547**	**1 567**	**1 587**	**1 547**	**1 447**	**1 400**	**1 398**	**1 398**	**1 398**
				Total, long-range bombers and missiles: USA	**2 140**	**2 140**	**2 100**	**2 079**	**2 058**	**2 058**	**2 058**	**2 057**	**1 976**	**2 000**
				USSR	**2 152**	**2 280**	**2 384**	**2 464**	**2 496**	**2 460**	**2 445**	**2 475**	**2 504**	**2 504**
Nuclear warheads														
Independently targetable warheads on missiles:				USA	3 858	5 210	5 678	6 410	6 842	7 130	7 274	7 273	7 000	7 032
				USSR	1 996	2 124	2 228	2 308	3 160	3 894	4 393	4 937	5 920	6 848
Total warheads on bombers and missiles, official US estimates:				USA	5 700	6 784	7 650	8 500	8 400	8 500	9 000	9 200*	9 200*	9 000*
				USSR	2 500	2 200	2 500	2 500	3 300	4 000	4 500	5 000*	6 000*	7 000*

* 1 January.

Sources and notes for appendix 8A (pages 274–275)

Sources: The main sources and methodology of this appendix are described in the *SIPRI Yearbook 1974*, pp. 108–109, where a comparable table for the decade 1965–74 appears.

The earlier table has been updated on the basis of material published in the *Annual Report* of the US Secretary of Defense for the fiscal years 1976 through 1982 (US Government Printing Office, Washington, D.C., 1975–1981) and the statements on *US Military Posture* by the Chairman of the Joint Chiefs of Staff for the same seven years.

The version of this table for 1967–76 which appeared in the *SIPRI Yearbook 1976*, pp. 24–27, included revised estimates of the numbers of US strategic submarines and SLBMs of various types, based on the dates of overhaul and conversion of each submarine given in *Jane's Fighting Ships* (Macdonald & Co., London, annual), *Ships and Aircraft of the US Fleet* (Naval Institute Press, Annapolis, Maryland, recent editions), and US Senate Committee on Appropriations annual *Hearings* on naval appropriations. The revised series has been continued, based on the same sources.

The estimates of the numbers of US strategic bombers were revised in the table for 1968–77 which appeared in the *SIPRI Yearbook 1977*, pp. 24–28. The revised series, continued here, is based on a narrow definition of 'active aircraft'—the only definition which permits a consistent time series to be constructed from public data—taking the authorized 'unit equipment' (number of planes per squadron) of the authorized numbers of squadrons of each type of plane and adding a 10 per cent attrition and pipeline allowance (or lower when it is known that adequate numbers of spare aircraft are lacking).

A version of the table covering the period 1967–78 appeared in the brochure containing the SIPRI Statement on World Armaments and Disarmament, presented at the UN General Assembly Special Session devoted to Disarmament on 13 June 1978. That table listed three configurations of Soviet submarine, also shown here ('Hotel III', 'Yankee II' and 'Delta III'), which had not been previously reported. Reference to these configurations, as well as to the 'Hotel IV' and 'Golf IV' SS-N-8 test conversions shown this year for the first time, are given in the defence statements of the US Secretary of Defense and Joint Chiefs.

Notes:

Dates of deployment

The estimates for the year 1981 are planned or expected deployments.

In the case of the official US estimates of total warheads on bombers and missiles (the last three rows of the table), the estimates for 1979–81 refer to 1 January. All other estimates in the table follow the more usual practice of official US accounts—which are the main source of the data—by referring to the closing date of the US government fiscal year.

US SLBMs and submarines

The number of US submarines and the corresponding SLBMs are derived by treating all submarines under conversion as though they carry their former load until the conversion is completed (shipyard work finished), and they take on their new load from the date of completion. This method, the only exact procedure feasible with public data, differs from the practice in some official US accounts of excluding from the estimates of *total force loadings* (warheads on bombers and missiles) the loads that would be carried by submarines undergoing conversion and treating the submarines as under conversion until the date of their first subsequent operational deployment at sea.

The first of 12 Poseidon-equipped submarines which are to be backfitted with the Trident I (C-4) missile began conversion in the autumn of 1978 and became operational in October 1979. The first Trident submarine, with 24 launch tubes for the Trident I or Trident II missile (the latter now under development), is currently scheduled to begin sea trials in 1981 and is therefore considered operational as of 31 September 1981.

The maximum payload of the Poseidon missile is 14 warheads, rather than the 10 shown in the table. It is estimated that, today, these missiles actually carry only 10 warheads each, an off-loading undertaken to compensate for poorer-than-expected performance by the missile propulsion system, so that the design range of 2 500 nautical miles can be reached. (In *Combat Fleets of the World 1978/79* (US Naval Institute Press, Annapolis, Maryland, 1978) Jean Labayle Couhat suggests that a range of 2 500 nautical miles can be reached with a 14-warhead payload and that reduction of the payload to 10 warheads increases the range to 3 200 nautical miles.) An article in the *New York Times* and an unofficial US Defense Department report, both from the autumn of 1980, have stated that, as the longer-range Trident missiles are phased in, covering more distant targets, the payload of the remaining 304 Poseidon missiles will revert to the originally designed 14 warheads. This will add a total of 1 216 warheads to the US SLBM force in the early 1980s.

US ICBMs

Starting in 1980 or 1981, 300 of the 550 Minuteman III missiles are to be backfitted with the Mark 12A re-entry vehicle, each of which will carry a 350-kt warhead. Moreover, NS-20 improvements in Minuteman III guidance have brought the expected accuracy (circular error probability) of this missile to about 600 ft. This gives the current 170-kt Minuteman III warhead a better than 50 : 50 chance of destroying a Soviet missile silo hardened to 1 000–1 500 psi, and two such warheads in succession (barring 'fratricide' effects) about an 80 per cent probability of kill. The hard-silo kill probability of the new 350-kt warhead, given 600-ft accuracy, will be about 57 per cent for one shot and close to 95 per cent for two shots.

MIRVed warheads on Soviet ICBMs

The original Soviet ICBM MIRVing programme is coming to an end, with a total of 818 ICBM silos converted to MIRV-capable launchers. The last of 309 SS-9 silos converted to hold the SS-18 were completed in 1980, and the 60 last SS-11 silos converted to hold the SS-19 are expected to be equipped with the SS-19 missile in 1981.

The exact numbers of MIRVed and unMIRVed versions of the SS-17, -18 and -19 are not known. All launchers for these missiles are counted as MIRV launchers for the purpose of the current understanding between the USA and the USSR to abide by the terms of the unratified SALT II Treaty.

Soviet and US bomber aircraft

The long-standing estimate of 140 Soviet long-range bombers has been revised upwards to 156 to conform with Soviet official data made public at the time of the signing of the SALT II Treaty. In past years, the designation 'Tu-20' has been given for the 'Bear' bomber in *SIPRI Yearbooks*. The SALT II Treaty states that the 'Bear' bomber is designated 'Tu-95' in the Soviet Union. Similarly, the Soviet designation for the medium-range bomber known in the West as 'Backfire' is referred to in the table as 'Tu-22M' (as opposed to 'Tu-26' in previous *SIPRI Yearbooks*) to conform with the designation used in the Soviet Backfire statement given to the USA before the signing of the SALT II Treaty.

US medium-range FB-111 strategic bombers are shown in parentheses, and long-range bombers only are included in the bomber totals, to clarify the number of delivery vehicles counted against SALT II limitations.

'Backfire' is included in the table only because much attention is given to this aircraft in the United States as a potential strategic delivery vehicle. It is the only weapon system in the table which is not officially recognized—indeed, disavowed—by the deploying government as a strategic weapon system. Moreover, it has been publicly recognized in US intelligence estimates as having less than intercontinental range in normal combat flight profile and as having been deployed at bases with peripherally oriented medium-range bombers and with naval aviation forces. As in the case of the Tu-95 'Bear', the naval aviation-assigned 'Backfires' are not included in the table at all. The medium-range bomber-assigned units, about half of production to date, shown in the table because of their prominence in the debate, are not included in the Soviet bomber totals.

For the past several years, the *Annual Report* of the US Secretary of Defense has included estimates of the total inventory of US bomber aircraft, including a large number of B-52s (about 220) in inactive storage. These aircraft will be counted against the SALT II delivery vehicle totals, even though many of them, perhaps most, are not in operating condition, and some may have been cannibalized or allowed to rust. (Almost all are older B-52 C/E/F models.)

Nuclear warheads

The estimates of independently targetable missile warheads can generally be reconciled with the official US estimates of total bomber and missile warheads if the following steps are taken: (*a*) bomber warhead loads are based on one bomb per 8 000–10 000 kg payload, using Unit

Equipment (UE) aircraft for the USA and adding SRAMs (1 140 operational missiles deployed on the bombers during 1972–75) to the internal payload; (*b*) in the case of US SLBMs, load on submarines under conversion and in overhaul are excluded altogether; and (*c*) for some early years, individual MRVs and not just MIRVs are counted separately in the force load total. The official US estimate of 7 000 independent nuclear warheads on Soviet strategic forces in 1981 can be obtained only if one or both of the following assumptions are made: that the most recent 'Delta III' submarines have been deployed with a 7-warhead version of the SS-N-18 rather than the 3-warhead version shown in the table as deployed on 'Delta IIIs'; or that a Soviet programme is under way to replace some of the 1-warhead SS-18s deployed in the last few years with a MIRVed version.

9. Military use of outer space

Square-bracketed numbers, thus [1], *refer to the list of references on page* 293.

The rate at which military satellites are launched has not changed significantly in the past decade or so (see chapter 5). In 1980, 103 military satellites were launched by the USA and the USSR. A summary of these satellites by mission is given in table 9.1 and details about the satellites are given in tables 9.2–9.9. It can be seen that nearly 40 per cent of the satellites are of the photographic reconnaissance type, and while most of these were launched by the Soviet Union, photographic reconnaissance from space is also performed extensively by the USA. The reason that only two US photographic reconnaissance satellites were launched in the past year is that these satellites remain in orbit for a very long time (see chapter 5). The extent of coverage during 1980 by such satellites for both nations is shown in figure 9.1. No new satellite was launched by the USA until February, but coverage was obtained in January by a KH-11 satellite launched in June 1978 and still in orbit in early 1981.

The use of photographic reconnaissance satellites for verifying the implementation of certain arms control agreements has become well established. Another use of such satellites has been to monitor conflict areas, for example, the 1973 Middle East War [1] and the Turkish invasion of Cyprus in 1974 [2]. The behaviour of some of the photographic reconnaissance satellites launched in 1980 indicates that the conflict between Iran and Iraq was monitored, at least during its initial phase.

A satellite is usually manoeuvred for two reasons; one is to extend its orbital life and the second is to scan a particular area on the Earth in greater detail. While these manoeuvres can usually be studied by plotting the ground tracks of a satellite, the amount of information that can be derived from them depends on whether the satellite is a long-lived or a short-lived one. For a long-lived satellite, it is difficult to identify the cause of manoeuvre. In the following section, therefore, only a Soviet satellite is discussed since most of these are short-lived with a lifetime of about 13 days. This does not mean that the US reconnaissance satellites did not perform similar orbital manoeuvres to observe the Iran–Iraq conflict.

I. Possible observation of the Iran–Iraq conflict by Cosmos satellites

The recent conflict between Iran and Iraq began on 22 September 1980. During this time Cosmos 1210, launched on 19 September, was already in

Figure 9.1. Coverage by US and Soviet photographic reconnaissance satellites launched during 1980

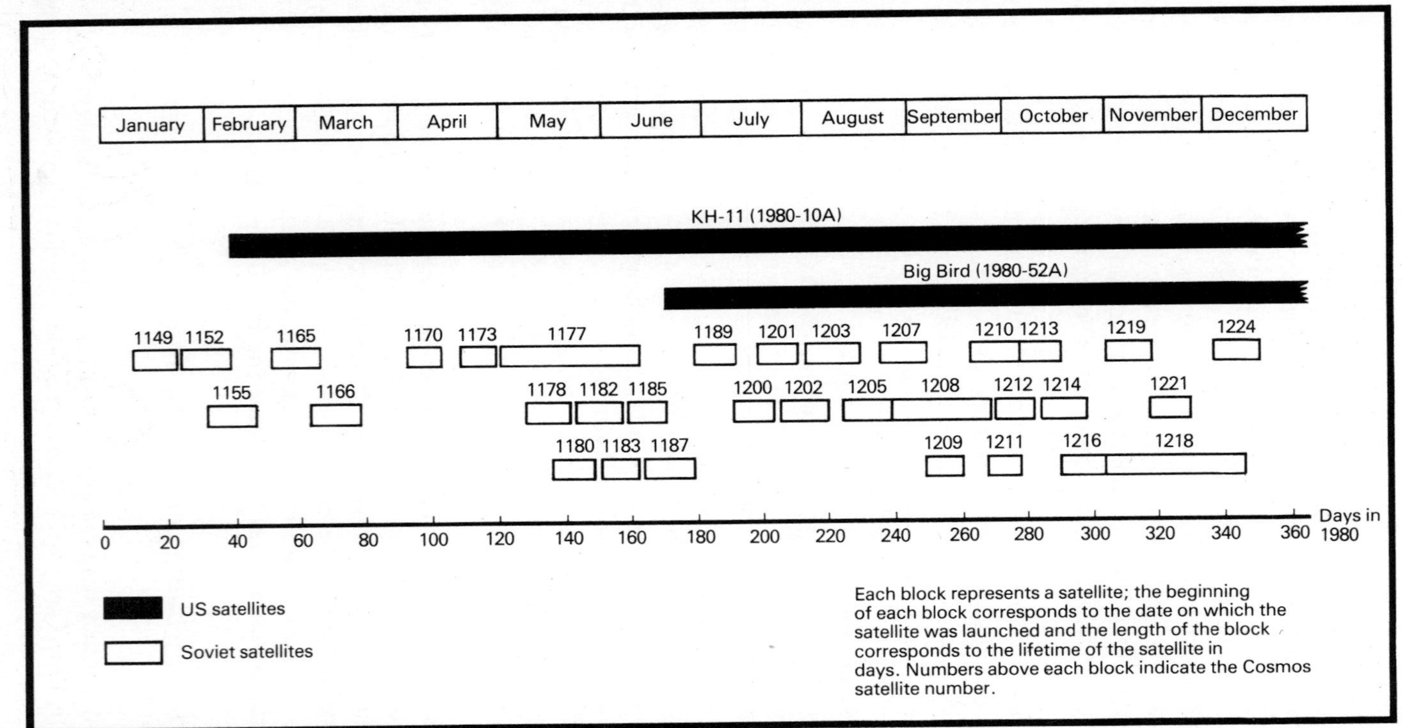

orbit; Cosmos 1211 was launched on 23 September, a day after the conflict began; and Cosmos 1212 was launched on 26 September. Of these three, Cosmos 1210 is that which most probably made observations of the conflict.

One indication of the area of interest on the Earth's surface for observation by a satellite is the position of the perigee of its orbit, since it is at this point that the satellite is closest to the Earth's surface. The perigee is a function of an orbital parameter called the argument of the perigee (ω). Normally the perigee and hence ω change because the Earth's uneven gravitational field causes the satellite orbit to rotate in its own plane. For a particular orbital inclination i, the rate of change of ω is given by

$$\frac{d\omega}{dt} = 4.9\ a^{7/2}(1-e^2)^{-1}(5\cos^2 i - 1)\ \text{degrees/day.}$$

This quantity does not change with time. In the formula, a, the semi-major axis of the orbit, and e, the eccentricity of the orbit, are constant for a given orbit. Therefore, if the values of ω are plotted against time a straight line should be obtained. Any discontinuity in the line would indicate that the satellite has been manoeuvred. For an orbital inclination of 63.4 degrees, the rate of change of ω is zero so that the perigee remains stationary. In figure 9.2, values of ω are plotted as a function of time for Cosmos 1210, 1211 and 1212. In all three cases discontinuity in the lines appears, suggesting some manoeuvring of the satellites. Since for orbits of high inclination ω is slightly greater than latitude, it can be seen from figure 9.2 that Cosmos 1211 and Cosmos 1212 have their perigees at very high latitudes, while the perigee of Cosmos 1210 comes over the area of interest during the satellite's lifetime. It should be noted that the orbits of Cosmos 1211 and 1212 are nearly circular.

Cosmos 1210

From figure 9.3 it can be seen that the ground tracks of Cosmos 1210 are closely spaced until the 158th orbit, after which the spacing between two consecutive tracks becomes greater. This change appears to occur after the 141st orbit, where discontinuity in the line of figure 9.2 is also apparent. Closeness of the tracks would indicate detailed observation of the area beneath the satellite. It must be noted here that such close spacing of the tracks and the position of the perigee occur elsewhere on the Earth's surface so that the areas of observation in figure 9.3 are not the exclusive ones. Other regions of particular interest for the Soviet Union are the United States and the People's Republic of China. The satellite ground tracks considered here pass over these countries too—at about midnight local time over the USA and in the late afternoon over China. Moreover,

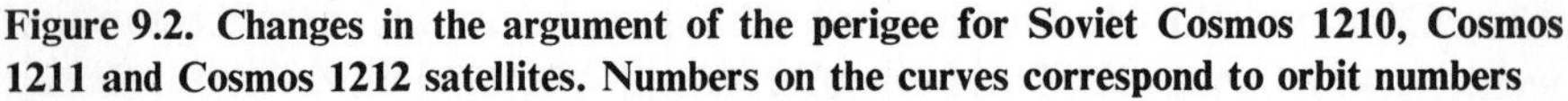

Figure 9.2. Changes in the argument of the perigee for Soviet Cosmos 1210, Cosmos 1211 and Cosmos 1212 satellites. Numbers on the curves correspond to orbit numbers

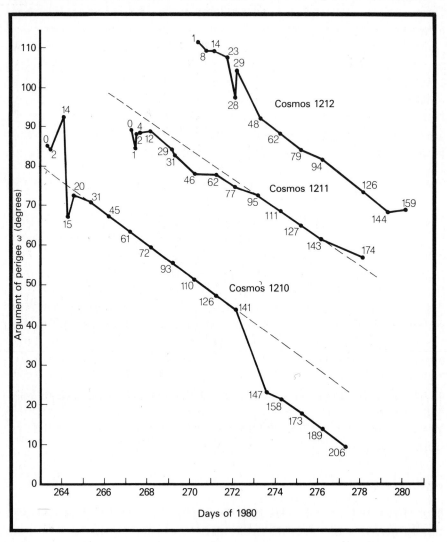

several of the orbital changes made for this satellite appear just before the satellite passes over Iran and Iraq. It was found that the perigee moved across Iran and Iraq and it was over the border of the two countries on 24 and 25 September, over Khorramshahr and Abadan, respectively. The local time during the passes in figure 9.3 was about 1115 hours.

In reality the altitude of the satellite did not vary much since its orbit was nearly circular. The satellite, therefore, could have taken photographs of events in the region considered during the initial period of the conflict.

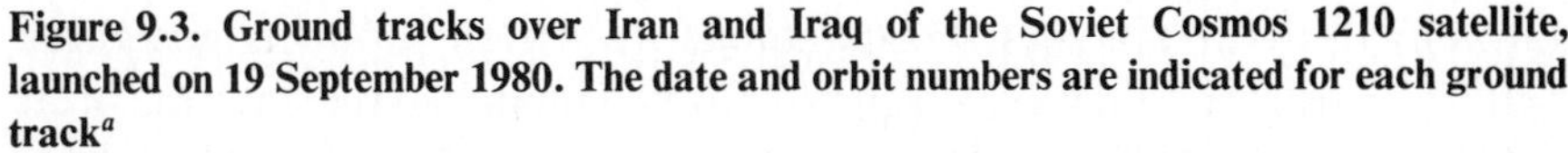

Figure 9.3. Ground tracks over Iran and Iraq of the Soviet Cosmos 1210 satellite, launched on 19 September 1980. The date and orbit numbers are indicated for each ground track[a]

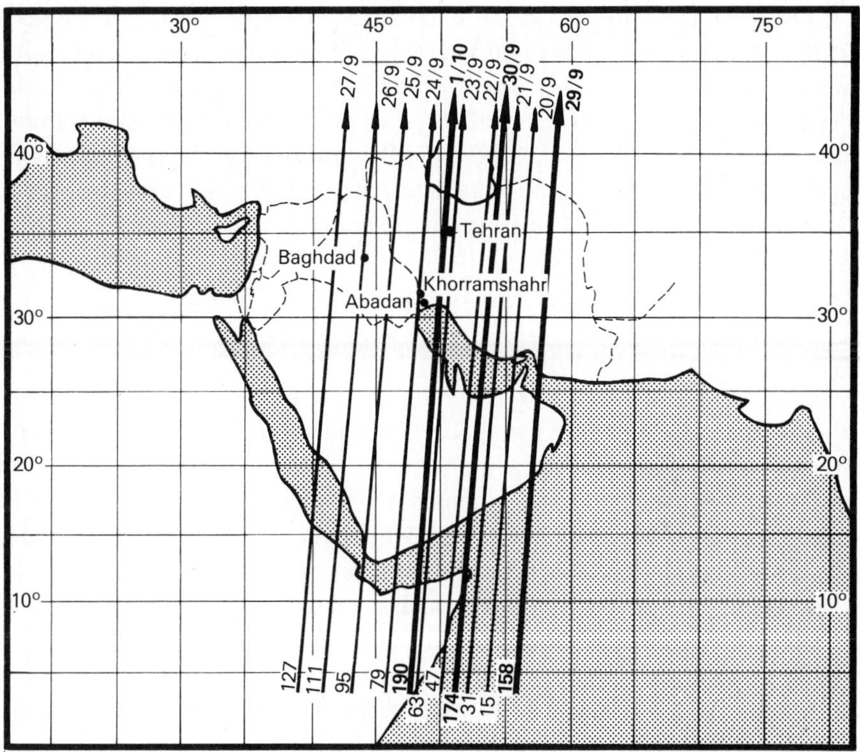

[a] It is interesting to briefly review the progress of the conflict during the initial period. It was reported that on 22 September Iraq attacked some Iranian cities including Tabriz, Tehran and Khorramshahr. Naval fighting in the Shatt al-Arab also took place. On 23 September, Iraqi troops crossed the Iraq–Iran border and attacked Abadan, Khorramshahr and Ahwas. Iran also bombed Iraqi cities including Baghdad and Basra. On 24 September the Kharg Island, Kirkuk, Mosul, Basra and Bandar Khomeini were under attack. On 25 September Baghdad was among the cities to be bombed. The conflict continues.

II. Ocean surveillance satellites

Of the reconnaissance satellites, the launch of Cosmos 1176 on 29 April 1980 was of special interest. This is an ocean surveillance satellite similar to Cosmos 954, which crash-landed in Canada in January 1978, contaminating part of the Earth's surface and possibly the atmosphere with radioactive materials. Such satellites carry a nuclear reactor to power the radar on board the satellite. After about two or three months in low orbit, such satellites are manoeuvred into high orbits of about 900-km altitude. At high altitude, the satellites will remain in orbit for some 500 years, a sufficient time for the short-lived radioactive fission products generated within the reactor to decay. Cosmos 1176 was manoeuvred into an orbit with a perigee of 870 km.

While a radar sensor can detect a naval vessel on the surface of the sea, it may not be possible to distinguish it from, for example, a large merchant ship or tanker. Normally, ocean surveillance satellites perform their mission in conjunction with satellites used to monitor electronic signals emitted from ships. This would help to distinguish a merchant ship from a naval vessel. Another purpose is to determine the direction and the speed of the vessel. Cosmos 1167 and Cosmos 1220 are probably naval electronic reconnaissance satellites [3].

III. Anti-satellite (ASAT) activities

Besides such satellites developed for observation of the Earth's surface, satellites to destroy other satellites in orbit have been tested. The Soviet Union appears to be developing such an ASAT capability. In the US ASAT system, however, a small missile would be launched from a high-altitude aircraft for the destruction of an Earth-orbiting satellite (see chapter 5). While the USA is expected to test such a system in the near future, the Soviet Union appears to have carried out its test in April 1980 when two satellites—a target (Cosmos 1171) and a hunter–killer (Cosmos 1174)—were launched. Other such tests were made during 1968–71 and during 1976–79.

It is interesting to note here that the concepts of peaceful uses of outer space seem to have been abandoned. 'Peaceful' is generally accepted to mean non-aggressive [4]. The development of the ASAT systems cannot be regarded as non-aggressive.

Apart from the ASAT systems in which satellite destruction would be achieved using conventional explosives, other methods, such as the use of high-energy laser beams and particle beams, are being investigated for ASAT applications. A method of destruction which has other applications is more likely to become a reality. High-energy beams belong to this category since, for example, they may in future be used for submarine communications. A high-energy laser beam could be used for the design of new nuclear weapons and for the study of the effects of nuclear weapons. High-energy particle and laser beams may already be used for these purposes. Above all, such high-energy beams are also thought to be suitable for ballistic missile defence (see chapter 8). Moreover, measures, such as an ASAT treaty or a Comprehensive Test Ban Treaty, to halt the development of such technologies are not under preparation.

IV. Tables

Table 9.1. Summary of satellites launched by the USSR and the USA during 1980

Satellite types	Number of satellites	
	USA	USSR
Photographic reconnaissance satellites	2	35
Electronic reconnaissance satellites	1	2
Ocean surveillance and oceanographic satellites	4	4
Early-warning satellites	–	5
Navigation satellites	2	6
Communications satellites	3	28
Meteorological satellites	2	6
Interceptor/destructor satellites	–	3
Totals	**14**	**89**
	103	

Table 9.2. Photographic reconnaissance satellites launched during 1980[a]

Country, satellite name and designation	Launch date and time (GMT)	Orbital inclination (deg) and period (min)	Perigee and apogee heights (km)	Comments
USA				
USAF (1980-10A)	7 Feb 2107	97.05 92.69	309 501	A KH-11 very long-lived digital imaging satellite
USAF (1980-52A)	18 Jun 1829	96.46 88.87	169 265	Big Bird satellite
USSR				
Cosmos 1149 (1980-01A)	9 Jan 1214	72.87 90.32	118 392	Lifetime 13.8 days; third-generation; high-resolution; manoeuvrable; TF recovery beacon
Cosmos 1152 (1980-06A)	24 Jan 1550	67.14 89.66	173 345	Lifetime 12.8 days; fourth-generation; high-resolution
Cosmos 1155 (1980-09A)	7 Feb 1102	72.86 90.45	195 397	Lifetime 13.7 days; third-generation; high-resolution; manoeuvrable
Cosmos 1165 (1980-17A)	21 Feb 1200	72.87 89.72	170 350	Lifetime 12.8 days; third-generation; TF recovery beacon
Cosmos 1166 (1980-20A)	4 Mar 1034	72.85 90.32	198 382	Lifetime 13.8 days; third-generation; high-resolution; manoeuvrable; TF recovery beacon
Cosmos 1170 (1980-25A)	1 Apr 0810	70.37 89.92	174 366	Lifetime 10.9 days; third-generation
Cosmos 1173 (1980-29A)	17 Apr 0838	70.30 89.59	155 354	Lifetime 10.9 days; third-generation; high-resolution; manoeuvrable; TF recovery beacon
Cosmos 1177 (1980-35A)	29 Apr 1312	67.14 89.69	174 346	Lifetime 44 days; fourth-generation; high-resolution; manoeuvrable

Country, satellite name and designation	Launch date and time (GMT)	Orbital inclination (deg) and period (min)	Perigee and apogee heights (km)	Comments
Cosmos 1178 (1980-36A)	7 May 1258	72.85 90.38	200 386	Lifetime 14.8 days; third-generation; high-resolution; manoeuvrable
Cosmos 1180 (1980-38A)	15 May 0546	62.81 89.79	238 291	Lifetime 11.7 days; third-generation; TL recovery beacon
Cosmos 1182 (1980-40A)	23 May 0712	82.34 89.14	211 251	Lifetime 12.9 days; third-generation
Cosmos 1183 (1980-42A)	28 May 1200	72.89 90.42	201 389	Lifetime 13.8 days; third-generation; high-resolution; manoeuvrable; TF recovery beacon
Cosmos 1185 (1980-46A)	6 Jun 0658	82.34 89.49	214 282	Lifetime 13.9 days; third-generation; high-resolution; manoeuvrable; TF recovery beacon
Cosmos 1187 (1980-48A)	12 Jun 1229	72.85 89.57	199 307	Lifetime 13.8 days; third-generation; high-resolution; manoeuvrable
Cosmos 1189 (1980-54A)	26 Jun 1229	72.88 89.55	198 305	Lifetime 13.8 days; third-generation; TF recovery beacon
Cosmos 1200 (1980-59A)	9 Jul 1243	72.86 89.57	198 307	Lifetime 13.8 days; third-generation; high-resolution; manoeuvrable; TF recovery beacon
Cosmos 1201 (1980-61A)	15 Jul 0735	82.33 89.12	213 247	Lifetime 12.9 days; third-generation; TK recovery beacon; also Earth resources mission
Cosmos 1202 (1980-65A)	24 Jul 1243	72.85 89.57	198 307	Lifetime 13.8 days; third-generation; TF recovery beacon
Cosmos 1203 (1980-66A)	31 Jul 0755	82.32 89.36	213 270	Lifetime 13.9 days; third-generation; high-resolution; manoeuvrable; TF recovery beacon
Cosmos 1205 (1980-68A)	12 Aug 1200	72.82 89.56	199 306	Lifetime 13.8 days; third-generation; high-resolution; manoeuvrable; TF recovery beacon
Cosmos 1207 (1980-70A)	22 Aug 1005	82.32 89.19	211 256	Lifetime 12.9 days; third-generation; TK recovery beacon
Cosmos 1208 (1980-71A)	26 Aug 1536	67.14 89.60	173 339	Lifetime 28.5 days; fourth-generation; high-resolution
Cosmos 1209 (1980-72A)	3 Sep 1019	82.34 89.44	211 280	Lifetime 13.9 days; third-generation; high-resolution; manoeuvrable; TF recovery beacon
Cosmos 1210 (1980-76A)	19 Sep 1019	82.33 88.76	180 244	Lifetime 13.8 days; third-generation; high-resolution; manoeuvrable; TF recovery beacon
Cosmos 1211 (1980-77A)	23 Sep 1033	82.35 89.11	216 242	Lifetime 10.9 days; third-generation; TL recovery beacon
Cosmos 1212 (1980-78A)	26 Sep 1019	82.34 89.11	209 249	Lifetime 12.8 days; third-generation; TK recovery beacon; also Earth resources mission
Cosmos 1213 (1980-80A)	3 Oct 1200	72.87 89.69	229 289	Lifetime 13.8 days; third-generation; high-resolution; manoeuvrable; TF recovery beacon
Cosmos 1214 (1980-82A)	10 Oct 1312	67.15 89.67	174 345	Lifetime 12.8 days; third-generation

Country, satellite name and designation	Launch date and time (GMT)	Orbital inclination (deg) and period (min)	Perigee and apogee heights (km)	Comments
Cosmos 1216 (1980-84A)	16 Oct 1229	72.87 90.29	198 379	Lifetime 13.8 days; third-generation; high-resolution; manoeuvrable; TF recovery beacon
Cosmos 1218 (1980-86A)	30 Oct 1005	64.89 89.73	171 353	Lifetime 43 days; fourth-generation; manoeuvrable; high-resolution
Cosmos 1219 (1980-88A)	31 Oct 1200	72.85 89.70	228 291	Lifetime 13 days; third-generation; TF recovery beacon
Cosmos 1221 (1980-90A)	12 Nov 1229	72.90 90.49	196 399	Lifetime 14 days; third-generation; high-resolution; manoeuvrable; TF recovery beacon
Cosmos 1224 (1980-96A)	1 Dec 1214	72.87 90.29	198 378	Lifetime 14 days; third-generation; high-resolution; manoeuvrable; TF recovery beacon
Cosmos 1227 (1980-101A)	16 Dec 1214	72.80 89.50	109 300	Lifetime 12 days; third-generation; TF recovery beacon
Cosmos 1236 (1980-105A)	26 Dec 1912	67.15 89.70	169 363	Lifetime about 6 weeks; third-generation

[a] Recovery beacon data supplied by the Kettering Group.

Table 9.3. Possible electronic reconnaissance satellites launched during 1980

Country, satellite name and designation	Launch date and time (GMT)	Orbital inclination (deg) and period (min)	Perigee and apogee heights (km)	Comments
USA				
USAF (1980-52C)	18 Jun 1829	96.62 112.31	1 331 1 333	Satellite was ejected from the Big Bird spacecraft (1980-52A)
USSR				
Cosmos 1186 (1980-47A)	6 Jun 1102	74.02 94.54	473 519	Lifetime 18 months; lower orbital period than usual; does not fit the orbital plane spacing of the main group[a]
Cosmos 1215 (1980-83A)	14 Oct 2038	74.04 95.12	498 550	Lifetime 10 years

[a] Information from G. E. Perry, private communication.

Table 9.4. Ocean surveillance and oceanographic satellites launched during 1980

Country, satellite name and designation	Launch date and time (GMT)	Orbital inclination (deg) and period (min)	Perigee and apogee heights (km)	Comments
USA				
NOSS-3 (1980-19A)	3 Mar 1117	63.03 107.12	1 035 1 150	Navy ocean-surveillance satellites; quadruple launch; sub-satellites are SSU satellites
NOSS-3 (1980-19C)	3 Mar 1117	63.49 107.40	1 048 1 166	
NOSS-3 (1980-19D)	3 Mar 1117	63.49 107.40	1 048 1 166	
NOSS-3 (1980-19E)	3 Mar 1117	63.49 107.40	1 048 1 166	
USSR				
Cosmos 1151 (1980-05A)	23 Jan 0658	82.52 97.78	637 666	Oceanographic satellite; lifetime 60 years
Cosmos 1167 (1980-21A)	14 Mar 1048	65.03 93.31	426 442	Equipped with ion-thrusters to maintain a near circular orbit; thought to be performing naval electronic reconnaissance[a]
Cosmos 1176 (1980-34A)	29 Apr 1005	65.02 89.65	250 266	Jettisoned rocket and platform; manoeuvred into circular orbit with a perigee of 870 km
Cosmos 1220 (1980-89A)	4 Nov 1507	65.04 93.3	427 440	Similar satellite to Cosmos 1167 above; these two are working as a pair[a]

[a] See reference [3].

Table 9.5. Possible early-warning satellites launched during 1980

Country, satellite name and designation	Launch date and time (GMT)	Orbital inclination (deg) and period (min)	Perigee and apogee heights (km)	Comments
USSR				
Cosmos 1172 (1980-28A)	12 Apr 2024	62.77 726.03	608 40 155	
Cosmos 1188 (1980-50A)	14 Jun 2053	62.92 725.53	609 40 129	
Cosmos 1191 (1980-57A)	2 Jul 0058	62.67 725.41	605 40 127	
Cosmos 1217 (1980-85A)	24 Oct 1229	62.92 725.33	596 40 131	
Cosmos 1223 (1980-95A)	27 Nov 2317	62.87 717.73	605 39 749	

Table 9.6. Meteorological satellites launched during 1980

Country, satellite name and designation	Launch date and time (GMT)	Orbital inclination (deg) and period (min)	Perigee and apogee heights (km)	Comments
USA				
NASA/NOAA 7 (1980-43A)	29 May 1048	92.23 102.05	264 1 445	National Oceanographic and Atmospheric Administration satellite; intended orbit not achieved
NASA/GOES-4 (1980-74A)	9 Sep 2234	0.19 1 436.2	35 776 35 800	Geostationary Operational Environmental Satellite; planned initial location at longitude 90°W
USSR				
Cosmos 1154 (1980-08A)	30 Jun 1258	81.23 97.48	630 644	
Cosmos 1184 (1980-44A)	4 Jun 0735	81.25 97.43	623 647	
Meteor 30 (1980-51A)	18 Jun 0614	97.94 97.24	584 667	
Cosmos 1206 (1980-69A)	15 Aug 0531	81.21 97.37	630 634	
Meteor 2-06 (1980-73A)	9 Sep 1102	81.25 102.39	848 894	
Cosmos 1222 (1980-93A)	21 Nov 1200	81.23 97.38	631 633	

Table 9.7. Communications satellites launched during 1980

Country, satellite name and designation	Launch date and time (GMT)	Orbital inclination (deg) and period (min)	Perigee and apogee heights (km)	Comments
USA				
Fleetsatcom 3 (1980-04A)	18 Jan 0126	2.40 1 423.00	35 405 35 661	Third of a series designed to provide communication links between small ground stations in 200–400 MHz band; located above longitude 172°E
Fleetsatcom 4 (1980-87A)	31 Oct 0350	2.40 1 418.72	34 903 35 991	Fourth of five Defense Department communications satellites
USAF (1980-100A)	13 Dec —	— —	— —	Orbital elements unannounced; it has been reported as a probable Satellite Data System launched by T-3B in a 64°, 250 km × 39 127 km orbit [5]
USSR				
Molniya 1-46 (1980-02A)	11 Jan 1229	62.88 717.87	442 39 920	
Cosmos 1156 (1980-12A)	11 Feb 2331	74.02 114.64	1 400 1 475	Octuple launch
Cosmos 1157 (1980-12B)	11 Feb 2331	74.02 114.85	1 417 1 477	
Cosmos 1158 (1980-12C)	11 Feb 2331	74.02 115.05	1 435 1 478	
Cosmos 1159 (1980-12D)	11 Feb 2331	74.02 115.26	1 453 1 481	
Cosmos 1160 (1980-12E)	11 Feb 2331	74.02 115.47	1 467 1 486	
Cosmos 1161 (1980-12F)	11 Feb 2331	74.02 115.71	1 469 1 505	
Cosmos 1162 (1980-12G)	11 Feb 2331	74.02 115.94	1 472 1 523	
Cosmos 1163 (1980-12H)	11 Feb 2331	74.02 116.20	1 472 1 545	
Cosmos 1164 (1980-13A)	12 Feb 0058	62.82 763.87	435 40 858	Failed to replace Molniya 1-43[a]
Statsionar-2 (1980-16A)	20 Feb 0810	0.60 1 486.15	36 087 37 438	
Cosmos 1175 (1980-31C)	18 Apr 1731	62.81 92.30	313 463	Failed to replace Molniya 3-9[a]
Statsionar-4 (1980-49A)	14 Jun 0058	0.81 1 436.1	35 744 35 828	
Molniya 1-47 (1980-53A)	21 Jun 2010	62.83 737.68	631 40 703	
Cosmos 1190 (1980-56A)	1 Jul 0712	74.05 100.86	792 806	Store–dump communications satellite?

Country, satellite name and designation	Launch date and time (GMT)	Orbital inclination (deg) and period (min)	Perigee and apogee heights (km)	Comments
Cosmos 1192 (1980-58A)	9 Jul 0043	74.02 114.61	1 398 1 476	Octuple launch
Cosmos 1193 (1980-58B)	9 Jul 0043	74.02 115.21	1 452 1 477	
Cosmos 1194 (1980-58C)	9 Jul 0043	74.01 114.82	1 414 1 479	
Cosmos 1195 (1980-58D)	9 Jul 0043	74.02 115.41	1 470 1 477	
Cosmos 1196 (1980-58E)	9 Jul 0043	74.02 115.63	1 473 1 494	
Cosmos 1197 (1980-58F)	9 Jul 0043	74.02 115.83	1 475 1 510	
Cosmos 1198 (1980-58G)	9 Jul 0043	74.02 116.08	1 475 1 533	
Cosmos 1199 (1980-58H)	9 Jul 0043	74.01 115.01	1 433 1 478	
Ekran 5 (1980-60A)	15 Jul 0307	0.36 ~1 420	~35 474 ~35 474	Statsionar T
Molniya 3-13 (1980-63A)	18 Jul 1048	62.81 736.48	457 40 818	
Statsionar 3 (1980-81A)	5 Oct 1717	0.33 1 436.0	35 730 35 840	
Molniya 1-48 (1980-92A)	16 Nov 0434	62.78 736.23	601 40 662	
Cosmos 1228 (1980-102A)	24 Dec 2248	74.02 114.41	1 391 1 464	Octuple launch
Cosmos 1229 (1980-102B)	24 Dec 2248	73.82 115.05	1 416 1 498	
Cosmos 1230 (1980-102C)	24 Dec 2248	74.17 114.51	1 412 1 452	
Cosmos 1231 (1980-102D)	24 Dec 2248	74 04 114.59	1 410 1 461	
Cosmos 1232 (1980-102E)	24 Dec 2248	74.01 114.60	1 414 1 458	
Cosmos 1233 (1980-102F)	24 Dec 2248	74.02 114.07	1 372 1 452	
Cosmos 1234 (1980-102G)	24 Dec 2248	73.99 114.44	1 404 1 454	
Cosmos 1235 (1980-102H)	24 Dec 2248	73.74 114.32	1 392 1 455	
Ekran 6 (1980-104A)	26 Dec 1326	0.07 1 439.85	35 859 35 859	Statsionar T

[a] Information from G. E. Perry, private communication.

Table 9.8. Navigation satellites launched during 1980

Country, satellite name and designation	Launch date and time (GMT)	Orbital inclination (deg) and period (min)	Perigee and apogee heights (km)	Comments
USA				
USAF/ Navstar 5 (1980-11A)	9 Feb 2317	63.72 717.23	20 083 20 147	Fifth in a network of 18 satellites
USAF/ Navstar 6 (1980-32A)	26 Apr 2150	62.88 707.73	19 628 30 232	Sixth in a network of 18 satellites
USSR[a]				
Cosmos 1150 (1980-03A)	14 Jan 1938	82.95 105.01	971 1 017	Number 3 to replace Cosmos 1011 which was renumbered 8
Cosmos 1153 (1980-07A)	25 Jan 2219	82.93 105.00	967 1 020	Number 4 to replace Cosmos 1091 which was renumbered 7
Cosmos 1168 (1980-22A)	17 Mar 2136	82.95 104.92	964 1 015	Number 11 to replace Cosmos 883
Cosmos 1181 (1980-39A)	30 May 0922	82.95 104.97	976 1 008	Number 5 to replace Cosmos 1072 which was renumbered 8; Cosmos 1011 became obsolete
Cosmos 1225 (1980-97A)	5 Dec 0419	82.9 104.93	950 1 031	Number 2 to replace Cosmos 1089 which was renumbered 7; Cosmos 1091 became obsolete
Cosmos 1226 (1980-99A)	10 Dec 2234	82.94 104.92	966 1 014	Number 13 to replace Cosmos 1000 which stopped functioning

[a] Numbers are the Soviet identity numbers (G. E. Perry, private communication).

Table 9.9. Possible interceptor/destructor satellites launched during 1980

Country, satellite name and designation	Launch date and time (GMT)	Orbital inclination (deg) and period (min)	Perigee and apogee heights (km)	Comments
USSR				
Cosmos 1169 (1980-23A)	27 Mar 0735	65.84 94.52	477 515	Probably served as a calibration target for ground radars
Cosmos 1171 (1980-26A)	3 Apr 0735	65.84 104.89	947 1 033	Target satellite like Cosmos 400 and 967; orbital heights similar to Soviet navigation satellites
Cosmos 1174 (1980-30A)	18 Apr 0058	65.84 98.63	362 1 025	Interceptor

References

1. *World Armaments and Disarmament, SIPRI Yearbook 1974* (Almqvist & Wiksell, Stockholm, 1974, Stockholm International Peace Research Institute), pp. 289–96.
2. *World Armaments and Disarmament, SIPRI Yearbook 1975* (Almqvist & Wiksell, Stockholm, 1975, Stockholm International Peace Research Institute), pp. 385–91.
3. Perry, G. E., Sharpling, T. A. and Grahn, S., 'Ocean Elint Cosmos satellites', *Flight International*, Vol. 118, No. 3737, 20 December 1980, p. 2278.
4. Jasani, B. and Lunderius, M. A., 'Peaceful uses of outer space—legal fiction and military reality', *Bulletin of Peace Proposals*, Vol. 11, No. 1, March 1980, pp. 57–70.
5. 'USAF Titan launch', *Aviation Week & Space Technology*, Vol. 114, No. 2, 12 January 1981, p. 18.

Part III. Developments in arms control in 1980

10. The Second NPT Review Conference

Square-bracketed numbers, thus [1], *refer to the list of references on page* 336.

I. Introduction

The second conference to review the 1968 Treaty on the Non-Proliferation of Nuclear Weapons (NPT) met in Geneva from 11 August to 7 September 1980, in accordance with Article VIII of the Treaty. The First Review Conference was held in 1975.

The Preparatory Committee for the Second NPT Review Conference, composed of the parties to the Treaty which were serving on the Board of Governors of the International Atomic Energy Agency (IAEA) or were represented on the Committee on Disarmament (CD), met in three sessions during 1979–80. The Preparatory Committee prepared the agenda, the rules of procedures and a schedule for the division of the costs of the Conference—all following the precedents set by the First Review Conference. It also issued background documents prepared by the UN Secretariat, the IAEA, and the Agency for the Prohibition of Nuclear Weapons in Latin America (OPANAL).

Since the First Review Conference, 21 additional states had joined the Treaty. The newcomers included countries with significant nuclear activities, such as Japan, the second largest producer of nuclear electricity in the world, and Switzerland, a country with the largest share of nuclear-supplied electrical power. However, attendance at the Conference was poor. Of a total of 114 NPT parties, only 75 or two-thirds attended. Egypt, a signatory state which had not ratified the Treaty, participated in the deliberations of the Conference without taking part in its decisions,[1] while 11 states that had neither signed nor ratified the NPT were present as observers without the right to address the Conference: Algeria, Argentina, Brazil, Chile, Cuba, Israel, Mozambique, Spain, Tanzania, the United Arab Emirates and Zambia.

The Conference opened with a general debate, in which 52 delegations took part and during which the Director General of the IAEA addressed the plenary. The Conference then pursued its work in two Main Committees. Committee I was given the task of reviewing the NPT provisions relating to non-transfer and non-acquisition of nuclear weapons, as well as the disarmament obligations and the question of security assurances.

[1] Egypt became party to the NPT only in 1981.

Committee II dealt with the provisions for the peaceful applications of nuclear energy, including nuclear safeguards.

Informal consultations at the Conference took place in three distinct groups: a Western group, a group of Socialist states, and a group of Third World countries, called 'the Group of 77'. This last group, which originally assembled 77 Third World states at the United Nations Conference on Trade and Development (UNCTAD) and which now includes over 110 states and other political entities, has become a well-known caucus on economic issues at the United Nations. But at the Second NPT Review Conference, the group was formed to deal with arms control matters. Approximately 40 NPT parties participated in its meetings, which were attended also by Egypt, as well as by most of the observers at the Conference.[2]

The Review Conference ended without making any substantive statement. The Final Document adopted [1] merely recorded the proceedings of the Conference and contained the recommendation that the NPT depositary governments (the UK, the USA and the USSR) convene a third review conference in 1985. The Secretary-General of the United Nations was requested to include in the provisional agenda of the 38th UN General Assembly (in 1983) an item dealing with the establishment of a preparatory committee for this Conference. (For the full text of the Final Document, see appendix 10A.)

Intense negotiations did, however, take place in an attempt to draft a substantive consensus declaration. Numerous proposals for such a declaration were included in official Conference documents. Moreover, informal working papers were produced which reviewed the implementation of the NPT provisions and contained specific recommendations. Although these working papers had no official status, they adequately reflected both the extent of the agreement reached and the magnitude of the outstanding differences. (For the texts of the working papers, see appendices 10B–10E.)

II. Non-transfer and non-acquisition of nuclear weapons

Article I of the NPT states that *Each nuclear-weapon State Party to the Treaty undertakes not to transfer to any recipient whatsoever nuclear weapons or other nuclear explosive devices or control over such weapons or explosive devices directly, or indirectly; and not in any way to assist, encourage, or induce any non-nuclear-weapon State to manufacture or*

[2] The Group of 77 often acted at the Conference as the spokesman for non-aligned states, although the two groups are not identical in spite of a large overlap in membership.

otherwise acquire nuclear weapons or other nuclear explosive devices, or control over such weapons or explosive devices.

The first part of Article I gave rise to relatively few questions. No complaints were made about transfer of nuclear explosive devices or transfer of control over these devices (even though, reportedly, attempts had been made to purchase them directly from nuclear weapon powers). However, the view was recorded that the deployment of nuclear weapons on the territories of non-nuclear weapon states and in international waters was "contrary to the nuclear non-proliferation objective of the Treaty" (see appendix 10B, review of Article I, para. 4). And, informally, certain delegations expressed fears that further sophistication of tactical nuclear weapons in Europe, and concomitant doctrines for their use, might require transfer of control over such weapons to members of the military alliance.

The extent to which the second part of Article I had been implemented proved to be more controversial, due to divergent interpretations of this clause.

Because there exists a significant overlap between the technologies for civilian nuclear energy and those useful for military and, specifically, explosive purposes, and because nuclear material and technology, nominally destined for nuclear power programmes, are exported by the parties to countries which have kept their nuclear weapon option open, it can be argued that the obligation not in *any way* to assist non-nuclear weapon states to manufacture nuclear explosive devices has not been observed. Indeed, many participants at the Review Conference expressed their concern that certain forms of nuclear co-operation contributed to the development of a nuclear weapon capability by non-parties to the Treaty (see appendix 10B, review of Article I, para. 5a). Nevertheless, there was considerable reluctance to specify all the cases where this danger existed. The Group of 77 asserted that such 'oblique proliferation' had taken place in regard to Israel and South Africa [2] and insisted that exporters of nuclear materials should terminate all nuclear contracts and co-operation with these two countries. Other delegations remarked that the problem was not limited to two states alone and expressed concern over similar developments in other regions, stressing that selective embargoes would not suffice. Some argued that to prevent oblique proliferation effectively, nuclear material and equipment would have to be denied to any country which is not bound by a legal commitment not to acquire nuclear weapons.

Under the NPT, only nuclear weapon states are prohibited to assist, encourage or induce non-nuclear weapon states to manufacture nuclear devices. The Treaty does not expressly prohibit the provision of such assistance, encouragement or inducement by a non-nuclear weapon state. But, as early as 1968, in response to a proposal to close this apparent loophole in the NPT, the Soviet Union made it clear that if a non-nuclear weapon state party to the Treaty were to assist another non-nuclear weapon state to manufacture and acquire nuclear weapons, such a case should be regarded as a violation of the Treaty. (This understanding was reiterated during the 1975 NPT Review Conference.)[3] The USA argued that a non-nuclear weapon state which had accepted the Treaty's restrictions would have no reason to assist a country not accepting the same restrictions to gain advantages in the field of nuclear weapon development. The USA also stated that if a non-nuclear weapon party nevertheless attempted to provide such assistance to a non-party, the presumption would immediately arise that it acted for the purpose of developing nuclear weapons for itself, in violation of the Treaty. These interpretations, made by the powers responsible for the formulation of the relevant provisions of the NPT, were not contested by any state. The question came up again at the Second Review Conference, and there was support for the view that the obligation not to "assist, encourage, or induce" under Article I should apply to both nuclear and non-nuclear weapon states.

Whatever the assurances given by states about the observance of the second part of Article I, there is ample proof that NPT parties are guilty of having brought certain non-parties to the nuclear weapon threshold.

It is known that India's nuclear explosion in 1974 was made possible by the availability of fissile material produced in a Canadian-supplied reactor and the use of heavy water supplied by the USA. Canada cut off its nuclear co-operation with India after the explosion, but the US government, contradicting its own non-proliferation policy, decided to continue to provide India with enriched uranium [4] and obtained Congressional approval of the sale, in spite of the US Nuclear Regulatory Commission recommendation to withhold the exports.

A perceived nuclear threat from India may have prompted Pakistan to attempt to acquire a nuclear weapon capability.[4] Pakistan announced that it was already manufacturing nuclear fuel (based on natural uranium) for a heavy water reactor and had thereby "joined the select group of technologically advanced nations which were self-reliant" in this respect [5]. Pakistan is also building a uranium enrichment plant, modelled on a plant at Almelo, Netherlands, having obtained the bulk of its components from several suppliers in states party to the NPT, including the Federal Republic of Germany, Switzerland and the United Kingdom. Reports about the construction of a facility to reprocess spent fuel [6],

[3] In the view of the USSR, the commitment not to encourage the proliferation of nuclear weapons is now a "recognized rule of contemporary international law" [3].

[4] There have also been reports that Pakistan started its nuclear weapon programme well before the Indian nuclear explosion.

apparently based mainly on French-supplied technology, indicate that indigenous production of plutonium by Pakistan may soon also be a reality. (As of 1979, the estimated amount of plutonium contained in spent fuel from a Canadian-built heavy water reactor in Pakistan was about 170 kg [7], or enough to make roughly 35 bombs of the Nagasaki type.) A good part of this enterprise is allegedly financed by Libya [8].

South Africa, which is suspected of already having carried out a nuclear explosion, had received considerable help in the nuclear field from several countries. The USA stopped its supplies to South Africa, but others continued nuclear co-operation with this country. There have been reports that a French–Belgian company has contracted to fabricate fuel rods for the French-supplied South African power plants [9]. South Africa has also built a uranium enrichment facility, based mainly on West German technologies, which is unsafeguarded and which by now could have produced a sufficient quantity of weapon-grade uranium for at least a few nuclear weapons [10].

Brazil and Argentina insist on their right to carry out nuclear explosions for peaceful purposes. Not only have they refused to sign the NPT, but the Treaty of Tlatelolco, prohibiting nuclear weapons in Latin America, is not in force for either country. Nevertheless, the Federal Republic of Germany has undertaken to supply Brazil with a complete nuclear fuel cycle, including enrichment and reprocessing facilities [11]. Argentina, which is building a fuel fabrication plant and which will complete the construction of a plutonium reprocessing facility in the early 1980s [12], is importing a heavy water reactor from FR Germany and a heavy water production plant from Switzerland.

Israel, which has been reported to possess several untested nuclear bombs, acquired its nuclear weapon capability due to a reactor supplied by France many years before the NPT and not covered by international controls, as well as heavy water supplied by Norway.

Cuba and North Korea are supplied with Soviet nuclear equipment and material, even though they have not become parties to the NPT.

It is, of course, unlikely that any of the suppliers mentioned above are intentionally seeking to promote the development of nuclear weapons in the recipient states. In most cases, they are motivated by a mixture of political and largely commercial interests. The nuclear industry is facing serious problems in nearly all supplier states. During 1979, the total number of nuclear power plants on order decreased, and this trend continued in the first half of 1980: more plants were cancelled than ordered [13]. Increasing costs and public resistance to nuclear energy in a number of countries are rendering nuclear industry less profitable, and a dwindling market has placed its viability in doubt, at least in North America and a good part of Western Europe. It is not surprising, therefore, to find this highly capital-intensive industry, which faces declining internal demand, in fierce competition in the export area.

International efforts to stop the spread of nuclear weapons are endangered by commercial pressures; long-term security problems are being created by short-term economic interests. To argue that the importing non-NPT countries would develop nuclear weapon capabilities even without aid from the parties, by using their own domestic resources or in co-operation with other non-parties, does not obviate the need for restraint. Acquiring indigenous technologies requires considerably more time than using imported technologies; and since it might also represent an unacceptable economic burden, the effort to reach a nuclear weapon capability might in some cases have to be abandoned. If the NPT parties themselves speed up proliferation by making it easier and less costly for non-parties to traverse the route towards a nuclear bomb, they must bear the responsibility for undermining the Treaty.

The more than 10 years that have passed since the entry into force of the NPT have demonstrated its wide international acceptance: two-thirds of the world's states have joined the Treaty. They include three nuclear weapon powers—the UK, the USA and the USSR—as well as many highly developed, industrialized and militarily significant non-nuclear weapon countries. Even France, a non-party, stated that it would behave as a state adhering to the Treaty [14] and that it would follow a policy of strengthening appropriate arrangements and safeguards relating to nuclear equipment, material and technology [15], while the People's Republic of China, though formally opposed to the NPT, has in practice not acted contrary to non-proliferation objectives. As a matter of fact, no arms control agreement has attracted so many adherents as has the NPT. In this situation, it is difficult to accept, at face value, the argument put forward by a handful of non-parties to the NPT, which in most cases are heavily dependent on other countries, that the Treaty is both objectionable on account of its discriminatory provisions and incompatible with the sovereign rights of states. It is more reasonable to assume that in refusing to join the Treaty the non-nuclear weapon countries with civilian nuclear activities, especially those operating unsafeguarded nuclear facilities, wish to preserve the possibility of acquiring a nuclear weapon. Continuation of nuclear supplies to these countries must be regarded as contradictory to the aims of the NPT.

Article II of the NPT states that *Each non-nuclear-weapon State Party to the Treaty undertakes not to receive the transfer from any transferor whatsoever of nuclear weapons or other nuclear explosive devices or of control over such weapons or explosive devices directly, or indirectly; not to manufacture or otherwise acquire nuclear weapons or other nuclear explosive*

Table 10.1. Parties to the Non-Proliferation Treaty, as of 31 December 1980[a]

Afghanistan (1970)
Australia (1973)
Austria (1969)
Bahamas (1976)
Bangladesh (1979)
Barbados (1980)
Belgium (1975)
Benin (1972)
Bolivia (1970)
Botswana (1969)
Bulgaria (1969)
Burundi (1971)
Canada (1969)
Cape Verde (1979)
Central African Republic (1970)
Chad (1971)
Congo (1978)
Costa Rica (1970)
Cyprus (1970)
Czechoslovakia (1969)
Democratic Kampuchea (1972)
Democratic Yemen (Southern Yemen) (1979)
Denmark (1969)
Dominican Republic (1971)
Ecuador (1969)
El Salvador (1972)
Ethiopia (1970)
Fiji (1972)
Finland (1969)
Gabon (1974)
Gambia (1975)
German Democratic Republic (1969)
Germany, Federal Republic of (1975)
Ghana (1970)
Greece (1970)
Grenada (1975)
Guatemala (1970)
Guinea-Bissau (1976)
Haiti (1970)
Holy See (Vatican City) (1971)
Honduras (1973)
Hungary (1969)
Iceland (1969)
Indonesia (1979)
Iran (1970)
Iraq (1969)
Ireland (1968)
Italy (1975)
Ivory Coast (1973)
Jamaica (1970)
Japan (1976)
Jordan (1970)
Kenya (1970)
Korea, South (1975)
Lao People's Democratic Republic (1970)
Lebanon (1970)
Lesotho (1970)
Liberia (1970)
Libya (1975)
Liechtenstein (1978)
Luxembourg (1975)
Madagascar (1970)
Malaysia (1970)
Maldives (1970)
Mali (1970)
Malta (1970)
Mauritius (1969)
Mexico (1969)
Mongolia (1969)
Morocco (1970)
Nepal (1970)
Netherlands (1975)
New Zealand (1969)
Nicaragua (1973)
Nigeria (1968)
Norway (1969)
Panama (1977)
Paraguay (1970)
Peru (1970)
Philippines (1972)
Poland (1969)
Portugal (1977)
Romania (1970)
Rwanda (1975)
Saint Lucia (1979)
Samoa (1975)
San Marino (1970)
Senegal (1970)
Sierra Leone (1975)
Singapore (1976)
Somalia (1970)
Sri Lanka (1979)
Sudan (1973)
Suriname (1976)
Swaziland (1969)
Sweden (1970)
Switzerland (1977)
Syria (1969)
Taiwan (1970)
Thailand (1972)
Togo (1970)
Tonga (1971)
Tunisia (1970)
Turkey (1980)
Tuvalu (1979)
Union of Soviet Socialist Republics (1970)
United Kingdom (1968)
United Republic of Cameroon (1969)
United States of America (1970)
Upper Volta (1970)
Uruguay (1970)
Venezuela (1975)
Yugoslavia (1970)
Zaire (1970)

[a] The following states have signed but not ratified the Treaty: Colombia, Kuwait, Trinidad and Tobago, and Yemen (Northern Yemen). Egypt ratified in 1981.

devices; and not to seek or receive any assistance in the manufacture of nuclear weapons or other nuclear explosive devices.

In regard to this Article, the Conference confirmed that the obligations undertaken by the non-nuclear weapon states had been observed (see appendix 10B, review of Article II, para. 7). There was no evidence that any non-nuclear weapon party to the NPT had manufactured or otherwise acquired nuclear explosive devices.

It should be noted, however, that certain non-nuclear weapon states may have designed nuclear weapons and perhaps even developed their non-nuclear components, since there is nothing in the NPT or in the existing agreements on nuclear transfers to prevent these activities. If such a state ever made a political decision to produce a nuclear weapon, it would only need the necessary amount of weapon-grade material.

The very acquisition of the capability to manufacture a nuclear weapon gives rise to suspicions and fears that the weapon will be produced. Some non-nuclear weapon countries, non-parties to the NPT, have chosen deliberately to create an ambiguity about their nuclear intentions in order to obtain a bargaining advantage in interstate politics. Such a posture could be perceived as a threat to neighbouring states and generate a regional arms race with global repercussions damaging to the cause of non-proliferation. It is therefore important, in addition to preventing the spread of nuclear weapons, to control the spread of nuclear weapon production capabilities.

III. Nuclear safeguards

Article III, dealing with nuclear safeguards, reads as follows: *1. Each non-nuclear-weapon State Party to the Treaty undertakes to accept safeguards, as set forth in an agreement to be negotiated and concluded with the International Atomic Energy Agency in accordance with the Statute of the International Atomic Energy Agency and the Agency's safeguards system, for the exclusive purpose of verification of the fulfilment of its obligations assumed under this Treaty with a view to preventing diversion of nuclear energy from peaceful uses to nuclear weapons or other nuclear explosive devices. Procedures for the safeguards required by this Article shall be followed with respect to source or special fissionable material whether it is being produced, processed or used in any principal nuclear facility or is outside any such facility. The safeguards required by this Article shall be applied on all source or special fissionable material in all peaceful nuclear activities within the territory of such State, under its jurisdiction, or carried out under its control anywhere.*

2. Each State Party to the Treaty undertakes not to provide: (*a*) *source or special fissionable material, or* (*b*) *equipment or material especially designed or prepared for the processing, use or production of special fission-*

able material, to any non-nuclear-weapon State for peaceful purposes, unless the source or special fissionable material shall be subject to the safeguards required by this Article.

3. The safeguards required by this Article shall be implemented in a manner designed to comply with Article IV of this Treaty, and to avoid hampering the economic or technological development of the Parties or international co-operation in the field of peaceful nuclear activities, including the international exchange of nuclear material and equipment for the processing, use or production of nuclear material for peaceful purposes in accordance with the provisions of this Article and the principle of safeguarding set forth in the Preamble of the Treaty.

4. Non-nuclear-weapon States Party to the Treaty shall conclude agreements with the International Atomic Energy Agency to meet the requirements of this Article either individually or together with other States in accordance with the Statute of the International Atomic Energy Agency. Negotiation of such agreements shall commence within 180 days from the original entry into force of this Treaty. For States depositing their instruments of ratification or accession after the 180-day period, negotiation of such agreements shall commence not later than the date of such deposit. Such agreements shall enter into force not later than eighteen months after the date of initiation of negotiations.

Safeguards constitute the control element of the NPT. Therefore, the conclusion of a safeguards agreement with the IAEA, in accordance with paragraph 1 of Article III, is the basic obligation of every non-nuclear weapon party to the Treaty. In the pre-NPT period, safeguards were applied by the IAEA to specific materials and to individual plants exported under bilateral nuclear co-operation agreements [16]. However, since the NPT requires broader measures to cover all the nuclear activities of the importing countries, a set of recommendations was drawn up by the IAEA for the contents of the safeguards agreements to be concluded with the non-nuclear weapon parties to the NPT. These recommendations have formed the basis for every safeguards agreement concluded in accordance with the NPT [17]. Pursuant to a safeguards agreement, the IAEA also concludes subsidiary arrangements with the state, which contain technical and operational details.

NPT safeguards consist of three main elements: material accountancy, containment and surveillance. These should enable "timely" detection of diversion of "significant" quantities of nuclear material from peaceful activities to the manufacture of nuclear explosive devices, as well as deterrence of diversion by creating the risk of early detection.[5] Following

[5] A Standing Advisory Group on safeguards implementation, established in 1975, provides the IAEA with recommendations on the formulation of basic safeguards criteria, such as "timely" detection and "significant" quantities, in order to make it possible to measure the effectiveness of safeguards activities.

a statement by the IAEA [18], the Review Conference participants noted that no such diversion had been reported. Some delegates drew attention to reports that significant quantities of special nuclear material were unaccounted for in "a nuclear-weapon State" (i.e., the USA) (see appendix 10C, review of Article III, para. 16), thereby implying that this material could have found its way to a non-nuclear weapon state. It was also noted that a large number of safeguards agreements had been concluded in recent years between the IAEA and non-nuclear weapon parties to the NPT; the countries that had still not fulfilled this obligation were urged to do so as soon as possible.

According to paragraph 4 of Article III, safeguards agreements must be concluded within the prescribed time-limits of 24 months for the original parties and 18 months for states acceding later. By mid-1980, these deadlines had passed for all but six parties to the NPT; 42 parties still did not have safeguards agreements in force. It is true that most of them had no significant nuclear activities, and those who had were covered by safeguards under previous agreements, but any failure to comply with treaty provisions must be regarded as an unsatisfactory state of affairs.

There was consensus that safeguards did not hamper the economic, scientific or technological developments of the parties, that they contributed to the maintenance of mutual confidence, and that, in applying them, the IAEA respected the sovereign rights of states. (It was somewhat surprising to learn from the Director General of the IAEA that discrimination was practised by certain states in the acceptance of inspectors [19].) Belgium, however, pointed out that inspections and controls complicated the production process and were a significant burden for enterprises in terms both of money and of protection of industrial secrets. Belgium therefore considered it premature to state categorically that such a burden had no effect on the economic activities or competitive positions of enterprises [20].

The Conference participants expressed satisfaction with the current safeguards procedures for existing facilities.[6] However, they emphasized that these procedures would need continued improvement to deal with the increasing amounts of nuclear material and increasingly complex nuclear fuel cycle facilities. It was recognized that in order to cope with its growing tasks the IAEA would need adequate human and financial resources for research and development of safeguards techniques. States were requested to design and construct new nuclear facilities in such a way as to facilitate the efficient application of safeguards [21].

[6] During the Conference, IAEA experts demonstrated a new computer-based communication system for remote continual verification (known as RECOVER) which had been designed to provide timely, centralized reporting of any operational failure of, or tampering with, devices installed to monitor activities or material flows at nuclear facilities under IAEA safeguards.

It should be added that effective safeguards for the most sensitive parts of the fuel cycle—enrichment and reprocessing—still remain to be elaborated. Although optimistic statements have been made about the accuracy of material accountancy in enrichment plants, there has not been much experience with international safeguarding of these plants. Similarly, the only IAEA experience to date in safeguarding reprocessing facilities has been with small or pilot plants. The large quantities of plutonium involved in commercial reprocessing will considerably complicate material accountancy, casting doubt on the feasibility of effective safeguards.

The implementation of Article III, paragraph 2, was more controversial than the actual application of safeguards by the IAEA. This clause, which sets forth the conditions for nuclear trade, has since its inception been applied in discriminatory fashion. As distinct from NPT parties, which are subject to safeguards comprehensively covering their nuclear activities, safeguards applied in the territories of non-parties continue to be facility-oriented, which means that only imported items are placed under IAEA safeguards and that at least part of the nuclear fuel cycle may consequently remain unsafeguarded. Some suppliers concerned about the dangers of proliferation inherent in this artificial distinction between imported and domestic technology have sought to impose full-scope safeguards, as extensive as NPT safeguards, also on non-parties. Other suppliers have been reluctant to change their export requirements. The Conference participants were agreed that non-nuclear weapon states not parties to the Treaty should submit all their nuclear activities to IAEA safeguards, but there were fundamental differences over whether the suppliers were under obligation to require such comprehensive safeguards of their customers. On this question, the Conference split three ways.

One group (Australia, Austria, the USA, Sweden, Canada, Norway, Finland and Denmark) consisted of supplier states wishing the Conference to recommend that exports be conditional upon acceptance of full-scope safeguards by recipient states. Some in this group of suppliers had already adopted this policy unilaterally. Two formulations were proposed: the USA urged that all nuclear suppliers require, as a condition of future nuclear supply commitments to non-nuclear weapon states not party to the NPT, that the latter accept the "same safeguards obligations" as had been undertaken by non-nuclear weapon states party to the Treaty pursuant to Article III [22]; Sweden and seven other states (Austria, Australia, Canada, Denmark, Finland, Norway and New Zealand) urged that parties require, as a condition of all future nuclear supply commitments to non-parties, "the application of IAEA safeguards to all source or special fissionable material in all peaceful nuclear activities, then existing and subsequent" [23]. In this connection, a model agreement, drawn up in the IAEA, which would enable non-parties to the NPT to accept safeguards voluntarily on all their nuclear activities, was specifically referred to [24]. It is noteworthy that while this model agreement, formally unrelated to the NPT, has been in existence for several years, no state has expressed interest in signing it.

A second group of supplier states (the UK, FR Germany, Belgium, Italy, Switzerland and Japan), while favouring full-scope safeguards for non-parties, was unwilling to make categorical demands in this respect. Italy urged parties to "work for" the extension of IAEA safeguards to all peaceful nuclear activities in importing states that are not party to the Treaty [25]. The UK was slightly more imperative in urging that states work "resolutely" and as a "matter of urgency" on this question [26]. In particular, the United Kingdom, supported by the Netherlands, felt that non-parties should participate in the discussion about their safeguards obligations. The Federal Republic of Germany and Switzerland expressed similar views, but both preferred the weaker Italian proposal. Japan also hesitated to impose full-scope safeguards on non-parties. Although Czechoslovakia, Poland and the German Democratic Republic had already decided to require safeguards on all nuclear activities in non-nuclear weapon states recipients of their exports [18], the GDR joined Bulgaria and Hungary in recommending only "the continuation of efforts" towards full-scope safeguards for non-parties [27–28], taking a position similar to that of the Soviet Union. An interesting aspect of this discussion among the suppliers is the distinction made between *de facto* full-scope safeguards and full-scope safeguards required by the agreements concluded in accordance with the NPT. Certain countries, not parties to the NPT, although having only facility-oriented safeguards, have in fact accepted control over all their present nuclear activities; Argentina and Brazil provide two such examples. However, as distinct from NPT safeguards, the *de facto* safeguards do not preclude the future development of an unsafeguarded domestic nuclear fuel cycle. Therefore, most suppliers seeking full-scope safeguards were careful to specify that they meant the same safeguards as those required by the NPT, or safeguards on nuclear activities "existing and subsequent". States satisfied with *de facto* controls, such as Belgium, urged safeguards only on nuclear materials "present" in non-party states [29]. The important distinction between the two types of safeguards was confirmed by the US delegation, which also clarified that safeguards required under the US Non-Proliferation Act (see section IV) were *de facto* full-scope safeguards, and were meant to be only an interim measure until the same safeguards as those required by the NPT were accepted [30].

The third position, that of the Group of 77, differed from these points of view. The Group was, of course, asking for preferential treatment for NPT parties—subject to full-scope safeguards—in access to or transfer of nuclear equipment, materials, services, and scientific and technological information for the peaceful uses of nuclear energy, but it was opposed to the imposition of full-scope safeguards as a condition of supply to non-parties. In effect, it no longer objected to the discriminatory application of safeguards under Article III, that is, full-scope for parties and partial for non-parties. In his statement made at the Conference, the representative of the Philippines implied that discrimination in the field of safeguards was not a matter of particular concern to most developing countries [31]. Only with regard to South Africa and Israel was a cut-off in supplies requested pending acceptance of full-scope safeguards by these countries.

Many speakers expressed the view that withholding co-operation from non-parties was unlikely to gain their adherence to the NPT. Nevertheless, it was strange for the Group of 77 to oppose measures devised to set the same safeguards criteria for non-parties as for the parties. If, at all, different standards were to be envisaged, more comprehensive and more stringent safeguards than those applied to the parties would be justified with regard to states that have chosen to keep the nuclear weapon option open.

Thus, no agreement was reached concerning full-scope safeguards for all non-nuclear weapon states. Such an agreement would be of utmost importance because it could provide a means of extending the non-proliferation regime to include non-parties to the NPT.[7] The supplier states split, while the Group of 77 adopted a selective approach, as if certain proliferators were better than others. But proliferation is, by its very nature, a problem that cannot for long be met by partial solutions. If one or more additional states should acquire nuclear weapons, certain other states would find it politically difficult to remain committed to not acquiring them. For instance, Nigeria, a party to the NPT, has warned that it could not remain indifferent to South Africa's acquisition of a nuclear weapon [32]. Under Article X of the NPT, any state may withdraw from the Treaty on short notice (only three months) if it concludes that its "supreme interests" have been jeopardized.

The main reason why the NPT has not yet gained universal acceptance is that non-parties have had no incentive to join it: they have been supplied with nuclear equipment and material under the same and sometimes even more advantageous conditions than the parties. Acceptance by non-parties of full-scope nuclear safeguards would, of course, not substitute for adherence to the international political commitment under the NPT, but it could at least give some assurance that nuclear weapon proliferation was being hindered. Categorical opposition to this minimum requirement

[7] The non-proliferation regime is a notion larger than the NPT; it encompasses all rules, norms and institutions which discourage nuclear weapon proliferation.

cannot but arouse suspicion that the countries in question want to hide some internationally objectionable activities. About a dozen significant nuclear facilities in non-NPT non-nuclear weapon states remain unsafeguarded. Some of these facilities are important from the point of view of production of weapons-usable material, and are situated in regions of political tension. There is little advantage in applying safeguards to materials supplied to these states as long as they are free to divert materials from unsafeguarded installations to weapon purposes.

A concerted denial of nuclear material deliveries to any state unwilling to accept full-scope safeguards would be a step consistent with the purposes of the NPT. Some might call it a punitive measure, but nuclear items are not ordinary items of trade. Since their acquisition may affect international

Table 10.2. Operating nuclear facilities not subject to IAEA or bilateral safeguards, as of 31 December 1980[a]

Country	Facility	Indigenous or imported	First year of operation
Egypt	Inshas research reactor	Imported (USSR)[b]	1961
India	Apsara research reactor	Indigenous	1956
	Cirus research reactor	Imported (Canada/USA)[c]	1960
	Purnima research reactor	Indigenous	1972
	Fuel fabrication plant at Trombay	Indigenous	1960
	Fuel fabrication plant, CANDU-type of fuel elements, at the Nuclear Fuel Cycle complex, Hyderabad	Indigenous	1974
	Reprocessing plant at Trombay	Indigenous	1964
	Reprocessing plant at Tarapur	Indigenous	1977
Israel	Dimona research reactor	Imported (France/Norway)[d]	1963
	Reprocessing plant at Dimona	Indigenous (in co-operation with France)[e]	..
Pakistan	Fuel fabrication plant at Chashma	Indigenous (in co-operation with Belgium)[f]	1980
South Africa	Enrichment plant at Valindaba	Indigenous (in co-operation with FR Germany)[g]	1975
Spain	Vandellos power reactor	Operation in co-operation with France[h]	1972

[a] Significant nuclear activities outside the five nuclear weapon states recognized by the NPT. The list is based on the best information available to SIPRI.

[b] Egypt also has a small-scale reprocessing facility not subject to safeguards. Operability and current status is unknown. In view of Egypt's recent adherence to the NPT, all its nuclear activities will have to be safeguarded by the IAEA.

[c] The reactor is of Canadian origin; heavy water was supplied by the USA.

[d] French-supplied reactor running on heavy water from Norway.

[e] Assistance by Saint Gobain Techniques Nouvelles.

[f] Assistance at an early stage by Belgo-Nucléaire. In addition, Pakistan is about to establish significant reprocessing and enrichment capacities. The status of these programmes is unknown.

[g] Co-operation between STEAG (FR Germany) and UCOR (South Africa).

[h] Negotiations with the IAEA on safeguarding of this reactor were being held.

security, they require special policies. Refusing international co-operation in the peaceful uses of nuclear energy can provide a leverage; a few countries have already been pressured into acceding to the NPT and accepting full-scope safeguards in order to receive nuclear materials.

Another important issue, mentioned in many statements, concerned safeguards on the civilian nuclear activities of the nuclear weapon states. Although, under the NPT, these states are not obligated to accept safeguards, they have frequently been urged to do so by the non-nuclear weapon states, which argue that they have been placed at a commercial disadvantage, either because of the costs associated with safeguards or because of a risk of exposure of proprietary information.

Since the First Review Conference, the United Kingdom and the United States, following up promises made at the time of the signing of the NPT, decided voluntarily to submit those nuclear installations not directly significant for their national security to IAEA safeguards, including inspection. France did the same, although it is not party to the Treaty. Many Conference participants welcomed these steps and expressed the hope that the USSR would adopt the same policy. It should be noted that the right of the nuclear powers to use their nuclear material for military purposes remains unaffected. Thus, while the argument about unfair advantage of the great powers' civilian industry has been somewhat defused, safeguarding peaceful activities in selected facilities in countries unrestricted in their military nuclear programmes continues to be pointless for non-proliferation, as it amounts to verifying the fulfilment of non-existing obligations. However, nuclear items imported by the nuclear weapon powers should be safeguarded to ensure that they do not add to a further build-up of nuclear weapon arsenals. For example, Australia decided that its exports of uranium for peaceful purposes to nuclear weapon states would be subject to undertakings that the uranium would not be diverted for military or explosive purposes and would be covered by IAEA safeguards.

The Conference participants welcomed the Convention on the physical protection of nuclear material, which had been negotiated under the auspices of the IAEA in fulfilment of the recommendations of the First Review Conference and which was opened for signature in March 1980. The Convention applies to "international nuclear transport", meaning the carriage of a consignment of nuclear material by any means of transport intended to go beyond the territory of the state where the shipment originates, "beginning with the departure from a facility of the shipper in that State and ending with the arrival at a facility of the receiver within the State of ultimate destination". The provisions of the Convention oblige the parties to ensure that, during international transport across their territory or on ships or planes under their jurisdiction, nuclear material for peaceful purposes as categorized in a special annex (plutonium, uranium-235, uranium-233 and irradiated fuel) is protected at the agreed level. For example, the transport of two or more kilograms of plutonium or five or more kilograms of uranium enriched to above 20 per cent uranium-235 must take place under constant surveillance of escorts and under conditions which assure close communication with "response forces". Storage of such nuclear material, incidental to international transport, must be within an area under constant surveillance by guards or electronic devices and surrounded by a physical barrier with a limited number of points of entry.

Furthermore, the parties undertake not to export or import nuclear material or allow its transit through their territory unless they have received assurances that this material will be protected during international transport in accordance with the levels of protection determined by the Convention, and to apply these levels of protection also to material which, during transit from one part of their territory to another, will pass through international waters or airspace.

The parties to the Convention agree to share information on missing nuclear material to facilitate recovery operations. Robbery, embezzlement or extortion in relation to nuclear material, and acts without lawful authority involving nuclear material which cause or are likely to cause "death or serious injury to any person or substantial damage to property", are to be treated as offences punishable by penalties which take into account their grave nature. The scheme of prosecution—or extradition—and related procedural clauses are meant to ensure that sanctuary will not be given to 'nuclear terrorists' in the territories of the parties.

Uniform application of measures of physical protection of nuclear material for peaceful purposes in international transport, as well as international co-operation in the case of its theft or misuse, may reduce the risks of its diversion to non-peaceful purposes. For this reason the Review Conference urged all states to become party to this Convention at an early date. It seems, however, equally vital that internationally agreed levels of physical protection should be applied to nuclear material in domestic use, storage and transport. (The importance of such protection was stressed in the preamble of the Convention.) This view was widely supported at the Review Conference.[8]

A question that was not discussed at the Review Conference, but which concerned many, was the physical protection both of nuclear material

[8] Belgium, however, considered that such an extension of the physical protection measures would be unacceptable interference in the domestic affairs of states, and a new element of discrimination, because it was unlikely that all the nuclear powers party to the NPT would accept the required control in their territories [33].

used for military purposes and of the nuclear weapons themselves. Accidents or negligence, especially with regard to weapons stationed outside the territories of the nuclear weapon states, may create proliferation risks much more serious than diversion of nuclear material used for peaceful purposes. The responsibility for reducing such risks to a minimum lies squarely with the nuclear powers, even though the Convention on the physical protection of nuclear material is not explicit on this subject.[9]

While it is generally recognized that safeguards, complemented by measures of physical protection of nuclear material, play an important role in demonstrating compliance with the NPT, in a world of rapid political and technological developments they cannot guarantee that proliferation will not occur. First, they can only deter a country from misusing its peaceful nuclear energy programme; they can detect but not prevent the misuse. Second, IAEA inspectors may be prevented from carrying out their safeguards duties by *force majeure* circumstances, such as violent internal upheavals in the recipient countries or interstate armed conflicts, not to speak of the risks to which nuclear material itself would be exposed in a war zone. Third, countries can abrogate their safeguards agreements; they may then need, in the case of plutonium or highly enriched uranium, no more than a few weeks or even days, depending on their technical capabilities, to transform nuclear material into an explosive. Time would most probably be insufficient for a successful international counteraction. Fourth, to be effective even in their deterrence role, safeguards must be full-scope in all non-nuclear weapon states, which they are not. And, fifth, certain nuclear technologies, such as enrichment and reprocessing, present proliferation dangers which cannot, as yet, be met by safeguards measures. It is therefore of utmost importance that, independently of safeguards, account be taken of the very nature of the nuclear material and equipment supplied for peaceful uses.

IV. Peaceful uses of nuclear energy

Article IV, dealing with the peaceful uses of nuclear energy, reads as follows: *1. Nothing in this Treaty shall be interpreted as affecting the inalienable right of all the Parties to the Treaty to develop research, production and use of nuclear energy for peaceful purposes without discrimination and in conformity with Articles I and II of this Treaty.*

[9] The Convention recognizes in its preamble the importance of physical protection of nuclear material used for military purposes, and records an understanding that such material "is and will continue to be accorded stringent physical protection".

2. All the Parties to the Treaty undertake to facilitate, and have the right to participate in, the fullest possible exchange of equipment, materials and scientific and technological information for the peaceful uses of nuclear energy. Parties to the Treaty in a position to do so shall also co-operate in contributing alone or together with other States or international organizations to the further development of the applications of nuclear energy for peaceful purposes, especially in the territories of non-nuclear-weapon States Party to the Treaty, with due consideration for the needs of the developing areas of the world.

This article, reaffirming the right of all parties to develop nuclear energy for peaceful purposes, obligates those parties which are "in a position to do so" (i.e., not only the nuclear weapon powers) to contribute to this development in non-nuclear weapon states. In agreed language (see appendix 10C, review of Article IV), the Conference participants stressed the specific needs of developing states and called for continued and substantially increased assistance through bilateral and multilateral channels, such as the IAEA and the UN Development Programme (UNDP). They appealed to the parties to meet the "technically sound" requests from developing countries for technical assistance, which the IAEA was unable to finance from its own resources.

In fact, figures attest to the general increase in assistance consistent with Article IV. From 1975 to 1979, technical assistance provided by the IAEA to member states (not all of whom, however, are parties to the NPT) amounted to $54.5 million; that is, it more than doubled as compared with the preceding five years. The target for voluntary contributions to the IAEA General Fund for Technical Assistance in 1980 was set at $10.5 million, also more than double the amount for 1975, and was to be raised to $13 million in 1981. Bilateral assistance increased and, in the opinion of the IAEA, has been "responsive to the specific needs of developing countries at least to a limited extent" [34].

These increases are less spectacular when inflation and exchange-rate fluctuations are taken into account, and the overall volume is still very modest. Conference participants were agreed that much more needed to be done. They expressed their readiness to consider the establishment of a special fund in order to assist research in, and development and practical application of, nuclear energy for peaceful purposes in developing non-nuclear weapon parties to the NPT (see appendix 10C, review of Article IV, para. 18). It is noteworthy that none of the world's 244 nuclear power reactors operating in 1980 was in a developing country party to the Treaty (see table 10.3).

Attention at the Review Conference was focused on certain events which had taken place since 1975 and which seemed to affect the implementation of Article IV. Not only had the spread of civilian nuclear power been

Table 10.3. Power reactors in the world, as of 1 June 1980[a]

Country	Operating		Under construction		Share of nuclear in total electricity (per cent)
	Number units	Total MW(e)	Number units	Total MW(e)	
Argentina	1	335	1	600	7.5
Belgium	3	1 665	4	3 807	22
Brazil	–	–	3	3 116	–
Bulgaria	2	816	2	828	19
Canada	11	5 495	14	9 751	11
Cuba	–	–	1	408	–
Czechoslovakia	2	801	6	2 520	~3
Finland	3	1 740	1	420	~20
France	18	9 983	31	30 950	~20
German Democratic Republic	5	1 695	4	1 632	~10
Germany, Federal Republic of	14	8 607	10	10 636	~10
Hungary	–	–	2	816	–
India	3	602	5	1 087	2.5
Italy	4	1 382	2	1 930	~2
Japan	23	14 466	9	7 274	10
Korea, South	1	564	6	4 954	8
Mexico	–	–	2	1 308	–
Netherlands	2	499	–	–	6
Pakistan	1	125	–	–	0.3
Philippines	–	–	1	621	–
South Africa	–	–	2	1 843	–
Spain	3	1 073	7	6 259	6
Sweden	6	3 700	5	4 686	23
Switzerland	4	1 940	1	942	26
Taiwan	3	2 158	1	950	17
UK	33	6 982	6	3 714	13
USA	70	50 900	88	96 254	12
USSR	32	11 616	15	13 680	~5
Yugoslavia	–	–	1	632	–
Total	**244**	**127 144**	**230**	**211 618**	

[a] Construction in Austria and Iran has been interrupted and the plants are not included.

slowed by environmental, health and economic factors, but nuclear suppliers had imposed restrictions on nuclear supplies for non-proliferation purposes.

In view of the different safeguards conditions for parties and non-parties to the Treaty (see above), and because India, a non-party, had taken advantage of the more lenient safeguards applied to its nuclear activities to explode a nuclear device, the major nuclear suppliers started meeting in London in 1975 to attempt to establish common guidelines for their nuclear exports. The original idea was to reduce competition between suppliers on safeguards requirements, which was damaging to the non-proliferation regime. In 1977, this nuclear supplier group, the so-called London Club which eventually comprised 15 countries (Belgium, Canada, Czechoslovakia, France, the German Democratic Republic, the Federal

Republic of Germany, Italy, Japan, the Netherlands, Poland, Sweden, Switzerland, the UK, the USA and the USSR), drew up a common catalogue of materials, equipment and technology which, when provided to any non-nuclear weapon state, would 'trigger' IAEA safeguards [35]. This document extended the list, agreed upon in the so-called Zangger Committee of suppliers (which did not include France) and communicated to the IAEA in 1974 [36], specifying the "equipment or material expressly designed or prepared for the processing, use or production of special fissionable material" and requiring safeguards under NPT Article III, paragraph 2b, when exported to non-parties (the parties being already covered by safeguards on all their nuclear activities). The London guidelines also required the recipients of the trigger-list items to pledge not to use these items for the manufacture of nuclear explosives and to provide effective physical protection of the imported materials. The safeguards requirements are to be applied also to facilities utilizing technologies directly transferred by the supplier or derived from transferred facilities, as well as to any facility of the same type as that imported and which was constructed indigenously during an agreed period. Retransfers of trigger-list items were made subject to the same conditions as those applied to the original transfer. In the event of diversion of materials or violation of supplier–recipient understandings, suppliers were to consult promptly on possible common action.

But irrespective of safeguards, there was increasing concern over the ease with which materials from a peaceful nuclear programme could be diverted to military purposes with the help of uranium enrichment or plutonium reprocessing plants, capable of producing fissile materials directly usable for weapons.[10] Therefore, the London Club suppliers recommended restraint in the transfer of these sensitive facilities. Subsequently, France and FR Germany announced that, until further notice, new deals for exports of reprocessing equipment and technology would not be allowed, while Canada and Australia established a requirement of prior consent for retransfer of their nuclear material supplies and for reprocessing or enrichment (over 20 per cent) of these supplies.

In 1978 the USA set even stricter unilateral restrictions by adopting the Nuclear Non-Proliferation Act. In addition to confirming the US embargo on enrichment and reprocessing plants, the Act stated that new commitments to export significant amounts of separated plutonium and highly enriched uranium were to be avoided. Other conditions included the

[10] Plutonium derived from the spent fuel rods of nuclear power reactors, so-called reactor-grade plutonium, has a higher content of undesired plutonium isotopes than weapon-grade plutonium produced in special facilities committed to military use. Nevertheless, it can be used to manufacture nuclear explosive devices, although there may be complications in the design and fabrication of a powerful device.

requirement of prior US consent for retransfer of any US-supplied materials or any fissionable material produced through the use of US equipment; prior US approval for reprocessing, enrichment (over 20 per cent) or alteration of nuclear materials supplied by the USA or derived from these supplies; and a guarantee of physical security for any special nuclear material transferred. The Act also required full-scope safeguards as a condition for receiving US nuclear supplies. Because its provisions were made retroactive, the Act entailed renegotiation of existing US nuclear co-operation agreements.[11] All these measures were taken to strengthen the non-proliferation regime, particularly to ensure control over plutonium-producing technologies. At the same time, the USA launched the International Nuclear Fuel Cycle Evaluation (INFCE) to devise measures which could "minimize the danger of the proliferation of nuclear weapons without jeopardizing energy supplies or the development of nuclear energy for peaceful purposes" [38]. The hope was that some alternative to a plutonium-producing cycle would be found.

INFCE concluded its work in February 1980, having achieved a wide measure of agreement on complex technical problems. It was, therefore, generally regarded as a useful exercise; its report gained support from nuclear suppliers and recipients. (For the INFCE report text dealing with non-proliferation aspects, see appendix 10F.) However, the main conclusion was not encouraging: although certain measures could make misuse of the fuel cycle more difficult, there is no technical way to produce nuclear energy without at the same time producing fissile material usable for weapons. In other words, there are close links between peaceful and military uses of nuclear energy.

The countries of the Third World viewed the restrictive measures taken by the suppliers as serving the latter's economic interests rather than non-proliferation goals. They considered these measures as an infringement on their rights to co-operation and supplies promised under Article IV. The debate on the implementation of Article IV centred, therefore, on the resentment of the developing countries against what they considered to be discriminatory obstructions to the development of nuclear energy for peaceful purposes. Many countries felt that since they had accepted the safeguards provided for in Article III, no further limitations should be placed on their peaceful nuclear programmes. They protested against the technological restrictions introduced by the London Club, and against the fact that the list of "sensitive" items, requiring additional measures of control, had been drawn up without consultation with other NPT parties. They also protested against control requirements unilaterally imposed by

[11] The legality of imposing upon recipients more stringent safeguards than originally agreed, as a condition for receiving nuclear supplies already validly contracted for, is questionable [37].

exporting countries and insisted on their right to assured long-term supplies, as well as the right to choose their own fuel cycle policies. They inveighed especially against any cut-off of supplies and violation of supply contracts "under the pretext" of preventing nuclear proliferation [39].

The Conference could agree to note concern over the technological restraints adopted by the London Club and the more stringent non-proliferation requirements (in some cases with retroactive effect) which had been imposed in bilateral agreements. Many delegations were ready to recognize that the suppliers had been motivated by the non-adherence to the NPT of a number of countries with nuclear programmes and the explosion of a nuclear device by one of them, but these motivations were not shared by "some importing countries which have undertaken full-scope safeguards" (see appendix 10C, review of Article IV, para. 6). All the Conference participants were agreed on the importance of improving the predictability of nuclear supplies and avoiding their interruption.

The potentially explosive confrontation on the issue of supply assurances versus technological restrictions was avoided by the fact that an additional forum had been created to continue this dialogue. In June 1980, as a follow-up to INFCE, the IAEA Board of Governors established a Committee on Assurances of Supply (CAS), open to all members of the IAEA, to consider and advise on "ways and means in which supplies of nuclear material, equipment and technology and fuel cycle services can be assured on a more predictable and long-term basis in accordance with mutually acceptable considerations of non-proliferation" [40]. This new committee is to provide an opportunity to air the differing views on the subject, but agreement could still remain elusive. In the discussion that followed its establishment there was a clear difference in emphasis. The developing countries mentioned only the importance of supply assurances while the supplier states insisted on non-proliferation considerations. It may not be easy to reconcile the two points of view, especially since important non-parties to the NPT were sponsors of the resolution setting up CAS and will be among its members. For the moment, however, the establishment of this body spared the Review Conference an impasse over the issue of supplies. The Conference participants urged support for the objectives of CAS.

It was perhaps inevitable that the restrictive export policies recommended by the London Club and imposed by individual suppliers in the name of non-proliferation would provoke such profound resentment at the NPT Conference. One of the fears of the non-nuclear weapon states has always been that the acquisition by them of civilian nuclear technology might be frustrated by the NPT. Article IV was to allay these fears by guaranteeing the right of all parties to peaceful nuclear programmes, and by obligating the nuclear suppliers to provide assistance in this respect, especially to the developing countries. But nuclear suppliers, concerned with the military implications of civilian programmes, seemed to have moved in the opposite direction, while the developing countries, in insisting on their rights, pushed the pendulum to the other extreme, turning non-proliferation into a secondary objective.

Continuing the policy adopted at the 1978 UN Special Session on Disarmament, the Third World countries stressed mainly, if not exclusively, the promises of nuclear co-operation contained in the NPT. Their position at the Second Review Conference may have been prepared at a meeting of non-aligned countries on the peaceful uses of nuclear energy, held in Buenos Aires in July 1980. A number of delegations participating in this meeting expressed the view that the NPT had had no real impact on nuclear weapon proliferation, and that it had been used rather to "hinder the transfer of nuclear material, equipment and technology" [41]. Non-NPT states at the meeting, including Algeria, Argentina, Brazil (as observer), Cuba, Egypt, Pakistan and India, had visibly influenced the policy of the non-aligned parties to the NPT. It was not surprising, then, that the London Guidelines for nuclear transfers, which were not even particularly harsh for the importers but had been devised specifically to bring non-parties closer to the non-proliferation requirements, were subjected to severe criticism at the Review Conference. Attention focused on the need to withdraw any technological restraints, and no distinction was made in this regard between parties and non-parties to the Treaty. The Group of 77 was preoccupied mainly with preparations for the UN conference "for the promotion of international co-operation in the peaceful uses of nuclear energy", scheduled to be held by 1983, outside the framework of the NPT [42].

In placing exclusive emphasis on nuclear supplies, the Group of 77 seemed to imply that the NPT was mainly an instrument for the promotion of the peaceful uses of nuclear energy; they therefore often tended to ignore an important proviso contained in Article IV of the Treaty, namely, that nuclear co-operation should be in conformity with Articles I and II. Both the obligation to provide and the right to obtain equipment, materials and scientific and technological information for the peaceful uses of nuclear energy are not without limits: any such supplies are clearly subordinated to non-proliferation goals, which means that they must not in any way facilitate the acquisition of nuclear weapons. In case of a collision between these arms control goals and the economic interests of the suppliers or recipients, it is the arms control aspect that must prevail, because the NPT is an arms control agreement. In other words, Article IV has no relevance without the overriding non-proliferation commitment.

The prevailing opinion at the Review Conference was that constraints mutually agreed between supplier and consumer states were preferable to unilateral restrictions, and that parties to the NPT should meet annually at the IAEA to discuss the implementation of Article IV in the context of Article III of the Treaty (see appendix 10C, review of Article IV, para. 8). It seems that such discussions should also deal with proliferation implications of certain supplies, irrespective of safeguards required by Article III. For example, there can be no justification for shipments of large quantities of weapon-grade nuclear material to countries having no immediate need for such material, even if they are subject to full-scope international controls. (It has been recognized in INFCE that even research reactors can operate on uranium of lower enrichment, involving lesser proliferation and physical security risks than highly enriched uranium.) Neither can one argue that refusal to supply plutonium reprocessing facilities to a country with a nuclear industry still in an embryonic state hampers the civilian uses of nuclear energy. Equally, an unrestricted right to retransfer nuclear material, especially to non-parties, safeguards notwithstanding, would run counter to the objectives of non-proliferation.

As a matter of fact, few non-nuclear weapon states party to the NPT were negatively affected by the London Guidelines, designed mainly to broaden safeguards coverage in non-NPT states, or by subsequent unilateral measures of restraint taken by certain suppliers with regard to all recipients.

Imposition of prior consent for alteration and retransfer of imported nuclear items was especially resented by Switzerland, itself a member of the London Club, because Swiss requests for retransfer licences to have spent fuel reprocessed abroad were held up for a long time by the exporters. Switzerland suggested, therefore, that implementation of Article IV should be subject to verification and that a monitoring mechanism be established to provide the parties with an annual report [43]. In addition, "to strengthen the confidence" in the NPT, Switzerland submitted a proposal for the establishment of a system for the peaceful settlement of disputes arising among parties over the interpretation or implementation of Articles I to V of the Treaty [44]. US legislation also affected Yugoslavia and the Philippines, causing delays and cost increases in the nuclear programmes of these two countries.

In recognition of the above grievances, the USA proposed that the Conference request nuclear supplier states, where necessary, to streamline procedures governing the issuance of export licences or authorizations and especially to "avoid creation of obstacles or administrative complications which unduly delay the issuance of such licences and authorizations, in order to permit stable and long-term planning of nuclear activities" [45].

Restrictions on exports of reprocessing and enrichment technologies have not significantly affected the parties to the NPT. In fact, for peaceful purposes, neither technology will be needed by most countries for the next

20 years. Enrichment capacity far exceeds demand; annual world demand may not catch up to planned capacity until the mid-1990s [46]. Reprocessing of spent fuel to extract plutonium for use in reactors will be necessary only when the fast breeder becomes commercially operational; this is foreseen for five or six countries only, and not before the end of the century.[12] And because uranium production is sufficient to satisfy current demands and could even substantially increase if there were sufficient incentives, reprocessing for plutonium recycling in the existing types of nuclear reactors is not economical. Neither is reprocessing necessary as a precondition to waste disposal. At this time, the clamour for reprocessing facilities, especially by countries with incipient nuclear programmes, can only arouse suspicion about the motives.

In view of the dangers of a 'plutonium economy', it would seem advisable to adopt the so-called once-through fuel cycle in which the fuel elements, when discharged from the reactors, are disposed of without separating the plutonium from the waste products [47].

Although the once-through cycle offers a solution to the proliferation threat, there is considerable reluctance to adopt it. To solve this dilemma the Conference turned to possible international institutional arrangements. In this connection, satisfaction was expressed with the work of the IAEA expert group on international plutonium storage (IPS). The Conference supported efforts to establish an effective scheme for such storage on the basis of Article XII.A(5) of the IAEA Statute, which entitles the IAEA to require the deposit with it of "any excess of any special fissionable materials". The scheme should help to alleviate the risk that plutonium accumulated as a result of growing reactor programmes would be misused. However, if reprocessing itself—that is, the very activity where diversion is most likely to take place—is not internationalized, an agreement on storage might create a false sense of security that the dangers of plutonium had been overcome.

A more delicate problem will be to identify the conditions under which the stored plutonium would be released. Since only a very small amount of this material is needed to make a weapon, it is essential that all plutonium not in use should be in international storage unless it is in transport. Conditions for its release would have to be strict, requiring detailed justification by the requesting state as well as control of whether the request is in accordance with non-proliferation objectives. Otherwise, the international storage area might serve only as a depot for temporarily unused plutonium. These concerns are especially relevant in light of the recommendation issued by the 1980 Buenos Aires meeting of the non-aligned

[12] It will be noted that in 1977 the USA suspended commercial nuclear fuel reprocessing and deferred development of the breeder reactor.

states to the effect that interested countries should insist on the right of free disposal of nuclear materials "including their own excess plutonium".

As regards reactor fuel supplies, there was recognition of the need for energy backup mechanisms, such as a uranium emergency safety network and an international nuclear fuel bank. Parties in a position to do so were called upon to make available on a commercial basis "an interim uranium stockpile", sufficient for one annual light water reactor reload of enriched uranium and one annual heavy water reactor reload of natural uranium, to parties which were unable to secure fuel supplied under existing contracts for reasons of "contract default that were not the result of a breach of the non-proliferation undertakings stipulated in the relevant agreement" (see appendix 10C, review of Article IV, para. 22).

International arrangements for assured fuel supplies could be an essential part of the non-proliferation regime as well as appropriate compensation for the technological restrictions necessitated by non-proliferation goals. However, it is important that a fuel bank limit its membership to NPT parties so that the implementation of Article IV of the Treaty would be reinforced and incentive for joining the NPT would be generated.

Little has been done in the area of the internationalization of nuclear fuel facilities since 1977, when the IAEA issued its report on regional nuclear fuel cycle centres [48], probably because of lack of interest on the part of those who could contribute most to such an undertaking. At the Review Conference many felt that it was time to give serious consideration to this question. Indeed, enrichment and reprocessing services, if internationalized, could be made available to all NPT parties, while the proliferation dangers inherent in national facilities would be avoided. Nuclear safeguards would be easier to apply and more reliable. The extent of internationalization would depend on future modes of nuclear energy production, especially on the degree of use of plutonium fuels. But for a start, the small number of existing enrichment and reprocessing facilities could perhaps form the core of an international scheme and facilitate its elaboration. The present limited need for reprocessing would make a multinational arrangement particularly manageable. Association of countries from both the developed and developing worlds in any such arrangement would alleviate the feeling of discrimination prevalent in the nuclear energy area today, and ensure that the scheme did not bring commercial advantage to any group. While technology must remain restricted for non-proliferation purposes, the users should be able to share the benefits.

V. Peaceful nuclear explosions

Article V states that *Each Party to the Treaty undertakes to take appropriate measures to ensure that, in accordance with this Treaty, under appropriate international observation and through appropriate international procedures, potential benefits from any peaceful applications of nuclear explosions will be made available to non-nuclear-weapon States Party to the Treaty on a non-discriminatory basis and that the charge to such Parties for the explosive devices used will be as low as possible and exclude any charge for research and development. Non-nuclear-weapon States Party to the Treaty shall be able to obtain such benefits, pursuant to a special international agreement or agreements, through an appropriate international body with adequate representation of non-nuclear-weapon States. Negotiations on this subject shall commence as soon as possible after the Treaty enters into force. Non-nuclear-weapon States Party to the Treaty so desiring may also obtain such benefits pursuant to bilateral agreements.*

The above provision, dealing with "potential" benefits of peaceful applications of nuclear explosions, was included in the Treaty in exchange for the surrender by non-nuclear weapon states of their right to conduct any nuclear explosions. For 'peaceful' devices could also be used as weapons: they are transportable and the amount of energy they are able to release could cause mass destruction.

The First NPT Review Conference noted that the technology for nuclear explosions for peaceful purposes was still at the stage of development and study. It nevertheless asked the IAEA (considered by the Conference as an appropriate international body through which any potential benefits of peaceful nuclear explosions were to be made available under Article V of the NPT) to examine the legal issues involved in, and to commence consideration of, the structure and content of the special international agreement or agreements contemplated in Article V of the Treaty. Accordingly, the IAEA established an *ad hoc* advisory group which, in a report submitted in 1977 to the IAEA Board of Governors, proposed four alternative international legal instruments dealing with nuclear explosions for peaceful purposes. In addition, the group examined health and safety matters related to peaceful nuclear explosions, economic aspects, including comparisons with non-nuclear alternatives, as well as the state of the art of various individual applications of such explosions [49]. Since then, scepticism as to the technical feasibility and economic viability of nuclear explosions for peaceful purposes has grown considerably. Apart from the economics and the environmental problems which would render such explosions unacceptable to the public in many countries, an agreement regulating nuclear explosive services would hamper efforts to reach a comprehensive prohibition of nuclear weapon testing because, as mentioned above, it is not possible to develop nuclear explosive devices which would be capable only of peaceful application.

The Second NPT Review Conference seemed to share the view of the IAEA Director General that Article V had been "overtaken by events", and that peaceful uses of nuclear explosions might entail greater risks than the benefits they would bring [19]. As opposed to the 1975 Review Conference, there was no pressure for establishing the international procedures envisaged in Article V. By tacit agreement, the implementation of this provision is kept in abeyance.

VI. Disarmament obligations

Under Article VI *Each of the Parties to the Treaty undertakes to pursue negotiations in good faith on effective measures relating to cessation of the nuclear arms race at an early date and to nuclear disarmament, and on a treaty on general and complete disarmament under strict and effective international control.*

The obligations under Article VI are considered to be of fundamental importance. The NPT is the only existing international document under which the major nuclear powers are legally committed to nuclear disarmament. The Review Conference therefore devoted much time and effort to assessing progress in disarmament negotiations and to formulating recommendations for the future. On both counts, agreement proved impossible to reach.

The Group of 77 found that Article VI had not been fulfilled. It concluded that despite some limited agreements "no effective measures relating to the cessation of the nuclear arms race at an early date and to nuclear disarmament have materialized" [2]. Rather, it noted with alarm the intensification of the nuclear arms race and the emerging strategy for limited use of nuclear weapons. A Swedish working paper was equally emphatic regarding the failure to achieve any results under Article VI, stressing that the continuation of the qualitative and quantitative arms race "will adversely affect the efforts to prevent further spread of nuclear explosive capability" [50].

Western assessments were more positive. They welcomed the arms control agreements reached, in particular the signing of the SALT II Treaty, and cited other efforts towards achieving the objectives of Article VI, expressing at the same time regret that more progress had not been possible (see, for example, the Canadian working paper [51] and the British and US statements [52]). These views were echoed by the Socialist states (see the Soviet statement [53] and the working paper of Hungary and Poland [54]).

There have, in fact, been some cautious advances in arms control negotiations since 1975. The SALT II Treaty, though intended mainly to regulate the nuclear arms competition between the two great powers, was more ambitious than the SALT I Interim Agreement. It would set equal numerical ceilings for the strategic delivery vehicles and equal subceilings for multiple independently targetable re-entry vehicles (MIRVs). It would also require some dismantling of nuclear delivery systems and establish an exchange of data regarding strategic forces. Above all, it prepared the ground for further negotiations under SALT III. However, the failure of the USA to ratify the SALT II Treaty has delayed the envisaged talks on actual nuclear arms reductions, a development which is not conducive to strengthening the NPT regime.

In the area of nuclear testing, a sombre assessment is even more justified. A comprehensive nuclear test ban treaty is considered by most countries as a very important measure to halt the nuclear arms race and an essential part of the non-proliferation regime. This is why the NPT preamble expressed the determination of the parties to achieve "the discontinuance of all test explosions of nuclear weapons for all time". Indeed, while an experimental explosion may not be absolutely necessary for constructing a simple fission device, it could be difficult for any country to develop a reliable nuclear arsenal without testing; at the same time, development of new designs of nuclear weapons by the nuclear powers would be practically impossible, while modification of existing weapon designs would be constrained. Yet, the UK, the USA and the USSR, meeting in private trilateral talks since 1977, have not been able to produce an agreed text for a comprehensive test ban treaty. It will be noted in this context that the 1980 report of the UN Secretary General [55], which identified the unresolved issues in the test ban negotiations, concluded that verification of compliance, which had been the major issue for many years, "no longer seems to be an obstacle to reaching agreement". It also emphasized the need for a permanent ban rather than one limited in time, as that negotiated by the three powers, in order to ensure the widest possible adherence, and pointed out that resumption of tests upon the expiration of a short-lived ban might be a serious setback to the cause of arms limitation and disarmament.

In comparison to these halting arms control efforts, the arms race has been accelerating at a rapid pace. The list of qualitative advances is voluminous. New types of nuclear weapon, including so-called Euro-strategic weapons, have been or are planned to be deployed within the next few years. Improvements in strategic weapons, such as the fixed land-based Minuteman III missile with its new guidance system, the submarine-launched Trident missile, and the projected MX mobile missile system (including a basing scheme to make the missile invulnerable), as well as air- and ground-launched cruise missiles being developed, will considerably upgrade the US nuclear capability. The same applies to Soviet strategic SS-18 and SS-19 missiles which are being equipped with new, more accurate MIRVs. Both powers are raising the quality of their strategic nuclear submarines and are developing means for anti-submarine warfare. Quantitatively, more than 4 000 nuclear warheads (on bombers and missiles) had been added to the strategic arsenals of the USA and the USSR between 1975, the year of the First Review Conference, and 1980. Nuclear testing had continued steadily. The number of explosions conducted by the USA and the USSR in 1979 was 40 per cent higher than that in 1975, in defiance of the appeal made by the First NPT Review Conference that the number of nuclear weapon tests should be limited to a minimum.

A few days before the opening of the 1980 Review Conference an announcement was made that the USA had revised its nuclear doctrine. The so-called countervailing strategy, formulated in Presidential Directive 59, put more stress than heretofore on the ability to employ strategic nuclear forces selectively by attacking political and military control centres, military forces, both nuclear (including missile bases) and conventional (including troop concentrations), as well as the industrial capability to sustain a war. The reason given for this targeting concept was that the threat of massive retaliation was losing credibility as a deterrent to a limited nuclear strike or an aggression with conventional arms.

The US Secretary of Defense emphasized that PD-59 represented only an evolutionary change in US strategic policy [56]. Indeed, over a period of years, one could observe in the USA a gradual departure from the 'mutual assured destruction' doctrine, designed to attack major population centres, towards a 'counterforce' doctrine, designed to destroy enemy forces. Already in 1974 the 'new strategic doctrine' (set forth in US National Security Decision Memorandum 242) envisaged so-called limited options to permit termination of a nuclear conflict at lower levels of destruction, avoiding large-scale damage to urban areas. The shift reflected advances in technology, especially in missile accuracy. New targets were probably 'needed' for ever more nuclear weapons having pin-point precision. Long before PD-59, the bulk of US strategic weapons must have been aimed at military targets, thousands of warheads being considerably in excess of what might be necessary to cover all the important 'soft' targets in the Soviet Union.

Proclaimed as official doctrine, the policy of selective strikes carries with it dangerous implications. It may resuscitate the spectre of a first strike wiping out the adversary forces by surprise. It weakens the inhibitions about the use of nuclear weapons by signalling acceptance of a prolonged but limited nuclear exchange as a rational option with expectation of success. And since it is based on the assumption that the adversary would follow the rules of behaviour set by the other side, it underestimates the risk of escalation of a limited nuclear war (which itself could cause immense casualties and destruction) into a full-scale nuclear holocaust. It should be borne in mind that attacks on political and military leadership centres, many of which are located in or near major urban areas, would be indistinguishable from counter-city attacks. Moreover, by enlarging the range of nuclear targets, the countervailing strategy provides an impetus to, or rationale for, unlimited increases in warhead inventories and continuous improvement in weapon systems, as well as reconnaissance and communications facilities, to buttress war-fighting capabilities. It raises serious doubts about the prospects of scaling down the numbers of nuclear weapons and limiting their qualitative characteristics and therefore appears incompatible with the letter and spirit of NPT Article VI.

As in 1975, the Western and Socialist groups were in 1980 content to rest on their disarmament records and to promote their respective proposals, urging essentially 'more of the same' in the CD and in bilateral negotiations. Recommendations for strengthening the implementation of Article VI came from the Group of 77, which sought clear commitments from the nuclear powers to specific actions, and proposed measures that would reaffirm the direct relationship between 'vertical' and 'horizontal' proliferation [2]. Thus, the nuclear powers were asked to agree to the creation in the CD of an *ad hoc* working group to start the negotiation envisaged in paragraph 50 of the Final Document of the UN Special Session on Disarmament, namely, on the cessation of the qualitative improvement and development of nuclear weapon systems; cessation of the production of all types of nuclear weapons and their means of delivery, and of the production of fissionable material for weapon purposes; and a comprehensive, phased programme with agreed time-frames, whenever feasible, for progressive and balanced reduction of stockpiles of nuclear weapons and their means of delivery, leading to their ultimate and complete elimination [57].

The USA and the USSR were urged by the Group of 77 to ratify the SALT II agreements and initiate immediately SALT III negotiations for limitations and reductions of both strategic and medium-range nuclear armaments; pending ratification, the two powers were asked to commit themselves to abide by the provisions of the SALT II Treaty "as if it had already formally entered into force". Furthermore, the nuclear weapon states were requested to support the creation of an *ad hoc* working group in the CD to start multilateral negotiations on a comprehensive test ban treaty, and to proclaim simultaneous unilateral moratoria or a trilateral moratorium on nuclear testing. With the exception of the moratorium on tests, these were mostly steps of a procedural nature. Yet, even on such modest demands the Group of 77 received no satisfaction.

Regarding SALT II agreements, the USA had already declared its intention not to take any action in the pre-ratification period that would be inconsistent with these agreements [52]. Nine countries of the Western group submitted a working paper urging the signatories of SALT II to adopt this policy [58], which would be in accordance with international law. However, the proposal that parties should "abide" by the SALT II agreements pending their entry into force proved unacceptable to both signatories. For the USSR, it would mean the dismantling of a number of nuclear delivery vehicles without any certainty that the agreements would ever enter into force.

A comprehensive test ban is considered basic to an acceptable balance between the responsibilities and obligations of the NPT parties. Nevertheless, the call for a moratorium on tests was rejected by the powers engaged in trilateral talks, who insisted that a verifiable treaty was preferable. But even the establishment of a CD working group to negotiate a multilateral test ban could not be agreed upon, in spite of the argument put forward by the non-nuclear weapon states that trilateral and multilateral negotiations could supplement each other. All the USA could accept, after strenuous negotiations, was the creation of a CD group, without fixing a specific date for its establishment and without giving it a mandate to draft a treaty text. This proved to be too little. Neither could agreement be reached on the initiation of multilateral negotiations in the CD for nuclear disarmament.

Different disarmament items were mentioned during the debate, but those dealing with nuclear matters received special attention. Thus, the need for limiting the medium-range nuclear systems in Europe was recognized by many. Norway, for example, considered the increased emphasis on nuclear weapons in the "management of security in Europe" as incompatible with the consolidation of the non-proliferation regime in the global context [33]. There was also support for a cut-off of production of fissionable material for weapon purposes as a separate arms control measure. The cut-off would set a limit on the availability of fissionable material for weapons and would thereby not only contribute to curbing the 'vertical' proliferation of nuclear weapons, but also impose a barrier to the 'horizontal' spread of such weapons. It would make it possible for the nuclear weapon states to accept the same IAEA safeguards that are required of the non-nuclear weapon states under the NPT, because future production of fissionable material would have to be only for civilian purposes. Thus, one of the elements of inequality between the nuclear and non-nuclear weapon states could be eliminated. However, prospects for achieving this goal are dim, especially in light of the recent US decision to increase production of plutonium to meet the requirements for new nuclear weapons [59].

Article VI embodies the basic bargain of the NPT; it represents the *quid pro quo* for the commitments of the non-nuclear weapon states. But no time limit was ever set by the nuclear powers for keeping their part of the bargain. They emphasized the complicated and sensitive nature of the problems involved and pleaded for patience on the part of other states. The demands of the Group of 77 at the Second NPT Review Conference were, in fact, minimal. They did not insist on instant nuclear disarmament but insisted only on some tangible evidence of the nuclear powers' commitment to reach agreements leading to such disarmament. However, the nuclear powers had come essentially empty-handed to the Conference, obviously unprepared for the vehemence of the debate on this article.

VII. Nuclear weapon-free zones

Regional denuclearization is dealt with in Article VII, which states: *Nothing in this Treaty affects the right of any group of States to conclude regional treaties in order to assure the total absence of nuclear weapons in their respective territories.*

The Conference participants recognized that nuclear weapon-free zones, properly constituted, could effectively curb the spread of nuclear weapons and contribute to the security of the states in the region. The nuclear weapon states were invited to undertake binding commitments to refrain from the use or threat of use of nuclear weapons against states in such zones. In this connection satisfaction was expressed with the prohibition of nuclear weapons in Latin America under the Treaty of Tlatelolco and, in particular, with the adherence of all the five nuclear weapon powers to Additional Protocol II of the Treaty, by which these powers committed themselves to respect the status of military denuclearization of the area (see appendix 10E, para. 1 and 2).

It will be noted that the ultimate goal of the Treaty of Tlatelolco, that of denuclearizing the whole Latin American continent, has not yet been achieved. Argentina, Brazil and Chile, countries with substantial nuclear activities, are still not bound by the Treaty; neither is Cuba, which is in the process of developing a nuclear power industry. Moreover, Additional Protocol I of the Treaty, according to which the status of military denuclearization extends also to Latin American territories under the responsibility of extra-continental or continental states, has not yet been adhered to by all the countries to which it applies.

To the extent that the incentive to acquire nuclear weapons may emerge from regional considerations, the establishment of denuclearized regions in various parts of the world would certainly be an asset for the cause of non-proliferation. If modelled after the Treaty of Tlatelolco, such zones would require full-scope safeguards agreements to be signed between individual states and the IAEA, and could therefore effectively complement the NPT. (The terms of the safeguards agreements under the Treaty of Tlatelolco are practically identical to those of the NPT-type safeguards agreements.)[13] There is consensus that states not parties to the NPT but with safeguards commitments equal to those required under Article III, paragraph 1, of the Treaty should be accorded the same treatment in regard to nuclear supplies as are parties to the NPT.

However, it is difficult to see where, outside Latin America, a nuclear weapon-free zone treaty could be concluded in the foreseeable future. Proposals for denuclearized zones concern mainly regions which are rife with political tension and where countries have not joined the NPT, that is, have not formally renounced the nuclear weapon option, as the Middle East, Africa or South Asia. It would be unrealistic to expect them to do so under a zonal arrangement: in proscribing the presence of foreign nuclear forces in a given geographical region, in addition to the prohibition of the possession of nuclear weapons by the countries of the zone, a nuclear weapon-free zone agreement is considerably wider in scope than the NPT and, judging by the Treaty of Tlatelolco, is more comprehensive because it bans *any* military use of nuclear material (not only for the manufacture of nuclear weapons) and provides for both special inspections by the countries in the region and international IAEA safeguards.

Furthermore, zonal agreements require intergovernmental negotiations, and it is difficult to envisage negotiations in conflict areas where governments are unwilling to communicate with each other. If and when the countries in question decide to give up the nuclear weapon option, they may find it easier to do so directly, through an act of adherence to the NPT, if necessary simultaneously with neighbouring states. The prohibition of foreign nuclear presence, though important, could come at a later stage, as a separate arrangement complementing the non-proliferation obligations.

[13] One reason why Argentina and Brazil refuse to be bound by the Treaty of Tlatelolco is their unwillingness to submit their nuclear activities to full-scope IAEA safeguards.

VIII. Security assurances

Strengthening the security of the non-nuclear weapon states that have surrendered their nuclear option is an intrinsic part of an effective non-proliferation regime, even though no specific obligation to this effect was laid down in the NPT (with the exception of a reference in the preamble to the obligation of states under the UN Charter to refrain from the threat or use of force). From the mid-1960s when the NPT was negotiated, this issue has never been properly resolved. The first attempt to deal with security assurances was Security Council Resolution 255, adopted in 1968, in which the three depositary governments of the NPT pledged immediate assistance to any non-nuclear weapon state party to the NPT which was a "victim of an act or an object of a threat of aggression in which nuclear weapons are used". These so-called positive assurances were, in fact, nothing more than reiterated obligations of UN members under the UN Charter. Moreover, they have hardly any practical value since all the nuclear weapon powers with the right of veto are now members of the Security Council. Some neutral European states stated that they could not accept positive guarantees because these were incompatible with their status of neutrality [60].

In recent years, the discussion was centred on 'negative assurances', that is, formal guarantees by the nuclear weapon states that nuclear weapons would not be used against non-nuclear weapon states. Steps in this direction were taken at the 1978 UN Special Session on Disarmament when the USA, the UK and the USSR each made an official policy statement giving such assurances. The USSR declared that it would never use nuclear weapons against those states which "renounce the production and acquisition of such weapons and do not have them on their territories" [61]. The USA announced that it would not use nuclear weapons against any non-nuclear weapon state which is party to the NPT or "any comparable internationally binding agreement not to acquire nuclear explosive devices", except in the case of an attack on the USA or its allies by a non-nuclear weapon state "allied to" or "associated with" a nuclear weapon state in carrying out or sustaining the attack [62]. A similar statement was issued by the UK [63].[14] This was a considerable advance as compared with the situation at the First NPT Review Conference, when

[14] France and China, which are not parties to the NPT, also made statements on this subject at the UN Special Session on Disarmament. The position of France was that it would give assurances of non-use of nuclear weapons, in accordance with arrangements to be negotiated, only to those states which have "constituted among themselves non-nuclear zones" [64] while China reiterated its commitment made long ago not to be the first to use nuclear weapons at any time and under any circumstances [65].

the nuclear powers refused even to discuss such undertakings. However, the assurances offered showed significant disparities and contained qualifications which could be subject to divergent interpretations. Doubts were also expressed as to the binding force of unilateral statements. Most countries saw the need to develop a uniform formula of security assurances and to incorporate it in an international legal instrument. The issue had been referred to the CD, where it was discussed for two years in a special working group.

At the Second NPT Review Conference there was agreement to confirm the continued validity of Security Council Resolution 255 and to note that states should have the right to decide if, and under what conditions, the assistance envisaged in that resolution might be granted. It was also agreed to note the declarations on the non-use of nuclear weapons of the three depositary governments at the 1978 UN Special Session, as well as the view that effective international arrangements to assure non-nuclear weapon states against the use or threat of use of nuclear weapons would further efforts to halt the proliferation of nuclear weapons (see appendix 10E, paragraph 5). Considering, apparently, that the threat of use of nuclear weapons in the area of North-East Asia should not be eliminated, South Korea warned against "arbitrary and indiscriminate" imposition of negative security assurances which, depending upon the actual situation in a particular region, could turn into a "negation of assurance" [66].

Differences remained on the scope and nature of the negative security assurances. These were precisely the issues before the CD where proposals had been made for non-use commitments to be extended to all non-nuclear weapon states, without any conditions or limitations, or only to those states which were not party to the nuclear security arrangements of some nuclear powers.

Other proposals would further limit the recipients of security assurances to non-nuclear weapon states party to the NPT or to a comparable internationally binding agreement (such as the Treaty of Tlatelolco), or to those countries which not only had renounced nuclear weapons for themselves but also did not have them on their territories [67].

There were divergent positions regarding the form of the assurances. Both the Soviet Union and Pakistan had tabled draft texts for international conventions. The United States and the United Kingdom favoured a General Assembly resolution which would record the unilateral statements made by each of the nuclear powers. Pakistan also proposed an interim measure in the form of a Security Council resolution [68].

Security assurances are the responsibility of the nuclear weapon states. The only condition which can be required of other states is that they remain committed to their non-nuclear weapon status by adhering to the NPT or a comparable agreement, and by keeping their nuclear activities under comprehensive international controls. There is no justification for asking these states to join yet another international instrument. There could be difficulties in making the guarantees conditional upon the physical absence of foreign nuclear weapons or non-adherence to security pacts. The burden of new obligations falls entirely on the nuclear weapon powers. Their assurances could take the form of identically worded national policy statements to be formalized internationally in a Security Council resolution. A multilateral treaty entered into by the nuclear weapon powers alone is yet another possibility.

The non-nuclear weapon states recognize that formal assurances, in whatever form, cannot guarantee their security. Only nuclear disarmament can remove the risk that nuclear weapons will be used. Nuclear war is unlikely to respect the borders between states that benefit from negative security guarantees and those that do not. Nevertheless, security assurances must be considered within the context of the NPT as a legitimate minimum *quid pro quo* for renouncing nuclear weapons.

IX. Summary and conclusions

The Second NPT Review Conference failed to adopt a consensus declaration. The main reasons lay outside the conference halls: in the uncertain future of the strategic arms limitation talks; in the inability of the US government to take major decisions during a presidential campaign; in the Soviet intervention in Afghanistan; in the ever more acute conflict in the Persian Gulf area; in the brewing social unrest in Poland, with its potential threat to security in Europe; in the controversy over Euro-strategic missiles; and in the continuous buildup of military strength. In an international situation, characterized by growing East–West tension, it was hardly possible for the Review Conference to produce a meaningful political document acceptable to the major powers. Moreover, Third World countries could not condone the complete standstill in nuclear disarmament negotiations. The Conference took place at the 'wrong' time. In the best case, with general good will (which was not always evident) one could perhaps have achieved a bland consensus paper; but such a paper would have most certainly contained ambiguous formulations, concealing divergent opinions and subject to different interpretations. This would hardly have been a success.

On the other hand, there is nothing in the text of the NPT compelling a review conference to issue a final declaration. The relevant clause requires only that a review of the operation of the Treaty be made (there exists a separate procedure for amendments) "with a view to assuring that the purposes of the Preamble and the provisions of the Treaty are being realized", which is what the Conference did. The in-depth discussion in two specialized committees and the detailed working documents submitted by the delegates provided a fairly accurate picture of the state of implementation of the NPT. They also revealed a convergence of views on a series of points concerning the assessment of the present situation as well as the measures to be taken in the future. These can be summarized as follows:

(*a*) The NPT continues to play a vital role in the efforts to prevent further proliferation of nuclear weapons. No party is known to be planning a withdrawal from the Treaty.[15] The parties are interested in ensuring its universality.

(*b*) No direct violation of the NPT has been recorded.

(*c*) Nuclear co-operation contributing to the development of a nuclear weapon capability by non-parties to the NPT should be avoided.

(*d*) The current safeguards procedures are adequate for existing facilities, but they need continued improvement to deal with increasing amounts of nuclear material and more complex nuclear facilities.

(*e*) It is desirable that non-nuclear weapon states not party to the NPT submit their nuclear activities to the same safeguards as those applied to the parties.

(*f*) The conclusion of the Convention on the physical protection of nuclear material was an important achievement; the Convention should be adhered to by all states.

(*g*) More assistance should be provided to developing non-nuclear weapon parties to the NPT in the field of application of nuclear energy for peaceful purposes.

(*h*) Conditions of nuclear supplies should be discussed between supplier and recipient states, in order to improve the predictability of supplies and avoid their interruption. These subjects are to be dealt with in the IAEA Committee on Assurances of Supply.

(*i*) The IAEA's efforts towards the establishment of a scheme for international plutonium storage and the management of spent fuel should continue.

(*j*) The establishment of nuclear weapon-free zones in different parts of the world would promote non-proliferation objectives.

(*k*) International arrangements to assure non-nuclear weapon states against the use of nuclear weapons would further non-proliferation efforts.

[15] At the beginning of the Review Conference, Peru warned that if the Conference did not give satisfaction to all the NPT parties, and in particular to the developing countries, those countries "could seriously consider the possibility of denouncing" the Treaty [3]. There is no indication that this view was shared by others.

However, the points of disagreement were more weighty. They concerned, first of all, the NPT provision dealing with disarmament. This provision was included in the Treaty at the insistence of non-nuclear weapon states, with a view to matching the cessation of horizontal proliferation of nuclear weapons with the cessation of vertical proliferation. It thus embodied the basic bargain of the NPT. The idea was that the NPT should become a transitional stage in a process of nuclear disarmament, but the nuclear weapon powers seem to regard it as an end in itself.

The NPT is certainly an unequal treaty in the sense that the non-nuclear weapon states, in renouncing the nuclear weapon option, have assumed the main burden of obligation, while the nuclear powers, in committing themselves not to transfer nuclear weapons, have sacrificed relatively little. Nevertheless, it would not be correct to maintain that the NPT only serves the interests of the great powers. The non-nuclear weapon states, which more than two decades ago formally proposed an international undertaking to prevent the wider dissemination of nuclear weapons [69–70], benefit at least to the same degree as the great powers from the renunciation of these weapons by the parties to the NPT. Conversely, the security of *all* states could be jeopardized if new states acquired nuclear weapons; even planning for nuclear arms control would then become much harder. But without a process of actual disarmament, which would de-emphasize the role and utility of nuclear weaponry in world diplomacy and military strategy, the future of the NPT may be at risk. The arms race undermines the credibility of the Treaty in the eyes of its non-nuclear weapon parties and provides an excuse to non-parties for not joining the Treaty. Under these conditions, it may be difficult to contain the nuclear ambitions of certain non-nuclear weapon states. This is why the demands put forward by the majority of the participants that the nuclear weapon parties to the NPT should undertake concrete commitments to halt the arms race were fully justified. Obviously, a review conference is not a forum where arms control agreements can be negotiated, but the nuclear powers could at least have signalled their readiness to step up the pace of ongoing negotiations and to agree to procedures for new negotiations. Their unwillingness to accede even to such minimum demands was bound to lead to an impasse.

Another major controversy was more directly related to the operation of the NPT. It arose in connection with the application of safeguards under Article III of the Treaty. While all the participants in the Review Conference were, in principle, in favour of applying full-scope NPT safeguards also in states which are not party to the Treaty, there was no agreement as to whether such safeguards should be required as a *condition* of supplies. On this issue, divisions appeared even within groups of countries that on many other matters took identical positions.

Full-scope safeguards cannot replace a political commitment not to acquire a nuclear weapon, but they could provide a way of extending the non-proliferation regime to states which have not joined the NPT. On the other hand, continued supplies to non-parties, especially to those having unsafeguarded facilities, constitute a direct danger to the survival of the NPT. For such countries are the most likely next candidates for membership in the 'nuclear club'. And if further proliferation takes place, withdrawals from the treaty by certain present parties may prove unavoidable. The inability to settle the question of safeguards was a regrettable failure. Evidently, more efforts are needed to ensure comprehensive controls of nuclear activities of all states.

The forceful arguments, put forward by the majority of states in favour of the strengthening of the NPT, cannot be ignored. They are bound to stimulate concrete actions, even though they were not recorded in a common statement of the Review Conference. In this sense, the Conference may not have been a useless exercise.

References

1. NPT Review Conference document NPT/CONF.II/22.
2. NPT Review Conference document NPT/CONF.II/C.I/2.
3. NPT Review Conference document NPT/CONF.II/SR.2.
4. Executive Order, White House, 19 June 1980.
5. *Pakistan Horizon*, Quarterly, Vol. 33, No. 3, 1980.
6. *International Herald Tribune*, 24 September 1980.
7. *Hearing before the Subcommittee on Energy, Nuclear Proliferation and Federal Services of the Committee on Governmental Affairs*, US Senate, 96th Congress, first session, May 1, 1979 (US Government Printing Office, Washington, D.C., 1979).
8. 'Panorama', BBC Broadcast, 16 June 1980.
9. *Washington Post*, 12 September 1980.
10. UN document A/35/402.
11. *World Armaments and Disarmament, SIPRI Yearbook 1980* (Taylor & Francis, London, 1980, Stockholm International Peace Research Institute), pp. 318–20.
12. *International Herald Tribune*, 17 October 1978.
13. IAEA General Conference, Press Release C/XXIV/2, 22 September 1980.
14. UN document A/PV.1672.
15. UN document A/C.1/31/PV.32.
16. IAEA document INFCIRC/66.
17. IAEA document INFCIRC/153.
18. NPT Review Conference document NPT/CONF.II/6.
19. NPT Review Conference document NPT/CONF.II/SR.1.
20. NPT Review Conference document NPT/CONF.II/C.II/8.
21. NPT Review Conference document NPT/CONF.II/C.II/4.

22. NPT Review Conference document NPT/CONF.II/C.II/29.
23. NPT Review Conference document NPT/CONF.II/C.II/30.
24. IAEA document GOV/1744 and Add. 1.
25. NPT Review Conference document NPT/CONF.II/C.II/26.
26. NPT Review Conference document NPT/CONF.II/C.II/22.
27. NPT Review Conference document NPT/CONF.II/C.II/6.
28. NPT Review Conference document NPT/CONF.II/C.II/10.
29. NPT Review Conference document NPT/CONF.II/C.II/7.
30. NPT Review Conference document NPT/CONF.II/C.II/SR.5.
31. NPT Review Conference document NPT/CONF.II/C.II/SR.4.
32. *Dagens Nyheter* (Stockholm), 22 October 1980.
33. NPT Review Conference document NPT/CONF.II/SR.3.
34. NPT Review Conference document NPT/CONF.II/7.
35. IAEA document INFCIRC/254 and Add. 1.
36. IAEA document INFCIRC/209.
37. Szegilongi, E., 'Unilateral revisions of international nuclear supply arrangements', *International Lawyer*, Vol. 12, No. 4.
38. INFCE document INFCE/TCC/1/2.
39. NPT Review Conference document NPT/CONF.II/C.II/34.
40. IAEA document GOV/1997, 20 June 1980.
41. Final Document, First Regular Meeting of non-aligned co-ordinating countries on the peaceful uses of nuclear energy, Buenos Aires, Argentina, 30 June–4 July, 1980.
42. UN document, General Assembly Resolution 34/63.
43. NPT Review Conference document NPT/CONF.II/C.II/11.
44. NPT Review Conference document NPT/CONF.II/C.I/4.
45. NPT Review Conference document NPT/CONF.II/C.II/32.
46. 'Enriched uranium makers face overcapacity', *Chemical & Engineering News*, 28 April 1980, p. 18.
47. *Nuclear Energy and Nuclear Weapon Proliferation* (Taylor & Francis, London, 1979, Stockholm International Peace Research Institute), pp. 413–15.
48. *Regional Nuclear Fuel Cycle Centres*, Vol. 1–3 (International Atomic Energy Agency, Vienna, 1977).
49. IAEA document GOV/1854.
50. NPT Review Conference document NPT/CONF.II/C.I/1.
51. NPT Review Conference document NPT/CONF.II/C.I/7.
52. NPT Review Conference document NPT/CONF.II/C.I/SR.4.
53. NPT Review Conference document NPT/CONF.II/C.I/SR.5.
54. NPT Review Conference document NPT/CONF.II/C.I/10 and Add. 1.
55. UN General Assembly document A/35/257.
56. Office of the US Assistant Secretary of Defense, News Release No. 344-80, Washington, D.C., 20 August 1980.
57. UN document A/RES/S-10/2.
58. NPT Review Conference document NPT/CONF.II/C.I/6.
59. *International Herald Tribune*, 29 September 1980.

60. NPT Review Conference document NPT/CONF.II/C.I/SR.6.
61. UN document A/S-10/PV.5.
62. UN document A/S-10/AC.1/30.
63. UN document A/S-10/PV.26.
64. UN document A/S-10/PV.27.
65. UN document A/S-10/PV.7.
66. NPT Review Conference document NPT/CONF.II/SR.7.
67. Committee on Disarmament document CD/139.
68. Committee on Disarmament document CD/SA/WP.3.
69. UN document A/C.1/L.206, October 1958.
70. UN document A/RES/1380 (XIV), November 1959.

Appendix 10A

*Final Document of the Second Review Conference of the parties to the Treaty on the Non-Proliferation of Nuclear Weapons**

7 September 1980

ORGANIZATION AND WORK OF THE CONFERENCE

Introduction

1. The Final Declaration of the first Review Conference of the Parties to the Treaty on the Non-Proliferation of Nuclear Weapons, which was held in 1975, in section entitled "Review of Article VIII" contains the following recommendation:

> "The States Party to the Treaty participating in the Conference propose to the Depositary Governments that a second Conference to review the operation of the Treaty be convened in 1980.
>
> The Conference accordingly invites States Party to the Treaty which are Members of the United Nations to request the Secretary-General of the United Nations to include the following item in the provisional agenda of the thirty-third session of the General Assembly: 'Implementation of the conclusions of the first Review Conference of the Parties to the Treaty on the Non-Proliferation of Nuclear Weapons and establishment of a preparatory committee for the second Conference'."

2. At its thirty-third session the General Assembly of the United Nations, in resolution 33/57, noted that, following appropriate consultations, a Preparatory Committee for such a Conference had been formed of Parties to the Treaty (a) serving on the Board of Governors of the International Atomic Energy Agency or (b) represented on the Committee on Disarmament.

3. Thus, at its first session the Preparatory Committee was composed of the following 39 States Parties: Australia, Austria, Belgium, Bulgaria, Canada, Czechoslovakia, Ecuador, Ethiopia, Finland, German Democratic Republic, Germany, Federal Republic of, Ghana, Greece, Guatemala, Hungary, Iran, Italy, Japan, Kenya, Korea, Republic of, Mexico, Mongolia, Morocco, Netherlands, Nigeria, Norway, Peru, Poland, Romania, Sri Lanka, Sweden, Thailand, Tunisia, Union of Soviet Socialist Republics, United Kingdom of Great Britain and Northern Ireland, United States of America, Venezuela, Yugoslavia and Zaire. At the second session Indonesia, having ratified the Treaty and being a member of the Committee on Disarmament, also participated in the work of the Preparatory Committee. Further, at the third session, Ireland, the Philippines and Switzerland, having been elected to the Board of Governors of the International Atomic Energy Agency, also served on the Preparatory Committee.

4. The Preparatory Committee held three sessions at Geneva: the first from 17 to 20 April 1979; the second from 20 to 24 August 1979; and the third from 24 March to 1 April 1980. Progress reports on the first two sessions of the Committee were issued as

---

* *Source:* Review Conference document NPT/CONF.II/22.

documents NPT/CONF.II/PC.I/3 and NPT/CONF.II/PC.II/12, which were circulated to the States Parties.

5. At the first session, on 17 April 1979, the Preparatory Committee decided to have a different Chairman for each of its three sessions. These three together would constitute the Bureau of the Committee; the two who were not Chairmen of a given session would act as Vice-Chairmen of the Committee at that session. At its first session, the Committee elected Mr R. R. Fernandez of Australia to serve as Chairman of that session. At the second session, the Committee elected Ambassador G. Herder of the German Democratic Republic as Chairman of that session. At the third session, the Committee elected Ambassador C. G. Maina of Kenya as Chairman of that session. The Committee decided that the Chairman of the third session should open the Review Conference.

6. The Preparatory Committee decided to issue, as pre-session Conference documentation, a number of background papers pertaining to the implementation of various provisions of the Treaty. The papers, which were originally submitted to the Committee by the Secretary-General of the United Nations, by the Director-General of the IAEA and by the Agency for the Prohibition of Nuclear Weapons in Latin America in response to an invitation from the Committee, were subsequently updated and revised and circulated as documents of the Conference, as follows:

(a) by the Secretariat of the United Nations:
— Background Paper on the basic facts within the framework of the United Nations in connexion with the realization of the purposes of the tenth preambular paragraph of the Treaty on the Non-Proliferation of Nuclear Weapons. (NPT/CONF.II/2).
— Background Paper on basic facts within the framework of the United Nations in connexion with the realization of the purposes of Articles I and II of the Treaty on the Non-Proliferation of Nuclear Weapons. (NPT/CONF.II/3).
— Background Paper on basic facts within the framework of the United Nations in connexion with the realization of the purpose of Articles IV and V of the Treaty on the Non-Proliferation of Nuclear Weapons. (NPT/CONF.II/4).
— Background Paper on basic facts within the framework of the United Nations in connexion with the realization of the purposes of Article VI of the Treaty on the Non-Proliferation of Nuclear Weapons. (NPT/CONF.II/5).

(b) by the International Atomic Energy Agency:
— IAEA's activities under Article III of the NPT. (NPT/CONF.II/6* and Add 1 and 2).
— IAEA's activities under Article IV of the NPT. (NPT/CONF.II/7).
— IAEA's activities under Article V of the NPT. (NPT/CONF.II/8).

(c) by the Agency for the Prohibition of Nuclear Weapons in Latin America (OPANAL).
— Memorandum from the Secretariat of OPANAL in response to the request of the Preparatory Committee for the Second Review Conference of the Parties to the Treaty on the Non-Proliferation of Nuclear Weapons. (NPT/CONF.II/9).

7. The Final Report of the Preparatory Committee for the Second Review Conference of the Parties to the Treaty on the Non-Proliferation of Nuclear Weapons (NPT/CONF.II/1) was also issued as a document of the Conference prior to its opening. The report included, *inter alia*, the Provisional Agenda for the Conference, the Draft Rules of Procedure, and a Schedule for the Division of Costs of the Conference.

Organization of the Conference

8. In accordance with the decision of the Preparatory Committee, the Conference was convened on 11 August 1980 at the Palais des Nations in Geneva, for a period of up to four weeks. After the opening of the Conference by Ambassador C. G. Maina of Kenya, Chairman of the Third Session of the Preparatory Committee, the Conference elected by acclamation as its President Mr Ismat T. Kittani, Under-Secretary of the Ministry of Foreign Affairs of Iraq. The Conference unanimously also confirmed the nomination of Mr Allessandro Corradini as Secretary-General of the Conference. The nomination had been made by the Secretary-General of the United Nations, following an invitation by the Preparatory Committee.

9. At the same meeting, Mr Mikhail D. Sytenko, Under-Secretary-General, Department of Political and Security Council Affairs, United Nations, conveyed to the Conference a message of the Secretary-General of the United Nations, and Mr Sigvard Eklund, Director-General of the IAEA, addressed the Conference.

10. A message was addressed to the participants in the Conference by Mr Leonid I. Brezhnev, Secretary-General of the Communist Party of the USSR and Chairman of the Presidium of the Supreme Soviet of the USSR (NPT/CONF.II/10).

11. A message was also addressed to the Conference by President Jimmy Carter of the United States of America (NPT/CONF.II/11).

12. At the opening meeting, the Conference adopted its agenda (NPT/CONF.II/14) as recommended by the Preparatory Committee.

13. At the fourth plenary meeting on 13 August, the Conference adopted its rules of procedure (NPT/CONF.II/15) as recommended by the Preparatory Committee. The rules of procedure established (a) two Main Committees; (b) a General Committee, chaired by the President of the Conference and composed of the Chairmen of the Conference's two Main Committees, its Drafting Committee and its Credentials Committee, as well as the 26 Vice-Presidents of the Conference; (c) a Drafting Committee, composed of representatives of the 31 States Parties represented on the General Committee, but open to representatives of other delegations when matters of particular concern to them were under discussion; and (d) a Credentials Committee, composed of a Chairman and two Vice-Chairmen elected by the Conference, and six other members appointed by the Conference on the proposal of the President.

14. At its tenth plenary meeting, on 18 August, the Conference unanimously elected the Chairman and Vice-Chairman of the two Main Committees, the Drafting Committee, and the Credentials Committee, as follows:

Main Committee I	Chairman	Mr C. G. Maina (Kenya)
	Vice-Chairman	Mr B. Grinberg (Bulgaria)
	Vice-Chairman	Mr N. Boel (Denmark)
Main Committee II	Chairman	Mr R. R. Fernandez (Australia)
	Vice-Chairman	Mr J. Beránek (Czechoslovakia)
	Vice-Chairman	Mr D. L. Siazon (Philippines)
Drafting Committee	Chairman	Mr G. Herder (German Democratic Republic)
	Vice-Chairman	Mr A. Pouyiouros (Cyprus)
	Vice-Chairman	Mr O. Vaernø (Norway)

Credentials Committee	Chairman	Mr R. Valdez (Ecuador)
	Vice-Chairman	Mr I. Kömives (Hungary)
	Vice-Chairman	Mr A. Onkelinx (Belgium)

The Conference also unanimously elected 26 Vice-Presidents from the following States Parties:

Canada
Congo
Costa Rica
Czechoslovakia
Ethiopia
Hungary
Indonesia
Japan
Mexico
Mongolia
Netherlands
Nigeria
Peru
Poland
Republic of Korea
Romania
Sri Lanka
Switzerland
Syria
Turkey
Union of Soviet Socialist Republics
United Kingdom of Great Britain and Northern Ireland
United States of America
Venezuela
Yugoslavia
Zaire

15. At the same meeting, the Conference also appointed, on the proposal of the President, the following six States Parties as members of the Credentials Committee: Jordan, Malaysia, Senegal, Tunisia, Union of Soviet Socialist Republics and the United States of America.

Participation in the Conference

16. Seventy-five States Parties to the Treaty on the Non-Proliferation of Nuclear Weapons participated in the Conference, as follows:

Australia
Austria
Bangladesh
Belgium
Bulgaria
Burundi
Canada
Congo
Costa Rica
Cyprus
Czechoslovakia
Democratic Yemen
Denmark
Ecuador
Ethiopia
Finland
Gabon
German Democratic Republic
Germany, Federal Republic of
Ghana
Greece
Holy See
Honduras
Hungary
Iceland
Indonesia
Iran
Iraq
Ireland
Italy
Ivory Coast
Japan
Jordan
Kenya
Korea, Republic of
Lebanon
Libyan Arab Jamahiriya
Liechtenstein
Luxembourg
Malaysia
Malta
Mexico

Mongolia
Morocco
Netherlands
New Zealand
Nicaragua
Nigeria
Norway
Panama
Peru
Philippines
Poland
Portugal
Romania
San Marino
Senegal
Sierra Leone
Somalia
Sri Lanka
Sudan
Sweden
Switzerland
Syrian Arab Republic
Thailand
Tunisia
Turkey
Union of Soviet Socialist Republics
United Kingdom
United Republic of Cameroon
United States of America
Uruguay
Venezuela
Yugoslavia
Zaire

17. In addition, Egypt, a signatory State which has not yet ratified the Treaty, participated in the Conference without taking part in its decisions, as provided for in paragraph 1 of rule 44 of the Rules of Procedure.

18. Eleven additional States, neither Parties nor Signatories of the Treaty, namely, Algeria, Argentina, Brazil, Chile, Cuba, Israel, Mozambique, Spain, United Arab Emirates, United Republic of Tanzania and Zambia, applied for observer status in accordance with paragraph 2 of rule 44. Such status was granted to them by the Conference.

19. The United Nations and the International Atomic Energy Agency participated in the Conference under paragraph 3 of rule 44.

20. Two regional organizations, the Agency for the Prohibition of Nuclear Weapons in Latin America (OPANAL) and the League of Arab States, were granted Observer Agency status under paragraph 4 of rule 44.

21. Several Non-Governmental Organizations attended the Conference under paragraph 5 of rule 44.

22. A list of all delegations to the Conference, including States Parties, Signatories, Observer States, the United Nations, the IAEA, Observer Agencies and Non-Governmental Organizations is contained in Annex II to this report.

23. The Credentials Committee held two meetings on 29 August and 4 September. At the latter date it adopted its report to the Conference on the credentials of States Parties (NPT/CONF.II/17). At its 19th plenary meeting on 7 September the Conference took note of the report.

Financial Arrangements

24. Concerning the schedule for the division of costs of the Conference, at its thirteenth plenary meeting, on 19 August, the Conference decided to adopt the cost-sharing formula proposed by the Preparatory Committee embodied in the Appendix to rule 12 of the Rules of Procedure (NPT/CONF.II/1, Annex III, Appendix). The final schedule based on the actual participation of States Parties and Signatories in the Conference was set out in document NPT/CONF.II/18.

Work of the Conference

25. The Conference held 19 plenary meetings between 11 August and 7 September, when it concluded its work.

26. The general debate in plenary, in which 51 States Parties and one Signatory took part, was held from 12 to 19 August.

27. The General Committee, at its first meeting on 18 August, considered item 1 of the Agenda entitled "Programme of Work", and decided to recommend that the following items be allocated to the two Main Committees, with the understanding that remaining items would be considered in the plenary.

(a) to Main Committee I:

— item 13. Review of the operation of the Treaty as provided for in its Article VIII (3):

A. Implementation of the provisions of the Treaty relating to non-proliferation of nuclear weapons, disarmament and international peace and security:
(1) Articles I, II and III (1, 2 and 4) and preambular paragraphs 1–5
(2) Article VI and preambular paragraphs 8–12
(3) Article VII

C. Other provisions of the Treaty

D. Security Assurances
(1) Resolution 255 (1968) of the United Nations Security Council
(2) Effective international arrangements to assure non-nuclear-weapon States against the use or threat of use of nuclear weapons.

— item 14. Role of the Treaty in the promotion of non-proliferation of nuclear weapons and of nuclear disarmament and in strengthening international peace and security:

A. Acceptance of the Treaty by States

B. Measures aimed at promoting a wider acceptance of the Treaty.

(b) to main Committee II:

— item 13. Review of the operation of the Treaty as provided for in its Article VIII (3):

B. Implementation of the provisions of the Treaty relating to peaceful applications of nuclear energy:
(1) Articles III and IV
(2) Article V and preambular paragraphs 6 and 7.

In connexion with the allocation of item 13 B (1) to Main Committee II, the General Committee recommended that discussion on Article III need not be limited to paragraph 3. With regard to the allocation of sub-item 14 B to Main Committee I, it was further recommended that Committee II should be free to discuss also this sub-item.

28. In connexion with the allocation of items to the two Main Committees, the General Committee recommended that the Committees should complete their work by 29 August.

29. The recommendations contained in paragraphs 27 and 28 above were approved by the Conference at its 13th meeting on 19 August. Subsequently, the Conference extended the deadline for completion of the Committees' work to 4 September.

30. Main Committee I held 12 meetings from 19 August to 4 September. Its report (NPT/CONF.II/19) was submitted to the Conference at its 19th meeting on 7 September. Main Committee II held 10 meetings from 19 August to 4 September. Its report (NPT/CONF.II/20) was submitted to the Conference at its 19th meeting on 7 September. At the same meeting the Conference decided to take note of the two reports.

Documentation

31. A list of the documents of the Conference is attached as Annex I.*

Conclusion of the Conference

32. At its final plenary meeting, on 7 September, the Conference proposed to the Depositary Governments that a third conference to review the operation of the Treaty be convened in 1985. The Conference accordingly invited States Parties to the Treaty which are Members of the United Nations to request the Secretary-General of the United Nations to include the following item in the provisional agenda of the thirty-eighth session of the General Assembly: "Implementation of the conclusions of the Second Review Conference of the Parties to the Treaty on the Non-Proliferation of Nuclear Weapons and Establishment of a Preparatory Committee for the Third Conference."

33. All the proposals submitted to the Conference as well as the various views expressed, which are fully reflected in the summary records and the documents of the Conference, form part of this Final Document and are forwarded as such for the consideration of Governments of States Parties to the Treaty on the Non-Proliferation of Nuclear Weapons.

* This annex is not reproduced in the Yearbook.

Appendix 10B

Informal working paper reviewing Articles I and II of the Non-Proliferation Treaty, prepared during the Second NPT Review Conference, August–September 1980

Consensus was not reached on the wording given in brackets.

4 September 1980

Article I

1. (a) [The Conference confirms that the obligations undertaken by the Nuclear Weapon States Parties under Article I have been [faithfully] observed.]

1. (b) [The Conference affirms that the obligation assumed by the Nuclear Weapon States Parties not to transfer to any recipient whatsoever nuclear weapons or other nuclear explosive devices or control over such weapons or explosive devices has been fulfilled to the extent that there has been no such direct transfer.]

2. [The Conference considers that emphasis must be placed on the obligation assumed by Nuclear-Weapon States Parties to the Treaty not in any way to assist, encourage, or induce any non-nuclear-weapon State to manufacture or acquire such weapons or devices, or control over such weapons or explosive devices.]

3. [The Conference believes that, in the interest of promoting the purpose and objective of the Treaty, no state should in any way assist, encourage or induce any non-nuclear-weapon State, particularly not party to the Treaty, to manufacture or otherwise acquire nuclear weapons or other nuclear explosive devices, or control over such weapons or explosive devices. This should in no way be interpreted as affecting the provisions of Article IV of the Treaty.]

4. [The Conference also believes that it is [not] contrary to the nuclear non-proliferation objective of the Treaty to deploy nuclear weapons and nuclear explosive devices on the territories of non-nuclear-weapon States and in international waters.]

5. (a) The Conference expresses its deep concern that certain forms of nuclear co-operation contribute to the development of a nuclear weapon capability by certain States, non-parties to the Treaty, which have not assumed appropriate international obligations [especially situated in (regions of tension or conflict) (Southern Africa, Middle East [and South Asia.])]

5. (b) [The Conference expresses further its concern with respect to the impact which co-operation supposedly for peaceful purposes has had on the development of the nuclear weapon capability of the non-NPT parties Israel and South Africa and the consequent growing alarm of African and Middle Eastern States in particular and the international community in general. The Conference further takes note of the concern expressed by the General Assembly of the United Nations about the nuclear weapon capabilities of Israel and South Africa, and that the Assembly has condemned the nuclear collaboration between Israel and South Africa.]

6. [The Conference is convinced that the strict observance of Article I remains central to the shared objectives of averting the further proliferation of nuclear weapons.]

Article II

7. The Conference confirms that the obligations undertaken by the non-nuclear-weapon States Parties under Article II have been [faithfully] observed.

8. [The Conference is convinced that the strict observance of Article II remains central to the shared objective of averting the further proliferation of nuclear weapons.]

Appendix 10C

Informal working paper reviewing Articles III, IV and V of the Non-Proliferation Treaty, prepared during the Second NPT Review Conference, August–September 1980

Consensus was not reached on the wording given in brackets.

6 September 1980

Article III

1. The Conference expresses the conviction that IAEA safeguards play a key role in preventing proliferation of nuclear weapons or other explosive devices by way of deterring diversion of nuclear materials from peaceful activities to explosive purposes through the risk of early detection and will thereby contribute to promoting further confidence among States.

2. The Conference notes with satisfaction that as a result of its verification activities, the Agency has not detected any diversions, anomalies or misuses of safeguarded material to nuclear weapons or other nuclear explosive devices.

3. The Conference considers that the undertaking under Article III (1) to verify commitments under the Treaty of NNWSP is fully met by the conclusion and implementation of agreements in accordance with IAEA document INFCIRC 153. The Conference notes with satisfaction the conclusion of an increasing number of these safeguards agreements in compliance with the undertaking in Article III.1 of the Treaty. The Conference urges the non-nuclear-weapon States Parties to the Treaty that have not concluded the agreements required under Article III (4) to conclude such agreements with the IAEA as soon as possible.

4. The Conference attaches great importance to the continued application of safeguards in accordance with Article III (1) on a non-discriminatory basis for the equal benefit of all States Parties to the Treaty.

5. The Conference considers that in the application of safeguards the IAEA should accord any non-nuclear-weapon State Party to the Treaty treatment with respect to safeguards not less favourable than the treatment it accords to other States or a group of States, provided that the Agency is satisfied that the national system of such a State achieves and maintains a degree of functional independence and technical effectiveness equivalent to that of such other States or groups of States. The Conference regards such a development as a measure to facilitate and complement the safeguards activities of the IAEA.

6. The Conference believes that all non-nuclear-weapon States not Parties to the Treaty should submit all their source or special fissionable material in all their nuclear activities to IAEA safeguards, with a view to preventing diversion of nuclear material to nuclear weapons or other nuclear explosive devices, and appeals to such States to do so.

[7. The Conference urges that States Parties to the Treaty participate actively in joint efforts with States concerned to adopt as a common requirement for the international exchange of nuclear materials and equipment, that non-nuclear-weapon States not Party to the Treaty accept the same safeguards obligations as have been accepted by non-nuclear-weapon States Parties to the Treaty.]

8. The Conference calls upon the Parties to work actively towards this end, including by participation in the forthcoming meetings of the IAEA Committee on Assurances of Supply.

[9. The Conference calls upon all nuclear-weapon States as well as non-nuclear-weapon States concerned, to cease all co-operation and to cut off supplies to Israel and South Africa, unless these countries submit all their nuclear programmes to IAEA full-scope safeguards, in order to prevent contributing further to these countries' capability to acquire or manufacture nuclear weapons or nuclear explosive devices.]

10. The Conference notes that the safeguards activities of the IAEA under Article III of the Treaty continue to respect the sovereign rights of States, that there are no indications that IAEA safeguards have hampered the economic, scientific or technological development of the Parties to the Treaty or international co-operation in peaceful nuclear activities, and that they contribute to the maintenance of confidence between States. It urges that this situation be maintained and that in further developing the Agency's safeguards activities, the promotion of the peaceful uses of nuclear energy should be fully taken into account.

11. The Conference, noting that existing IAEA safeguards approaches are capable of adequately dealing with current facility types, emphasizes the importance of continued improvements in the effectiveness and efficiency of IAEA safeguards. The Agency's responsibilities in the future can be expected to grow, *inter alia*, from the increasing amounts of nuclear material and the increasing number and complexity of facilities. The Conference calls for the continuing support of States Parties for the IAEA safeguards system.

12. The Conference calls upon States Parties to take IAEA safeguards requirements fully into account in planning, designing and developing nuclear fuel cycle facilities.

13. The Conference notes that more regard needs to be paid to the importance of recruiting and training staff for the safeguards activities of the Agency on as wide a geographical basis as possible in accordance with Article VIID of the Statute of the IAEA and the recommendation of the First Review Conference. It calls upon States to exercise the right of accepting or rejecting proposals for the designation of particular IAEA inspectors in such a way as to facilitate the effective implementation of safeguards.

14. The Conference recommends that during the review of the arrangements relating to the financing of safeguards in the IAEA which is to be undertaken by the Board of Governors at an appropriate time in 1983 the less favourable financial situation of the developing countries be fully taken into account.

15. The Conference welcomes the opening for signature of the Convention on the Physical Protection of Nuclear Material, which has been negotiated under the auspices of the IAEA in fulfilment of the recommendations of the First Review Conference. The Conference urges all States that have not done so to become party, as soon as possible, to this Convention.

[16. The Conference expresses concern on the reports alleging that significant quantities of special nuclear material are unaccounted for in a nuclear-weapon State Party to the Treaty.]

17. The Conference in its review of Articles III and IV welcomes the work of the IAEA expert group on international plutonium storage, and supports efforts directed at the early establishment of an internationally agreed effective scheme for international plutonium storage on the basis of Article XII A5 of the IAEA Statute. The Conference considers that such a scheme for excess plutonium, if well designed, should not jeopardize the promotion of the peaceful uses of nuclear energy, and would make a substantial contribution to non-proliferation as well as to the improvement of the assurance of nuclear supply and the development of common approaches and generally agreed arrangements for international nuclear trade. In addition, the Conference considers that such a scheme should not affect the free technological development of the countries concerned and the disposal of plutonium in accordance with internationally adopted arrangements, including the application of IAEA safeguards.

Article IV

1. The Conference re-emphasizes its conviction that nothing in the Treaty shall be interpreted as affecting the inalienable right of all the Parties to the Treaty to develop research, production and use of nuclear energy for peaceful purposes without discrimination and in conformity with Article I and II of this Treaty.

2. The Conference urges further efforts to ensure that the benefits of peaceful applications of nuclear energy are made available to all Parties to the Treaty. In this context it recognizes the growing needs of developing States and calls for continued and substantively increased assistance to such States through bilateral and multilateral channels such as the IAEA and the UNDP.

3. The Conference is of the view that the activities of the IAEA directed towards the broadening of world-wide co-operation in the field of the peaceful uses of nuclear energy are of central importance.

4. The Conference confirms that each country's choices and decisions in the field of peaceful uses of nuclear energy should be respected without jeopardizing their respective fuel cycle policies or international co-operation agreements and contracts for peaceful uses of nuclear energy, provided that agreed safeguards measures are applied.

5. The Conference notes that there has been continued growth in the use of nuclear energy for peaceful purposes among Parties since the 1975 Review Conference.

6. The Conference notes the concern of many countries that, after the First Review Conference of Parties to the Treaty, a group of countries in closed consultations between themselves on nuclear supply conditions adopted and applied, including amongst themselves, common guidelines for the export of nuclear material, equipment and technology (INFIRC/254). While largely designed to broaden safeguards coverage in non-Parties to the NPT, these guidelines also called for "restraint in the transfer of sensitive facilities, technology and weapons-usable materials" which may also apply to non-nuclear-weapon States Party to the Treaty. In addition, some countries have decided to introduce in their bilateral arrangements more stringent non-proliferation requirements beyond the provisions of Article III of the Treaty. In a few cases these

had retroactive effect. Also, in a few cases there have been instances of delays and added costs with adverse consequences for economic planning and development of the importing States. Non-adherence to the Treaty by a number of countries with nuclear programmes and the explosion of a nuclear device by an additional State were seen by these supplier countries as important reasons when they sought agreement on the guidelines and modified export requirements. These motivations, however, have not been shared by some importing countries, which have undertaken full-scope safeguards.

7. States participating in the Conference, while reaffirming their adherence to the principle of non-proliferation, note that the introduction unilaterally of supply conditions without consultation among the Parties has been a cause of concern. The Conference notes the view of some importing States that the application of measures of control and supervision beyond the IAEA safeguards under Article III as a condition of international nuclear co-operation does not allow the full implementation of Article IV of the Treaty. However, States applying such measures do not share this view. The Conference considers that the introduction of new non-proliferation measures should be the subject of consultation and the broadest possible consensus among the Parties to the Treaty, *inter alia*, through the IAEA.

8. States Parties propose to meet annually in Vienna at the Headquarters of the IAEA to discuss the implementation of Article IV in the context also of Article III of the Treaty. In this connexion, the Parties will request the IAEA to make the necessary arrangements.

9. The Conference welcomes the establishment of an IAEA Committee on Assurances of Supply to consider and advise the Board of Governors on ways and means in which supplies of nuclear material equipment and technology and fuel cycle services can be assured on a more predictable and long-term basis in accordance with mutually acceptable considerations of non-proliferation and the Agency's role and responsibilities in relation thereto.

10. The Conference stresses the importance of using the Committee on Assurances of Supply to develop as wide a consensus as possible and urges States Parties to the Treaty to give their full support towards the early attainment of the objectives of the Committee on Assurances of Supply.

11. The Conference requests States Parties to consider and make recommendations where appropriate, within the framework of the Committee on Assurances of Supply and other relevant fora on proposed institutional arrangements ranging from multinational ventures to regional fuel cycle centres and to continue the consideration begun in INFCE of suitable emergency backup mechanisms including a uranium emergency safety network and an international nuclear fuel bank.

12. The Conference considers that international agreements on the peaceful uses of nuclear energy amongst States Party to the Treaty should be fulfilled in accordance with international law and with a view also to facilitating the fulfilment of contracts. The Conference urges that, in adopting relevant national legislation and regulations, States Parties to the Treaty take fully into account, by consultations or otherwise, the obligations, rights and mutual responsibilities contained in the Treaty and in their nuclear agreements, as required by principles of international law.

13. The Conference affirms that where one or other party to a bilateral agreement wishes to seek the renegotiation of non-proliferation conditions, it is desirable that

means be devised to achieve such renegotiation equitably, without resort to the unilateral interruption of supply or import, or the threat of such interruption, and with each party avoiding to the extent possible the unilateral imposition of additional costs on the other or of new conditions retroactively applied.

14. The Conference confirms the significance of peaceful uses of nuclear energy for economic development and the important contribution it can make in accelerating the economic growth of developing countries and overcoming the technological and economic disparities among States.

15. The Conference recognizes that due to their weaker infrastructure and financial base, the developing countries are more vulnerable to changing conditions. The Conference therefore considers that effective measures can and should be taken to meet the specific needs of developing countries in the peaceful uses of nuclear energy.

16. The Conference suggests the continuation of the study of financing the technical assistance programme of the IAEA in accordance with the decision taken by the last General Conference of the IAEA.

17. The Conference calls further on all States Party to the Treaty in a position to do so to meet the "technically sound" requests for technical assistance submitted by developing States Party to the Treaty that the IAEA is unable to finance from its own resources as well as such "technically sound" requests as may be made by developing States Party to the Treaty which are not members of the IAEA.

18. The Conference calls on States Parties to the Treaty to give consideration to the establishment on the basis of voluntary contributions of a Special Fund to be administered by the IAEA, or otherwise provide special contributions for the provision of technical assistance to developing non-nuclear-weapon States Parties to the Treaty in order to encourage and assist research in, and development and practical application of, nuclear energy for peaceful purposes. The Fund could be utilized to contribute to research reactor programmes.

19. The non-nuclear-weapon States Parties to the Treaty and those States that have safeguards commitments equal to those required under Article III.1 of the Treaty should be provided preferential treatment in access to or transfer of equipment, materials, services and scientific and technological information for the peaceful uses of nuclear energy, taking particularly into account needs of developing countries.

20. States Parties to the Treaty should promote the establishment of more favourable conditions in national, regional and international financial institutions for the financing of nuclear energy projects in developing countries.

21. The Conference notes with satisfaction the technical study by the International Nuclear Fuel Cycle Evaluation (INFCE) as an important exercise in the search for ways of making nuclear energy widely available consistent with non-proliferation.

22. The Conference notes that energy backup mechanisms such as a uranium emergency safety network or an international nuclear fuel bank are to be considered. As an interim measure, the Conference calls on States Parties in a position to do so (including particularly one or more Depositaries) to make available, on a commercial basis, an interim uranium stockpile sufficient for one annual LWR reload of enriched uranium and one annual HWR reload of natural uranium together with specific arrangements and conditions under which this uranium would be available to Parties which are unable to secure fuel supplied under existing contracts for reasons of contract

default that were not the result of a breach of the non-proliferation undertakings stipulated in the relevant agreement.

23. The Conference notes there is a growing need for storage of spent nuclear fuel and therefore welcomes the ongoing studies in the IAEA concerning the management of spent nuclear fuel.

24. The Conference calls on all Parties to give serious consideration to the establishment of international nuclear fuel cycle facilities, including multinational participation on a sound economic basis.

25. The Conference also recommends that the IAEA extend its study to cover the whole of the nuclear fuel cycle, in accordance with the recommendations made by the First Review Conference.

26. The Conference expects that the convening of the International Conference for the promotion of international co-operation in the peaceful uses of nuclear energy, decided by the United Nations General Assembly resolution 34/63, bearing in mind the terms of the United Nations General Assembly resolution 32/50, will be of importance to the nuclear co-operation matters addressed by the Conference.

Article V

1. The Conference reaffirms the obligation of Parties to the Treaty to take appropriate measures to ensure that potential benefits from any peaceful application of nuclear explosions are made available to non-nuclear-weapon States which are Party to the Treaty in accordance with the provisions of Article V of the Treaty and other relevant international obligations.

2. The Conference confirms that the IAEA is the appropriate international body through which any potential benefits of peaceful nuclear explosions could be made available to non-nuclear-weapon States under the terms of Article V of the Treaty.

3. The Conference notes that the IAEA has received no information in the past few years from the nuclear-weapon States and urges the IAEA to regularly include in its annual reports for the information of all States Parties to the Treaty, pursuant to its central role in arrangements for peaceful applications of nuclear explosions, a listing of all reports and information regarding the development of peaceful applications of nuclear explosions received from nuclear-weapon States during the period under review. The Conference calls on the nuclear-weapon States Parties to the Treaty to continue to provide the Agency with any such information which may become available to them. The Conference further urges the IAEA to continue to submit to the United Nations General Assembly information on the peaceful uses of nuclear explosions and on the prospects for their use.

4. The Conference supports the work of the IAEA Procedures Group and notes that existing procedures have been adequate to deal with requests which have been made so far to the IAEA for assistance in this area and that the special machinery called for at the First Review Conference has yet to be formed.

5. The Conference notes the extensive work of the *Ad Hoc* Advisory Group on Nuclear Explosions set up by the IAEA in accordance with the requirements of the terms of the Treaty and commends its report which was adopted by consensus and noted with appreciation by the IAEA Board of Governors and subsequently forwarded to the Secretary-General of the United Nations [in 1977]. The Conference notes that

the IAEA Board of Governors decided to keep the matter of peaceful uses of nuclear explosions under review.

6. The Conference further notes that peaceful uses of nuclear explosions are at an early stage of development and no application has reached the stage at which projects can be subjected to the economic assessment judged appropriate by the *Ad Hoc* Advisory Group. The Conference notes that potential benefits from peaceful applications of nuclear explosions have not been demonstrated.

Appendix 10D

Informal working paper reviewing Articles VI, VIII and IX of the Non-Proliferation Treaty, prepared during the Second NPT Review Conference, August–September 1980

Consensus was not reached on the wording given in brackets.

4 September 1980

I. REVIEW OF ARTICLE VI

1. The Conference recalls that under the provisions of Article VI of the Treaty all Parties have undertaken to pursue negotiations in good faith:

— on effective measures relating to cessation of the nuclear arms race at an early date;
— on effective measures relating to nuclear disarmament;
— on a Treaty on general and complete disarmament under strict and effective international control.

2. The Conference stresses that the implementation of Article VI is [a basic requirement] [of basic importance] to maintain the effectiveness of the Treaty as an instrument for non-proliferation of nuclear weapons. The Conference also stresses that all Parties to the Treaty, and particularly the nuclear-weapon States Party should reaffirm their commitment to the implementation of this Article and to the objectives referred to in the tenth preambular paragraph closely related thereto, and by achieving [further] concrete results demonstrate this commitment.

[3. The Conference is aware that some limited agreements have been reached in the period since the NPT came into force. Nevertheless no effective measures relating to the cessation of the nuclear arms race at an early date and to nuclear disarmament have materialized.]

[4. While welcoming the efforts in the field of arms limitation and disarmament since the first Review Conference, aimed at the implementation of Article VI of the Treaty, the Conference expresses its serious concern that the arms race, in particular the nuclear arms race, has continued unabated.] [The Conference notes the fact that, in conformity with Article VI, negotiations have been and continue to be conducted in various fora on arms limitation and disarmament. It is aware that some limited agreements have been reached in the period since the NPT came into force. Nevertheless no effective measures relating to the cessation of the nuclear arms race at an early date and to nuclear disarmament have materialized.] New technological developments in the military field [especially the possible] [and the] deployment of new generations of nuclear weapons, pose the danger that the nuclear arms race may enter into a qualitatively new phase. Mankind feels deeply alarmed by this threatening prospect.

5. The Conference notes that the tenth special session of the General Assembly of the United Nations concluded, in paragraph 50 of its Final Document, that "the achievement of nuclear disarmament will require urgent negotiations of agreements

at appropriate stages and with adequate measures of verification satisfactory to the States concerned for:

(a) Cessation of the qualitative improvement and development of nuclear-weapon systems;

(b) Cessation of the production of all types of nuclear weapons and their means of delivery, and of the production of fissionable material for weapons purposes;

(c) A comprehensive, phased programme with agreed time-tables, whenever feasible, for progressive and balanced reduction of stockpiles of nuclear weapons and their means of delivery, leading to their ultimate and complete elimination at the earliest possible time. ["]

[Consideration can be given in the course of the negotiations to mutual and agreed limitation or prohibition without prejudice to the security of any State, of any types of nuclear armaments."]

6. The Conference stresses that very little has been [done] [achieved] to realize these objectives and therefore urges all States, particularly the nuclear-weapon States [Party], to undertake urgent measures to implement the above-mentioned objectives.

[7a. The Conference underlines that instead of cessation there has been an intensification of the nuclear arms race. Thus between 1970 and 1980 the total of nuclear warheads in the strategic arsenals of the United States and the Soviet Union has almost tripled, jumping from 5,800 to 16,000.

Likewise, world military expenditure during the same period has increased from 180 thousand million dollars to 500 thousand million dollars.

New technological developments have occurred in the military field. New generations of nuclear weapons have been developed and deployed at a faster rate.

Increasing deployment of new nuclear weapons in the territories of non-nuclear-weapon States and in the oceans has taken place.]

[7b. Instead of cessation there has been an intensification of important aspects of the nuclear arms race. Thus between 1970 and 1980 the total of nuclear warheads in strategic arsenals has considerably increased. Likewise world military expenditures during the same period have also increased. New technological developments have occurred in the military field and new generations of nuclear weapons have been developed.]

8. [An alarming trend has also developed lately favouring a so-called "new strategy" for the use of nuclear weapons, based on the theory of a limited nuclear war which could be won by one of the parties in conflict. Such a theory is doubtless illusory, but it does involve the very real danger of making "thinkable" and bringing closer the hypothesis of a nuclear world war, which according to the General Assembly may well mean the end of the human species.]

9. The Conference expresses the conviction that the prohibition of all nuclear [weapon tests] [explosions] by all States in all environments is a basic requirement to halt the nuclear arms race, the qualitative improvement of nuclear weapons and the spread of nuclear weapons.

10. The Conference recalls the determination expressed in the Treaty "to seek to achieve the discontinuance of all test explosions of nuclear weapons for all time and to continue negotiations to this end". The Conference also recalls that in the Final Declaration of the first Review Conference, the Parties expressed the view that the

conclusion of a treaty banning all nuclear-weapon tests was one of the most important measures to halt the nuclear arms race and expressed the hope that the nuclear-weapon States Party to the Treaty would take the lead in reaching an early solution of the technical and political difficulties of this issue.

11. The Conference also stresses the important contribution that such a treaty would make toward strengthening and extending the international barriers against the proliferation of nuclear weapons. It further notes that adherence to such a treaty by all States would contribute substantially to the full achievement of this objective.

12. The Conference considers that for maximum effectiveness the treaty should be [a treaty prohibiting nuclear-weapon test explosions in all environments and should have a protocol covering nuclear explosions for peaceful purposes] [comprehensive, covering all kinds of nuclear explosions in any environment] [be of unlimited duration], be provided with an adequate verification system, be capable of attracting the widest possible adherence [, leading to discontinuance of all test explosions of nuclear weapons for all time.] and that it should be concluded most urgently.

13. The Conference deeply regrets that until now a comprehensive multilateral nuclear test-ban treaty has not been concluded, [and that the three nuclear-weapon States Party to the NPT have not discharged their obligation in this respect.] The Conference recalls the appeal made at the first Review Conference that the nuclear-weapon States signatories of the Treaty on the Limitation of Underground Nuclear Weapons Tests limit the number of such tests to a minimum. In this connexion, it notes that nuclear weapon tests have been proceeding at an [enhanced] [undiminished] pace [as proved by the fact that between 1970 and the end of 1979 there have been 154 nuclear explosions by the United States and 191 by the Soviet Union, of which in the year 1979 alone 15 were conducted by the United States and 28 by the Soviet Union.] [: a total of 421 nuclear explosions were reported during the 1970s, out of which the Soviet Union made 191, the United States 154, France 55, China 15, the United Kingdom 5 and India [1]].

14. The Conference nevertheless [welcomes] [notes] the considerable progress in the trilateral negotiations [which, according to the report submitted] [reported] to the Committee on Disarmament by the three nuclear-weapon States Party to the NPT [was attained] on a treaty prohibiting nuclear-weapon test explosions in all environments and its protocol covering nuclear explosions for peaceful purposes.

15. The Conference regrets, however, that these negotiations have [not] proceeded [at a pace] [at a slower pace than had been] [as rapidly as] expected by the international community, [particularly in the light of the fact that the completion of a comprehensive test ban has been a high priority issue for the last 25 years.]

16. [The Conference further notes that much of the technical and scientific problems involved in such a treaty have been solved and that the requisite political will needs to be demonstrated by all concerned for achievement of this important measure.]

17. [The Conference urges the negotiating parties to bring those negotiations to a successful conclusion at the earliest possible date.]

18. The Conference recognizes the indispensable role of the Committee on Disarmament in [negotiating] [achieving] a treaty that could attract the widest possible international support and adherence, and notes the extensive deliberations which have

taken place within the Committee on Disarmament on the various aspects of the multilateral treaty.

19. It appreciates the valuable work which has been carried out under the auspices of the Committee on Disarmament on the development of national and international co-operative measures to detect seismic events aimed at setting up a global verification system.

20a. [However, the Conference regrets that multilateral negotiations on a comprehensive test ban treaty have not yet commenced in the Committee on Disarmament, in spite of the insistence of the overwhelming majority of its members.]

20b. [The Conference regrets that it has not yet been feasible for the Committee on Disarmament to initiate negotiations on such a Treaty.]

20c. [The Conference notes that multilateral negotiations on a comprehensive test ban treaty have not yet taken place.]

21. [The Conference considers that negotiations in the Committee on Disarmament on the same subject as the separate trilateral negotiations of the nuclear-weapon States Party to the NPT, are not mutually exclusive: on the contrary, they should supplement and encourage each other.]

22. [The Conference expresses the hope that at the earliest feasible date the Committee will give full consideration to the achievement of such a treaty.]

* * *

23a. [The Conference therefore appeals, in particular to the three nuclear-weapon States Party to the Treaty, to support the creation of an *ad hoc* working group of the Committee at the beginning of its 1981 session and urgently to conclude their trilateral preparatory talks on a comprehensive test-ban treaty and submit the results thereof to the Committee on Disarmament.]

23b. [The Conference calls on the Committee on Disarmament to take urgent steps in order to facilitate the attainment of the goal of a comprehensive test-ban treaty.]

24. [The accomplishment of a comprehensive test-ban treaty which has been constantly identified as worthy of the highest priority, would create a very favourable international climate for the second special session of the General Assembly devoted to disarmament which is to be held in 1982. Pending such an accomplishment, the three nuclear-weapon States Party to the NPT should proclaim the immediate cessation of all their nuclear-weapon tests, either through simultaneous unilateral moratoria or through a trilateral moratorium.]

* * *

25. The Conference recognizes the importance, in this connexion, of the 1963 Treaty banning nuclear weapons tests in the atmosphere, in outer space and under water and urges all States which have not yet done so to adhere to that Treaty.

26a. [The Conference notes with satisfaction the signature in 1979 of the SALT II Treaty and [expects] [expresses the view] [expresses the hope] that the Treaty will make a substantial contribution to strengthening international peace and security and to reducing the risk of outbreak of nuclear war and will be a major step in fulfilling the obligations contained in Article VI of the NPT. It urges the States that have signed the SALT II Treaty to bring the Treaty into force at the earliest feasible date.]

26b. [The Conference expresses the hope that pending the entry into force of the SALT II Treaty, the nuclear-weapon States that are signatories to the Treaty will take no action inconsistent with any of its provisions.]

26c. [The Conference has noted that the treaty known as SALT II has been signed but expresses regret that it has not yet been brought into force despite the fact that more than a year has elapsed since the date of the signature. The Conference also regrets that, contrary to what both parties had agreed in their Joint Statement of principles and basic guidelines for subsequent negotiations on the limitation of strategic arms, there has not been any continuation of the negotiations with a view to achieving, *inter alia*, significant and substantial reductions in the numbers of strategic offensive arms, as well as qualitative limitations thereon, including restrictions on the development, testing and deployment of new types of such arms and on the modernization of existing strategic offensive arms.]

26d. The Conference expresses regret that SALT II has not yet been brought into force. [It considers that the third phase of the SALT negotiations should begin promptly after the Treaty has been brought into force.]

27a. [The Conference expresses the hope that the third phase of SALT negotiations will begin promptly after entry into force of the SALT II Treaty with the objective of reaching agreement, as soon as possible, in accordance with the principle of equality and equal security, on further measures for their further qualitative limitation. The Conference notes with satisfaction the agreement reached by the States concerned that their objectives for the third phase of the SALT negotiations will include significant and substantial reductions in the numbers of strategic offensive arms and qualitative limitations on strategic offensive arms, including restrictions on the development, testing and deployment of new types of strategic offensive arms.]

27b. The Conference [considers] [expresses the hope] that the third phase of the SALT negotiations [will] [should] begin promptly after the entry into force of the SALT II Treaty with the objective of reaching agreement, as soon as possible, in accordance with the principle of equality and equal security, on further measures for the limitation and reduction in the number of strategic arms, as well as for their further qualitative limitation.

27c. The Conference [welcomes] [takes note of] [notes with satisfaction] the agreement reached by the States concerned that their objectives for the third phase of the SALT negotiations will include significant and substantial reductions in the numbers of strategic offensive arms and qualitative limitations on strategic offensive arms, including restrictions on the development, testing and deployment of new types of strategic offensive arms [and on the modernization of existing strategic offensive arms.]

28a. [The Conference also expresses the hope that the Parties concerned will begin without delay [preliminary exchanges which will subsequently be included in the framework of the third phase of the SALT process on limitations on certain other nuclear weapon systems] [negotiations concerning middle-range nuclear missiles in Europe and the United States forward-based systems which would make it possible to prevent a new spiral in the nuclear arms race on the European continent.]]

28b. [The Conference calls upon the nuclear-weapon States, which are engaged in the process of negotiating limitations on strategic nuclear arms, to ensure the early ratification of the SALT II agreements and to undertake to abide by them pending their entering into force. The Conference considers that further measures should include significant and substantial reductions in the number of strategic arms and major qualitative restraint in the development and deployment of nuclear-weapon systems and that negotiations be started at an early date with the view of limiting the medium-range tactical nuclear systems in Europe.]

28c. The Conference also expresses the hope that the Parties concerned will begin without delay [negotiations concerning middle-range nuclear missiles in Europe and the US nuclear forward-based systems which could make it possible to prevent a new spiral in the nuclear arms race on the European continent.] [preliminary exchanges, which will subsequently be included in the framework of the third phase of the SALT process, on limitations on certain other nuclear-weapon systems.]

29. The Conference recognizes the importance of implementing the measures contained in the programme of action adopted by the Tenth Special Session of the United Nations General Assembly and notes the value of developing a comprehensive programme of disarmament as a practical means of facilitating the realization of the objectives of Article VI of the Treaty. With this in mind the Conference expresses its satisfaction that the Committee on Disarmament has commenced, through an *ad hoc* working group, and on the basis of the recommendations of the United Nations Disarmament Commission, the elaboration of the Comprehensive Programme of Disarmament which will encompass all measures thought to be advisable in this respect. The Conference appeals to all States to support in an active manner the elaboration of such a programme.

30. [The Conference urges negotiations at the earliest possible date, at appropriate stages and with adequate measures of verification, on the cessation of the production of fissionable material for weapons purposes.]

31. [The Conference welcomes the progress achieved so far in negotiating a treaty prohibiting the development, production, stockpiling and use of radiological weapons, and urges the Committee on Disarmament to continue the negotiations and to accomplish the elaboration of such a treaty.] [without prejudice to negotiations on other items of very high priority which have been under consideration by the negotiating body for a considerable period of time.]

* * *

32a. [In its review of Article VI the Conference arrived at the conclusion that its provisions have not been fulfilled. The Conference recalls that the conclusion of the NPT was only possible due to the fact that the Treaty was originally conceived as an instrument which should embody "an acceptable balance of mutual responsibilities and obligations of the nuclear and non-nuclear Powers". This meant, in effect, the prohibition, not only of the horizontal, but also of the vertical proliferation of nuclear weapons.]

32b. [In its review of Article VI the Conference, while welcoming the steps taken and progress made has nevertheless arrived at the conclusion that the goals identified in the Article have not been fulfilled.]

32c. [In reviewing Article VI, the Conference was of the view that progress achieved towards the objectives stated therein fell considerably short of what had been desired by the international community; the Conference therefore calls upon all States, especially the nuclear-weapon States, to intensify their efforts to accomplish the universally desired objectives of the Article.]

33. [The Conference stresses therefore that the implementation of the Article VI is one of the most important elements for strengthening of the NPT and the universal adherence to it. This can only be achieved through concrete measures and tangible deeds for halting the further spread of both the horizontal and the vertical proliferation of nuclear weapons, as well as for the cessation of the nuclear arms race and for undertaking of steps towards nuclear disarmament.]

34. [The Conference therefore adopts the following recommendations:]

35. [Multilateral negotiations on nuclear disarmament as envisaged in paragraph 50 of the Final Document of the first special session of the General Assembly devoted to disarmament should be commenced without delay. In this connexion the Committee on Disarmament constitutes the most appropriate forum and the three nuclear-weapon States Party to the NPT should give to the second Review Conference a joint undertaking to support the creation of an *ad hoc* working group of the Committee.]

36. [Parties to the SALT negotiations should ratify most urgently the SALT II agreements and commence immediate negotiations for the conclusion of a new agreement—SALT III—which would provide for important qualitative limitations and substantial reductions of nuclear armaments, both strategic as well as theatre or medium-range. Pending ratification of the SALT II Treaty, and without prejudice to the overriding priority of the procedure established in its article XIX, the two contracting parties should adopt a solemn Joint Declaration, to be appended to the Final Document of the second NPT Review Conference, committing themselves to abide by the provisions of the Treaty as if it had already formally entered into force.]

37. [Multilateral negotiations on the comprehensive test-ban treaty should be commenced in the Committee on Disarmament at the beginning of its 1981 session. To this end, the three nuclear-weapon States Party to the NPT should jointly undertake to support the creation of an *ad hoc* working group of the Committee. The same three nuclear-weapon States should conclude urgently their trilateral negotiations on a comprehensive test-ban treaty and submit the results thereof to the Committee on Disarmament early in its 1981 session.]

38. [The accomplishment of a comprehensive test-ban treaty which has been constantly identified as worthy of the highest priority, would create a very favourable international climate for the second special session of the General Assembly devoted to disarmament which is to be held in 1982. Pending such an accomplishment, the three nuclear-weapon States Party to the NPT should proclaim the immediate cessation of all their nuclear-weapon tests, either through simultaneous unilateral moratoria or through a trilateral moratorium.]

39. The concrete disarmament negotiations envisaged in Article VI should be conducted in such a manner as will lead to general and complete disarmament under effective international control. The Conference calls on all States, particularly the nuclear-weapon States, to ensure that the Comprehensive Programme on Disarmament will provide an effective framework for negotiations leading at an early date to general and complete disarmament under strict and effective international control.

40. [The Conference is of the view that the Committee on Disarmament is the most suitable forum for the preparation and conduct of such negotiations, and calls on it to undertake immediately preparatory consultation in accordance with United Nations General Assembly resolution 34/83J, with the aim of identifying the prerequisites and the fundamental elements for subsequent negotiations.]

41. [The Conference underlines the importance of the view expressed by the Tenth Special Session of the United Nations General Assembly in paragraph 54 of its Final Document that significant progress in nuclear disarmament would be facilitated both by parallel political or international legal measures to strengthen the security of States and by progress in the limitation and reduction of armed forces and conventional armaments of the nuclear-weapon States and other States in the regions.]

II. REVIEW OF ARTICLE VIII

1. The Conference is of the opinion that the Review Conference invites States Party to the Treaty which are members of the United Nations to request the Secretary-General of the Organization to include the following item in the provisional agenda of the thirty-sixth session of the General Assembly: "Implementation of the conclusions of the second Review Conference of the Parties to the Treaty on the Non-Proliferation of Nuclear Weapons".

2. States Party to the Treaty participating in the Conference proposed to the Depositary Governments that a third Conference to review the operation of the Treaty be convened in 1985.

3. The Conference accordingly invites States Party to the Treaty which are members of the United Nations to request the Secretary-General of the Organization to include the following item in the provisional agenda of the thirty-eighth session of the General Assembly: "Implementation of the conclusions of the second Review Conference of the Parties to the Treaty on the Non-Proliferation of Nuclear Weapons and establishment of a preparatory committee for the third Conference".

III. REVIEW OF ARTICLE IX

[The Conference, having expressed great satisfaction that the overwhelming majority of States have acceded to the Treaty on the Non-Proliferation of Nuclear Weapons and having recognized the urgent need for further ensuring the universality of the Treaty, appeals to all States, particularly the nuclear-weapon States and other States advanced in nuclear technology, which have not yet done so, to adhere to the Treaty at the earliest possible date.]

[The ten years that have passed since the entry into force of the Treaty have demonstrated its wide international acceptance. The Conference welcomes the recent progress towards achieving wider adherence. At the same time, the Conference notes with concern that the Treaty has not as yet achieved universal adherence. Therefore, the Conference expresses the hope that States that have not already joined the Treaty will do so at the earliest possible date.]

88. Although some common approaches to this task were discussed in the TCC, each working group adopted its own methodology. In general, they have all followed the guidance from the TCC and considered

time required,
resource required, and
detectability,

together with safeguardability, using factors such as

the number of sites with significant quantities of weapons-usable materials and the importance of those quantities;
the form of the material, its accessibility (varying with its radioactivity) and the isotopic mixture; and
the nature of the facility, which determines the resources required for different diversion routes.

89. The risks of diversion identified by the working groups on this basis are associated with: fresh fuel containing enriched uranium or plutonium; uranium enrichment; reactors; spent fuel storage; reprocessing, including plutonium storage and mixed oxide fuel fabrication; and spent fuel or waste disposal. Transportation was considered as involving primarily risks of theft, which, as noted, is a matter of national responsibility. But it was also pointed out by Working Group 4 that one possible scenario for misuse of fuel cycle facilities would be a theft simulated by a national government.

III-A. Sensitive points in the nuclear fuel cycle

III-A-1. Fresh fuel

90. Fresh fuel for natural uranium fuelled reactors is not of particular concern from a proliferation perspective. For the low-enriched uranium cycles considered, for LWRs, HWRs and HTRs, and the medium-enriched (less than 20% ^{235}U) uranium/thorium cycles considered for HWRs and HTRs, the uranium in the fresh fuel itself would not be weapons-usable without further enrichment. Less separative work would be required, however, to gain weapons-usable material than from natural uranium fuels. For the HEU/Th fuel cycle and for most research reactors, highly enriched uranium is present at the enrichment, fuel fabrication and fresh fuel transport and storage stages. Mixed oxide fuel containing plutonium will be required for thermal and fast reactors when operating on uranium cycles in a recycle mode; for example, mixed oxide fuel for fast reactors would contain up to 20% plutonium. The separation of weapons-usable material from such fuel would require chemical processing.

III-A-2. Uranium enrichment facilities

91. All reactor types and fuel cycle options considered, except HWRs fuelled with natural uranium and FBRs, require enriched uranium in the fresh fuel and therefore the existence of enrichment facilities. Proliferation risk is inherent in enrichment technologies. Three aspects of the activity deserve consideration:

92. *Nuclear materials in enrichment facilities.* Almost all uranium enrichment facilities based on proven technologies (i.e. diffusion and gas centrifuge) and all facilities under construction based on technologies which are not yet in the stage of commercial application (nozzle, chemical) are designed and constructed to produce low-enriched uranium in the range of 3–4% ^{235}U for nuclear power programmes, a material which cannot be used as such for nuclear weapons.

93. The proliferation risk associated with nuclear material within this assay range lies in its possible diversion for use in other facilities for the production of weapons-usable material. Such production may be made easier, the higher the assay of the material diverted.

94. *Enrichment technologies.* The same basic technology utilized for LEU production might be used to produce HEU, a weapons-usable material. Enrichment technologies made available might be utilized to build and operate an undeclared or unsafeguarded facility with the aim of producing such material. In evaluating the proliferation risks associated with a given technology, one must take into account the fact that the time, resources and difficulties of various proliferation pathways based on this technology may be reduced over time. On the other hand, the various means to minimize proliferation risks may also be improved with time. Concerning advanced enrichment processes such as laser or plasma, the technologies are at too early a stage of development for their possible proliferation implications to be properly assessed.

95. The choice of an enrichment technology for the construction of an undeclared HEU-producing facility would be influenced by a large variety of factors associated with the various technologies. These factors include purely technical features and factors related to the access to and the application of these technologies. Purely technical features such as separation factor, size of separation element, power consumption, uranium hold-up and equilibrium time, may be factors in assessing the proliferation risks of existing enrichment technologies. To different extents, these features make enrichment technologies susceptible to a potential misuse by the construction and operation of non-declared facilities or the diversion of nuclear material. Factors concerning the access to and application of an enrichment technology include:

(a) Knowledge of and possibly experience with feasible technologies and availability of or access to key components and/or experts;

(b) The technical complexity and resource commitment involved;

(c) The availability of undeclared nuclear materials (natural uranium and, in particular, LEU).

For any enrichment technology it is difficult not only to develop the sensitive components but also to master the associated problems of manufacturing them and assembling them in a workable system. An approximate measure of the degree of difficulty is provided by the R&D efforts, investment costs and development times involved, which are of the same order of magnitude with proven enrichment technologies.

96. As regards the influence of the technical features, many members of Working Group 2 expressed the view that they could not draw conclusions as to their relevance to the construction of non-declared HEU-producing facilities. Others expressed the view that a conjunction of several process features such as high separation factor, small size of separation element, small power consumption, small uranium hold-up and short equilibrium time offer significant advantages for the construction of a small HEU-producing facility. Features of that kind are characteristic of the centrifuge technology and may be so for the laser method when developed.

97. Other members expressed the view that the differences resulting from these purely technical features in assessing proliferation risks (e.g. difficulties, detectability, time and resources) are too small to be of real importance in a decision for the construction of a small clandestine facility, but that other factors concerning the access to and

application of a technology are more significant. In particular as regards experience and status of development it is noted that, for the past 30 years, only the diffusion process has been used for large-scale production of enriched uranium including HEU.

98. In states where no technology has been developed, non-declared facilities may be constructed by using rather primitive and simple technologies because, owing to control on access to sensitive know-how by technology holders, sophisticated technologies may not be available. In this case, such facilities might have larger physical dimensions and so be more easily detected. But size is not the only factor which could lead to detection; in particular, better performance in such a facility could be achieved for example by acquisition of know-how and components from technology holders which would be difficult to conceal.

99. *Operating enrichment facilities.* One way to acquire weapons-usable material would be to use an enrichment facility designed and operated for low-enriched uranium to produce HEU by modifying the plant and/or its method of operation, for example by rearrangement of cascade equipment, changes of operating conditions or by adoption of a batch recycle operating mode. However, these modifications would entail varying degrees of difficulties, depending on the enrichment process used and the extent of the modification. Such basic changes from the original design would require activities and fundamental changes of operation mode which are subject to detection, particularly if the plant was under safeguards from its inception.

100. The different ways of misuse of an existing enrichment plant:

diverting LEU within a plant,

altering a declared LEU plant so as to make it produce HEU,

which both might be undertaken either covertly under safeguards or possibly following a withdrawal from safeguards, are influenced in different directions by some technical process features such as the size of the separation factor and hold-up, the length of equilibrium time and the mode of connection of elements. Where these factors operate to reduce the difficulties, they would in some cases simultaneously operate to increase the effectiveness of safeguards through earlier detection of diversion of nuclear material and through timely detection of possible deviation from the defined design. With the centrifuge process this means that features such as high separation factors, small uranium hold-up, and parallel mode of connection of small separation elements, which are technically advantageous for HEU production, would, in some cases, facilitate the effectiveness of safeguards. In the diffusion and chemical enrichment processes, their special features, small separation factor, large separation elements in series arrangements, high uranium hold-up, which reduce the convertibility of a plant, would at the same time make difficult the application of effective safeguards based only on present materials accountancy and require further development also of containment and surveillance techniques.

III-A-3. Reactors (LWRs, HWRs, FBRs and advanced reactors)

101. In general, the phase when the fuel elements are in an operating reactor was considered a less important area than the other parts of the fuel cycle from the proliferation point of view. All reactors require safeguards, but the effective safeguarding of continuous-refuelling systems requires different procedures and is currently more difficult than that of batch-refuelling systems. New approaches incorporating containment and surveillance devices currently under development could provide effective safeguards more easily.

102. On the whole, it appears that an adequate degree of proliferation resistance can be attained, at least in the short and medium term, with present thermal reactors in the once-through mode, provided that appropriate safeguards are applied to enrichment, fuel fabrication and irradiated fuel storage facilities.

103. Working Group 5 pointed out that the degree of risk depends in a complicated way on the different parts of the fuel cycle, their stage of development, on specific local circumstances, and in particular on what measures, such as safeguards or others, have been implemented to eliminate or reduce the risks. In this context Working Group 5 estimates that the diversion risks encountered in the various stages of the FBR fuel cycle present no greater difficulties than in the case of the LWR with the U/Pu cycle, or even in the case of the once-through cycle, in the long term.

104. In relation to HWRs, the use of natural uranium removes the need for enrichment facilities. Though some countries believe that the availability of heavy water adds to the concerns presented by the availability of natural uranium and reprocessing facilities, it appears that, when appropriate safeguards are applied to this cycle, an adequate degree of proliferation resistance can be attained. Some countries do not believe that heavy water presents a specific concern because of the ready availability of other moderating materials such as graphite.

105. As for the closed thorium cycles, it was recognized that they require considerably higher uranium enrichment levels than the U/Pu cycles and that less separative work would be required to produce highly enriched uranium from the denatured uranium/thorium fuel than from the low-enriched uranium. On the other hand, in the denatured uranium/thorium cycles, no directly weapons-usable material is present during transportation and storage of the fabricated fuel. Those thorium-based fuel cycles that require highly enriched uranium show a particularly important need for appropriate safeguarding systems associated with the enrichment, storage, transportation and fabrication stages.

III-A-4. Spent fuel storage

106. The high radiation level inherent in spent fuel is an important factor against proliferation. As such levels decrease, the safeguards techniques applied may require adjustment or replacement by other existing techniques. No significant changes would be expected in the inherent proliferation resistance of the spent fuel during the interim storage time envisaged by Working Group 6. The Working Group determined that the existing legal and institutional framework for spent fuel management is adequate to minimize the risk of proliferation. However, at present there is no international legal framework that provides states with an assurance of access to or management of their spent fuel. The needs identified with respect to the legal framework include *inter alia*: the application of IAEA safeguards to all nuclear material contained in spent fuel in interim storage and transport; harmonization of national licensing frameworks regarding spent fuel storage and transport, based on the related IAEA guides; adherence to an international convention on physical protection; review of clauses in legally binding instruments perceived to be causing difficulty with the implementation of national programmes to consider possible revision in a manner designed to meet energy needs consistent with non-proliferation objectives.

III-A-5. Reprocessing, plutonium storage and mixed oxide fuel fabrication

107. Plutonium is inevitably produced when operating nuclear power plants. The problem is therefore not how to avoid such production, but how to manage the

plutonium once it has been created. In that respect, two main choices can be considered: leaving the plutonium in stored spent fuel elements without reprocessing; and reprocessing of the spent fuel elements followed by the storage of separated plutonium or the recycling of the separated plutonium in thermal or fast breeder reactors.

108. The most sensitive part of these fuel cycle activities appears to be a function of the particular threat of diversion being considered:

(a) In the case of subnational theft, the transport element;

(b) In the case of overt diversion by national governments, in a situation where international safeguards are not operating or have been abrogated, the plutonium store;

(c) In the case of covert diversion by national governments, where international safeguards are operating, the elements of the fuel cycle which require the greatest safeguarding effort: Safeguarding a reprocessing plant or a MOX fuel fabrication plant requires a relatively greater effort than safeguarding a store of separated plutonium.

109. The concern for the future is thus, in the event that reprocessing develops, to adopt the best technical, safeguards and institutional measures to increase the protection of such material against diversion.

110. The use of commercial-grade plutonium is an unattractive route to the manufacture of nuclear weapons as compared with weapons-grade plutonium produced by a dedicated programme. It is considered therefore that a given amount of plutonium-239, whatever use it is prepared for, is a more serious proliferation risk than an equal amount of commercial-grade plutonium, but this cannot be quantified without a detailed knowledge of weapon design, which INFCE does not have. However, it should be noted that the United States government has declared that commercial-grade plutonium can be used for weapon purposes and that this statement has not been challenged by other nuclear-weapon states. From the outset, the IAEA has safeguarded plutonium as a special nuclear material without distinction as to its isotopic content.

111. Although in some deployment modes there could be an advantage in the use of denatured fuel (^{233}U and ^{238}U), it was noted that the proliferation potential of thorium fuel cycles operating with recycle of ^{233}U, with or without plutonium, is similar to that of the uranium fuel cycle operating with recycle of plutonium.

III-A-6. Disposal of waste and spent fuel

112. Waste disposal was not regarded as a sensitive step in the fuel cycle since the materials concerned are relatively unattractive for the production of a nuclear weapon. Depleted uranium would require either enrichment (in which case it would be inferior to natural uranium) or irradiation and reprocessing. Plutonium in vitrified waste or in concrete would be very dispersed and difficult to recover. Consequently, only spent fuel from once-through fuel cycles will be an item to be considered as regards the possibility of diversion, as its underground repositories would become an increasingly attractive target for diversion owing to their large content of fissile material and their decreasing radioactivity.

113. The study concluded that, as stated in the Washington Communiqué, measures could and should be taken to minimize the risks identified, without jeopardizing energy supplies or the development of nuclear energy for peaceful purposes.

11. Nuclear explosions

Square-bracketed numbers, thus [1], *refer to the list of references on page* 378.

Of the 1 271 nuclear explosions reported to have been conducted between 1945 and 1980, 783 were carried out after the signing in 1963 of the Partial Test Ban Treaty (PTBT) prohibiting atmospheric tests. Thus, the rate was, on average, 46 explosions per year after the Treaty as against 27 before it. The nuclear weapon powers party to the PTBT—namely, the UK, the USA and the USSR—are responsible for conducting over 90 per cent of all nuclear explosions (see appendix 11B).

In 1980 the USSR carried out 20 explosions, of which two took place outside the Soviet weapon testing sites known to be in the region of Semipalatinsk, east Kazakhstan, and on Novaya Zemlya in the Arctic Ocean; these two are therefore presumed to have served non-weapon purposes. Continuation of this programme of so-called peaceful nuclear explosions (as many as eight explosions were conducted outside the usual testing sites by the USSR in 1979) may indicate that the Soviet Union does not share the widespread scepticism about the usefulness of such explosions. In 1980 the USA conducted 14 nuclear weapon test explosions; France conducted 11; the UK, 3; and China, 1—all in the usual sites (see appendix 11A). India has not tested a nuclear device since 1974.

The French, British, US and Soviet tests were made underground and, according to the data obtained from the Hagfors Observatory in Sweden, all had a yield below or around 150 kilotons.

The USA complained that two Soviet explosions had exceeded the 150-kiloton limit set by the 1974 US–Soviet Threshold Test Ban Treaty (TTBT). Conclusive proof of such a breach would have to be based on world-wide seismic recordings, but these recordings were apparently not concordant. In any event, the US assertion that the tests in question were the largest made by the USSR in the past four years does not seem to be justified. Since 1976, when the two powers agreed to abide by the terms of the TTBT (which is formally not yet in force), seven Soviet explosions produced seismic signals of the same or even greater magnitude than those produced by the above-mentioned controversial events. In this connection, it should be borne in mind that exact yield determination of underground explosions requires knowledge about the environment in which the explosions have been carried out, as well as about explosions previously performed at the same site. The exchange of information, envisaged by the TTBT and necessary to establish a correlation between yields of explosions at specific sites and the seismic signals produced, so as to improve each side's assessments of the yields of explosions based on the measurements derived from its own seismic instruments, has not taken place pending ratification of the treaty.

The nuclear testing activity of France is particularly noteworthy. The figure for 1980 was the highest since the beginning of the French testing programme. The yield of these explosions is estimated at 100 kilotons or lower. Also the United Kingdom, whose testing activity has remained relatively modest, conducted more nuclear explosions last year than in any other year since 1963.

China, not a party to the PTBT, made its 1980 thermonuclear test in the atmosphere. The explosion, having a yield between 200 kilotons and 1 megaton, produced a radioactive cloud which passed in the stratosphere over North America around 20 October and over Europe one week later. Several countries protested against this explosion.

The mysterious event, which on 22 September 1979 was detected by a US satellite in the Southern hemisphere and which may have been a low-yield nuclear explosion in the atmosphere (see *SIPRI Yearbook 1980*, page 360), has not been cleared up. South Africa, which was accused by many members of the United Nations of being the testing nation, denied having any knowledge of a nuclear explosion occurring in its vicinity. France, recently suspected of having conducted this explosion in the Indian Ocean to test a neutron bomb [1], also rejected the allegation as baseless, and recalled that since 1975 all its nuclear tests had been carried out underground [2].

Since 1977, the UK, the USA and the USSR have been engaged in trilateral talks for the achievement of a test ban treaty. In the meantime, the rate of testing has increased, as shown below.

Average annual number of Soviet, US and British explosions in 1973–80

	USSR	USA	UK
1973–76	16.25	12.75	0.50
1977–80	23.00	13.25	1.50

On 13 August 1980, the three powers submitted to the Committee on Disarmament (CD) a report on the status of the test ban negotiations [3], which was subsequently transmitted for the information of the Second NPT Review Conference [4]. The main points of agreement reached among the negotiators can be summarized as follows.

1. The treaty should prohibit any nuclear weapon test explosion at any place under the jurisdiction or control of the parties in any environment; the parties should also refrain from encouraging or in any way

participating in the carrying out of any nuclear weapon test explosion anywhere. The treaty would be accompanied by a protocol on nuclear explosions for peaceful purposes, which would establish a moratorium on such explosions until arrangements for conducting them were worked out consistent with the treaty being negotiated, the Partial Test Ban Treaty and the Non-Proliferation Treaty.

2. Any amendments to the test ban treaty would require the approval of a majority of all parties, which majority should include all parties that are permanent members of the UN Security Council. The treaty should enter into force upon ratification by 20 signatory governments, including those of the UK, the USA and the USSR, and withdrawal from the treaty would be possible on the grounds of "supreme national interests". A conference would be held at an "appropriate time" to review the operation of the treaty.

3. The parties would use national technical means of verification at their disposal to verify compliance with the treaty, and would undertake not to interfere with such means of verification. An international exchange of seismic data would be established, and each party would contribute data from designated seismic stations on its territory and receive the seismic data made available through the exchange. The data would be transmitted through the Global Telecommunications System of the World Meteorological Organization or through other agreed communications channels. International seismic data centres would be established in agreed locations, taking into account the desirability of appropriate geographical distribution. A committee of experts would be set up to consider questions related to the international seismic data exchange, to facilitate the implementation of the exchange and review its operation, as well as consider technological developments that have a bearing on its operation.

4. The treaty would provide for consultations to resolve questions that may arise concerning compliance. Any party would have the right to request an on-site inspection for the purpose of ascertaining whether or not an event on the territory of another party was a nuclear explosion. The requesting party should state the reasons for its request, including appropriate evidence. The party receiving the request should state whether or not it was prepared to agree to an inspection on its territory; if it was not, it should provide the reasons for its decision.

5. Any two or more treaty parties would be permitted, because of special concerns or circumstances, to take, by mutual consent, additional measures to facilitate verification. The three negotiating parties agreed that it was necessary to develop such additional measures for themselves in order to specify in greater detail the procedures under which on-site inspection would be conducted. In addition, the three parties were

negotiating an exchange of supplemental seismic data. This would involve the installation and use by them of high-quality national seismic stations of agreed characteristics. (For the text of the report, see appendix 11C.)

Despite the accomplishments described above, a number of problems remain to be solved. The most important of them are as follows.

1. To be really comprehensive, the test ban would have to cover all nuclear explosions without exception, including laboratory tests, such as, for example, very low-yield nuclear experiments, or the so-called inertial confinement fusion.[1] On the other hand, laboratory tests are contained and not verifiable, and some may have civilian applications, including the development of new sources of energy.

2. The co-operative seismic monitoring measures proposed in the tripartite report are based on the recommendations of the *ad hoc* group of scientific experts, established by the CD. One of these recommendations is that the verification system should comprise about 50 globally distributed teleseismic stations, selected in accordance with seismological requirements. However, to render such a seismic network fully operative, there is a need for more stations in the Southern hemisphere, the world-wide distribution of the existing ones being unequal. Moreover, the equipment for data acquisition should be modern and of high quality, which is not the case with all stations that may be included in a global network, and the same applies to data communications facilities.

3. Since the partners in the tripartite negotiations agree on the possibility of having on-site inspection, a detailed procedure for setting the inspection process in motion must be worked out. The rights and functions of the personnel carrying out the inspection, as well as the role to be played by the host party during the inspection, would also have to be defined. A question remaining to be answered is whether on-site inspection on the territory of the three great powers would be conducted with the participation of other states as well.

4. Additional verification arrangements to be used by the UK, the USA and the USSR would include special, nationally manned but tamper-proof seismic stations, transmitting the data recorded by them continuously and directly outside the host country. These national seismic stations (NSS) could help lower the detection threshold, reduce the risk of mistaking earthquakes for nuclear explosions, and also serve to deter

[1] A very low-yield nuclear experiment could involve an explosion of a device which may have the characteristics of a nuclear device but uses fissile material of an amount or kind that produces only a very small fraction of the yield of the chemical explosion that sets off the release of the nuclear energy.

The inertial confinement concept is to use lasers or other high-power sources to heat and compress small pellets containing fusionable fuel (deuterium and tritium). If a properly shaped pulse of sufficient energy can be delivered to the pellet, the density and temperature may become high enough for fusion.

evasion if they were placed in areas in which the geological structure might be considered suitable for conducting clandestine tests. There are problems concerning the instrumentation of the NSS, their number in each of the negotiating states (the USA and the USSR have agreed on having 10 such stations installed in their territories, but the number for the UK has not yet been settled), specific locations, procedures for their emplacement and maintenance, as well as the transmission of data. It is not clear whether the treaty would be allowed to enter into force before the NSS became fully operative; it may take a few years for the stations (which are still in the stage of development) to start functioning. Neither is it known whether the data from the NSS would be generally available or reserved solely for the three powers.

5. While the ultimate goal is to bring about a cessation of nuclear explosions by all states, the partners in the tripartite talks have agreed that the treaty could become effective even without China and France joining it. However, if the latter powers decide to accede to the treaty at a later stage, a question may arise whether they should be allowed to become parties simply by depositing their instruments of accession, or whether they should be required to work out special control arrangements with the UK, the USA and the USSR, such as the establishment of NSS, in addition to the generally applicable verification measures. For states that are already engaged in testing may have special interests in controlling each other.

6. The duration of the comprehensive test ban which is being negotiated trilaterally would be limited to three years. The review conference of the parties which is envisaged to be held before the expiration of the treaty may discuss its possible extension, and the protocol to the treaty covering peaceful nuclear explosions would most certainly get the same treatment as the treaty itself. However, a test ban of fixed duration would not fulfil the pledge included in the Partial Test Ban Treaty, and reiterated in the Non-Proliferation Treaty, "to achieve the discontinuance of all test explosions of nuclear weapons for all time". Moreover, a treaty of short duration would create a problem with respect to the adherence of non-nuclear weapon states, particularly parties to the Non-Proliferation Treaty, which have renounced the possession of nuclear explosive devices for a much longer period. And, finally, resumption of tests upon the expiration of a short-lived comprehensive test ban might be a serious setback to the cause of arms limitation and disarmament.

The UN Secretary-General's report on a comprehensive nuclear test ban [5], published in 1980, concludes that the cessation of nuclear tests would be an important measure of non-proliferation of nuclear weapons, "both vertical and horizontal". (For the text of the conclusions of the report, see appendix 11D.) However, to achieve this goal, more intensive negotiations are needed, not only trilateral but also multilateral.

References

1. *France-Soir*, 28 January 1981.
2. *Le Monde*, 29 January 1981.
3. Committee on Disarmament document CD/130.
4. NPT Review Conference document NPT/CONF.II/13.
5. UN document A/35/257.

Appendix 11A

Nuclear explosions, 1979–80 (known and presumed)

Note

1. The following sources were used in compiling the list of nuclear explosions:

(*a*) US Geological Survey,

(*b*) US Department of Energy,

(*c*) Hagfors Observatory of the Research Institute of the Swedish National Defence, and

(*d*) press reports.

2. Unless otherwise indicated, the explosions were carried out underground.

3. Events marked with an asterisk * may be part of a programme for peaceful uses of nuclear energy in view of their location outside the known weapon testing sites.

4. m_b (body wave magnitude) indicates the size of the event; the data have been provided by the Hagfors Observatory of the Research Institute of the Swedish National Defence.

5. In the case of very weak events, it is impossible to distinguish, through seismological methods alone, between chemical and nuclear explosions.

I. Nuclear explosions in 1979 (revised data)

Date (GMT)	Latitude (deg)	Longitude (deg)	Region	m_b
USA				
24 Jan	37.105 N	116.011 W	Nevada	4.7
8 Feb	37.101 N	116.054 W	Nevada	5.8
15 Feb	37.152 N	116.072 W	Nevada	5.2
14 Mar	37.028 N	116.039 W	Nevada	
11 May	36.981 N	116.034 W	Nevada	
11 Jun	37.290 N	116.455 W	Nevada	5.7
20 Jun	37.107 N	116.015 W	Nevada	
28 Jun	37.142 N	116.087 W	Nevada	5.4
3 Aug	37.084 N	116.070 W	Nevada	5.3
8 Aug	37.036 N	116.031 W	Nevada	5.2
6 Sep	37.087 N	116.052 W	Nevada	6.2
8 Sep	37.154 N	116.038 W	Nevada	
26 Sep	37.229 N	116.364 W	Nevada	6.0
29 Nov			Nevada	
14 Dec			Nevada	
USSR				
10 Jan			W Kazakh*	5.0
17 Jan	47.985 N	48.212 E	W Kazakh*	6.5
1 Feb	50.125 N	78.944 E	E Kazakh	6.4
16 Feb	50.018 N	77.781 E	E Kazakh	5.8
6 May	49.869 N	78.247 E	E Kazakh	5.6
24 May			E Kazakh	4.9
31 May	49.837 N	78.237 E	E Kazakh	5.4
23 Jun	49.935 N	78.971 E	E Kazakh	7.2
7 Jul	50.062 N	79.110 E	E Kazakh	6.7
14 Jul	47.835 N	48.249 E	W Kazakh*	6.2
18 Jul	49.966 N	77.927 E	E Kazakh	5.2
4 Aug	49.886 N	78.957 E	E Kazakh	7.2
12 Aug	61.909 N	122.087 E	Central Siberia*	5.4
18 Aug	49.961 N	79.020 E	E Kazakh	7.2
6 Sep	64.126 N	99.554 E	Central Siberia*	4.6
14 Sep			E Kazakh	5.2
15 Sep			E Kazakh	4.6
24 Sep	73.335 N	54.729 E	Novaya Zemlya	6.5
27 Sep			E Kazakh	5.0
4 Oct	60.650 N	71.525 E	W Siberia*	5.8
7 Oct	61.839 N	113.059 E	Central Siberia*	5.3
18 Oct			E Kazakh	5.4
18 Oct			Novaya Zemlya	6.6
24 Oct	47.769 N	48.177 E	W Kazakh*	6.4
28 Oct	49.941 N	79.041 E	E Kazakh	6.6
30 Nov	49.840 N	78.269 E	E Kazakh	4.9
2 Dec	49.868 N	78.824 E	E Kazakh	7.2
21 Dec			E Kazakh	5.0
23 Dec			E Kazakh	7.2
UK				
29 Aug	37.120 N	116.066 W	Nevada	5.2
France				
1 Mar			Mururoa	
9 Mar			Mururoa	
24 Mar	22.054 S	139.263 W	Mururoa	
4 Apr			Mururoa	
18 Jun			Mururoa	
29 Jun	22.106 S	139.401 W	Mururoa	
25 Jul	21.842 S	139.026 W	Mururoa	
28 Jul			Mururoa	
22 Nov			Mururoa	

II. Nuclear explosions in 1980 (preliminary data)

Date (GMT)	Latitude (deg)	Longitude (deg)	Region	m_b
USA				
28 Feb	37.126 N	116.088 W	Nevada	
8 Mar	37.180 N	116.083 W	Nevada	
3 Apr	37.149 N	116.082 W	Nevada	5.2
16 Apr	37.101 N	116.031 W	Nevada	5.6
2 May	37.056 N	116.019 W	Nevada	
22 May			Nevada	
12 Jun	37.281 N	116.454 W	Nevada	5.6
24 Jun	37.023 N	116.034 W	Nevada	
25 Jul	37.255 N	116.477 W	Nevada	5.6
31 Jul	37.012 N	116.023 W	Nevada	
25 Sep	37.056 N	116.048 W	Nevada	4.9
25 Sep	37.115 N	116.065 W	Nevada	
31 Oct	37.211 N	116.205 W	Nevada	5.3
14 Nov	37.109 N	116.002 W	Nevada	
USSR				
4 Apr	49.968 N	77.777 E	E Kazakh	5.1
10 Apr	49.813 N	78.140 E	E Kazakh	5.3
25 Apr	49.946 N	78.808 E	E Kazakh	6.5
22 May	49.759 N	78.102 E	E Kazakh	5.8
12 Jun	49.990 N	79.027 E	E Kazakh	6.1
29 Jun	49.923 N	78.860 E	E Kazakh	6.8
13 Jul			E Kazakh	5.0
31 Jul	49.812 N	78.169 E	E Kazakh	5.5
14 Sep	49.979 N	78.883 E	E Kazakh	7.3
20 Sep			E Kazakh	4.9
25 Sep	49.713 N	77.986 E	E Kazakh	4.9
30 Sep			E Kazakh	4.6
30 Sep			E Kazakh	5.2
8 Oct	46.748 N	48.288 E	W Kazakh*	5.7
11 Oct	73.313 N	55.021 E	Novaya Zemlya	6.6
12 Oct	49.912 N	79.050 E	E Kazakh	6.2
1 Nov	61 N	98 E	Central Siberia*	4.7
14 Dec			E Kazakh	7.0
26 Dec			E Kazakh	4.6
27 Dec			E Kazakh	6.9
UK				
26 Apr	37.247 N	116.422 W	Nevada	5.8
24 Oct	37.075 N	115.999 W	Nevada	
17 Dec			Nevada	5.3
France				
23 Feb			Mururoa	
3 Mar			Mururoa	
23 Mar	21.872 S	139.066 W	Mururoa	
1 Apr	21.881 S	138.809 W	Mururoa	
4 Apr			Mururoa	
16 Jun	21.979 S	138.905 W	Mururoa	
21 Jun			Mururoa	
6 Jul			Mururoa	
19 Jul	21.871 S	139.004 W	Mururoa	
25 Nov			Mururoa	
3 Dec			Mururoa	
China				
16 Oct			Lop Nor (in atmosphere)	

Appendix 11B

Nuclear explosions, 1945–80 (known and presumed)

I. 16 July 1945–5 August 1963 (the signing of the Partial Test Ban Treaty)

USA	USSR	UK	France	Total
293	164	23	8	**488**

II. 5 August 1963–31 December 1980

a atmospheric
u underground

	USA		USSR		UK		France		China		India		
Year	a	u	a	u	a	u	a	u	a	u	a	u	Total
5 Aug–31 Dec 1963	0	14	0	0	0	0	0	1					**15**
1964	0	28	0	6	0	1	0	3	1	0			**39**
1965	0	29	0	9	0	1	0	4	1	0			**44**
1966	0	40	0	15	0	0	5	1	3	0			**64**
1967	0	29	0	15	0	0	3	0	2	0			**49**
1968	0	39[a]	0	13	0	0	5	0	1	0			**58**
1969	0	28	0	15	0	0	0	0	1	1			**45**
1970	0	33	0	12	0	0	8	0	1	0			**54**
1971	0	15	0	19	0	0	5	0	1	0			**40**
1972	0	15	0	22	0	0	3	0	2	0			**42**
1973	0	11	0	14	0	0	5	0	1	0			**31**
1974	0	9	0	19	0	1	7	0	1	0	0	1	**38**
1975	0	16	0	15	0	0	0	2	0	1	0	0	**34**
1976	0	15	0	17	0	1	0	4	3	1	0	0	**41**
1977	0	12	0	16	0	0	0	6	1	0	0	0	**35**
1978	0	12	0	27	0	2	0	7	2	1	0	0	**51**
1979	0	15	0	29	0	1	0	9	0	0	0	0	**54**
1980	0	14	0	20	0	3	0	11	1	0	0	0	**49**[b]
Total	**0**	**374**	**0**	**283**	**0**	**10**	**41**	**48**	**22**	**4**	**0**	**1**	**783**

III. 16 July 1945–31 December 1980

USA	USSR	UK	France	China	India	Total
667	447	33	97	26	1	**1 271**

[a] Five devices used simultaneously in the same test are counted here as one.
[b] The data for 1980 are preliminary.

Appendix 11C

*Tripartite report to the Committee on Disarmament**

1. This report on the status of the negotiations between the Union of Soviet Socialist Republics, the United Kingdom of Great Britain and Northern Ireland and the United States of America on a treaty prohibiting nuclear weapon test explosions in all environments and its protocol covering nuclear explosions for peaceful purposes has been jointly prepared by the three parties to the negotiations.

2. The three negotiating parties are well aware of the deep and long-standing commitment to the objective of this treaty that has been demonstrated by the Committee on Disarmament and its predecessor bodies. They recognize the strong and legitimate interest of the Committee on Disarmament in their activities, and they have reported to the Committee on Disarmament previously, most recently on 31 July 1979. They welcome the opportunity to do so again, just as they welcome the continued support and encouragement that their negotiations derive from the interest of the Committee on Disarmament.

3. Since the last report to the Committee on Disarmament, the three delegations have completed two rounds of negotiations. The negotiations reconvened on 16 July 1980.

4. The negotiating parties are seeking a treaty that for decades has been given one of the highest priorities in the field of arms limitation, and the Soviet Union, the United Kingdom and the United States continue to attach great importance to it. The desire to achieve an early agreement, which is so widely shared by the international community, has been repeatedly expressed at the highest level of all three governments.

5. Global interest in the cessation of nuclear weapon tests by all States has been recorded by a succession of resolutions of the United Nations General Assembly and by the Final Document of the Special Session on Disarmament of the United Nations General Assembly. It has been stated in the preambles to a number of international arms limitation treaties now in force, and its significance will again be underlined in the forthcoming second Review Conference of the Treaty on the Non-Proliferation of Nuclear Weapons.

6. The objectives which the negotiating parties seek to achieve as a result of this treaty are important to all mankind. Specifically, they seek

* *Source:* Committee on Disarmament document CD/130, 30 July 1980.

to attain a treaty which will make a major contribution to the shared objectives of constraining the nuclear arms race, curbing the spread of nuclear weapons, and strengthening international peace and security.

7. Given the importance of these objectives, it is understandable that the international community has repeatedly called for the earliest possible conclusion of the treaty. At the same time, it is important to note that this treaty is, in many respects, a difficult one to negotiate. Many of the issues are novel, sensitive and intricate. The treaty directly affects vital national security concerns and the process of negotiation requires considerable and painstaking work.

8. In spite of these challenges, however, the Soviet Union, the United Kingdom and the United States have made considerable progress in negotiating the treaty.

9. The negotiating parties have agreed that the treaty will require each party to prohibit, prevent and not to carry out any nuclear weapon test explosion at any place under its jurisdiction or control in any environment; and to refrain from causing, encouraging or in any way participating in the carrying out of any nuclear weapon test explosion anywhere.

10. The negotiating parties have agreed that the treaty will be accompanied by a protocol on nuclear explosions for peaceful purposes, which will be an integral part of the treaty. The protocol will take into account the provisions of Article V of the Treaty on the Non-Proliferation of Nuclear Weapons. In the protocol, the parties will establish a moratorium on nuclear explosions for peaceful purposes and accordingly will refrain from causing, encouraging, permitting or in any way participating in, the carrying out of such explosions until arrangements for conducting them are worked out which would be consistent with the treaty being negotiated, the Treaty Banning Nuclear Weapon Tests in the Atmosphere, in Outer Space and Under Water and the Treaty on the Non-Proliferation of Nuclear Weapons. Without delay after entry into force of the treaty, the parties will keep under consideration the subject of arrangements for conducting nuclear explosions for peaceful purposes, including the aspect of precluding military benefits. Such arrangements, which could take the form of a special agreement or agreements, would be made effective by appropriate amendment to the protocol.

11. To ensure that the treaty does not detract from previous arms limitation agreements, there will be a provision stating that the treaty does not affect obligations compatible with it that have been assumed by parties under other international agreements. Such other agreements include the Treaty Banning Nuclear Weapon Tests in the Atmosphere, in Outer Space and Under Water and the Treaty on the Non-Proliferation of Nuclear Weapons. The three negotiating parties have agreed that the treaty will provide procedures for amendment, and that any amendments

will require the approval of a majority of all parties, which majority shall include all parties that are permanent members of the Security Council of the United Nations. They have also agreed that, as in other arms limitation agreements, there will be provision for withdrawal from the treaty on the grounds of supreme national interests. They have also agreed that the treaty should enter into force upon ratification by twenty signatory governments, including those of the Soviet Union, the United Kingdom and the United States.

12. The parties are considering formulations relating to the duration of the treaty. They envisage that a conference will be held at an appropriate time to review the operation of the treaty. Decisions at the conference will require a majority of the parties to the treaty, which majority shall include all parties that are permanent members of the Security Council of the United Nations.

13. The negotiating parties, recognizing the importance of verification, have agreed that a variety of verification measures should be provided to enhance confidence that all parties to the treaty are in strict compliance with it. Such measures in the treaty itself, and the additional measures under negotiation to facilitate verification of compliance with the treaty, must first be agreed in principle, and then drafted in detail, which is of course a laborious process. It must be done with care because the implementation of these measures will have important impact not only on ensuring compliance with the treaty, but also on political relations among its parties.

14. It has been agreed that the parties will use national technical means of verification at their disposal in a manner consistent with generally recognized principles of international law to verify compliance with the treaty, and that each party will undertake not to interfere with such means of verification.

15. It has long been recognized that co-operative seismic monitoring measures can make an important contribution to verifying compliance with the treaty. The Committee on Disarmament and its predecessors have played a leading role in developing such measures. On the basis of the work done in the past few years under those auspices, the negotiating parties have agreed to provisions establishing an International Exchange of Seismic Data. Each treaty party will have the right to participate in this exchange, to contribute data from designated seismic stations on its territory, and to receive all the seismic data made available through the International Exchange. Seismic data will be transmitted through the Global Telecommunications System of the World Meteorological Organization or through other agreed communications channels. International seismic data centres will be established in agreed locations, taking into account the desirability of appropriate geographical distribution.

16. A Committee of Experts will be established to consider questions related to the International Seismic Data Exchange and all treaty parties will be entitled to appoint representatives to participate in the work of the Committee. The Committee of Experts will be responsible for developing detailed arrangements for establishing and operating the International Exchange, drawing on the recommendations of the *Ad Hoc* Group of Scientific Experts, which was established under the auspices of the Conference of the Committee on Disarmament and has continued its work under the Committee on Disarmament. Arrangements for establishing and operating the International Exchange will include the development of standards for the technical and operational characteristics of participating seismic stations and international seismic data centres, for the form in which data are transmitted to the centres, and for the form and manner in which the centres make seismic data available to the participants and respond to their requests for additional seismic data regarding specified seismic events.

17. In addition to its role in setting up the International Exchange, the Committee of Experts will have ongoing responsibility for facilitating the implementation of the International Exchange, for reviewing its operation and considering improvements to it, and for considering technological developments that have a bearing on its operation. The Committee will serve as a forum in which treaty parties may exchange technical information and co-operate in promoting the effectiveness of the International Exchange. The Committee of Experts will hold its first meeting not later than 90 days after the entry into force of the treaty and will meet thereafter as it determines.

18. The negotiating parties have agreed to other co-operative measures as well. There will be provision in the treaty for direct consultations, and for the exchange of inquiries and responses among treaty parties in order to resolve questions that may arise concerning treaty compliance. If a party has questions regarding an event on the territory of any other party, it may request an on-site inspection for the purpose of ascertaining whether or not the event was a nuclear explosion. The requesting party shall state the reasons for its request, including appropriate evidence. The party which receives the request, understanding the importance of ensuring confidence among parties that treaty obligations are being fulfilled, shall state whether or not it is prepared to agree to an inspection. If the party which receives the request is not prepared to agree to an inspection on its territory, it shall provide the reasons for its decision. Tripartite agreement on these general conditions with regard to on-site inspections represents an important achievement by the negotiating parties in resolving issues regarding verification of compliance with the treaty.

19. The three negotiating parties believe that the verification measures

being negotiated—particularly the provisions regarding the International Exchange of Seismic Data, the Committee of Experts, and on-site inspections—break significant new ground in international arms limitation efforts and will give all treaty parties the opportunity to participate in a substantial and constructive way in the process of verifying compliance with the treaty.

20. The treaty will also contain a provision permitting any two or more treaty parties, because of special concerns or circumstances, to agree by mutual consent upon additional measures to facilitate verification of compliance with the treaty. The three negotiating parties have agreed that it is necessary to develop such additional measures for themselves in connexion with the treaty under negotiation.

21. The additional measures to facilitate verification of compliance with the treaty, while paralleling those of the treaty itself, will specify in greater detail the procedures under which on-site inspection would be conducted, and will incorporate a list of the rights and functions of the personnel carrying out the inspection. They will also contain a description of the role to be played by the host party during an inspection.

22. In addition, the three parties are negotiating an exchange of supplemental seismic data. This would involve the installation and use by the three parties of high-quality national seismic stations of agreed characteristics.

23. Despite significant accomplishments, there are important areas where substantial work is still to be done.

24. The three negotiating parties have demonstrated their strong political commitment to completion of this treaty by achieving solutions to problems that for many years made a treaty difficult to attain. Most notable in this regard are the agreements concerning the prohibition of any nuclear weapon test explosion in any environment, the moratorium on nuclear explosions for peaceful purposes, the general conditions with regard to on-site inspections, and a number of important seismic verification issues.

25. The negotiating parties are mindful of the great value for all mankind that the prohibition of nuclear weapon test explosions in all environments will have, and they are conscious of the important responsibility placed upon them to find solutions to the remaining problems. The three negotiating parties have come far in their pursuit of a sound treaty and continue to believe that their trilateral negotiations offer the best way forward. They are determined to exert their best efforts and necessary will and persistence to bring the negotiations to an early and successful conclusion.

Appendix 11D

*Comprehensive nuclear test ban, Report of the UN Secretary-General**

Excerpt

CONCLUSIONS

151. A main objective of all efforts of the United Nations in the field of disarmament has been to halt and reverse the nuclear-arms race, to stop the production of nuclear weapons and to achieve their eventual elimination.

152. In this connexion, a comprehensive test ban is regarded as the first and most urgent step towards a cessation of the nuclear-arms race, in particular, as regards its qualitative aspects.

153. Over the years, enormous efforts have been invested in achieving a cessation of all nuclear-weapon tests by all States for all time. These efforts have occupied the uninterrupted attention of the Members of the United Nations for a longer period of time than any other disarmament issue.

154. The trilateral negotiations have now been going on for nearly three years, while in the Committee on Disarmament negotiations have still not commenced. In order to bring the achievement of a comprehensive test ban nearer to realization, much more intensive negotiations are essential. Verification of compliance no longer seems to be an obstacle to reaching agreement.

155. A comprehensive test ban could serve as an important measure of non-proliferation of nuclear weapons, both vertical and horizontal.

156. A comprehensive test ban would have a major arms limitation impact in that it would make it difficult, if not impossible, for the nuclear-weapon States parties to the treaty to develop new designs of nuclear weapons and would also place constraints on the modification of existing weapon designs.

157. A comprehensive test ban would also place constraints on the further spread of nuclear weapons by preventing nuclear explosions, although a test explosion may not be absolutely essential for constructing a simple fission device.

158. In the view of the parties to the non-proliferation Treaty, a comprehensive test ban would reinforce the Treaty by demonstrating the

---

* *Source:* UN document A/35/257, 23 May 1980.

awareness of the major nuclear Powers of the legal obligation under the Treaty "to pursue negotiations in good faith on effective measures relating to cessation of the nuclear arms race at an early date".

159. The arms limitation benefits of a comprehensive test ban could be enhanced, and the channels of arms competition among the great Powers further narrowed, if the comprehensive test ban were followed by restrictions on the qualitative improvement of nuclear delivery vehicles.

160. To achieve its purpose, the comprehensive test ban must be such as to endure. With the passage of time, even non-parties to the comprehensive test ban may feel inhibited from engaging in nuclear-weapon testing.

161. A permanent cessation of all nuclear-weapon tests has long been demanded by the world community and its achievement would be an event of great international importance.

12. United Nations General Assembly resolutions, 1980

I. UN member states and year of membership

The following list of names of the 154 UN member states is provided for convenience in reading the record of votes on the UN resolutions listed in section II below.

Afghanistan, 1946
Albania, 1955
Algeria, 1962
Angola, 1976
Argentina, 1945
Australia, 1945
Austria, 1955
Bahamas, 1973
Bahrain, 1971
Bangladesh, 1974
Barbados, 1966
Belgium, 1945
Benin, 1960
Bhutan, 1971
Bolivia, 1945
Botswana, 1966
Brazil, 1945
Bulgaria, 1955
Burma, 1948
Burundi, 1962
Byelorussia, 1945
Cameroon: see United Republic of Cameroon
Canada, 1945
Cape Verde, 1975
Central African Republic, 1960
Chad, 1960
Chile, 1945
China, 1945
Colombia, 1945
Comoros, 1975
Congo, 1960
Costa Rica, 1945
Cuba, 1945
Cyprus, 1960
Czechoslovakia, 1945
Democratic Kampuchea, 1955
Democratic Yemen,[a] 1967
Denmark, 1945
Djibouti, 1977
Dominica, 1978
Dominican Republic, 1945
Ecuador, 1945
Egypt, 1945
El Salvador, 1945
Equatorial Guinea, 1968
Ethiopia, 1945
Fiji, 1970
Finland, 1955
France, 1945
Gabon, 1960
Gambia, 1965
German Democratic Republic, 1973
Germany, Federal Republic of, 1973
Ghana, 1957
Greece, 1945
Grenada, 1974
Guatemala, 1945
Guinea, 1958
Guinea-Bissau, 1974
Guyana, 1966
Haiti, 1945
Honduras, 1945
Hungary, 1955
Iceland, 1946
India, 1945
Indonesia, 1950
Iran, 1945
Iraq, 1945
Ireland, 1955
Israel, 1949
Italy, 1955
Ivory Coast, 1960
Jamaica, 1962
Japan, 1956
Jordan, 1955
Kampuchea: see Democratic Kampuchea
Kenya, 1963
Kuwait, 1963
Lao People's Democratic Republic, 1955
Lebanon, 1945
Lesotho, 1966
Liberia, 1945
Libya, 1955

Luxembourg, 1945
Madagascar, 1960
Malawi, 1964
Malaysia, 1957
Maldives, 1965
Mali, 1960
Malta, 1964
Mauritania, 1961
Mauritius, 1968
Mexico, 1945
Mongolia, 1961
Morocco, 1956
Mozambique, 1975
Nepal, 1955
Netherlands, 1945
New Zealand, 1945
Nicaragua, 1945
Niger, 1960
Nigeria, 1960
Norway, 1945
Oman, 1971
Pakistan, 1947
Panama, 1945
Papua New Guinea, 1975
Paraguay, 1945
Peru, 1945
Philippines, 1945
Poland, 1945
Portugal, 1955
Qatar, 1971
Romania, 1955
Rwanda, 1962
Saint Lucia, 1979
Saint Vincent and the Grenadines, 1980
Samoa, 1976
Sao Tome and Principe, 1975
Saudi Arabia, 1945
Senegal, 1960
Seychelles, 1976
Sierra Leone, 1961
Singapore, 1965
Solomon Islands, 1978
Somalia, 1960
South Africa, 1945
Spain, 1955
Sri Lanka, 1955
Sudan, 1956
Suriname, 1975
Swaziland, 1968
Sweden, 1946
Syria, 1945
Tanzania: see United Republic of Tanzania
Thailand, 1946
Togo, 1960
Trinidad and Tobago, 1962
Tunisia, 1956
Turkey, 1945
Uganda, 1962
Ukraine, 1945
Union of Soviet Socialist Republics, 1945
United Arab Emirates, 1971
United Kingdom, 1945
United Republic of Cameroon, 1960
United Republic of Tanzania, 1961
United States, 1945
Upper Volta, 1960
Uruguay, 1945
Venezuela, 1945
Viet Nam, 1977
Yemen,[a] 1947
Yugoslavia, 1945
Zaire, 1960
Zambia, 1964
Zimbabwe, 1980

[a] The name Democratic Yemen refers to the People's Democratic Republic of Yemen (Southern Yemen). The name Yemen refers to the Yemen Arab Republic (Northern Yemen).

II. *Resolutions on disarmament matters adopted in 1980*

Note

The list includes those resolutions which exclusively concern disarmament, as well as those which deal with other questions but refer to disarmament matters. In the latter case, the negative votes or abstentions listed do not necessarily reflect the positions of states on the disarmament paragraphs of the relevant resolutions.

Only the essential parts of each resolution are given here. The texts have been abridged, but the wording is close to that of the resolution.

The resolutions are grouped according to disarmament subjects, irrespective of the agenda items under which they were discussed.

Subject, number, date of adoption and contents of resolution	Voting results
Nuclear weapons	
35/156 F 12 December 1980	
Takes note, with satisfaction, of the report of the Secretary-General on a comprehensive study on nuclear weapons as a highly significant statement on present nuclear arsenals, on the trends in their technological development and the effects of their use, as well as on the various doctrines of deterrence and the security implications of the continued quantitative and qualitative development of nuclear weapon systems, and also as a reminder of the need for efforts to increase the political will necessary for effective disarmament measures, *inter alia*, through the promotion of public awareness of the need for disarmament; notes the conclusions of the report and expresses the hope that all states will consider them carefully; and recommends the wide distribution of the report so as to acquaint public opinion with its contents.	*In favour* 126 *Against* 0 *Abstaining* 19: Belgium, Bulgaria, Byelorussia, Czechoslovakia, France, German Democratic Republic, Federal Republic of Germany, Greece, Hungary, Italy, Lao People's Democratic Republic, Luxembourg, Mongolia, Poland, Portugal, Ukraine, UK, USA, USSR *Absent*: Albania, Botswana, Dominica, Equatorial Guinea, Guinea-Bissau, Saint Vincent, Seychelles, Solomon Islands
35/156 K 12 December 1980	
Deplores that the Treaty between the USA and the USSR on the limitation of strategic offensive arms (SALT II) has not yet been ratified; trusts that, pending the entry into force of the Treaty, the	Adopted without vote

Subject, number, date of adoption and contents of resolution	Voting results
signatory states, in conformity with the provisions of the Vienna Convention on the Law of Treaties, will refrain from any act which would defeat the object and purpose of the Treaty; reiterates its satisfaction at the agreement reached by both parties in the joint statement of principles and basic guidelines for subsequent negotiations on the limitation of strategic arms, signed the same day as the Treaty, to the effect of continuing negotiations on measures for the further limitation and reduction in the number of strategic arms, as well as for their further qualitative limitation, which should culminate in the SALT III treaty; and invites the governments of the USSR and the USA to keep the General Assembly appropriately informed of the results of their negotiations.	
35/156 H 12 December 1980 Requests the Committee on Disarmament, at an appropriate stage of its work on the item entitled "Nuclear weapons in all aspects", to pursue its consideration of the question of adequately verified cessation and prohibition of the production of fissionable material for nuclear weapons and other nuclear explosive devices and to keep the General Assembly informed of the progress of that consideration.	*In favour* 125[a] *Against* 11: Bulgaria, Byelorussia, Czechoslovakia, German Democratic Republic, Hungary, Lao People's Democratic Republic, Mongolia, Poland, Ukraine, USSR, Viet Nam *Abstaining* 8: Afghanistan, Argentina, Bhutan, Brazil, Cuba, France, India, UK *Absent*: Albania, Botswana, China, Dominica, Equatorial Guinea, Guinea-Bissau, Saint Vincent, Seychelles, Solomon Islands
35/156 C 12 December 1980 Requests the Committee on Disarmament to proceed without delay to talks with a view to elaborating an international agreement on the non-stationing of nuclear weapons on the territories of states where there are no such weapons at present; and requests the Committee to submit a report on this question to the General Assembly at its thirty-sixth session.	*In favour* 95 *Against* 18: Australia, Belgium, Canada, Denmark, France, Federal Republic of Germany, Greece, Iceland, Italy, Luxembourg, Netherlands, New Zealand, Norway, Portugal, Spain, Turkey, UK, USA *Abstaining* 27: Algeria, Austria, Brazil, Burma, Central African Republic, Congo, Costa Rica, Cyprus, Democratic Kampuchea, Gabon, Ghana, Guatemala, Ireland, Israel, Japan,[b] Morocco, Niger, Pakistan, Peru, Samoa, Senegal, Singapore, Sudan, Sweden, Upper Volta, Yugoslavia, Zaire *Absent*: Albania, Botswana, China, Dominica,

Equatorial Guinea, Guinea-Bissau, Haiti, Mali,[c] Saint Lucia, Saint Vincent, Seychelles, Solomon Islands, Swaziland

Nuclear tests

35/145 A
12 December 1980

Reiterates once again its grave concern that nuclear weapon testing continues unabated against the wishes of the overwhelming majority of member states; reaffirms its conviction that a treaty to achieve the prohibition of all nuclear test explosions by all states for all time is a matter of the highest priority and constitutes a vital element for the success of efforts to prevent both vertical and horizontal proliferation of nuclear weapons and a contribution to nuclear disarmament; and urges all states that have not yet done so to adhere without further delay to the Treaty banning nuclear weapon tests in the atmosphere, in outer space and under water and, meanwhile, to refrain from testing in the environments covered by that Treaty.

Urges all states members of the Committee on Disarmament to support the creation by the Committee, upon initiation of its session in 1981, of an *ad hoc* working group which should begin the multilateral negotiation of a treaty for the prohibition of all nuclear weapon tests, and to use their best endeavours in order that the Committee may transmit to the General Assembly at its thirty-sixth session the multilaterally negotiated text of such a treaty.

Calls upon the states depositaries of the Treaty banning nuclear weapon tests in the atmosphere, in outer space and under water and the Treaty on the non-proliferation of nuclear weapons, by virtue of their special responsibilities under those two treaties and as a provisional measure until the new comprehensive test-ban treaty enters into force, to bring to a halt without delay all nuclear test explosions, either through a trilaterally agreed moratorium or through three unilateral moratoria.

In favour 111
Against 2: UK, USA
Abstaining 31: Australia, Belgium, Bulgaria, Byelorussia, Canada, Central African Republic, China, Cuba, Czechoslovakia, Denmark, France, German Democratic Republic, Federal Republic of Germany, Greece, Hungary, Iceland, Israel, Italy, Japan, Lao People's Democratic Republic, Luxembourg, Mongolia, Netherlands, New Zealand, Norway, Poland, Portugal, Turkey, Ukraine, USSR, Viet Nam
Absent: Albania, Botswana, Democratic Kampuchea, Dominica, Equatorial Guinea, Guinea-Bissau, Saint Vincent, Solomon Islands, Zimbabwe

35/145 B
12 December 1980

Noting with appreciation the report of the Secretary-General on a comprehensive test ban, reaffirms its conviction that a treaty to achieve the prohibition of all nuclear test explosions by all states for all time is a matter of the greatest urgency and priority; calls upon the three negotiating nuclear weapon states to exert their best efforts to bring their negotiations to a successful conclusion in time for consideration during the next session of the Committee on Disarmament; expresses the conviction that such a treaty is a vital requirement to halt the nuclear arms race and the qualitative improvement of nuclear weapons and to prevent the spread of nuclear weapons to additional countries; requests the Committee on Disarmament to take the necessary steps, including the establishment of a working group, to initiate substantive negotiations on a comprehensive test ban treaty as a matter of the highest priority at the beginning of its session to be held in 1981; further requests this Committee to determine, in the context of its negotiations on such a treaty, the institutional and administrative steps necessary for establishing, testing and operating an international seismic monitoring network

In favour 129
Against 0
Abstaining 16: Argentina, Bulgaria, Byelorussia, China, Czechoslovakia, France, German Democratic Republic, Hungary, Lao People's Democratic Republic, Mongolia, Poland, Ukraine, UK, USA, USSR, Viet Nam
Absent: Albania, Botswana, Dominica, Equatorial Guinea, Guinea-Bissau, Papua New Guinea, Saint Vincent, Solomon Islands

Subject, number, date of adoption and contents of resolution	Voting results
and effective verification system; and calls upon the Committee to exert all efforts in order that a draft comprehensive nuclear test ban treaty may be submitted to the General Assembly no later than at its second special session devoted to disarmament, to be held in 1982.	
35/12 3 November 1980 Requests the UN Scientific Committee on the effects of atomic radiation to continue its work, including its important coordinating activities, to increase knowledge of the doses, effects and risks of ionizing radiation from all sources.	Adopted without vote
Non-use of nuclear weapons	
35/152 D 12 December 1980 Declares once again that: (*a*) the use of nuclear weapons would be a violation of the Charter of the United Nations and a crime against humanity; and (*b*) the use or threat of use of nuclear weapons should therefore be prohibited, pending nuclear disarmament. Requests all states that have so far not submitted their proposals concerning the non-use of nuclear weapons, avoidance of nuclear war and related matters, to do so, in order that the question of an international convention or some other agreement on the subject may be further considered at the thirty-sixth session of the General Assembly.	*In favour* 112 *Against* 19: Australia, Belgium, Denmark, France, Federal Republic of Germany, Greece, Iceland, Ireland, Israel, Italy, Japan, Luxembourg, Netherlands, New Zealand, Norway, Portugal, Turkey, UK, USA *Abstaining* 14: Austria, Bulgaria, Byelorussia, Canada,[b] Czechoslovakia, German Democratic Republic, Hungary, Malawi, Mongolia, Poland, Spain, Sweden, Ukraine, USSR *Absent*: Albania, Botswana, Dominica, Equatorial Guinea, Guinea-Bissau, Saint Vincent, Seychelles, Solomon Islands
35/154 12 December 1980 Welcomes the conclusion of the Committee on Disarmament that there is continuing recognition of the urgent need to reach agreement on effective international arrangements to assure non-nuclear weapon states against the use or threat of use of nuclear weapons; notes with satisfaction that in the Committee there was no objection, in principle, to the idea of an international convention; requests the Committee to continue on a priority basis, during its session in 1981, the negotiations on the question of strengthening the security guarantees of non-nuclear weapon states; calls upon all nuclear	*In favour* 110 *Against* 2: Albania, USA *Abstaining* 31: Australia, Austria, Belgium, Bhutan, Burma, Canada, Central African Republic, Denmark, France, Federal Republic of Germany, Greece, Guatemala, Haiti, Iceland,

weapon states to make solemn declarations, identical in substance, concerning the non-use of nuclear weapons against non-nuclear states having no such weapons on their territories, as a first step towards the conclusion of an international convention; and recommends that the Security Council should examine declarations which may be made by nuclear states regarding the strengthening of security guarantees for non-nuclear states and, if all these declarations are found consistent with the above-mentioned objective, should adopt an appropriate resolution approving them.

India, Ireland, Israel, Italy, Japan, Luxembourg, Netherlands, New Zealand, Niger, Norway, Portugal, Spain, Sweden, Turkey, UK, United Republic of Cameroon, Zaire
Absent: Botswana, China, Colombia, Democratic Kampuchea, Dominica, Equatorial Guinea, Guinea-Bissau, Saint Vincent, Seychelles, Solomon Islands

35/155
12 December 1980

Reaffirms the urgent need to reach agreement on effective international arrangements to assure non-nuclear weapon states against the use or threat of use of nuclear weapons; appeals to all states, in particular the nuclear weapon states, to demonstrate the political will necessary to reach agreement on a common approach which could be included in an international instrument of a legally binding character; and recommends that the Committee on Disarmament should actively continue negotiations with a view to reaching agreement and concluding effective international arrangements during its next session to assure non-nuclear weapon states against the use or threat of use of nuclear weapons, taking into account the widespread support for the conclusion of an international convention and giving consideration to any other proposals designed to secure the same objective.

In favour 121
Against 0
Abstaining 24: Australia, Austria, Belgium, Bhutan, Central African Republic, Denmark, France, Federal Republic of Germany, Greece, Grenada, Iceland, India, Ireland, Israel, Italy, Japan, Luxembourg, Netherlands, New Zealand, Norway, Portugal, Sweden, UK, USA
Absent: Albania, Botswana, Dominica, Equatorial Guinea, Guinea-Bissau, Saint Vincent, Seychelles, Solomon Islands

Nuclear weapon-free zones

35/143
12 December 1980

Regrets that the signatures of Additional Protocol I of the Treaty of Tlatelolco by the United States and France, which the General Assembly duly noted and which took place on 26 May 1977 and 2 March 1979, respectively, have not yet been followed by the corresponding ratifications.

In favour 138
Against 0
Abstaining 5: Central African Republic, Cuba, France, Guyana, USA
Absent: Albania, Argentina, Botswana, Dominica, Equatorial Guinea, Guinea-Bissau, Liberia, Saint Vincent, Solomon Islands, Zimbabwe

35/146 B
12 December 1980

Strongly reiterates its call upon all states to consider and respect the continent of Africa, comprising the continental African states, Madagascar and other islands surrounding Africa, as a nuclear weapon-free zone; reaffirms that the nuclear programme of South Africa constitutes a very grave danger to international peace and security and, in particular, jeopardizes the security of African

In favour 133
Against 0
Abstaining 12: Belgium, Canada, France, Federal Republic of Germany, Greece, Israel,

Subject, number, date of adoption and contents of resolution	Voting results
states and increases the danger of the proliferation of nuclear weapons; condemns any form of nuclear collaboration by any state, corporation, institution or individual with the racist regime of South Africa since such collaboration frustrates, *inter alia*, the objective of the declaration of the Organization of African Unity to keep Africa a nuclear weapon-free zone; calls upon such states, corporations, institutions or individuals, therefore, to terminate forthwith nuclear collaboration between them and the racist regime of South Africa; requests the Security Council to prohibit all forms of cooperation and collaboration with the racist regime of South Africa in the nuclear field; and demands that South Africa submit all its nuclear installations to inspection by the IAEA.	Italy, Luxembourg, Netherlands, Portugal, UK, USA *Absent*: Argentina, Botswana, Dominica, Equatorial Guinea, Guinea-Bissau, Paraguay, Saint Vincent, Solomon Islands
35/147 12 December 1980	
Urges all parties directly concerned to consider taking the practical and urgent steps required for the implementation of the proposal to establish a nuclear weapon-free zone in the Middle East and, as a means of promoting this objective, invites the countries concerned to adhere to the Treaty on the non-proliferation of nuclear weapons; invites those countries, pending the establishment of such a zone in the Middle East and during the process of its establishment, to declare solemnly that they will refrain, on a reciprocal basis, from producing, acquiring or in any other way possessing nuclear weapons and nuclear explosive devices; calls upon those countries to refrain, on a reciprocal basis, from permitting the stationing of nuclear weapons on their territory by any third party and to agree to place all their nuclear activities under IAEA safeguards; further invites those countries, pending the establishment of a nuclear weapon-free zone in the Middle East to declare their support for establishing such a zone in the region and to deposit those declarations with the Security Council for consideration as appropriate; and reaffirms again its recommendation to the nuclear weapon states to refrain from any action contrary to the spirit and purpose of the present resolution and the objective of establishing in the region of the Middle East a nuclear weapon-free zone under an effective system of safeguards and to extend their cooperation to the states of the region in their efforts to promote these objectives.	Adopted without vote
35/148 12 December 1980	
Reaffirms its endorsement, in principle, of the concept of a nuclear weapon-free zone in South Asia; urges once again the states of South Asia and such other neighbouring non-nuclear weapon states as may be interested to continue to make all possible efforts to establish a nuclear weapon-free zone in South Asia and to refrain, in the meantime, from any action contrary to this objective, and calls upon those nuclear weapon states which have not done so to respond positively to this proposal and to extend the necessary cooperation in the efforts to establish a nuclear weapon-free zone in South Asia.	*In favour* 96 *Against* 3: Bhutan, India, Mauritius *Abstaining* 44: Afghanistan, Algeria, Angola, Argentina, Australia, Austria, Bahamas, Benin, Bolivia, Brazil, Bulgaria, Burma, Byelorussia, Central African Republic, Congo, Cuba, Cyprus,

Czechoslovakia, Denmark, Ethiopia, Fiji, France, German Democratic Republic, Greece, Hungary, Indonesia, Israel, Italy, Lao People's Democratic Republic, Malawi, Mongolia, Morocco, Mozambique, Nicaragua, Norway, Poland, Sao Tome and Principe, Seychelles, Sweden, Ukraine, UK, USSR, Viet Nam, Yugoslavia
Absent: Albania, Botswana, Dominica, Equatorial Guinea, Guinea-Bissau, Madagascar, Saint Vincent, Solomon Islands, Suriname, Syria

Indian Ocean as a zone of peace

35/150
12 December 1980

Requests the *Ad Hoc* Committee on the Indian Ocean, in pursuance of the decision contained in resolution 34/80 B, to convene a conference on the Indian Ocean during 1981 at Colombo, and requests the conference to submit its report to the General Assembly.

Adopted without vote

Non-proliferation of nuclear weapons

35/17
6 November 1980

Commends the IAEA for its efforts to ensure the safe use of nuclear energy for peaceful purposes, notes the steady improvement of the Agency's safeguards system and welcomes the conclusion that in 1979 nuclear material under Agency safeguards remained in peaceful nuclear activities or was otherwise adequately accounted for. Notes with satisfaction that there is continuing progress in the studies by the IAEA aimed at establishing a system of international storage of plutonium and the international management of spent fuel, and that the Committee on assurances of supply, open to all states members of the IAEA, held its first session in September 1980 and will reconvene at the beginning of March 1981; and urges all states that have not already done so to ratify the Convention on the physical protection of nuclear material, which was opened for signature on 3 March 1980.

Adopted without vote

35/146 A
12 December 1980

Expresses its appreciation to the Secretary-General for his report on South Africa's plan and capability in the nuclear field; expresses its deep alarm that the report has established South Africa's capability to manufacture nuclear weapons; also expresses its deep concern that South Africa's nuclear capability is being developed to preserve white supremacy by intimidating neighbouring

In favour 132
Against 0
Abstaining 13: Belgium, Canada, France, Federal Republic of Germany, Greece, Israel,

Subject, number, date of adoption and contents of resolution	Voting results
countries and blackmailing the entire continent of Africa; reaffirms that the racist regime's nuclear plans and capability constitute a very grave danger to international peace and security; requests the Security Council to prohibit all forms of cooperation and collaboration with the racist regime of South Africa in the nuclear field; calls upon all states, corporations, institutions or individuals to terminate forthwith such nuclear collaboration between them and the racist regime of South Africa; requests the Security Council to institute effective enforcement action against the racist regime of South Africa, so as to prevent it from endangering international peace and security through its acquisition of nuclear weapons; and demands that South Africa submit all its nuclear installations to inspection by the IAEA.	Italy, Japan, Luxembourg, Netherlands, Portugal, UK, USA *Absent*: Argentina, Botswana, Dominica, Equatorial Guinea, Guinea-Bissau, Paraguay, Saint Vincent, Solomon Islands
35/119 (Resolution relating to decolonization matters) 11 December 1980 Strongly condemns all collaboration, particularly in the nuclear and military fields, with the government of South Africa and calls upon the states concerned to cease forthwith all such collaboration.	*In favour* 134 *Against* 3: France, UK, USA *Abstaining* 9: Belgium, Canada, Federal Republic of Germany, Guatemala, Israel, Italy, Luxembourg, Mauritius, Portugal *Absent*: Dominica, Grenada, Haiti, Paraguay, Saint Vincent, Solomon Islands, Upper Volta
35/157 12 December 1980 Takes note of the progress report of the Secretary-General on the work of the Group of experts to prepare a study on Israeli nuclear armament and requests the Secretary-General to pursue his efforts in this regard and to submit his report to the General Assembly at its thirty-sixth session.	*In favour* 99 *Against* 6: Denmark, Iceland, Israel, Netherlands, Norway, USA *Abstaining* 38: Argentina, Australia, Austria, Belgium, Bolivia, Burma, Canada, Central African Republic, Chile, Colombia, Costa Rica, Dominican Republic, Fiji, Finland, France, Federal Republic of Germany, Greece, Guatemala, Honduras, Ireland, Italy, Ivory Coast, Japan, Liberia, Luxembourg, Malawi, Nepal, New Zealand, Papua New Guinea, Paraguay, Portugal, Saint Lucia, Samoa, Spain, Swaziland, Sweden, Thailand, UK *Absent*: Botswana, Dominica, Equatorial Guinea, Guinea-Bissau, Haiti, Lesotho, Saint Vincent, Seychelles, Singapore, Solomon Islands

35/28 (Resolution relating to decolonization matters)
11 November 1980

Strongly condemns the states and transnational corporations which continue their investments in, and supply of armaments and oil and nuclear technology to, the racist South African regime, thus buttressing it and aggravating the threat to world peace; strongly condemns the collusion of France, the Federal Republic of Germany, Israel and the United States with South Africa in the nuclear field and calls upon all other governments to continue to refrain from supplying the racist minority regime of South Africa, directly or indirectly, with installations that might enable it to produce uranium, plutonium and other nuclear materials, reactors or military equipment.

In favour 103
Against 15: Australia, Belgium, Canada, France, Federal Republic of Germany, Ireland, Israel, Italy, Japan, Luxembourg, Netherlands, New Zealand, Portugal, UK, USA
Abstaining 28: Austria, Central African Republic, Chile, Denmark, El Salvador, Finland, Gabon, Gambia, Greece, Guatemala, Honduras, Iceland, Ivory Coast, Lesotho, Liberia, Norway, Papua New Guinea, Rwanda, Samoa, Senegal, Singapore, Spain, Swaziland, Sweden, Thailand, Togo, Turkey, Upper Volta
Absent: Congo, Democratic Kampuchea, Djibouti, Dominica, Paraguay, Saint Vincent, Solomon Islands

35/112
5 December 1980

Decides to convene in 1983 a UN conference for the promotion of international cooperation in the peaceful uses of nuclear energy, and requests the preparatory committee for the Conference to submit its report to the General Assembly at its thirty-sixth session.

Adopted without vote

Biological and chemical weapons

35/144 A
12 December 1980

Welcomes the final declaration of the Review Conference of the parties to the Convention on the prohibition of the development, production and stockpiling of bacteriological (biological) and toxin weapons and on their destruction, in which the states parties to the Convention, *inter alia*: (*a*) reaffirmed their strong determination to exclude completely the possibility of bacteriological (biological) agents and toxins being used as weapons; (*b*) expressed the belief that article I had proved sufficiently comprehensive to have covered recent scientific and technological developments relevant to the Convention; (*c*) considered that the flexibility of the provisions concerning consultations and cooperation on any problems which might arise in relation to the objective, or in the application of the provisions of, the Convention enabled interested states parties to use various international procedures which would make it possible to ensure effectively and adequately the implementation of the provisions of the Convention, taking into account the concern expressed by the participants in the Conference to this effect—these procedures include, *inter alia*, the right of any state party subsequently to request that a consultative meeting open to all parties be convened at expert level—and,

Adopted without vote

Subject, number, date of adoption and contents of resolution	Voting results
having noted the concerns and differing views expressed on the adequacy of article V, believed that this question should be further considered at an appropriate time; (*d*) reaffirmed the obligation assumed by the states parties to the Convention to continue negotiations in good faith towards the recognized objectives of an early agreement on complete, effective and adequately verifiable measures for the prohibition of the development, production and stockpiling of chemical weapons and for their destruction; and (*e*) noted that during the first five years of the operation of the Convention the provisions of articles VI, VII, XI and XIII had not been invoked. Calls upon all signatory states which have not ratified the Convention to do so without delay and upon those states which have not yet signed the Convention to consider acceding to it at an early date as a significant contribution to international confidence.	
35/144 C 12 December 1980 Calls upon all states parties to the 1925 Protocol for the prohibition of the use in war of asphyxiating, poisonous, or other gases, and of bacteriological methods of warfare to reaffirm their determination strictly to observe all their obligations under the Protocol; calls upon all states which have not yet done so to accede to the Protocol; appeals to all states to comply with the principles and objectives of the Protocol; decides to carry out an impartial investigation to ascertain the facts pertaining to reports regarding the alleged use of chemical weapons and to assess the extent of the damage caused by the use of chemical weapons; requests the Secretary-General to carry out such investigation, *inter alia*, taking into account proposals advanced by the states on whose territories the use of chemical weapons has been reported, with the assistance of qualified medical and technical experts who shall: (*a*) seek relevant information from all concerned governments, international organizations and other sources necessary; and (*b*) collect and examine evidence, including on-site with the consent of the countries concerned, to the extent relevant to the purposes of the investigation. Invites the governments of states where chemical weapons were used to provide the Secretary-General with all relevant information they may have in their possession; calls upon all states to co-operate in this investigation and to provide any relevant information they may have in their possession; and requests the Secretary-General to submit a report on this matter to the General Assembly at its thirty-sixth session.	*In favour* 78[d] *Against* 17: Afghanistan, Benin, Bulgaria, Byelorussia, Cuba, Czechoslovakia, Democratic Yemen, German Democratic Republic, Hungary, Lao People's Democratic Republic, Mongolia, Poland, Romania, Syria, Ukraine, USSR, Viet-Nam *Abstaining* 36: Argentina, Bangladesh, Barbados, Bhutan, Bolivia, Brazil, Burma, Congo, Cyprus, Ecuador, Finland, Grenada, Guinea, India, Indonesia, Iraq, Jamaica, Lebanon, Madagascar, Maldives, Mexico, Nepal, Nicaragua, Nigeria, Peru, Qatar, Saint Lucia, Saudi Arabia, Somalia, Sri Lanka, Trinidad and Tobago, Uganda, United Republic of Cameroon, Venezuela, Yemen, Yugoslavia *Absent*: Albania, Algeria, Angola, Bahrain, Botswana, Cape Verde, Dominica, Equatorial Guinea, Ethiopia, Guinea-Bissau, Iran, Jordan, Kuwait, Libya, Mozambique, Saint Vincent, Sao Tome and Principe, Seychelles, Solomon Islands, United Arab Emirates, United Republic of Tanzania, Zimbabwe

35/144 B
12 December 1980

Taking note of the joint report on the progress in the bilateral negotiations on the prohibition of chemical weapons, submitted by the USSR and the USA to the Committee on Disarmament on 7 July 1980, which regrettably have not yet resulted in the elaboration of a joint initiative, notes with satisfaction the work of the Committee on Disarmament during its session held in 1980 regarding the prohibition of chemical weapons, in particular the work of its *ad hoc* working group on that question, and urges the Committee to continue, as from the beginning of its session in 1981, negotiations on a multilateral convention as a matter of high priority, taking into account all existing proposals and future initiatives.

Adopted without vote

Radiological weapons

35/156 G
12 December 1980

Calls upon the Committee on Disarmament to continue negotiations with a view to elaborating a treaty prohibiting the development, production, stockpiling and use of radiological weapons and to report on the results to the General Assembly at its thirty-sixth session.

Adopted without vote

New weapons of mass destruction

35/149
12 December 1980

Requests the Committee on Disarmament, in the light of its priorities, to continue negotiations, with the assistance of qualified governmental experts, with a view to preparing a draft comprehensive agreement on the prohibition of the development and manufacture of new types of weapons of mass destruction and new systems of such weapons, and to draft possible agreements on particular types of such weapons, and urges all states to refrain from any action which could adversely affect the talks aimed at working out an agreement or agreements to prevent the emergence of new types of weapons of mass destruction and new systems of such weapons.

In favour 117
Against 0
Abstaining 26: Australia, Austria, Belgium, Canada, Central African Republic, Denmark, France, Gambia, Federal Republic of Germany, Greece, Iceland, Ireland, Israel, Italy, Japan, Luxembourg, Malawi, Netherlands, New Zealand, Norway, Portugal, Spain, Sweden, Turkey, UK, USA
Absent: Albania, Botswana, China, Congo, Democratic Kampuchea, Dominica, Equatorial Guinea, Guinea-Bissau, Saint Vincent, Solomon Islands

Subject, number, date of adoption and contents of resolution	Voting results
Conventional weapons	
35/153 12 December 1980	
Welcomes the successful conclusion of the conference, which resulted in the adoption, on 10 October 1980, of the following instruments: (*a*) Convention on prohibitions or restrictions on the use of certain conventional weapons which may be deemed to be excessively injurious or to have indiscriminate effects; (*b*) Protocol on non-detectable fragments (Protocol I); (*c*) Protocol on prohibitions or restrictions on the use of mines, booby traps and other devices (Protocol II); and (*d*) Protocol on prohibitions or restrictions on the use of incendiary weapons (Protocol III). Takes note of article 3 of the Convention, which stipulates that the Convention shall be open for signature on 10 April 1981; commends the Convention and the three annexed Protocols to all states, with a view to achieving the widest possible adherence to these instruments; and takes note that, under article 8 of the Convention, conferences may be convened to consider amendments to the Convention or any of the annexed Protocols, to consider additional protocols relating to other categories of conventional weapons not covered by the existing Protocols, or to review the scope and operation of the Convention and the Protocols.	Adopted without vote
35/152 G 12 December 1980	
Calls upon the states permanent members of the Security Council and the countries which have military agreements with them to exercise restraint both in the nuclear and conventional fields and to resolve not to increase their armed forces and conventional armaments, effective from an agreed date, as a first step towards a subsequent reduction of their armed forces and conventional armaments.	*In favour* 104[e] *Against* 19: Australia, Belgium, Canada, Denmark, France, Federal Republic of Germany, Iceland, Israel, Italy, Japan, Luxembourg, Netherlands, New Zealand, Norway, Portugal, Spain, Turkey, UK, USA *Abstaining* 17: Austria, Burma, Chile, Fiji, Greece,[b] Guatemala, Ireland, Malaysia, Morocco, Niger, Papua New Guinea, Philippines, Samoa, Singapore, Sri Lanka, Sweden, Thailand *Absent*: Albania, Botswana, China, Democratic Kampuchea, Djibouti, Dominica, Equatorial Guinea, Guinea-Bissau, Paraguay, Saint Vincent, Senegal, Seychelles, Solomon Islands
35/156 A 12 December 1980	
Approves, in principle, the carrying out of a study on all aspects of the conventional arms race and on disarmament relating to conventional weapons and armed forces, to be undertaken by the Secretary-	*In favour* 101 *Against* 14: Afghanistan, Brazil, Bulgaria,

General with the assistance of a group of qualified experts appointed by him on a balanced geographical basis; agrees that the Disarmament Commission, at its forthcoming substantive session, should work out the general approach to the study, its structure and scope; requests the Commission to convey to the Secretary-General the conclusions of its deliberations, which should constitute the guidelines for the study; and further requests the Secretary-General to submit a progress report on the study to the General Assembly at its second special session devoted to disarmament, and a final report at its thirty-eighth session.

Byelorussia, Czechoslovakia, German Democratic Republic, Hungary, India, Lao People's Democratic Republic, Mongolia, Poland, Ukraine, USSR, Viet Nam
Abstaining 27: Algeria, Bahrain, Benin, Bhutan, Cape Verde, Comoros, Congo, Cuba, Democratic Yemen, Egypt, Ghana, Guatemala, Guinea, Iran, Iraq, Ivory Coast, Jordan, Mozambique, Nicaragua, Oman, Qatar, Sao Tome and Principe, Syria, Tunisia, United Arab Emirates, Yemen, Yugoslavia
Absent: Albania, Angola, Botswana, Dominica, Equatorial Guinea, Guinea-Bissau, Libya, Saint Lucia, Saint Vincent, Seychelles, Solomon Islands

35/71 (Resolution relating to the economic and financial problems of remnants of war
5 December 1980

Recognizing that the presence of material remnants of war, particularly mines, on the territories of certain developing countries seriously impedes their development efforts and entails loss of life and property, and convinced that the removal of those remnants of war should be the responsibility of the countries that implanted them and should be carried out at their expense, calls upon states which took part in those wars to make available forthwith to the affected states all information on the areas in which such mines were placed, including maps indicating the position of those areas, and information concerning the types of mines; and supports the demand of the states affected by the implantation of mines on their lands for compensation for the losses incurred from the states which planted the mines.

In favour 119
Against 0
Abstaining 29
(States are not specified because the votes were not recorded)

Regional disarmament

35/156 D
12 December 1980

Having examined the report of the Secretary-General containing the study prepared by the Group of Governmental Experts on regional disarmament, takes note with appreciation of the report and the study; commends the study and its conclusions to the attention of all states; invites all member states to inform the Secretary-General, at the latest by 1 June 1981, of their views regarding the study and its conclusions; and expresses the hope that the study will encourage governments to take initiatives and to consult within the different regions with a view to agreeing upon appropriate measures of regional disarmament.

Adopted without vote

Subject, number, date of adoption and contents of resolution	Voting results
Military expenditures	
35/142 A 12 December 1980	
Reaffirms the urgent need to reinforce the endeavours in the area of the reduction of military budgets, with a view to reaching international agreements to freeze, reduce or otherwise restrain military expenditures; reiterates the appeal to all states, in particular the most heavily armed states, pending the conclusion of agreements on the reduction of military expenditures, to exercise self-restraint in their military expenditure with a view to reallocating the funds thus saved to economic and social development, particularly for the benefit of developing countries; and requests the Secretary-General to invite member states to express their views and suggestions on the principles which should govern their actions in the field of the freezing and reduction of military expenditures and to prepare on this basis a report to be submitted to the Disarmament Commission at its session in 1981.	Adopted without vote
35/142 B 12 December 1980	
Recognizing with satisfaction that a carefully elaborated instrument for international reporting of military expenditures has now become available for general and regular implementation, and convinced that systematic reporting of military expenditures is an important first step in the move towards agreed and balanced reductions in military expenditures, recommends that all member states should make use of the reporting instrument and report annually to the Secretary-General their military expenditures of the latest fiscal year, for which data are available, presenting their first report preferably not later than 30 April 1981; and requests the Secretary-General, with the assistance of an *ad hoc* group of qualified experts in the field of military budgets: (*a*) to refine further the reporting instrument on the basis of future comments and suggestions received from states during the general and regular implementation of the reporting instrument; and (*b*) to examine and suggest solutions to the question of comparing military expenditures among different states and between different years as well as to the problems of verification that will arise in connection with agreements on reduction of military expenditures.	*In favour* 113 *Against* 0 *Abstaining* 21: Afghanistan, Bulgaria, Byelorussia, Cape Verde, Cuba, Czechoslovakia, Democratic Yemen, Ethiopia, German Democratic Republic, Ghana, Guinea, Hungary, India, Lao People's Democratic Republic, Mongolia, Mozambique, Poland, Sao Tome and Principe, Ukraine, USSR, Viet Nam *Absent*: Albania, Algeria, Angola, Botswana, China, Dominica, Dominican Republic,[f] El Salvador, Equatorial Guinea, Guinea-Bissau, Israel, Liberia, Libya, Nicaragua, Saint Vincent, Seychelles, Solomon Islands, Syria, Zimbabwe
Outer space	
35/14 3 November 1980	
Invites states which have not yet become parties to the international treaties governing the uses of outer space to give consideration to ratifying or acceding to those treaties.	Adopted without vote

35/15
3 November 1980

Endorses the recommendations contained in the report of the Preparatory Committee for the Second UN Conference on the exploration and peaceful uses of outer space and decides to accept the offer of the government of Austria to be host to the Conference at Vienna from 9 to 21 August 1982.

Adopted without vote

Disarmament and international security

35/156 E
12 December 1980

Takes note of the report of the Secretary-General containing a letter from the chairman of the Group of Experts on the relationship between disarmament and international security, informing the Secretary-General that, owing to the vast area to be covered and the complexity and sensitivity of the issues involved, the Group would need more time to complete its work; and requests the Secretary-General to continue the study and to submit the final report to the General Assembly at its thirty-sixth session.

Adopted without vote

35/156 J
12 December 1980

Calls upon all states to proceed towards measures under the Charter of the United Nations for a system of international security and order concurrently with efforts at effective disarmament measures; recommends that the main organs of the United Nations responsible for the maintenance of international peace and security should give early consideration to the requirements for halting the arms race, particularly the nuclear arms race, and developing the modalities for the effective application of the system of international security provided for in the Charter; and requests the permanent members of the Security Council to facilitate the work of the Council towards carrying out this essential responsibility under the Charter.

Adopted without vote

35/160
15 December 1980

Considers that the question of the peaceful settlement of disputes should represent one of the central concerns for states and that, to this end, the efforts for examining and further developing the principle of the peaceful settlement of disputes and the means of consolidating its full observance by all states in their international relations should be continued; considers also that the elaboration, as soon as possible, of a declaration of the General Assembly on the peaceful settlement of international disputes is likely to contribute to the strengthening of the role and the efficiency of the United Nations in preventing conflicts and settling them peacefully; and requests the Special Committee on the Charter of the United Nations and on the strengthening of the role of the Organization to continue the elaboration of the draft declaration on the peaceful settlement of international disputes with a view to submitting it for further consideration to the General Assembly at its thirty-sixth session.

Adopted by consensus

Subject, number, date of adoption and contents of resolution	Voting results
35/50 (Resolution relating to legal matters) 4 December 1980 Decides that the Special Committee on enhancing the effectiveness of the principle of non-use of force in international relations shall continue its work with the goal of drafting, at the earliest possible date, a world treaty on the non-use of force in international relations as well as the peaceful settlement of disputes or such other recommendations as the Committee deems appropriate.	*In favour* 107 *Against* 16: Belgium, Canada, Denmark, France, Federal Republic of Germany, Iceland, Israel, Italy, Japan, Luxembourg, Netherlands, Norway, Portugal, Spain, UK, USA *Abstaining* 12: Australia, Austria, Brazil, China, Greece, Ireland, Ivory Coast, Liberia, Malawi, New Zealand, Sweden, Turkey *Absent*: Botswana, Cape Verde, Chad,[f] Colombia, Democratic Kampuchea, Dominica, El Salvador, Guatemala, Guinea-Bissau, Guyana, Mali,[f] Saint Lucia, Saint Vincent, Solomon Islands, Thailand, Uganda, Zimbabwe Albania announced that it was not participating in the vote.
35/158 (Resolution on the strengthening of international security) 12 December 1980 Urges all states, particularly the permanent members of the Security Council, to take all the necessary steps to prevent further erosion or disruption of the process of détente and to refrain from any act which may aggravate the international situation, impede the resolution of crises and the elimination of focal points of tension in various regions of the world and hamper the implementation of the decisions and recommendations adopted at the Tenth Special Session of the General Assembly on halting and reversing the arms race, particularly the nuclear arms race, which are essential for the preservation of international peace and security; reaffirms the decision, taken at its Tenth Special Session, by which it called upon the Security Council to take appropriate effective measures to prevent the non-fulfilment of the objectives of the denuclearization of Africa, and notes with alarm that the nuclear capability of South Africa poses a serious danger to the security of African states and to international peace and security; reaffirms the objectives of the Declaration of the Indian Ocean as a zone of peace and commends the decision of the permanent members of the Security Council and major maritime users of the Indian Ocean to serve on the expanded *Ad Hoc* Committee on the Indian Ocean for the preparation of the Conference on the Indian Ocean scheduled to be held in 1981 at Colombo; commends the convening at Madrid of the Conference on Security and Co-operation in Europe and expresses the hope that it will result in further strengthening the security and cooperation of states in Europe in all spheres, including the reduction of armaments and	*In favour* 120 *Against* 0 *Abstaining* 24: Australia, Austria, Belgium, Canada, Denmark, France, Federal Republic of Germany, Greece, Guatemala, Iceland, Ireland, Israel, Italy, Japan, Luxembourg, Netherlands, New Zealand, Norway, Portugal, Spain, Sweden, Turkey, UK, USA *Absent*: Albania, Botswana, Dominica, Equatorial Guinea, Paraguay, Saint Vincent, Seychelles, Solomon Islands, Zimbabwe

armed forces and the halting of the arms race in both nuclear and conventional fields, thus contributing to the preservation and furtherance of the process of détente in Europe and to peace and stability in the world; and urges all states to cooperate in efforts aimed at transforming the region of the Mediterranean into a zone of peace and cooperation.

Confidence-building measures

35/156 B
12 December 1980

Takes note with satisfaction of the report of the Secretary-General on a comprehensive study on confidence-building measures, to which was annexed the report of the Group of Governmental Experts, and requests the Secretary-General to continue the work in this regard and to submit the study to the General Assembly at its thirty-sixth session.

Adopted without vote

Disarmament machinery

35/152 J
12 December 1980

Urges the Committee on Disarmament to continue or undertake, during its session to be held in 1981, substantive negotiations on the priority questions of disarmament on its agenda; invites the members of the Committee involved in separate negotiations on specific priority questions of disarmament to intensify their efforts to achieve a positive conclusion of those negotiations for submission to the Committee; and requests the Committee to continue negotiations on the elaboration of a comprehensive programme of disarmament, and to submit the programme in time for consideration by the General Assembly at the second special session devoted to disarmament.

In favour 132
Against 0
Abstaining 13: Bulgaria, Byelorussia, Czechoslovakia, German Democratic Republic, Hungary, Israel, Lao People's Democratic Republic, Mongolia, Poland, Ukraine, UK, USA, USSR
Absent: Albania, Botswana, Dominica, Equatorial Guinea, Guinea-Bissau, Saint Vincent, Seychelles, Solomon Islands

35/152 B
12 December 1980

Calls upon the Committee on Disarmament to consider the establishment of an *ad hoc* working group on the cessation of the nuclear arms race and on nuclear disarmament, with a clearly defined mandate.

In favour 118
Against 18: Australia, Belgium, Canada, Denmark, France, Federal Republic of Germany, Greece, Iceland, Italy, Japan, Luxembourg, Netherlands, New Zealand, Norway, Portugal, Turkey, UK, USA
Abstaining 7: Brazil, Ireland, Israel, Malawi, Morocco, Spain, Zaire
Absent: Albania, Botswana, China, Democratic Kampuchea, Dominica, Equatorial Guinea, Guinea-Bissau, Saint Vincent, Seychelles, Solomon Islands

Subject, number, date of adoption and contents of resolution	Voting results
35/152 C 12 December 1980 Urges the Committee on Disarmament to establish, upon initiation of its session to be held in 1981, an *ad hoc* working group on the item which, in its agenda for 1979 and 1980, was entitled "Cessation of the nuclear arms race and nuclear disarmament", and considers that it would be advisable that the working group begin its negotiations by addressing the question of the elaboration and clarification of the stages of nuclear disarmament envisaged in paragraph 50 of the Final Document of the Tenth Special Session of the General Assembly, including the identification of the responsibilities of the nuclear weapon states and the role of the non-nuclear weapon states in the process of achieving nuclear disarmament.	*In favour* 124 *Against* 4: France, Israel, UK, USA *Abstaining* 17: Australia, Belgium, Canada, Denmark, Federal Republic of Germany, Greece, Iceland, Italy, Japan, Luxembourg, Malawi, Netherlands, New Zealand, Norway, Portugal, Spain, Turkey *Absent*: Albania, Botswana, Dominica, Equatorial Guinea, Guinea-Bissau, Saint Vincent, Seychelles, Solomon Islands
35/156 I 12 December 1980 Requests the Committee on Disarmament to continue to consider the modalities of the review of the membership of the Committee and to report on this subject to the General Assembly at its thirty-sixth session; recommends that the first review of the membership of the Committee should be completed, following appropriate consultations among member states, during the next special session of the General Assembly devoted to disarmament; and reaffirms that states not members of the Committee, upon their request, should be invited to participate in the work of the Committee when the particular concerns of those states are under discussion.	*In favour* 135 *Against* 0 *Abstaining* 10: Bulgaria, Byelorussia, Czechoslovakia, German Democratic Republic, Hungary, Lao People's Democratic Republic, Mongolia, Poland, Ukraine, USSR *Absent*: Albania, Botswana, Dominica, Equatorial Guinea, Guinea-Bissau, Saint Vincent, Seychelles, Solomon Islands
35/152 E 12 December 1980 Urges all states, particularly nuclear-weapon and other major military powers, immediately to take steps leading to effective halting and reversing of the arms race and to disarmament; urges those states also to intensify efforts to bring to a successful end the negotiations in the Committee on Disarmament and other international forums or to proceed with negotiations on effective international agreements according to the priorities of the programme of action in section III of the Final Document of the Tenth Special Session; calls upon states to refrain from actions which have or may have negative effects on the implementation of the recommendations and decisions of the Tenth Special Session; and invites states engaged in disarmament or arms limitation negotiations outside the UN framework to keep the General Assembly and the Committee on Disarmament informed of the results.	Adopted without vote
35/152 F 12 December 1980 Requests the Disarmament Commission to continue its work in accordance with its mandate, with emphasis on the preparation of a report to the Assembly at its second special session devoted to disarmament.	Adopted without vote

Resolution	Vote
35/151 12 December 1980 Renews the mandate of the *Ad Hoc* Committee on the World Disarmament Conference and requests it to maintain close contact with the representatives of the nuclear weapon states in order to remain informed of their attitudes, as well as with all other states, and to consider any relevant proposals and observations.	Adopted without vote
35/47 3 December 1980 Decides to establish a preparatory committee for the second special session of the General Assembly composed of 78 member states appointed by the President of the General Assembly on the basis of equitable geographic distribution; and requests the committee to prepare a draft agenda, to examine all relevant questions and to submit to the General Assembly at its 36th session its recommendations.	Adopted without vote
Information, research and training	
35/152 I 12 December 1980 Recalling that at its Tenth Special Session it stressed the importance of mobilizing public opinion on behalf of disarmament, requests the Secretary-General to carry out, with the assistance of a small group of experts, a study on the organization and financing of a world disarmament campaign under the auspices of the United Nations.	*In favour* 128 *Against* 0 *Abstaining* 17: Belgium, Canada, Colombia, France, Gabon, Federal Republic of Germany, Ghana, Greece, Israel, Luxembourg, Netherlands, Portugal, Togo,[f] Turkey, UK, USA, Yugoslavia *Absent*: Albania, Botswana, Dominica, Equatorial Guinea, Guinea-Bissau, Saint Vincent, Seychelles, Solomon Islands
35/152 A 12 December 1980 Decides to continue the United Nations programme of fellowships on disarmament and requests the Secretary-General to make adequate arrangements relating to the programme for 1981, in accordance with the guidelines approved by the General Assembly at its thirty-third session.	Adopted without vote
35/152 H 12 December 1980 Welcomes the establishment at Geneva of the UN Institute for Disarmament Research within the framework of the UN Institute for Training and Research as an interim arrangement for the period until the second special session of the General Assembly devoted to disarmament.	Adopted without vote
35/141 12 December 1980 Requests the Secretary-General to bring up to date, with the assistance of qualified experts, the report entitled *Economic and Social Consequences of the Arms Race and of Military Expenditures*, covering the basic topics of that report, and to transmit it to the General Assembly at its 37th session.	Adopted without vote

Subject, number, date of adoption and contents of resolution	Voting results
Disarmament Decade	
35/46 3 December 1980 Adopts the Declaration of the 1980s as the Second Disarmament Decade. The goals of the Decade should be the following: (*a*) halting and reversing the arms race, particularly the nuclear arms race; (*b*) concluding and implementing effective agreements on disarmament, particularly nuclear disarmament, which will contribute significantly to the achievement of general and complete disarmament under effective international control; (*c*) developing on an equitable basis the limited results obtained in the field of disarmament in the 1970s; (*d*) strengthening international peace and security in accordance with the UN Charter; and (*e*) making available a substantial part of the resources released by disarmament measures to promote the attainment of the objectives of the Third UN Development Decade and, in particular, the economic and social development of developing countries. All efforts should be exerted by the Committee on Disarmament urgently to negotiate: (*a*) a comprehensive nuclear test ban treaty; (*b*) a treaty on the prohibition of the development, production and stockpiling of all chemical weapons and their destruction; (*c*) a treaty on the prohibition of the development, production and use of radiological weapons; and (*d*) effective international arrangements to assure non-nuclear weapon states against the use or threat of use of nuclear weapons. The same priority should be given to the following measures which are dealt with outside the Committee on Disarmament: (*a*) ratification of the SALT II Treaty and commencement of negotiations for a SALT III agreement; (*b*) ratification of Additional Protocol I of the Treaty of Tlatelolco; (*c*) signature and ratification of the agreement negotiated by the UN Conference on prohibitions or restrictions of use of certain conventional weapons which may be deemed to be excessively injurious or to have indiscriminate effects; (*d*) achievement of an agreement on mutual reduction of armed forces and armaments and associated measures in central Europe; (*e*) negotiations on effective confidence-building and disarmament measures in Europe among the states participating in the Conference on Security and Co-operation in Europe; and (*f*) achievement of a more stable situation in Europe at a lower level of military potential on the basis of approximate equality and parity by agreement on appropriate mutual reduction and limitation of armaments and armed forces.	Adopted without vote

[a] Mozambique later advised the Secretariat it had intended to abstain.
[b] Later advised the Secretariat it had intended to vote against.
[c] Later advised the Secretariat it had intended to abstain.
[d] Guyana and Mali later advised the Secretariat they had intended to abstain.
[e] Togo and Zaire later advised the Secretariat they had intended to abstain.
[f] Later advised the Secretariat it had intended to vote in favour.

13. The implementation of multilateral arms control agreements

The eight major multilateral arms control treaties and conventions in force on 31 December 1980 were concluded with the following objectives:

(*a*) to prevent militarization or military nuclearization of certain areas or environments (Antarctica, Latin America, outer space and the sea-bed);

(*b*) to restrict nuclear weapon tests;

(*c*) to prevent the spread of nuclear weapons;

(*d*) to prohibit the production and eliminate the stockpiles of biological weapons; and

(*e*) to prevent the use of environmental forces for military ends.

Section I of this chapter summarizes the essential provisions of the agreements, while Section II lists information on ratifications, accessions or successions to these agreements.

I. Summary of the essential provisions of the agreements

Antarctic Treaty

Signed at Washington on 1 December 1959.
Entered into force on 23 June 1961.
Depositary: US government.

Declares the Antarctic an area to be used exclusively for peaceful purposes. Prohibits any measure of a military nature in the Antarctic, such as the establishment of military bases and fortifications, and the carrying out of military manoeuvres or the testing of any type of weapon. Bans any nuclear explosion as well as the disposal of radioactive waste material in Antarctica, subject to possible future international agreements on these subjects.

Treaty banning nuclear weapon tests in the atmosphere, in outer space and under water (Partial Test Ban Treaty—PTBT)

Signed at Moscow on 5 August 1963.
Entered into force on 10 October 1963.
Depositaries: UK, US and Soviet governments.

Prohibits the carrying out of any nuclear weapon test explosion, or any other nuclear explosion: (*a*) in the atmosphere, beyond its limits, including outer space, or under water, including territorial waters or high seas; or (*b*) in any other environment if such explosion causes radioactive debris to be present outside the territorial limits of the state under whose jurisdiction or control the explosion is conducted.

Treaty on principles governing the activities of states in the exploration and use of outer space, including the moon and other celestial bodies (Outer Space Treaty)

Signed at London, Moscow and Washington on 27 January 1967.
Entered into force on 10 October 1967.
Depositaries: UK, US and Soviet governments.

Prohibits the placing in orbit around the Earth of any objects carrying nuclear weapons or any other kinds of weapons of mass destruction, the installation of such weapons on celestial bodies, or the stationing of them in outer space in any other manner. The establishment of military bases, installations and fortifications, the testing of any type of weapons and the conduct of military manoeuvres on celestial bodies are also forbidden.

Treaty for the prohibition of nuclear weapons in Latin America (Treaty of Tlatelolco)

Signed at Mexico, Federal District, on 14 February 1967.

The Treaty enters into force for each state that has ratified it when the requirements specified in the Treaty have been met—that is, that all states in the region which were in existence when the Treaty was opened for signature deposit the instruments of ratification; that Additional Protocols I and II be signed and ratified by those states to which they apply (see below); and that agreements on safeguards be concluded with the IAEA. The signatory states have the right to waive, wholly or in part, those requirements.

The Treaty came into force on 22 April 1968 as between Mexico and El Salvador, on behalf of which instruments of ratification, with annexed declarations wholly waiving the above requirements, were deposited on 20 September 1967 and 22 April 1968, respectively.

Depositary: Mexican government.

Prohibits the testing, use, manufacture, production or acquisition by any means, as well as the receipt, storage, installation, deployment and any form of possession of any nuclear weapons by Latin American countries.

The parties should conclude agreements with the International Atomic Energy Agency (IAEA) for the application of safeguards to their nuclear activities.

Additional Protocols

The Additional Protocols enter into force for the states that have ratified them on the date of the deposit of their instruments of ratification.

Depositary: Mexican government.

Under *Additional Protocol I*, annexed to the Treaty, the extra-continental or continental states which, *de jure* or *de facto*, are internationally responsible for territories lying within the limits of the geographical zone established by the Treaty (France, the Netherlands, the UK and the USA), undertake to apply the statute of military denuclearization, as defined in the Treaty, to such territories.

Under *Additional Protocol II*, annexed to the Treaty, the nuclear weapon states undertake to respect the statute of military denuclearization of Latin America, as defined in the Treaty, and not to contribute to acts involving a violation of the Treaty, nor to use or threaten to use nuclear weapons against the parties to the Treaty.

Treaty on the non-proliferation of nuclear weapons (Non-Proliferation Treaty —NPT)

Signed at London, Moscow and Washington on 1 July 1968.
Entered into force on 5 March 1970.
Depositaries: UK, US and Soviet governments.

Prohibits the transfer by nuclear weapon states to any recipient whatsoever of nuclear weapons or other nuclear explosive devices or of control over them, as well as the assistance, encouragement or inducement of any non-nuclear weapon state to manufacture or otherwise acquire such weapons or devices. Prohibits the receipt by non-nuclear weapon states from any transferor whatsoever, as well as the manufacture or other acquisition by those states, of nuclear weapons or other nuclear explosive devices.

Non-nuclear weapon states undertake to conclude safeguards agreements with the International Atomic Energy Agency (IAEA) with a view to preventing diversion of nuclear energy from peaceful uses to nuclear weapons or other nuclear explosive devices.

The parties undertake to facilitate the exchange of equipment, materials and scientific and technological information for the peaceful uses of nuclear energy and to ensure that potential benefits from peaceful applications of nuclear explosions will be made available to non-nuclear weapon parties to the Treaty. They also undertake to pursue negotiations on effective measures relating to cessation of the nuclear arms race and to nuclear disarmament, and on a treaty on general and complete disarmament.

Treaty on the prohibition of the emplacement of nuclear weapons and other weapons of mass destruction on the sea-bed and the ocean floor and in the subsoil thereof (Sea-Bed Treaty)

Signed at London, Moscow and Washington on 11 February 1971.
Entered into force on 18 May 1972.
Depositaries: UK, US and Soviet governments.

Prohibits emplanting or emplacing on the sea-bed and the ocean floor and in the subsoil thereof beyond the outer limit of a sea-bed zone (coterminous with the 12-mile outer limit of the zone referred to in the 1958 Geneva Convention on the Territorial Sea and the Contiguous Zone) any nuclear weapons or any other types of weapons of mass destruction as well as structures, launching installations or any other facilities specifically designed for storing, testing or using such weapons.

Convention on the prohibition of the development, production and stockpiling of bacteriological (biological) and toxin weapons and on their destruction (BW Convention)

Signed at London, Moscow and Washington on 10 April 1972.
Entered into force on 26 March 1975.
Depositaries: UK, US and Soviet governments.

Prohibits the development, production, stockpiling or acquisition by other means or retention of microbial or other biological agents, or toxins whatever their origin or method of production, of types and in quantities that have no justification for prophylactic, protective or other peaceful purposes, as well as weapons, equipment or means of delivery designed to use such agents or toxins for hostile purposes or in armed conflict. The destruction of the agents, toxins, weapons, equipment and means of delivery in the possession of the parties, or their diversion to peaceful purposes, should be effected not later than nine months after the entry into force of the Convention.

Convention on the prohibition of military or any other hostile use of environmental modification techniques (ENMOD Convention)

Signed at Geneva on 18 May 1977.
Entered into force on 5 October 1978.
Depositary: UN Secretary-General.

Prohibits military or any other hostile use of environmental modification techniques having widespread, long-lasting or severe effects as the means of destruction, damage or injury to states party to the Convention. The term 'environmental modification techniques' refers to any technique for changing—through the deliberate manipulation of natural processes—the dynamics, composition or structure of the Earth, including its biota, lithosphere, hydrosphere and atmosphere, or of outer space.

II. Parties to multilateral arms control treaties, as of 31 December 1980

Number of parties

Antarctic Treaty	21	
Partial Test Ban Treaty	112	
Outer Space Treaty	82	
Treaty of Tlatelolco	22	
Additional Protocol I	2	
Additional Protocol II	5	
Non-Proliferation Treaty	114[a]	
NPT safeguards agreements	69	non-nuclear weapon states
Sea-Bed Treaty	70	
BW Convention	91	
ENMOD Convention	31	

Note

1. The list of parties records ratifications, accessions and successions.

2. The Partial Test Ban Treaty, the Outer Space Treaty, the Non-Proliferation Treaty, the Sea-Bed Treaty and the Biological Weapons Convention provide for three depositaries—the governments of the UK, the USA and the USSR. The dates given in the list are the earliest dates on which countries deposited their instruments of ratification, accession or succession—whether in London, Washington or Moscow.
Under the Antarctic Treaty, the only depositary is the US government; under the Treaty of Tlatelolco, the Mexican government; and under the ENMOD Convention, the UN Secretary-General.

3. Key to abbreviations used in the table:
S: signature without further action
PI: Additional Protocol I to the Treaty of Tlatelolco
PII: Additional Protocol II to the Treaty of Tlatelolco
SA: Safeguards agreement in force with the International Atomic Energy Agency under the Non-Proliferation Treaty or the Treaty of Tlatelolco

4. The footnotes are listed at the end of the table and are grouped separately under the heading for each agreement.

[a] Egypt ratified in 1981, bringing the total number of parties to the NPT to 115.

State	Antarctic Treaty	Partial Test Ban Treaty	Outer Space Treaty	Treaty of Tlatelolco	Non-Proliferation Treaty	Sea-Bed Treaty	BW Convention	ENMOD Convention
Afghanistan		12 Mar 1964	S		4 Feb 1970 SA: 20 Feb 1978	22 Apr 1971	26 Mar 1975	
Algeria		S						
Argentina	23 Jun 1961	S	26 Mar 1969	S[1]		S[1]	27 Nov 1979	
Australia	23 Jun 1961	12 Nov 1963	10 Oct 1967		23 Jan 1973[1] SA: 10 Jul 1974	23 Jan 1973	5 Oct 1977	S
Austria		17 Jul 1964	26 Feb 1968		27 Jun 1969 SA: 23 Jul 1972	10 Aug 1972	10 Aug 1973[1]	
Bahamas		16 Jul 1976[1]	11 Aug 1976[1]	26 Apr 1977[2]	11 Aug 1976[2]			
Bangladesh					31 Aug 1979			3 Oct 1979
Barbados			12 Sep 1968	25 Apr 1969[2]	21 Feb 1980		16 Feb 1973	
Belgium	26 Jul 1960	1 Mar 1966	30 Mar 1973		2 May 1975 SA: 21 Feb 1977	20 Nov 1972	15 Mar 1979	S
Benin		15 Dec 1964[2]			31 Oct 1972	S	25 Apr 1975	S
Bhutan		8 Jun 1978					8 Jun 1978	

Bolivia		4 Aug 1965	S	18 Feb 1969[2]	26 May 1970	S	30 Oct 1975	S
Botswana		5 Jan 1968[1]	S		28 Apr 1969	10 Nov 1972	S	
Brazil	16 May 1975	15 Dec 1964	5 Mar 1969[2]	29 Jan 1968[3]		S[2]	27 Feb 1973	S
Bulgaria		13 Nov 1963	28 Mar 1967		5 Sep 1969 SA: 29 Feb 1972	16 Apr 1971	2 Aug 1972	31 May 1978
Burma		15 Nov 1963	18 Mar 1970			S	S	
Burundi		S	S		19 Mar 1971	S	S	
Byelorussia		16 Dec 1963[3]	31 Oct 1967[3]			14 Sep 1971	26 Mar 1975	7 Jun 1978
Cameroon: see United Republic of Cameroon								
Canada		28 Jan 1964	10 Oct 1967		8 Jan 1969 SA: 21 Feb 1972	17 May 1972[3]	18 Sep 1972	S
Cape Verde		24 Oct 1979			24 Oct 1979	24 Oct 1979	20 Oct 1977	3 Oct 1979
Central African Republic		22 Dec 1964	S		25 Oct 1970	S	S	

State	Antarctic Treaty	Partial Test Ban Treaty	Outer Space Treaty	Treaty of Tlatelolco	Non-Proliferation Treaty	Sea-Bed Treaty	BW Convention	ENMOD Convention
Chad		1 Mar 1965			10 Mar 1971			
Chile	23 Jun 1961	6 Oct 1965	S	9 Oct 1974[4]			22 Apr 1980	
China				PII: 12 Jun 1974[5]				
Colombia		S	S	4 Aug 1972[2]	S	S	S	
Congo					23 Oct 1978	23 Oct 1978	23 Oct 1978	
Costa Rica		10 Jul 1967		25 Aug 1969[2] SA[15]	3 Mar 1970 SA: 22 Nov 1979	S	17 Dec 1973	
Cuba			3 Jun 1977[4]			3 Jun 1977[4]	21 Apr 1976	10 Apr 1978
Cyprus		15 Apr 1965	5 Jul 1972		10 Feb 1970 SA: 26 Jan 1973	17 Nov 1971	6 Nov 1973	12 Apr 1978
Czechoslovakia	14 Jun 1962	14 Oct 1963	11 May 1967		22 Jul 1969 SA: 3 Mar 1972	11 Jan 1972	30 Apr 1973	12 May 1978
Democratic Kampuchea					2 Jun 1972	S	S	
Democratic Yemen*		1 Jun 1979	1 Jun 1979		1 June 1979	1 June 1979	1 Jun 1979	12 Jun 1979

Denmark	20 May 1965	15 Jan 1964	10 Oct 1967		3 Jan 1969 SA: 21 Feb 1977	15 Jun 1971	1 Mar 1973	19 Apr 1978
Dominican Republic		3 Jun 1964	21 Nov 1968	14 Jun 1968[2] SA[15]	24 Jul 1971 SA: 11 Oct 1973	11 Feb 1972	23 Feb 1973	
Ecuador		6 May 1964	7 Mar 1969	11 Feb 1969[2] SA[15]	7 Mar 1969 SA: 10 Mar 1975		12 Mar 1975	
Egypt		10 Jan 1964[4]	10 Oct 1967		S		S	
El Salvador		3 Dec 1964	15 Jan 1969	22 Apr 1968[2] SA[15]	11 Jul 1972 SA: 22 Apr 1975		S	
Equatorial Guinea						S		
Ethiopia		S	S		5 Feb 1970 SA: 2 Dec 1977	12 Jul 1977	26 May 1975	S
Fiji		14 Jul 1972[1]	18 Jul 1972[1]		21 Jul 1972[2] SA: 22 Mar 1973		4 Sep 1973	
Finland		9 Jan 1964	12 Jul 1967		5 Feb 1969 SA: 9 Feb 1972	8 Jun 1971	4 Feb 1974	12 May 1978
France	16 Sep 1960		5 Aug 1970	PI: S[6] PII: 22 Mar 1974[7]				
Gabon		20 Feb 1964			19 Feb 1974		S	

P

State	Antarctic Treaty	Partial Test Ban Treaty	Outer Space Treaty	Treaty of Tlatelolco	Non-Proliferation Treaty	Sea-Bed Treaty	BW Convention	ENMOD Convention
Gambia		27 Apr 1965[1]	S		12 May 1975 SA: 8 Aug 1978	S	S	
German Democratic Republic	19 Nov 1974[1]	30 Dec 1963[5]	2 Feb 1967[5]		31 Oct 1969[3] SA: 7 Mar 1972	27 Jul 1971	28 Nov 1972	25 May 1978
Germany, Federal Republic of	5 Feb 1979[2]	1 Dec 1964[6]	10 Feb 1971[6]		2 May 1975[4] SA: 21 Feb 1977	18 Nov 1975[5]	S	S
Ghana		27 Nov 1963	S		4 May 1970 SA: 17 Feb 1975	9 Aug 1972	6 Jun 1975	22 Jun 1978
Greece		18 Dec 1963	19 Jan 1971		11 Mar 1970 SA: 1 Mar 1972	S	10 Dec 1975	
Grenada				20 Jun 1975[2]	2 Sep 1975[2]			
Guatemala		6 Jan 1964[2]		6 Feb 1970[2]	22 Sep 1970	S	19 Sep 1973	
Guinea						S		
Guinea-Bissau		20 Aug 1976	20 Aug 1976		20 Aug 1976	20 Aug 1976	20 Aug 1976	
Guyana			S				S	

Haiti		S	S	23 May 1969[2]	2 Jun 1970		S	
Holy See (Vatican City)			S		25 Feb 1971[5] SA: 1 Aug 1972			S
Honduras		2 Oct 1964	S	23 Sep 1968[2] SA[15]	16 May 1973 SA: 18 Apr 1975	S	14 Mar 1979	
Hungary		21 Oct 1963	26 Jun 1967		27 May 1969 SA: 30 Mar 1972	13 Aug 1971	27 Dec 1972	19 Apr 1978
Iceland		29 Apr 1964	5 Feb 1968		18 Jul 1969 SA: 16 Oct 1974	30 May 1972	15 Feb 1973	S
India		10 Oct 1963	S			20 Jul 1973[6]	15 Jul 1974[2]	15 Dec 1978
Indonesia		20 Jan 1964	S		12 Jul 1979[6] SA: 14 Jul 1980		S	
Iran		5 May 1964	S		2 Feb 1970 SA: 15 May 1974	26 Aug 1971	22 Aug 1973	S
Iraq		30 Nov 1964	4 Dec 1968		29 Oct 1969 SA: 29 Feb 1972	13 Sep 1972[4]	S	S
Ireland		18 Dec 1963	17 Jul 1968		1 Jul 1968 SA: 21 Feb 1977	19 Aug 1971	27 Oct 1972[3]	S
Israel		15 Jan 1964	18 Feb 1977					
Italy		10 Dec 1964	4 May 1972		2 May 1975[7] SA: 21 Feb 1977	3 Sep 1974[7]	30 May 1975	S

State	Antarctic Treaty	Partial Test Ban Treaty	Outer Space Treaty	Treaty of Tlatelolco	Non-Proliferation Treaty	Sea-Bed Treaty	BW Convention	ENMOD Convention
Ivory Coast		5 Feb 1965			6 Mar 1973	14 Jan 1972	S	
Jamaica		S	6 Aug 1970	26 Jun 1969[2] SA[15]	5 Mar 1970 SA: 6 Nov 1978	S	13 Aug 1975	
Japan	4 Aug 1960	15 Jun 1964	10 Oct 1967		8 Jun 1976[8] SA: 2 Dec 1977	21 Jun 1971	S	
Jordan		29 May 1964	S		11 Feb 1970 SA: 21 Feb 1978	17 Aug 1971	30 May 1975	
Kampuchea: see Democratic Kampuchea								
Kenya		10 Jun 1965			11 Jun 1970		7 Jan 1976	
Korea, South		24 Jul 1964[2]	13 Oct 1967[4]		23 Apr 1975[9, 10] SA: 14 Nov 1975	S[4]	S[4]	
Kuwait		20 May 1965[7]	7 Jun 1972[7]		S		18 Jul 1972[5]	2 Jan 1980[1]
Lao People's Democratic Republic		10 Feb 1965	27 Nov 1972		20 Feb 1970	19 Oct 1971	20 Mar 1973	5 Oct 1978
Lebanon		14 May 1965	31 Mar 1969		15 Jul 1970 SA: 5 Mar 1973	S	26 Mar 1975	S

Lesotho			S		20 May 1970 SA: 12 Jun 1973	3 Apr 1973	6 Sep 1977	
Liberia		19 May 1964			5 Mar 1970	S	S	S
Libya		15 Jul 1968	3 Jul 1968		26 May 1975 SA: 8 Jul 1980			
Liechten-stein					20 Apr 1978[11] SA: 4 Oct 1979			
Luxembourg		10 Feb 1965	S		2 May 1975 SA: 21 Feb 1977	S	23 Mar 1976	S
Madagascar		15 Mar 1965	22 Aug 1968[8]		8 Oct 1970 SA: 14 Jun 1973	S	S	
Malawi		26 Nov 1964[1]					S	5 Oct 1978
Malaysia		15 Jul 1964	S		5 Mar 1970 SA: 29 Feb 1972	21 Jun 1972	S	
Maldives					7 Apr 1970 SA: 2 Oct 1977			
Mali		S	11 Jun 1968		10 Feb 1970	S	S	
Malta		25 Nov 1964[1]			6 Feb 1970	4 May 1971	7 Apr 1975	
Mauritania		6 Apr 1964						

State	Antarctic Treaty	Partial Test Ban Treaty	Outer Space Treaty	Treaty of Tlatelolco	Non-Proliferation Treaty	Sea-Bed Treaty	BW Convention	ENMOD Convention
Mauritius		30 Apr 1969[1]	16 Apr 1969[1]		8 Apr 1969 SA: 31 Jan 1973	23 Apr 1971	7 Aug 1972	
Mexico		27 Dec 1963	31 Jan 1968	20 Sep 1967[2, 8] SA: 6 Sep 1968	21 Jan 1969[12] SA: 14 Sep 1973		8 Apr 1974[6]	
Mongolia		1 Nov 1963	10 Oct 1967		14 May 1969 SA: 5 Sep 1972	8 Oct 1971	5 Sep 1972	19 May 1978
Morocco		1 Feb 1966	21 Dec 1967		27 Nov 1970 SA: 18 Feb 1975	26 Jul 1971	S	S
Nepal		7 Oct 1964	10 Oct 1967		5 Jan 1970 SA: 22 Jun 1972	6 Jul 1971	S	
Netherlands	30 Mar 1967	14 Sep 1964	10 Oct 1969	PI: 26 Jul 1971[9]	2 May 1975 SA: 21 Feb 1977	14 Jan 1976	S	S
New Zealand	1 Nov 1960	10 Oct 1963	31 May 1968		10 Sep 1969 SA: 29 Feb 1972	24 Feb 1972	13 Dec 1972	
Nicaragua		26 Jan 1965	S	14 Oct 1968[2,10] SA[15]	6 Mar 1973 SA: 29 Dec 1976	7 Feb 1973	7 Aug 1975	S
Niger		3 Jul 1964	17 Apr 1967			9 Aug 1971	23 Jun 1972	
Nigeria		17 Feb 1967	14 Nov 1967		27 Sep 1968		3 Jul 1973	

Norway	24 Aug 1960	21 Nov 1963	1 Jul 1969		5 Feb 1969 SA: 1 Mar 1972	28 Jun 1971	1 Aug 1973	15 Feb 1979
Pakistan		S	8 Apr 1968				25 Sep 1974	
Panama		24 Feb 1966	S	11 Jun 1971[2]	13 Jan 1977	20 Mar 1974	20 Mar 1974	
Papua New Guinea		27 Oct 1980[1]	27 Oct 1980[1]				27 Oct 1980	28 Oct 1980
Paraguay		S		19 Mar 1969[2] SA[15]	4 Feb 1970 SA: 20 Mar 1979	S	9 Jun 1976	
Peru		20 Jul 1964	28 Feb 1979	4 Mar 1969[2]	3 Mar 1970 SA: 1 Aug 1979		S	
Philippines		10 Nov 1965[2]	S		5 Oct 1972 SA: 16 Oct 1974		21 May 1973	
Poland	8 Jun 1961	14 Oct 1963	30 Jan 1968		12 Jun 1969 SA: 11 Oct 1972	15 Nov 1971	25 Jan 1973	8 Jun 1978
Portugal		S			15 Dec 1977 SA: 14 Jun 1979	24 Jun 1975	15 May 1975	S
Qatar						12 Nov 1974	17 Apr 1975	
Romania	15 Sep 1971[3]	12 Dec 1963	9 Apr 1968		4 Feb 1970 SA: 27 Oct 1972	10 Jul 1972	25 Jul 1979	S
Rwanda		22 Oct 1963	S		20 May 1975	20 May 1975	20 May 1975	
Saint Lucia					28 Dec 1979[2]			

State	Antarctic Treaty	Partial Test Ban Treaty	Outer Space Treaty	Treaty of Tlatelolco	Non-Proliferation Treaty	Sea-Bed Treaty	BW Convention	ENMOD Convention
Samoa		15 Jan 1965			17 Mar 1975 SA: 22 Jan 1979			
San Marino		3 Jul 1964	29 Oct 1968		10 Aug 1970[9]		11 Mar 1975	
Sao Tome and Principe						24 Aug 1979	24 Aug 1979	5 Oct 1979
Saudi Arabia			17 Dec 1976			23 Jun 1972	24 May 1972	
Senegal		6 May 1964			17 Dec 1970 SA: 14 Jan 1980	S	26 Mar 1975	
Seychelles			5 Jan 1978			29 Jun 1976	11 Oct 1979	
Sierra Leone		21 Feb 1964	13 Jul 1967		26 Feb 1975	S	29 Jun 1976	S
Singapore		12 Jul 1968[1]	10 Sep 1976		10 Mar 1976 SA: 18 Oct 1977	10 Sep 1976	2 Dec 1975	
Somalia		S	S		5 Mar 1970		S	
South Africa	21 Jun 1960	10 Oct 1963	30 Sep 1968			14 Nov 1973	3 Nov 1975	
Spain		17 Dec 1964	27 Nov 1968				20 Jun 1979	19 Jul 1978
Sri Lanka		5 Feb 1964	S		5 Mar 1979		S	25 Apr 1978

Sudan		4 Mar 1966			31 Oct 1973 SA: 7 Jan 1977	S		
Suriname				10 Jun 1977[2] SA[15]	30 Jun 1976[2] SA: 2 Feb 1979			
Swaziland		29 May 1969			11 Dec 1969 SA: 28 Jul 1975	9 Aug 1971		
Sweden		9 Dec 1963	11 Oct 1967		9 Jan 1970 SA: 14 Apr 1975	28 Apr 1972	5 Feb 1976	
Switzerland		16 Jan 1964	18 Dec 1969		9 Mar 1977[11] SA: 6 Sep 1978	4 May 1976	4 May 1976[7]	
Syria		1 Jun 1964	14 Nov 1968[9]		24 Sep 1969[9]		S	S
Taiwan		18 May 1964	24 Jul 1970		27 Jan 1970	22 Feb 1972[8]	9 Feb 1973[8]	
Tanzania: see United Republic of Tanzania								
Thailand		15 Nov 1963	5 Sep 1968		7 Dec 1972 SA: 16 May 1974		28 May 1975	
Togo		7 Dec 1964	S		26 Feb 1970	28 Jun 1971	10 Nov 1976	
Tonga		22 Jun 1971[1]	22 Jun 1971[1]		7 Jul 1971[2]		28 Sep 1976	

State	Antarctic Treaty	Partial Test Ban Treaty	Outer Space Treaty	Treaty of Tlatelolco	Non-Proliferation Treaty	Sea-Bed Treaty	BW Convention	ENMOD Convention
Trinidad and Tobago		14 Jul 1964	S	3 Dec 1970[2]	S			
Tunisia		26 May 1965	28 Mar 1968		26 Feb 1970	22 Oct 1971	18 May 1973	11 May 1978
Turkey		8 Jul 1965	27 Mar 1968		17 Apr 1980[13]	19 Oct 1972	25 Oct 1974	S[2]
Tuvalu					19 Jan 1979[2]			
Uganda		24 Mar 1964	24 Apr 1968					S
Ukraine		30 Dec 1963[3]	31 Oct 1967[3]			3 Sep 1971	26 Mar 1975	13 Jun 1978
Union of Soviet Socialist Republics	2 Nov 1960	10 Oct 1963	10 Oct 1967	PII: 8 Jan 1979[11]	5 Mar 1970	18 May 1972	26 Mar 1975	30 May 1978
United Arab Emirates							S	
United Kingdom	31 May 1960	10 Oct 1963[8]	10 Oct 1967	PI: 11 Dec 1969[12] PII: 11 Dec 1969[12]	27 Nov 1968[14] SA: 14 Aug 1978[15]	18 May 1972[9]	26 Mar 1975[9]	16 May 1978
United Republic of Cameroon		S[2]	S		8 Jan 1969	S		
United Republic of Tanzania		6 Feb 1964				S	S	

United States	18 Aug 1960	10 Oct 1963	10 Oct 1967	PI: S PII: 12 May 1971[13]	SA: 9 Dec 1980[16] SA[15]	18 May 1972	26 Mar 1975	[3]
Upper Volta		S	18 Jun 1968		3 Mar 1970			
Uruguay	11 Jan 1980[4]	25 Feb 1969	31 Aug 1970	20 Aug 1968[2] SA[15]	31 Aug 1970 SA: 17 Sep 1976	S		
Venezuela		22 Feb 1965	3 Mar 1970	23 Mar 1970[2,14]	25 Sep 1975		18 Oct 1978	
Viet Nam			20 June 1980			20 June 1980[10]	20 June 1980	26 Aug 1980
Yemen*		S			S		S	20 Jul 1977
Yugoslavia		15 Jan 1964	S		4 Mar 1970[17] SA: 28 Dec 1973	25 Oct 1973[11]	25 Oct 1973	
Zaire		28 Oct 1965	S		4 Aug 1970 SA: 9 Nov 1972		16 Sep 1975	S
Zambia		11 Jan 1965[1]	20 Aug 1973			9 Oct 1972		

* Yemen refers to the Yemen Arab Republic (Northern Yemen), Democratic Yemen refers to the People's Democratic Republic of Yemen (Southern Yemen).

Postscript: Egypt ratified the Non-Proliferation Treaty on 26 February 1981. It declared that it expected assistance from industrialized nations with a developed nuclear industry and expressed the view that the Middle East should be free of nuclear weapons.

The Antarctic Treaty

[1] The German Democratic Republic stated that in its view Article XIII, paragraph 1 of the Antarctic Treaty was inconsistent with the principle that all states whose policies are guided by the purposes and principles of the United Nations Charter have a right to become parties to treaties which affect the interests of all states.
[2] The Federal Republic of Germany stated that the Treaty applies also to Berlin (West).
[3] Romania stated that the provisions of Article XIII, paragraph 1 of the Antarctic Treaty were not in accordance with the principle according to which multilateral treaties whose object and purposes concern the international community, as a whole, should be open for universal participation.
[4] In acceding to the Antarctic Treaty, Uruguay proposed the establishment of a general and definitive statute on Antarctica in which the interests of all states involved and of the international community as a whole would be considered equitably. It also declared that it reserved its rights in Antarctica in accordance with international law.

The Partial Test Ban Treaty

[1] Notification of succession.
[2] With a statement that this does not imply the recognition of any territory or régime not recognized by this state.
[3] The United States considers that Byelorussia and Ukraine are already covered by the signature and ratification by the USSR.
[4] On ratifying the Treaty, Egypt stated that its ratification did not mean or imply any recognition of Israel or any treaty relation with Israel. On 28 April 1980, Egypt informed the US government, the depositary of the Treaty, that its position contained in the above statement was no longer in force.
[5] The United States did not accept the notification of signature and deposit of ratification of the Treaty in Moscow by the German Democratic Republic, which it then did not recognize as a state. On 4 September 1974, the two countries established diplomatic relations with each other.
[6] The Federal Republic of Germany stated that the Treaty applies also to *Land* Berlin.
[7] Kuwait stated that its signature and ratification of the Treaty do not in any way imply its recognition of Israel, nor oblige it to apply the provisions of the Treaty in respect of the said country.
[8] The UK stated its view that if a régime is not recognized as the government of a state, neither signature nor the deposit of any instrument by it nor notification of any of those acts will bring about recognition of that régime by any other state.

The Outer Space Treaty

[1] Notification of succession.
[2] The Brazilian government interprets Article X of the Treaty as a specific recognition that the granting of tracking facilities by the parties to the Treaty shall be subject to agreement between the states concerned.
[3] The United States considers that Byelorussia and Ukraine are already covered by the signature and ratification of the USSR.
[4] With a statement that this does not imply the recognition of any territory or régime not recognized by this state.
[5] The USA stated that this did not imply recognition of the German Democratic Republic. On 4 September 1974, the two countries established diplomatic relations with each other.
[6] The Federal Republic of Germany stated that the Treaty applies also to *Land* Berlin.
[7] Kuwait acceded to the Treaty with the understanding that this does not in any way imply its recognition of Israel and does not oblige it to apply the provisions of the Treaty in respect of the said country.
[8] Madagascar acceded to the Treaty with the understanding that under Article X of the Treaty the state shall retain its freedom of decision with respect to the possible installation of foreign observation bases in its territory and shall continue to possess the right to fix, in each case, the conditions for such installation.
[9] Syria acceded to the Treaty with the understanding that this should not mean in any way the recognition of Israel, nor should it lead to any relationship with Israel that could arise from the Treaty.

The Treaty of Tlatelolco

[1] Argentina stated that it understands Article 18 as recognizing the right of parties to carry out, by their own means or in association with third parties, explosions of nuclear devices for peaceful purposes, including explosions which involve devices similar to those used in nuclear weapons.
[2] The Treaty is in force for this country due to a declaration, annexed to the instrument of ratification in accordance with Article 28, paragraph 2, which waived the requirements specified in paragraph 1 of that Article: namely, that all states in the region deposit the instruments of ratification; that Additional Protocol I and Additional Protocol II be signed and ratified by those states to which they apply; and that agreements on safeguards be concluded with the IAEA. Colombia made this declaration subsequent to the deposit of ratification (on 6 September 1972), as did Nicaragua (on 24 October 1968) and Trinidad and Tobago (on 27 June 1975).
[3] On signing the Treaty, Brazil stated that, according to its interpretation, Article 18 of the Treaty gives the signatories the right to carry out, by their own means or in association with third parties, nuclear explosions for peaceful purposes, including explosions which involve devices similar to those used in nuclear weapons. This statement was reiterated at the ratification. Brazil stated also that it did not waive the requirements laid down in Article 28 of the Treaty. The Treaty is therefore not yet in force for Brazil. In ratifying the Treaty, Brazil reiterated its interpretation of Article 18, which it made upon signing.
[4] Chile has not waived the requirements laid down in Article 28 of the Treaty. The Treaty is therefore not yet in force for Chile.

[5] On signing Protocol II, China stated, *inter alia:* "China will never use or threaten to use nuclear weapons against non-nuclear Latin American countries and the Latin American nuclear-weapon-free zone; nor will China test, manufacture, produce, stockpile, install or deploy nuclear weapons in these countries or in this zone, or send her means of transportation and delivery carrying nuclear weapons to cross the territory, territorial sea or airspace of Latin American countries. It is necessary to point out that the signing of Additional Protocol II to the Treaty for the Prohibition of Nuclear Weapons in Latin America by the Chinese Government does not imply any change whatsoever in China's principled stand on the disarmament and nuclear weapons issue and, in particular, does not affect the Chinese Government's consistent stand against the treaty on non-proliferation of nuclear weapons and the partial nuclear test ban treaty . . ."

"The Chinese Government holds that, in order that Latin America may truly become a nuclear-weapon-free zone, all nuclear countries, and particularly the super-powers, which possess huge numbers of nuclear weapons, must first of all undertake earnestly not to use or threaten to use nuclear weapons against the Latin American countries and the Latin American nuclear-weapon-free zone, and they must be asked to undertake to observe and implement the following: (1) dismantling of all foreign military bases in Latin America and refraining from establishing any new foreign military bases there; (2) prohibition of the passage of any means of transportation and delivery carrying nuclear weapons through Latin American territory, territorial sea or airspace."

[6] On signing Protocol I, France made the following reservations and interpretative statements: the Protocol, as well as the provisions of the Treaty of Tlatelolco to which it refers, will not affect the right of self-defence under Article 51 of the UN Charter; the application of the legislation referred to in Article 3 of the Treaty relates to legislation which is consistent with international law; the obligations under the Protocol shall not apply to transit across the territories of the French Republic situated in the zone of the Treaty, and destined to other territories of the French Republic; the protocol shall not limit, in any way, the participation of the populations of the French territories in the activities mentioned in Article 1 of the Treaty, and in efforts connected with national defence of France; the provisions of Articles 1 and 2 of the Protocol apply to the text of the Treaty of Tlatelolco as it stands at the time when the Protocol is signed by France, and consequently no amendment to the Treaty that might come into force under Article 29 thereof would be binding on the government of France without the latter's express consent.

[7] On signing Protocol II, France stated that it interprets the undertaking contained in Article 3 of the Protocol to mean that it presents no obstacle to the full exercise of the right of self-defence enshrined in Article 51 of the United Nations Charter; it takes note of the interpretation of the Treaty given by the Preparatory Commission and reproduced in the Final Act, according to which the Treaty does not apply to transit, the granting or denying of which lies within the exclusive competence of each state party in accordance with the pertinent principles and rules of international law; it considers that the application of the legislation referred to in Article 3 of the Treaty relates to legislation which is consistent with international law. The provisions of Articles 1 and 2 of the Protocol apply to the text of the Treaty of Tlatelolco as it stands at the time when the Protocol is signed by France. Consequently, no amendment to the Treaty that might come into force under the provision of Article 29 thereof would be binding on the government of France without the latter's express consent. If this declaration of interpretation is contested in part or in whole by one or more contracting parties to the Treaty or to Protocol II, these instruments would be null and void as far as relations between the French Republic and the contesting state or states are concerned. On depositing its instrument of ratification of Protocol II, France stated that it did so subject to the statement made on signing the Protocol. On 15 April 1974, France made a supplementary statement to the effect that it was prepared to consider its obligations under Protocol II as applying not only to the signatories of the Treaty, but also to the territories for which the statute of denuclearization was in force in conformity with Article 1 of Protocol I.

[8] On signing the Treaty, Mexico said that if technological progress makes it possible to differentiate between nuclear weapons and nuclear devices for peaceful purposes, it will be necessary to amend the relevant provisions of the Treaty, according to the procedure established therein.

[9] The Netherlands stated that Protocol I shall not be interpreted as prejudicing the position of the Netherlands as regards its recognition or non-recognition of the rights of or claims to sovereignty of the parties to the Treaty, or of the grounds on which such claims are made. With respect to nuclear explosions for peaceful purposes on the territory of Suriname and the Netherlands Antilles, no other rules apply than those operative for the parties to the Treaty. Upon Suriname's accession to independence on 25 November 1975, the obligations of the Netherlands under the Protocol apply only to the Netherlands Antilles.

[10] Nicaragua stated that it reserved the right to use nuclear energy for peaceful purposes such as the removal of earth for the construction of canals, irrigation works, power plants, and so on, as well as to allow the transit of atomic material through its territory.

[11] The Soviet Union signed and ratified Additional Protocol II with the following statement:

The Soviet Union proceeds from the assumption that the effect of Article 1 of the Treaty extends, as specified in Article 5 of the Treaty, to any nuclear explosive device and that, accordingly, the carrying out by any party to the Treaty of explosions of nuclear devices for peaceful purposes would be a violation of its obligations under Article 1 and would be incompatible with its non-nuclear status. For states parties to the Treaty, a solution to the problem of peaceful nuclear explosions can be found in accordance with the provisions of Article V of the NPT and within the framework of the international procedures of the IAEA. The signing of the Protocol by the Soviet Union does not in any way signify recognition of the possibility of the force of the Treaty as provided in Article 4(2) being extended beyond the territories of the states parties to the Treaty, including airspace and territorial waters as defined in accordance with international law. With regard to the reference in Article 3 of the Treaty to "its own legislation" in connection with the territorial waters, airspace and any other space over which the states parties to the Treaty exercise sovereignty, the signing of the Protocol by the Soviet Union does not signify recognition of their claims to the exercise of sovereignty which are contrary to generally accepted standards of international law. The Soviet Union takes note of the interpretation of the Treaty given in the Final Act of the Preparatory Commission for the Denuclearization of Latin America to the effect that the transport of nuclear weapons by the parties to the

Treaty is covered by the prohibitions envisaged in Article 1 of the Treaty. The Soviet Union reaffirms its position that authorizing the transit of nuclear weapons in any form would be contrary to the objectives of the Treaty, according to which, as specially mentioned in the preamble, Latin America must be completely free from nuclear weapons, and that it would be incompatible with the non-nuclear status of the states parties to the Treaty and with their obligations as laid down in Article 1 thereof.

Any actions undertaken by a state or states parties to the Tlatelolco Treaty which are not compatible with their non-nuclear status, and also the commission by one or more states parties to the Treaty of an act of aggression with the support of a state which, in possession of nuclear weapons or together with such a state, will be regarded by the Soviet Union as incompatible with the obligations of those countries under the Treaty. In such cases the Soviet Union reserves the right to reconsider its obligations under Protocol II. It further reserves the right to reconsider its attitude to this Protocol in the event of any actions on the part of other states possessing nuclear weapons which are incompatible with their obligations under the said Protocol. The provisions of the articles of Protocol II are applicable to the text of the Treaty for the Prohibition of Nuclear Weapons in Latin America in the wording of the Treaty at the time of the signing of the Protocol by the Soviet Union, due account being taken of the position of the Soviet Union as set out in the present statement. Any amendment to the Treaty entering into force in accordance with the provisions of Articles 29 and 6 of the Treaty without the clearly expressed approval of the Soviet Union shall have no force as far as the Soviet Union is concerned.

In addition, the Soviet Union proceeds from the assumption that the obligations under Protocol II also apply to the territories for which the status of the denuclearized zone is in force in conformity with Protocol I of the Treaty.

[12] When signing and ratifying Additional Protocol I and Additional Protocol II, the United Kingdom made the following declarations of understanding:

In connection with Article 3 of the Treaty, defining the term "territory" as including the territorial sea, airspace and any other space over which the state exercises sovereignty in accordance with "its own legislation", the UK does not regard its signing or ratification of the Additional Protocols as implying recognition of any legislation which does not, in its view, comply with the relevant rules of international law.

The Treaty does not permit the parties to carry out explosions of nuclear devices for peaceful purposes unless and until advances in technology have made possible the development of devices for such explosions which are not capable of being used for weapon purposes.

The signing and ratification by the UK could not be regarded as affecting in any way the legal status of any territory for the international relations of which the UK is responsible, lying within the limits of the geographical zone established by the Treaty.

Should a party to the Treaty carry out any act of aggression with the support of a nuclear weapon state, the UK would be free to reconsider the extent to which it could be regarded as committed by the provisions of Additional Protocol II.

In addition, the UK declared that its undertaking under Article 3 of Additional Protocol II not to use or threaten to use nuclear weapons against the parties to the Treaty extends also to territories in respect of which the undertaking under Article 1 of Additional Protocol I becomes effective.

[13] The United States signed and ratified Additional Protocol II with the following declarations of understanding:

In connection with Article 3 of the Treaty, defining the term "territory" as including the territorial sea, airspace and any other space over which the state exercises sovereignty in accordance with "its own legislation", the US ratification of the Protocol could not be regarded as implying recognition of any legislation which did not, in its view, comply with the relevant rules of international law.

Each of the parties retains exclusive power and legal competence, unaffected by the terms of the Treaty, to grant or deny non-parties transit and transport privileges.

As regards the undertaking not to use or threaten to use nuclear weapons against the parties, the United States would consider that an armed attack by a party, in which it was assisted by a nuclear weapon state, would be incompatible with the party's obligations under Article 1 of the Treaty.

The definition contained in Article 5 of the Treaty is understood as encompassing all nuclear explosive devices; Articles 1 and 5 of the Treaty restrict accordingly the activities of the parties under paragraph 1 of Article 18.

Article 18, paragraph 4 permits, and US adherence to Protocol II will not prevent, collaboration by the USA with the parties to the Treaty for the purpose of carrying out explosions of nuclear devices for peaceful purposes in a manner consistent with a policy of not contributing to the proliferation of nuclear weapon capabilities.

The United States will act with respect to such territories of Protocol I adherents, as are within the geographical area defined in Article 4, paragraph 2 of the Treaty, in the same manner as Protocol II requires it to act with respect to the territories of the parties.

[14] Venezuela stated that in view of the existing controversy between Venezuela on the one hand and the United Kingdom and Guyana on the other, Article 25, paragraph 2 of the Treaty should apply to Guyana. This paragraph provides that no political entity should be admitted, part or all of whose territory is the subject of a dispute or claim between an extra-continental country and one or more Latin American states, so long as the dispute has not been settled by peaceful means.

[15] Safeguards under the NPT cover the Treaty of Tlatelolco.

The Non-Proliferation Treaty

[1] On signing the Treaty, Australia stated, *inter alia*, that it regarded it as essential that the Treaty should not affect security commitments under existing treaties of mutual security.

[2] Notification of succession.

[3] On 25 November 1969, the United States notified its non-acceptance of notification of signature and ratification by the German Democratic Republic which it then did not recognize as a state. On 4 September 1974, the two countries established diplomatic relations with each other.

[4] On depositing the instrument of ratification, the Federal Republic of Germany reiterated the declaration made at the time of signing: it reaffirmed its expectation that the nuclear weapon states would intensify their efforts in accordance with the undertakings under Article VI of the Treaty, as well as its understanding that the security of FR Germany continued to be ensured by NATO; it stated that no provision of the Treaty may be interpreted in such a way as to hamper further development of European unification; that research, development and use of nuclear energy for peaceful purposes, as well as international and multinational co-operation in this field, must not be prejudiced by the Treaty; that the application of the Treaty, including the implementation of safeguards, must not lead to discrimination of the nuclear industry of FR Germany in international competition; and that it attached vital importance to the undertaking given by the United States and the United Kingdom concerning the application of safeguards to their peaceful nuclear facilities, hoping that other nuclear weapon states would assume similar obligations.

In a separate note, FR Germany declared that the Treaty will also apply to Berlin (West) without affecting Allied rights and responsibilities, including those relating to demilitarization. In notes of 24 July, 19 August, and 25 November 1975, respectively, addressed to the US Department of State, Czechoslovakia, the USSR and the German Democratic Republic stated that this declaration by FR Germany had no legal effect.

[5] On acceding to the Treaty, the Holy See stated, *inter alia*, that the Treaty will attain in full the objectives of security and peace and justify the limitations to which the states party to the Treaty submit, only if it is fully executed in every clause and with all its implications. This concerns not only the obligations to be applied immediately but also those which envisage a process of ulterior commitments. Among the latter, the Holy See considers it suitable to point out the following:

(*a*) The adoption of appropriate measures to ensure, on a basis of equality, that all non-nuclear weapon states party to the Treaty will have available to them the benefits deriving from peaceful applications of nuclear technology.

(*b*) The pursuit of negotiations in good faith on effective measures relating to cessation of the nuclear arms race at an early date and to nuclear disarmament, and on a treaty on general and complete disarmament under strict and effective international control.

[6] On signing the Treaty, Indonesia stated, *inter alia*, that the government of Indonesia attaches great importance to the declarations of the USA, the UK and the USSR affirming their intention to provide immediate assistance to any non-nuclear weapon state party to the Treaty that is a victim of an act of aggression in which nuclear weapons are used. Of utmost importance, however, is not the action *after* a nuclear attack has been committed but the guarantees to prevent such an attack. The Indonesian government trusts that the nuclear weapon states will study further this question of effective measures to ensure the security of the non-nuclear weapon states. On depositing the instrument of ratification, Indonesia expressed the hope that the nuclear countries would be prepared to co-operate with non-nuclear countries in the use of nuclear energy for peaceful purposes and implement the provisions of Article IV of the Treaty without discrimination. It also stated the view that the nuclear weapon states should observe the provisions of Article VI of the Treaty relating to the cessation of the nuclear arms race.

[7] Italy stated that in its belief nothing in the Treaty was an obstacle to the unification of the countries of Western Europe; it noted full compatibility of the Treaty with the existing security agreements; it noted further than when technological progress would allow the development of peaceful explosive devices different from nuclear weapons, the prohibition relating to their manufacture and use shall no longer apply; it interpreted the provisions of Article IX, paragraph 3 of the Treaty, concerning the definition of a military nuclear state, in the sense that it referred exclusively to the five countries which had manufactured and exploded a nuclear weapon or other nuclear explosive device prior to 1 January 1967, and stressed that under no circumstance would a claim of pertaining to such category be recognized by the Italian government to any other state.

[8] On depositing the instrument of ratification, Japan expressed the hope that France and China would accede to the Treaty; it urged a reduction of nuclear armaments and a comprehensive ban on nuclear testing; appealed to all states to refrain from the threat or use of force involving either nuclear or non-nuclear weapons; expressed the view that peaceful nuclear activities in non-nuclear weapon states party to the Treaty should not be hampered and that Japan should not be discriminated against in favour of other parties in any aspect of such activities. It also urged all nuclear weapon states to accept IAEA safeguards on their peaceful nuclear activities.

[9] A statement was made containing a disclaimer regarding the recognition of states party to the Treaty.

[10] On depositing the instrument of ratification, the Republic of Korea took note of the fact that the depositary governments of the three nuclear weapon states had made declarations in June 1968 to take immediate and effective measures to safeguard any non-nuclear weapon state which is a victim of an act or an object of a threat of aggression in which nuclear weapons are used. It recalled that the UN Security Council adopted a resolution to the same effect on 19 June 1968.

[11] On depositing the instruments of accession and ratification, Liechtenstein and Switzerland stated that activities not prohibited under Articles I and II of the Treaty include, in particular, the whole field of energy production and related operations, research and technology concerning future generations of nuclear reactors based on fission or fusion, as well as production of isotopes. Liechtenstein and Switzerland define the term "source or special fissionable material" in Article III of the Treaty as being in accordance with Article XX of the IAEA Statute, and a modification of this interpretation requires their formal consent; they will accept only such interpretations and definitions of the terms "equipment or material especially designed or prepared for the processing, use or production of special fissionable material", as mentioned in Article III of the Treaty, that they will expressly approve; and they understand that the application of the Treaty, especially of the control measures, will not lead to discrimination of their industry in international competition.

[12] On signing the Treaty, Mexico stated, *inter alia*, that none of the provisions of the Treaty shall be interpreted as affecting in any way whatsoever the rights and obligations of Mexico as a state party to the Treaty for the Prohibition of Nuclear Weapons in Latin America (Treaty of Tlatelolco).

It is the understanding of Mexico that at the present time any nuclear explosive device is capable of being used as a nuclear weapon and that there is no indication that in the near future it will be possible to manufacture nuclear explosive devices that are not potentially nuclear weapons. However, if technological advances modify this situation, it will be necessary to amend the relevant provisions of the Treaty in accordance with the procedure established therein.

[13] The ratification was accompanied by a statement in which Turkey underlined the non-proliferation obligations of the nuclear weapon states, adding that measures must be taken to meet adequately the security requirements of non-nuclear weapon states. Turkey also stated that measures developed or to be developed at national and international levels to ensure the non-proliferation of nuclear weapons should in no case restrict the non-nuclear weapon states in their option for the application of nuclear energy for peaceful purposes.

[14] The United Kingdom recalled its view that if a régime is not recognized as the government of a state, neither signature nor the deposit of any instrument by it, nor notification of any of those acts, will bring about recognition of that régime by any other state.

[15] This agreement, signed between the United Kingdom, Euratom and the IAEA, provides for the submission of British non-military nuclear installations to safeguards under IAEA supervision.

[16] Together with the notification by the USA that the statutory and constitutional requirements for the entry into force of the agreement for the application of safeguards to US civilian nuclear installations had been met, the IAEA received a list of facilities in the USA eligible to be safeguarded.

[17] In connection with the ratification of the Treaty, Yugoslavia stated, *inter alia*, that it considered a ban on the development, manufacture and use of nuclear weapons and the destruction of all stockpiles of these weapons to be indispensable for the maintenance of a stable peace and international security; it held the view that the chief responsibility for progress in this direction rested with the nuclear weapon powers, and expected these powers to undertake not to use nuclear weapons against the countries which have renounced them as well as against non-nuclear weapon states in general, and to refrain from the threat to use them. It also emphasized the significance it attached to the universality of the efforts relating to the realization of the NPT.

The Sea-Bed Treaty

[1] On signing the Treaty, Argentina stated that it interprets the references to the freedom of the high seas as in no way implying a pronouncement of judgement on the different positions relating to questions connected with international maritime law. It understands that the reference to the rights of exploration and exploitation by coastal states over their continental shelves was included solely because those could be the rights most frequently affected by verification procedures. Argentina precludes any possibility of strengthening, through this Treaty, certain positions concerning continental shelves to the detriment of others based on different criteria.

[2] On signing the Treaty, Brazil stated that nothing in the Treaty shall be interpreted as prejudicing in any way the sovereign rights of Brazil in the area of the sea, the sea-bed and the subsoil thereof adjacent to its coasts. It is the understanding of the Brazilian government that the word "observation", as it appears in paragraph 1 of Article III of the Treaty, refers only to observation that is incidental to the normal course of navigation in accordance with international law.

[3] In depositing the instrument of ratification Canada declared: Article I, paragraph 1 cannot be interpreted as indicating that any state has a right to implant or emplace any weapons not prohibited under Article I, paragraph 1 on the sea-bed and ocean floor, and in the subsoil thereof, beyond the limits of national jurisdiction, or as constituting any limitation on the principle that this area of the sea-bed and ocean floor and the subsoil thereof shall be reserved for exclusively peaceful purposes. Articles I, II and III cannot be interpreted as indicating that any state but the coastal state has any right to implant or emplace any weapon not prohibited under Article I, paragraph 1 on the continental shelf, or the subsoil thereof, appertaining to that coastal state, beyond the outer limit of the sea-bed zone referred to in Article I and defined in Article II. Article III cannot be interpreted as indicating any restrictions or limitation upon the rights of the coastal state, consistent with its exclusive sovereign rights with respect to the continental shelf, to verify, inspect or effect the removal of any weapon, structure, installation, facility or device implanted or emplaced on the continental shelf, or the subsoil thereof, appertaining to that coastal state, beyond the outer limit of the sea-bed zone referred to in Article I and defined in Article II. On 12 April 1976, the Federal Republic of Germany stated that the declaration by Canada is not of a nature to confer on the government of this country more far-reaching rights than those to which it is entitled under current international law, and that all rights existing under current international law which are not covered by the prohibitions are left intact by the Treaty.

[4] A statement was made containing a disclaimer regarding recognition of states party to the Treaty.

[5] On ratifying the Treaty, the Federal Republic of Germany declared that the Treaty will apply to Berlin (West).

[6] On the occasion of its accession to the Treaty, the government of India stated that as a coastal state, India has, and always has had, full and exclusive sovereign rights over the continental shelf adjoining its territory and beyond its territorial waters and the subsoil thereof. It is the considered view of India that other countries cannot use its continental shelf for military purposes. There cannot, therefore, be any restriction on, or limitation of, the sovereign right of India as a coastal state to verify, inspect, remove or destroy any weapon, device, structure, installation or facility, which might be implanted or emplaced on or beneath its continental shelf by any other country, or to take such other steps as may be considered necessary to safeguard its security. The accession by the government of India to the Sea-Bed Treaty is based on this position. In response to the Indian statement, the US government expressed the view that, under existing international law, the rights of coastal states over their continental shelves are exclusive only for purposes of exploration and exploitation of natural resources, and are otherwise limited by the 1958 Convention on the Continental Shelf and other principles of international law. On 12 April 1976, the Federal Republic of Germany stated that the declaration by India is not of a nature to confer on the government of this country more far-reaching rights than those to which it is entitled under current international law, and that

all rights existing under current international law which are not covered by the prohibitions are left intact by the Treaty.

[7] On signing the Treaty, Italy stated, *inter alia*, that in the case of agreements on further measures in the field of disarmament to prevent an arms race on the sea-bed and ocean floor and in their subsoil, the question of the delimitation of the area within which these measures would find application shall have to be examined and solved in each instance in accordance with the nature of the measures to be adopted. The statement was repeated at the time of ratification.

[8] Romania stated that it considered null and void the ratification of the Treaty by the Taiwan authorities.

[9] The United Kingdom recalled its view that if a régime is not recognized as the government of a state, neither signature nor the deposit of any instrument by it, nor notification of any of those acts, will being about recognition of that régime by any other state.

[10] Viet Nam stated that no provision of the Treaty should be interpreted in a way that would contradict the rights of the coastal states with regard to their continental shelf, including the right to take measures to ensure their security.

[11] On 25 February 1974, the Ambassador of Yugoslavia transmitted to the US Secretary of State a note stating that in the view of the Yugoslav government, Article III, paragraph 1 of the Treaty should be interpreted in such a way that a state exercising its right under this Article shall be obliged to notify in advance the coastal state, in so far as its observations are to be carried out "within the stretch of the sea extending above the continental shelf of the said state". On 16 January 1975, the US Secretary of State presented the view of the USA concerning the Yugoslav note, as follows: "Insofar as the note is intended to be interpretative of the Treaty, the United States cannot accept it as a valid interpretation. In addition, the United States does not consider that it can have any effect on the existing law of the sea". In so far as the note was intended to be a reservation to the Treaty, the United States placed on record its formal objection to it on the grounds that it was incompatible with the object and purpose of the Treaty. The United States also drew attention to the fact that the note was submitted too late to be legally effective as a reservation. A similar exchange of notes took place between Yugoslavia and the United Kingdom. On 12 April 1976, the Federal Republic of Germany stated that the declaration by Yugoslavia is not of a nature to confer on the government of this country more far-reaching rights than those to which it is entitled under current international law, and that all rights existing under current international law which are not covered by the prohibitions are left intact by the Treaty.

The BW Convention

[1] Considering the obligations resulting from its status as a permanently neutral state, Austria declares a reservation to the effect that its co-operation within the framework of this Convention cannot exceed the limits determined by the status of permanent neutrality and membership with the United Nations.

[2] In a statement made on the occasion of the signature of the Convention, India reiterated its understanding that the objective of the Convention is to eliminate biological and toxin weapons, thereby excluding completely the possibility of their use, and that the exemption in regard to biological agents or toxins, which would be permitted for prophylactic, protective or other peaceful purposes, would not in any way create a loophole in regard to the production or retention of biological and toxin weapons. Also any assistance which might be furnished under the terms of the Convention would be of a medical or humanitarian nature and in conformity with the Charter of the United Nations. The statement was repeated at the time of the deposit of the instrument of ratification.

[3] Ireland considers that the Convention could be undermined if reservations made by the parties to the 1925 Geneva Protocol were allowed to stand, as the prohibition of possession is incompatible with the right to retaliate, and that there should be an absolute and universal prohibition of the use of the weapons in question. Ireland notified the depositary government for the Geneva Protocol of the withdrawal of its reservations to the Protocol, made at the time of accession in 1930. The withdrawal applies to chemical as well as to bacteriological (biological) and toxin agents of warfare.

[4] The Republic of Korea stated that the signing of the Convention does not in any way mean or imply the recognition of any territory or régime which has not been recognized by the Republic of Korea as a state or government.

[5] In the understanding of Kuwait, its ratification of the Convention does not in any way imply its recognition of Israel, nor does it oblige it to apply the provisions of the Convention in respect of the said country.

[6] Mexico considers that the Convention is only a first step towards an agreement prohibiting also the development, production and stockpiling of all chemical weapons, and notes the fact that the Convention contains an express commitment to continue negotiations in good faith with the aim of arriving at such an agreement.

[7] The ratification by Switzerland contains the following reservations:

1. Owing to the fact that the Convention also applies to weapons, equipment or means of delivery designed to use biological agents or toxins, the delimitation of its scope of application can cause difficulties since there are scarcely any weapons, equipment or means of delivery peculiar to such use; therefore, Switzerland reserves the right to decide for itself what auxiliary means fall within that definition.

2. By reason of the obligations resulting from its status as a perpetually neutral state, Switzerland is bound to make the general reservation that its collaboration within the framework of this Convention cannot go beyond the terms prescribed by that status. This reservation refers especially to Article VII of the Convention as well as to any similar clause that could replace or supplement that provision of the Convention (or any other arrangement).

In a note of 18 August 1976, addressed to the Swiss Ambassador, the US Secretary of State stated the following view of the US government with regard to the first reservation: The prohibition would apply only to (*a*) weapons, equipment and means of delivery, the design of which indicated that they could have no other use than that specified, and (*b*) weapons, equipment and means of delivery, the design of which indicated that they were specifically intended to be capable of the use specified. The government of the United States shares the view of the government of Switzerland that there are few weapons, equipment or means of delivery peculiar to the uses referred to. It does not, however, believe that it would be appropriate, on this ground alone, for states to reserve unilaterally the right to decide which weapons, equipment or means of delivery fell within the definition. Therefore, while acknowledging the entry into force of the Convention between itself and the government of Switzerland, the United States government enters its objection to this reservation.

[8] The USSR stated that it considered the deposit of the instrument of ratification by Taiwan as an illegal act because the government of the Chinese People's Republic is the sole representative of China.

[9] The United Kingdom recalled its view that if a régime is not recognized as the government of a state, neither signature nor the deposit of any instrument by it nor notification of any of those acts will bring about recognition of that régime by any other state.

The ENMOD Convention

[1] Kuwait made the following reservation and understanding: This Convention binds Kuwait only towards states parties thereto; its obligatory character shall *ipso facto* terminate with respect to any hostile state which does not abide by the prohibition contained therein. It is understood that accession to this Convention does not mean in any way recognition of Israel by Kuwait; furthermore, no treaty relation will arise between Kuwait and Israel.

On 23 June 1980, the UN Secretary-General, the depositary of the Convention, received from the government of Israel a communication stating that Israel would adopt towards Kuwait an attitude of complete reciprocity.

[2] On signing the Convention, Turkey declared that the terms "widespread", "long-lasting" and "severe effects" contained in the Convention need to be more clearly defined, and that so long as this clarification was not made, Turkey would be compelled to interpret itself the terms in question and, consequently, reserved the right to do so as and when required. Turkey also stated its belief that the difference between "military or any other hostile purposes" and "peaceful purposes" should be more clearly defined so as to prevent subjective evaluations.

14. US–Soviet strategic arms limitation agreements

Treaty on the limitation of anti-ballistic missile systems (SALT ABM Treaty)

Signed at Moscow on 26 May 1972.
Entered into force on 3 October 1972.

Prohibits the deployment of ABM systems for the defence of the whole territory of the USA and the USSR or of an individual region, except as expressly permitted. Permitted ABM deployments are limited to two areas in each country—one for the defence of the national capital, and the other for the defence of some intercontinental ballistic missiles (ICBMs). No more than 100 ABM launchers and 100 ABM interceptor missiles may be deployed in each ABM deployment area. ABM radars should not exceed specified numbers and are subject to qualitative restrictions. National technical means of verification are to be used to provide assurance of compliance with the provisions of the Treaty.

The ABM Treaty is accompanied by agreed interpretations and unilateral statements made during the negotiations.

Interim Agreement on certain measures with respect to the limitation of strategic offensive arms (SALT I Interim Agreement)

Signed at Moscow on 26 May 1972.
Entered into force on 3 October 1972.

Provides for a freeze for a period of five years of the aggregate number of fixed land-based intercontinental ballistic missile launchers and ballistic missile launchers on modern submarines. The parties are free to choose the mix, except that conversion of land-based launchers for light ICBMs, or for ICBMs of older types, into land-based launchers for modern heavy ICBMs is prohibited. National technical means of verification are to be used to provide assurance of compliance with the provisions of the Agreement.

A protocol, which is an integral part of the Interim Agreement, specifies that the USA may have not more than 710 ballistic missile launchers on submarines and 44 modern ballistic missile submarines, while the USSR

may have not more than 950 ballistic missile launchers on submarines and 62 modern ballistic missile submarines. Up to those levels, additional ballistic missile launchers—in the USA over 656 launchers on nuclear-powered submarines and in the USSR over 740 launchers on nuclear-powered submarines, operational and under construction—may become operational as replacements for equal numbers of ballistic missile launchers of types deployed before 1964, or of ballistic missile launchers on older submarines.

The Interim Agreement is accompanied by agreed interpretations and unilateral statements made during the negotiations.

In September 1977 the USA and the USSR formally stated that, although the Interim Agreement was to expire on 3 October 1977, they intended to refrain from any actions incompatible with its provisions, or with the goals of the ongoing talks on a new agreement.

Agreement on basic principles of negotiations on the further limitation of strategic offensive arms

Signed at Washington on 21 June 1973.

Provides that the two powers will continue negotiations in order to work out a permanent agreement on more complete measures for the limitation of strategic offensive arms, as well as their subsequent reduction. Both powers will be guided by the recognition of each other's equal security interests and by the recognition that efforts to obtain unilateral advantage, directly or indirectly, would be inconsistent with the strengthening of peaceful relations between the USA and the USSR. The limitations placed on strategic offensive weapons could apply both to their quantitative aspects as well as to their qualitative improvement. Limitations on strategic offensive arms must be subject to adequate verification by national technical means. The modernization and replacement of strategic offensive arms would be permitted under conditions formulated in the agreements to be concluded. Pending a permanent agreement, both sides are prepared to reach agreements on separate measures to supplement the SALT Interim Agreement of 26 May 1972. Each power will continue to take necessary organizational and technical measures for preventing accidental or unauthorized use of nuclear weapons under its control in accordance with the Nuclear Accidents Agreement of 30 September 1971.

Protocol to the Treaty on the limitation of anti-ballistic missile systems (see above)

Signed at Moscow on 3 July 1974.
Entered into force on 25 May 1976.

Provides that each party shall be limited to a single area for deployment of anti-ballistic missile systems or their components instead of two such areas as allowed by the SALT ABM Treaty (see above). Each party will have the right to dismantle or destroy its ABM system and the components thereof in the area where they were deployed at the time of signing the Protocol and to deploy an ABM system or its components in the alternative area permitted by the ABM Treaty, provided that, before starting construction, notification is given during the year beginning on 3 October 1977 and ending on 2 October 1978, or during any year which commences at five-year intervals thereafter, those being the years for periodic review of the ABM Treaty. This right may be exercised only once. The deployment of an ABM system within the area selected shall remain limited by the levels and other requirements established by the ABM Treaty.

Joint US–Soviet Statement on the question of further limitations of strategic offensive arms (Vladivostok Agreement)

Signed in the area of Vladivostok on 24 November 1974.

States that a new US–Soviet agreement on the limitation of strategic offensive arms will incorporate the relevant provisions of the SALT Interim Agreement of 26 May 1972 and will cover the period from October 1977 to 31 December 1985. Based on the principle of equality and equal security, it will include the following limitations: both powers will be entitled to have a certain agreed aggregate number of strategic delivery vehicles and to have a certain agreed aggregate number of intercontinental ballistic missiles (ICBMs) and submarine-launched ballistic missiles (SLBMs) equipped with multiple independently targetable warheads. The Agreement will include a provision for further negotiations beginning no later than 1980–81 on the question of further limitations and possible reductions of strategic arms after 1985.

Soviet Statement on the Backfire bomber

Handed, on 16 June 1979, by the Soviet President to the US President.

The USSR informs the USA that the Soviet 'Tu-22M' aircraft, called 'Backfire' in the USA, is a medium-range bomber. The Soviet Union does not intend to give this bomber an intercontinental capability and will not increase its radius of action to enable it to strike targets on US territory. It also pledges to limit the production of the Backfire to the current (1979) rate.

Treaty on the limitation of strategic offensive arms (SALT II Treaty)

Signed at Vienna on 18 June 1979.
Not in force by 31 December 1980.

Sets, for both parties, an initial ceiling of 2 400 on intercontinental ballistic missile (ICBM) launchers, submarine-launched ballistic missile (SLBM) launchers, heavy bombers, and air-to-surface ballistic missiles capable of a range in excess of 600 kilometres (ASBMs). This ceiling will be lowered to 2 250 and the lowering must begin on 1 January 1981, while the dismantling or destruction of systems which exceed that number must be completed by 31 December 1981. A sublimit of 1 320 is imposed upon each party for the combined number of launchers of ICBMs and SLBMs equipped with multiple independently targetable re-entry vehicles (MIRVs), ASBMs equipped with MIRVs, and aeroplanes equipped for long-range (over 600 kilometres) cruise missiles. Moreover, each party is limited to a total of 1 200 launchers of MIRVed ICBMs and SLBMs, and MIRVed ASBMs, and of this number no more than 820 may be launchers of MIRVed ICBMs. A freeze is introduced on the number of re-entry vehicles on current types of ICBMs, with a limit of 10 re-entry vehicles on the one new type of ICBM allowed each side, a limit of 14 re-entry vehicles on SLBMs and a limit of 10 re-entry vehicles on ASBMs. An average of 28 long-range air-launched cruise missiles (ALCMs) per heavy bomber is allowed, while current heavy bombers may carry no more than 20 ALCMs each. Ceilings are established on the throw-weight and launch-weight of light and heavy ICBMs. There are bans: on the testing and deployment of new types of ICBMs, with one exception for each side; on building additional fixed ICBM launchers; on converting fixed light ICBM launchers into heavy ICBM launchers; on heavy mobile ICBMs, heavy SLBMs, and heavy ASBMs; on surface-ship ballistic missile launchers; on systems to launch missiles from the sea-bed or the beds of internal waters; as well as on systems for delivery of nuclear weapons from Earth orbit, including fractional orbital missiles. National technical means will be used to verify compliance. Any interference with such means of verification, or any deliberate concealment measures which impede verification, are prohibited. The Treaty is to remain in force until 31 December 1985.

The parties also signed a series of agreed statements and common understandings clarifying their obligations under particular articles of the Treaty and of the Protocol to the Treaty (see below).

Protocol to the Treaty on the limitation of strategic offensive arms

Signed at Vienna on 18 June 1979.
Not in force by 31 December 1980.

Bans until 31 December 1981: the deployment of mobile ICBM launchers or the flight-testing of ICBMs from such launchers; the deployment (but not the flight-testing) of long-range cruise missiles on sea-based or land-based launchers; the flight-testing of long-range cruise missiles with multiple warheads from sea-based or land-based launchers; and the flight-testing or deployment of ASBMs. The Protocol is an integral part of the Treaty.

Memorandum of understanding between the USA and the USSR regarding the establishment of a data base on the numbers of strategic offensive arms

Signed at Vienna on 18 June 1979.

States that the parties have agreed, for the purposes of the SALT II Treaty, on the number of arms in each of the 10 categories of strategic offensive weapons limited by the Treaty, as of 1 November 1978. In separate statements of data, each party declares that it possesses the stated number of strategic offensive arms subject to the Treaty limitations as of the date of signature of the Treaty (18 June 1979).

Joint Statement of principles and basic guidelines for subsequent negotiations on the limitation of strategic arms

Signed at Vienna on 18 June 1979.

States that the parties will pursue the objectives of significant and substantial reductions in the numbers of strategic offensive arms, qualitative limitations on these arms, and resolution of the issues included in the Protocol to the SALT II Treaty. To supplement national technical means of verification, the parties may employ, as appropriate, co-operative measures.

15. The prohibition of inhumane and indiscriminate weapons

Square-bracketed numbers, thus [1], *refer to the list of references on page* 456.

I. Introduction

The laws of war and international humanitarian law have developed over the past century in two broad streams: restrictions on targets ("targetry") and restrictions on weapons ("weaponry"). During the period 1968–77 a major effort was made to reaffirm and develop international humanitarian law applicable in armed conflict, with both these broad streams brought together in a single process of negotiation.[1] With the encouragement of the United Nations General Assembly, but without at that stage the direct involvement of the UN itself, this process went forward first at expert level, culminating in four Conferences of Government Experts convened by the International Committee of the Red Cross (ICRC) in Geneva, 1971 and 1972; in Lucerne, 1974; and in Lugano, 1976. Into these sessions were introduced the findings and concerns not only of governments but also of non-governmental organizations, including SIPRI, and of expert consultants retained by the World Health Organization. From 1974 to 1977 the process was parallelled at the higher level of intergovernmental negotiation, in the Diplomatic Conference on the Reaffirmation and Development of International Humanitarian Law Applicable in Armed Conflicts, which was held in Geneva under the auspices of the Swiss Government and ran to four sessions.[2]

The final product of this process was the opening for signature, in Bern on 12 December 1977, of two Additional Protocols to the Geneva Conventions of 1949. The Additional Protocols of 1977 deal with the protection of victims respectively of international armed conflict (Protocol I) and armed conflict not of an international character (Protocol II), it being understood that only large-scale hostilities between entities willing and

[1] 1968 is a convenient starting-point as far as the UN is concerned, because of its Teheran Conference for International Human Rights Year and the follow-up resolution [1] of the same year in the General Assembly. Outside the UN *strictu senso*, however, the International Committee of the Red Cross had long recognized that the humanitarian enterprise must now encompass both streams, and had been pressing more particularly since 1955 for a new international agreement [2a].

[2] The two Geneva conferences had the broader mandate "Reaffirmation and development of the international humanitarian law applicable to armed conflicts", while the Lucerne and Lugano conferences were concerned with "Weapons that may cause unnecessary suffering or have indiscriminate effects" or "Use of certain conventional weapons". For an historical summary see reference [3a].

able to honour their obligations under the laws of war are the subject of Protocol II.

However, the content of these Additional Protocols was exclusively[3] concerned with the 'targetry' stream of restrictions, which had proved more amenable to negotiation in the Diplomatic Conference of 1974–77 than had 'weaponry'.

The question of restrictions on "certain conventional weapons", which had been the subject of the ICRC Conferences of Government Experts at Lucerne and Lugano, was referred by the Diplomatic Conference to an Ad Hoc Committee on Conventional Weapons. By the time the Diplomatic Conference ended, this committee was still some way from reaching agreement on any 'weaponry' restrictions. Accordingly, in Resolution 22, which it adopted on 9 June 1977, the Diplomatic Conference noted the main possibilities for restriction which its Ad Hoc Committee on Conventional Weapons had considered, listed these in the preamble in such a way as to indicate which ones it thought the most fruitful to pursue and which less likely to be agreed, and recommended that the UN General Assembly pursue these possibilities in a separate conference under UN auspices.[4]

The General Assembly accepted this recommendation of the Diplomatic Conference and, on 19 December 1977 [5], resolved that a UN Conference on Specific Conventional Weapons should be held in 1979, preceded by a preparatory conference. The preparatory conference held two sessions, in 1978 and 1979, and the UN conference another two sessions (since one proved insufficient for agreement to be reached) from 10 to 28 September 1979 and from 15 September to 10 October 1980.

Various abbreviated terms were used to give a name to this conference on "inhumane weapons", "wicked weapons", "dirty weapons", and so on. Its full title was long and derived from General Assembly Resolution 32/152, which called it

> a United Nations conference with a view to reaching agreement on prohibitions or restrictions on the use of specific conventional weapons, including those which may be deemed to be excessively injurious or have indiscriminate effects, taking into account humanitarian and military considerations, and on the question of a system of periodic review of the matter and for the consideration of further proposals. [5]

Just over half the states in the world were represented at some stage of these negotiations at Geneva, although the attendance declined steadily: 85 states attended the preparatory conference, 81 attended the first session of the UN conference, and 76 attended the second session.

[3] With the exception of certain articles reaffirming general principles, e.g. Article 35 (*Basic rules*) in Protocol I which provides that "in any armed conflict, the right of the Parties to the conflict to choose methods or means of warfare is not unlimited" and that "it is prohibited to employ weapons, projectiles and material and methods of warfare of a nature to cause superfluous injury or unnecessary suffering".

[4] Resolution 22 is reproduced in reference [4a].

II. Convention and protocols

The Final Act of the UN conference was adopted on 10 October 1980 and a convention and protocols were forwarded to the UN General Assembly for commendation (see appendices 15A–15D). Entry into force requires 20 states to have ratified or acceded.

It was Mexico which originally, at the preparatory conference, tabled an 'umbrella treaty' or 'framework convention' as the instrument under which specific agreements should be subsumed [6]. This proposal looked to the adoption of successively more far-reaching restrictions and provided a means for cumulative progress in this area, as well as economizing on final clauses and other general provisions by avoiding the need to repeat them in each prohibition. Having begun to find favour at the preparatory conference, the umbrella-treaty concept was taken up by the UK and the Netherlands 12 months later. Their joint draft of 1979 [7] provided the basis for the eventual convention.

Three specific protocols were also agreed, in the first instance, and the form of the convention is such that more can be added in the future. The initiative for review, amendment or addition to the convention or its protocols, or for the negotiation of further restrictions, can come from the UN General Assembly, the UN Disarmament Commission, the Committee on Disarmament, or any 18 states parties to the convention. Although indicated only tangentially, at the end of the preamble to the convention, this flexibility of procedure represents a diplomatic breakthrough of some potential significance, further discussed in section III.

Protocol on non-detectable fragments (Protocol I)

The one concrete achievement of the first (1979) session of the UN conference was agreement among all 81 participating states that there should be an outright prohibition of the use, whether against civilians or against combatants, of weapons (such as plastic-coated bombs) intended to injure by means of dispersing fragments not detectable in the human body by X-ray. This single-sentence prohibition was carried forward to the 1980 session where, without further discussion, it was adopted as a protocol. Only 26 words in length, it must be one of the most concise expressions ever formulated of an international legal norm.

The principle invoked here was that of excessive injury, and the criterion that of primary effect. This was a clear case of medical and humanitarian considerations being allowed, for once, to outweigh any argument for the military advantages of keeping enemy casualties *hors de combat* for longer. In the celebrated phrase of the 1868 Declaration of St Petersburg, "the necessities of war ought to yield to the demands of humanity".

It must, however, be regretted that a comprehensive ban on the use of fragmentation weapons as such was not attainable at this juncture. Several non-governmental organizations (NGOs) had campaigned for many years to persuade governments to ban not just plastic but also metallic fléchettes discharged at high velocity from 'claymore' or 'pineapple' bombs. Using the criteria of indiscriminacy and excessive injury together, NGOs and sympathetic governments may be expected to press for the extension of this protocol to embrace fléchettes regardless of the material used.

Protocol on prohibitions or restrictions on the use of mines, booby-traps and other devices (Protocol II)

The notion that "treacherous" weapons fall foul of the laws of war is well established, but its detailed specification required considerable effort on the part of the conference since some of the norms invoked involve fine distinctions—as, it might be argued, does the traditional prohibition of *perfidy* but not of *ruses de guerre* in international law up to and including the 'targetry' protocols of 1977.[5]

In the course of the Diplomatic Conference of 1974–77 the UK, with strong support from the Netherlands, proposed restrictions on landmines and booby-traps; a draft treaty co-sponsored by the UK, the Netherlands and France was tabled.[6] A high degree of consensus on what these restrictions should be was achieved at the first session of the UN conference, in 1979, but Yugoslavia in particular was unhappy with the provision for notifying the location of minefields to enemy forces still in occupation of part of the national territory.[7] This aspect of the problem required further negotiation at the 1980 session, in the course of which Yugoslavia received support, understandably in the light of their experience of foreign occupation following invasion, from Cyprus and from Egypt. The revised text recognizes these sensitivities: publication of records is only required upon the termination of occupation by enemy forces, and the emphasis is placed instead on the obligation to keep full and accurate records of minefields and other deployments of the weapons in question.

The protocol eventually agreed prohibits the use on land of mines and booby-traps against civilian populations and their indiscriminate use

[5] Bailey [2b] notes "the near impossibility of distinguishing between a 'ruse of war', which is permitted under the Hague Regulations (Article 24), and to 'kill or wound treacherously', which are among the acts 'especially prohibited' (Article 23b)"; he comments that "A more precise rule is needed on this".

[6] "A great deal of attention was paid" to this proposal at the Lugano experts' conference in 1976 [3b].

[7] The reservation made by the Yugoslav delegation is noted in reference [8].

against enemy combatants. It also requires the location of minefields, mines and booby-traps to be recorded, in order to diminish the danger of accidental injury to civilians. Not only civilians have suffered, as witness the deaths and other casualties sustained by soldiers of the United Nations Disengagement Observer Force among the minefields left on the Golan Heights from the Israeli–Syrian war of 1973: this explains the provisions of Article 8, designed expressly for the protection of UN forces and missions from minefields, mines and booby-traps. Mines are defined as any munitions placed under, on or near the ground or other surface area and designed to be detonated or exploded by the presence, proximity or contact of a person or vehicle. Remotely delivered mines are those delivered by artillery, rocket, mortar or similar means, or dropped from an aircraft. Booby-traps are defined as any devices or materials designed, constructed or adapted to kill or injure, and which function unexpectedly when a person disturbs or approaches an apparently harmless object or performs an apparently safe act. Other devices covered by this protocol are defined as manually emplaced munitions and devices designed to kill, injure or damage which are activated by remote control or automatically after a lapse of time.

The use of mines, remotely delivered mines, booby-traps and other devices against the civilian population as such, or against individual civilians, is prohibited in all circumstances, whether in offence or defence or even as reprisals. Also prohibited is the indiscriminate use of these devices against military objectives in conditions which may be expected to cause incidental loss of civilian life, injury to civilians, damage to civilian objects, or a combination of these outcomes excessive in relation to the concrete and direct military advantage anticipated. Booby-traps designed to cause superfluous injury or unnecessary suffering are prohibited in all circumstances.

The protocol also contains guide-lines for the recording (for eventual notification) of the location of pre-planned minefields, mines and booby-traps, and provides for international co-operation in their removal in the last of its nine intricately drafted articles.

Protocol on prohibitions or restrictions on the use of incendiary weapons (Protocol III)

This protocol on protection of civilians was agreed as a second-best formula, after it became clear towards the end of the conference that consensus could not be reached on a general prohibition of the use of incendiary weapons in war. The aim of Mexico, Sweden and Switzerland, in particular, with widespread support, had been to secure a complete ban on the use of napalm and other especially injurious or indiscriminate weapons in this category.[8] However, military considerations proved too strong for the humanitarian argument to prevail. The proponents of a complete ban are able only to point to a consensus that consideration of the question of evolving rules for the protection of combatants from incendiary warfare shall be resumed in the course of follow-up to the conference. It is not specified however, when, where, or by whom precisely this will be considered afresh.

The central principle of the protocol is that the use of incendiary weapons against civilians is prohibited. This immunity of the civilian population is, however, qualified in several respects. For example, military objectives which are situated within populated areas but which are nevertheless clearly separated from concentrations of civilians are excluded from the restriction in respect of incendiary weapons delivered otherwise than from the air. The protocol does provide that, in the event of such an attack, all feasible precautions are to be taken to limit the incendiary effects to the military objective concerned and to minimize (and, if possible, avoid altogether) incidental loss of civilian life, injury to civilians and damage to civilian objects. However, the definition of 'feasible precautions' invokes both humanitarian and military considerations in such terms as to seem to rob the provision of much of its substantive significance.

The protocol also, at the initiative of the Soviet Union, prohibits incendiary attacks on forests and other plant cover, except in cases where these are used as camouflage or for concealment of combatants or are themselves military objectives.

It is difficult to assess the degree of protection that this protocol will afford in practice, since so much must depend upon the way in which its provisions are translated into field manuals and operating procedures within armed forces. In defining the incendiary weapons with which it deals, the protocol adopts the criterion of primary intention. It therefore excludes from its scope those munitions which may have incidental incendiary effects. These include smoke, tracers, illuminants and signalling systems. It also excludes from the purview of its restrictions on use those munitions which are designed to combine penetration, blast or fragmentation effects with an additional incendiary effect. Examples of such munitions would be armour-piercing projectiles, fragmentation shells, explosive bombs and similar combined-effects munitions in which the incendiary effect is not specifically intended to cause burn injury to persons but is designed to set fire to military objectives, such as armoured vehicles,

[8] "The use of incendiary weapons is prohibited" was the categorical first clause of the draft proposal submitted to the Preparatory Conference by these three countries together with Austria, Egypt, Ghana, Jamaica, Romania, Sudan, Yugoslavia and Zaire. Mexico and Jamaica also wanted combined-effect munitions included in the prohibition [9].

aircraft and military installations or facilities (rather than to people inside them).

Such a notional distinction may smell to many of pedantry, or even casuistry. About the only thing which can be said in favour of this criterion of the main intended effect, and it is not much, is that, like the classification of napalm as an incendiary rather than a chemical weapon (on the somewhat macabre grounds that it kills more people by burning than by asphyxiation), it makes possible piecemeal and limited prohibitions which some governments might otherwise be even more wary of concluding for fear of depriving themselves unwittingly of more than they had bargained for.

The most glaring deficiency of the protocol, however, must be its failure to restrict in any way the use of even the most injurious incendiary weapons against combatants. It is a far cry from the erstwhile recognition in customary international law of incendiary weapons as falling under the same interdict as chemical weapons. The failure to get beyond a limited protection of civilians in 1980 demonstrates all too clearly how hard it will be to restore this long-broken link and subject incendiary weapons to a comparable ban while they remain militarily attractive for "close air support" against military objectives (other than those now subject to the Protocol III restrictions).

Provisions of the convention

Most problems in the diplomacy of arms control and disarmament treaties have to do with verification and scope. (The protracted negotiations for a comprehensive prohibition of chemical weapons [10] provide a good example.)

To this pattern the Convention on Specific Conventional Weapons offers a total contrast. There are no provisions for verification, complaint or even consultation in handling suspicions of non-compliance with obligations; several delegations did, however, announce their intention of pursuing the idea of adding subsequent provision for a Consultative Committee of Experts to handle suspicions and allegations of non-compliance. As for scope, Article 1 applies the convention and its annexed protocols to the situations referred to in Article 2 common to the Geneva Conventions of 1949, including those described in Article 1 of Additional Protocol I, signed in 1977, which defines the scope of the international humanitarian law applicable in armed conflict.

The convention allows for review and amendment, requires the dissemination of its provisions to the armed forces of the parties, and permits denunciation of the convention or any of its protocols on one year's notice in time of peace or after the end of armed conflict or occupation in time of war. To enter into force for any party, its acceptance of the convention must be accompanied by acceptance of at least two (any two) of its protocols. The Secretary-General of the United Nations is designated as Depositary.

Exclusions and disappointments

The significance of the new convention and protocols is severely, some would say crucially, limited by the deliberate exclusion of nuclear weapons from the negotiations, as indeed from the major effort of 1968–77 which produced the 'targetry' restrictions of the 1977 protocols additional to the Geneva Conventions of 1949. The other types of weapons of mass destruction were also excluded from consideration.

The other most important negative point that must be made about the 1980 agreement is that it leaves the use of incendiary weapons against combatants as unrestricted as before, while even the protection of civilians against incendiary attack is left incomplete. The hope that there would be a ban on the use in war of napalm and at least some other types of incendiary weapon, if not incendiary weapons as an entire class, has been referred to subsequent consideration with no certainty that it will be fulfilled; yet this was the category of conventional weapons most prominently identified, for example, in UN and SIPRI reports of the early 1970s, as "inhumane" and urgently in need of prohibition [11–13].

It is also a cause for disappointment that no agreement could be reached on the prohibition of certain small-calibre projectiles. Modern developments in rifle ammunition have produced bullets whose action is widely considered to cause excessive injury and thereby to meet one of the criteria for prohibition. The prohibition of flattening and expanding bullets adopted in the Hague Declaration[9] of 1899 (the 'dum-dum' rule) has been seen as an expression of the same principle, and any reaffirmation and progressive development of international legal norms might reasonably have been expected to succeed in placing the small-calibre projectiles in question in the category of excessively injurious weapons.

That this has not happened is due in part to the inability of the relevant wound-ballistics experts to agree on just how injurious to human tissue particular types of ammunition are, and in part (it will be widely believed) to the reluctance of military authorities to forgo the possibility of equipping their respective armies with 'superior' firepower. The shallowness of such an argument is readily demonstrated once it is recalled that the same soldier whose confidence is supposedly to be boosted by being equipped

[9] Declaration IV.3, signed at The Hague on 29 July 1899, the text of which is reproduced in reference [4b].

with the ammunition in question is also liable to suffer the aggravated wounds inflicted by enemy use of comparably destructive ammunition.

It may be indicative of a certain loss of momentum in 1979–80, compared with the Lucerne–Lugano period, that the most lively controversy at the UN conference regarding small-calibre projectiles in 1979 turned on the issue of whether the next Gothenburg symposium on wound ballistics should receive UN sponsorship, as desired by the Swedish delegation.[10] At the final, 1980 session Sweden kept the question of prohibition alive through an informal working group of interested delegations. There will be another Gothenburg symposium on wound ballistics in 1981, and the original proposal made in 1978 by Mexico, Sweden and Zaire may eventually be revived [15].[11]

Another, if less widely shared, cause for disappointment is that no restriction was placed on fuel–air explosives. The case for considering these to be excessively injurious or, alternatively, analogous to the category of projectiles for the diffusion of deleterious gases which was also prohibited in 1899,[12] was set out by SIPRI [3]. There was, however, too little acceptance of these arguments in governmental circles for fuel–air explosives to be taken on to the agenda for restriction or prohibition; the draft prohibition tabled in 1978 by Mexico, Sweden and Switzerland has since received only perfunctory attention.[13]

III. Follow-up to the conference

Much will now turn on the prospects for energetic follow-up of the UN conference by those concerned to make further advances in the categories of 'weaponry' with which it started to deal: for example, extending the ban on incendiary weapons to give more complete protection to civilians and provide some restrictions on their use against combatants, extending

[10] Although opposition to formal UN sponsorship of the Gothenburg symposium proved insuperable, the conference did adopt a resolution submitted by Egypt, Ireland, Jamaica, Mexico, Sweden, Switzerland and Uruguay which "welcomes the announcement that an international scientific symposium on wound ballistics will be held at Gothenburg, Sweden, in late 1980 or in 1981; and [in a further revision to the text] hopes that the results will be made available to the UN Disarmament Commission, the Committee on Disarmament and other interested fora" [14].

[11] Among its conclusions was a proposal for "a new rule or understanding ensuring that the weapons developments in this field do not bring more severe injuries than those connected with the traditional standard weapons in this category".

[12] Declaration IV.2, signed at The Hague on 29 July 1899, the text of which is reproduced in reference [4b].

[13] The proposed agreement was "to abstain from the use of munitions which rely for their effects on shock waves caused by the detonation of a cloud created by a substance spread in the air, except when the aim is exclusively to destroy material objects, such as the clearance of mine fields" [16].

the ban on non-detectable fragmentation weapons to cover metallic fléchettes as well, and adding further protocols on small-calibre projectiles and, conceivably, fuel–air explosives. This process may well be facilitated by the indirect effects which the UN conference and its precursors have had upon governmental thinking in the realm of military planning. There is already some evidence of 'voluntary restraint' in the procurement of new rifle ammunition (e.g., the M-16) which may be attributable in part to the lengthy discussions of possible restrictions on small-calibre projectiles. Similarly, future use of land-mines may be influenced in the direction of restraint by the conference's agreement to an explanatory text, and further discussions should be the easier for states having come this far. There is also ample room for consultative procedures to be negotiated to strengthen the whole regime.

The prospects for such follow-up are brighter than they appeared to be in 1979, when the UN conference at its first session was riven with disagreement over the role (if any) to be allowed to the Committee on Disarmament in this regard. It was pointed out earlier that the flexibility of procedure eventually enshrined in the follow-up provisions of the new convention represents a diplomatic breakthrough of some significance. This is because the increasingly unrealistic distinction (jealously guarded in the past by diplomats and lawyers of a rather conservative disposition) between the international realm of disarmament and the international realm of the laws of war has now been laid to rest, with the Committee on Disarmament formally recognized as one of four sources from which proposals may properly be received for the further development of prohibitions and restraints in war. Eventually one may hope for a measure of parallelism or integration, in respect of the work done if not of the institutions through which it is done, so that these two formerly separate realms may give each other some positive reinforcement. Regimes of disarmament and of non-use may come to be seen as mutually supportive in the hitherto generally neglected area of conventional weapons, just as in the area of weapons of mass destruction the Biological Weapons Convention of 1972 and the long-sought chemical weapons convention in the realm of disarmament are already seen as complementary to the regime of CBW non-use, represented by the Geneva Protocol of 1925 and the corresponding norm of international customary law.[14]

[14] The principle of complementarity referred to in this paragraph is more fully expounded in reference [17], and is alluded to in the ninth preambular paragraph of the convention agreed in 1980: "*Wishing* to prohibit or restrict further the use of certain conventional weapons and believing that the positive results achieved in this area may facilitate the main talks on disarmament with a view to putting an end to the production, stockpiling and proliferation of such weapons".

IV. Conclusions

Modest though their significance must be judged to be in the total context of world armaments and warfare, the agreements of 1980 represent a solid achievement and one which had long proved elusive: indeed, it looked like continuing to elude the negotiators until the United States and the Soviet Union were persuaded to join in the emergent consensus on the banning of air-delivered incendiary weapons in populated areas, as the UN conference, already running a year behind schedule, entered its final fortnight. Seen in that narrower context of repeated disappointment and despondency, there is some reason for modest gratification over the extent of the October 1980 agreements.

No one could pretend that all use of weapons which cause unnecessary suffering or excessive injury, or have indiscriminate effects, has now been prevented; or that the intentions of the Hague Conferences of 1899 and 1907 (when the aim of the *maux superflus* criterion "was not primarily to spare civilians, but to avoid causing suffering to combatants in excess of what is essential to place an adversary *hors de combat*" [2c]) have been fulfilled. There is now a precise framework within which further advances on this humanitarian front can be made. The UN Conference of 1979–80 has provided the appropriate legal instruments and categories, of which fuller use can henceforth be made. The 'weaponry' area of restrictions need no longer lag behind that of 'targetry', and this will be incidentally of service to the latter: for in terms of legal analysis and state practice, the discrepancy between the two areas or streams of law has long been a source of weakness. Using more traditional categories (which it should be said do not correspond perfectly to the distinction between 'targetry' and 'weaponry' restrictions), Bailey and Pictet have pointed out that: "One difficulty of securing full implementation of the Law of Geneva is that the Law of The Hague is so out of date . . . 'belligerents necessarily consider this law as a single whole, and the inadequacy of the [Hague] rules relating to the conduct of hostilities has a negative impact on the observance of the Geneva Conventions.' " [2a]. At least there is now no institutional reason why both streams of law should not develop *pari passu* and in a mutually supportive relationship.

It remains to be seen how rapidly the new convention with its protocols enters into force. In the meantime, it behoves all states and other potential parties to armed conflict to recall the principle made famous by the Russian jurist Martens. The 'Martens clause' was inserted into the preambles to the Hague Conventions of 1899 and 1907 (and is paraphrased in the fifth preambular paragraph of the new convention):

Until a more complete code of the laws of war has been issued, the High Contracting Parties deem it expedient to declare that, in cases not included in the Regulations adopted by them, the inhabitants and the belligerents remain under the protection and the rule of the principles of the law of nations, as they result from the usages established among civilised peoples, from the laws of humanity and the dictates of the public conscience.

References

1. UN General Assembly Resolution 2444 (XXIII), 19 December 1968.
2. Bailey, S. D., *Prohibitions and Restraints in War* (Oxford University Press for the Royal Institute of International Affairs, London, 1972).
   (a) —, p. 75, quoting J. Picket, *Review of the International Commission of Jurists*, March 1969, p. 8.
   (b) —, p. 101.
   (c) —, p. 79.
3. *Anti-personnel Weapons* (Taylor & Francis, London, 1978, Stockholm International Peace Research Institute).
   (a) —, chapter 9, pp. 211–67.
   (b) —, p. 233.
4. *Arms Control: A Survey and Appraisal of Multilateral Agreements* (Taylor & Francis, London, 1978, Stockholm International Peace Research Institute).
   (a) —, pp. 137–38.
   (b) —, p. 54.
5. UN General Assembly Resolution 32/152.
6. UN document A/CONF.95/PREP.CONF./L.8, 11 September 1978.
7. UN document A/CONF.95/CW/WG.1/L.1, 12 September 1979.
8. UN document A/CONF.95/6 (*Report of the Committee of the Whole*), paragraph 7, 28 September 1979.
9. UN document A/CONF.95/PREP.CONF./L.1, 8 September 1978.
10. *Chemical Weapons: Destruction and Conversion, Current Disarmament Problems* (Taylor & Francis, London, 1980, Stockholm International Peace Research Institute), p. 4.
11. *Napalm and other Incendiary Weapons and all aspects of their possible use: Report of the Secretary-General* (United Nations, New York, 1973).
12. *Napalm and Incendiary Weapons: A SIPRI Interim Report* (Almqvist & Wiksell, Stockholm, 1972, Stockholm International Peace Research Institute).
13. *Incendiary Weapons* (Almqvist & Wiksell, Stockholm, 1975, Stockholm International Peace Research Institute).
14. UN document A/CONF.95/CW/L.2/Rev.1, 27 September 1979.
15. UN document A/CONF.95/PREP.CONF./L.3 (*Working paper on certain small calibre weapons and projectiles*), 11 September 1978.
16. UN document A/CONF.95/PREP.CONF./L.2/Rev.1, 11 September 1978.
17. Sims, N. A., *Approaches to Disarmament* (QPS, London, 1979), pp. 95–97.

Appendix 15A

Draft Convention on the prohibition or restrictions of the use of certain conventional weapons which may be deemed to be excessively injurious or to have indiscriminate effects

THE HIGH CONTRACTING PARTIES,

RECALLING that every State has the duty, in conformity with the Charter of the United Nations, to refrain in its international relations from the threat or use of force against the sovereignty, territorial integrity or political independence of any State, or in any other manner inconsistent with the purposes of the United Nations,

FURTHER RECALLING the general principle of the protection of the civilian population against the effects of hostilities,

BASING THEMSELVES on the principle of international law that the right of the parties to an armed conflict to choose methods or means of warfare is not unlimited, and on the principle that prohibits the employment in armed conflicts of weapons, projectiles and material and methods of warfare of a nature to cause superfluous injury or unnecessary suffering,

ALSO RECALLING that it is prohibited to employ methods or means of warfare which are intended, or may be expected, to cause widespread, long-term and severe damage to the natural environment,

CONFIRMING THEIR DETERMINATION that in cases not covered by this Convention or by other international agreements, the civilian population and the combatants shall at all times remain under the protection and authority of the principles of international law derived from established custom, from the principles of humanity and from the dictates of public conscience,

DESIRING to contribute to international détente, the ending of the arms race and the building of confidence among States, and hence to the realization of the aspiration of all peoples to live in peace,

RECOGNIZING the importance of pursuing every effort which may contribute to progress towards general and complete disarmament under strict and effective international control,

REAFFIRMING the need to continue the codification and progressive development of the rules of international law applicable in armed conflict,

WISHING to prohibit or restrict further the use of certain conventional weapons and believing that the positive results achieved in this area may facilitate the main talks on disarmament with a view to putting an end to the production, stockpiling and proliferation of such weapons,

EMPHASIZING the desirability that all States become parties to this Convention and its annexed Protocols, especially the militarily significant States,

BEARING IN MIND that the General Assembly of the United Nations and the United Nations Disarmament Commission may decide to examine the question of a possible broadening of the scope of the prohibitions and restrictions contained in this Convention and its annexed Protocols,

FURTHER BEARING IN MIND that the Committee on Disarmament may decide to consider the question of adopting further measures to prohibit or restrict the use of certain conventional weapons,

HAVE AGREED as follows:

ARTICLE 1 *Scope of application*

This Convention and its annexed Protocols shall apply in the situations referred to in Article 2 common to the Geneva Conventions of 12 August 1949 for the Protection of War Victims, including any situation described in paragraph 4 of Article 1 of Additional Protocol I to these Conventions.

ARTICLE 2 *Relations with other international agreements*

Nothing in this Convention or its annexed Protocols shall be interpreted as detracting from other obligations imposed upon the High Contracting Parties by international humanitarian law applicable in armed conflict.

ARTICLE 3 *Signature*

This Convention shall be open for signature by all States at United Nations Headquarters in New York for a period of twelve months from 10 April 1981.

ARTICLE 4 *Ratification, acceptance, approval or accession*

1. This Convention is subject to ratification, acceptance or approval by the Signatories. Any State which has not signed this Convention may accede to it.
2. The instruments of ratification, acceptance, approval or accession shall be deposited with the Depositary.
3. Expressions of consent to be bound by any of the Protocols annexed to this Convention shall be optional for each State, provided that at the time of the deposit of its instrument of ratification, acceptance or approval of this Convention or of accession thereto, that State shall notify the Depositary of its consent to be bound by any two or more of these Protocols.
4. At any time after the deposit of its instrument of ratification, acceptance or approval of this Convention or of accession thereto, a State may notify the Depositary of its consent to be bound by any annexed Protocol by which it is not already bound.
5. Any Protocol by which a High Contracting Party is bound shall for that Party form an integral part of this Convention.

ARTICLE 5 *Entry into force*

1. This Convention shall enter into force six months after the date of deposit of the twentieth instrument of ratification, acceptance, approval or accession.
2. For any State which deposits its instrument of ratification, acceptance, approval or accession after the date of the deposit of the twentieth instrument of ratification, acceptance, approval or accession, this Convention shall enter into force six months after the date on which that State has deposited its instrument of ratification, acceptance, approval or accession.
3. Each of the Protocols annexed to this Convention shall enter into force six months after the date by which twenty States have notified their consent to be bound by it in accordance with paragraph 3 or 4 or Article 4.
4. For any State which notifies its consent to be bound by a Protocol annexed to this Convention after the date by which twenty States have notified their consent to be bound by it, the Protocol shall enter into force six months after the date on which that State has notified its consent so to be bound.

ARTICLE 6 *Dissemination*

The High Contracting Parties undertake, in time of peace as in time of armed conflict, to disseminate this Convention and those of its annexed Protocols by which they are bound as widely as possible in their respective countries and, in particular, to include the study thereof in their programmes of military instruction, so that those instruments may become known to their armed forces.

ARTICLE 7 *Treaty relations upon entry into force of this Convention*

1. When one of the parties to a conflict is not bound by an annexed Protocol, the parties bound by this Convention and that annexed Protocol shall remain bound by them in their mutual relations.

2. Any High Contracting Party shall be bound by this Convention and any Protocol annexed thereto which it has accepted, in any situation contemplated by Article 1, in relation to any State which is not a party to this Convention or bound by the relevant annexed Protocol, if the latter accepts and applies this Convention or the relevant Protocol, and so notifies the Depositary.

3. The Depositary shall immediately inform the High Contracting Parties concerned of any notification received under this Article.

4. This Convention, and the annexed Protocols by which a High Contracting Party is bound, shall apply with respect to an armed conflict against that High Contracting Party of the type referred to in Article 1, paragraph 4, of Additional Protocol I to the Geneva Conventions of 12 August 1949 for the Protection of War Victims:

(a) where the High Contracting Party is also a party to Additional Protocol I and an authority referred to in Article 96, paragraph 3, of that Protocol has undertaken to apply the Geneva Conventions and Protocol I in accordance with Article 96, paragraph 3, of the said Protocol, and undertakes to apply this Convention and the relevant annexed Protocols in relation to that conflict; or

(b) where the High Contracting Party is not a party to Additional Protocol I and an authority of the type referred to in sub-paragraph (a) above accepts and applies the obligations of the Geneva Conventions and of this Convention and the relevant annexed Protocols in relation to that conflict. Such an acceptance and application shall have in relation to that conflict the following effects:

(i) the Geneva Conventions and this Convention and its relevant annexed Protocols are brought into force for the parties to the conflict with immediate effect;

(ii) the said authority assumes the same rights and obligations as those which have been assumed by a High Contracting Party to the Geneva Conventions, this Convention and its relevant annexed Protocols; and

(iii) the Geneva Conventions, this Convention and its relevant annexed Protocols are equally binding upon all parties to the conflict.

The authority and the High Contracting Party may also agree to accept and apply the obligations of Additional Protocol I to the Geneva Conventions on a reciprocal basis.

ARTICLE 8 *Review and amendments*

1. (a) At any time after the entry into force of this Convention any High Contracting Party may propose amendments to this Convention or any annexed Protocol by which it is bound. Any proposal for an amendment shall be communicated to the Depositary, who shall notify it to all the High Contracting Parties and shall seek their views on whether a conference should be convened to consider the proposal. If a majority, that shall not be less than 18, of the High Contracting Parties so agree, he shall promptly convene a conference to which all High Contracting Parties shall be invited. States not parties to this Convention shall be invited to the conference as observers.

(b) Such a conference may agree upon amendments which shall be adopted and shall enter into force in the same manner as this Convention and the annexed Protocols, provided that amendments to this Convention may be adopted only by the High Contracting Parties and that amendments to a specific annexed Protocol may be adopted only by the High Contracting Parties which are bound by that Protocol.

2. (a) At any time after the entry into force of this Convention any High Contracting Party may propose additional protocols relating to other categories of conventional weapons not covered by the existing annexed Protocols. Any such proposal for an additional protocol shall be communicated to the Depositary, who shall notify it to all the High Contracting Parties in accordance with sub-paragraph 1(a) of this Article. If a majority, that shall not be less than 18, of the High Contracting Parties so agree, the Depositary shall promptly convene a conference to which all States shall be invited.

(b) Such a conference may agree, with the full participation of all States represented at the conference, upon additional protocols which shall be adopted in the same manner as this Convention, shall be annexed thereto and shall enter into force as provided in paragraphs 3 and 4 of Article 5.

3. (a) If, after a period of ten years following the entry into force of this Convention, no conference has been convened in accordance with sub-paragraph 1(a) or 2(a) of this Article, any High Contracting Party may request the Depositary to convene a conference to which all High Contracting Parties shall be invited to review the scope and operation of this Convention and the Protocols annexed thereto and to consider any proposal for amendments of this Convention or of the existing Protocols. States not parties to this Convention shall be invited as observers to the conference. The conference may agree upon amendments which shall be adopted and enter into force in accordance with sub-paragraph 1(b) above.

(b) At such a conference consideration may also be given to any proposal for additional protocols relating to other categories of conventional weapons not covered by the existing annexed Protocols. All States represented at the conference may participate fully in such consideration. Any additional protocols shall be adopted in the same manner as this Convention, shall be annexed thereto and shall enter into force as provided in paragraphs 3 and 4 of Article 5.

(c) Such a conference may consider whether provision should be made for the convening of a further conference at the request of any High Contracting Party if, after a similar period to that referred to in sub-paragraph 3(a) of this Article, no conference has been convened in accordance with sub-paragraph 1(a) or 2(a) of this Article.

ARTICLE 9 *Denunciation*

1. Any High Contracting Party may denounce this Convention or any of its annexed Protocols by so notifying the Depositary.

2. Any such denunciation shall only take effect one year after receipt by the Depositary of the notification of denunciation. If, however, on the expiry of that year the denouncing High Contracting Party is engaged in one of the situations referred to in Article 1, the Party shall continue to be bound by the obligations of this Convention and of the relevant annexed Protocols until the end of the armed conflict or occupation and, in any case, until the termination of operations connected with the final release, repatriation or re-establishment of the persons protected by the rules of international law applicable in armed conflict, and in the case of any annexed Protocol containing provisions concerning situations in which peace-keeping, observation or similar functions are performed by United Nations forces or missions in the area concerned, until the termination of those functions.

3. Any denunciation of this Convention shall be considered as also applying to all annexed Protocols by which the denouncing High Contracting Party is bound.

4. Any denunciation shall have effect only in respect of the denouncing High Contracting Party.

5. Any denunciation shall not affect the obligations already incurred, by reason of an armed conflict, under this Convention and its annexed Protocols by such denouncing High Contracting Party in respect of any act committed before this denunciation becomes effective.

ARTICLE 10 *Depositary*

1. The Secretary-General of the United Nations shall be the Depositary of this Convention and of its annexed Protocols.

2. In addition to his usual functions, the Depositary shall inform all States of:

(a) signatures affixed to this Convention under Article 3;

(b) deposits of instruments of ratification, acceptance or approval of or accession to this Convention deposited under Article 4;

(c) notifications of consent to be bound by annexed Protocols under Article 4;

(d) the dates of entry into force of this Convention and of each of its annexed Protocols under Article 5; and

(e) notifications of denunciation received under Article 9 and their effective date.

ARTICLE 11 *Authentic texts*

The original of this Convention with the annexed Protocols, of which the Arabic, Chinese, English, French, Russian and Spanish texts are equally authentic, shall be deposited with the Depositary, who shall transmit certified true copies thereof to all States.

Source: UN document A/CONF.95/DC/CRP.3, 10 October 1980.

Appendix 15B

Draft Protocol concerning non-detectable fragments (Protocol I)

It is prohibited to use any weapon the primary effect of which is to injure by fragments which in the human body escape detection by X-rays.

Source: UN document A/CONF.95/14/Add.2, 10 October 1980.

Appendix 15C

Draft Protocol on prohibitions or restrictions on the use of mines, booby-traps and other devices (Protocol II)

ARTICLE 1 *Material scope of application*

This Protocol relates to the use on land of the mines, booby-traps and other devices defined herein, including mines laid to interdict beaches, waterway crossings or river crossings, but does not apply to the use of anti-ship mines at sea or in inland waterways.

ARTICLE 2 *Definitions*

For the purpose of this Protocol:

1. "Mine" means any munition placed under, on or near the ground or other surface area and designed to be detonated or exploded by the presence, proximity or contact of a person or vehicle, and "remotely delivered mine" means any mine so defined delivered by artillery, rocket, mortar or similar means or dropped from an aircraft.

2. "Booby-trap" means any device or material which is designed, constructed or adapted to kill or injure and which functions unexpectedly when a person disturbs or approaches an apparently harmless object or performs an apparently safe act.

3. "Other devices" means manually-emplaced munitions and devices designed to kill, injure or damage and which are actuated by remote control or automatically after a lapse of time.

4. "Military objective" means, so far as objects are concerned, any object which by its nature, location, purpose or use makes an effective contribution to military action and whose total or partial destruction, capture or neutralization, in the circumstances ruling at the time, offers a definite military advantage.

5. "Civilian objects" are all objects which are not military objectives as defined in paragraph 4.

6. "Recording" means a physical, administrative and technical operation designed to obtain, for the purpose of registration in the official records, all available information facilitating the location of minefields, mines and booby-traps.

ARTICLE 3 *General restrictions on the use of mines, booby-traps and other devices*

1. This Article applies to:
(a) mines;
(b) booby-traps; and
(c) other devices.

2. It is prohibited in all circumstances to direct weapons to which this Article applies, either in offence, defence or by way of reprisals, against the civilian population as such or against individual civilians.

3. The indiscriminate use of weapons to which this Article applies is prohibited. Indiscriminate use is any placement of such weapons:
(a) which is not on, or directed at, a military objective; or
(b) which employs a method or means of delivery which cannot be directed at a specific military objective; or
(c) which may be expected to cause incidental loss of civilian life, injury to civilians, damage to civilian objects, or a combination thereof, which would be excessive in relation to the concrete and direct military advantage anticipated.

4. All feasible precautions shall be taken to protect civilians from the effects of weapons to which this Article applies. Feasible precautions are those precautions which are practicable or practically possible taking into account all circumstances ruling at the time, including humanitarian and military considerations.

ARTICLE 4 *Restrictions on the use of mines other than remotely delivered mines, booby-traps and other devices in populated areas*

1. This Article applies to:
(a) mines other than remotely delivered mines;
(b) booby-traps; and
(c) other devices.

2. It is prohibited to use weapons to which this Article applies in any city, town, village or other area containing a similar concentration of civilians in which combat between ground forces is not taking place or does not appear to be imminent, unless either:
(a) they are placed on or in the close vicinity of a military objective belonging to or under the control of an adverse party; or
(b) measures are taken to protect civilians from their effects, for example, the posting of warning signs, the posting of sentries, the issue of warnings or the provision of fences.

ARTICLE 5 *Restrictions on the use of remotely delivered mines*

1. The use of remotely delivered mines is prohibited unless such mines are only used within an area which is itself a military objective or which contains military objectives, and unless:
(a) their location can be accurately recorded in accordance with Article 7(1)(a); or
(b) an effective neutralizing mechanism is used on each such mine, that is to say, a self-actuating mechanism which is designed to render a mine harmless or cause it to destroy itself when it is anticipated that the mine will no longer serve the military purpose for which it was placed in position, or a remotely-controlled mechanism which is designed to render harmless or destroy a mine when the mine no longer serves the military purpose for which it was placed in position.

2. Effective advance warning shall be given of any delivery or dropping of remotely delivered mines which may affect the civilian population, unless circumstances do not permit.

ARTICLE 6 *Prohibition on the use of certain booby-traps*

1. Without prejudice to the rules of international law applicable in armed conflict relating to treachery and perfidy, it is prohibited in all circumstances to use:
(a) any booby-trap in the form of an apparently harmless portable object which is specifically designed and constructed to contain explosive material and to detonate when it is disturbed or approached, or
(b) booby-traps which are in any way attached to or associated with:
(i) internationally recognized protective emblems, signs or signals;
(ii) sick, wounded or dead persons;
(iii) burial or cremation sites or graves;
(iv) medical facilities, medical equipment, medical supplies or medical transportation;
(v) children's toys or other portable objects or products specially designed for the feeding, health, hygiene, clothing or education of children;
(vi) food or drink;

(vii) kitchen utensils or appliances except in military establishments, military locations or military supply depots;
(viii) objects clearly of a religious nature;
(ix) historic monuments, works of art or places of worship which constitute the cultural or spiritual heritage of peoples;
(x) animals or their carcasses.

2. It is prohibited in all circumstances to use any booby-trap which is designed to cause superfluous injury or unnecessary suffering.

ARTICLE 7 *Recording and publication of the location of minefields, mines and booby-traps*

1. The parties to a conflict shall record the location of:
(a) all pre-planned minefields laid by them; and
(b) all areas in which they have made large-scale and pre-planned use of booby-traps.

2. The parties shall endeavour to ensure the recording of the location of all other minefields, mines and booby-traps which they have laid or placed in position.

3. All such records shall be retained by the parties who shall:
(a) immediately after the cessation of active hostilities:
(i) take all necessary and appropriate measures, including the use of such records, to protect civilians from the effects of minefields, mines and booby-traps; and either
(ii) in cases where the forces of neither party are in the territory of the adverse party, make available to each other and to the Secretary-General of the United Nations all information in their possession concerning the location of minefields, mines and booby-traps in the territory of the adverse party; or
(iii) once complete withdrawal of the forces of the parties from the territory of the adverse party has taken place, make available to the adverse party and to the Secretary-General of the United Nations all information in their possession concerning the location of minefields, mines and booby-traps in the territory of the adverse party;
(b) when a United Nations force or mission performs functions in any area, make available to the authority mentioned in Article 8 such information as is required by that Article;
(c) whenever possible, by mutual agreement, provide for the release of information concerning the location of minefields, mines and booby-traps, particularly in agreements governing the cessation of hostilities.

ARTICLE 8 *Protection of United Nations forces and missions from the effects of minefields, mines and booby-traps*

1. When a United Nations force or mission performs functions of peacekeeping, observation or similar functions in any area, each party to the conflict shall, if requested by the head of the United Nations force or mission in that area, as far as it is able:
(a) remove or render harmless all mines or booby-traps in that area;
(b) take such measures as may be necessary to protect the force or mission from the effects of minefields, mines and booby-traps while carrying out its duties; and
(c) make available to the head of the United Nations force or mission in that area, all information in the party's possession concerning the location of minefields, mines and booby-traps in that area.

2. When a United Nations fact-finding mission performs functions in any area, any party to the conflict concerned shall provide protection to that mission except where, because of the size of such mission, it cannot adequately provide such protection. In that case it shall make available to the head of the mission the information in its possession concerning the location of minefields, mines and booby-traps in that area.

ARTICLE 9 *International co-operation in the removal of minefields, mines and booby-traps*

After the cessation of active hostilities, the parties shall endeavour to reach agreement, both among themselves and, where appropriate, with other States and with international organizations, on the provision of information and technical and material assistance—including, in appropriate circumstances, joint operations—necessary to remove or otherwise render ineffective minefields, mines and booby-traps placed in position during the conflict.

Technical Annex to the Protocol on Prohibitions or Restrictions on the Use of Mines, Booby-traps and Other Devices (Protocol II)

Guidelines on Recording

Whenever an obligation for the recording of the location of minefields, mines and booby-traps arises under the Protocol, the following guidelines shall be taken into account.

1. With regard to pre-planned minefields and large-scale and pre-planned use of booby-traps:

(a) maps, diagrams or other records should be made in such a way as to indicate the extent of the minefield or booby-trapped area; and

(b) the location of the minefield or booby-trapped area should be specified by relation to the co-ordinates of a single reference point and by the estimated dimensions of the area containing mines and booby-traps in relation to that single reference point.

2. With regard to other minefields, mines and booby-traps laid or placed in position:

In so far as possible, the relevant information specified in paragraph 1 above should be recorded so as to enable the areas containing minefields, mines and booby-traps to be identified.

Source: UN document A/CONF.95/14/Add.3, 10 October 1980.

Appendix 15D

Draft Protocol on prohibitions or restrictions on the use of incendiary weapons (Protocol III)

ARTICLE 1 *Definitions*

For the purpose of this Protocol:

1. "Incendiary weapon" means any weapon or munition which is primarily designed to set fire to objects or to cause burn injury to persons through the action of flame, heat, or a combination thereof, produced by a chemical reaction of a substance delivered on the target.

   (a) Incendiary weapons can take the form of, for example, flame throwers, fougasses, shells, rockets, grenades, mines, bombs and other containers of incendiary substances.

   (b) Incendiary weapons do not include:

      (i) Munitions which may have incidental incendiary effects, such as illuminants, tracers, smoke or signalling systems;

      (ii) Munitions designed to combine penetration, blast or fragmentation effects with an additional incendiary effect, such as armour-piercing projectiles, fragmentation shells, explosive bombs and similar combined-effects munitions in which the incendiary effect is not specifically designed to cause burn injury to persons, but to be used against military objectives, such as armoured vehicles, aircraft and installations or facilities.

2. "Concentration of civilians" means any concentration of civilians, be it permanent or temporary, such as in inhabited parts of cities, or inhabited towns or villages, or as in camps or columns of refugees or evacuees, or groups of nomads.

3. "Military objective" means, so far as objects are concerned, any object which by its nature, location, purpose or use makes an effective contribution to military action and whose total or partial destruction, capture or neutralization, in the circumstances ruling at the time, offers a definite military advantage.

4. "Civilian objects" are all objects which are not military objectives as defined in paragraph 3.

5. "Feasible precautions" are those precautions which are practicable or practically possible taking into account all circumstances ruling at the time, including humanitarian and military considerations.

ARTICLE 2 *Protection of civilians and civilian objects*

1. It is prohibited in all circumstances to make the civilian population as such, individual civilians or civilian objects the object of attack by incendiary weapons.

2. It is prohibited in all circumstances to make any military objective located within a concentration of civilians the object of attack by air-delivered incendiary weapons.

3. It is further prohibited to make any military objective located within a concentration of civilians the object of attack by means of incendiary weapons other than air-delivered incendiary weapons, except when such military objective is clearly separated from the concentration of civilians and all feasible precautions are taken with a view to limiting the incendiary effects to the military objective and to avoiding, and in any event to minimizing, incidental loss of civilian life, injury to civilians and damage to civilian objects.

4. It is prohibited to make forests or other kinds of plant cover the object of attack by incendiary weapons except when such natural elements are used to cover, conceal or camouflage combatants or other military objectives, or are themselves military objectives.

Source: UN document A/CONF.95/14/Add.4, 10 October 1980.

Appendix 15E

Resolution on small-calibre weapon systems

Adopted by the Conference at its 7th plenary meeting, 23 September 1979

THE UNITED NATIONS CONFERENCE ON PROHIBITIONS OR RESTRICTIONS OF USE OF CERTAIN CONVENTIONAL WEAPONS,

RECALLING United Nations General Assembly resolution 32/152 of 19 December 1977,

AWARE of the continuous development of small-calibre weapon systems (i.e., arms and projectiles),

ANXIOUS to prevent an unnecessary increase of the injurious effects of such weapon systems,

RECALLING the agreement embodied in The Hague Declaration of 29 July 1899, to abstain, in international armed conflict, from the use of bullets which expand or flatten easily in the human body,

CONVINCED that it is desirable to establish accurately the wounding effects of current and new generations of small-calibre weapon systems including the various parameters that affect the energy transfer and the wounding mechanism of such systems,

1. *Takes note* with appreciation of the intensive research carried out nationally and internationally in the area of wound ballistics, in particular relating to small-calibre weapon systems, as documented during the Conference;

2. *Considers* that this research and the international discussion on the subject has led to an increased understanding of the wounding effects of small-calibre weapon systems and of the parameters involved;

3. *Believes* that such research, including testing of small-calibre weapon systems, should be continued with a view to developing standardized assessment methodology relative to ballistic parameters and medical effects of such systems;

4. *Invites* Governments to carry out further research, jointly or individually, on the wounding effects of small-calibre weapon systems and to communicate, where possible, their findings and conclusions;

5. *Welcomes* the announcement that an international scientific symposium on wound ballistics will be held in Gothenburg, Sweden, in late 1980 or in 1981, and hopes that the results of the symposium will be made available to the United Nations Disarmament Commission, the Committee on Disarmament and other interested fora;

6. *Appeals* to all Governments to exercise the utmost care in the development of small-calibre weapon systems, so as to avoid an unnecessary escalation of the injurious effects of such systems.

16. The role of the United Nations in the field of disarmament

Square-bracketed numbers, thus [1], *refer to the list of references on page* 478.

I. Introduction

In the Final Document of the first Special Session of the General Assembly Devoted to Disarmament, held in 1978, the members of the United Nations affirmed that the UN "has a central role and primary responsibility in the sphere of disarmament". The United Nations, accordingly, should actively promote disarmament; it should facilitate and encourage all disarmament measures—unilateral, bilateral, regional or multilateral—and be kept duly informed of disarmament initiatives outside its aegis, without prejudice to the progress of negotiations [1a].

This concept of the UN disarmament role is based on the recognition of the fact that disarmament, in the nuclear age, stands at the heart of any solution to the problem of international order and security. As the General Assembly stated in its Final Document, the existing stockpiles of weapons, in particular nuclear weapons, the constant build-up of arms and armed forces and the endless competition for qualitative superiority posed incalculable threats to peace and, indeed, to the very survival of mankind. Hence, it is imperative that international peace and security be sought through arms reductions within the framework of the United Nations, where all countries are represented and can play an active role.

The Secretary-General of the United Nations referred in 1978 to four main functions which the United Nations should perform in the discharge of its responsibilities in the field of disarmament. First, the United Nations must continue to provide a forum in which disarmament can be given the necessary prominence on the international agenda. Second, it should be a focal point for disarmament deliberations, that is to say, for setting the goals to be achieved and imparting a sense of direction to the multilateral negotiating process, a process the "pace, direction and priorities" of which should be influenced, more than in the past, by contributions coming from all sides and not only from the major nuclear weapon powers. Third, it should serve as a major source of information on disarmament, develop a programme of studies oriented to specific disarmament and security goals and to that end conduct research as necessary. Fourth, it should use its capacity, "which has not yet been fully exploited", to supervise arms limitation and disarmament agreements, by assisting in their follow-up and implementation. It is in this context that the present and potential effectiveness of the United Nations on disarmament matters should be viewed [2a].

The question has received considerable attention in recent years. In 1975, for instance, the General Assembly established an *Ad Hoc* Committee to Review the Role of the United Nations in the Field of Disarmament for the purpose of strengthening that role, thereby making it more closely related to current needs. The Committee recommendations, which were endorsed by the General Assembly in 1976, represented a first step towards the desired goals, namely: more effective procedures and organization of work to enable the United Nations to exercise its full role in multilateral disarmament efforts; improvement of the UN facilities for the collection, compilation and dissemination of information on disarmament issues; and strengthening of the resources of the UN Secretariat to enable it to provide assistance as required at all stages of the disarmament process. One of the results of the *Ad Hoc* Committee's review and recommendations was the establishment, early in 1977, of the Centre for Disarmament as the executive arm of the UN Secretary-General in all disarmament-related matters [3].

Further and bigger steps were taken at the Special Session of the General Assembly Devoted to Disarmament, when the UN member states agreed, by consensus, on principles for disarmament and on priorities for a programme of action. It was also decided to revitalize the disarmament machinery and make it more representative.

II. Deliberative and negotiating bodies

On the question of machinery, the General Assembly, at the Special Session, started from the premise that, while the decisive factor for achieving real measures of disarmament was the "political will" of states, especially nuclear weapon states, an effective international disarmament machinery was also necessary. Further, the Assembly held that there should be two kinds of disarmament bodies—deliberative and negotiating. All member states should be represented in the former, whereas the latter, although representative in character, should, for the sake of efficiency, have a relatively small membership.

Concerning the deliberative bodies, it was decided at the Special Session that (*a*) the General Assembly should remain the main deliberative organ of the United Nations on disarmament matters and the First (Political) Committee of the Assembly should henceforth deal solely with questions of disarmament and related international security questions; and (*b*) the reactivated Disarmament Commission, composed of all the members of the United Nations, should act as the Assembly's sub-subsidiary intersessional deliberative organ.

As for the negotiating body—the very core of the delicately balanced disarmament mechanism—it was agreed at the Special Session that there would be a single multilateral disarmament negotiating forum open to the participation of the five nuclear weapon states and 32 to 35 non-nuclear weapon states; that it would conduct its business by consensus; and that it would submit a report to the General Assembly annually, or more frequently if appropriate.

The Committee on Disarmament, the negotiating body that emerged from the Special Session, has been in existence for more than two years and has settled down to work in accordance with the mandate contained in the Final Document. The Committee is composed of the five nuclear weapon states, who for the first time find themselves together at the disarmament negotiating table, and 35 other states representing all geographical regions and political groupings. Twenty-one of the 35 members of the Committee do not belong to either of the two major alignments.

In 1979, at its first session, the Committee on Disarmament adopted its rules of procedure, an agenda and a programme of work. As agreed at the Special Session, the rules of procedure have established that the Committee will conduct its work and adopt its decisions by consensus, on substantive as well as procedural matters.

Will the new set-up help in making progress towards disarmament? The United Nations experience of the past 35 years tends to prove that it has not been the lack of appropriate machinery that has stood in the way of disarmament agreements. Over the years, numerous bodies with a variety of flexible procedures, which fully reflect the needs of the situation, have been established to deal with disarmament. The real question has been one of how and for what purpose the available resources would be utilized. When the problem is seen in these terms, inevitably the answer is that, in the last analysis, machinery "can only be as effective as national policies permit" [2b]. Of course, the weight of national policies is being felt more and more as the disarmament process advances from identification of the problems towards negotiations.

III. Deliberations on disarmament

The General Assembly has been rather successful in identifying the problems as they have arisen and in making appropriate recommendations on them. Some of the Assembly resolutions represent real landmarks in the deliberative process. This is true, for instance, of the very first resolution of the General Assembly, adopted on 24 June 1946, calling for the use of atomic energy exclusively for peaceful purposes, the elimination from national armaments of atomic weapons and all other weapons adaptable to mass destruction, the establishment of an effective system of inspection against violations and evasions, and the exchange of information on atomic energy for peaceful purposes for the benefit of all nations. Another of these landmarks was the first General Assembly resolution on general and complete disarmament, adopted on 20 November 1959, which recognized that the question of general and complete disarmament "is the most important one facing the world today". Equally significant were the numerous Assembly resolutions which prepared the ground for the negotiations of the Treaty on the Non-Proliferation of Nuclear Weapons (NPT), and the many resolutions calling for a comprehensive nuclear test ban, a goal that has been pursued by the international community for more than two decades. These are just a few examples from nearly 400 resolutions on disarmament matters adopted by the General Assembly since the founding of the United Nations in 1945. Of these, more than 250 were adopted in the last 10 years, 122 in the last three years alone.

Given the vast and increasing number of issues dealt with by the General Assembly over the years, particularly since the beginning of the 1970s, it would be illusory to pretend that its recommendations on disarmament are the result of a well co-ordinated plan or of a single concept. The deliberative process would gain significantly if efforts were made to bring into it a greater clarity and precision and if the main issues, particularly those related to the arms race, were kept sharply in focus. Also, there is need for streamlining the process by reducing as much as possible, through consolidation, the number of items on the disarmament agenda and the number of resolutions. A vast number of recommendations does not necessarily indicate productivity on the part of the disarmament machinery. On the other hand, the adoption of relatively few clear-cut decisions by the General Assembly on key priority issues would greatly increase the effectiveness of the deliberative process and help to strengthen the General Assembly's ability to influence the course of the disarmament negotiations.

The attainment of such a goal, it is increasingly felt, could be facilitated if the Secretary-General were to present annually, at the request of the General Assembly, a report surveying and assessing world developments on armaments, disarmament and their impact on international security. The task would pose complex and delicate problems, given the present limited availability of information on armaments and military expenditures. Undoubtedly, the problems would be much greater than those encountered in the preparation of other UN periodical publications, for instance, the World Economic Survey and the Report on the World Social Situation. It should, nonetheless, be possible for the Secretary-General, without recourse to highly technical arguments, to call attention to major events and trends and to current and newly emerging problems, so as to provide the General Assembly with a point of reference and a basis for its deliberations on disarmament.

Full advantage should also be taken of the preparations for the second Special Session of the General Assembly Devoted to Disarmament, to be held in 1982, to move closer to the goal of starting a real process of reduction in the present level of armaments. At the first Special Session, a consensus was reached on principles, priorities and machinery for disarmament. The second Special Session offers an opportunity to build on that foundation. That opportunity should not be missed, even though developments since 1978 have not been encouraging.

One way to build on the foundation of the first Special Session would be to focus attention on *how* the arms race can be stopped. Hardly any attempt has been made so far to determine what is really meant by the expression "stopping the arms race". Attention should be given, in particular, to ensuring that the adoption of limited measures of disarmament will not simply deflect the arms race in other directions.

If this were done, the way would be open for the adoption of a concrete programme of action. As to the contents of such a programme, it may be possible to adopt at the next Special Session a comprehensive programme which would provide a general framework for long-range negotiations. This should in no way preclude, however, the simultaneous adoption of a limited and realistic short-range programme to give substance to the recommendation, in paragraph 1 of the Final Document of the first Special Session, for a gradual but effective process of disarmament beginning with a reduction in the present level of armaments.

IV. Negotiating disarmament

The most significant aspect of the provision of the Final Document dealing with the negotiating body is the way in which the subject is introduced: "The General Assembly welcomes the agreement reached following appropriate consultations among the Member States during the Special Session of the General Assembly Devoted to Disarmament that the Committee on Disarmament will . . ." [1b]. This rather anodyne wording reflects the fact that highly divergent views on the question of the position of the negotiating body within the overall disarmament framework were maintained by the nuclear weapon powers until the end of the Special Session. As far as the Soviet Union, the United Kingdom and the United States were concerned, the reference to an agreement reached among the member states and *welcomed* by the General Assembly was intended to convey that the Committee on Disarmament is not a subsidiary organ of the General Assembly. On the other hand, China maintained that the negotiating body must be "responsible to the deliberative organ" [4]. And the position of France was that the body entrusted with negotiations should have "concrete ties to the United Nations system" [5].

Ultimately, numerous ties with the United Nations were created. The Committee on Disarmament, it was agreed, would adopt its own agenda, taking into account the recommendations made to it by the General Assembly and the proposals presented by the members of the Committee [1b]. Every year, the Assembly adopts resolutions which are addressed to the Committee on Disarmament and are transmitted to it by the UN Secretary-General. Also, as indicated earlier, the Committee submits reports to the General Assembly on a regular basis. The Committee's budget is part of the budget of the United Nations. The Committee holds its meetings on UN grounds, and all its members belong to the United Nations. Also, the secretary of the Committee is appointed by the UN Secretary-General and acts as his personal representative. All the Committee meetings are serviced by UN personnel.

There can be no doubt, therefore, that the United Nations has a central role in the negotiating process, even though the Committee on Disarmament, like its predecessors, namely, the Eighteen Nation Committee on Disarmament (1962–69) and the Conference of the Committee on Disarmament (1969–78), was not formally recognized as an organ of the General Assembly. Indeed, progress in disarmament is a primary concern and responsibility of the United Nations.

There are both reasons and precedents[1] for suggesting that the multilateral negotiating body should be inside the United Nations. One must admit, however, that the crucial question—at least at present—is not so much one of form, but of substance, namely, to ensure that deliberations are related to negotiations in a meaningful way.

Negotiation is usually facilitated when the number of parties involved is relatively small. This was recognized by the Special Session when it stated that the negotiating body "should have a relatively small membership" [1c]. It should be noted, however, that even taking into account the increase in the membership of the United Nations through the years, the long-range trend has been to set up ever larger negotiating bodies.

[1] Initially the multilateral disarmament negotiating body was an organ of the United Nations. For instance, in 1946 the UN established the Atomic Energy Commission, and, later, the Sub-Committee of the Disarmament Commission, which was active from 1954 to 1957. It was only with the Ten Nation Committee on Disarmament, in 1960, that the negotiating body was set up outside the UN, though linked with it.

The General Assembly agreed, in the Final Document, that the membership of the Committee on Disarmament will be reviewed at regular intervals. This may mean 'rotation' among the non-nuclear weapon states—an idea that was put forth by some member states at and after the first Special Session—but may also open the way to a further enlargement of the negotiating body, given the well-known reluctance for rotation on the part of incumbents. The enlargement of the Committee would seem undesirable because of the increased danger of the multilateral negotiating body sliding into the practices of a debating forum.

V. Studies, research and training

There can be no better introduction to the subject of disarmament studies than the words of Dag Hammarskjöld who once stated: "The very study of disarmament may be the vehicle for progress towards greater international political understanding." Hammarskjöld strongly believed that expert technical studies and exchange of information on disarmament-related matters could help in "making an effective dent in the hitherto rather intractable problem of disarmament", the words with which he welcomed, in 1958, the agreed report of the Conference of Experts to study the Possibility of Detecting Violations of a Possible Agreement on Suspension of Nuclear Tests [6].

Studies on the arms race and disarmament prepared under the auspices of the United Nations since the early 1960s have been intended to facilitate better understanding of the issues involved and to give assistance and support to the disarmament process, and in particular the negotiating process, through an analysis of specific questions. To enable the United Nations to draw on the widest range of expertise and political outlook, most of the studies have been conducted with the assistance of consultant or governmental experts appointed by the Secretary-General or by experts appointed directly by governments. In a number of cases, the UN Secretariat itself has made analyses which could be considered studies.

Interest in such studies has been growing in recent years. In 1976, the *Ad Hoc* Committee on the Review of the Role of the United Nations in the Field of Disarmament considered the possibility of additional functions which the UN might assume in that field and recommended, *inter alia*, that the General Assembly should consider making more use of in-depth studies by the Secretary-General on the arms race, disarmament and related matters, on an *ad hoc* basis. Later, the subject occupied a prominent place in the preparations for the first Special Session of the General Assembly Devoted to Disarmament, as well as at the Special Session itself.

In his statement at the opening meeting of the Special Session, the Secretary-General proposed the establishment of an advisory board of eminent persons, selected on the basis of their personal expertise and taking into account the principle of equitable geographical representation, to advise him on various aspects of the studies to be undertaken by the United Nations on disarmament and arms limitation.

Concerning research, France advanced a proposal at the Special Session for the establishment, within the framework of the United Nations, of an international institute for disarmament research. Nigeria proposed that a UN programme be established to provide expertise on disarmament matters to public officials, particularly to officials from developing countries which were short of such expertise.

As a result of these initiatives and decisions, the Advisory Board on Disarmament Studies held its first session in November 1978. The United Nations programme of fellowships on disarmament began in June 1979. The United Nations Institute for Disarmament Research was established in Geneva on 1 October 1980, within the framework of the United Nations Institute for Training and Research (UNITAR), as an interim arrangement for the period until the second Special Session, to be held in 1982.

At its first session, in November 1978, the Advisory Board on Disarmament Studies discussed the purposes to be served by UN studies in the area of disarmament and arms limitation, and agreed that they include: (*a*) assisting in ongoing negotiations on disarmament and arms limitation; (*b*) assisting in the identification of specific topics with a view to initiating new negotiations; (*c*) providing the general background to current deliberations and negotiations; and (*d*) assessing and promoting public awareness of the threat to the very survival of mankind posed by the existence of nuclear weapons and the continuing arms race as well as its impact on both international security and development.

In 1979 and 1980, the Board devoted its attention primarily to the consideration of a comprehensive programme of disarmament studies. It also considered specific proposals for studies. In 1979, the Board agreed to recommend that a study on a comprehensive nuclear test ban be carried out by the Secretary-General of the United Nations. This recommendation was endorsed by the General Assembly. The following year, the Board reported to the Secretary-General that, from the discussions and consultations among the members, a broad agreement had emerged reflecting the view of most of the members of the Board that four studies should be undertaken on the following subjects: (*a*) conduct and financing of a world-wide disarmament campaign; (*b*) the question of zones of peace and cooperation; (*c*) the verification problem; and (*d*) cessation of the production of all types of nuclear weapon and means of delivery and of the production of fissionable material for weapon purposes. The study under (*a*) above was endorsed by the General Assembly at its 1980 session.

A list of the UN studies is provided in appendix 16A.

As to the United Nations Institute for Disarmament Research, in 1980 the Secretary-General informed the General Assembly about the establishment of the Institute, which it had been agreed would have "a simple, pragmatic mandate to carry out research for the purpose of assisting in ongoing negotiations in the area of disarmament and arms limitation, stimulating initiatives for new negotiations and providing a general insight into the problems involved". It was understood that the Institute would carry out this mandate on the basis of the provisions of the Final Document of the first Special Session of the General Assembly Devoted to Disarmament.

The United Nations programme of fellowships on disarmament, which is organized and supervised by the United Nations Centre for Disarmament, draws on expertise from the UN system, including UNITAR, and from academic and research institutes, in particular SIPRI. Its usefulness has been recognized by the General Assembly which, in 1979, noted with satisfaction the report of the Secretary-General on its first year of operation. The following year the Secretary-General was commended by the Assembly for the diligence with which the programme was being conducted. The Assembly decided that the programme should be continued.

VI. Information activities

The UN Centre for Disarmament maintains a continuing programme of public information on the arms race and disarmament. As part of its programme, the Centre prepares a number of publications, including the *United Nations Disarmament Yearbook* and the periodical entitled *Disarmament, a periodic review by the United Nations*. Both publications resulted from the recommendations of the *Ad Hoc* Committee on the Review of the Role of the United Nations in the Field of Disarmament, which were endorsed by the General Assembly in 1976. At its Special Session, in 1978, the General Assembly requested the UN Centre for Disarmament to intensify its information activities and called for closer liaison between the United Nations and the non-governmental organizations (NGOs) that were active on disarmament matters. It was the Assembly's way of recognizing that the United Nations, as well as the governments of member states, needed the support and stimulus of an informed and concerned public opinion.

Concerted efforts are being made by the Centre to reach the public through a clear and realistic disarmament message. If there is a clear understanding of the real problems involved, the pressure of public opinion can increasingly be brought to bear on the disarmament effort. In this connection, it should be recalled that at its first Special Session, the General Assembly decided to invite 25 international NGOs and six peace research institutes, including SIPRI, to address the *Ad Hoc* Committee of the Special Session. The experiment was not only sound, but productive, as the NGOs and the research institutes made a valuable contribution to the Special Session. One hopes that an initiative along the same lines will be taken in conjunction with the second Special Session in 1982.

VII. Conclusions

The disarmament role of the United Nations has been fully acknowledged and, on the whole, strengthened by the adoption of the Final Document of the first Special Session. There is, however, an urgent need to build on that foundation. The mechanisms made available by the Special Session are, by and large, adequate and, if used constructively, can be effective. The question is one of ensuring that they are so used. This is a task for which the UN General Assembly bears a major responsibility.

It may be asked whether, with the First Committee acting as the disarmament committee of the Assembly, there is need for a deliberative body, additional to the General Assembly, namely, the Disarmament Commission. This is a question on which there continues to be some difference of opinion among member states.

Concerning the negotiating process, it should be noted that during the past 35 years, the results of multilateral negotiations have constantly fallen far short of the goals set by the General Assembly and the consequences are too well known to require lengthy comments. It has been proposed from time to time that a special disarmament organization should be set up. This view is not shared by all. Those who oppose it argue *inter alia* that the idea is premature, since no decisive progress has yet been made towards disarmament. In any event, changes in the organizational arrangements for negotiations cannot, by themselves, solve the basic problem, which is essentially political, namely, the assurance of national security on a firmer basis than the ongoing competition in arms build-up.

References

1. *Official Records of the General Assembly, Tenth Special Session, Supplement No. 4* (A/S-10/4), Resolution S/10-2.
   (a) —, para. 114.
   (b) —, para. 120.
   (c) —, para. 113.

2. Kurt Waldheim, "Who is responsible?" *Building the Future Order* (The Free Press, New York, 1980).
   (a) —, pp. 79–80.
   (b) —, p. 78.
3. *Official Records of the General Assembly, Thirty-First Session, Supplement No. 36* (A/31/36).
4. United Nations document A/S-10/AC.1/17, para. 11.
5. Provisional Verbatim Record of the Third Plenary Meeting of the Tenth Special Session, A/S-10/PV.3, pp. 13–15.
6. Brian Urquhart, *Hammarskjold* (Knopf, New York, 1972), pp. 316, 321–22.

Appendix 16A

UN disarmament studies

Studies already completed

1962 Economic and social consequences of disarmament, E/3593/Rev.1 (United Nations publication, Sales No. 62.IX.1).

1967 Effects of the possible use of nuclear weapons and the security and economic implications for States of the acquisition and further development of these weapons, A/6858 (United Nations publication, Sales No. E.68.IX.1).

1969 Chemical and bacteriological (biological) weapons and the effects of their possible use, A/7575/Rev.1-S/9292/Rev.1 (United Nations publication, Sales No. E.69.I.29).

1971 Economic and social consequences of the arms race and of military expenditures, A/8469/Rev.1 (United Nations publication, Sales No. E.72.IX.16).

1972 Napalm and other incendiary weapons and all aspects of their possible use, A/8803/Rev.1 (United Nations publication, Sales No. E.73.I.3).

Disarmament and development: report of the group of experts on the economic and social consequences of disarmament, ST/ECA/174 (United Nations publication, Sales No. E.73.IX.1).

1974 Declaration of the Indian Ocean as a zone of peace: factual statement pursuant to General Assembly resolution 3080 (XXVIII), A/AC.159/1/Rev.1.

Reduction of the military budgets of States permanent members of the Security Council by 10 per cent and utilization of part of the funds thus saved to provide assistance to developing countries, A/9770/Rev.1 (United Nations publication, Sales No. E.75.I.10).

1975 Comprehensive study of the question of nuclear-weapon-free zones in all its aspects: special report of the Conference of the Committee on Disarmament, A/10027/Add.1 (United Nations publication, Sales No. E.76.I.7).

1976 Reduction of military budgets—Measurement and international reporting of military expenditures, A/31/222/Rev.1 (United Nations publication, Sales No. E.77.I.6).

1977 Reduction of military budgets: report of the Secretary-General with the assistance of an intergovernmental group of budgetary experts, A/32/194 and Add.1.

Economic and social consequences of the arms race and of military expenditures, A/32/88/Rev.1 (United Nations publication, Sales No. E.78.IX.1).

1978 Report to the Conference of the Committee on Disarmament of the *Ad Hoc* Group of Scientific Experts to consider international co-operative measures to detect and to identify seismic events (*Official Records of the General Assembly, Thirty-third Session Supplement No. 27* (A/33/27), vol. II, document CCD/558 and Add. 1.

1979 Second report of the *Ad Hoc* Group of Scientific Experts to consider international co-operative measures to detect and to identify seismic events, document CD/43 and Add.1.

1980 Study on a comprehensive nuclear test ban: report of the Secretary-General, A/35/257 and CD/86.[1]

Comprehensive study on nuclear weapons: report of the Secretary-General, A/35/392.[2]

South Africa's plan and capability in the nuclear field: report of the Secretary-General, A/35/402 and Corr.1.[2]

Study on all the aspects of regional disarmament: report of the Secretary-General, A/35/416.[2]

Reduction of military budgets—Reporting of military expenditures: report of the Secretary-General, A/35/479.[2]

Studies in progress

In the course of 1981, expert studies on the following subjects will be completed and submitted to the General Assembly pursuant to Assembly decisions adopted prior to 1980.

(*a*) Relationship between disarmament and development;
(*b*) Relationship between disarmament and international security;
(*c*) Technical, legal and financial implications of the establishment of an international satellite monitoring agency;
(*d*) Confidence-building measures;
(*e*) Israeli nuclear armament;
(*f*) Institutional arrangements relating to the process of disarmament.

[1] A study proposed by the Advisory Board on Disarmament Studies in 1979.
[2] To be issued as a United Nations publication in the course of 1981.

Studies requested by the General Assembly at its 1980 session

At its 35th session, in 1980, the General Assembly decided that export studies on the following subjects be undertaken:

(*a*) Study on all aspects of the conventional arms race and on disarmament relating to conventional weapons and armed forces;[3]
(*b*) Reporting of military expenditures;[4]
(*c*) Economic and social consequences of the arms race and of military expenditures;[4]
(*d*) Organization and financing of a world disarmament campaign under the auspices of the United Nations.[5]

Studies proposed in 1980 in the Advisory Board on Disarmament Studies

(*a*) The conduct and financing of a world-wide disarmament campaign;[6]
(*b*) The question of zones of peace and co-operation;
(*c*) The verification problem;
(*d*) The cessation of the production of all types of nuclear weapons and means of delivery and of the production of fissionable material for weapons purposes.

Other proposals to be considered in the Advisory Board on Disarmament Studies at a later stage

(*a*) The question of the consequences of the military uses of science and technology on the free access of States to science and technology for peaceful purposes;
(*b*) Further prohibition of military or any other hostile use of environmental modification techniques;
(*c*) Further measures in the field of disarmament to prevent the arms race on the seabed or the ocean floor or in the subsoil thereof;
(*d*) Further measures to prevent an arms race in outer space;
(*e*) The Indian Ocean as a zone of peace (military presence in the Indian Ocean);[7]
(*f*) The denuclearization of Africa: a study on the declaration of Africa, comprising continental Africa, Madagascar and other islands surrounding Africa, as a nuclear-weapon-free zone and its relationship with the nuclear capability of South Africa.

[3] To be completed in 1983.
[4] To be completed in 1982.
[5] To be completed in 1981.
[6] This proposal was taken up by the General Assembly in 1980. See Studies requested by the General Assembly (*d*) above.
[7] This proposal was subsequently withdrawn on the understanding that the member who had initially advanced it might wish to bring the matter up again at an appropriate moment.

17. European security and the Madrid Conference

Square-bracketed numbers, thus [1], *refer to the list of references on page* 494.

The second follow-up meeting of the 35-nation Conference on Security and Co-operation in Europe (CSCE) opened in Madrid on 11 November 1980. During the first phase, which ended on 19 December, the implementation of the Helsinki Final Act was reviewed, much attention being given to human rights issues. The second phase, starting on 27 January 1981, was devoted largely to discussion of new proposals, *inter alia* for more effective confidence-building measures (CBMs) and for a European Disarmament Conference.

I. The function of confidence-building measures

A basic virtue of effective CBMs is increased openness. Increased openness is needed in order to enhance predictability; predictability is essential for the development of mutual confidence; and mutual confidence is needed in order to curb the dynamics of arms build-ups and to embark on arms restraint and disarmament. This is, in essence, the logic and the *raison d'être* of so-called first-generation CBMs. It must, however, be recognized that, particularly for the big powers, such CBMs can be only minor supplements to the various means of intelligence collection (for an evaluation of first-generation CBMs, see *SIPRI Yearbook 1980*).[1]

The exchange of information provided by the CBMs applied today serves, to some small extent, to reduce the convertibility of military force to political utility. For example, prior notification of military manoeuvres removes the option of declaring them, at very short notice, exercises in order to camouflage preparations for an invasion. And the longer the notification time, the greater is the reassurance that an exercise is neither cover for deployment to war positions nor designed to be a show of power to exert political pressure. However, for CBMs to become of real military significance, provisions for exchange of information should be supplemented by verifiable measures of military restraint and disengagement, affecting military postures. In particular, CBMs should be designed to curtail the option of surprise military action; hence, confidence would be enhanced to the extent that the threat of surprise attack recedes into the background. In Madrid, some suggestions for such second-generation

[1] See also references [1–3].

CBMs were made, mostly in connection with proposals to convene a European Disarmament Conference (see section IV below).

Militarily significant CBMs constrain the *use* rather than the *magnitude* of military force. However, the rationale for CBMs does not stop there. The role of CBMs is also to prepare the ground, politically and psychologically, for real arms control and disarmament measures. To the extent that decision makers obtain more realistic perceptions of each other's intentions and capabilities, and are reassured of the absence of threats, some of the driving forces of the arms race will be removed and the possibilities for real disarmament may improve. Thus, CBMs should lead from reduction of fears to reduction of the objective grounds for such perceptions, and it is important that the link between CBMs and efforts to restrain and reduce military capabilities is maintained. Today, this link is all too evident in the reverse: the spiralling arms build-up has feed-back on the whole CBM enterprise, leaving us essentially at square one. While the Helsinki Final Act recognized that the experience gained by the implementation of its provisions could "together with further efforts . . . lead to developing and enlarging measures aimed at strengthening confidence", it has, to date, not been possible to move beyond the confines of the Final Act.

While CBMs are usually referred to in the context of the CSCE Document on confidence-building measures and certain aspects of security and disarmament (see *SIPRI Yearbook 1976* for the text of this document) and in connection with the negotiations on Mutual Force Reductions (MFR) in Vienna—where they are called 'collateral constraints' or 'associated measures' and are directly linked with the verification of troop reductions—it should be emphasized that confidence can also be created in other realms, such as in economic co-operation, in human contacts, in diplomatic and political acts, and so on. Generally, what is unknown tends to be perceived as hostile and threatening, whereas the dissemination of enemy images and threats will be more difficult between peoples who have some acquaintance and understanding of one another. Broader interaction also provides improved opportunities for public opinion to counteract tension-producing behaviour. All main parts or baskets of the Final Act are therefore important for eliminating unfounded suspicion and worst-case assumptions and for fostering mutual confidence.

II. CBM proposals in Madrid

In Madrid, separate proposals to extend the present system of CBMs were submitted by a group of neutral and non-aligned states (Austria, Cyprus, Finland, Liechtenstein, San Marino, Sweden, Switzerland and Yugoslavia;

see appendix 17C) and by Romania. Other proposals, less specific but more far-reaching, were included in the proposals for a European Disarmament Conference.

The activity displayed by neutral and non-aligned states in this field—to help bridge the gap between 'maximalist' and 'minimalist' positions in the preparation of the Final Act, and in forwarding more ambitious proposals in Belgrade and Madrid—reflects in large measure their international position. CBMs are only indirectly related to the size of military forces, so, in a sense, these states can take part in the deliberations on an equal footing. A high profile on CBMs is all the more natural since the bulk of arms control negotiations are characterized by bilateralism, between either the two major powers or the alliances led by them, who are among the first to benefit from CBMs.

The scope of CBMs

Concerning the scope of CBMs, it is widely held that the current force threshold for notification of military manoeuvres is somewhat high in relation to the magnitude of the threat experienced in many parts of Europe and the rather high number of smaller-scale manoeuvres in WTO countries. At their meeting on 5–6 December 1979, the WTO Ministers of Foreign Affairs proposed to reduce the threshold to 20 000 troops. In Madrid, the neutral and non-aligned states proposed a threshold of 18 000 troops. The Western countries preferred the division level which, although not specified by them, implies a noticeably lower threshold (approaching 10 000 troops).

An upper limit on the size of manoeuvres remains an unpopular concept within NATO. In October 1979, the Soviet Union suggested an upper limit of 40 000–50 000 troops. Since the signature of the Helsinki Final Act, four manoeuvres involved between 40 000 and 50 000 troops—two Western, one Eastern and one non-aligned. Nine had more than 50 000 participants, all of them Western manoeuvres (see appendix 17B). Comprising more states and more substantial contributors to overall alliance strength, NATO arguably needs to exercise larger numbers of troops than the WTO in order to function effectively in a unitary fashion. The argument seems valid, but only to some extent. It certainly cannot be used to justify manoeuvres of any size, and NATO has recently staged some very large exercises. The Spearpoint manoeuvre in FR Germany on 15–25 September 1980, involving 90 000 troops, is the largest that has been held since the signing of the Final Act in 1975, and in the same period, other manoeuvres also took place on the territory of FR Germany.

All states furthermore agree, in principle, on prior notification of major military movements. The Western, neutral and non-aligned states prefer the same threshold as that applied for manoeuvres. So far, the WTO states have not been explicit on this.

The CSCE Final Act attaches special military significance to amphibious forces, on the understanding that, even on a rather small scale, exercises involving such forces may give rise to tension. To meet this concern, the neutral and non-aligned states proposed notification of naval exercises involving more than 5 000 troops and/or more than 10 major amphibious warfare vessels—the latter being indicative of a capacity roughly corresponding to 5 000 troops, but with great variations: 5 000 men more than cover a Soviet Marine Infantry Regiment or a US Marine Amphibious Unit—both of somewhat more than 2 000 men. On the other hand, it is well below the level often considered necessary for so-called 'opposed landings': one Marine Infantry Regiment and one Motorized Infantry Division for the USSR and one Marine Amphibious Brigade for the USA, both of approximately 15 000 men.

It was also proposed that endeavours should continue with a view to developing CBMs in relation to other naval exercises, seeking *inter alia* a definition of the term 'major naval exercise' (by neutral and non-aligned states), and that multinational manoeuvres should not be carried out near the frontiers of other participating states (by Romania). The participating states were urged to display greater openness with regard to their military expenditures (by neutral and non-aligned states), and a freeze on military budgets was proposed pending conclusion of an agreement to reduce them (by Romania). The suggestions for more significant, second-generation CBMs included in the proposals to convene a European Disarmament Conference contained references to measures such as military disengagement (proposed by Romania); military restraint and disengagement in sensitive border areas (by Sweden); transitional measures comprising limitation of military activities, halting of the arms race and military disengagement, an adequate zone and other conditions of application being decided for each transitional measure in accordance with its character and scope (by Yugoslavia); and political and legal steps to reduce the danger of war, together with measures aimed at lowering the level and intensity of military confrontation (by Poland). The French proposal for a European Disarmament Conference, which in its first version (of 1978) had focused on conventional weapons, now concentrated on more binding, appropriately verifiable and militarily significant CBMs, but without specifying the contents of measures to be negotiated.

Area of applicability

In his speech before the Party Congress on 20 February 1981, Leonid Brezhnev declared that the Soviet Union was willing to apply CBMs "to the entire European part of the USSR, provided the Western states, too, extend the confidence zone accordingly". The statement was made in response to a cardinal demand by France and other Western countries that CBMs should be applicable to all of Europe, from the Atlantic to the Urals.

The WTO states have argued that in limiting the area of participating states whose territories extend beyond Europe to 250 kilometres from the frontiers faced or shared with other European participating states, the Final Act struck a balance which cannot be changed unilaterally. Other states claim that the area of application for European CBMs ought to be just 'Europe'. However, the delimitation of the area of application at sea is an issue which must be faced sooner or later anyhow, in connection with the proposals for notification of naval exercises. In their proposal for prior notification of naval exercises involving amphibious forces, the neutral and non-aligned states suggested that notification shall be given of any such exercise which takes place in 'European waters', defined as "the inner seas of Europe, i.e. the Baltic, the North Sea and the Black Sea, the Mediterranean and the ocean areas adjacent to the territorial waters of European participating States". The notion of the inner seas of Europe, as offered in this proposal, is a new and interesting proposition.

The concurrence of the MFR talks and the CSCE endeavours may be seen as indicative of a European-wide area embracing an inner zone with more far-reaching yet compatible CBMs. Arrangements for the inner zone might then be designed on the premise that forces stationed in it should not be capable of launching a successful attack upon the other side without major reinforcements—which would have to come from or pass through the wider area and be subject to prior notification and appropriate verification. To what extent the MFR reduction area fits such a concept can, however, be questioned.

Notification time, guide-lines for observers, and exchange of information

The Eastern and neutral and non-aligned countries have proposed to extend the notification time from 21 to 30 days. Western states always favoured notification of manoeuvres much longer in advance than the minimum stipulated in the Final Act. In fact, most Western states pre-announce their exercises earlier anyhow, *inter alia* because of the need to inform local communities which will be affected by the manoeuvres. To the extent that notification through diplomatic channels appears *after* preannouncement for other reasons, the status of the CSCE provisions can only deteriorate.

At times, there has been irritation over the restrictions placed on observers invited to attend manoeuvres. To avoid unduly constraining observers and to establish uniform practices, it would therefore be desirable to develop guide-lines for how much invited observers should be allowed to observe. In Madrid, the neutral and non-aligned states proposed a set of rules to ensure that observers acquire a good overall picture of the purpose and progress of the manoeuvre, that they can follow the activities of command staffs and field units and have personal contact with troops, and that observers attending the same manoeuvre will have equal opportunities to carry out their functions.

There have also been requests for more information, to be extended together with the notification, on the purpose and characteristics of exercises and movements.

Some states furthermore asked for a regular exchange of information on the nature, designation and garrison location of all major military formations, against the background of which notification should be made whenever any of these formations is moved from its garrison area, together with a statement on the purpose of the movement. As expressed by the United Kingdom, "not only would the standard posture of major military units over the whole map of Europe [then] become public property, but so would any changes in that posture and the reasons given for these changes" [4]. This line of thought, which bears great similarity to the NATO proposal for associated measures in Vienna of 20 December 1979, contains elements which are controversial, especially since there are diverging views on how to ensure appropriate verification. In Madrid, the need for effective verification has been strongly underlined by the Western states in particular, although in general terms only. However, the set of on-site inspection rights proposed by the NATO participants in the MFR talks triggered a tepid response from the WTO negotiators.

Verification

Verification is a necessary ingredient in any militarily significant confidence-building arrangement. Especially at times of high tension, adequate techniques for verification of commitments are important for mutual assurance. The need for more far-reaching control in the implementation of an extended system of CBMs therefore not only arises with the nature of the new measures being contemplated, but also reflects the general deterioration of East–West relations.

Involving 35 nations with greatly differing verification capabilities, the task at the CSCE is much more complex than in the bloc-to-bloc MFR setting. Only an all-European agency, properly equipped for the purpose, could give equal assurance to all. Some airborne systems equipped with radar and other sensors would, moreover, facilitate verification in an inner (MFR) zone, but less so in the wider European area. AWACS (the

Western Airborne Warning and Control System) can detect movements of armoured units on the ground by listening to their radio emissions, of helicopters even when hovering, and of aircraft at whatever height out to a distance of 350–400 km. Other airborne systems, such as the TR-1 (a tactical reconnaissance version of the U-2) and the EC-135 may also be of use—and much the same would go for the Eastern side.

The overall effectiveness of national technical means of verification, primarily satellite monitoring, is hard to establish with precision. Satellite monitoring is, for instance, affected by cloud formations, which are relatively frequent in certain parts of Europe. Whether such means will suffice, or to what extent and in which forms on-site inspection will prove necessary, depends, of course, on the CBMs to be adopted. In this connection, it has been recalled that paragraph 31 of the Final Document of the 1978 UN Special Session on Disarmament states that: "The form and modalities of the verification to be provided for in any specific agreement depend upon and should be determined by the purposes, scope and nature of the agreement" [5]. While an extended system of CBMs is hard to imagine without more far-reaching controls, differing approaches and evaluations regarding verification of the provisions should not be allowed to halt further negotiations on CBMs.

III. Obstacles to extended CBMs

To some extent, voluntary implementation over and above the minimum requirements of the Document on CBMs was, from the very beginning, an important precondition for developing and enlarging CBMs. Thus, the provisions concerning the exchange of observers at manoeuvres, notification of smaller-scale manoeuvres, and notification of military movements and exchange of military visits were formulated in such a way as to move ahead of statutory requirements, with an awareness of the cumulative nature of confidence-building and of directions in which CBMs could be enlarged. These provisions, however, have been unevenly applied, and no significant increase in their application can be discerned over the five-year period since Helsinki (see appendix 17B). The parties have, in other words, not succeeded in giving momentum to the effort, so today we are left with a few measures providing rather insignificant information about certain routine military activities. The above-mentioned proposals to extend first-generation CBMs and move on to more significant second-generation measures therefore appear against a bleak background. To implement them, a number of difficulties must be overcome, which have been aggravated of late by the deterioration of relations between the major powers.

Peace is divisible—all rhetorics to the contrary notwithstanding—but *confidence* between states is not. Armed conflict and major power rivalry in the Third World have had increasingly adverse effects on international relations in Europe. The rules of behaviour agreed upon by the USA and the USSR a decade ago have been broken; competition for power and positions throughout the world has been intensified; the policies pursued by the major powers in various parts of the world are linked together by more extensive application of global logic; and European nations have become more involved in contests for control and influence elsewhere. 1980 saw a further deterioration of East–West relations, but also some efforts by European states to alleviate tension between the two major powers, and to stem its repercussions on European affairs.

For some years, détente and rearmament co-existed in Europe. In the long run, however, it is difficult to treat one's 'opponent' as a collaborator and partner in economic, scientific and political affairs, and as an enemy worthy of total extinction as far as military dispositions are concerned [6]. Since the mid-1970s, there has been a gradual deterioration of East–West relations, spurred by the growing arms race. Arms races always have a high potential for fuelling hostility and suspicion, and in the shadow of another great leap upwards on the arms spiral, the governments represented at the Madrid Conference naturally found it hard to convince each other of their benign intentions.

Two characteristics of modern weaponry, in particular, give ground for suspicion and anxiety: first, the multi-purpose nature of new weapon systems, which provide more options and greater flexibility for the possessor and which, correspondingly, make his behaviour less predictable for potential adversaries; and second, the speed with which modern weapons can be activated and the resulting reduction of warning time. Together, they tend to accentuate the danger of surprise attack, in time and space as well as operational mode. The magnitude and nature of contemporary arms build-ups therefore tend to undermine and undo any confidence that has been created.

Modern military technology furthermore tends to defy quantitative restrictions. This is proven by logic and supported by many years of arms control experience. In Europe, it is of great importance to limit options for surprise attack and pre-emptive strikes, but quantitative restrictions are largely inadequate for the purpose, and the manpower figures discussed at the MFR talks are particularly ill-suited. Over the past centuries, the outcome of war has been determined less and less by the relative number of troops at the disposal of the warring entities, and more by the armaments, deployment patterns, organization and training. Short of great differences in the size of forces employed, superiority in numbers has been a less important determinant of victory than the advantage of striking first [7].

Given the insufficiency of numerical limitations on military input, curtailments on the output side, particularly on missions of surprise attack, have been all the more emphasized [8]. This is exactly what a number of proposals for associated measures at the MFR talks in Vienna and CBMs within the framework of the CSCE aim at. In the MFR context, associated measures may contribute more to stability than the marginal reductions of aggregate troop levels proposed for phase one. Within the CSCE, an extended system for prior notification and observation of military manoeuvres and movements, combined with new measures of military restraint and disengagement, could, likewise, be a valuable contribution to thwarting the dangers of surprise attack. As indicated above, the CSCE arrangements might, furthermore, provide a general framework for integration of particular constraints to be applied in an 'inner' (MFR) area into a broader context. Hence, compatibility between CBMs in the two diplomatic fora should be ensured, and the coherence and cohesion of the security order in Europe preserved.

However, to curtail options of surprise attack, some basic obstacles must be overcome that are rather peculiar to Europe. Nowhere in the world is there such a massive deployment of military forces, equipped with sophisticated weapons, standing face to face. Both sides have adopted doctrines of forward defence, being prepared to meet an attacker as close to the boundary as possible. Efforts to constrain the perceived offensive, quick reaction capabilities on the other side, are therefore tantamount to blunting the opponent's defences as defined by his own doctrine. CBMs and arms reduction in Europe must therefore be designed and pursued in ways which weaken the grounds for maintenance of strong forward defence postures. However, for reasons of geography, this is particularly hard to work out on the Western side.

A related difficulty is posed by the general shift of emphasis from deterrence to war fighting. To threaten one another with ever more effective weapons for the sake of mutual deterrence is hard to reconcile with confidence building; increased emphasis on the possibilities for fighting and winning a war, by all the means available, makes it even worse. Associated with this is a drive for greater readiness—and in the eyes of the adversary, measures to increase military readiness are the opposite of confidence building. For major military powers, readiness to defend is almost indistinguishable from readiness to attack. The moves toward greater readiness are therefore largely irreconcilable with measures to make more transparent the preparations for war.

In the present climate of mistrust, confidence in the ability to defend oneself takes precedence over mutual confidence that neither side in fact intends to attack or threaten to attack. *Self*-confidence is best served by more binding and clearly verifiable measures constraining the *capabilities* of the opponent. Such measures may certainly also be conducive to enhancing *mutual* confidence, but the latter can be approached from the 'softer' and 'easier' end as well, by adopting measures affecting perceived *intentions* [9].

At present, part of the dilemma in negotiating CBMs is that the prevailing mistrust tends to dictate tangible measures that can enhance self-confidence, but which are particularly hard to achieve precisely under circumstances of deep suspicion and intense rivalry, while political and legal measures bearing on intentions are often discarded as useless. It might be observed, however, that the CBMs enshrined in the Helsinki Final Act relate to capabilities as well as intentions, and therefore offer a suitable, although weak, basis for building a bridge over troubled waters.

A certain interest in military stability in Europe also derives from the fact that the magnitude of military capabilities amassed on the continent no longer bears any relationship to the remaining conflict potentials in the region. The strains on European security to a large extent come from outside the continent, through a globalization of major power military doctrines and, partly as a consequence of it, by the involvement of European nations in the politics and conflicts of other regions. It would therefore be in the interest of European nations to shield themselves from certain repercussions of conflicts elsewhere, and stabilization through confidence building is a meaningful pursuit also in this regard.

IV. A European Disarmament Conference

The discussion of CBMs at the Madrid follow-up meeting did not centre on the proposals to extend first-generation CBMs, but rather on guide-lines for more far-reaching measures in connection with the proposals to convene a European Disarmament Conference.

The proposals for such a conference—submitted by France, Poland, Romania, Sweden and Yugoslavia—reflect a growing concern for the security of Europe by a number of small and medium-sized countries in particular, and an increasing will to take initiatives and be subjects, not only objects, in high politics between East and West. In many countries, giving higher priority to arms restraint and disarmament efforts is underpinned and pressed forward by an active public opinion, geared especially to the problems posed by nuclear weapons. Not only are arms build-ups more intense than ever before, but in many parts of Europe, public opinion against them is also becoming stronger than it has been for decades. Today, discussion of European disarmament matters therefore takes place in a dynamic setting with dialectic ingredients, holding out a glimpse of hope for stronger political control of military affairs, and more effective endeavours to bring the arms race to a halt.

There was broad agreement that the Conference ought to be a *phased* process, and that the first phase should be devoted to an elaboration of more significant CBMs. It is certainly high time to proceed, not only by extending the present system of CBMs, but also by elaborating militarily significant second-generation measures, defining more substantial constraints on the uses of military force. Without further progress in the near future, the modest beginning that was made five years ago may in reality dwindle and the CBM undertaking launched in Helsinki therefore fail. This would affect the balance of the CSCE undertaking and have adverse effects on the entire process.

A number of proposals to extend first-generation CBMs are specific, and on some of them, positions do not differ very much. However, in the tense international climate of today, a step-by-step enlargement of present arrangements for information exchange relating primarily to intentions—communication of more adequate messages of non-aggressive intent—is by many states found unattractive or of questionable utility. While a number of single steps may seem negotiable, consideration is rather given to package solutions aiming at a well-balanced sum of CBMs, comprising militarily significant measures affecting military postures and constraining the use of force to a larger extent than heretofore.

The tentative nature of the proposals for second-generation CBMs submitted in Madrid would indicate that, in order to succeed, political will to establish appropriate machinery for the exploration of possibilities and the negotiation of new arrangements is required. In this connection, there was broad agreement that a new conference ought to be separate from, yet closely linked to, the CSCE. This might have the advantage of ensuring effective working methods and would also make it easier to take due account of other questions of relevance to the basic issues of détente and disarmament.

Finally, there should be a link between CBMs and efforts at arms control and disarmament. In Helsinki, only a vague connection was made. A new conference, concentrating on CBMs in phase one, ought to have a clear mandate in this regard and, after achievement of positive results in the first phase, lead on to questions of arms reduction in phase two. This would be in conformity with the nature and rationale of CBMs, and of some importance for future endeavours. CBMs should *encourage* arms control and disarmament measures; they can never *substitute* for them, and should by no means be allowed to absorb attention at the expense of real disarmament initiatives.

The scope of disarmament issues to be addressed should also comprise nuclear weapons planned for use in Europe. Both doctrinally and technically, these weapons are to a large extent connected with conventional weapons, and for that reason logical elements of European disarmament talks. Above all, the challenge posed by the presence of about 10 000 nuclear warheads planned for use in Europe is so formidable that it should be moved to the top of the European political agenda as soon as possible. That would also be the best way to create a stronger link between the CSCE and public opinion, which is so important for any disarmament initiative to succeed.

Should the Madrid Conference fail, other possibilities must be tried.

References

1. Alford, J., *The Future of Arms Control: Part III—Confidence-building Measures*, Adelphi Paper No. 149 (International Institute for Strategic Studies, London, 1979).
2. Holst, J. J. and Melander, K. E., 'Dealing with the military aspects of European security: the CBM approach', paper prepared for the Belgrade meeting within the follow-up of the CSCE and the military aspects of European security (Institute of International Politics and Economics, Belgrade, 9–10 May 1977).
3. IPRA Disarmament Study Group, 'Building confidence in Europe', *Bulletin of Peace Proposals*, No. 2, 1980.
4. Intervention by the Head of the UK Delegation at the plenary session of the Madrid CSCE Follow-Up Meeting, 2 February 1981.
5. Intervention at the plenary session of the Madrid CSCE Follow-Up Meeting, 9 February 1981.
6. Kissinger, H., *Hearings on Detente before the Senate Foreign Relations Committee* (US Government Printing Office, Washington, D.C., 19 September 1974).
7. Record, J., *Force Reductions in Europe: Starting Over* (Institute for Foreign Policy Analysis, Washington, D.C., 1980).
8. Bertram, C., *The Future of Arms Control: Part II—Arms Control and Technological Change: Elements of a New Approach*, Adelphi Paper No. 145 (International Institute for Strategic Studies, London, 1978).
9. Birnbaum, K. E., 'Confidence building as an approach to cooperative arms regulation in Europe', in K. E. Birnbaum (ed.), *Arms Control in Europe: Problems and Prospects*, Laxenburg Papers No. I/March 1980.

Appendix 17A

Notifications of military manoeuvres in 1980, in compliance with the Final Act of the Conference on Security and Co-operation in Europe

State giving notification	Date of notification	Duration of manoeuvre	Designation of manoeuvre	Number of troops involved*	Area of manoeuvre
Norway	12 Feb	14–19 Mar	Anorak Express[1]	18 200	Troms, northern Norway
USSR	19 Jun	10–16 Jul	. .	30 000	German DR: Stendal – Magdeburg – Cottbus – Brandenburg
German DR	13 Aug	First half of Sep	Waffen-brüderschaft 80[2]	c. 40 000	German DR and adjacent parts of the Baltic
USA	21 Aug	15–24 Sep	Certain Rampart[3]	c. 40 000	FR Germany: Southwest of Nürnberg
Norway	21 Aug	18–24 Sep	Team Work 80[4]	16 800	North Möre – South Tröndelag, central Norway
UK	22 Aug	15–25 Sep	Spearpoint[5]	90 000	FR Germany: Osnabrück – Minden – Nienburg – Wolfsburg – Braunlage – Unna
FR Germany	22 Aug	15–25 Sep	Spearpoint[5]	. .	Osnabrück – Minden – Nienburg – Wolfsburg – Braunlage – Unna
FR Germany	22 Aug	15–24 Sep	Certain Rampart[3]	. .	Feuchtwangen – Nürnberg – Freising – Augsburg – Dinkelscherben
FR Germany	22 Aug	15–19 Sep	St Georg[6]	c. 48 000	Dillenburg – Eschwege – Bamberg – Heilbronn
Canada	28 Aug	15–24 Sep	Certain Rampart[3]	. .	FR Germany
France	25 Sep	6–10 Oct	Marne 80[7]	17 000	Aube, Marne, Meuse

* It may be incorrect to add together the number of troops in different manoeuvres taking place within the same time period, as some troops may participate in more than one manoeuvre.

[1] 'Anorak Express'—a multinational field manoeuvre in the 'Express' series.

Purpose of the manoeuvre: routine exercise of NATO plans and procedures for the deployment of reinforcement forces and co-operation with Norwegian troops under winter conditions. The combined forces supported by Marine and Air Force units. Command level: Commander, North Norway.

Participating units: 6th Division, Combined Regiment No. 15 and smaller national units; Mobile force of the Euro Command, army and air elements; 3rd Commando Brigade Royal Marines, including units from the Netherlands Marine infantry (Royal Netherlands Marine Commando); 36th Marine Amphibious Unit, US Marine Corps. In addition, Norwegian air defence, smaller allied air force units and small Norwegian and allied marine units will participate.

Absence from garrisons: 5 March until a few days after the end of the manoeuvre.

[2] 'Waffenbrüderschaft'—a routine exercise of staffs and troops of ground and air forces as well as amphibious forces of the navies of the WTO participating states.

Purpose of the manoeuvre: to exercise co-operation between staffs and units of the allied armies.

[3] 'Certain Rampart'—a multinational manoeuvre in the context of the Autumn Forge field training and command post exercises, being conducted by members of NATO. It includes US troops being transported to Europe in the 'Reforger 80' movement.

Purpose of the manoeuvre: to provide combined arms training of US and allied forces in defence, river-crossing and counter-attack operations. Command level: Headquarters 7th US Corps.

Participating units: 3rd Infantry Division (USA), 2nd Armoured Cavalry Regiment (USA), 1st Infantry Division (USA); 35th Panzer Brigade (FRG); 4th Canadian Mechanized Brigade; Belgian Mechanized Battalion.

Foreign observers invited to attend.

[4] 'Team Work 80'—a multinational field manoeuvre in the 'Team Work' series.

Purpose of the manoeuvre: to train NATO procedures for deployment of reinforcement units and to exercise combat training with Norwegian forces. Command level: Commander, South Norway.

Participating units: Combined Regiment No. 12 and other smaller national ground units; 4th US Marine Amphibious Brigade; 3rd Commando Brigade Royal Marines (UK) including one Amphibious Combat Group of the Netherlands Marine infantry (Royal Netherlands Marine Commando). In addition to the Norwegian air defence, allied air force and Norwegian and allied naval defence units will participate.

Absence from garrisons: 18 September until a few days after the end of the manoeuvre.

Foreign observers invited to attend.

[5] 'Spearpoint'—a field training exercise forming the main tactical phase of the national exercise 'Crusader 80'. ('Crusader 80' also embraces Exercise 'Square Leg', which will practise plans for mobilization and defence of the UK; and Exercise 'Jog Trot', which will practise the movement of reinforcements to the continent.)

Purpose of the manoeuvre: to practise the deployment of 1st British corps, reinforced by regular and territorial army units and reservists from the UK for defensive operations. Command level: Headquarters 1st British Corps.

Participating units: 1st British Corps (reinforced); 2nd US Armoured Division; 3rd FRG Armoured Brigade.

Absence from garrisons: 1 September–3 October.

Foreign observers invited to attend.

[6] 'St Georg'—an exercise with opposing ground forces supported by air force units.

Purpose of the manoeuvre: to train troops in co-operation with large allied forces, the territorial army and air force units. Command level: 3rd FRG Corps.

Participating units: FRG: 2nd 'Jägerdivision', 12th Armoured Division, parts of the 5th and 10th Armoured Division; USA: 2nd Brigade/8th Infantry Division, 3rd Brigade/8th Infantry Division. Air support supplied by tactical air force units of participating states.

Absence from garrisons: 13–19 September.

Foreign observers invited to attend.

[7] 'Marne 80'—an army corps field manoeuvre with the participation of one armoured division and one infantry division of the 1st Army Corps with support from the air force. A reconnaissance phase to follow with river-crossing operations and air–ground actions.

Appendix 17B

Notified military manoeuvres in Europe, 1975–80

Year	NATO[a] Notification time[b]	Manoeuvres < 25 000 troops	Manoeuvres ⩾ 50 000 troops	Total no. of manoeuvres	WTO Notification time[b]	Manoeuvres < 25 000 troops	Manoeuvres ⩾ 50 000 troops	Total no. of manoeuvres
1975	24.3[c]	4	2	6	–	–	–	–
1976	21.9	3	1[d]	7	21.0[e]	2[f]	–	5
1977	23.4	5	1	7	21.5	–	–	2
1978	27.4	2	2	6	21.0	–	–	3
1979	24.3	4	2	7	18.6[g]	1	–	5
1980	23.2	3	1	6	20.0[h]	–	–	2
Total	24.1	21	9	39	20.1	3	–	17

Year	Non-aligned countries Notification time[b]	Manoeuvres < 25 000 troops	Manoeuvres ⩾ 50 000 troops	Total no. of manoeuvres	Total Notification time[b]	Manoeuvres < 25 000 troops	Manoeuvres ⩾ 50 000 troops	Total no. of manoeuvres
1975	26.0	1	–	2	24.5	5	2	8
1976	32.0	2	–	2	22.9	7	1	14
1977	42.3	3	–	3	27.2	8	1	12
1978	21.0	1	–	1	25.7	3	2	10
1979	34.7	–	–	3	24.4	5	2	15
1980	–	–	–	–	22.6	3	1	8
Total	33.5	7	–	11	24.6	31	9	67

[a] Including France, a member of NATO with special status.
[b] The average number of days between the date of notification (inclusive) and the start of the manoeuvre (exclusive). Calculated on the basis of the separate national notifications (for NATO only, there may be several notifications made by separate countries for the same manoeuvre).
[c] The 'Reforger 75' manoeuvre was officially to start in "early October", which has been calculated here as 1 October.
[d] The 'Grosser Bär' manoeuvre, with approximately 50 000 troops.
[e] Not including two Hungarian manoeuvres, for which only one was given notification (one day).
[f] The two Hungarian exercises mentioned in note *e*.
[g] On 3 May Hungary gave notification of a manoeuvre (of fewer than 25 000 troops) to take place in "mid-May", which has been calculated here as 15 May.
[h] The 'Waffenbrüderschaft 80' manoeuvre in the German Democratic Republic was to take place in the "first half" of September, which has been calculated here as 1 September.

Appendix 17C

*Proposal submitted to the Madrid Conference by the delegations of Austria, Cyprus, Finland, Liechtenstein, San Marino, Sweden, Switzerland and Yugoslavia on Confidence-Building Measures**

Excerpt

1. *Prior notification of major military manoeuvres*

The participating States will notify their major military manoeuvres exceeding a total of 18,000 troops 30 days or more in advance of the start of the manoeuvre in accordance with the relevant provisions of the Final Act of the CSCE.

The term "major military manoeuvres" is applicable also to smaller-scale military manoeuvres which are carried out close to each other in time and space under the same command and which, together, exceed a total of 18,000 troops.

They will also, in their notification of major military manoeuvres, include additional information as referred to in the Final Act on the number and types of participating major units, the level of command, the estimated starting and finishing dates of the movements of the forces involved, as well as the period of absence from their regular duty stations.

2. *Prior notification of other military manoeuvres*

The participating States recognize, furthermore, that the prior notification of manoeuvres encompassing less than 18,000 troops will contribute further to reducing tension and to confidence-building.

3. *Exchange of observers*

The participating States have agreed to adopt the following as guide-lines when inviting observers in accordance with the relevant provisions of the Final Act to attend military manoeuvres:

—Observers will be given ample and continuous information as well as the opportunity of acquiring a good over-all picture of the purpose and progress of the manoeuvre;

—Observers will be given the opportunity, if feasible, to follow the activities of command staffs and field units and to have personal contacts with troops;

—Observers from different participating States attending the same manoeuvre will be offered equal opportunities to carry out their functions.

4. *Prior notification of major military movements*

The participating States will notify their major military movements to all other participating States through usual diplomatic channels in accordance with the following provisions:

—Notification will be given of major military movements exceeding a total of 18,000 troops (in this context the word "troops" includes amphibious and airborne troops).

* *Source:* Madrid Conference document CSCE/RM.21, 12 December 1980.

—Notification will be given of major military movements within or into the area of application as defined in the Final Act concerning prior notification of major military manoeuvres, when the movement extends over a straight-line distance of more than 100 km from the point of origin.

—The term "major military movements" is applicable also to smaller-scale military movements which are undertaken sequentially, in units or not in units, as part of the same basic operation, and heading for the same general area of destination, and which within 60 days from the start of the first movement in the aggregate exceed a total of 18,000 troops.

—Notification will be given 30 days or more in advance of the start of the movement or, in the case of a movement arranged at shorter notice, at the earliest possible opportunity prior to its starting date.

—Notification will contain information of the general purpose of and the States involved in the movement, the number and types of the participating major units and the numerical strength of the forces engaged, the estimated time-frame and direction of the movement and its place or places of origin and destination if located within the applicable area. The participating States will also, if possible, provide additional relevant information.

5. *Prior notification of naval exercises involving amphibious forces*

Taking into account the special military significance attached in the Final Act to amphibious forces and recognizing that naval exercises involving a significant number of amphibious forces near the territorial waters of other participating States may give rise to particular concern and tension, the participating States will notify their naval exercises involving amphibious forces in accordance with the following provisions:

—Notification will be given of naval exercises involving more than 5,000 troops and/or more than 10 major amphibious warfare vessels.

—Notification will be given of any such naval exercise which takes place in European waters. For the purposes of this measure, the term "European waters" is defined as the inner seas of Europe, i.e. the Baltic, the North Sea and the Black Sea, the Mediterranean and the ocean areas adjacent to the territorial waters of the European participating States.

—Notification will be given 30 days or more in advance of the start of the exercise or, in the case of an exercise arranged at shorter notice, at the earliest possible opportunity prior to its starting date.

—Notification will be given to all other States participating in the CSCE through usual diplomatic channels.

—Notification will contain information of the general purpose of the exercise and the States involved, the number and types of the participating naval units, particularly as regards amphibious warfare vessels, the number of troops involved, the area and estimated time-frame of the conduct of the exercise, as well as, if feasible, other relevant information.

6. *Prior notification of major naval exercises*

The participating States recognize that by notifying major naval exercises which take place in European waters they will contribute further to reducing tension and to confidence-building. When notifying such naval exercises they will apply the same provisions *mutatis mutandis* as agreed upon concerning naval exercises involving amphibious forces.

They have agreed, furthermore, to continue endeavours with a view to developing confidence-building measures in the field of naval exercises, seeking *inter alia* a definition of the term "major naval exercise".

7. *Openness of information concerning military expenditures*

Recognizing that increased openness in military matters contributes to the strengthening of confidence among them, the participating States will display openness with regard to their military expenditures, taking also into account ongoing efforts in a multilateral context.

8. *Other confidence-building measures*

The participating States recognize that there exist additional measures which may usefully serve the common objectives as contained in the Final Act. They have agreed therefore to continue endeavours with a view to developing and enlarging such measures.

18. Chronology of major events concerning disarmament issues

January-December 1980

3 January The US President requests the Senate to delay consideration of the ratification of the SALT II Treaty.

25 January In a statement issued after its first meeting the special NATO Consultative Group on Arms Control says that the Alliance is still formally committed to the "parallel approaches" of modernizing its long-range theatre nuclear forces (LRTNF) in Europe while seeking an agreement with the Soviet Union to limit the number of such weapons on either side.

5 February The People's Republic of China participates, for the first time, in the work of the Committee on Disarmament in Geneva.

25–27 February The two-year International Nuclear Fuel Cycle Evaluation (INFCE) programme is concluded at a conference held in Vienna.

3 March The Convention on the physical protection of nuclear material is opened for signature.

3–21 March The Review Conference of the parties to the Convention on the prohibition of the development, production and stockpiling of bacteriological (biological) and toxin weapons and on their destruction is held in Geneva.

13 March The Indian Prime Minister states in the Indian Parliament that India would not hesitate to carry out nuclear explosions in the national interest, and that it is necessary for India to keep in touch with the latest developments in the nuclear technology field.

18 March A US State Department spokeman says that the outbreak of a disease, believed to be anthrax, in a Soviet city, Sverdlovsk, has raised questions concerning compliance by the USSR with the 1972 Convention prohibiting biological weapons.

17 April In a letter addressed to the UN Secretary-General concerning the tasks of the Second Disarmament Decade, the Soviet Foreign Minister proposes, *inter alia*, an agreement on renunciation of the expansion of the armies and of increases in the conventional weapons of powers which are permanent members of the UN Security Council, as well as of countries allied with them under military agreements. Curtailment of sales and deliveries of conventional weapons is also proposed.

15 May In a declaration issued in Warsaw at the conclusion of the meeting of the WTO Political Consultative Committee, the Warsaw Treaty states suggest that, in the interest of ensuring reliable and unimpeded use of the principal international sea lanes, an examination be made, for example, within the UN framework, of the question of limiting and scaling down the level of military presence and military activity in the areas concerned, be it in the Atlantic, Indian or Pacific Oceans, the Mediterranean Sea, or the Persian Gulf.

18 May China announces that it has launched an intercontinental ballistic missile on a target situated in the South Pacific.

3–4 June At a meeting of the NATO Nuclear Planning Group, held in Bodö, Norway, the participating ministers call on the Soviet Union to accept the repeated offer by the USA to negotiate verifiable limitations on US and Soviet long-range theatre nuclear forces (LRTNF). The ministers also note that the withdrawal of 1 000 US nuclear warheads from Europe as an integral part of the LRTNF modernization and arms control decision has begun. They recall that the new LRTNF warheads, decided upon on 12 December 1979, would be accommodated within the reduced level.

9–13 June The World Congress on Disarmament Education takes place at UNESCO Headquarters in Paris.

17–19 June A conference of non-governmental organizations is held at UN Headquarters to discuss the current status of the arms race and the strategies to halt it.

19 June The US President authorizes nuclear exports to India, determining that withholding the exports would be prejudicial to the achievement of US non-proliferation objectives.

25–26 June At a meeting of the North Atlantic Council, held in Ankara, the attending Foreign Ministers express their regret that the current international crisis has delayed the process of ratification of the SALT II Treaty. They recall their agreement to work towards the adoption of a mandate for negotiations, under the aegis of the Conference on Security and Co-operation in Europe, on militarily significant and verifiable confidence-building measures, applicable to the entire continent of Europe, that is, including the whole of the European part of the Soviet Union, as proposed by the government of France.

26 June The French President announces that at the meeting of the French Defence Council on 10 June he decided to start the development of a mobile strategic missile launcher. He also says that a possible decision concerning the production of the neutron bomb (on which research has already begun) will not be taken before 1982–83.

30 June–4 July The first regular meeting of non-aligned co-ordinating countries on the peaceful uses of nuclear energy is held in Buenos Aires.

7 July The USA and the USSR submit to the Committee on Disarmament a joint report on the progress in their bilateral negotiations on the prohibition of chemical weapons.

10 July The Socialist countries, participating in the Vienna talks on the reduction of forces in Central Europe, propose that in the first stage of troop reductions 20 000 Soviet and 13 000 US troops be withdrawn, irrespective of the unilateral withdrawal of 20 000 Soviet troops and 1 000 tanks, which has already begun.

25 July The US President signs Presidential Directive 59, formulating the so-called countervailing strategy. The new US strategy puts more stress than heretofore on the ability to employ strategic nuclear forces selectively by attacking political and military control centres, military forces, both nuclear and conventional, as well as the industrial capability to sustain a war.

31 July The UK, the USA and the USSR transmit to the Committee on Disarmament their tripartite report on the status of the negotiations on a treaty prohibiting nuclear weapon test explosions in all environments.

1 August The USSR concludes the unilateral withdrawal of 20 000 Soviet troops and 1 000 tanks from the German Democratic Republic, as it decided in 1979.

11 August–7 September The Second Review Conference of the parties to the Treaty on the non-proliferation of nuclear weapons is held in Geneva.

20 August An agreement is signed in Brasilia, under which Argentina will supply Brazil with 240 tons of natural uranium in return for help on nuclear technology.

21 August Pakistan announces that it now manufactures its own nuclear fuel.

19 September A US Titan strategic missile explodes accidentally in its silo in Arkansas.

30 September The Iraki centre for nuclear research is damaged by air-launched bombs.

10 October A UN Conference concludes its work by adopting the following instruments: (*a*) Convention on prohibitions or restrictions on the use of certain conventional weapons which may be deemed to be excessively injurious or to have indiscriminate effects; (*b*) Protocol on non-detectable fragments (Protocol I); (*c*) Protocol on prohibitions or restrictions on the use of mines, booby-traps and other devices (Protocol II); and (*d*) Protocol on prohibitions or restrictions on the use of incendiary weapons (Protocol III).

16 October US–Soviet talks on medium-range nuclear delivery vehicles in Europe open in Geneva.

11 November The follow-up Conference on Security and Co-operation in Europe opens in Madrid.

18 November France tests the prototype of a three-stage missile with multiple nuclear warheads.

3 December The UN General Assembly adopts the Declaration of the 1980s as the Second Disarmament Decade.

5 December The UN General Assembly decides to convene in 1983 a conference for the promotion of international co-operation in the peaceful uses of nuclear energy.

9 December The US–IAEA agreement submitting US civilian nuclear facilities to international safeguards enters into force.

11–12 December The North Atlantic Council, meeting in ministerial session in Brussels, states that the withdrawal of 1 000 US nuclear warheads from Europe has been completed.

12 December The UN General Assembly declares that the use of nuclear weapons would be a violation of the UN Charter.

12 December The UN General Assembly decides to carry out an impartial investigation to ascertain the facts pertaining to reports of the alleged use of chemical weapons and to assess the extent of the damage caused by the use of these weapons.

Errata

World Armaments and Disarmament, SIPRI Yearbook 1980

Page XXXV.	Title of Appendix A should read "Modernization of strategic nuclear weapons".
Page XXXVII, line 8 from bottom.	Read "the others should be ready by 1982" for ". . . by 1984".
Page XXXVII, line 5 from bottom.	Line should read "operational in 1981."
Page XXXVII, line 2 from bottom.	Line should read "at a rate of one per year through 1984 and three every two years thereafter."
Page XXXVIII, line 8 from bottom.	Line should read "The missile, a two-stage solid propellant rocket, is provided with a stellar-aided".
Page XXXIX, second paragraph.	Paragraph should read: "Only six Tridents, with 144 MIRVed SLBMs, can be deployed before the SALT II ceiling of 1 200 launchers of MIRVed missiles is reached. When the seventh Trident begins sea trials, some older MIRVed launchers will, according to the SALT II Treaty, have to be scrapped."
Page XXXIX, line 16.	Read "300 Mt" for "290 Mt".
Page XXXIX, line 19.	Read "50 per cent" for "56 per cent".
Page XXXIX, line 12 from bottom.	Read "As of 18 June 1979, 144 SS-N-18s had been put to sea" for "So far, 144 SS-N-18s have been put to sea".
Page XXXIX, lines 7–8 from bottom.	Lines should read "and a single 1-Mt warhead. Three hundred and twenty SS-N-8s are deployed on 23 Delta-class submarines."
Page XL, line 14.	Read "Boeing AGM-86" for "Boeing MGM-86".
Page 65, table 3.1.	Ireland should be omitted from the table.
Page 75, line 20.	Read "South Yemen" for "North Yemen".
Page 130.	Delete line of information indicating supply of Patton tanks by Italy to FR Germany.
Page 183, last sentence.	Sentence should read "The launch-points assumed were close to the borders with the German Democratic Republic and Czechoslovakia in the case of the Federal Republic of Germany, and the Norfolk/Suffolk region in the UK."

Page 190, line 4.	Read "2.5 times" for "1.4 times".
Page 196, line 6.	Read "December 1976" for "December 1975".
Page 207, end of page.	Insert a final reference: "14. 'GPS to test nuclear detonation sensor', *Aviation Week & Space Technology*, Vol. 111, No. 9, 27 August 1979, p. 51."
Page 294, figure 7.1.	The Soviet tracking site indicated in the Dominican Republic is actually located on Cuba.
Page 296, table 7.1.	In the Sensors column, fifth entry should read "Seismograph, microbarograph"; sixth entry should read "VHF–UHF–SHF receivers, precision tracking radar".
Page 299, figure 7.3.	The distance between the surface of the Earth and the trajectory should be 1 200–1 500 km.

INDEX

Index